CREATIVITY AND POWER MANAGEMENT: A CONCISE PROGRAM OF EMOTIONAL EDUCATION

CLINICAL DELIVERY OF THE POWER MANAGEMENT TRAINING

Based on the Conflict Analysis Battery:
A Didactic, Diagnostic and Therapeutic Self-Assessment

MORAL SCIENCE NORMATIVE PUBLICATION: VOLUME FIVE

By Albert Levis, M.D. & Maxwell Levis, Ph.D.

COVER IMAGE: GORSKI'S 'CRUCIFIXION'

Gorski's 'Crucifixion' canvas depicts the critical point of decision making: a person caught between the pleasure of kisses and the pain of the cross. In this canvas the artist makes a moral decision and expands it to other contemporary heroes who chose sacrifice rather than yielding to temptation. Power management is this critical faculty of humans in regulating behaviors and attitudes. Pursuit of conflict resolution is a more powerful motivation than pleasurable gratifications.

Choosing the cross and sacrifice reflects identifying with the set of Christian norms. Other Gorski canvases present his face as illuminated in its interface with the cross. They are labeled 'Identity' and 'Eye-dentity'. The cross wins. The artist elevated his personal moral dilemma to the Christian role model of self-sacrifice in his paintings, which he renamed 'pain-things'. Odysseus in a similar way exercised self-restraint asking his sailors to tie him on the mast of his boat so he can listen to the sirens but resist their power of seduction and associated destructiveness.

The canvas is helpful in demonstrating morality as the quest for conflict resolution by conforming to the prevailing cultural norms.
Another aspect of this canvas is in examining alternatives to conforming to norms such as rebelling at them. Other personality types and other cultural systems will differ in resolving conflict by following alternative choices of power management. Indeed Odysseus freed himself from the mast and enjoyed encounters with the sirens in his many Mediterranean island sojourns. The Greek way is choosing pleasure challenging authorities and norms but then experiencing pain in the unfolding of tragedies. Managing power is the key to finding the balance between pleasure and pain.

DEDICATION

The book is dedicated to my wife Georgette and our four children: Tajlei, Melissa, Oliver and Max

The Formal Theory evolved with the support of my family. Georgette, my wife who passed away in 2014, had been my companion almost 50 years through all the tribulations of my thinking big, seeking to heal the world, revolutionizing psychology, and taking risks like acquiring the Wilburton Inn to evolve a training center. She was down to earth, unpretentious, caring, funny, welcoming, patient and supportive. While I promised the sky, she delivered the earth. She was the one to work hard to manage the inn until I developed a following, which took a very long time to happen. She made the Wilburton a great destination for celebrating life, the seasons and beautiful family reunions. She bonded with our guests and made their stays unforgettable caring experiences.

While Georgette was the spirit of our home and the inn our four children contributed in the developments of the Formal Theory into art and science projects, which eventually led to the creation of the Museum of the Creative Process on the grounds of the inn.

My older daughter Tajlei upon her informal bat mitzvah contributed skits on the history of the bible as a walk around our extensive back yard. This experience was the inspiration of the 'Sculptural Trail in the History of Love' retracing all religions as a sequence of discoveries of science completed by the Moral Science.

My younger and outgoing daughter Melissa helped in evolving and delivering the self-assessment tests as playful art exercises introducing them to her friends and developing our training activities at the inn with programs like 'Hikers, thinkers and singers'. An illustration of her remarkable activities is a mural of the Sanctuary of the Wizard contrasting the two relational modalities, dominance and subordinacy. She also composed a dramatization of the Formal Theory with her musical Eurika as her thesis at Brown. One song starts as 'I am Prometheus and I am bringing Fire'. She also choreographed the six-role process as a song, and composed a song on 'Power Management'. She did not become a psychologist because she was too talented as a song-writer, but she blended her experiences as her songs were children's empowerment music.

My older son Oliver assisted me in developing and delivering the Gorski Retrospective as we constructed five panels of lifetime conflict resolutions for one of his grammar school science projects. These panels became the principle study of the integration of an artist's symbolic universe into the key exhibit of the Museum of the Creative Process. Oliver eventually became a farmer, baker and singer and popularized the name of my first training center, 'Earth Sky Time' into his brand of artisan bread. While very few people understood my interpretation of the Greek Cosmogony's figures, everybody loves his breads.

My younger son Max has been my associate as a fellow researcher. He started as my traveling companion attending conferences on psychological topics spanning from Cape Town to St. Petersburg and eventually becoming a presenter in professional conferences traveling without me. He contributed a great deal to the research on my assessment battery at an early age. He used the animal metaphor test in a grammar school science project to identify the structure of the thought process in stories of his fellow students, and then later he used the personality inventory test as a high school science project to study the inheritance of relational modalities by delivering the assessment to his friends' families. He also challenged me to study the Wizard of Oz story and that became one more of the exhibits of the Museum of the Creative Process. It was thanks to his initiatives that we evolved a training program at the museum recruiting interns as our research associates, who were helpful in completing their own case studies thus contributing to the research effort.

Max graduated from Harvard Divinity School and continued for a PhD at Boston University with his thesis examining the effectiveness of the online delivery of the assessment as an educational, diagnostic and therapeutic instrument. He has coauthored with me the volume on the Museum Art Exhibits and has contributed much to this volume.

So I wish to thank all of you, Levis kids, for being my partners and for continuing the project on your own.

NOTE: The publication of creativity and power management in two volumes retraces the evolution of the testing from the clinical to the pschoeducational delivery of the battery. Volume five is about its clinical delivery by a therapist to a patient. Volume six is about its delivery by a teacher to students and by a computer software to the general public online.

CONTENTS

3 ❖ Clinical Delivery Case Studies:
The Dominance Relational Modality: All About Lions 329

Introduction And Definition Of Dominance
Identifying Characteristics Of Dominant Persons' Artwork and of the Relational Modality

Cases Of The Dominant Relational Syndrome

Dominant Case Study #1:
Hannah, The Story Of A Holocaust Survivor

Dominant Case Study # 2 : The Transformation Of The Handicapped Flea And Ant Into The Disabled Lion And Eagle

Intern Cases

Dominant Cases

Submissive Cases

Chapter 1: The Impact to Psychotherapy Upon Rethinking Psychology as the Moral Science

Chapter 2: Findings and Validations

Chapter 3: Therapy Outcome Studies

Chapter 4: The Role of Therapists in Self-Assessment

Chapter 5: Traditional Psychotherapies Integrated into Psycho-Education

|1|

Introduction to the Moral Science

Creativity and Power Management:
A Concise Program of Emotional Education
Benefitting from
Moral Science's Conceptual Innovations

Major Scientific Breakthrough

Conflict Analysis: The Formal Theory of Behavior

introduces the unconscious Conflict Resolution Process as the atomistic Unit of the social sciences. The Unit, by focusing on process rather than content, interfaces art and science.

Art: The Unit was observed as a reoccurring pattern in the five generations of the Greek Creation Myths.

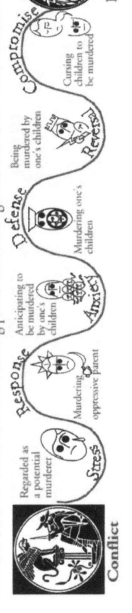

Regarded as a potential murderer — **Stress**

Murdering oppressive Parent — **Response**

Anticipating to be murdered by one's children — **Anxiety**

Murdering one's children — **Defense**

Being murdered by one's children — **Reversal**

Cursing children to be murdered — **Compromise**

Conflict

Resolution

Science: This phenomenon was abstracted into a 6-role formal transformation process that resolves conflict.

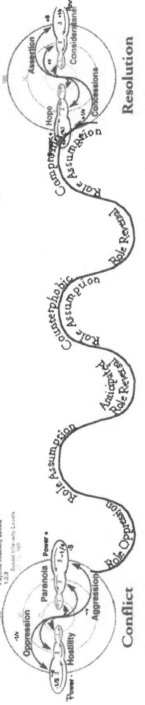

Role Oppression

Role Assumption

Anticipation of Role Reversal

Counterphobic Role Assumption

Role Reversal

Compromise — Role Assumption

Conflict

Resolution

Psychotic Intensity Levels
1,2,3
Sadistic Intensity Levels

Power + — Paranoia

Oppression

Power - — Hostility

Aggression

Assertion

Hope — Compromise

Concessions

Consideration?

Power

- Three Art as Evidence of Science Exhibits
- Power Management--a journey to self-discovery and personal transformation.
- The Epistemology of The Unit.
- Collaborative Project: Is behavior predictable, qualifiable, quantifiable and graphically portrayable?

- The Psychology of The Unit.
- Assessment of The Unit.
- The Unit as a moral paradigm.

Introduction: Creativity and Power Management, A Concise program of Emotional Education Benefitting from Moral Science's Conceptual Innovations

A Paradigm Shift

This is a case-study book introducing a paradigm shift in the study of behavior, of the humanities in general. The shift is from art to science, from trusting the content of stories, theories, in the quest for insights in human behavior to identifying science, what is universal in all stories as the orderly nature of their plot. The plot is analyzed as a harmonic, a circumscribed entity that has a scientific structure and a moral order function. This plot phenomenon reflects the unconscious need for resolution, normative adjustment, as an emotional dialectic. As a natural science entity the plot is a measurable conflict resolution process.

Identifying this scientific entity as universal represents a shift of paradigms. It helps to understand art, the creative process as a measurable, and also moral communication. The case studies of this volume use art, metaphors, creativity for self-discovery and accelerate the process of healing as founded on rational principles that everybody can understand and agree upon.

This book of case studies examines the creative process as a scientific and moral order phenomenon and the means to help the client to readily become conscious of the unconscious. It demonstrates that the mind is both predictable, measurable and also moral, where morality is defined as conflict resolution.

We will be examining samples of creativity, metaphors, utilizing a creativity-based psycho-assessment to identify their scientific interpretation in terms of formal relational and physical dimensions. We will see the features of the new paradigm: the clear dialectic structure of the mental process and its moral directionality as alternative ways of resolving conflict. Validation of the Formal Theory transforms psychology. It is no longer agnostic and vague as we identify the unit entity of behavior as both morally directed and as fathomable. Psychology is no longer an elusive domain; it has become a science and the evidence is in the cases of this volume. It is in the statements of how clearly people understand themselves and are able to evolve insights and directives for healing.

The plot of stories, conflict resolution, represents a physiological adjustment mechanism of the individual in the social environment as a normative structure. Conflicts are generated as the individual deviates from the center of the normative gravity. Moral stories, such as the scriptures represent normative institutions determining what is acceptable and what is not. Moral values bring the person back to the center of moral gravity.

The new moral explanation examines how the unconscious follows automatically principles of conflict resolution redefining morality as a scientific phenomenon superseding religions as narrow normative institutions of conflict resolution. The new unconscious accounts for morality as the innate and universal adjustment mechanism, which we show to have a scientific organization that is detected in all samples of creativity.

The Conflict Analysis Battery is an assessment that identifies, measures, the assumed orderly process in the personal symbolic universe. It is founded on Formal Theory's shift of paradigms in the sense that it departs from art, creativity exercises, to achieve accurate measurement, science. Studying samples of creativity the test taker identifies the underlying scientific organization of one's emotions as particular ways of resolving conflicts, their strengths and their shortcomings.

The case studies illustrate the science but also the advantages of utilizing it for didactic, diagnostic and therapeutic objectives. A distinct program Creativity and Power Management has been developed, which is shown to serve as a concise and comprehensive program of emotional education that can be delivered for patients as psychotherapy, for students in academic settings as training, and also online for self-discovery without professional supervision.

The case studies introduce four innovations in the study of psychology that revamp the social sciences, integrating the humanities and the sciences, psychology and religions into the Science of Conflict Resolution, the Moral Science. These four innovations:

- Identifying the conflict resolving process as the scientific and moral order unconscious, the universal harmonic, the common denominator of the social sciences manifested as a six-role state and three formal operations mechanism in all samples of creativity.

- Identifying four relational modalities, alternative ways of resolving conflict, as a wellness personality typology that recognizes the syndromal psychodynamic organization of emotions and that is accountable for psychopathology and for psychotherapeutic interventions.

- Evolving the Conflict Analysis Battery, a self-assessment technology that is didactic, diagnostic, and therapeutic

- And delivering knowledge and insights through the Creativity and Power Management emotional education program that clarifies moral values as the scientific principles of conflict resolution. This program changes both the delivery of therapy and of education.

I arrived to this conceptualization in my quest for meaning that started as I witnessed as a child the atrocities of the Second World War, the Holocaust and the Communist inspired Civil War in Athens Greece. I have been seeking to learn from history so humanity can avert the destructive conflicts of the

WWII's ideologies and religions. My findings give me satisfaction as they introduce the scientific understanding of morality as originating in the unconscious need for social or normative adjustment. The implication from this observation is the need for shifting the moral and normative authority from stories of revelation to the scientific analysis of the unconscious, as observed in the plot of all stories, as the scientific moral order entity.

This book of case studies then has a wider pertinence to healing. It heals the individual by teaching her to resolve conflicts, conforming to the environment, but it also dares explore healing the divided world, by reconciling its multiple paradigms into the Moral Science. Can science introduce moral consensus so that all people and all cultures agree on moral matters?

The far-reaching goal of the Moral Science is peace of mind but also peace in the world. We explore with the case studies attaining the first objective, wellness but we must not forget that conflict is a normative deviation and that cultures establish norms that are partial discoveries of the science of conflict resolution, and thus that humanity is trapped to alternative normative worlds inducing perennial strife; this will be the case until the world establishes the science based consensus on moral paradigms.

Validating the Formal Theory through an assessment, which measures the creative process as a scientific moral or conflict resolution process
These are volumes five and six of the Normative Publications series consisting in the delivery of *Creativity and Power Management,* CPM, a concise program of emotional education based on the Formal Theory's concept of the unconscious as a natural science measurable conflict resolving entity.

Case studies in this book illustrate the nature of the scientific unconscious studying the creative process as a *Conflict Resolution Process* (CRP) utilizing a self-assessment, the *Conflict Analysis Battery* (CAB) (*Conflict Analysis Training,* Normative Publications, 1988, Volume 3). The significance of this study is in that it demonstrates the practical clinical value of the abstractions advanced by *Conflict Analysis, the Formal Theory of Behavior,* (Normative Publications, 1988, Volume one) and that in doing so it validates the concepts and the related assessment technology.

Creativity and Power Management (CPM) is shown to be an effective psychotherapy (volume five) but also a program of psycho-education (volume six). It is presented as a concise wellness emotional education integrating but considerably modifying a number of psychotherapeutic modalities. It is based on the self-assessment accompanied by an educational introduction. The self-assessment is educational, diagnostic and therapeutic. It works well assisting therapy as well as an emotional education without a therapist, without the need for a therapeutic relationship.

Creativity and Power Management
The Power Management program combines the introduction to the concepts with a self-assessment, the *Conflict Analysis Battery* applying them to clinical practice by measuring the creative process for self-discovery and personal growth.

The battery has two types of tests:

- A personality inventory, which identifies the relational modality, the formal dimensions of one's way of resolving conflicts.

- And a set of projective tests, the metaphors, which capture the conflict resolution process reconstructing the six-role process as a symbolic system.

Both test types help the test taker to become conscious of the unconscious as one's relational modality diagnosis. The Conflict Analysis Battery's inventory identifies the relational modality, and the set of projectives illustrating its emotional syndromal or dialectic manifestation.

Moral Science's Four Conceptual Innovations

The first component of *Creativity and Power Management*, the educational information sums up Formal Theory's four key concepts. It is important for the reader of this volume to identify these key-conceptual changes introduced by the Formal Theory. They pertain to redefining the concepts of the unconscious, of diagnostic categories, of assessment technology, and of the nature of moral values.

- The unconscious is introduced as a natural science morality driven conflict resolution process.

- The diagnostic categories are the alternative ways of resolving conflicts, four psychodynamic relational modalities.

- The Formal Theory rethinks assessments by combining a personality inventory with a set of projectives measuring the unconscious as a conflict resolution mechanism.

- Finally moral values are identified as three formal operations, the principles of conflict resolution.

The introduction to this clinical case studies volume reviews these new concepts contrasting them to the equivalent current conceptualizations. We will examine each of these concepts in depth in four chapters of the introductory segment.

The four chapters:

- On Epistemology: We will examine Formal Theory's unconscious as an exact natural science phenomenon, the unit order of the Moral Science, the Science of Conflict Resolution. We will review the unconscious contrasting it with Freud's multiple models.

- On Diagnosis: We will review a new set of wellness diagnostic categories, the relational modalities as syndromes of six emotions leading predictably to conflict resolutions. We will do so in two separate chapters on dominance and subordinacy relating to identify the differences between the relational modalities' syndromal psychodynamics. We will examine diagnostic categories contrasting Formal Theory's personality typology, the relational modalities, to DSM 5's clinical symptoms nosology.

- On Assessment: The studies demonstrate the new *Conflict Analysis Battery*, a self-assessment combining a personality inventory, the *Relational Modality Evaluation Scale* (RMES) which is diagnostic, with the Metaphor tests, reconstructing the syndromal sequence of emotions which is therapeutic. We will contrast Formal Theory's CAB to traditional assessments.

- On Therapy and Education: The studies illustrate how the well-structured manual driven self-assessment program changes the traditional delivery of therapy into a psycho-education. The studies illustrate the battery's versatility in its delivery to a number of cohorts always fulfilling its three key functions: didactic, diagnostic, and therapeutic. This therapy understands moral values as the innate motivational forces, three formal operations, driving the unconscious mind spontaneously to conflict resolution. We will discuss Power Management and compare this procedure to traditional therapies.

Three Types of Delivery of Creativity and Power Management

The two volumes contrast three cohorts for the delivery of *Creativity and Power Management.* Volume five contains the transcribed testing records of 15 clinical case studies. Volume six contains case studies delivered as a training program without therapy; additionally the study contains partially transcribed case studies generated through the online delivery of the cognitive information and the CAB testing.

The three cohorts:

- First, a group of fifteen patients from my psychiatric practice (volume five).

- Second, a group of seven college students, interns at the Museum of the Creative Process, conducting research projects (volume six).

- Third, a group of online test takers, who never encountered us or benefited from personalized services whatsoever.

The 15 Patients (Volume Five)

The program evolved at an outpatient clinic, The Center for the Study of Normative Behavior in Hamden, Connecticutt. The center operated as a research and training institution from 1970 to 2000. The research led to the publication of *Conflict Analysis, the Formal Theory of Behavior* along with the *Conflict Analysis Training, A Program of Emotional Education*, a workbook containing the self-assessment identified as the *Conflict Analysis Battery* (Normative Publications, 1988).

In this psychiatric practice the program was applied to clinically identified patients but also to the well public as psychological evaluations of police cadets, clergymen and the training of schoolteachers. The delivery of the battery to patients, police cadets and seminarians proved to be tremendously effective as a therapeutic evaluation.

The Cohort of Seven Interns as Well Individuals (Volume Six)

In 1987, upon the publication of the Formal Theory textbook and its companion workbook, I acquired the Wilburton Inn as a potential training center to deliver from there the educational program. I established there the Institute of Conflict Analysis and the Museum of the Creative Process. I used the battery for training of interns without engaging them into a therapeutic relationship. The conclusion was that the assessment represented a wellness educational program that did not depend on a therapeutic relationship but on a brief educational presentation.

The Cohort of the Online Test Takers

In 2013, my son Max formatted the assessment for its online delivery precluding any personalized professional services. One of the deliveries occurred on January 2014 to a cohort of 33 test takers stemming from the domain of the Mechanical Turk. A query to the online test takers upon completion of this self-assessment confirmed that the experience was educational, diagnostic and therapeutic. It was effective without any therapeutic intervention whatsoever.

All Case Studies Illustrate Conceptual and Technological Developments
The case studies exemplify the assessment's diagnostic and therapeutic value for the test taker; they examine the relational modalities as wellness diagnostic categories, and introduce the usefulness of the assessment through three alternative modes of delivery. Self-reports composed by the test takers document the consistently positive therapy outcome of the cases. The query responses offered by the online assessment-takers also demonstrate the effectiveness of the program and validate the assumptions of the Formal Theory.

These testing protocols feature the measurements of the unconscious process combining the relational diagnoses with their syndromal manifestation as the six-role state template. Each case study includes the assessment record of the test-taker illustrating how the information is organized along the two tests: first by reproducing the relational profile summarized in one page, and then by utilizing the metaphor tests in reconstructing the six role syndromal process.

The battery's projective tests are therapeutic. The projective tests are structured into identifying one's pattern and then eliciting behavior modification insights. They help the testee to become instantly conscious of the unconscious as a relational dynamic and to recognize its six-part emotional dialectic pattern reflecting its syndromal psychodynamic nature connecting one's behaviors with one's emotions along the six role-state conflict resolution process.

Awareness of this connection evokes insights into making the appropriate corrective behavioral changes in order to optimize one's mode of resolving conflicts and thus diminishing one's psychic tension and any related clinical symptoms.

All cases in this volume show that this unconscious process unfolds predictably along the four diagnostic alternative types of conflict resolution, the relational modalities and along the syndromal six-emotions dialectic pathway from a conflict to its resolution. The case studies also show that the assessment works equally well through three types of delivery: with a therapist, without a therapist but with an educator and finally without intermediaries through the online delivery.

Another feature of this assessment record is a companion essay completed by the test taker upon termination of therapy and of the online delivery of the assessment. This essay is elicited as a test: 'a Letter to Oneself' reflecting thoughts spelled out by the test takers of the relevance of the testing, and therapy in the clinical case studies, in evoking insights for behavior changes and for the relief of clinical symptoms.

Chapter One

Epistemology: The Unconscious as a Scientific Conflict Resolution or Moral Order Phenomenon

On Methodology

The theoretical position, articulated in *Conflict Analysis, the Formal Theory of Behavior*, 1988, identified the nature of the unconscious by analyzing the formal relationship between emotions predictably leading to the completion of a story as a conflict resolution.

The Formal Theory's contribution to science is methodological. Both creationists and evolutionists have erred methodologically focusing on the veracity or falsity of the content of the story of Genesis. Both analyses of the story are axiomatic assumptions, methodologically incorrect procedures. Genesis is correct as the metaphor of the creative process correlating the six days of creation into the totality of an act of creation. Genesis is an appropriate metaphor of the six-role process as a symbolic universe, not a cosmic one. The unconscious mind, like its projection on Gods, creates order; it achieves in six emotions the state of rest. Divinities are projections of the unconscious process. The attributes of the conflict resolution process have been ascribed to the nature of Gods, the morality aspiring divine.

The Formal Theory introduced the scientific study of the unconscious based on two premises:

- First, studying the proper object, the realm of the plot of stories as a circumscribed totality of formal energetic transformations and

- Second, utilizing the appropriate method, the physics of two mechanical equilibrial phenomena: the pendulum oscillation and the formal operations correcting imbalance in the trays of a scale.

The structure of the unconscious was conceived as a natural science measurable phenomenon following the laws of the oscillation of a pendulum and of the equilibrial trays of a scale. The moral function of conflict resolution was identified as the individual's normative reconciliation or social adjustment.

Science then reduced the complexity of behavior to the simplicity of two natural science equilibrial phenomena. This premise is validated in this book by detecting multiple manifestations of this order by sampling the creative process.

The Formal Theory identified the plot of stories as a conflict resolution totality consisting of a six-part, six-role-state, six formally interrelated emotions: stress and response, anxiety and defense, reversal and compromise. These were guided by three formal operations from a conflict to its resolution: passivity was transformed to activity, antagonism to cooperation and alienation to mutual respect. The unconscious then was seen as a unit entity that has a physical structure and conflict resolution as its moral function.

This methodological change in the social sciences represents a paradigm shift from stories we believe in that divide scientists and believers, to identifying the plot of stories as a universal psychological entity with a sociological adaptive function. The plot of stories reflects the scientific unconscious as the unit of the social sciences. This order is meaningful as it resonates with the inner quest for the reduction of painful psychic tension.

The New Unconscious
The Formal Theory studies the creative process, the formal organization of emotions in the plot of every story, as a natural science conflict-resolving or psychic tension reducing phenomenon. This is the accurate reflection of the structure and the function of the unconscious. We know the structure of the plot and as the moral of stories as a dramatic totality. The new concept is described by constructs and formulas of the Simple Harmonic Motion, an energy transforming phenomenon, and of the Kleinian group of four formal equilibrial operations of the scale.

Creativity as the choice of an object combines then rigorous science and moral determinism originating in the unconscious. Science and moral purpose or determinism are two foreign notions in the realm of current psychology. The Formal Theory allows us to introduce constructs and formulas from the rigorous sciences as binding emotions in the predictable moral or conflict resolution unconscious as a periodic energy upgrading phenomenon, the unit of the social sciences.

This definition of the unconscious radically revamps the social sciences. This unit order is the foundation of a totally revamped psychology, the Science of Conflict Resolution or the Moral Science. The psyche becomes a rigorous and morality driven measurable phenomenon instead of the currently perceived agnostic, amoral, and unfathomable unconscious. The principle unconscious motivational force is the quest for reduction of psychic tension through attitude change as moral order; it is not libido and thanatos but the predictability of the moral determinism, the directedness of conflict resolution, the pursuit for justice. We know this motivational force as the driving power of faiths and of ideologies, manifested as patriotism and as idealism, surpassing the love of life.

The Scientific Definition of the Unconscious
The unconscious is no longer a vague psychological term. It is identified as a natural science and moral order energy conserving but also upgrading unit entity. The unit entity has rigorous constructs and formulas and the moral function of conflict resolution. We identify the unconscious as a natural science entity studying the creative process. We detect its presence as the universal harmonic. This is the object for the scientific and moral study of behavior.

The unconscious is defined as a conflict resolution process integrating emotions and behaviors into syndromes of six interrelated role states predictably leading to social adjustment following three conflict resolution scientific principles as the innate motivational forces. These principles operating unconsciously steer the person to social adjustment as conflict reducing normative reconciliation.

Conflict Analysis, the Formal Theory of Behavior introduced the unconscious as reflected in the structure of the creative process as a scientific conflict resolution mechanism combining two natural science phenomena: *the formal operations of the equilibrial scale and the energetic constructs and formulas of the Simple Harmonic Motion.* Several studies including the clinical applications in this volume's case studies validate the Formal Theory into the Moral Science, which unifies the multiple psychological theories and the many religions into the exact Science of Conflict Resolution.

This conceptualization of the unconscious as a scientific conflict resolution measurable entity with relational and moral dimensions radically departs from its psychoanalytic definition as an amoral, indeed libidinal and aggressive, conflict inducing, and non-rational entity. The new unconscious is a totally rigorous humanistic entity. It is conceived as a scientific and moral concept that guides the person to conflict resolution pursuing instinctively one's adjustment to societal norms.

The unconscious process may be graphically portrayed as a six-part harmonic oscillation. Its cross section allows portraying the place of the person in its deviation from the normative center, the point of moral gravity.

The diagrams illustrate the physical structure of the conflict resolution process as a natural science measurable oscillatory phenomenon. The orderly nature of the unconscious was observed examining the structure and function of the creative process, the plot of stories, as a natural science phenomenon studying a pattern that repeated itself five times in the Greek Cosmogony. This order shapes the structure of associations as a series of formally interrelated emotions. The function of this physiological process is the reduction of psychic tension coinciding with social or normative adjustment.

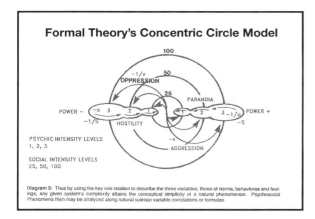

According to the Formal Theory morality originates in the unconscious as a natural science conflict resolution phenomenon. This process is the origin of religions as partial and complementary discoveries of the three formal operations and of the creative process.

The jacket of the volume illustrates the three formal operations that guide the emotions in the conflict resolution process

The Physics and the Logic of the Process
This theoretical insight originated in the observation of a pattern that repeated five times in the Greek Cosmogony's five generations; I identified the process as an equilibrial natural science phenomenon, as an energetic transformation that upgrades order. I then introduced the two equilibrial models: one from the realm of physics, the energetic model of the Simple Harmonic Motion, and one from the realm of mathematics and logic, the Kleinian group of four formal operations illustrated in the model of a scale.

The model of formal operations governing the equilibrial trays of a scale has been studied by Piaget as pertaining to the conservation of intellectual constructs. I used the formal operations method to explain conservation of emotional energy instead of that of cognitive or intellectual constructs. It is this physical energy that we are concerned about, key to the emotional continuity of the process from the beginning to the end of a conflict resolution process. The process is about the transformations of the conserved emotional energy.

I assumed that conservation of energy leads one directionally to resolution as a state of stable energies that is of negative entropy, the state referred to as the rest position, a story's moral conclusion. The unconscious transforms energy from chaos, or unstable energy, to sociological and emotional order, a stable energetic state. Order is identified as the normative conciliation, the individual experiencing mutual respect with the social system. This reconciliation reduces the psychic tension experienced by the individual and by her environment. This mutual respect compatibility defines the concept of moral order as a psychological development based on the redefined conflict resolving unconscious.

Differences Between Mind and Machines
The consequence of identifying the structure of the mental process with the two mechanical models allows us to introduce their constructs and formulas into the study of behavior. Science of physics and logic become the conceptual language or epistemology of the social sciences. Although the mind abides by the natural laws of these two equilibrial machines, the pendulum and the scale, it differs from these machines.

- **The mental equilibrial oscillation differs from the mechanical simple Harmonic Motion in that the mental oscillation is circumscribed.** The emotional dialectic of a six-part conflict resolution process achieves its goal in six exchanges and then it stops oscillating. Its goal of resolution is completed upon the third cycle, as the mind transforms the energy of conflict to order and goes to the state of rest.

- **The formal mental process is guided by the three formal operations irreversibly restoring the equilibrium.** The equilibrial trays of the mental scale self-correct by transforming the role states energy along three formal operations: negation, reciprocity and correlation. These operations transform emotional states of passivity into activity, its reciprocal, of antagonism to cooperation, its opposite, and of alienation to mutual respect, its correlative. The mental scale seeks a one directional restoration of the equilibrium. Hence the three formal mental operations lead irreversibly to psychosocial adjustment.
  The six roles suffice to complete the attitudinal change and energetic transformation advancing a conflict to its resolution.

The Unconscious as a Natural Science Periodic Phenomenon

The unconscious as a conflict resolving process is about emotions conceived as energetic quantities generated through induction, like electricity generated in a spool opposing changes experienced through rotation in a magnetic field. The unconscious generates psychic tension as the individual resists change upon her/his shift within the societal magnetic/normative field. A person being oppressed generates hostility, while one transgressing experiences guilt; both emotions oppose the respective social shifts. Conflict then may be defined as the energy generated by the deviaton of the self within the normative field. The forces and energies are defined by the following formulas:

$E = S \times F$
Conflict energy (E) is equal to the normative deviation (S) times one's dependency needs (F) or one's attachment to the state of normative rest (F).

$F = A$ acceleration emotions $= -K \times S$
Accelleration (F or A) corresponds to emotions. It is a force proportional and opposite to the normative deviation (S).

There are three variables constructs in the physics of the pendulum oscillation that help to understand normative deviations, emotions and behaviors as interrelated. These are the concepts of displacement (S) corresponding to the normative deviation within a social system, Accelleration (A) to emotions and velocity (V) corresponding to behaviors.

These are in formal relation to each other specified by the trigonometric formulas of

S, normative deviation,$= R \sin (w)$,
F or A, acceleration or emotions$=$negative $R \sin w$ and
V, behaviors $= R$ cosine W Where R corresponds to a deviaton from the norm as a choice 'role' behavior.

Resolution occurs as the energy E is discharged transformed into work performed mentally or socially as a creation, an attitude and/or a normative change. The transformation of a conflict to a resolution is an emotional and energetic process that has the characteristics of the Simple Harmonic Motion, the pendulum oscillation. The pendulum differs from the mind in the sense that the mind converts the energy of the oscillation into useful work, usually in the course of three oscillations, whereas the pendulum oscillates till its energy is dissipated.

Conflict Resolution is an equilibrial operation abiding by the simple formal relational dynamics of another phenomenon of physics and logic. This is the four equilibrial operations of the trays of a scale: an *Identity* operation as a weight placed on a tray may be offset or balanced out by three different operations: *Reciprocity*, adding an equal weight on the other tray, opposition or *Negation*, removing the weight, and third by *Correlation*, a shift of the weight on the fulcrum. The equilibrial dynamics of the unconscious seek to restore the state of rest in three pendulum oscillations. $I = R \times N \times C$.

The Measurable Parameters of the Unconscious
The variables of this unconscious are determined by the physical energetic structure of the oscillation and by its formally determined equilibrial orientation. This phenomenon as one of physics abides by the law of the conservation of energy and as one of formal organization it abides by the laws of mathematics and logic of the equilibrial trays of a scale.

The physics model consists of a simple harmonic motion, three oscillations, corresponding to the dialectic of a six part emotional and formally defined rollercoaster: stress, response, anxiety, defense, reversal and compromise. These role states are emotions as energetically charged states of mind; they are intertransformable types of energy; passivity is experienced as a state of dynamic energy and activity as the reciprocal state of kinetic energy.

The scale model is an equilibrial mechanism of the six formally related emotions evolve spontaneously from a conflict defined as passivity, antagonism and alienation to resolution as mastery, cooperation and mutual respect. At that point the trays of the mental scale are in an equilibrial balance and the person experiences it as the restoration of the state of rest.

The conflict resolution process is defined as an energetic transformational entity coinciding with the performance of a creation as work. The energy generated upon a normative deviation: the individual deviating within the gravitational or magnetic field of her culture, is transformed to order, negative entropy, entelechy, meaning, creations, and resolution through normative compliance. Resolution coincides with arresting the mental oscillation by completing it as a six-step three formal operations unit entity. Upon conflict resolution the motion stops and its energy is conveyed into the performance of moral transformation work. The work consists in the individual's change of attitude: embracing the normative order, alternatively in the individual negotiating a social or normative change, as the condition for the completion of a resolution.

The Integrative Quality of the Unconscious Process
The physical structure and the moral function of the dramatic totality define the unconscious as a universal psychological entity; it is the engine upgrading order but also the atomistic unit of the social sciences. The study of the dramatic plot of stories leads then to the bridging of psychology with morality. The unconscious is identified examining the creative or dramatic process with the correct method: the formal analysis of parts in the energetically conserved totality of the story.

Formal analysis applied to the totality of a story identifies the order in the realm of the unconscious as the processing of emotions accounting for human motivation pursuing meaning and justice. The Formal Theory applies physics and logic, the sciences of method, to the realm of emotions as a dramatic and hence as a moral transformative process. It therefore demonstrates that morality is the unconscious determinism of conflict resolution as manifested in all samples of creativity.

Methodological Issues: Relational Versus Propositional Method

Josiah Royce pointed out that truth is not in the veracity of assumptions postulated by a theory, but in the formal relation of parts within the totality considered. The Formal Theory advanced the notion that the parts in any story are six emotions bound together by three formal operations as a totality reflecting the universality of the unconscious as a conflict resolution process. Aristotle identified this order in Greek tragedies. The Formal Theory recognized this dramatic process and introduced physics and logic to its study identifying the unconscious as a periodic natural science, moral order phenomenon, the unit of the social sciences.

Aristotle, in his *Poetics,* detected this processing of emotions in Greek tragedies as cycles of *pathos,* passivity, states of suffering, offset by *drasis* or states of activity integrated in the dramatic totality he identified as the Teleion Holon, Greek for the perfect universe. This totality has a beginning, middle and a moral end, justice, deke, imparting catharsis to the audience. He observed tragedies as characterized by continuity of action, ending with the punishment of the hero, through the verdict pronounced by the emissary of the Olympians, the dues ex machina. This setback or role reversal, incurred cleansing, catharsis, expiation, coinciding with the upgrading of social order, the creation of a new social norm, the higher order of entelechy or inner meaning or moral purpose.

This natural science phenomenon has also a moral function: conflict resolution. This unit entity integrates the humanities: psychology and religions with science. This process of moral order is the universal harmonic. There are two assumptions about this unit order. The principles of physics and logic are appropriate method applied to the realm of emotions as conserved energetic entities processed by the unconscious in every story's unfolding drama.

- First, it is an energetic entity that is conserved, but upgraded from chaos to order in a six-part continuum of emotional exchanges corresponding to the physics of the Simple Harmonic Motion, as three oscillations between formally related emotional states such as passivity and activity ones.

- And second, this order follows the three formal operations of the equilibrial scale guiding the process from a conflict as a normative deviation to resolution as the normative reconciliation corresponding to the restoration of the emotional rest state.

The case studies demonstrate the universality of this process by identifying its presence integrating fragments of information into formally interrelated relational modalities as distinct and as six role syndromal entities. We will see affirmations of these distinctions in every case.

- The relational modality is presented graphically as the <u>relational modalities profile,</u> a table reproducing the multiple-choice scorings of the five relational scales scored along an original set of distinctions with values varying from -3 to +3. The computerized version of the assessment integrates the relational dimensions of each relational modality and the psychic tension scale numerically as variations along the Likert scoring with numbers from 1 to 6. The highest scores reveal the person's diagnostic distinctions along the four relational modalities. The psychic tension score reflects the degree of wellness versus illness.

- A second diagram, the *Metaphor Profile*, reconstructs the relational six role state process. The template of the six-role process is illustrated pictorially by inserting the images of the metaphors along the six role states. In each case study the six-role state template integrates the fragments of emotional experiences captured through the metaphor testing into meaningful dramatic continua.

Accordingly the scientific explanation on the nature of the unconscious is in the formal organization of parts/emotions/role-states in the totality of one's stories. Methodologically the focus of psychology as a science is in detecting the formal relationship between the constellation of six emotions in the predictable plot of stories as a conserved energetic continuum integrated by the three formal operations into a resolution. Our quest in the case studies is to identify this order in conceptualizing the nature of the personal symbolic system reflecting the universal syndromal organization of emotions. Do the templates reflect conflict resolution? They do. Then the cases present evidence reflecting the scientific nature of the unconscious as a system of six interrelated emotions or role states within every story. They also illustrate how each relational modality evolves alternative syndromal conflict resolving states.

The Formal Theory advances the relational method and refutes axiomatic pronouncements on the nature of the psyche and of morality. The psychoanalytic assumptions on the primacy of sexuality and aggression are arbitrary propositions that have misled psychological research. The Formal Analysis of a story as the dramatic processing of emotions redefines the Oedipus complex. Instead of considering axiomatically or dogmatically with Freud the unconscious driven by libido and thanatos reflecting the universal unconscious, we examine the Oedipus Rex play's dramatic totality of correlated emotions. The resolution of the drama is in the punishment of the hero as the transgressor. His punishment, the condemnation of his hubris of incestuous-family relations, is the formal resolution of his arrogant, disrespectful, transgressive behavior.

The moral significance of the *Oedipus Rex* play is in correcting the antagonistic gender relations reported in the Greek Cosmogony where mothers undermine fathers in alliances with their offspring. This relation between domestic partners evolved from Cosmogony's antagonistic power struggles to cooperative relations upon the completion of the culture's Odyssey and several dramas like the one of *Oedipus Rex*. The culture shifted to cooperation in domestic relations and to mutual respect between men and women.

Formality dismisses the axiomatic or propositional method used in the debate on the descriptive explanation advanced by Freud on the Oedipus Complex, the universality of a sexually and aggressively driven unconscious. Propositional or axiomatic method has been the method of analysis that has characterized the debate on Genesis, as creationism versus evolution, religion versus science.

Both the explorations on the Oedipus Complex and on Genesis are methodologically incorrect as axiomatic arbitrary non relational pronouncements. The Formal Theory introduces the relational method, for the analysis of the process as a circumscribed periodic entity. This coincides with the Aristotelian dramatic totality as the origin of moral thought. It identifies what is universal in all stories as the formal correlation of six parts/emotions within a conflict resolving morality driven totality. Conflict resolution then is viewed as a psychological physiological sociological homeostatic natural science phenomenon. Simply said the unconscious seeks automatically the social adjustment of the individual.

Social adjustment, normative compliance, defines conflict resolution morality as originating in the scientific unconscious phenomenon. Morality is not determined by religions as normative nomothetic institutions but by the peace and justice-seeking unconscious. Religions have been generated by the unconscious need for social justice as normative revolutions, but their norms should not be referred to as the definitive statement of morality, as their norms become dated and their morality becomes immoral. Religions are normative institutions but their norms become outgrown by societal innovations seeking more inclusive concepts of justice.

The Science of Conflict Resolution studies how the unconscious mechanism predictably resolves conflicts by following certain science based equilibrial principles. It transforms passivity to activity, antagonism to cooperation and alienation to mutual respect. Morality is then in these formal operations. Conflict resolution is the morality driven process.

Moral Psychology

The Formal Theory reduces the unconscious into a natural science homeostatic physiological equilibrial phenomenon governed by the inner need of the individual to adjust to external or societal normative realities. The process of adjustment is reflected in the orderly structure of our associations, representing the organization of emotions from a conflict to its resolution.

Conflict resolution is the circumscribed entity beginning with a normative deviation and completed with normative compliance or normative change. This conceptualization of the unconscious explains behavior as predictable and as morality or normatively driven notion. Morality is a mental and also a natural science system of forces defining humans as justice-pursuing animals.

The Significance of the Moral Process

The conflict resolving process defines the nature of the psyche as an orderly periodic morality driven phenomenon abiding by the well-established laws of two natural science phenomena. Emotions are organized by the conflict resolution needs or by morality and are interdependent and inseparable as a syndrome of six role-states, the totality of the unconscious mental process. This process is the unit periodic spontaneous phenomenon, which operates as the compass steering the person to adapt to and alternatively to change the norms of the societal environment. This entity is the origin of moral behavior and of all religious institutions identifiable as particular ways of resolving conflict.

This entity is of great clinical significance as the syndromal organization of all mental states. It is significant because it reconciles the humanities: psychology with morality, and the sciences. It represents the unconscious as a homeostatic social adjustive physiological mechanism that has the measurable structures of the two natural science phenomena: the pendulum oscillation and the equilibrial scale.

The Moral Science differs radically from traditional psychology and religions by recognizing the unconscious as a scientifically fathomable unit entity integrating the realms of psychology and morality. The orderly and moral unconscious redefines the current theories of the unconscious. The rigorous conceptualization of the unconscious differs from the Freudian unconscious generating conflicts, driven by prohibited drives of sexuality and aggression, whose repression leads to neuroses. Psychoanalysis identified the process but conceiving it as amoral and as amorphous or erratic, not abiding by laws of nature.

The Unconscious is a Physiological and Sociological Homeostatic Phenomenon

The syndromal organization of emotions as a conflict resolution mechanism is the origin of all psychological and moral behavior. Conflicts are experienced upon an individual's normative deviation.

Normative structures generate personal conflicts, psychic tension, to the individual upon his/her normative deviation. The motivation to resolution stems from the need to reduce social and psychic tension or discomfort and experience relief upon normative conciliation. Relief of tension, as resolution is experienced as conflict energy is transformed to order, the pleasure of the rest state. The unconscious process is a homeostatic physiological mechanism reducing psychic and social tension through normative conciliation. This mechanism, as the inner need for mastery, cooperation and mutual respect, targets peace of mind as well as social justice.

The Unconscious is the Automatic Adjustment Response to a Normative Deviation
How do we explain the unconscious need for conflict resolution? Conflict, defined as deviation from a key norm, the rest state, represents the generation of psychic tension, which is perceived as pain. The conflict's resolution may be defined as the restoration of the rest state, the personal return to the norm experienced emotionally both as pleasure but also as reinforcement of moral order. This is achievable either through compliance to the norm or alternatively the revamping of the social norm.

The resolution represents the social or normative adjustment of the individual. The plot of stories reflects the unconscious evolving from a conflict to its resolution. As the universal structure of the process driven by the need or motivation for social adjustment, that is for moral behavior. The plot of stories reflects the organization of emotions as a homeostatic psychological mechanism generated by the need to preserve the rest state, continuity or stability, resisting deviant change. Free will is the escape from norms.

The social reality is a magnetic field and individuals moving within the field are subject to forces positioning them in orbits of social adjustment. Norms generate emotional gravity. This is the power of religions and civil laws structuring the social reality governing individual behavior. The free will is compromised by the power of norms. The individual finds a personal balance between deviating and conforming.

Contrasting Freud's versus Formal Theory's Definitions of the Unconscious
It is very important to comprehend that the unconscious motivation is morality driven, where morality is defined as normative conciliation. The new psychology is no longer amoral or agnostic, but it is not theistic either. On the contrary the Conflict Resolution Process is the unit of the Science of Conflict Resolution, the Moral Science. The key human motivation is not libido and thanatos but the need for conflict resolution. The case studies validate Formal Theory's assumption on the scientific moral nature of the unconscious.

The conflict resolution concept on the nature of the unconscious is different from Freud's several inconclusive conceptual models. The new unconscious integrates Freud's fragmented psychodynamic perspectives into a cohesive and meaningful natural science relational entity.

- Unlike the Freudian unconscious, the formal theoretical one is a natural science measurable entity, a dialectic/syndromal continuum of six emotions evolving predictably from a conflict to its resolution following three formal operations. The pleasure principle coincides with the need for reduction of psychic tension, the driving force for the process.

- The Freudian Oedipus complex identifying the unconscious motivation driven by instincts or drives for sexuality and aggression is fallacious. Freud's universal Oedipal Complex with its libidinal and aggressive motivations is contradicted by Formal Theory's conflict resolving moral and formalized unconscious.

- The Formal perspective counters the Oedipal complex by introducing the lifetime six role cyclic pattern of the father-son relationship repeated five times in the Greek Cosmogony as a six-part conflict resolution dialectic. This pattern is a dramatic process, beginning with a stressor followed by a transgression: hubris or arrogance as normative deviation, a father murdering a son, and ending with a compromise following one's punishment. The punished father curses his son to the same predicament that he in his turn be killed by his children.

- Freud's *structural model*, the descriptively defined triad of the id, ego and super ego find a psychodynamic integration in Formal Theory's cyclic six-role state entity: stress/response, anxiety/defense, and reversal/compromise. This natural science three cycle psychodynamic process as a periodic phenomenon is the alternative to Freud's fragmented psyche.

- The descriptive psychoanalytic *defense mechanisms* such as denial, projection, reaction formation and sublimation are accounted for by *the three formal relational operations* of the process as a systemic equilibrium guiding the mental experiences from a conflict to its resolution: sublimation.

- The vague Freudian *transference* is offset by the concepts of the innateness of *relational modalities* as alternative ways of resolving conflicts. These can be readily identified and precisely measured with the new assessment's personality inventory without the need for a laborious therapeutic relationship.

- Freud's identifying one's conflicts utilizing *the free associations generated on the couch* through long-term psychotherapy is replaced by Formal Theory's expeditious *projective creativity based self-assessment instrument*.

- Freud's *energy concepts of cathexis, catharsis and sublimation* are understood with Formal Theory's *mental process as energetic transformations*. Energy is conserved and transformed from chaos to order diminishing chaos or disorder by transforming entropy to negative entropy.

- Freud's theory of the *Oedipal dynamics determining religion as advanced in 'Moses and Monotheism' is countered by Formal Theory's understanding the unconscious need for conflict resolution as the psychological origin of religions*. Religions are viewed as motivated by the political task of resolving societal conflicts by improving social justice; their function is the normative restructuring of societies to alleviate public suffering as inequities.

Formal Theory's Hypotheses are Testable
All assumptions on the nature of the process merge into a new Epistemology, which considers the following:

- The unconscious is a periodic phenomenon abiding by the formulas of the Simple Harmonic Motion and the operations of the equilibrial scale. It is a natural science six-role state harmonic guided by three formal operations.

- Behavior's object of study is this unconscious formal organization of associations in any sample of creativity.

- The creative process is then a moral, meaningful, directional natural science phenomenon; is the object for the scientific analysis of behavior.

- The process is both a natural science and a universal moral or conflict resolution phenomenon.

- As both a scientific and moral order entity it reconciles the rigorous sciences with the humanities and transforms psychology into the Science of Conflict Resolution, the Moral Science.

The Exhibits of the Museum Of the Creative Process Validate the Process

It has been my objective to demonstrate the validity of Formal Theory's thesis on the nature of the unconscious in order to introduce the new conceptualization in behavior. Validation of the Formal Theory transforms it into the Moral Science, the Science of Conflict Resolution. This science then revamps psychology as morality driven and understands religions as psychologically generated normative institutions; it integrates them and advances the science as knowledge that may integrate the religions of the world hence heal the world from its disparate moral quandaries in conflict with each other.

Several approaches have been used to validate the Formal Theory into the exact Moral Science.

To support the thesis of the unconscious as a conflict resolution scientific phenomenon, I founded the Museum of the Creative Process. The art exhibits present art as evidence of science introducing the syndromal organization of emotions and of associations as a universal harmonic. The task of the museum is displaying exhibits illustrating the unconscious studying the creative process as a moral and scientific phenomenon. The exhibits are reproduced and discussed in the volume: Science Stealing the Fire of the Gods and Healing the World. They demonstrate the organization of the unconscious as a scientific conflict-resolving or moral order phenomenon attesting that the mind is predictable, orderly and moral. Establishing this entity contradicts the Freudian assumption that the unconscious is irrational, sexual and aggressive that is generating conflicts rather than resolving them.

There is a unifying element in all exhibits: the sine curve of the process. It integrates diversity into the orderly entity, a six part harmonic of the rollercoaster of emotions: *stress, response, anxiety, defense, reversal and compromise*, the conflict resolution totality. The exhibits also show how this cyclic transformation is guided by three formal operations: *Conflict as passivity, antagonism, and alienation is transformed to resolution as activity, cooperation and mutual respect.*

This harmonic is the mental heartbeat. It is the new way of looking at art, at associations, at metaphors, at religions, to detect continuity and meaning as the dialectic progression to order. The person unconsciously seeks a homeostatic adjustment to stress. The individual oscillates emotionally three times in the magnetic field of norms, from a normative deviation to a normative conciliation, the state of rest. Analysis of the harmonic shows that this unconscious is an equilibrial phenomenon abiding by the laws of physics and logic.

This harmonic order, the organizing force of our feelings corresponds to a formula. It is a formula true for any value of its variables. It is the formula of the plot and the moral of all stories. It is the unit of the social sciences introducing order into the realm of psychology; it represents the syndromal organization of emotions following the alternative paths of three formal operations.

The process's universality affirms that this entity is a purely natural science system, graphically portrayable and measurable. The syndromal organization of emotions leads to four relational modalities, based on the variation between passivity and activity, cooperation and antagonism and also modulated quantitatively by psychic tension, conflict, along the distinctions of alienation versus mutual respect.

This concept is of extraordinary significance. It presents the human mind striving for reduction of conflict, peace, rest, justice, as the driving motivational force of the individual and also of humanity. This entity manifested as the familiar plot and moral of all stories integrates meaningfully parts, be those the canvases of an artist and the religions of the world, into a unified continuum, which is also a natural science measurable entity. This moral and measurable unconscious totally revamps the way we understand psychology, believe religions as revealed truths and deliver education and therapy. Each of the five exhibits serves a complementary function. The importance of the exhibits is that they demonstrate this order as the integrative paradigm, as the unit of the social sciences, making behavior into an exact science, the Science of Conflict Resolution or the Moral Science.

The Scientific Concept of the Process is Illustrated and Demonstrated with the Art Exhibits of the Museum of the Creative Process
The process is identified as a scientific phenomenon in the Metaphoria Murals, the Gorski Retrospective and the Wizard of Oz Panels.

The **Metaphoria Murals** feature the six-role process unfolding on six tiles. The emotions are shown to evolve following the three formal operations. The first mural presents three creation stories describing with three different metaphors the six-step conflict resolution process. The third mural presents how the Ten Commandments correspond to the three formal operations guiding our unconscious to four alternative conflict resolutions, the relational modalities, and how these vary from culture to culture and person to person.

The **Gorski Retrospective** studies the formal organization of symbolic languages and shows how the process integrates the lifetime canvases into units of conflict resolution of increasingly abstract spirituality. Each phase leads to a redefinition of how to achieve peace of mind: from political justice, to religious beliefs and then to spirituality and finally assertiveness of the individual in spite of one's limitations.

The **Wizard of Oz Panels** illustrate the scientific interpretation of four key metaphors, each corresponding to a social science disciplines: epistemology, diagnosis, transformation and morality. The exhibit integrates the disciplines into the comprehensive scientific Moral Science.

The scientific concept's relevance in demystifying, integrating and reconciling the religions of the world is presented in the sculptural trail through the history of love.
It retraces the history of religions as partial discoveries of science, identifying the conflict resolution principles, one at a time. Religions according to the Formal Theory evolved as charismatic individuals discovering alternative ways of resolving conflict, which then were espoused by a community evolved as the cultural norms. Cultural religions and norms evolved regulating domestic relations. Religions evolved as discoveries of the process increasing in fairness of domestic role relations and in the abstract definition on the nature of gods. In doing so religions discovered partially the universal harmonic order, but ritualized and deified it. The trail integrates the epics of the goddess and the scriptures of the one god, also the ideologies of the 20th century as formally interrelated societal conflict resolutions dealing with the need to settle family and intergroup conflicts in an equitable or just manner. The Moral Science clarifying the divine as the formal and physical understanding of the unconscious process completes the mission of religions by integrating them into the exact Moral Science.

The clinical value of the concept is illustrated in the case study exhibit. Seven murals, presents case studies illustrating how tapping creativity leads to self-discovery as a complete program of emotional education. Case studies utilizing the self-assessment instrument, the Conflict Analysis Battery, validate the theory and demonstrate that we have a valid and reliable user-friendly psycho-assessment (see volume six).

Chapter Two

The Qualifications of the Unconscious as Four Relational Modalities: Syndromal Wellness Diagnostic Categories

Diagnoses Qualify the Natural Science Unconscious as a Relational Syndromal Mechanism
The unconscious as a physiological processor of tension/energy is a process that converts conflict energy into emotional and social adjustment or personal growth. The unconscious self-adjustment process, conflict resolution / moral order system propels the individual one directionally to increased inner order transforming stress energy into internalized and also externally reinforced organization along a series of independent conflict resolution syndromes.

A new personality typology examines the range of relational systemic or syndromal formal alternative responses to stress. These vary along the formal distinctions of passivity versus activity and cooperation versus antagonism. The intensity of these responses is addressed by a third dichotomy, alienation versus mutual respect.

Relational Modalities as Wellness Diagnostic Categories
The Formal Theory introduced four alternative ways of resolving conflict as wellness syndromal diagnoses. These are the relational modalities: two dominance, cooperative and antagonistic modalities complemented by two subordinacy alternatives: cooperative and antagonistic modes of relating. These formal distinctions identify a simple personality typology.

The wellness diagnoses are syndromes of behaviors and emotions that explain the psychodynamic development of most psychopathologies. The case studies validate this set of four alternative syndromal ways of resolving conflict introduced as wellness diagnoses. A personality inventory identifies the modalities and also makes a quantitative distinction, psychic tension, as unresolved conflicts leading to increases of the psychic tension experienced as pathology leading potentially to decompensation of the wellness state.

The relational diagnostic categories are useful in predicting the type of emotional responses. The wellness personality types are of importance because they determine the nature of alternative relational adjustment profiles. Decompensation of the wellness state can lead to distinct patterns of psychopathology and it is important that people recognize the pathologies and their respective therapeutic interventions to restore efficiently the state of wellness. Psychotherapy consists in determining the relational modalities diagnosis using creativity for self discovery, to evolve insights into his/her relational make up and the requisite approaches in managing power appropriately.

Thus the formal operations as principles of conflict resolution lead to detecting a new wellness range of formally interrelated diagnostic categories pertaining to wellness but also accounting for psychopathology. These offer the etiological explanation of illness in that the syndromal organization clarifies the psychodynamic formulation of psychological and pathological conditions. Pathology occurs as the psychic tension rises under stress and the emotional reserves are exhausted. The wellness syndromes may decompensate and manifest as distinct patterns of psychopathology.

The Syndromal Nature of Relational Modalities

The sequence of the conflict resolution unconscious manifests clinically as a syndrome of interrelated emotions and behaviors. These correspond to the six role states. This sequence of six role states may be reduced to the formal variations of one key activity that may unfold intra-psychically as thoughts or associations and interpersonally as a system of reciprocal interactions. Syndromes then consist of the constellation of the six formally interrelated role states as emotions and behaviors bound together as a perfect totality, a relational pattern, elicited upon dealing with a stressor. Measuring personality targets first, identifying this entity as a relational modality and second, as a symbolic system of the formal inclinations of one key action.

Relational modalities are six role-emotional syndromes, sociological psychological constellations. They are systemically interrelated choices of power position as social deviations incurring balancing psychological forces, as emotional corrective correlates. All these emotions and actions are in formal and systemic relation to each other.

Syndromes are emotional and behavioral constellations existing as circumscribed patterns, consisting of six role states: stress, response, anxiety, defense reversal and compromise guided by three formal operations. The six role state emotional continuum predictably unfolds upon any stressor as associations in one's mind as well as interpersonal exchanges. The associations and interactions within a story may be viewed as constituting the six component syndromal continuum. In their intrapsychic and interpersonal unfolding syndromes constitute psychological sociological self-fulfilling entities. Hence syndromes are not a single emotion but a sequence, a rollercoaster of emotions and behaviors due to a particular attitude or way of engaging the environment leading to specific predictable outcomes.

The Function of the Syndromal Structure of Emotions

The function of the unconscious process is in converting conflict or chaos, displeasure, maladjustment, psychic tension, to order as rest, adjustment, and reduction of psychic tension. The oscillations, driven by psychic adjustment needs, are guided by three of the four formal equilibrial operations seeking relief of tension. Passivity is converted to its reciprocal, activity, antagonism to its opposite, cooperation, and alienation to its correlative: mutual respect. We conclude then that the unconscious is a natural science conflict resolution or moral/formal order equilibrial phenomenon that has energetic physical and formal relational dimensions allowing its qualitative and quantitative measurement.

The new diagnoses of wellness understand psychopathology purely psychodynamically in the context of increased psychic tension affecting wellness relational diagnoses. The formal distinctions understand clinical symptoms as generated by relational intensity leading to particular disturbances of wellness. The relational diagnoses entail interventions on behaviors for the management of emotions and the automatic reduction of symptoms. Of course we recognize the medical nature of certain major psychopathologies independently of the psychodynamic make up of illness.

Contrasting Formal Theory's Wellness Relational Modalities with Diagnostic Statistical Manual V's Mental Illnesses

The concept of diagnosis in the realm of behavior is about identifying predictable behavioral emotional entities, their etiology or pathogenesis and their treatment for the restoration of wellness. There has been a trend in the medicalization of mental diagnoses, a move away from psychodynamic formulations, and a shift toward chemotherapeutic rather than relational therapies. The diagnostic philosophy favored by contemporary psychiatry, codified in the Diagnostic Statistical Manual, DSM, is establishing mental diagnoses of illness as clusters of clinical symptoms, preferably recognizing a neurobiological causation and amenable to a most appropriate chemotherapy.

The formal theoretical perspective strongly opposes this trend of diagnosis and of therapeutic interventions. It places emphasis on the psychodynamic understanding of wellness and illness as alternative ways of resolving conflict. It identifies a set of four syndromal wellness diagnostic categories that also account for psychopathology and psychotherapeutic interventions as appropriate power management attitude changes.

The Formal Theory innovates in the area of diagnosis introducing wellness syndromal diagnostic categories, which are predictive, psychodynamic, accounting for pathogenesis, psychopathology and psychotherapy.

The Formal Theory's set of wellness personality types differs from the illness diagnoses of the DSM V's identified as symptom clusters. The diagnostic manual does not recognize wellness diagnoses focusing on illnesses instead. DSM V identifies illnesses without psychodynamic analysis of emotions and behaviors. This methodological position medicalizes psychology by recognizing illness as clusters of symptoms and attributing these problems to chemical disorders and brain pathology. The relational modalities diagnostic categories challenge the illness-based model of the Diagnostic Statistical Manual, DSM V. The current diagnostic distinctions identify clinical symptoms without comprehending their generation and potential elimination through psychodynamic causality. This is the significance in the change of diagnostic perspectives.

The Genetic Origin of Modalities, Pathogenesis and Treatment of Relational Modalities

The public needs to know this personality typology as the diagnoses determine the personal emotional strengths and weaknesses in interpersonal relationships potentially leading to minor and major psychopathologies.

We recognize relational modalities as genetically transmitted and determined personality types. They manifest upon the beginning of one's life. Individuals are born with their relational modalities like computers bundled with their software. We speculate that the cooperative and antagonistic qualifications are environmentally and culturally determined; we do not know the level of hereditary transmission of the cooperative and antagonistic distinctions.

The Four Formal Relational Categories Identify Wellness and Illness
The typology is determined by characterizations of formal alternative ways of resolving conflicts dependent on the three relational operations transforming conflict to resolutions. Three operations determine the formal range of relational modalities. Passivity is transformed to activity, antagonism to cooperation and alienation to mutual respect. According to how the person resolves conflict along the three formal operations we distinguish four relational modalities. The third dimension pertains to each one addressing the intensity of unresolved conflict as psychic tension or neuroticism. The modalities unfold as dialectic sequences of conflict resolution, as syndromes. We identify clinical variations qualifying wellness, while allowing a dynamic understanding of illness.

The distinctions of modalities provide alternative clinical wellness and illness profiles along the dichotomies of passivity versus activity, and cooperation versus antagonism. We identify four diagnostic categories, the syndromes of dominance and subordinacy with the subcategories of cooperation and antagonism. Nosological distinctions are made along the same modalities, compounded by the third relational operation of alienation versus mutual respect or affiliation, which pertains to the psychic tension or distress level.

The same typology, four relational categories apply in the formal analysis of cultures. Relational diagnosis detects the syndromal organization of emotions and behaviors as manifestations of the unconscious equilibrial, homeostatic syndromal response.

Four Alternative Cultural or Normative Ways of Dealing with Temptation, the Apple as Symbol of a Desirable Object. Judea represents the dominant cooperative paradigm, Greece the dominant antagonistic counterpart. India represents the submissive cooperative modality and Mexico the submissive antagonistic disposition.

The Four Relational Modalities
Syndromal sequences vary as conflict resolutions; they differ qualitatively along the three guiding formal operations: reciprocity, negation and correlation. These equilibrial operations vary in determining the individual's responses along the range of four relational modalities. There is always an equilibrium between the change inflicted by the identity operation and the three operations offsetting the stress: reciprocity, negation and correlation.

Accordingly the formal operation of reciprocity determines two alternative responses: the dominant and submissive relating; the formal operation of negation qualifies each one of the two along the opposite directions of cooperation and antagonism. The change in the operation of correlation corresponds to alienation, high versus mutual respect with low psychic tension.

Thus we recognize four relational modalities, dominance and subordinacy and their cooperative and antagonistic variations. These four entities represent four diagnostic categories, the personality types. The third formal operation, correlation, reflecting how the individual relates to the public, as alienated versus mutually respectful allows a quantitative measurement of the individual's psychic tension, reflecting the intensity of conflict experienced as maladjustment or neuroticism. Psycic tension is measured by the mental status scale, pertaining to the intensity of conflict experienced. This variable is independent of the four relational modalities. While operations may be viewed as qualitative distinctions, they are also modified to reflect intensity of responses, as the quantitative determination of dominance, submission, cooperation, antagonism and psychic tension.

Assessment and Graphic Representation of the Modalities
The nature of the conflict resolution process is identified by two types of measurement: first, by the sequence of three formal operations; second by the syndromal condition consisting of a six role-state chain of emotional events. The case studies provide relational distinctions but also the syndromal six-part unfolding of the personal pattern.

Identifying the psychic and the social system with a natural science entity confers to behavior the constructs and the formulas of the natural science SHM and scale phenomena and allows the graphic representation of the process as a universal harmonic. The harmonic's cross-section represents the individual within the normative social system; within the periphery of this sociogram we place the interacting individuals portrayed as ellipses in reciprocal orbital positions.

The Three Relational Operations as Dichotomies of Syndromal Dynamics
Three alternative formal operations were detected leading the mental process from a conflict to its resolution along three relational pathways providing three dichotomies of personality relational characteristics. These are measurable providing clear diagnostic categories for the characterization of personality. The four types are attributed to two relational alternatives: the reciprocal dominance versus subordinacy and the opposites of cooperation versus antagonism. Intensity of unresolved conflict,

quantitative variations of conflict, are attributed to the correlative distinction: alienation versus mutual respect. The modalities and the psychic tension are measurable through the relational inventory test, which also includes a mental status questionnaire. The formal distinctions pertain to the normative deviations of the individual in the social system. They also pertain to cultural relational choices.

These diagnostic categories are of great predictive value, identifying strengths and weaknesses of the person, health and potential pathologies. The assessment information is pertinent to the person as self-knowledge and accordingly preparing the individual to cope with adversity by knowing her responses.

The Graphic Representation of Social and Emotional Dynamics of Relational Modalities

Submissive Cooperative	Submissive Antagonistic	Dominant Cooperative	Dominant Antagonistic
Clockwise Directed to Powerlessness	Counterclockwise Directed to Powerlessness	Clockwise Towards Power	Counterclockwise Towards Power
Hope for love	Hostility	Trust	Distrust paranoia

TWO FORMAL OPERATIONS LEAD TO FOUR ALTERNATIVE WAYS OF RESOLVING CONFLICT

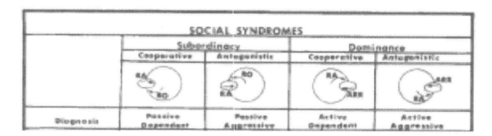

THE FOUR RELATIONAL MODALITIES AS SYNDROMES: THE DIAGNOSTIC CATEGORIES OF WELLNESS

Relational modality Evaluation Scale
Submissive Cooperative Syndrome

Role model: Scarecrow, Charlie Brown

Relational characteristics, pleaser, accepts norms, gets depressed, develops hostility, escapism, dependencies

Assessment questions

Compassion, Considerateness, Respect for Limits ....I respect and obey rules and regulations

- **Cooperation, Trust** ....I never express my anger. People think that I am very modest
- **Recessivity**....I am a non-assertive person
- In my relationships, I am usually dominated by others
- I am not rebellious, I find it futile arguing, I do things to please others rather than myself

The judge's relational modality and his Transparent Mask covering his feeling like a lamb

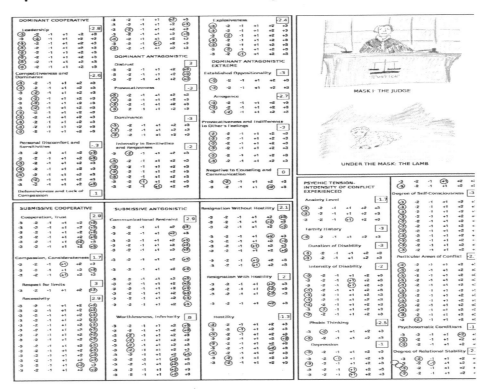

The metaphor tests cross-validating the relational diagnosis

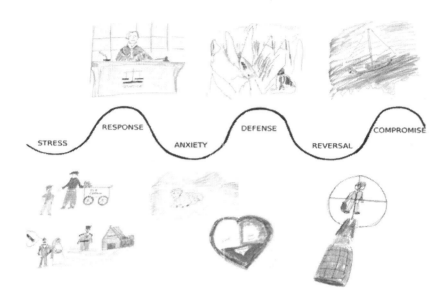

Submissive Antagonistic syndrome

Role model: Tin Man
Relational characteristics
- **Communicational Restraint, Worthlessness, Inferiority**

Assessment questions
- I don't know how to express myself without upsetting people
- I keep my anger under control. I don't let myself fly off the handle, I hold everything in
- I brood about things that bother me, If I have a complaint, it takes a long time for me to bring it up
- Frequently, I am mad and I don't let anyone know it, I am an extremely private person
- People don't care about what I think and how I feel

Dominant Cooperative Syndrome

Role model: Dorothy

Relational characteristics, challenges norms and rules

- **Leadership Competitiveness and Dominance**
- **Personal Discomfort and Sensitivities, anxiety disorders, performance anxiety, scared.**
- **Defensiveness and Compassion**

Assessment questions

- I get my way more than I give into others
- I am a dominant person, I have a comment all the time, I am easily frustrated when I don't get my way

Dominant Antagonistic Syndrome

Role model: The Cowardly lion

Relational characteristics

- **Distrust Provocativeness Dominance Intensity In Sensitivities and Responses Explosiveness**

Assessment questions

- I hardly ever compromise
- You are wise not to trust people
- I have a tendency to provoke people
- I attack people with little or no provocation

The Significance of the Syndromal Diagnosis
The four relational personality modalities are wellness distinctions, not stigmatizing psychiatric diagnoses. The relational modalities are genetically determined qualifiers of wellness. Yet these wellness states account for psychopathology, illness. The formal structure of the syndromes establishes a cause effect interrelation of emotions and behaviors. This personality typology clarifies individual emotional perceptions and distortions, as well as choice of behavioral responses. The formal connection of emotions intensified by stressors explains pathogenesis.

Thus the diagnostic categories account for the etiological formulation of pathology. Dominance may lead to anxiety and defensiveness, while submissiveness may lead to depression and hostility. This interrelation accounts for psychopathology as the intensification or polarization of relational responses, defensiveness and hostility, experienced intra-psychically and interpersonally. The psychic tension unlike the rest of the inventory generates clinical symptoms as intensification of wellness relational states.

The Psycho-Educational Function of the Relational Diagnoses: The Possibility for the Person to Initiate Changes
The relational diagnoses explain experiences, behaviors and emotions, wellness and symptoms, along the syndromal organization of emotions. They place the individual as able to make choices determining her/his emotional condition. The DSM illness diagnoses instead present the individual as helpless, victim of a chemical imbalance, or a brain anomaly and present the solution in medical management of one's condition. The success of insight and power management of one's relational condition through the self-assessment approach informs the person how to deal with one's emotional experiences by managing her power.

Self-awareness of the relational diagnostic categories eliciting symptoms reduces the perception of helplessness and passivity in dealing with one's emotions. The patient/and well person, who realizes the syndromal interconnection of emotions, will assume responsibility for the experience and will seek deliberately to correct it. Relational diagnoses entail responsibility to make relational changes to reduce symptoms. Self-awareness of one's relational modality entails the individual becoming responsible for her/his emotional and social experiences. To reduce symptoms and conflicts one must modify one's attitude, his/her relational disposition. The aware person seeks to address the social interactional power-managing component affecting one's state of distress.

Syndromes, Relational Modality Diagnostic Categories, and Healing
Recognizing one's relational pattern explains the personal experiences, as emotions as well as symptoms, constituting parts of a totality, the relational modality syndrome. Dominant people are vulnerable to become both overactive and also anxious, while submissive people readily repress their feelings and evolve hostility and depression.

One's sensitivities, actions, reactions, anxieties, defenses, reversals and resolutions or compromises are components of the syndrome. The relational diagnosis connects disparate personal and interpersonal experiences; it makes them meaningful by explaining their connection as syndromally interrelated emotions, defenses, reversals, following the underlying pattern of the six role states.

This structure of emotions entails the direction for making responsible changes in dealing with stressors, averting helplessness, while assuming corrective intervention in power-management. Relational diagnosis provides the direction of emotional behavioral changes in terms of what one can do to change one's emotional adjustment.

The Sociological Result of Conflict Resolutions
The rest state is a spiritual, pleasurable state. The psychological accomplishment has sociological impact. Resolutions from personal conflict support social norms or alternatively question them. From personal discoveries of rest they may evolve to social celebrated norms. The emotional creation of order and its periodic occurrence may have inspired the concept of Genesis as a six-part event. Creativity leading to resolutions may have inspired the notion of Creation as an act of God and Sabbath, the seventh day as the day of rest.

Illustration of the Modalities in the Case Study Volume
In the volume of case studies featuring the Conflict Analysis Battery as the diagnostic and therapeutic interventions we differentiate cases along the relational syndromal distinctions of dominance and submissiveness and how these differ in their respective social and psychological adjustments.

All case studies validate the relational distinctions combining the inventory and the projective tests. The two types of tests cross-validate each other demonstrating the correctness of the formal relational distinctions. The case studies report on the assessment protocols clearly identify the relational modalities as four major wellness diagnostic categories. While results show that a person may score high at several modalities, usually individuals score high on one set of scales score low on the reciprocal ones. Dominant individuals are not submissive and vice versa. The testing rediscovers the five factors of psychological assessments as relational diagnoses. The fifth factor corresponding to alienation versus mutual respect accounts for intensity of conflict coincides with neuroticism.

Psychology and Pathology of Relational Modalities
The case studies are organized under the headings of two key distinctions, the alternative personality types of dominance and subordinacy. Nuances of cooperation and antagonism are discussed where appropriate. The two segments present the characteristics of the major alternative modalities. Dominance and subordinacy determine a person's responses; they have not been identified by the DSM classifications. Freud identified relationship issues as transference but he did not identify relational diagnostic categories. Jung identified them as extraversion versus introversion. The Formal Theory identifies the relational modalities as genetically determined personality syndromes, and introduces their measurement and modification with the Conflict Analysis Battery.

- In the dominance cases individuals assume leadership roles. They also act out impulsively, manipulatively, occasionally conduct antisocial and limit testing behaviors. Emotionally they experience anger, arrogance, but also on the reverse side they experience fears of reversal of roles as anxiety, paranoia, guilt, leading to performance anxiety, and social phobias.

- The submissive individuals present relational perseverance versus withdrawal, resilience under stress alternatively escapism, acting out behaviors such as dependencies, eroticism and eating disorders, self-mutilation and hostile acting out.

The two major types of personality diagnosis are complementary compatible opposites; and as such they pair themselves in social systems such as the spousal self-selection. We have a very typical case study of a marital dyad reflecting this self-selection. While this constellation manifests in wellness, there is potential pathology under stress. Such relations decompensate leading to pathologies. In this case study characteristically dominance turns to violence and submissiveness to escapism, anxiety and depression. The case study of the judge, case #1, in the section of subordinacy, describes the compensation of the spousal self-selection in more detail.

Chapter Three

Measuring the Unconscious with The Conflict Analysis Battery (CAB):
A Didactic, Diagnostic and Therapeutic Self-Assessment

Introduction

The Conflict Analysis Battery, is a theory-based self-assessment; it measures objectively the unconscious process with two complementary instruments: an inventory and a set of projectives leading to the identification of a test taker's relational modality and its unfolding along the six role state syndromal process.

- The battery's personality inventory measures the formal relational dimensions of the modalities and the psychic tension of the process.

- The battery's projectives, the metaphor creation tests, identify the syndromal unfolding of the process as six formally interrelated emotions, the mental oscillation, predictably evolving from a conflict, the stress state, to its resolution, as the compromise one.

- Insights are generated in the testing process, which elicit corrective consequences spelled out by the test-taker. The test taker can measure this unconscious utilizing the self-assessment and can identify the changes required to alleviate symptoms and related suffering.

- Interpretations by therapists are certainly welcome and useful for further understanding one's testing and the study of one's mental process. The assessment simply helps the person through the analysis of samples of creativity to become conscious of the unconscious and to assume responsibility in rectifying the unconscious automatism by resolving conflicts deliberately following the three rational principles of conflict resolution: mastery, cooperation and mutual respect, the innate moral values.

Contrasting Conflict Analysis Battery with Traditional Assessments

- In great contrast to widely used instruments, it is a theory based self-assessment that helps the test taker to identify both her/his relational modality and its syndromal unfolding manifested as the orderly six-role states bound into a dramatic continuum.

- Current psychological diagnostic instruments identify traits, which do not explain psychodynamically the pathogenetic origin of symptoms or serve a therapeutic function for the test taker. The CAB identifies patterns and also generates insights and directives for changes.

- The focus on unrelated traits is exemplified with the statistical analysis of all assessments identifying five factors of personality held together not relationally but simply with acronyms; one of them is *Ocean* for the five factors of statistical analysis of all assessments. The letters correspond to Openness to Experience, Conscientiousness, Extraversion, Agreeableness, and Neuroticism.

- The Battery's diagnostic entities, the relational modalities and the psychic tension, are equivalent to the *ocean* five factors of unrelated clusters of traits. The difference is that four of the factors correspond to the four interrelated relational modalities, while the fifth factor identifies neuroticism corresponding to the psychic tension scale.

Formal Theory's Conflict Analysis Battery identifies patterns whereas traditional psychological assessments identify traits.

- Openness corresponds to the dominant cooperative relational modality

- Conscientiousness to the submissive antagonistic relational modality

- Extraversion to the dominant antagonistic modality

- Agreeableness to the submissive cooperative relational modality

- Neuroticism corresponds to the psychic tension scale.

The Conflict Analysis Battery identifies patterns as relational modalities examining the inventory responses along the three formal dichotomies and also along the six role-states process of their syndromal unfolding as alternative conflict resolution processes. The three formal dichotomies are the measurable dimensions of the unconscious process. These are the dichotomies of passivity/activity, antagonism/cooperation and alienation versus mutual respect. These identify four formally interrelated conflict resolution alternatives: the relational modalities, diagnostic categories of wellness, and the psychic tension corresponding to intensity of conflicts identifying psychopathology as qualification of wellness.

- The inventory is diagnostic. The observer or test taker can at a glance identify one's relational modality diagnosis. The inventory also measures psychic tension identifying the degree of illness or alienation.

- The projective metaphor construction protocols are therapeutic and validate the six-role state unfolding of the process from a conflict to its resolution.

- The completion of the battery tests is shown in this volume to be both diagnostic and therapeutic for the test taker. The metaphor tests elicit cathartic emotional responses. The diagnostic relational alternatives illustrated in the inventory and the metaphors elicit behavioral changes.

- The combination of cognitive information, self-discovery, and observation of relational differences compound the educational and therapeutic value of the assessment.

- The assessment is self-diagnostic and self-healing; it is both an emotional experience and a cognitive intellectual one. The assessment validates the theory and demonstrates the personal relevance of the abstract concepts as test takers understand the theoretical material and benefit emotionally and intellectually from the assessment. Test-takers upon completion of the assessment feel emotionally gratified by the insights generated by the experience.

- The outcome of the testing is a therapeutic emotional experience diminishing the need for a therapist. It shifts the burden of delivering this moral education from doctors and clergy to the skills of educators.

The History of Assessment Technologies
Psychological distinctions about personality types evolved through the ages from descriptive concrete to abstract formal parameters. Typologies of personality originally attributed differences to biological factors such as elements of nature: earth, water, air, temperatures variables: hot and cold, then the humors of the body.

Quotations from Wikipedia 2013 (in Italics)
*Galen mapped the Four Temperaments to a matrix of **hot/cold** and **dry/wet.** The sanguine temperament showed quick, impulsive and relatively brief reactions. (hot/wet; air). The choleric temperament manifested a short response time-delay, but the response was sustained for a relatively long time. (hot/dry; fire). The melancholic temperament exhibited a long response time-delay, and the response was sustained at length, if not, seemingly, permanently. The phlegmatic temperament was characterized by a longer response-delay, but the response was also short-lived. (cold/wet; water)*

Distinctions evolved to the abstractions of formal factors such as passivity and activity, cooperation and antagonism. These distinctions remained isolated from each other and evolved to become descriptive and dividing personality typologies to multiple complex categories. The Formal Theory has introduced three formal distinctions recognizing them as the system of interrelated equilibrial operations tied together with the Kleinian formula of the set theory. These distinctions represent a turning point in abstract methodology; they lead to a set of clear distinctions in developing a perfect personality typology.

In 1928, William Moulton Marston identified four primary emotions, each with an initial feeling tone of either pleasantness or unpleasantness. This led to his viewing people's behavior along two axes, with their attention being either "passive" or "active", depending on the individual's perception of his or her environment as either "favorable" or "antagonistic". By placing the axes at right angles, four quadrants form with each describing a behavioral pattern:

- *Dominance, which produces activity in an antagonistic environment; with a feeling of unpleasantness until stimulus is acted upon*

- *Compliance, which produces passivity in an antagonistic environment; with a feeling of unpleasantness until stimulus is reconciled*

- *Inducement, which produces activity in a favorable environment; with a feeling of pleasantness increasing as interaction increases*

- *Submission, which produces passivity in a favorable environment; with a feeling of pleasantness increasing as yielding increases*

*This would be further developed in the 1970s by John G. Geier [6] into the **DiSC assessment System**, which grades individual scales of **"Dominance"**, **"Influence"**, **"Steadiness"**, and **"Conscientiousness"**. By now, it would be classified in terms of the two factors; consisting of pairs of Extroverted or "Assertive" aspects (D, I), Introverted or "Passive" aspects (S, C), Task-oriented or "Controlled" aspects (D, C) and social or "Open" aspects (I, S).*

There is an overlap of the four DiSC categories and the relational modalities. Neuroticism is missing but the DiSC categories are descriptive. They are not viewed as formally interrelated.

Evolution of Considerations on the Unconscious as a Measurable Process
It is interesting to explore the evolution of distinctions characterizing the mental operations attributed to the unconscious. Freud's theories promoted understanding the unconscious with a variety of models.

- First he suggested the unconscious propelled by biological drives as libidinal desires and aggression. The early concept led to the recognition of three developmental phases of personality: oral, anal, phallic.

- Later he proposed the unconscious as the conflicts among a three-part structural entity: the id, ego and super ego. This later model led to observing transference issues addressing interpersonal relations.

- Freud's theories recognized the power of the unconscious and of personality dynamic distinctions but his theoretical models neither led to a personality typology nor to an assessment instrument.

- Freud's theories influenced the development by his disciples of psychodynamic personality typologies and of assessments instruments measuring them. His followers distinguished relational categories and evolved a number of assessment instruments. Jung described extraversion versus introversion, Horney identified categories of 'going away, inside, and towards people'; eventually such distinctions led to the enneogram assessment for the identification of measurable personality types.

- Timothy Leary's interpersonal check-list identified one formal relational distinction, the reciprocals of passivity and activity, and the non formal distinctions of love and hate, which are descriptive, rather than being identified relationally as opposites.

- Keirsey evolved formal alternative distinctions such as passive versus active, cooperative versus antagonistic, but these formal distinctions were contaminated by non formal ones such as functionality of people for work settings, sensing versus intuition, thinking versus feeling. Also he did not address the neuroticism factor.

Carl Jung in the early 20th century introduced the four factors that would become a part of the later MBTI, and these included extroversion/introversion, E/I, sensing and intuition, and thinking/feeling, which would be correlated to Agreeableness, with Judging-Perceiving roughly as Conscientiousness.

Keirsey also divided his temperaments by "Role-Informative"/"Role Directive" to form eight "intelligence types"; and finally by E/I, to yield the 16 types of the MBTI. It was when his former student Berens, paired the latter two factors separately that she yielded her Interaction Styles, discussed above. Keirsey also divided the intelligence types by I/E into "roles of interaction"[6].

Formal Theory's Differentiating Wellness From Illness Utilizing a Third Relational Distinction
Hans Eysenck (1916–1997) was one of the first psychologists to analyze personality differences using a psycho-statistical method (factor analysis), and his research led him to believe that temperament is biologically based. In his book Dimensions of Personality (1947) he paired Extraversion (E) which was "the tendency to enjoy positive events", especially social ones with Neuroticism (N) which was the tendency to experience negative emotions, and By pairing the two dimensions, Eysenck noted how the results were similar to the four ancient temperaments.

- *High N, High E = Choleric*

- *High N, Low E = Melancholy (also called "Melancholic")*

- *Low N, High E = Sanguine*

- *Low N, Low E = Phlegmatic*

He later added a third dimension psychoticism, resulting in his "P-E-N" three factor model of personality.

Eysenck identified factors of neuroticism and psychoticism seeking to make the distinction between well personality and illness. He was contaminating qualitative distinctions with quantitative parameters but was a pioneer in the personality taxonomy of the third formal distinction, the one we use in the Formal Theory as 'alienation versus mutual respect'; we introduce into typology a relational dimension that explains pathology as unresolved conflict, corresponding to psychic tension.

*The California Psychological Inventory's **CPI 260 Instrument** also has similar scales, of **Initiates action, Confident in social situations** versus **Focuses on inner life, Values own privacy**; and **Rule-favoring, Likes stability, Agrees with others** versus **Rule-questioning, has personal, value system, often disagrees with others** and the four "lifestyles" **Leader, Supporter, Innovator**, and **Visualizer**.*

The Thomas Kilmann Conflict Mode Instrument (TKI) used a version of this with "Assertiveness" and "Cooperativeness" as the two factors, also leading to a fifth mode:

- *Competing, (assertive, uncooperative)*

- *Avoiding (unassertive, uncooperative)*

- *Accommodating (unassertive, cooperative)*

- *Collaborating (assertive, cooperative)*

- *Compromising (intermediate assertiveness and cooperativeness).*

References

1. ^ http://webspace.ship.edu/cgboer/neurophysio.html
2. ^ (Evidence-based Research in Complementary and Alternative Medicine I: History Francesco Chiappelli, Paolo Prolo and Olivia S. Cajulis)[1]
3. ^ Kagan, Jerome (1998), Galen's Prophecy: Temperament In Human Nature, New York: Basic Books, ISBN 0-465-08405-2
4. ^ http://www.greekmedicine.net/b_p/Inherent_Temperament.html
5. ^ http://sun2.science.wayne.edu/~tpartrid/Manuscripts/HEETemperament1.25.02.doc
6. ^ http://www.keirsey.com/brains.aspx#
7. ^ Lutz, Peter L. (2002). The Rise of Experimental Biology: An Illustrated History. Humana Press. p. 60. ISBN 0896038351. OCLC 47894348.
8. ^ Why You Act the Way You Do, ch.7: "Uses of Temperament in the Workplace"

The Creative Process as a Measurable Phenomenon
The object for the scientific study of behavior has been identified clearly by the Formal Theory as the creative process, a natural science periodic phenomenon that has formal distinctions. The conflict-resolving unconscious is an operational equilibrial system. The process, the unit order of the social sciences, is a periodic formal and energetic transformation in the sense that emotional reactions are:

- Formally interrelated; and that

- They represent real energetic physical entities.

The unconscious then is measurable as the equilibrial balance of the trays of a scale and as the oscillations of a pendulum ball. These mechanical equivalents give to the creative process their scientific constructs and formulas. The mental order is measurable like any physical entity that has both formal and physical dimensions. The assessment measures these dimensions.

The Formal Theory's conceptualization of the unconscious introduced a purely natural science, formal relational mechanism with a moral or conflict resolution adjustive function.

This definition is in line with Aristotle's Teleion Holon, but goes beyond, as a periodic phenomenon with the scientific structure of energetic transformations, characterized by conservation of energy, and the moral directional end coinciding with reduction of psychic tension. The Formal Theory made this entity measurable by introducing into Aristotle's perfect universe the Simple Harmonic Motion's three-oscillation-harmonic, the six-role process and also by introducing the four formal equilibrial operations of the scale. The restoration of the equilibrium of the trays of the scale guides the mind to the upgrading of the emotional energy upon the conflict's resolution.

This conflict resolution unit order is the individual moral compass with a range of responses to the normative field. The unconscious has alternative preferences in dealing with societal norms. The mental entity has an innate moral/sociological normative adjustive setting.

Accordingly the unconscious has:

- The finite direction determined by the formal operations of the scale and

- The six-role structure determined by the harmonic motion's energetic transformations.

The three oscillations guided by the three moral/formal operations restore the mental/social relational balance. The assessment identifies the three formal operations with a personality inventory, and the six-role process by sampling creativity reflecting the dialectic of one's interrelated emotions.

The Formal Theory identifies the formal operations transforming psychic tension to adaptive changes. The process transforms energies as emotional states. Unlike Piajet's formal operations conserving intellectual constructs, in the Formal Analysis, they apply on emotions as interrelated forms of energy gradually upgrading conflict energy to moral order energy.

- The three formal operations of the equilibrial scale correct the disturbance generated by the Identity conflict creating operation by restoring the equilibrial state. The formal states defining conflict as passivity, antagonism, and alienation are transformed to resolution defined as activity, cooperation and mutual respect. These formal alternatives represent the grammar of the key role state as its activity passivity forms across any story's symbolic language

- The six-role sequence, the mental simple harmonic motion, represents the syntax of emotions: stress is followed by response, anxiety by defense, and reversal by compromise. These operations clarify motivation as reduction of relational instability. Conflict resolution completes the emotional task in every sample of creativity, in any story. This end accomplishment is the condition for a story to be meaningful and complete.

- The process then becomes the measurable periodic unit of the unconscious. The testing measures this morally teleological unconscious.

- Creativity is not only an artistic gift; it is the reflection of the physiology of the unconscious adjustment mechanism driven by the purpose of reducing the individual's psychic tension, coinciding with the restoration of the emotional equilibrium. Reduction of tension corresponds to the finality of moral determinism.

The Measurable Variables of the Creative Process
In the past, the distinctions judging personality types have relied on concrete criteria: Temperaments have been based on descriptive distinctions. These have evolved from concrete alternatives associated with physical juices, nature-based descriptive distinctions, to more abstract formal distinctions but these have never been interrelated as the four-equilibrial formal operations of one scientific system. While psychodynamic assessments introduced formal distinctions, these remained arbitrary, independent of each other, and evolved with many descriptive qualifications. They were never integrated into the formal operations of an equilibrial system like the trays of a scale leading to the set of four equilibrial operations of a closed scientific system with abstract concepts and formulas clarifying their systemic

interrelation as equilibrial operations.

Hence testing in the history of assessments has not been able to correctly measure personality types. The CAB by formalizing the psychological process along the relational operations of the scale grasps the dimensions of the mental equilibrial process. Formalization introduces the three formal operations with their respective dichotomies. These operations lead to the recognition of relational alternatives as diagnostic categories, the four syndromal relational modalities, each corresponding to a factor identified by the personality inventory, the <u>Relational Modality Evaluation Scale, RMES.</u> The formal distinctions lead to identifying the spectrum of relational types. The fifth factor of the instrument corresponds to the psychic tension reflecting degree of psychopathology.

The difference with the dichotomies of other theoretical assessments is that the Formal Theory introduces three formal operational distinctions examining the unconscious as an equilibrial system. This system abides by the laws of the Kleinian formal operations. These are portrayed in the balance formulas of the trays of a scale. This systemic perspective is in opposition to the descriptively applied formal dichotomies of a number of psychometric tests and leads to the determination of the process as a three dimensional system, a spiral, evolving as a function of time.

Formal relational distinctions are interrelated as an equilibrial system captured by the formula of the Kleinian group of four formal operations: I=RNC.

<u>Identity</u> is balanced off by the product of <u>Reciprocity, Negation and Correlation</u>

The Formal Theory identifies the Kleinian system of four formal equilibrial operations: Identity, Reciprocity, Negation, and Correlation, as constituting the psychic response equilibrial system. The Identity operation corresponds to the stress or disturbance of the equilibrium. Two operations: Negation and Reciprocity, account for four personality types as wellness relational alternatives restoring the psychic equilibrium.

- Reciprocity identifies the alternative poles of passivity and activity.

- Negation identifies the continuum of antagonism to cooperation.

These two operations yield the four personality types: submissiveness cooperative and antagonistic; dominance cooperative and antagonistic.

- The last operation, Correlation, identifies the polarity of Alienation versus Mutual Respect pertaining to the degree of conflict resolution experienced as psychic tension corresponding to psychopathology. It refers to illness rather than wellness, hence it corresponds to Eysenck's Neuroticism and Psychoticism but not overlapping to his definitions of these terms as referred to in the PEN system.

The formal operations equilibrial model was applied by Piaget to the conservation of intellectual constructs, not to emotions. He suggested that these operations are reversible; we see them in the operations of the unconscious as one directional propelled by the need to reduce the experience of conflict as psychic tension. He identified them as manifested developmentally; we detect them as present at birth in the emotional responses of an infant seeking to preserve the rest state of comfort.

The Formal Theory also Introduces the Six Role Energetic Transformations Concept. Creativity is the manifestation of the six role conflict resolution process. The process manifests itself in all samples of creativity. Creativity as the manifestation of the energetic process became the object for the study of personality allowing the introduction of a new focus in evolving an assessment technology. To observe the unconscious we study the creative process as a measurable circumscribed periodic well-structured energetic phenomenon.

We examine samples of creativity as perfect symbolic systems with clear measurable dimensions. We study creativity as a scientific phenomenon identical to the corresponding two natural science equilibrial entities: the physics of the SHM, the pendulum oscillation, and the formal relations of the equilibrial scale.

The abstract concept of the process is a distinct energetic symbolic system with clearly defined variables, the formal operations of the equilibrial scale and the physical constructs and formulas of the Simple Harmonic Motion, the pendulum oscillation. The conflict resolution entity, a syndrome of emotions and behaviors with a moral end, becomes the physical measurable structure. How does the assessment measure these dimensions of the conflict resolution process? The assessment measures the three formal operations and the six energetic role states as reflected onto the structure of the creative process as a measurable scientific phenomenon pointing out the moral end.

The Conflict Analysis Battery, CAB

The new assessment instrument: the Conflict Analysis Battery identifies the measurement of

- Four categories of wellness as the spectrum of the four relational modalities identified by the personality inventory

- And the syndromal six-role state process qualifying the relational modality diagnosis of the person utilizing a projective component consisting of several creativity tasks. These are a set of projective tests that reconstruct the syndromal sequence of role states as formally interconnected emotions and behaviors; this is a purely psychodynamic projective instrument.

The relevance of the conceptual definition of the unconscious process for personality assessment is that it is measurable both as a formal and as a natural science energetic phenomenon.

- It is a formal relational phenomenon that unfolds predictably as a conflict resolution process that varies along the three formal operations determined qualitatively and quantitatively.

- It is also a natural science oscillation with physical dimensions that may be determined as an emotional dialectic qualitatively and quantitatively as the unit periodic energetic phenomenon unfolding along the set of the six role states from a conflict to its resolution.

The Construction of the Assessment Measuring Natural Science Variables Bound by Laws of Nature

The battery combines two types of tests both measuring the Conflict Resolution Process: A personality inventory with a set of projectives.

- The personality inventory of categories of relational alternatives uses items reflecting the formal distinctions along five scales. The four scales identify the personality types according to two relational operations: reciprocity and opposition. The personality inventory measures the formal operations and identifies a person's relational modality along the three formal distinctions. The inventory identifies the formal relational operations leading to four relational modalities and along a fifth scale, correlation, which corresponds to one's psychic tension, the mental status, identifying degrees of conflict resolution and of psychopathology.

- The creativity tasks measure the physical six role state emotional oscillation as an energetic directional transformation. The six role states each one of the six emotions is identified with creativity metaphor generating tests integrated into a dramatic continuum.

The assessment then addresses how a person resolves conflict, a moral process, along its formal and physical dimensions. The inventory and the projectives help to recognize the qualitative and quantitative parameters of the unit system numerically and also metaphorically.

The Projective Tests Measure the Emotional Dialectic

The projective techniques sample creativity to measure the unfolding of the personal pattern by composing a number of stories, metaphors to identify the six role process, as how a person feels about oneself and how s/he resolves conflicts.

The difference between the mind and equilibrial machines is that the mental oscillation is not a perpetual motion but a finite directional journey; it completes its mission of the conversion and upgrading of order, or energies within a three-oscillation sequence. The three cycle dialectic of emotions is a physical natural science energetic phenomenon, which abides by the laws of the Simple Harmonic Motion, SHM; as such it is defined by the constructs and formulas of the SHM translated to equivalent constructs describing the measurable dimensions of the mental process.

The detection of the six-role process may be achieved by observing the creative process dealing with distinct aspects of the six role process leading to its reconstruction as a unit dramatic entity, the mental harmonic. The six emotions are readily measurable by testing the subject with appropriate emotion related simple creativity exercises.

- The Stress role state is identified by the three Conflictual Memories Tests.

- The Response role is identified by the Transparent Mask Test.

- Anxiety is depicted by the Underlying Feelings Mask revealing one's hidden emotions.

- Defense is identified through the Animal and Fairy Tale Metaphor Tests.

- Reversal is depicted in the Dream Metaphor Test and the Intensified Animal Metaphor Test.

- Compromise is identified by the Short Story Test.

The six-role process is evident in all sample stories as in the conversation between the two animals. The dialogue between the two parties in a conversation usually ends upon the sixth exchange. Each exchange corresponds to a role state leading to the manifestation of the six-role process.

Accordingly by sampling the creativity exercises we reconstruct the unit of the social sciences, the unconscious as a syndromal six-role state periodic entity. The three-oscillations entity is graphically portrayed as a six-part, six-emotions harmonic, or sine curve performing the moral or conflict resolution function of converting psychic tension to the typical conflict resolution.

This physical oscillatory process, a sequence of formally interrelated associations as emotions, guided by the three formal operations of the equilibrial scale of the Kleinian set theory, is the syndromal structure of the unconscious.

The Formal Theory applies these operations to emotions, as conserved energetic entities. While Piaget's formal intellectual operations are viewed as reversible, the formal operations on emotions are irreversible. They are transformed one-directionally, negentropicly to order, to the spiritual emotional state identified with the state of rest.

The Battery Identifies the Mental Process Quantitatively and Also Visually with Art and Text Along the Role Sequence

The Conflict Analysis Battery uses the relational inventory to determine the relational modality and a set of projective creativity tasks to identify a subject's syndrome, the six-role conflict resolution sequence. The inventory identifies the relational modality and the projective tests reconstruct the personalized sequence of emotions. This information delivers insights directly to the test taker. The questionaire guides the test taker to generate self-awareness, and self-correction guidelines as the healing path of conflict resolution. The battery combines diagnoses with therapeutic interventions by prompting the test-taker to detect the formal nature of the unconscious and how to modify it.

Thus the protocols of each case study address two tasks: the relational modality diagnosis and the syndromal reconstruction of the process reflecting the dynamics of the particular diagnosis. Psychopathology is reflected in the psychic tension experienced, also in the elevation of relational modality choices.

The Projective Testing

Ten creativity-based tests consist of art-tasks and their analytic evaluation. The tests begin with an artwork assignment. The topics include autobiographic experiences and projective metaphorical themes; the art tasks are followed by structured questionnaires seeking the identification of a relational pattern throughout a person's thinking. The questions develop a metaphor, its interpretation and insights for behavior modification. The questionnaires solicit developing dialogues, identifying conflicts, then becoming introspective, identifying a pattern, owning the pattern, examining its reoccurrence, and entailing deliberate consciously pursued changes to correct the ineffectiveness of the unconsciously evolving relational pattern. The testee becoming conscious of the unconscious explores changes to be made. These thoughts reflect on one's capacity to evolve insights and one's willingness to pursue them.

There are many creativity for self-discovery tests, each beginning with an art exercise and continued with a short or lengthy questionnaire. These tests are of several categories:
The projectives are subdivided into the factual, autobiographic sociological information gathering tests including:

- The Conflictual Memories: Childhood, Adolescent and Recent Conflictual Memories

- Family Portraits as Balloons and as Animals, the Zoo Portrait of the Family of Origin, Marital Family

- Dream Analysis

The second set consists of a number of metaphor creation stories:

- The Three Masks (Transparent, Feelings and What Is In Your Hear)

- The Animal Metaphors (Regular and Intensified Animal Metaphor)

- The Fairy Tale Metaphor

- The Short Story Test

The metaphor tests differ in evoking the manifestation of one's relational pattern examined under different degrees of stress, alternative symbolic systems, and by altering the depth of unconscious thinking.

Then we have two traditional but modified tests:

- The House Tree Person test

- The Scribble Metaphor

These traditional but modified tests are accompanied by questionnaires eliciting more information and also interpretation of the images by the test taker.

Each metaphor task is followed by a structured questionaire, the "Levis Metaphor Analysis Process" questions, which lead the test taker progressively to insights about one's pattern and then to awareness of optimization of the pattern's outcome. They yield information, which is integrated by identifying the perfect dramatic universe of the person's conflict resolution process.

The projective techniques validate the inventory diagnosis of a relational pattern by capturing the psychological and sociological manifestation of the syndromal category. The two types of tests cross-validate each other.

The metaphor tests also cross validate each other by eliciting the same pattern in two symbolic languages, the Animal and the Fairy Tale Metaphors. They also complement each other by examining the impact of different degrees of stress by eliciting responses intensifying the conflict, as in the Intensified Conflictual Metaphor Test.

They also explore the depth of unconscious thinking by starting the test with art versus prose. The Short Story starts with prose. Short stories are autobiographic, identifying conflict resolution compromises rather than simply restating the conflictual pattern and identifying the defense approach to resolving conflicts.

Each test informs on one of the six role-states. Stress is reflected in the states of Conflictual mMemories. The tests are used to reconstruct the emotional dialectic of the personal pattern. The autobiographic tests reflect the stress and the reversal states, while the metaphor tests provide the balance: Mask as the Response and Anxiety, the Animal Metaphor Test as the Defense. The Intensified Metaphor illustrates the Reversal State, while the Short Story reveals the Compromise. The projective tests unfold as the deployment of the six-role pattern guided by one's unconscious.

Prof. Donald Mosher's Description of the Entire CAB Upon a Copyright Infringement Suit

I will begin with a general description of Levis's Conflict Analysis Battery. The CAB was copyrighted in 1984, and has a lengthy and detailed manual, The Conflict Analysis Battery: Theory and Tests.

It consists of three chapters:
> *(1) The Formal Analysis Profile (70 pp.), (2) The Diagnostic Inquiry for the Determination of Relational Parameters (80 pp.), and (3) Testing (approx. 99 pp.) which contains the CAB itself.*

The Formal Analysis Profile presents an original scientific theory of behavior and a detailed discussion of ten levels of analysis applied to the CAB:

> *(1) Relational, (2) Variables, (3) Induction, (4) Energetic Transformation, (5) Conflict, (6) Syndromal, (7) Graphic, (8) Relational Modality, (9) Quantitative, and (10) Efficiency.*

After discussing its functions and advantages, Chapter 2 relates the ten levels of analysis to specific psychometric indicators on the CAB. Its rationales and procedures are unusually explicit and detailed.

The CAB, itself, contains:
> *(1) Personal Data and Biographical Information,*
> *(2) The Relational Modality Evaluation Scale,*
> *(3) The Animal Metaphor Test,*
> *(4) Balloon Portraits and Stories, of the Family of Origin, and of the Marital Family, Peer Group/Fellow workers,*
> *(5) Conflictual Memories Test (Childhood, Adolescence, and Recent),*
> *(6) Chronological List of Outstanding Conflicts,*
> *(7) Intensified Animal Metaphor Test AMT #2,*
> *(8) Transparent Mask Test,*
> *(9) Report of Dream Analysis,*
> *(10) Adapted Scribble Metaphor,*
> *(11) Short Story Metaphor,*
> *(12) Adapted Rorschach Response Process,*
> *(13) Adapted TAT Response Process,*
> *(14) Lifetime Repetitions of the Metaphor Cycle,*
> *(15) AMT #3, Resolution of Conflict Test,*
> *(16) Letter to Yourself, Know Thyself Statement,*
> *(17) AMT #4, Exploring Special Relationships and/or Patterns,*
> *(18) Hero and Villain Metaphor Test,*
> *(19) Fairy Tale Metaphor Story,*
> *(20) Adapted House-Tree-Person Test,*
> *(21) AMT #5 Beyond the Obsession, and*
> *(22) AMT #6, Special Relations Protocol*

In addition several other forms are included in the manual:

(1) Conflict in Psychodrama,
(2) Psychodrama Metaphor Analysis,
(3) Power Struggle Protocol (per-termination),
(4) Formal Analysis of Individual Therapy Session,
(5) Evaluation Format,
(6) General Feedback Information,
(7) Release and Feedback Form, and
(8) The CAB Supplement which is a form used to help convert insights into behavior modification in a specifically developed Formal Analysis Training Program.

The functions of the CAB include: (1) determining the structure of an individual's psychic and social systems, namely, degree of psychic tension, and relational modalities, (2) measuring the person's conflicts and their resolution patterns, (3) measuring sociometric and normative patterns, and (4) assessing conflicts, both past traumatic and recent conflicts, and as reviewed and changing in dreams.

The manual lists the following advantages of the CAB as a testing instrument: (1) the CAB's interpretation follows a rigorous methodological process, The Formal Analysis Profile, (2) the CAB has a comprehensive diagnostic function, (3) the CAB has a therapeutic function--(a) provides insight, (b) offers emotional release, (c) creates a personal mastery experience, and (d) places client in role of responsibility, (4) The CAB is cost effective, (5) the CAB has multiple applications, and (6) when used with therapy, achieves insight and behavior modification in a few sessions. In addition, the manual contains information about reliabilities and validity of the RMES.

From my study of the CAB, it is an innovative, useful, and significant test battery in my opinion as an expert on psychological tests and assessment. It integrates a thorough test battery with a formal theory and method of test analysis. Particularly noteworthy is Dr. Levis' process analysis--a set of questions designed to elicit psychological information about the drawing process itself. Also innovative is Dr. Levis's therapeutic use of questions that provoke insight, elicit adaptive strategies, and contract for change.

<u>*I would characterize the CAB most favorably as a state-of-the-art or state-of-the-science psychological test battery.*</u>

As one example of the level of sophistication involved, Dr. Levis systematically relates a model of simple harmonic motion taken from physics to the repetition of relational patterns across five generations of Greek cosmogony. Physical variables are assigned parallel psychological constructs, for example, displacement of the pendulum is equated to normative deviation. Further, normative deviation is related to location of animals from the AMT. Energy equations from physics are used to make predictions. Both graphic and sine wave systems are used to model psychological states and behavior.

The Features of the Conflict Analysis Battery: Innovations in Assessment

The Conflict Analysis Battery has several characteristics making it different from prior assessment instruments. The Conflict Analysis Battery represents a radical breakthrough in psychological assessment technology. It has the following differentiating characteristics:

1. **The assessment is theory based;** it measures the dimensions of the unconscious as a natural science conflict resolving entity with physical and formal dimensions. The findings validate the premise of the Formal Theoretical assumption that the unconscious resolves conflicts along a six-role sequence guided by three formal operations.

2. **It combines a personality inventory with a set of projectives.** The two tests are complementary in evaluating two different dimensions of the same entity. The personality inventory measures the three formal operations; the projective techniques identify the six roles of the dialectic process as syndromally interrelated emotions.

3. **These two types of testing cross validate each other as the relational variables are identified by two types of testing instruments.** The relational operations identified by the inventory are illustrated by the projective tests. The tests identify the test taker's relational modality abstractly and then concretely.

4. **The battery is a self-assessment;** the testee constructs metaphors and interprets them following a structured questionnaire; s/he integrates them on a template to identify the personal conflict resolution process, one's relational modality and how to modify one's adjustment.

5. **The battery is educational** confirming the scientific and moral organization of the unconscious. **It uses the constructs and formulas of the physics of the SHM** by organizing the syndromal dialectic of emotions as a six emotions sequence: stress, response, anxiety, defense, reversal and compromise.
   The battery measures the physical dimensions of the unconscious conflict resolution process, the three formal or relational variables, and their physical dimensions, while it illustrates them in the symbolic language of the person.

6. **The relational modality instrument is diagnostic.** It uses the Kleinian group of four formal transformations and not isolated formal distinctions. These measure relational distinctions, which identify modalities as reciprocal to each other, subordinacy versus dominance, and as opposite to each other as antagonism versus cooperation, and as correlative to each other corresponding to alienation versus mutual respect, low versus high psychic tension.

7. **The projective segment of the self-assessment is therapeutic as it represents an emotional experience.** It leads the person to create a conflict resolution and then to personalize the pattern, to see it as a metaphor of personal conflictual experiences, and to start rethinking how one deals with such responses. One draws insights about oneself and arrives at conclusions about how to make changes.

8. **The information is delivered directly to the test taker** to readily identify her relational modality. **The clinical record is meaningful to the test taker** without professional services; trained assistants' knowledge can reinforce and clarify the personal impressions. **The self-**

assessment being meaningful to the creator the test bypasses the need for an interpreter. The interpretation of the testing is very simple. A template integrates the artwork of the testing providing the personal pattern as an illustrated drama. We examine the power differential in every metaphor by pacing the heroes of stories on the concentric circles of a sociogram and identifying the cooperative versus antagonistic interactions with appropriate vectors within the circles.

9. **The assessment is cost-effective.** The interpretation of personality inventories can be complex as well with many traits considered independently from each other. The interpretation of projectives like Rorschach and TAT is a very elaborate technical procedure. The interpretation of the CAB is relatively easy and simple. It is a self-assessment; the test taker generates the art and its interpretation leading to insights and changes without requiring professional services.

10. **The assessment generates a valuable clinical record** useful for the testee and any observers, be that teachers or clinicians/therapists. The assessment represents a standardized valid and reliable clinical record that reflects the intellectual and emotional state of the testee, and her/his sociometric realities. The assessment is useful to the testee, the therapist, the educator in the classroom, the coach in an organizational setting.

11. **The tests are valid and reliable.** Its statistical profile scores surpass by far existing tests' validity and reliability ratings.

Interpreting of the Assessment

The goal of the assessment is the diagnosis of a person's relational modality. The identification of the relational modalities as diagnostic categories of wellness and the interpretation of the testing have been described in depth at the volume that launched the Formal Theory and its experimental validation. *'Conflict Analysis, the Formal Theory of Behavior'*, (Normative Publications, 1988.) Chapter Seven: Psychopathology as the Formal Syndromal Structuring of Relations. Chapter Eight: The Diagnostic Inquiry for the Determination of Relational Parameters. Here we are supplementing that information with a quick overview on conducting the scientific interpretation of the assessment.

Measuring Variables with the Formal Analysis Profile, FAP
In the above publication the interpretation of all battery tests has been based on the ten levels of the **Formal Analysis Profile, FAP**. These ten levels reduce symbolic systems into measurable natural science phenomena. The first level pertains to the formal analysis of a symbolic system utilizing the equilibrial dynamics of the Kleinian group of the four formal operations. These are exemplified in the operations of the equilibrium of the trays of a scale. The formal analysis model serves the interpretation of the personality inventory. The other nine levels measure metaphors' symbolic systems utilizing the constructs and formulas of the physics of the pendulum motion. The Simple Harmonic Motion model is applied to the analysis of the metaphors. Both natural science models allow the introduction of the rigorous constructs and formulas of the two scientific equilibrial phenomena into the analysis of the assessment. The tests of the assessment measure the unconscious as alternative ways of resolving conflicts along one of the four relational modalities.

The formal analysis profile, FAP, identifies ten formulas as levels for the analysis of any symbolic system. The SHM's constructs of displacement, velocity and acceleration pertain to normative deviation, activities and emotions respectively. These allow the graphic representation of the emotional social symbolic system of any personal story to be reduced to a set of measurable variables, an entity that is also graphically portrayable.

The Inventory Test

The Relational Modalities Evaluation Scales is a Personality Inventory That Measures the Three Formal Operations.

The RMES personality inventory identifies the alternative formal operations guiding the process to resolutions diagnosing the personality type as a relational modality. Resolutions are measured by the personality inventory as five scales corresponding statistically to the five factors of the assessment instrument. We distinguish four alternative ways of resolving conflicts along the two formal transformational operations: passivity versus activity and antagonism versus cooperation. We also identify neuroticism as measuring conflict resolution along the operation of alienation versus mutual respect. This is the fifth scale and corresponding factor of the diagnostic analysis.

The inventory consists of approximately 200 items evaluated according to a Likert scale of one to six as degrees of agreement; the items are distributed as clusters identified by name as relational scales. The items are grouped together for easy recognition of a person's pattern or modality of conflict resolution. The items may be also scattered to avoid manipulation by the testee's bias. There are four relational scales and a fifth independent of relational distinctions; the latter measures psychic tension as a mental status questionnaire corresponding to the degree of conflict resolution.

Formal Analysis of the Relational Modality Inventory

The relational modality inventory measures the three formal relational dichotomies objectively as five scales each corresponding to one of the inventory's factors. Four scales correspond to the four relational modalities as diagnostic syndromes, as alternative types of conflict resolution. The fifth scale reflects the person's psychic tension state differentiating a person along the alternatives of wellness versus illness. The fifth scale measures the unresolved emotional tension independently of the relational modality. In the case studies of this volume the inventory items are presented in the raw format as columns with the scores for each item and each subcategory. As the research got refined through the online delivery the scores were summarized by the software and presented numerically and graphically as diagrams. The findings are portrayed graphically through two types of diagrammatic illustrations: the grid and the scorecard.

The Relational Modalities Grid or Spectrum

This grid graph displays the scores of the 200-item personality inventory of the battery as a simple linear diagram reflecting the intensity of each modality and of the psychic tension. Along the horizontal axis of the table, we place the relational modalities and sub categories as features of the respective syndrome. Displayed on the vertical axis is the intensity of deviation from one to six. The testee and the test giver can identify at a glance both the relational modality variations and the psychic tension diagnoses of the person.

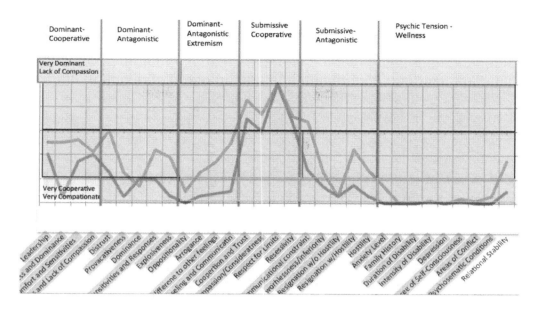

The graphic representation of relational modalities
The grid graph above illustrates the overlapping scores of two identical 56 year-old twin brothers scoring the same test separately. This finding reflects two scientific facts: the reliability of the testing instrument measuring correctly a set of personality traits and the genetic transmission of personality types, accounting for the overlap between the two identical brothers' scores.

Intense deviations in the four relational scales reflect potential relational communicational problems and also emotions/symptoms of different kinds. Strong polarization reflects potential difficulties in managing power in dealing with stressors. The scoring of the psychic tension is also of significance in detecting clinical diagnostic items. Elevations in psychic tension may be qualified and quantified along the subcategories to diagnose clinical pathology.

Both social and psychic intensity reflect that a person could experience emotional discomfort and social dysfunctions and they represent criteria that the test taker could benefit from counseling, potentially requiring meds management.

A software program integrates the modalities information both graphically and numerically automatically facilitating the visual interpretation of the tests. The linear graph and the scorecard numbers inform about the personality profile. The personality relational modalities grid reflects the scores in a linear graph, the cross section of the harmonic is the scorecard. The relational modalities are analyzed with statistical average numbers. The subcategories of the relational modalities are analyzed separately leading to attributions or qualifications about the person along the subset of each modality. The scores will be displayed on top of the grid.

The computerized statistical measurement of the person's responses leads to the numerical identification of the four relational modalities/scales and of the psychic tension experienced. The weighted averages of the person's relational modalities are presented on the top of the images below. They represent the diagnostic information for each diagnostic category. In the original online delivery the computer generated report placed the personality type assessment scores, on top of the six-column artwork. In some cases there are two rows of scores as reflected in two successive testings. The repeated scores reflect the high reliability of the instrument as successive measurements almost coincide.

Interpreting the Projective Tests

The Metaphor Tests Explore the Person's Responses to a Variety of Stressors — Prompts eliciting particular emotions. Both the projectives and the inventory are extraordinarily reliable and valid.

The Metaphors Measure the Syndromal Sequence as a Six-Role Process
The syndromal nature of the process is assessed with the projective tests by identifying the manifestation of the six-role process both in individual tests and also in the reconstruction of the syndromal organization of emotions. To this effect we utilize the template of the harmonic to integrate the set of art exercises as these pertain to the respective six emotions. We also use in the online delivery of the tests a six column table that allows the test taker to complete the drawings integrated automatically on their role state placement.

Integrating the Testing Information
The tests have been chosen to correspond to the six role state syndromal sequence. Stress is depicted by the Conflictual Memory Test, Response by the Mask Test, Anxiety by the image revealed as the mask becomes transparent. Defense corresponds to the Animal Metaphor Test; Reversal is reflected in the dream test and Compromise in the Short Story Test. There is correspondence of metaphors with one of the six emotions. The set of the metaphors identifies the dialectic unfolding of the mental process. Accordingly the set of tests reconstructs the six-part emotional dialectic visually.

The Processing of the Projective Testing by Establishing Correspondence of Tests and Role-States
The interpretation of the testing is conducted by the testee; the services of a professional are required in making the testing more meaningful and beneficial. The tests constitute challenges of interpretation at several levels of analysis.

First, the associations in each metaphor test are shown to follow the given formal structure along the six-role process.

Second, the tests as formally interrelated emotions are interpreted as the six-part syndromal continuum. The test taker examines the template of the process connecting the tests along the syndromal emotional dialectic:

- The Conflictual Memory and the Family of Origin Balloons identify one's stress state.

- The Transparent Mask and the marital family portrait identifies the response state.

- The Image behind the Mask reflects a person's related anxiety state; his feelings.

- The Animal Metaphor identifies the defense response to the anxiety state.

- The Dream Analysis test and the Intensified Animal Metaphor Test clarifies one's state of reversal.

- The Short Story Metaphor clarifies autobiographically one's state of compromise.

- The Animal Metaphor Test and the Fairy Tale Metaphor Test represent the regular personal stressor sensitivities.

- The Intensified Metaphor illustrates a more intense stress situation, while the Short Story Test presents a less stressful stimulus. The range of responses generated by these three levels of stimuli illustrates the personality's reactivity to the range of stressors.

The Metaphor Profile Template for the Reconstruction of the Six-Role Process

Six Roles	Stress	Response	Anxiety	Defense	Reversal	Compromise
Tests	Memories, Portrait of the Family of origin	Mask one Portrait of Marital Family	Masks 2 and Feeling in one's Heart	Animal Metaphor Fairy Tale Metaphor	Dream Intensified AMT	Short Story Letter to oneself

Correlation of Tests in the Six-Role Process

2. Response:	4. Defense:	6. Compromise:
Mask #1, *Marital Family Portrait* Mastery, choice of role	*Animal/ Fairy Tale Metaphors* Mastery, cooperation, respect and alternatives	*Short Story* Concession making as Mastery, cooperation and mutual respect
1. Stress:	**3. Anxiety:**	**5. Reversal:**
Conflictual Memory, Portrait of the Family of origin Passivity, antagonism, alienation	*Mask#2, #3* Passivity, antagonism or cooperation, alienation versus mutual respect	*Dream, Intensified Animal Metaphor* *Recent Memory*: passivity, antagonism, alienation or alternatives

Ten Tests, Six-Role States in More Detail

Stress

A person's stress state is portrayed in the conflicts depicted in four tests:

The three Conflictual Memories: childhood, adolescence, and recent identifying the key passivity state and related responses.

The Balloon Portrait of the Family of Origin portrays the formative experiences with members of the family of origin. Colors and shapes of the balloons, strings attached or separate, reflect the family constellation.

Response

The Transparent Mask represents the identity of the person.

The Marital Family configuration helps to identify one's making changes as opposed to the family of origin

Anxiety

Mask #2 as the hidden image reflects the true self-image as feelings of the person, negative and positive.

The Heart Mask #3 differentiates what conflicts one experiences, internal and interpersonal. Dominant persons present interpersonal conflicts, while submissive people present them as internal in the heart image.

The sequence of response and anxiety is discussed in the synthesis page of the mask protocol.

Defense

The Animal and Fairy Tale Metaphor Tests illustrate how a person resolves conflicts; the dialogue unfolds in a predictable conflict resolution sequence usually with six exchanges.

The person identifies with one or both animals and explains how and why.

Reversal

The Dream Test reveals a person's reversal as the manifestation of one's wishes and fears. The **Intensified Animal Metaphor** indicates the polarization in a person's thinking and the state of loosing control as opposed to seeking control.

Compromise

The Short Story is usually autobiographic. It begins with a text segment followed by art. It reflects how a person resolves conflicts making a compromise.

The Sine Curve Synthesis of the Projective Tests

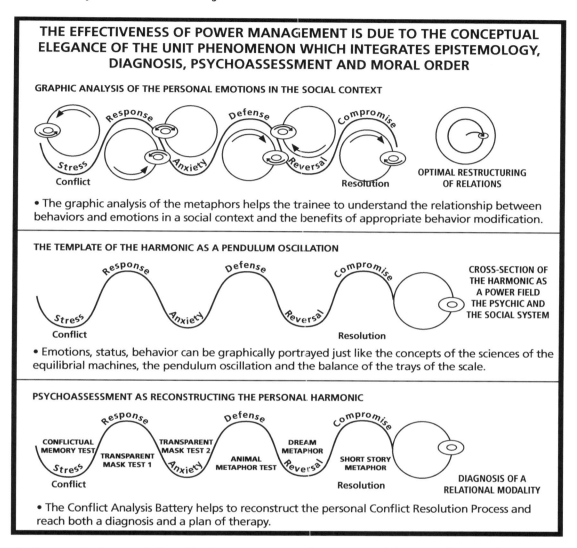

THE EFFECTIVENESS OF POWER MANAGEMENT IS DUE TO THE CONCEPTUAL ELEGANCE OF THE UNIT PHENOMENON WHICH INTEGRATES EPISTEMOLOGY, DIAGNOSIS, PSYCHOASSESSMENT AND MORAL ORDER

GRAPHIC ANALYSIS OF THE PERSONAL EMOTIONS IN THE SOCIAL CONTEXT

Response   Defense   Compromise

Stress
Conflict   Anxiety   Reversal   Resolution   OPTIMAL RESTRUCTURING OF RELATIONS

• The graphic analysis of the metaphors helps the trainee to understand the relationship between behaviors and emotions in a social context and the benefits of appropriate behavior modification.

THE TEMPLATE OF THE HARMONIC AS A PENDULUM OSCILLATION

Response   Defense   Compromise

Stress   Anxiety   Reversal
Conflict   Resolution   CROSS-SECTION OF THE HARMONIC AS A POWER FIELD THE PSYCHIC AND THE SOCIAL SYSTEM

• Emotions, status, behavior can be graphically portrayed just like the concepts of the sciences of the equilibrial machines, the pendulum oscillation and the balance of the trays of the scale.

PSYCHOASSESSMENT AS RECONSTRUCTING THE PERSONAL HARMONIC

Response   Defense   Compromise

CONFLICTUAL MEMORY TEST   TRANSPARENT MASK TEST 2   DREAM METAPHOR
TRANSPARENT MASK TEST 1   ANIMAL METAPHOR TEST   SHORT STORY METAPHOR
Stress   Anxiety   Reversal
Conflict   Resolution   DIAGNOSIS OF A RELATIONAL MODALITY

• The Conflict Analysis Battery helps to reconstruct the personal Conflict Resolution Process and reach both a diagnosis and a plan of therapy.

In the case study murals found in the next pages we have arranged the Metaphor Test (images and insights) according to the template of the Conflict Resolution Process. The template above indicates the correspondence between role-states and the various tests of the Conflict Analysis Battery.

A simple sine curve graph has been used to integrate the artwork along the six-role process, the syndromal dialectic of emotions, leading to conflict resolution. The six emotions, represented by the images of the projective tests, illustrate the personal drama unfolding metaphorically. The continuity of images confirms how the person evolves emotionally from passivity to activity, from antagonism to cooperation, and from alienation to mutual respect. There is continuity of dramatic action and conservation of energy along the process as the emotions evolve from chaos to order, from entropy to negative entropy.

The summary of the workbook metaphors: The sine curve of the six-role process is reconstructed by the patient, Cheshire Cat. It integrates meaningfully the metaphor tests accompanied by a summary of each respective text illustrating his conflict resolution syndrome. This is the second workbook of tests demonstrating the conflict resolution sequence reflecting the dominant cooperative power management choices in his triumphant dealing with authorities.

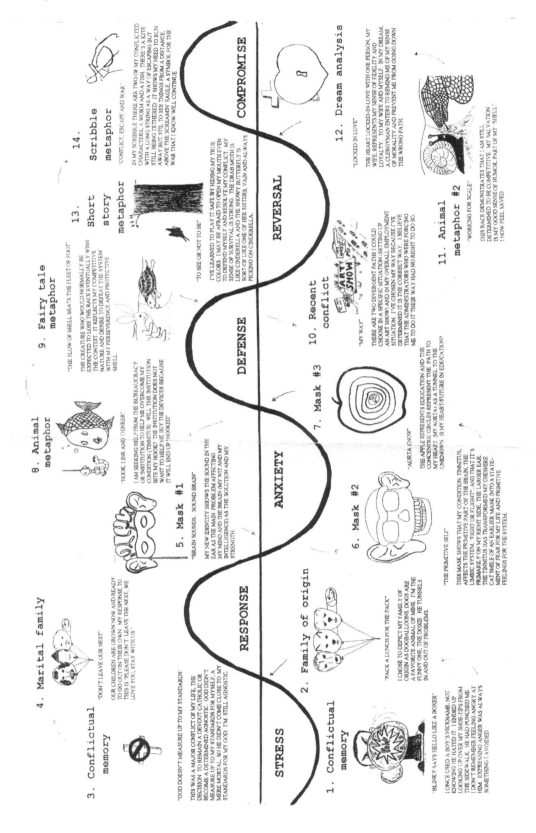

STRESS   RESPONSE   ANXIETY   DEFENSE   REVERSAL   COMPROMISE

1. Conflictual memory

"BLINKY SAYS HELLO LIKE A BOXER"

I ONCE USED A BOY'S NICKNAME. NOT KNOWING HE HATED IT. I ENDED UP LOOKING UP OVER MY SHOE-TIPS FROM THE SIDEWALK. HE HAD PUNCHED ME. I DON'T REMEMBER FEELING ANGRY AT HIM. EXPRESSING ANGER WAS ALWAYS SOMETHING I AVOIDED.

2. Family of origin

"PACK A LUNCH FOR THE PACK"

I CHOSE TO DEPICT MY FAMILY OF ORIGIN AS DOXIE BALLOONS. DOGS ARE A FAVORITE ANIMAL OF MINE. I'M THE FUNNY ONE. THE DOXIE. HE TUNNELS IN AND OUT OF PROBLEMS.

3. Conflictual memory

"GOD DOESN'T MEASURE UP TO MY STANDARDS"

THIS WAS A MAJOR CONFLICT OF MY LIFE. THE DECISION TO REMAIN A DEVOUT CATHOLIC OR BECOME A DETERMINED AGNOSTIC. GOD DIDN'T MEASURE UP TO MY STANDARDS FOR MYSELF. A MERE MORTAL. SO HE DIDN'T COME CLOSE TO MY STANDARDS FOR MY GOD. I'M STILL AGNOSTIC.

4. Marital family

"DON'T LEAVE OUR NEST"

OUR CHILDREN ARE GROWN NOW AND READY TO GO OUT ON THEIR OWN. MY RESPONSE TO THIS IS "PLEASE DON'T LEAVE THE NEST. WE LOVE YOU, STAY WITH US".

5. Mask #1 — SOUND BRAIN

"BRAIN SOUNDS"

MY NEW IDENTITY SHOWS THE SOUND IN THE EAR AS THE MAIN PROBLEM AFFECTING MY MIND AND THE BRAIN (MY WIT AND MY INTELLIGENCE) AS THE SOLUTION AND MY STRENGTH.

6. Mask #2 — "THE PRIMITIVE SELF"

THIS MASK SHOWS THAT MY CONDITION, TINNITUS, AFFECTS THE PRIMITIVE PART OF THE BRAIN, THE LIMBIC SYSTEM, "FIGHT OR FLIGHT", AND THAT IT'S PRIMARILY ON MY RIGHT SIDE. THE LARGER EAR. THE TINNITUS HAS TRANSFORMED MY CHESHIRE CAT SMILE OF AN EARLIER MASK INTO A STATE-MENT OF FEAR FOR MY LIFE AND PRIMITIVE FEELINGS FOR THE SYSTEM.

7. Mask #3

"AORTA KNOW"

THE APPLE REPRESENTS EDUCATION AND THE CONCENTRIC CIRCLES REPRESENT THE PATH TO MY HEART. (MY AORTA) AS A TUNNEL TO THE UNKNOWN. IS MY HEART/FUTURE IN EDUCATION?

8. Animal metaphor

"HOOK, LINE AND THINKER"

I AM SEEKING HELP FROM THE BUREAUCRACY OR INSTITUTION TO HELP ME OVERCOME MY CONDITION (TINNITUS). WILL THE INSTITUTION DOES NOT BITE MY HOOK? THE INSTITUTION DOES NOT WANT TO HELP ME BY THE DEVICES BECAUSE IT WILL END UP "HOOKED".

9. Fairy tale metaphor

"THE 'SLOW' OF SHELL BEATS THE FLEET OF FOOT"

THE CREATURE WHO WOULD NORMALLY BE EXPECTED TO LOSE THE RACE EVENTUALLY WINS THE CONTEST. IT REFLECTS MY COMPETITIVE NATURE AND DESIRE TO DEFEAT THE SYSTEM WITH MY PERSEVERENCE AND PROTECTIVE SHELL.

10. Recent conflict

"MY WAY"

THERE ARE TWO DIVERGENT PATHS I COULD CHOOSE IN A SPECIFIC SITUATION (SETTING UP AN ART SHOW) AND IN MY OVERALL EMPLOYMENT SITUATION. I'VE CHOSEN MY WAY BECAUSE I'VE DETERMINED IT'S THE CORRECT WAY. I BELIEVE THAT THE ADMINISTRATORS WHO WERE FORCING ME TO DO IT THEIR WAY HAD NO RIGHT TO DO SO.

11. Animal metaphor #2

"WORKING FOR SCALE"

THIS RACE DEMONSTRATES THAT I AM STILL DETERMINED TO BE COMPETITIVE. MY SALVATION IS MY GOOD SENSE OF HUMOR, PART OF MY "SHELL". I NOW FEEL SAVED.

12. Dream analysis

"LOCKED IN LOVE"

THE HEART LOCKED-IN-LOVE WITH ONE PERSON, MY WIFE, REPRESENTS MY SENSE OF FIDELITY AND LOYALTY. TO MY WIFE AND MYSELF. IN MY DREAM, A CLERGYMAN ENTERS TO REMIND ME OF MY SENSE OF MORALITY AND PREVENT ME FROM GOING DOWN THE WRONG PATH.

13. Short story metaphor

"TO SEE OR NOT TO BE"

I'VE LEARNED TO PLAY IT SAFE BY HIDING MY TRUE COLORS. I MAY BE AFRAID TO OPEN MY MOUTH TO DEFEND MYSELF AND RESOLVE MY CONFLICT. MY SENSE OF SURVIVAL IS STRONG. THE DRAB MOTH IS LIKE CINDERELLA AND THE SHOWY BUTTERFLY IS SORT OF LIKE ONE OF HER SISTERS, VAIN AND ALWAYS PICKING ON CINDERELLA.

14. Scribble metaphor

"CONFLICT: ESCAPE AND WAR"

IN MY SCRIBBLE THERE ARE TWO OF MY CONFLICTED CHARACTERS, A WORM AND A FISH. THERE'S A KITE WITH A LONG STRING, A WAY OF ESCAPING BUT STILL BEING TETHERED. IT SHOWS MY NEED TO RUN AWAY BUT STILL. TO SEE THINGS FROM A DISTANCE. ABOVE THE SCREAMIN' EAGLE, A SYMBOL FOR THE WAR THAT I KNOW WILL CONTINUE.

64

Analysis of the Battery Information

The battery, inventory and the projectives, evaluate the relational tendencies of the client, patient, along the same relational parameters: With the inventory we recognize one's relational choices for passivity versus activity, cooperation versus antagonism, and alienation versus mutual respect. The two types of tests cross-validate each other: The projectives help a testee to identify the key conflict integrating emotions and behaviors in the relational modality sequence. The test taker identifies one's relational modality; s/he becomes conscious of the ineffectiveness of the unconscious and assumes deliberately or consciously the initiative to modify the problem generating attitude.

The Conscious Informed About the Unconscious Assumes the Role of a Self-Correcting Faculty

The Formal Theory applies the relational method in the analysis of the thought process measuring the physical structure and relational or formal type of resolution of a given story. The relational or formal analysis of the process identifies the unconscious transformational totality as having a distinct structure consisting of six emotions, and a moral function identified by the choices along the three formal operations. We recognize the prevalent relational modality manifested in a story representing a diagnostic category. The syndromal dynamics account for wellness but also for psychopathology.

Conflict resolution occurs in every story as a dramatic totality. The story's conflict resolution structure is the object for the scientific analysis of behavior reflecting the adjustment-seeking unconscious. Any sample story, as a circumscribed phenomenon, qualifies to be examined as reflecting the personal unconscious. Its formal analysis allows to measure the sample story along its physical six-role dialectic of emotions and to identify the three formal operations transforming conflict to resolution. The formal operations as variables determine the personal way of resolving conflicts. They represent the personality characteristics leading to identifying one's diagnosis as a syndrome of relating.

The Formal Theory distinguishes the unconscious response as a predictable and measurable entity, a six-role state emotional response that is guided by three formal operations. The associations inform on the core pattern allowing one to be objective in observing its manifestation. The simple device of capturing the personal pattern sampling one's creativity is the model of the diagnostic and therapeutic intervention. Therapy is in the observation that leads to become conscious of the unconscious as a relational modality and then in allowing the person to assume responsibility for the optimal restructuring of relations. The person becoming self-aware spells out the changes needed in modifying any dysfunctional relational power choices.

The Assessment is Diagnostic

The person identifies her/his relational modality as a pattern of conflict resolution, observing the scales of the inventory and integrates the tests, the formally related art and content of the stories, by examining the psychodynamically interrelated six-role template.
The choice of metaphor animals and their exchanges reflect on the testee's relational modality.

The difference between relational modalities may be studied in the symbolic choices of the metaphor characters. The difference between wellness and illness is reflected in the intensity of relational deviations along all five scales. These disturbances are also reflected in the unfolding of the metaphor stories.

Dominant and submissive individuals choices are reflected in their choice of species and conflicts identified in the animals' traits and stories. A dominant case study starts with a damaged flea and a lame ant. These animals are cured and reemerge as a disabled eagle and lion able to dominate the world. A dominant person may choose to be a dog and a cat but these animals are powerful emotionally and physically. The 'Cheshire Cat' case study has the power of the wide triumphant smile; his dog is a vicious pit bull. By contrast the submissive person's dog and a cat choices identified in the case study of the 'The vulture and the snake', as her initial metaphor are powerless. The two do not communicate. They have their backs turned to each other. Her animals were unable to communicate. Her identities as animals evolved from being oppressed and secretive to become two giraffes able to talk about feelings and still be friends.

The Self-Assessment is Therapeutic

The testing has a therapeutic function. If the relational process is the mental heartbeat, the CAB is the mental stethoscope. Yet it is more than just diagnostic. It is the scalpel and the stent, the corrective interventions to normalize one's heartbeat and blood pressure by operating inside one's heart. The fact that the CAB is therapeutic reduces the need of a therapist and empowers the role of the educator, of the nurse and the social worker all of whom may be readily trained to deliver this instrument and monitor the insights generated to the test-takers.

What makes the battery different from other tests is that the testee processes the emotional information elicited by the assessments structured instructions. Processing the tests is an emotional, intellectual, and cathartic transformative but also safe experience. It leads to personal emotional and intellectual growth, empowerment, without the problematic development of a positive or negative transference of a dependency relationship. A peer group setting like the classroom, just like the AA self-help support system can be effective in making changes.

The test-taker gains diagnostic insights and therapeutic and behavior modification directives without professional intervention.

The testing is therapeutic. The test-taker analyzes the projective tests along the structured questionnaire and becomes conscious of the unconscious, increasing self-awareness and sense of potential personal therapeutic growth.

Insights connect the person spiritually within one's sociological perspective. S/he understands the social and cultural normative environment; morality as normative cultural definitions is expanded to understand the universal, and totally abstract principles of conflict resolution.

The Syndromal Organization of Metaphors within the Six Role-States Template (Computer Delivery) and Along a Sine Curve (Workbook Delivery)

The riddle of one's symptoms, emotions, behaviors, is solved by the diagnosis of one's relational modality through the inventory test. This diagnosis is corroborated by arranging the tests on the template of the six role-states. The testing may reveal the key role state, choice action, binding the several tests as formally interrelated in the template profile. The relational modality diagnosis helps to comprehend the psychodynamic integration of the projective tests. The relational modality clarifies / makes meaningful, the entirety of the symbolic system of the client from its inception to its conclusion. The formal and six-part organization of testing sheds light to the personal experiences as a drama highlighting the protagonist's conflict-resolving pattern by integrating the testing as fragmented experiences into a meaningful totality.

The inventory identifies one's modality abstractly, numerically; the reconstruction illustrated by the template of metaphors represents the clinical manifestation of the syndromal dialectic of emotions. The relational diagnosis clarifies the use of power; the student/patient realizes the importance of responsible power management in relations; the relational diagnosis entails changes commensurate to one's deviant tendencies; here we encounter the significance of power management in the context of wellness.

The art-work of each metaphor may be analyzed examining the metaphors' systemic variables corroborating in providing a detailed profile of the person evaluated. Each choice made contributes in evaluating the symbolic system of the test taker. The several metaphors have parallel relational dimensions, which pertain to the creator of the test. The equivalent choices confirm the relational characteristics of the person. In the animal, fairy tale metaphors, in the balloon portraits the figures reveal the reciprocal distinctions of the person's character. Family portraits as Balloons and Zoo choices reflect the family system culture but also the individuals' personal identities. Colors reflect particular emotions again significant as dichotomies pertaining to the person. Positioning of the balloons, their strings and their configurations reflect the closeness of members in the group, dependencies and alliances of the person's formative social system.

The creativity tests measure the relational modalities indirectly, utilizing the Simple Harmonic Motion, SHM, constructs, formulas and diagrams in the interpretation of symbolic systems. The metaphors identify a person's social bipole positions with the duality of the two animals symbolizing power alternatives. The characteristics of the animals indicate the points of differentiation between the opposite characters. According to the SHM the metaphors are interpreted as the person's deviations from the normative rest state, generating an opposite emotional psychic force in the ellipses representing the need to restore the rest state by cancelling the person's deviation. The sine curve of the mental harmonic and its cross section as the power field are borrowed from the study of the SHM.

The metaphors reflect social power position and movements within the power grid. The feelings are identified on the concentric ellipses. There are fine points illustrated in a table included in the textbook of the Formal Theory exploring the significance of aesthetic variables such as the direction of the animals, their size, the selection of species, the adjectives qualifying them reflecting on the specific personal choices in dealing with stress.

The Six Emotions Template
The images of templates below illustrate the insertion of art in a meaningful manner in the six columns, representing the syndromal structure of the six emotions involved in the unconscious mechanism of conflict resolution. The topics of the columns specify the six-role process as stress, response, anxiety, defense, reversal and compromise. The template integrates the images of the 10 art tasks into the 6 columns process as a totality; they integrate the fragments of one's emotional life into a dramatic continuum.

The observer can visually detect in each of these templates the evolution from a conflict to its resolution. The first column, stress, includes 4 vignettes of conflict, while the sixth, compromise, presents the resolution frequently as a hand shake, a couple with hearts, and the companion love story.

The Online Delivery Art as Captured in a Template of Columns
The template of the conflict resolution process integrates emotions portrayed by the images of the metaphors as six role states. The template is completed by the computer for the online test takers. Alternatively it is completed by the test taker using a workbook then inserting the tests into the conflict resolution profile. The testing images reflect at a glance the syndromal sequences beginning with conflicts and ending with resolutions.

The computer generates a relational modalities profile as a spectrum of scores and respectively of the interrelated traits for every score.

The sociogram consists of concentric circles representing the social normative system allowing us to indicate the individual's range of deviations and related emotional motivational equilibrial forces.

The sociogram is a graph positioning of the individual as a pendulum ball suspended in the normative field illustrated by a system of concentric circles. This graph utilizes a system of concentric circles and ellipses to illustrate the personality scores and the psychic tension scores as interrelated graphically. The psycho-sociogram allows presenting how the individual fits into the social power map. The two sets of concentric ellipses, placed on diametrically opposite positions on a set of concentric circles represent the individual states. The size of the circle is determined by the intensity of the weighted averages of the four relational modalities. The size of the ellipse is determined by the psychic tension score, the fifth weighted average of the grid. Both vary from 1-6.

This portrayal reveals at a glance the testee's relational modality as well as the psychic tension experienced. The graph of the social system clarifies the power/powerlessness intensity through the concentric circles. The individual extreme emotions are portrayed peripherally as two concentric ellipses in reciprocal positions. Vectors in the ellipses reflect the psychic forces, emotions. Vectors in the circles reflect behaviors. The diagram may be completed through information contributed by the inventory and corroborated by the metaphor tests. There is correspondence and complementarity between the relational inventory and the metaphor relational choices. The inventory provides clarity, when the pattern described in the metaphors is ambiguous.

The placement of the individual on the power side and the powerless side is determined by the scores of the relational modalities. The direction of vectors departing from the ellipses indicates the alternatives of cooperation, clockwise, versus antagonism, counterclockwise.

The scores of relational modalities determine the length of vectors attached to the individual's ellipse/s. The psychic tension of the individual determines the polarization level of the ellipses. The numbers of the four relational scales indicate the relational modalities corresponding to the individual. They determine where the individual is placed on the concentric circles and if his attitude is cooperative or antagonistic.

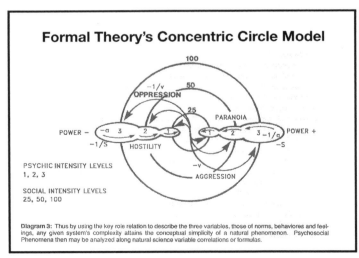

Formal Theory's Concentric Circle Model

PSYCHIC INTENSITY LEVELS
1, 2, 3

SOCIAL INTENSITY LEVELS
25, 50, 100

Diagram 3: Thus by using the key role relation to describe the three variables, those of norms, behaviors and feelings, any given system's complexity attains the conceptual simplicity of a natural phenomenon. Psychosocial Phenomena then may be analyzed along natural science variable correlations or formulas.

This graph conveys diagnostic information; it identifies the test taker's relational profile. It portrays the individual as dominant or submissive, cooperative or antagonistic, alternatively all the above. The graph simply presents the distribution of modalities visually.

The concentric circles diagram reflects the reciprocity between positions of power on the right and of the reciprocal positions of powerlessness on the left. The relational intensity is reflected in the polarization between the opposite states, as increasingly distant placement on the three concentric circles.

Four vectors within the circles qualify the person's attitude. Cooperative modalities are identified with clockwise vectors, antagonistic modalities with counterclockwise vectors attached on the ellipses and going along the perimeters of the concentric circles; at the end of the vectors we point the intensity of each corresponding modality; thus submissive cooperative relating would have a vector scored with the corresponding number along the clockwise direction, while the submissive antagonistic modality would be a vector departing from the ellipse going counterclockwise with a number reflecting the intensity of this submissive antagonistic modality.

There are three parameters to evaluate in the graphic portrayal of the power field. Its concentric structure indicates degrees of polarization. This diagram is used in scoring every test by placing a circle system next to the art-work analyzed and within it identifying three dichotomies:

   1. Passivity/activity polar opposite and reciprocal locations to place the individuals. These are indicated with ellipses positioned on the reciprocal posts on one of the social system's circumferences.

   2. Cooperation with clockwise vectors and antagonism with counterclockwise vectors within the social system's concentric circles and similarly in the psychic system's ellipses.

   3. Social and emotional interaction vectors and psychic tension placed within the social system may be used to reflect the dichotomy of alienation versus mutual respect.

Pathology is reflected in the numbers of the relational grid, the nature of the artwork and the companion text

Subject R_3q6nRZQaQUnyTAN Male r

Dominant Cooperative Weighed Average	Dominant Antagonistic Weighed Average	Submissive Cooperative Weighed Average	Submissive Antagonistic Weighed Average	Psychic Tension
2.303030303	1.972972973	4.041666667	5	3.960784314

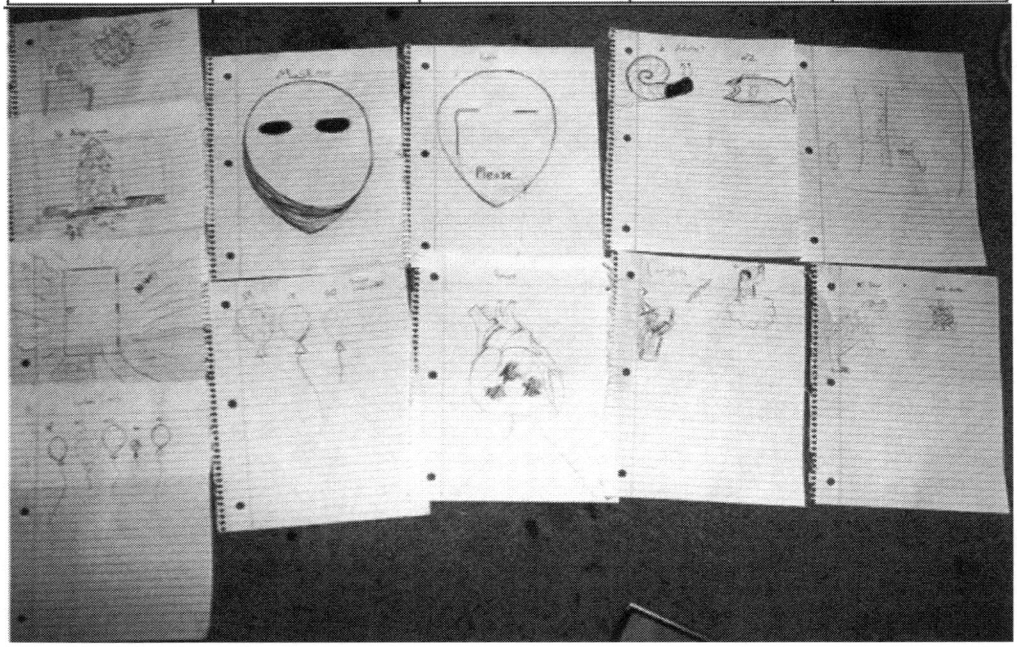

In the template above we see a dramatic elevation in the submissive antagonism modality, and the psychic tension scale 3.96 out of 6. The text of the protocols reveals that the individual is troubled throughout. In his Short Story an individual leaves a suicide note behind.

The sociogram of this individual should portray an elongated ellipse positioned on the left pole of the social system with a counterclockwise vector leading to that end. A similar vector should be introduced in the ellipse.

Simplifying the interpretation each test of the battery may be scored according to the three formal dichotomies recognized above. A diagram below the given art work sums up the relational dynamics identified in each metaphor be that an animal, memory, or dream study. The diagram summarizes the emotional and social constellation. The diagrams reduce the complexity of the stories and of the corresponding art-work into purely scientific abstractions. The graphic representation of the tests illustrates the linking of art and science. Science quantifies every emotional experience. Metaphors are shown to become natural science measurable entities.

The tests inserted in the template illustrate how the relational modality is experienced by the test taker. The template columns are viewed in dialectic continuity of cause effect evolving from the stress state to the compromise. Images reflect the continuity of emotions as a conflict resolving order. They may be shown to be in formal relation to each other, revealing the syndromal unfolding of the person's relational modality. Stress, a state of passivity, antagonism and alienation in each case study may be observed to evolve predictably to a compromise as the position of mastery, cooperation and mutual respect reflecting the mind's universal pathway yet modified by the test taker's particular way of resolving conflicts.

The template displays the individual's six sets of metaphor tests. The tests visualize the emotions as an oscillating energetic quantity conserved but transformed from the emotional or dynamic state to its kinetic or behavioral energetic counterpart and then to a spiritual, attitudinal change as the resolution, the return to the new rest state. The art is viewed as the dramatic unfolding of the personal relational modality pattern. The mental oscillation sometimes clearly shows how a conflict evolves to a resolution along the formal transformations of a key symbolic construct. The emotional continuum reflected in the templates underscores the significance of the stories as reflecting the circumscribed nature of the unconscious process.

Interpretations are not speculative and qualitative but objective and quantitative.

The fact that the Formal Theory represents a scientific breakthrough integrating the humanities and the sciences is well illustrated as we convert emotions into their graphic representation with constructs and formulas with systemic significance. Unlike other psychological tests, inventories of traits and projectives with given set of interpretation of images, here we readily translate emotions into natural science constructs and graphs. Interpretations are not speculative and qualitative but objective and quantitative.

The Computer Generated Report: Transcript of the Tests Plus Six Templates for the Interpretation of the Battery

A simple program is used to readily generate a report on the total battery testing provided it is entered on a digital format. The report besides containing the transcription of all tests delivers six templates.

1. The program addresses first, the relational inventory, the RMES.
It identifies results graphically and then with a verbal report on the prevalent relational modality, or mixture of modalities and their respective subcategories. The relational modality report identifies a single relational modality when appropriate or multiple relational diagnoses, when the impression is complex.

- The computer report informs the test taker on her/his relational diagnosis with set descriptions of each relational modality, each of the four modalities being described in totality as wellness resolutions of conflicts.

- Subcategories of each modality are also given weighted average scores.

- Significant items for each relational diagnosis are added to the report.

  The report will identify the very prominent items in the five scales with 4-6 items that are the most outstanding as scored highly intense.

- Psychic tension qualifies the wellness versus illness state of personal functioning. It will highlight the particular elevated items.

- Also depending on the intensity of agreement or disagreement along all scales the report should refer to concerns of certain related clinical psychopathologies.

2. The program organizes information provided by the projective tests. The report sums the following items across all metaphor tests finding commonalities.

- The report starts with the psychodynamic organization of the images on the template of the six roles. Stress elicits a response, the response elicits anxiety as anticipations of role reversal; anxiety elicits defenses and these the actual role reversal captured in dreams and intensified metaphors; resolutions are presented in Short Stories.

- The modality is illustrated by the artwork. The relational modality is exemplified by the person's particular emotional conflict and how this is resolved.

- The person's syndromal sequence of emotions in his/her lifecycle is bound on one key action with its transformations organized by the six-role process as illustrated in the template.

3. Insights Template

- The report combines answers to several tests in one summary statement. The report uses the words of the testee to describe each identity figure and their traits.

- The comparative display of similar tests, memories, masks and metaphors is presented in respective columns followed by the narrative. The report sums up the insights combining parallel items from all metaphors.

- The personal identities include these parallel distinctions: Animals, fairy tale heroes, intensified animals, and short story. This transcript includes the bipole of animal choices, fairy tales, etc. and indicates the animal a person identifies with.

4. The Suggested Changes Template

- The program identifies the test taker's pattern compiling the parallel responses in successive metaphors under the same question from 8-14.

  Step 8, Changes the animals need to make
  Items 10, pertinence of the animal drama to one's life
  Item 11 Changes a person needs to make.
  Item 12, pattern that one repeats
  Item 13 Responsibility for pattern
  Item 14 Willingness to make changes

5. The program includes a self evaluation of the assessment's insight evoking experience in 'The letter to oneself'. The synthesis in the words of the test taker are usually presented in one's letter to one self.

This exercise reinforces the insights derived from both types of tests, the diagnostic inventory and the emotional metaphors. The four questions of the letter explore the impact of the testing for the person.

6. The Query Report. The query is a list of statements regarding the testing experience. It solicits the impression generated by the tests as awareness of the level of knowledge, insights accomplished, and the issues of changes a person is willing to make based on the findings from the testing.

These six computer-generated reports should be very valuable to the test taking person and the professionals involved in the testee's education be those therapists or educators, who could discuss the findings with the client and develop a more meaningful integration of information.

Delivery of the Testing Information
The testing may be delivered once or repeated for diagnostic, therapeutic, and for monitoring therapy outcome objectives.

Therapy and wellness education consist in informing the person about the syndromal cause effect connection of power positioning and related emotions as syndromal entities and proceeding to identify them utilizing the creative process through the CAB. The assessment and correction of intrapsychic and interpersonal conflicts is the same for both educational wellness objectives and for therapeutic intervention in illness. The test taker identifies the personal relational modality and then addresses modifying one's relational social power conduct affecting the correlated emotional counterpart component.

The Tests Have Three Functions: Didactic, Diagnostic and Therapeutic
The first function of the battery is educational; an essay points out how the mind works along the structure and function of the creative process. It informs that the mind is predictable as a conflict resolution mechanism clarifying the need for normative social adjustment and informs on the nature of wellness diagnostic categories, the relational modalities, representing genetically determined, culturally influenced wellness diagnostic entities.

The second function is diagnostic; the tests reveal to the test taker the diagnosis of one's pattern along the range of alternative modalities of resolving conflicts. The relational modality diagnosis is made with both the REMS inventory and the projectives. The RMES detects the relational modality of a person and the traits, subcategories within the modalities. The inventory measures the third formal operation as distinctions of alienation versus mutual respect, corresponding to high psychic tension, identifying illness as distinct clinical symptoms: depression, anxiety, paranoia and a whole slew of pathologies or normative deviations such as need disorders, alcohol use, eating disorders, psychosomatic conditions, and performance, a range of relational adjustment issues.

Finally the testing is therapeutic by helping a person to get in touch with his hidden feelings, to become aware of his defenses and their ineffectiveness and to modify his conduct as power management changes. The tests are therapeutic along many levels of growth; they have a cathartic emotional significance by expressing feelings. The battery is integrative along the template by connecting power choices and emotional syndromal consequences thus giving the person insight in the cause effect integration of one's experiences. It helps a person to consider changes. The testee arrives to conclusions about one's diagnosis and one's need for particular changes, assertiveness for submissive and moderation for dominant individuals. The testing an emotional experience is processed intellectually.

The goal of therapy is to generate awareness in the person of the correlation of emotions and behaviors as circumscribed syndromes.

The self-knowledge consists in identifying one's relational pattern and realizing its ineffectiveness requiring that one modify it in order to reduce one's psychic tension. The Battery is therapeutic in the sense that it helps to identify emotions and to ease oneself into making changes in the personal conflict generating relational pattern. This conceptualization and identification of personal tendencies potentiates the reduction of emotional distress and dysfunctional behavior. The program reduces both intrapsychic and interpersonal conflict.

The Formal Theoretical diagnosis and therapy follows along two directions: one is cognitive, simple cognitive behavioral information on the nature of syndromal thinking. The second component is experiential; it consists in completing the workbook evoking insights and spelling one's need for changes.

CAB represents a standardized delivery of a number of therapeutic modalities integrated in one: It generates emotional release, generates insights and elicits corrective changes for behavioral changes spelled out by the test taker. More insights evolve upon organizing tests and emotions on a conflict resolution template. The meaningfulness of the assessment lowers the resistance of the patient to therapeutic interventions.

The assessment information consists of a thorough psychological evaluation. The task is artistically pleasing, socially meaningful and spiritually fulfilling. The assessment integrates many therapeutic interventions into an educational experience.

1. The testee becomes conscious of the unconscious power management relational modality as one's mode of processing emotions.

2. The projective tests begin with *art therapy* exercises tapping the unconscious.

3. The information of the several projective tests is organized along the *cognitive behavioral model*, by understanding emotions as a syndrome of choices unifying one's experiences along one's relational modality diagnostic category. The homework assignments consist in ongoing creativity tests.

4. *Psychodynamic insights* are generated by identifying the interrelation of behaviors and emotions as a person's relational pattern.

5. The assessment leads to *behavior modification* directives spelled out by the testee.

6. The *therapy outcome* may be identified by repeating the evaluation to measure the progress completed. In education the assessment should be repeated in periodic intervals.

7. The effectiveness of the educational, diagnostic, therapeutic assessment and behavior modification interventions reduce the need for *reliance on medications* and reduce the length of hospitalization, while they generate information that can be useful as a record for the continuation of therapy.

Summarizing the Functions of the Conflict Analysis Battery
This assessment instrument unlike other assessments has many functions:

1. It is educational as it demonstrates that the mind is predictably resolving conflict following certain natural science laws.

2. It is diagnostic by delivering information in simple language to the testee, who identifies her relational modality in both the inventory and the metaphors.

3. It is therapeutic guiding the test-taker to identify her emotions, their rational interrelation, and changes to make in order to optimize conflict resolution. The assessment has a clear diagnostic function. The two approaches to assessment, the inventory and the projectives, cross validate each other and complement each other into a valid and reliable personality profile.

4. The assessment leads to therapeutic benefits that facilitate the process of therapy. The findings can be further analyzed by the respective professionals to extract more therapeutically helpful information.

5. The testing is cost-effective and may be delivered bypassing the need for costly professional services. The testing demonstrates that the unconscious mind resolves conflict as a purely scientific phenomenon; hence the information and process may be used for educational purposes in the classroom rather than be monopolized either by psychologists or clergy.

6. The CAB instrument measures the unit of the unconscious as a relational diagnosis and identifies the physical and formal structure of the creative process as a natural science conflict resolving measurable entity, the unit of the social sciences. This phenomenon is measurable and generates a clear personality typology.

7. The CAB represents a new way of collecting, organizing and interpreting assessment information. The overarching order is recognizing a six role state dialectic of emotions proceeding universally to conflict resolution reflecting an inner need for justice. The assessment validates the Formal Theory's assumption on the nature of the unconscious. The assessment promotes awareness of the conflict resolution principles as moral values.

The Integrative Function of the Process
The unconscious process reconciling morality and psychology is shown through the testing as guiding the person to respect conflict resolution structuring the thought process and social relations. The testee is shown to instinctively value fairness in relations and to define the creative unconscious process as compelling one to think morally. This scientific and moral entity integrates the humanities and the sciences. As the psychological and moral order entity it unifies psychology, morality and science. As a physiological homeostatic and psychological moral entity the process integrates morality and psychology with physiology. As the conflict resolving moral organization of emotions in all creativity/stories this unit order of the social sciences integrates them into a single science, the Science of Conflict Resolution or the Moral Science.
The process integrates the social sciences:

*   Therapy as the modification of behavior with the moral direction of appropriate conflict

resolution.

- Education as the delivery of abstract personally relevant information.

- Sociology as information on the structuring of relations, norms.

- Politics as the sociological models of power management, individual rights and rules of social representation.

- Creativity, arts, literature as compositions, the casual creation of conflictual presentations with a moral outcome in several media.

- Religion as the moral redirection of behavior.

 SOUTHERN CONNECTICUT STATE UNIVERSITY New Haven,

I conducted Item Analysis, Reliability, and Validity Studies of the Conflict Analysis Battery which was constructed by Dr. Albert Levis.

The reliability study of the battery indicates that the different scales have high reliability coefficients to be used in individual diagnosis. The Dominant Cooperative, Dominant Antagonistic, Submissive Cooperative, Submissive Antagonistic, and Psychic Conflict Tension scales have reliability coefficients which range from .88 - .96. The Antagonistic/Cooperative Scale has a reliability coefficient of .79. This is due to the fact that it is the shortest scale. It has only ten items. The different reliability coefficients are much higher than those of the MMPI scales.

The different validity studies of the battery indicate that the scales have enough evidence of validity for its purpose.

In addition, factor analysis was conducted on the battery items. The factors which were extradited highly overlapped the original scales. The results of factor analysis are indicative of the factorial validity of the different battery scales.

The battery is comparable to the best available personality inventories in construction, reliability and validity. Also, it measures important personality dimensions based on Dr. Levis' Theory of Behavior. By continuing research, the battery will gain prominence   in personality assessment.

F-Karas

Shawky F. Karas, Ed.D.
Professor & Director of the Research &
Measurement Program

Reliability

As far as the reliabilities of the scales are concerned, the Conflict Analysis Battery scales are much better than the MMPI scales. "Several studies among psychiatric groups have reported coefficient within the range of .11 (Welsh, 1952) to .96 (Winfield, 1952)." (Kleinmuntz, 1967). The reliabilities of the Conflict Analysis Battery scales are comparable to the carefully constructed the California Psychological Inventory scales whose reliabilities are generally high, "in the upper .80's and lower .90's (Kleinmuntz, 1967). The Conflict Analysis Battery scales reliabilities are generally higher than those of the Guilford-Zimmerman Temperament Survey scales whose split-half reliabilities range from .75 to .87 (Kleinmuntz, 1967).

Validity

A of the "Conflict Analysis Battery" has a significant correlation with SA of the "Interpersonal Check List." The correlation is noticeably a high correlation (.778). While the correlations between SA of the "Conflict Analysis Battery" and other scale in the "Interpersonal Check List" is not significantly higher than zero. This is a very clear evidence of the concurrent validity and discriminant validity of SA.

Factorial Validity

To find the factorial structure of the Conflict Analyis Battery items, the intercorrelations among the items were computed, factor analysis of the correlation matrix was carried out using the Principle Component method, and the factors were rotated using the Varimax method. Three factors were extracted using the criterion that the sign values should not be less than one. The items of the three factors are highly overlapping with the items of the major three scales. When six factors were extracted, the six battery scales were almost reproduced. The results are clearly indicative of the factorial validity of the six scales of the battery.

Conclusion

There is enough evidence of the construct validity of the battery scales besides its ability to discriminate between the clinical groups. While "the greatest limitation of the MMPI, as critics have repeatedly indicated (Adock, 1965; Lingoes, 1965), is its lack of sensitivity in discriminating within abnormal or normal group themselves" (Kleinmuntz, 1967).

The Conflict Analysis Battery scales ere constructed around the framework of a new theory and have enough evidence of reliabilities and construct validity for each scale to identify clinical groups and discriminate among them. While the Conflict Analysis Battery is theoretical the MMPI is atheoretical. In addition, the Conflict Analysis Battery scales have enough high reliabilities to be used for the interpretation of individual scores; and enough evidence of construct validity for the purpose of each scale.

Chapter Four

Creativity and Power Management
A Concise Program of Emotional Education
Based on the Conflict Analysis Battery

Objectives of Therapy

Identifying the unconscious has been traditional psychodynamic therapies' classical objective. Identifying moral values and following them has been religions' mission. Power Management attains both objectives effortlessly in one concise program without either a therapist or a clergy person being involved.

Therapies have aspired to make the person conscious of the unconscious by identifying it through analysis of the transference relationship between the patient and the therapist. Religions have aspired to inspire the faithful imparting respect for a moral authority. The Moral Science's emotional education program, Creativity and Power Management, CPM, accomplishes insights and values, by making a person conscious of her/his unconscious without a therapist or clergyman simply by identifying natural science's moral authority in dictating values as the formal operations guiding the unconscious to conflict resolution.

The Program's Two Segments

'Creativity and Power Management' is a concise program of emotional education that uses the concepts and the technology of the Formal Theory. It has two components:

1. The cognitive or educational provides the meaningful integration of knowledge. The participant learns about the nature of the process, about the relational modality syndromes and about the principles of conflict resolution as the three formal operations. S/he also learns about the two test-types, the inventory and the projectives, and learns about using the imagery of the tests to reconstruct the six-role process template to identify the personal pattern.

2. The experiential segment consists in completing the self-assessment battery utilizing creativity for self-discovery. The assessment is inherently psychotherapeutic. It helps to identify one's relational modality and to evolve the meaningful integration of personal experiences. It allows the student of behavior to become conscious of the unconscious and to identify the syndromal interrelation of behaviors and emotions hence recognizing changes needed to reduce conflicts and symptoms.

Power Management integrating the didactic, diagnostic and therapeutic information becomes a very cohesive concise and comprehensive self-examination. It departs from traditional therapies as it relies on knowledge and on the self-assessment. The testing combined with educational material delivers a wholesome psycho-education.

While most current therapies are not bound to moral values the Formal Theory's Creativity and Power Management promotes awareness of them as the pivotal mental dynamic: They are redefined as the formal operations of the unconscious: mastery, cooperation and mutual respect as the science based conflict resolution unconscious principles that automatically propel to conflict resolution. Now moral values are adopted deliberately by the person, who becomes self aware on how to manage power. The program advancing knowledge on the nature of the unconscious advocates the deliberate pursuit of the formal operations as needed to restore emotional balance, the state of wellness.

The cognitive segment imparts information on the creative process. The abbreviated format for this information is simply reading an essay about the four key concepts of the Formal Theory: The essay about the Wizard of Oz story utilizing its four metaphors to understand the process as the Yellow Brick Road, the relational modalities as the four characters, the assessment as equivalent to killing the witch, and clarity of moral values by demystifying the authority of the Wizard. The essay leads to the meaningful integration of knowledge based on the concept of the conflict resolution process.

The experiential segment utilizes the Conflict Analysis Battery (CAB) to identify the personal wellness diagnosis as a relational modality syndrome. Insights lead to understanding oneself and exploring personal attitude changes. The combination of education and self-assessment consist in a powerful emotional education that delivers knowledge affirmed by its relevance in gaining personal insights by learning how to improve one's management of power. The case studies confirm the effectiveness of this program delivered within educational, clinical and on-line settings.

The principle element of this education is understanding the unifying process. It allows to progress from the encyclopedic unintegrated, fragmented information on emotions and behaviors to examine their logical integration imparted by the meaningful psychodynamic structure of the syndromal six-role process. Creativity is shown to be the language of the unconscious that the test taker learns to understand and gradually speak.

We identify this order as alternative relational modalities and seek to evolve self-awareness and power management skills. The concepts and the related assessment technology revamp psychology and education; we identify the delivery as psycho-education instead of psychotherapy because the emphasis is on learning actively by oneself rather than being a passive recipient of services.

The Cognitive Segment: The Curriculum of Emotional Education
The cognitive segment introduces the four new concepts: the unconscious, diagnostic categories, the

assessment instrument, and conflict resolution principles as moral values. These notions represent conceptual and technological innovations that literally revamp the field of psychology into that of a very different field; we call it the Moral Science or alternatively, the Science of Conflict Resolution. A lecture series provides cognitive information about the theory, its distinctions and their relevance. Below we review the four topics as the curriculum of an educational program for the academic and the school age public:

1. **Innovations in the field begin with a new method and object for the study of behavior**
   The unconscious is a measurable Conflict Resolution Process. The method is formal analysis; the object of formal analysis is the creative process. The methodological shift overlooks the content of stories to observe what is universal in all stories, their plot, as a concise one directional relation of emotions/ideas from a point of conflict to one of resolution. This order will be observed through the formal analysis of samples of personal creativity. The focus is in examining associations as a dialectic of emotions to identify the individual's unconscious as her way of resolving conflicts or managing power.

   The Formal Theory identifies the unconscious as a natural science conflict resolution or moral order phenomenon, where morality is defined as a sociologically adaptive function. The formal unconscious is the unit of the social sciences, methodologically a totally different concept from the contemporary agnostic, non-rational, non-holistic conflict-generating unconscious.

   The unconscious is a scientific mechanism identified by studying the creative process as a six-role state, three emotional oscillations, following three formal operations. The studies demonstrate this concept in organizing emotions into the universal, measurable and graphically portrayable harmonic.

2. **The formal theoretical position departs from the clinical symptoms based DSM diagnostic categories by identifying four wellness personality types, the relational modality syndromes.**
   The unit mechanism is a qualifiable and quantifiable relational modality providing new diagnostic categories, the four relational modalities as wellness syndromes of relating. These are unlike the illness based diagnostic categories. The relational modalities explain personality differences, pathogenesis and entail therapeutic changes as power management modifications. These wellness diagnoses account for clinical symptoms experienced upon increased psychic tension or stress.

3. **The Conflict Analysis Battery, CAB, self-assessment instrument is didactic, diagnostic and therapeutic.**
   The process is measurable by the self-assessment instrument. The objective of the assessment is to identify one's relational modality diagnosis, thus becoming conscious of the unconscious. It also leads to reconstruct the emotional dialectic guiding a person to identify changes in order to deliberately reduce one's conflicts.

   The CAB combines a personality inventory identifying the relational modality and a set of projective, creativity-tapping exercises leading to the reconstruction of the personal way of resolving conflicts. The two types of tests lead to insights and directives for changes.

4. **Processing of the assessment a personalized emotional education in the context of the new Moral Science.**

The formal role analysis processing of information is facilitated by using a template to organize the test-derived information. The learner recognizes the personal pattern and the repetitions of the pattern. This self-assessment is conducted by the client, be s/he a well and or a clinically identified person. It delivers insights directly to the test-taker.

The testing integrates various psychotherapeutic modalities: it combines cognitive behavioral principles, art therapy, psychodynamic analysis and behavior modification. The cumulative information is integrated by the test-taker. This intervention changes the authoritarian patient therapist relationship into that of a teacher student collaborative one. The self-discovery process is effective without a therapist or educator in its online delivery.

The test taker becomes conscious of the unconscious as a particular relational modality. The conscious mind seeks to guide the person to improved adjustment by deliberately resolving conflicts optimally. The conscious mind follows the principles of conflict resolution: mastery, cooperation and mutual respect deliberately. The relational insights guide a person to comply or alternatively defy her societal norms toward optimal adjustment. The next step is in the relational skills training by promoting the development of relational coping skills to improve personal emotional competence in dealing optimally with conflicts. Exercises depart from the diagnosis to evolve the corrective processing of emotions.

Science Empowers Therapy and Education

Science changes the practice of therapy. It becomes clear that studying and tapping creativity we can achieve clarity of behavior as a science. Therapy and education become meaningful as the complementary realms in the integration of knowledge, making knowledge personally relevant as diagnostic, therapeutic and spiritually empowering.

The recognition that the mental process is a scientific phenomenon transforms the field of the social sciences into that of the rigorous Moral Science. This development enables education to promote the study of the creative process as the scientific integrative paradigm that transforms education into being therapeutic and psychotherapy into becoming educational. The program changes both therapy and education by providing educational/cognitive information within the process of self-explorations.

Psychotherapy Versus Psycho-Education

Conflict Analysis Battery's therapeutic effectiveness is due to the testing's faculty to identify the unconscious objectively for the benefit of the test taker. The inventory findings are cross-validated by the metaphor tests. The tests are complementary identifying the unconscious as a measurable scientific, qualifiable and quantifiable phenomenon, predictable and readily identifiable as a relational modality.

The new therapy challenges traditional insight focused psychotherapies. The test taker becomes conscious of the unconscious attaining the objective by oneself without interpretations proposed by a therapist. The objectivity of the diagnostic insights generated by the assessment preempt the need for a therapist to interpret the test taker's protocols and the need for a relationship required for the accurate determination of one's transference type. The relational scales identify the relational modality of the testee thus canceling the diagnostic significance of transference. Transference is a misnomer for the relational modality diagnoses, which are readily identified using the personality inventory completed by a test taker in a half hour.

The effectiveness of the assessment changes the realm of psychotherapy into one of psycho-education. It is true though that the expert conflict-analyst can compound insights derived from the testing and of course nothing substitutes the healing significance of a model relationship between a patient and a great caring and norm respecting therapist.

The reason for the approach's effectiveness is in the fact that the program is based on science. Science foretells. Prometheus' name means foretelling. He stole the fire of the gods and gave it to the mortals. We consider this to mean that he stole the moral authority of gods by identifying patterns as independent of the power of gods, and he used this wisdom to foretell Zeus' fate. Zeus then respectfully released Prometheus from the rock and the related predicament to be attacked nightly by an eagle. The fire of the gods is identifying the conflict resolution process as the universal harmonic, the key to a new empowering order integrating the social sciences into the wisdom of the Moral Science and freeing humankind from the divisive wisdom of religions.

The Moral Science's object of study is conflict resolution. Science identifies the process and its relevance in healing the individual and the world as the path to resolution is as wide open and predictable as formulas and enlightening technology conferred through an educational program. The relevance of this scientific breakthrough is effectiveness in all aspects of conducting psychological services: diagnosis, formulation, delivery of therapy and measurement of the outcome of interventions.

Contrasting Power Management versus Traditional Therapies and Identifying Power Management as the Model Integrative Therapy
CPM represents a new concept in the realm of therapeutic interventions. It is an educational program that integrates many modalities of therapy. This program can be delivered by therapists but also by ordinary educators for the benefit of school age population.

Power Management like cognitive therapies has an educational component informing on the nature of the unconscious and on the revised diagnostic categories. This education is delivered to the online test takers through an essay, alternatively to patients and trainees by studying the exhibits of the Museum of the Creative Process. Cognitive therapies use assignments to the patients. Power Management's equivalent is the completion of the assessment as a workbook or through its online delivery.

The Power Management intervention qualifies as *Cognitive behavioral* due to the fact that it is based on an education on the nature of the process accompanied by homework, completing a manual for self-discovery. This manual is the thorough self-assessment workbook combining a personality inventory with a set of projectives to identify how the person resolves conflict along the psychodynamic pathway.

The didactic information clarifies that the unconscious is a natural science phenomenon, and that we have a set of wellness diagnostic categories, the four relational modalities. The cognitive piece explains the significance of syndromal causality of the interrelation of behaviors and emotions. Then the therapy uses a manual, the self-assessment, the CAB, tapping on the creative process for the measurement of the individual process. The test taker learns about the organization of emotions along the conflict resolution continuum of six emotions and using the testing identifies her own relational diagnosis and how to organize the information to achieve insights and directives for changes.

Cognitive therapies traditionally educate the patient on a variety of narrow behavioral conditions; they inform on symptom control or management, rather than the interrelation of behaviors and emotions as syndromally connected and allowing a person to modify feelings by modifying behaviors.

The cognitive message in Power Management therapy does not stop at identifying and modifying unpleasant emotions and behaviors. It clarifies the syndromal equilibrial structure of the conflict resolving function of the unconscious. Normative deviations from the comfort level result in the experience of psychic tension, which leads to the manifestation of symptoms.

Psychodynamic therapies identify insights by interpreting the transference relationship and understanding the use of defense mechanisms. The insights in Power Management are generated by identifying one's relational modality by completing the relational inventory and by identifying the syndromal emotional sequence by completing the metaphor tests.

Psychodynamic insights are generated by interrelating fragmented experiences into syndromal entities integrating predictably emotions and behaviors along the six-role process. The assessment identifies one's relational modality as a psychodynamic totality leading to insights on one's intrapsychic and interpersonal relations but without the need for an interpersonal relationship or even a therapist.

In CPM the patient becomes aware of her/his power management modality and assumes responsibility for making changes. Dominant and submissive relating are the diagnostic categories. Correction of social deviations through appropriate modification of one's power leads to relief from psychic tension and symptoms. A person's feelings are normalized as the dominant person reduces her anger and the submissive person asserts herself. Moderating acting out as restraint of one's demanding behaviors or aggression, leads to reduction of anxiety. Assertive expression of one's feelings reduces depression and hostility. The emotional relief experienced by relational adjustments reinforces changes in conduct.

Insight psychodynamic therapies focus on interpersonal relations and patterns studying the transference relationship. In Power Management we identify one's relational pattern through the personality inventory as a relational modality diagnosis. The relational modality diagnosis captures the transference pattern abstractly while the metaphors identify it as the pattern manifested across one's lifetime of conflicts and ineffective resolutions.

The battery confirms *the psychodynamic connection of behaviors and emotions* as a relational modality, one's wellness diagnosis. The six-role template connects the episodes in one's life into continua of resolutions. The meaningful connection of fragmented experiences seemingly unrelated episodes on the template helps to understand the psychodynamic integration of all emotions and to clarify the role of the person in generating the psychological and sociological problems experienced.

The completion of the test battery has a significant emotional cathartic impact on the person. The conflict is identified with the conflictual memories tests, the response with the transparent mask test, anxiety is the hidden feelings behind the mask. Defense is in the animal and fairy tale metaphors. Reversal is identified with the dream metaphor and compromise with the short story; this continuum constructs one's lifetime pattern. Completing the assessment is an emotional experience.

This syndrome indicates what changes a person needs to make to better resolve conflicts. Since the testing identifies the relational modality diagnosis therapy is not required to determine a person's transference relating. The relational modality is a person's transference. To identify it we do not need the patient therapist relationship though the ineffective relational pattern may be observed in that and other relationships. The relational modality is not due to formative childhood experiences. It is genetically determined. The diagnosis/insight helps one to understand one's relational modality's strengths and weaknesses.

In CPM *the therapist is active but with a simplified psychodynamic task*; he helps the client to identify her/his role system, meaningfully connecting the tests into a dramatic or conflict-resolving continuum. He is a teacher rather than the impersonator of a magical authority like the Wizard viewed by the four characters as a totally different entity.

Behavior modification therapies: Power Management includes behavior modification insights delivered through the assessment's emphasis in identifying directives for change.

Behavior modification therapies contain manuals for the recording of symptoms and how to deal with them utilizing particular techniques such as desensitization through gradual exposure therapies. The CAB provides insights on one's pattern as manifested in one's metaphors and the person identifies there the respective need for power management changes.

Power Management addresses behavior modification as indicated by one's relational deviation. CPM is clear in explaining the connection of symptoms and behaviors and the need accordingly to modify one's behavior. Dominance as abusing of power generates anxiety, fears of reciprocities. Hence to reduce one's anxiety one needs to moderate the abuse of power. Submissiveness, the lack of use of power generates depression and hostility. This person needs to assume power to reduce the hostile attitude.

Psychodynamics, cognition and behavior modification can be pursued together and possibly at an educational rather than a therapeutic setting.

Spiritual Therapies
While religions suggest moral values as general principles science suggests to deliberately follow the principles of conflict resolution: moderation, cooperation and mutual respect. This therapeutic approach may include reviewing the topic of the reconciliation of science and religion by recognizing that religions worship alternative approaches to conflict resolutions and that this therapeutic approach integrates all wisdoms into the unifying science of conflict resolution. All religions seek to control desires as power management to reduce the experience of conflict. But in the process they promote alternative approaches to conflict resolution focusing to either one of the scientific values: moderation, cooperation and mutual respect. This point helps to reconcile the traditional dogma-based partial knowledge into an all-inclusive moral perspective encouraging the person to integrate morality as conflict resolution and science.

'The sculptural trail in the history of love', one of the exhibits of the Museum of the Creative Process demonstrates the progression of moral discoveries by the great cultures of the world as the evolution of norms restructuring family role relations. Greece discovered mastery of patriarchy over matriarchy, India discovered men's cooperation and submission to women, and Judea neutralized women by focusing on mutual respect between father and son; the Messianic religions corrected this preference by introducing the political counterpart to Judaism's father-son covenant by favoring the mother-child alliance.

This evolution in the restructuring of gender relational norms emphasizes awareness of the progression to normative fairness and abstraction on the nature of the divine. The Moral Science concludes the unfinished business of religions by both completing normative transformation in family relations and in the redefinition of the divine. Science ascribes the attributes of the divine to the human unconscious orderly conflict resolution process.

Comparing Traditional Models of Diagnosis and Therapy with the Formal Theoretical Counterparts

Features of Psychotherapies	Psychodynamic Therapies	Power Management
The Unconscious	The Freudian definition of the unconscious is that of an irrational, sexual and aggressive set of drives, alternatively the focus is on relations	A conflict resolving natural science entity observed as the syndromal analysis of creativity, by utilizing the self-assessment battery
Diagnosis	DSM's distinctions identify clusters of clinical symptoms	Four wellness syndromal genetically determined relational modalities
Testing Procedures and Therapy Interventions	No routine tests. They utilize chemotherapies	Completing the self-assessment, which is diagnostic and therapeutic
Moral Values	Agnostic perspective	Moral values as the three scientific principles of resolving conflict
Therapist	The Authority making interpretations diagnosis and prescribing meds	Relationship of patient to therapist is modified to that of student to teacher
Principal Therapeutic Modality or Manual Driven Intervention	Cognitive, behavioral, and psychodynamic	The *Conflict Analysis Battery* integrates many psychotherapeutic modalities: psychometrics, cognitive behavioral, art therapy and psychodynamic formulation. It is completed with an essay

Comparison of Power Management to Other Therapeutic Modalities

	Formal Theory's Conflict Analysis, psychodynamic therapy	Cognitive Behavior Therapy	Behavior Modification Therapy	Psychodynamic therapy
Diagnosis	Relational modality as alternative to transference	Symptom based clinical diagnosis	Behaviors based diagnosis	Transference psychodynamic analysis
Pattern awareness	Six emotions syndrome defining the unconscious as a conflict resolving measurable process	Thought pattern that needs to be interrupted	Focus on Behavior pattern that needs to be interrupted	The unconscious as a relational and drive directed pattern
Origin of Symptom Evoking Thinking	Genetically determined relational disposition affected by stress	Self perpetuating pattern activated by stress		Developmentally evoked relational genesis of illness

Diagnostic Strategy	Connecting six emotions and behaviors as a lifetime pattern through the battery of tests	Monitoring symptoms emotions associations	Monitoring behaviors	Free associations combined with observing interaction with therapist
Therapeutic Interventions	Identifying diagnosis of relational modality and modifying power management mode to reduce psychic and interpersonal conflict	Controlling Emotions and behaviors without reference to psychic conflict	Controlling behaviors through a number of techniques	Analysis of transference, and of defenses
Manual Homework	CAB complete self assessment periodically repeated	Identifying and interrupting thought patterns	Interrupting behavior patterns	No homework
Termination	Essay upon completion of therapy and mural of integrated metaphors			
Duration of the Intervention	Evaluation 3 sessions Simple therapy 6, complex therapy 16 sessions	Contractually defined limited number of sessions		Unlimited; therapy as interminable
Cost Effectiveness and Therapeutic Thoroughness	Resolution of emotional conflicts with reduced need for professional services	Lengthy and expensive behavior and thought management programs		Unstructured and complex perspective relationship promoting dependence and ongoing work

Three Creativity and Power Management Programs

'Insight in one Hour', a brief self-assessment leading to knowing oneself
The person who wishes to find about oneself does not have to be in therapy. *Insight in one hour* consists in a brief creativity for self-discovery assessment exercise. By completing two tests of the *Conflict Analysis Battery: the Relational Personality Inventory, and the Animal Metaphor Test*. The two tests readily identify the most important information about oneself: one's relational modality, the pattern we repeat affecting our lives. This pattern is one's wellness diagnosis as one's way of resolving conflicts. The importance of this knowledge is in that we can identify, understand and optimize our way of resolving conflicts as our unconscious power management pattern.

The double exercise delivers instant insights. It takes about an hour to complete and interpret the two tests to identify one's relational modality and to consider the respective changes. One can detect one's wellness diagnosis through the inventory test numerically and recognize it as a pattern in one's metaphor test. The test taker quickly becomes conscious of the unconscious and identifies changes one needs to make for self-improvement.

Unlike psychoanalysis's transference the Formal Theory understands patterns as having measurable dimensions as personality types wellness diagnoses. There are four modalities, each having different relational scenarios. These are well illustrated with the four characters of the Wizard of Oz, and also the four children asking *what is special about this night?* upon the Passover ceremony. The modalities affect differently one's emotional and social experiences. It helps to know one's personality type as a wellness diagnosis so one can understand oneself, and how to manage power deliberately, consciously in dealing with adversity.

Modalities explain a person's six emotions and experiences as syndromal sequences evolving from a stress to a response generating anxieties and eliciting defenses, which lead to reversals and also to compromises. The testing captures this relational pattern both numerically through the inventory and also in the symbolic language of the metaphors.

- The inventory test identifies it along three formal alternatives: passivity versus activity, cooperation versus antagonism and alienation versus mutual respect.

- The metaphor test identifies the relational pattern along a dialogue on the six exchanges leading to a resolution.

This experience is beneficial, educational, diagnostic and therapeutic with minimal need of intervention from a therapist or an educator. At the end of the *Insight,* participants are encouraged to consider completing the entire *Creativity and Power Management* program.

This program has two segments: The first is the *Enlightenment in One Day*. It consists of the guided tour of the art exhibits of the Museum of the Creative Process, which helps to understand the universality of the conflict resolution process and how the world has gradually shifted from metaphors to the scientific interpretation. The Moral Science now radically revamps education, psychology and religion. *Enlightenment in one day* is the educational segment and *Wisdom in one Week* is the experiential segment of the *Power Management* program. The two segments combine knowledge with self-knowledge. They continue from self-discovery into healing as well as learning skills for the delivery of the program, be that in the classroom, the business and the psychotherapy worlds.

'Enlightenment in One Day' provides information on the concepts of the Formal Theory through the guided tour of the five permanent art exhibits of the Museum of the Creative Process

This workshop introduces the creative process as a scientific and moral order phenomenon, the integrative paradigm of the social sciences revealing the unconscious. A guided tour of the art exhibits of the *Museum of the Creative Process* helps to understand the moral and scientific nature of the process integrating the emotions in all samples of creativity.

Enlightenment may be summed up as comprehending the nature of the creative process reconciling meaningless fragmented knowledge into a unifying meaningful dynamic process. It understands the unconscious need for harmony, psychic comfort and social justice as a scientific conflict resolution mechanism, the unit of the social sciences. The workshop integrates knowledge, psychology, morality, religions, and art with science.

The adequate time to complete this enlightening education is one day; it is adequate to review the art exhibits of the Museum of the Creative Process and to understand the universal harmonic.

There are five exhibits on the grounds of the Wilburton Inn. The volume *'Science Stealing the Fire of the Gods and Healing the World'* (Normative Publications, 2011, Volume 4) reviews all the exhibits.

The Museum exhibits volume has three chapters. The first chapter is about the science of the process as the 'fire of the gods'; the second chapter 'stealing the fire from the gods' is about demystifying religions as partial and complementary discoveries of the science, and the third is about 'giving the fire to the mortals' pertaining to the educational delivery of *Creativity and Power Management* to the public.

Below we summarize the book's three topics:

Chapter One: The Fire, examines the scientific understanding of the creative process as the fire of the Gods. Three exhibits demonstrate and validate the scientific and moral nature of the creative process as an orderly conflict resolving mechanism.

The exhibits identify the unconscious mechanism as abiding by the natural laws of two orderly phenomena: the Simple Harmonic Motion and the formal operations characterizing the balance of the trays of a scale. The process is viewed as a system of three oscillations guided by three formal operations, the equilibrial principles of the scale. The unconscious resolves conflicts by restoring the emotional rest state disturbed by the conflict. The new unconscious is shown to be a measurable universal harmonic, the unit order of a new psychology: the Moral Science.

Three exhibits show the scientific nature of the process:

- The Metaphoria Murals begin with the study of cultural metaphors.

- The Gorski Retrospective recognizes the process integrating the abstract canvases of the artist into five sequential conflict resolution periods, and

- The 12 Wizard of Oz panels interpret the metaphors as the manifestations of the process uniting four social sciences into the Moral Science.

Chapter Two: "Stealing the Fire of the Gods" is illustrated by a fourth exhibit, the *Sculptural Trail in the History of Love.* It retraces the history of religions as partial and complementary discoveries of the science. It shows how religions evolved as discoveries of the process. They progressed from metaphors, believing concrete stories, to increasingly fair norms for family relations, and more abstract redefinitions of the divine.

The Moral Science is shown to complete the mission of religions by clarifying the nature of the divine as the unit process. The Moral Science reconciles the humanities: psychology and morality with science by placing them of the scientific foundation of the formal analysis of the creative process. Science identifies moral values as the three-equilibrial formal operations that lead the mind from a conflict to its resolution.

Chapter Three: "Giving the Fire to the Mortals" is illustrated by the fifth exhibit of the Museum, the standardized delivery of the Conflict Analysis Battery. The assessment makes the test taker conscious of the unconscious conflict resolution as a relational pattern or modality and engages the person to identify relational changes optimizing adjustment. The fifth exhibit is utilizing the creative process for self discovery as a program of emotional education. Seven case studies of this exhibit are reproduced at the end of this section of the book. Each mural portrays a key research issue.

Enlightenment, our need for knowing the divine, is shifted to gratitude for the creative process as respect for the orderly unconscious the universal harmonic. The experience may be viewed as a paradigm shift from believing the content of stories as fragmented and divisive knowledge to understanding meaning as what is universal in all stories, their plot, and as the mental software, the universal conflict resolution process now respected as the ultimate representation of the divine.

'Wisdom in One Week' is the experiential segment of the Creativity and Power Management Program.
Wisdom is an educational experience targeting self-knowledge; one attains personal growth as well as healing within a wellness environment. While the *Insight* is the initiation in this study and *Enlightenment* is about learning about the process and how it integrates knowledge, the *Wisdom* study is about learning about oneself and exploring both making changes and developing skills in utilizing the program in one's capacity as a councilor or educator.

The weeklong workshop consists in completing the Conflict Analysis Training workbook and integrating the metaphors as a set of six emotions into reconstructing the personal drama as a manageable totality. The creativity exercises represent an encounter with oneself, with one's past predicting the future. It is an emotional experience based on the recognition of the personal way of dealing with conflicts.

We see the manifestation of this personal process at the level of the individual metaphors; for instance the Animal Metaphor Test instructs the student of behavior to draw two animals and then to listen to their conversation. The sequence of exchanges of the conversation reflects the person's six role-state Conflict Resolution Process.

The exchanges become the prototype of the personal drama's predictable formal structure. We see the same six role-state dialectic connecting the several metaphors into the totality of each case study.

Science is presented first in the six formally interrelated exchanges of one's unconscious dialectic and second, in the six key metaphors connecting the exercises as a progression to conflict resolution. The simple creativity tasks depart from art and demonstrate science.

Creativity pursues conflict resolution in the span of three emotional oscillations from a state of conflict to one of resolution. The testing visualizes this pictorially contrasting the Conflictual Memories Tests and the Short Story, respectively illustrating the conflict and the resolution role states, while the other exercises complete the role states in between the conflict and the resolution into the six role state harmonic. The personal metaphor profile demonstrates this unconscious order validating the theory on the nature of the unconscious need for the conservation of the emotional rest state as the motivational imperative. This directionality generates continuity in each exercise and each mural case study may be examined as demonstrating conflict resolution.

The Formal Theory gives us natural laws, sound method, in deciphering symbolic systems. The case studies validate science, the theoretical assumptions, demonstrating that the theory-related testing is valid and reliable in measuring the unconscious conflict resolution dynamic.

The assessment puts the creative process on the couch as the object of analysis and observes meaning in detecting the universal order. Occasionally we need more skills in delivering the sophisticated analysis to the trainee of her underlying emotional dynamics.

The implication of the demonstrations is that this battery is a user-friendly instrument providing a standardized, emotional psychological and moral education experience, a rational alternative morality that reduces the reliance on propositional thinking in both the realms of psychology and morality. Science challenges the entrenched propositional axiomatic method and its conflict generating normative absolutes.

All workshops introduce reverence as piety for the universal order of the conflict resolution process. It is of paramount importance to experience deep respect for the process leading to harmony and happiness as the alternative to the ongoing experience of conflicts. Religions ritualize reverence. Humanity needs them but refocused to reverence of the magic of science.

Chapter Five

Seven Exemplary Case Studies Featured As An Exhibit of the Museum of The Creative *Process Illustrate Important Points in the Formal Interpretation of the Symbolic Language of Artistic Creations*

The sampler of the seven case studies addresses a number of insights useful in the sophisticated and detailed interpretation of the artwork of the assessment protocols. The case studies are displayed in the *Sanctuary of the Wizard and of Wisdom* located on the grounds of the Wilburton Inn, representing one of the five permanent exhibits of *the Museum of the Creative Process.* The Sanctuary's seven murals have been generated by completing the workbook tasks and then organizing the images of the tests in the template of the six-role process.

They present the test taker's personal Conflict Resolution Process. Each case study departs from a conflict and ends with its resolution. This organization of the tests reflects visually the orderly six-role process connecting the diversity of a person's life experiences into a meaningful dramatic conflict resolution totality.

In this case-studies exhibit we are focusing on the detailed scientific analysis of the symbolic language of the testing. The cases illustrate a series of important analytical insights that the sophisticated analyst should be aware of in observing the artwork and the exchanges as a scientific phenomenon. These insights are very important aspect in the consideration of the Power Management educational and therapeutic modality. They have not been dealt within this volume of case studies. The emphasis in this volume has been placed on the interpretation of the formal dialectic of emotions by the test taker rather than by the therapist. This dialectic is readily interpreted by the test taker, but the analysis of the symbolism requires the professional skills of the trained therapist.

In this segment of the book, we address the formal analysis of the artistic creations as the science of symbolic languages. These insights differ from the traditional interpretation of aesthetics. They are pertinent to making good use of the assessment's information in comprehending emotional matters.

The following seven case studies address the most complex issues involved in the formal analysis of the symbolic language of emotions. This sophistication is desirable for the delivery of education to the public; it can benefit the public and the professionals, the well person and the one clinically identified, to know about the underlying science as it pertains to the art work of the metaphors as a decipherable symbolic language. We show here that this language abides by scientific laws, underlying the grammar and the syntax of emotions.

The mural studies illustrate the delivery of this concise program of emotional education reducing the need for professional services. The self-assessment's usefulness can be compounded when monitored by trained professionals be they therapists, clergy, coaches or educators. While the assessment has implicit emotional educational value for the test taker, the supervised review of the testing can maximize the effectiveness of its meaningfulness for the test taker. The optimal utilization of the testing is its delivery within traditional therapeutic and educational settings.

The task of the teacher/therapist is to cultivate the analytical skills of the student/patient through the scientific understanding of creativity. The objective is to detect in the symbolic language of art the fine nuances of one's conflict resolution process. Analytical skills lead one to become a better observer, more empathetic and insightful.

These case studies amplify the manifestation of order in art symbolism.
While the six-role process is the unifying order in all samples of creativity it is also manifested in the aesthetic language of the images as well.

- In mural 4 the process connects the metaphors into a symbolic system.

- In mural 7 we are addressing the repair of stressful childhood experiences through formal reversal of passivity states into activity restructuring the same symbolisms in corresponding tasks. We see this formal reversal in the mask test, the balloon portraits, and the animal metaphors.

- In mural 8 we observe the directedness of imagery in the graphic field of the metaphor images reflecting emotions as physical forces of the Simple Harmonic Motion, the pendulum oscillation.

- In mural 9 we present the transformation of conflict to resolution through the cathartic release of emotional energy.

- In the last three murals we present the manifestation of relational modalities as alternative ways of expressing feelings manifested in one's art work; dominant cases are identified testing limits; submissive cases on the contrary suffer of non aggressiveness; they suffer of communicational blocks.

Mural 4: 'My Metaphors Myself' introduces the reconstruction of the personal conflict resolution pattern. The trainee completes the exercises of the workbook and then arranges them in the template of the six role states, corresponding to the reconstruction of the personal emotional process. This correspondence organizes information meaningfully; the completed template reflects the process.

This mural presents my own story of conflict resolution captured with the tests of the self-assessment. The unifying theme is my quest in understanding the path to peace in the world. I am resolving my childhood conflicts by detecting the science of the process, which allows us to use the metaphors for self-discovery and for the healing of the world.

- **Stress** is revealed in the Conflictual Memory Test, here the memory of my childhood experiences during the WWII and the Holocaust as the War of Metaphors.

- **Response** is captured in the Transparent Mask Test. Here the image reflects my identity with Pinocchio because of my awareness of lying about my identity, during the Holocaust, assuming a Christian name and religious identity. My Pinocchio is pursued by the killer whale of metaphors, symbolizing the world's ideologies and religions seeking to gabble up the wooden puppet.

- **Anxiety/hopes, the hidden emotions** are portrayed in the image behind the mask. In my case the anxiety, as the generic state of anticipations, refers to my hope that the puppet captured by the whale along with Geppetto, his carpenter creator, can be transformed into a real boy by freeing himself from the strings of metaphors. My Pinocchio tells Geppetto inside 'the killer whale of metaphors' that he has figured out metaphors as conflict resolutions and is no longer commandeered by puppeteers. Free from the strings that manipulate him, he is no longer a wooden puppet but a live human child.

- **Defense** is presented in the Animal Metaphor; here it is my Oedipus addressing the riddle of the Sphinx with a conflict resolution attitude. He tells the Sphinx: 'I know the answer to your riddle, but I do not want to tell it to you and see you jump off the cliff. Instead let us be partners; you take care of the sheep; protect them from wolfs'. This response promotes my concept of mutual respect as the answer to the riddle of the ongoing Greek war between the genders.

- **Reversal** is revealed in the Dream Metaphor. Here I am presenting my family in front of the Wilburton Inn delivering hospitality to the public.

- **Compromise** is identified in the Autobiographic Short Story Test. This exercise informs on a person's attitude. Here I am sharing my resolution of the conflict between reason and faith as the Jewish Fiddler on the roof of a Greek temple. It represents my integration of reason and faith into the Moral Science. The *Sanctuary of Wisdom* is encircled by the flags of the nations as a halo of the united metaphors celebrating the era of the *Moral Science*.

Mural 4: The Reconstruction of the Process through the Metaphor Tests

6. COMPROMISE is identified by the SHORT STORY TEST. My Judaic passion for justice and my Greek respect for reason as the fiddler on the temple roof unite the world metaphors in the cosmic dance of a universal moral order.

5. ROLE REVERSAL is identified by the DREAM TEST. It presents the daydream of my family working as a team delivering hospitality and wisdom to fellow travelers on the patio of my Art to Science Project, the Wilburton Inn.

4. MY METAPHORS, MYSELF: 1983

Validation #2: Here six metaphor creation tests help to reconstruct the personal six-role Conflict Resolution Process. The experimentally derived sequence validates the theory by showing that parts are formally interrelated within the dramatic totality. This totality also tells how its author, Dr. Levis, evolved from a stress, "The War of the Metaphors", through his response, anxiety, defense, reversal, to the compromise of "The Reconciliation of the Metaphors".

4. DEFENSE is identified by the ANIMAL METAPHOR TEST. Here the Formal Theory Oedipus is offering the Sphinx an olive branch, conflict resolution, as the new answer to the everlasting riddle on the nature of man.

3. ANXIETY is identified by the BEHIND THE MASK TEST. It presents Pinocchio trapped in the stomach of the killer whale with his creator, Geppetto. My Pinocchio is showing to a puzzled Gepetto the unit of the Conflict Resolution Process which has transformed him into a true human.

2. RESPONSE is identified by the MASK TEST which reveals a person's identity. I chose the image of the runaway Pinocchio, the wooden puppet lying about his identity, fleeing the killer whale of hot ideologies pursuing naive consumers.

1. STRESS is identified by the MEMORIES TEST. It represents my recollection of World War II as "The War of the Metaphors", the war of multiple cultural conflicts endangering everybody's survival.

Mural 4: MY METAPHORS, MYSELF: 1983

Here, six metaphor creation tests help to reconstruct the personal six-role Conflict Resolution Process. The experimentally derived sequence validates the theory by showing that parts are formally interrelated within the dramatic totality. This totality also tells how its author, Dr. Albert Levis, evolved from a stress, "The War of Metaphors," through his response, anxiety, defense, reversal, to the compromise of "The Reconciliation of the Metaphors."

RESPONSE is identified by the TRANSPARENT MASK TEST, which reveals a person's identity. I chose the image of the runaway Pinocchio, the wooden puppet lying about his identity, fleeing the killer whale of hot ideologies pursuing naive consumers.

DEFENSE is identified by the ANIMAL METAPHOR TEST. Here, the Formal Theory Oedipus is offering the Shpinx an olive branch–Conflict Resolution–as the new answer to the everlasting riddle on the nature of man.

COMPROMISE is identified by the SHORT STORY TEST. My Judaic passion for justice and my Greek respect for reason as the fiddler on the temple roof unites the world metaphors in the cosmic dance of an universal moral order.

STRESS is identified by the MEMORIES TEST. It represents my recollection of World War II as "The War of the Metaphors," the war of multiple cultural conflicts endangering everybody's survival.

ANXIETY is identified by the BEHIND THE MASK TEST. It presents Pinocchio trapped in the stomach of the killer whale with his creator, Geppetto. My Pinocchio is showing the Unit of the Conflict Resolution Process to Geppetto. This discovery has transformed him from a puppet into a true human.

ROLE REVERSAL is identified by the DREAM TEST. It presents the daydream of my family working as a team delivering hospitality and wisdom to fellow travelers on the patio of the Art to Science Project, the Wilburton Inn.

Mural 7: The case of an abused child becoming a mother scared of abusing her children illustrates the formal modification of symbols in the move from powerlessness to power

Mural 7 presents the very painful and dramatic story of an adult woman who as an adopted child was physically and sexually abused. The mural demonstrates the healing dynamics of the unconscious process by contrasting side-by-side formative traumatic childhood experiences with the formally-related corresponding adult experiences and/or fantasies. This demonstrates the healing of the person manifested in the formal reconfiguration of emotions captured in the symbolic systems.

The mural's imagery demonstrates the formal structure of emotions underlying conflict and resolution.

We examine each test-image reflecting a childhood experience in the context of another reflecting her adult healing as a formal reversal. We see the formal restructuring of childhood traumas with adult developmental adjustments. We observe a continuum of formally-related states of passivity, antagonism and alienation experienced in childhood as connected to the formally rearranged states of mind in adulthood: mastery, cooperation and mutual respect. The artwork presents the three formally related reversals within each one of the six equivalent symbolic systems.

Balloons of the Family of Origin versus Balloons of the Marital Family: This juxtaposition shows how the family balloons are colored, placed with short strings at a distance from each other in the Family of Origin, while the Marital Balloons are held together with long strings.

The baby balloon overlaps the maternal balloon reflecting the mother's protective stance toward her child. This image also reveals the mother's discomfort at being emotionally drained from being overprotective by making sure that she would not in anyway hurt her child.

The Mask of True Feelings reflects the traumas of her childhood as a landscape of mishaps offset by the cover-up of "a mask of serenity."

Her Dream Test corrects a trauma of her childhood, her mother intruding into the bathroom to slap her while she was sitting on the toilet in sight of her father. This trauma is corrected in a dream about her second husband and protector who attacked her first husband perceived as cruel as her mother. Instead of herself it is her ex-husband sitting on the toilet; he is presented being attacked by her second husband holding Cinderella's glass slipper in his hand. The patient was a foster/step-child like Cinderella.

Her Intensified Animal Metaphor portrays her being abused as a puppy by a cruel lion.

Her Animal Metaphor presents her accommodating the neediness of her own demanding child.

Her Childhood Metaphor depicts her experience of abuse in her childhood versus her assuming a protective stance rescuing an animal from a garbage bag in her Short Story exercise. The experience of abuse is offset by acts of kindness as she saves a life.

7. THE FORMALLY INTERRELATED METAPHORS YIELD THE PERSONAL SCENARIO OR SYNDROMAL POWER MANAGEMENT STYLE.

The CONFLICT ANALYSIS BATTERY elicits art along the opposite polarities of certain themes. The lower tier features passivity and DREAMS. The upper tier presents the reciprocal activity states, the MARITAL FAMILY, a MASK, the ANIMAL, FAIRY TALE and SHORT STORY METAPHORS. Contrasting Passivity vs. Activity states we reconstruct the PERSONAL CONFLICT RESOLUTION PROCESS here that of "Cinderella", a 34-year-old survivor of childhood abuse.

— MASTERY CONFLICT RESOLUTION — PHASE — ACTIVITY — COOPERATION — RESPECT

1. PARENTAL FAMILY BALLOONS portray the abusive mother as a black balloon, and the abused client as a small blue balloon. Family members are far apart from each other and have short independent strings.

2. THE MARITAL FAMILY BALLOONS portray the dramatic manifestation of closeness as balloons tightly held together; their strings are long and tightly intertwined. Indeed the infant is overlapping the maternal balloon.

4. MASK I Depicted as "Serenity" is a coverup or feelings. "I hide my feelings to appear unaffected. I have done so for so long that I don't recognize my feelings anymore."

6. DREAM - Slapping her ex-husband, a mother surrogate, while he was sitting on the toilet. "I pulled out a dress slipper made of emeralds. It I think id. My boyfriend said back it. I'll get him with that!!!"

8. RECENT MEMORY Illustrates the patient escaping hiding with baby while her foster mother is directing her husband to go after her and the baby.

10. ANIMAL METAPHOR TEST the Shepherd as mother represents the depressed client resenting her demanding infant.

"Would you stop hitting me?" "No I won't." "Why not?" "Because it feels good." "So what?" "It hurts!!!" "I don't want you to bother me." "Too!! Who cares!"

12. SHORT STORY - Snip rescuing a kitten thrown in the garbage. "Oh look at the poor thing. It is a kitten. It is just real sick. I am going to take it home and make it better."

"Look! It's not trash!"

CHILDHOOD CONFLICT INDUCTION PHASE — PASSIVITY — ANTAGONISM — ALIENATION

3. MASK II illustrates "anger, frustration, confusion, sorrow, hopelessness and emptiness." The HEART is labeled "Beauty with Mishap."

5. CHILDHOOD MEMORY OF ADOLESCENCE "My foster mother entered the bathroom and slapped my face while I was sitting on the toilet. I was embarrassed to be seen by my foster father topless and exposed."

7. RECENT MEMORY OF CONFLICT Illustrates first husband abusing "Cinderella."

9. ANIMAL METAPHOR TEST INTENSIFIED CONFLICT ...

"Didn't you tell me to do what I tell you or I'll cut you. The club your little one, etc." "Puppy: Neither... None don't hurt me." "I'll do anything you say." "Please stop you are hurting me."

11. CHILDHOOD MEMORY ...

MURAL VII: THE FORMALLY INTERRELATED METAPHORS

YIELD THE PERSONAL SCENARIO OR SYNDROMAL POWER MANAGEMENT STYLE.

THE *CONFLICT ANALYSIS BATTERY ELICITS ART AND TEXT AND TEXT ALONG THE OPPOSITE POLARITIES OF CERTAIN THEMES.*

The lower tier features passivity states, the PARENTAL FAMILY, MEMORIES OF CONFLICT, HIDDEN EMOTIONS and DREAMS.

The upper tier presents the reciprocal activity states, the MARITAL FAMILY, a MASK, the ANIMAL FAIRY TALE and SHORT STORY METAPHORS.

Contrasting Passivity vs. Activity States we reconstruct the PERSONAL CONFLICT RESOLUTION PROCESS of "Cinderella", a 34-year-old survivor of child abuse.

MASTERY CONFLICT RESOLUTION PHASE • ACTIVITY, COOPERATION, AND RESPECT.

2. *THE MARITAL FAMILY BALLOONS*

Portrays the dramatic manifestation of closeness as balloons tightly held together their strings are long and tightly intertwined. Indeed the infant is overlapping the maternal balloon .

4. *MASK I*

Depicted as "Serenity" is a cover up of feelings. "I hide my feelings to appear unaffected. I have done so for so long. I don't recognize my feelings anymore."

6. *DREAM*

Slapping her ex-husband, a mother surrogate, while he was sitting on the toilet. "I pulled out a dress slipper made of emeralds. It tinkled. My boyfriend said that's it. I'll get him with that."

8. *RECENT MEMORY*

Illustrates the patient escaping, hiding with her baby while her foster mother is directing her husband to go after her and the baby.

10. *ANIMAL METAPHOR TEST*

The Shepherd vs. Kitten metaphor represents the depressed client resenting her demanding infant.

"Would you stop licking me?" vs. "No I won't."

"Why not?" vs. "Because it feels good."

"To whom?" vs. "To both of us."

"I don't want you to bother me." vs. "Then I'll lay next to you." vs. "Okay."

12. *SHORT STORY*

She is rescuing a kitten thrown in the garbage. "Oh look at the poor thing. It is a kitten, it is just real sick, I am going to take it home and make it better."

CHILDHOOD CONFLICT INDUCTION PHASE • STATES OF PASSIVITY, ANTAGONISM, AND ALIENATION.

1. *PARENTAL FAMILY BALLOONS*

Portrays the abusive mother as a black and the abused client as a small blue balloon. Family members are far apart from each other and have short independent strings.

3. *MASK II*

Illustrates "anger, frustration, confusion, sorrow, hopelessness and emptiness. "

The HEART is labelled 'Beauty With Mishaps'.

5. *CHILDHOOD MEMORY OF ADOLESCENCE*

"My foster mother entered the bathroom and slapped my face while I was sitting on the toilet. I was embarrassed to be seen by my father helpless and exposed."

7. *RECENT MEMORY OF CONFLICT*

Illustrates first husband abusing "Cinderella."

9. *ANIMAL METAPHOR TEST-INTENSIFIED CONFLICT*

This Metaphor illustrates a passivity state her foster mother's abusive conduct. She is a vicious, manipulative, dominant Lion. The patient is a timid, loyal, humble puppy.

Lion: "You rotten mutt, you do what I tell you or I'll eat you up. I'll crush your little bones, etc."

Puppy: "No, no.... please don't hurt me. I'll do anything you say. Please stop, you are hurting me."

11. *CHILDHOOD MEMORY*

Portrays foster brother in his bed with patient underneath the covers. "I was two years old. He placed me between his knees and told me it was a baby's bottle. He didn't care about me, he used me as an object."

Mural 8: The directionality of images reflects the individual moving inside the normative power field. The direction of figures corresponds to the emotions as real natural science motivational forces.

Mural 8 is the case of a young seminarian in a routine screening for emotional pathology. The mural is valuable in reflecting the meaningfulness of the direction of the animals in the five sets of drawings. The aesthetics of the artwork, as the directionality of images, reflect the physical nature of his emotions coinciding with those of the pendulum oscillation. The directions of the movements of the animals in the artwork introduce information about the social emotional phenomena as physical forces within a given gravitational or morally ordered field.

1. Right-directed faces and bodies correspond to move towards power; right directed images may be associated with behaviors of impulsivity, competitiveness and aggression. Here the story pertains to transgression as the collaboration of two youths in a homosexual outing.

2. Left-directed animals portray depression and introspection; the metaphor here is of the "Prodigal Horse" returning to the farm.

3. Forward- facing animals reflect anxiety; this metaphor reflects concerns about issues of right and wrong originating in this homosexual experience.

8. THE PHYSICS OF AESTHETICS: THE ART CONFIGURATIONS HAVE SOCIAL EMOTIONAL MEANING AND NATURAL SCIENCE DIMENSIONS.

The evolving direction of metaphor figures of the "tempted seminarian" confirm the formal thesis that the self is like a pendulum ball oscillating in a morally polarized magnetic field whose right pole coincides with power, and left pole with powerlessness. As figures oscillate to power like a pendulum ball, we see their profiles representing the state of kinetic or action energy; when the figures face forward they represent potential or emotional energy. We then read his METAPHOR PROFILE as the motion of a sinner to power, a transgression, where he experiences anxiety, guilt, and anger and from where he oscillates back to powerlessness, repentence and social service.

2. RESPONSE - MASK I

The mask conveys the Seminarian's damaged identity as he, the youth, has become a bearded, grough map paradoxically labelled "Mona Lisa". A bug on the mask's cheek reflects a further blemish of his identity, his impression that he has become both effeminate and evil.

1A. STRESS - THE CONFLICTUAL MEMORY TEST

reveals that his adolescent homosexual play generated guilt: "I always assumed the more female role which felt perverted."

1B. STRESS - THE PARENTAL FAMILY PORTRAIT

is titled "Berlin Wall". It reflects the tremendous polarization, and lack of communication between the father and the members of the family, entailing elevated psychic tension experienced by the seminarian. This state corresponds to a pendulum ball suspended in a maximal left deviation as the state of maximal potential or emotional energy.

4. DEFENSE - ANIMAL METAPHOR TEST I

Assumption: The imbalance of two animals directed to the right corresponds to a person seeking power or taking liberties and experiencing anxiety.
Validation: His eagles transgress. Top Eagle: "Let's fly over there- this is fun, huh?"
Bottom Eagle: "Yeah this is fun! Let's go over here. - But it is kind of dangerous."

3. ANXIETY- MASK II Reflects hope that a smiling and winking face magically gets rid of the sense of guilt as the bug, seen descending below.

THE HEART ILLUSTRATES THE TOTAL FORCE SYSTEM: ANXIETY AND HOPE as a rainbow reflecting his alternative identities. On the right end of the rainbow (-S) the evil power tries to control him. He feels guilty (-1/a). On the left end he surrenders to God (+1/S), and feels empowered (+a) as a preacher saving people from evil and sin.

6. COMPROMISE - SHORT STORY:
Assumption: Two left directed animals reflect introspection and depression.
Validation: The "Prodigal Horse" didn't want to plow and followed the evil horse to another field where food was plentiful without having to work. But this food "poisoned his insides". Repenting, this Horse, returns home to plow.

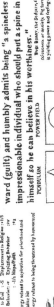

5. REVERSAL - FAIRY TALE METAPHOR
Assumption: The imbalance of two animals partially facing forward reflects different degrees of anxiety and action.
Validation: Bugs Bunny is a big bully setting the pig up for humiliation brandishing his menacing phallic carrot. (Hostility). While Porky Pig on the right field is moving to the left, and redfaced looks forward (guilt) and humbly admits being "a spineless impressionable individual who should put a spine in himself so he can believe in his worthiness."

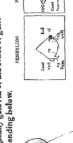

5. ROLE REVERSAL - INTENSIFIED CONFLICTUAL ANIMAL METAPHOR
Assumption: Forward directedness coincides with maximal psychic tension or anxiety.
Validation: The monkey, the good energy, defies the boxy gorilla, the evil power. Like a hero he picks up the sword and slays the mighty gorilla.

MURAL VIII. THE PHYSICS OF AESTHETICS:
THE ART CONFIGURATIONS HAVE SOCIAL EMOTIONAL MEANING AND NATURAL SCIENCE DIMENSIONS.

The evolving direction of metaphor figures of the "tempted seminarian" confirm the formal thesis that the self is like a pendulum ball oscillating in a morally polarized magnetic field whose right pole coincides with power, and left pole with powerlessness. As figures oscillate to power like a pendulum ball, we see their profiles representing the state of kinetic or action energy when the figures face forward they represent potential or emotional energy. We then read his METAPHOR PROFILE as the motion of a sinner to power, a transgression, where he experiences anxiety, guilt, and anger and from where he oscillates back to powerlessness, repentence and social service.

1A. STRESS - CONFLICTUAL MEMORY TEST

reveals that his adolescent homosexual play generated guilt: "I always assumed the more female role which felt perverted."

1B. STRESS

PARENTAL FAMILY PORTRAIT titled "Berlin Wall." It reflects the tremendous polarization, and lack of communication between the father and the members of the family, entailing elevated psychic tension experienced by the seminarian. This state corresponds to a pendulum ball suspended in a maximal left deviation as the state of maximal potential or emotional energy.

2. RESPONSE
MASK I

The mask conveys the Seminarian's damaged identity as he, the youth, has become a bearded, gruff man paradoxically labelled "Mona Lisa." A bug on the mask's cheek reflects a further blemish of his identity, his impression that he has become both effeminate and evil.

3. ANXIETY
MASK II

Reflects hope that a smiling and winking face magically gets rid of the sense of guilt as the bug, seen descending below.

THE HEART ILLUSTRATES THE TOTAL FORCE SYSTEM: ANXIETY AND HOPE as a rainbow reflecting his alternative identities. On the right end of the rainbow(-S) the evil power tries to control him. He feels guilty (-1/a). On the left end he surrenders to God (+1/S), and feels empowered (+a) as a preacher saving people from evil and sin.

4. DEFENSE
ANIMAL METAPHOR TEST

Assumption: The imbalance of two animals directed to the right corresponds to a person seeking power or taking liberties and experiencing anxiety.

Validation: His eagles transgress. Top Eagle: "Let's fly over there- this is fun, huh?"

Bottom Eagle: "Yeah this is fun! Let's go over here. But it is kind of dangerous."

5. REVERSAL
FAIRY TALE METAPHOR

Assumption: The imbalance of two animals partially facing forward reflects different degrees of anxiety and action.

Validation: Bugs Bunny is a big bully setting the pig up for humiliation brandishing his menacing phallic carrot. (Hostility). While Porky Pig on the right field is moving to the left, and red faced looks forward (guilt) and humbly admits being "a spineless impressionable individual who should put a spine in himself so he can believe in his worthiness."

6. COMPROMISE
SHORT STORY

Assumption: Two left directed animals reflect introspection and depression.

Validation: The "Prodigal Horse" didn't want to plow and followed the evil horse to another field where food was plentiful without having to work. But this food "poisoned his insides." Repenting, this Horse, returns home to plow.

5. ROLE REVERSAL
INTENSIFIED CONFLICTUAL ANIMAL METAPHOR

Assumption: Forward directedness coincides with maximal psychic tension or anxiety.

Validation: The monkey, the good energy, defies the bossy gorilla, the evil power. Like a hero he picks up the sword and slays the mighty gorilla.

9. THE METAPHOR PROCESS IS A COST-EFFECTIVE VEHICLE FOR SELF-DISCOVERY AND SELF-HEALING. THE WORKBOOK GUIDED HANNA, A 62 YEAR OLD HOLOCAUST SURVIVOR TO RECOGNIZE AND RESOLVE HER CONFLICTS.

IN ONLY THREE SESSIONS SHE WAS ABLE TO MAKE PEACE WITH HERSELF TO GET RID OF HER MASK AND TO FEEL ALIVE, VULNERABLE AND PASSIONATE AGAIN.

2a. RESPONSE. In her MARITAL BALLOON PORTRAITS she admits anger in her marital family.

My husband agreed to forgo his share so that his sisters could get more of the inheritance; we were all very angry.

2b. RESPONSE. *She hid her emotions behind strength. "Inscrutable", is the face of a 40-year-old woman who does not want to admit to weakness; this face is a well controlled mask.*

1a. STRESS. *Three MEMORIES OF CONFLICT reveal a proneness for power and guilt.*

a. A German soldiers forced the door, they took my mother to another room. I heard her crying and shouting. The next morning my mother had tried to hang herself. I felt guilty.

b. My grandparents were deported to Auschwitz, I thought to a "work-camp". Some part of me felt glad to be rid of their loving control. Later, when I realized they went to a "death-camp", I felt like a terrible person for enjoying a slight feeling of freedom.

c. I was taken to a foundling home. At night I tackled the way to the bathroom past waterbugs and cockroaches. Every morning the nuns combed each child for lice. Every day I got sick. I was a spoiled brat unable to cope with the new reality.

4a. DEFENSE. *Her ANIMAL TEST reveals her emerging from victimization by identifying with the oppressors' dominant behaviors.*

#1 "We shall see about that!"
#2 "Roar, growl, Grrr"
#1 "Get away thief, the catch is mine."
#2 "No way, by right, it's mine."

One lion killed an antelope. Another encroached on his territory. They must kill to live, they are territorial. I identify with the lions. The lions could be nations or persons who think they should have something somebody else has. It goes on constantly and I have to join in it if I want to survive.

4b. DEFENSE. *Her FAIRY TALE METAPHOR reconciles her with an unpleasant reality.* This fairytale is about Joshua, a 10-year-old boy. His friend Cerberus, an adventurous, trusting, wise, changeable, flying ageless dog is guiding him to the land that never ends. The boy is myself. The dog represents my grandfather.

Joshua: Will you take me to the land that never ends?
Cerberus: A strong belief of enough people propelled me into being again.
Cerberus: It's a wondrous realm; continents appear and vanish. That happens when believers and naysayers are just about even. Evil philosophies sometimes gain ascendancy and destroy gods and heavens. The guiding principle is to have balance.

6a. COMPROMISE. *Her SHORT STORY METAPHOR reveals her successfully restraining dominant and anxiety provoking strivings.*

Ava: My niece was on a farm this summer and when they wanted milk they went to Bessy the cow instead of the store.
Allan: This is the day I want to meet my first cow!
Ava: How much is the fare to the country? If it is more than I've got, cash!
Allan: There are alot of dames with cash!
Ava: You would not dare! There will be other weekends for cows.

Allan appears to be the bold unconventional facet of my personality. Ava keeps me honest and out of jail.

6b. COMPROMISE. *In A THANK YOU NOTE she shared her losing control and experiencing a profound emotional release.*

A mezzo-soprano sings to celebrate the Israeli Independence Day. I broke down sobbing and made a fool of myself, but I did not care. Her voice filled me with peace. I felt alive again.

3a. ANXIETY. *In her TRUE FEELINGS MASK she denounced herself as deception. She was a "Perfect Looking Poison Fruit!"*

Owl - Maternal Grandmother: clever, outgoing
Mule: Myself analytical, polite, private.
Songbird- Mother: Emotional, mezzo-soprano, vegetarian
Grandmother: Enterprising,
Porcupine: Aunt, critical.

3b. ANXIETY. *In her WHAT IS IN YOUR HEART DRAWING she denounces her good motives but then dismisses these concerns.*

They made lame excuses for murdering 12 million people. Ostrich: Grandfather, in denial. I may have inadvertently encouraged it. Before I died, I began to question all the stuff they taught me.

My heart is full of good intentions that pave the road to hell. I take things too seriously. It helps to laugh at your pain and confusion.

If I wish real hard maybe I can erase the Holocaust and take what I see at face value.

1b. STRESS. *In her ZOO FAMILY PORTRAIT she contrasted her Jewish mother's and her German father's families and wondered "Can we understand some of our persecutors and if so are they innocent?"*

Parrot: Uncle G., indoctrinated, idealistic, Nazi.
Coyote: German Father: Liked Bach, tossed me up in the air.

5a. REVERSAL. *Three DREAM METAPHORS reveal her fears of the impending destruction of her universe and of herself.*

5b. REVERSAL. *In a memorable DREAM AT AGE 40 she finally met her fate, death:* I remember being dead. I was killed but don't know how, and I was waiting for something to happen and nothing did. I told myself there is nothing after death afterall and kept watching the preparations for my funeral.

A CHILDHOOD DREAM: 9-years-old. A large black sinister crow sat on a wooden fence next to three sunflowers. Above the moon and the sun shone at the same time. This meant the end of the world the way I knew it. I was terrified. The sunflowers represent my mother and hope.

5c. REVERSAL. *A RECENT DREAM gave her relief, her grandmother had not died in Auschwitz. She was alive and well.*

Grandmother is still alive in Prague in a government shelter. She has not written me because she doesn't know my address.

MURAL 9. THE METAPHOR PROCESS IS A COST-EFFECTIVE VEHICLE FOR SELF-DISCOVERY AND SELF-HEALING.

The workbook guided Hanna, a 62-year-old holocaust-survivor to recognize and resolve her conflicts. In her three sessions she was able to make peace with herself to get rid of her inscrutable mask and to accept feeling alive vulnerable and passionate again.

1a.STRESS

3 MEMORIES OF CONFLICT reveal a proneness for power and guilt.

a. German soldiers forced the door, they took my mother to another room. I heard her crying and shouting. The next morning my mother had tried to hang herself. I felt guilty.

b. My grandparents were deported to Auschwitz, I thought to a "work-camp." Some part of me felt glad to be rid of their loving control. Later when I realized they went to a "death-camp", I felt like a terrible person for enjoying a slight feeling of freedom.

c. I was taken to a foundling home. At night I tackled the way to the bathroom past waterbugs and cockroaches. Every morning the nuns combed each child for lice. Every day I got sick. I was a spoiled brat unable to cope with the new reality.

1b. STRESS

ZOO FAMILY PORTRAIT

She contrasted her Jewish mother's and her German father's families and wondered "Can we understand some of our persecutors and if so are they innocent?"

Unicorn- Maternal grandfather: Honest, trusting, patient

Owl - Maternal grandmother: Enterprising, clever, outgoing

Ostrich- Paternal grandpa: Strict, fair, strong work ethic.

Mule- Myself: Analytical, polite, private.

Songbird- Mother: Emotional, mezzo-soprano, vegetarian

Porcupine- Aunt : Critical, protective

Griffin - Uncle : Scientific, versatile, loving.

Coyote-German Father: Liked garlic, tossed me up into the air

Parrot - Uncle G.: Indoctrinated, idealistic, Nazi

1. Unicorn: Shouldn't we have learned something since?
2. Owl: The wounds are emotional.
3. Mule: If I wish real hard maybe I can erase the Holocaust and take what I see at face value.
4. Porcupine:They made lame excuses for murdering 12 million people.
5.Ostrich:I may have inadvertently encouraged it.
6. Parrot: Before I died, I began to question all the stuff they taught me.

2a. RESPONSE

In her *MARITAL BALLOON PORTRAITS* she admits anger in her marital family. My husband agreed to forgo his share so that his sisters could get more of the inheritance; we were all very angry.

2b. RESPONSE

She hid her emotions behind strength. "Inscrutable" is the face of a 40-year-old woman who does not want to admit to weakness; thisface is a well controlled mask.

3a. ANXIETY

In her *TRUE FEELINGS MASK* she denounced herself as deceptive. She was a "Perfect Looking Poison Fruit." This image reflected my being suspicious, alternatively gullible, that is taking things at face value.

3b. ANXIETY

In *WHAT IS IN YOUR HEART DRAWING she denounces her good motives but then dismisses these concerns.* My heart is full of good intentions that pave the road to hell. I take things too seriously. It helps to laugh at your pain and confusion.

4a. DEFENSE.

Her ANIMAL METAPHOR TEST reveals her emerging from victimization by identifying with the aggressors' dominant behaviors.

#1 "Get away thief, the catch is mine."
#2"No way, by right, it's mine."
#1"We shall see about that!"
#2"Roar, growl, Grrr!"
#1" Grrr, grrr. They continue to growl and fight."

One lion killed an antelope. Another encroached on his territory. They must kill to live, they are territorial. I identify with the lions. The lions could be nations or persons who think they should have something somebody else has. It goes on constantly and I haveto join in it if I want to survive.

4b. DEFENSE. Her FAIRY TALE METAPHOR *reconciles her with an unpleasant reality.*

This fairytale is about Joshua, a 10-year-old boy. His friend Cerberus, an adventurous, trusting, wise, changeable, flying ageless dog is guiding him to the land that never ends. The boy is myself. The dog represents my grandfather.

Cerberus: A strong belief of enough people propelled me into being again.

Joshua: Will you take me to the land that never ends?

Cerberus: It's a wondrous realm, continents appear and vanish. That happens when believers and naysayers are just about even. Evil philosophies sometimes gain ascendancy and destroy gods and heavens. The guiding principleis to have balance.

5a. REVERSAL

Three DREAM METAPHORS reveal her fears of the impending destruction of her universe and of herself.

A CHILDHOOD DREAM: 9-years-old. A large black sinister crow sat on a wooden fence next to three sunflowers. Above the moon and the sun shone at the same time. This meant the end of the world the way I knew it. I was terrified. The sunflowers represent my mother and hope.

5 b. REVERSAL

In a memorable DREAM AT AGE 40 she finally met her fate, death: I remember being dead. I was killed but don't know how, and I was waiting for something to happen and nothing did. I told myself there is nothing after death afterall and kept watching the preparationsfor my funeral.

5 c. REVERSAL

A RECENT DREAM *gave her relief, her grandmother had not died in Auschwitz. She was alive and well.* Grandmother is still alive in a government shelter. She has not written me because she doesn'tknow my address.

6a.COMPROMISE

Her SHORT STORY METAPHOR reveals her successfully restraining dominant and anxiety provoking strivings.

Ava: My niece was on a farm this summer and when they wanted milk they went to Bessy the cow instead of the store.

Allan: This is the day I want to meet my first cow!

Ava: How much is the fare to the country? It is more than I've got.

Allan:There are alot of dames with cash!

Ava:You would not dare! There will be other weekends for cows. Allan appears to be the bold unconventional facet of my personality. Ava keeps me honest and out of jail.

6b. COMPROMISE.

In A THANK YOU NOTE she shared her losing control and experiencing a profound emotional release. A mezzo-soprano sings to celebrate the Israeli Independence Day. I broke down sobbing and made a fool of myself, but I did not care. Her voice filled me with peace. I felt alive again.

Mural 9: Demonstrating the cathartic healing effectiveness of the conflict analysis battery in a case of dominance

Mural 9 is about the speed of the insights generated through the testing contained in the workbook. This is the touching case of a holocaust survivor who by completing the workbook worked through her childhood drama. She came to terms with her guilt about the loss of her overprotective grandparents.

Studies of Alternative Relational Modalities

The last three murals illustrate four case studies exemplifying with artwork the diagnostic differences between relational modalities determining the respective social adjustments and emotional pathologies. These cases also exemplify the process of their therapeutic evolution to healing and wellness.

Mural 10: Contrasting the symbolism of alternative relational modalities: images of a dominant and a submissive trainee

This mural displayed in the case study of interns is about the two opposite relational modalities. Two students in training reveal the opposite personality types, the two major relational modalities. Here side-by-side we see the differences in relating manifested in the relational scales and artwork of two trainees. The metaphors of Melissa show her dominant, competitive and anxious personality while the metaphors of Chris show the counterpart disposition, his tendency to be submissive antagonistic, hostile, intolerant and how he could lose control of his well-restrained anger.

Murals 11 & 12: Monitoring the progress of two patients in long-term therapy utilizing the metaphor testing. The first is a dominant and the second a submissive person. The first is an acting out person, the second suffers from an eating disorder.

The two patients reflect the alternative relational modalities in long-term therapy monitored by the use of the metaphor testing. The first case is a dominant woman, who completed five workbooks. She is dealing with her aggressiveness and paranoid fears. The other is a submissive woman struggling with communicating her feelings. She suffered from an eating disorder and was also terrified of losing control of her anger and destroying her family. She enjoyed creativity utilizing only the Animal Metaphor Test.

Mural 12: An eating disorder masking the underlying communicational disorder
Gladys completed metaphors practically for each one of her many therapy sessions. These are reconstructed in a mural showing the progress in her therapy along four rows of metaphors integrated into four phases of conflict resolution growth.

1. The first row reproduces the evaluation documents, presenting the sequence of metaphors generated upon the initial phase of therapy. We identify here the nature of her conflict as an eating disorder with two of her tests: the Conflictual Memory presents her feeding her mother while her grandmother is objecting to her choice of a multi-layered sandwich. The first Mask presents her being feminine with lots of make-up. The second image, what is underneath the mask, presents her with her mouth blackened; it is the 'black hole' reflecting her binge-purge eating disorder; in the third mask we see the problem as a communication blockage. We see a moat separating smiles and bunnies from tears and dark clouds, lightning, and heavy rain, all signs of her unexpressed anger and depression. This difficulty in communicating feelings was the issue underlying her eating disorder. Gladys, a submissive person, could not express her feelings; this was the significance of the moat symbolizing her inability to vent her angry feelings. The problem of communications was confirmed in her first Animal Metaphor of a dog and a cat turning their backs to each other. The difficulty in venting her feelings was explained in the last metaphor, the Short Story, which presents a dragon breathing fire and burning her family. Expressing her anger was perceived as dangerous and unacceptable.

   The deep-seated communication problems were determined by her submissive antagonistic relational modality. Therapy helped her work through the expression of her emotions and the metaphors and associated poetry attest that she achieved substantial growth. This mural captures well the growth accomplished in long term therapy.

2. The second phase of metaphors, the moat series, presents animals in conflict in either side of the moat. The counterpart animals evolved as it became easier to express herself. She is transformed from a scared bunny stuck with big animals, to an ostrich with her head stuck in the sand, and then at the end state she is an eagle soaring above the moat.

3. The third series is about a phase of intensification of her eating disorder as bouts of anorexia and bulimia; this recurrence manifested upon a stressful encounter. This phase was characterized as a cycle of intense binge-purge behaviors worked on symbolically as the conflicts between a vulture and a snake battling each other. At the end of this series her new identity is a tiger, which kills both the snake and the vulture. Gladys evolved to a new identity, distancing herself from the self-destructive pattern.

4. The fourth series of her metaphors describes communication conflicts with the several key figures in her life. In each she was spelling out her feelings honestly. The particular individuals start with her mother and end with her husband. She is able to finally communicate with him. The end metaphors, two giraffes, represent herself and her husband talking to each other. The exchanges are pertinent: 'we can disagree and still be friends', the two giraffes face each other and are symmetrical which corresponds to mutual respect. What a transformation from the initial metaphor of a dog and a cat, turning their backs to each other and to the viewer and stating in a hostile manner 'Who cares about your feelings?'

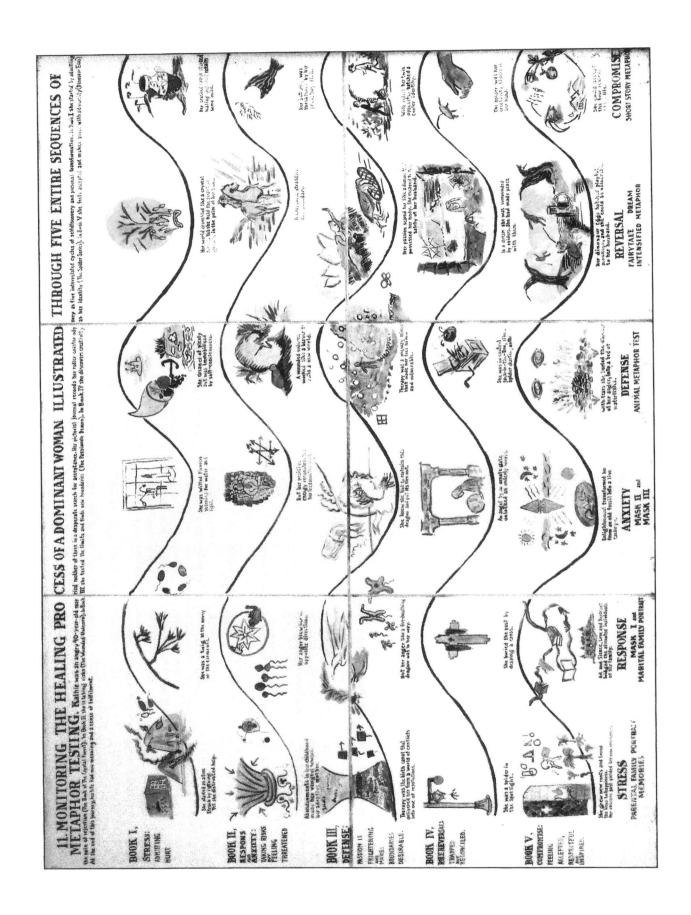

11. MONITORING THE HEALING PROCESS OF A DOMINANT WOMAN ILLUSTRATED THROUGH FIVE ENTIRE SEQUENCES OF METAPHOR TESTING.

Kathie was an angry 40-year-old married mother of three in a desperate search for acceptance. Her pictorial journal records her roller coaster odyssey as five interrelated cycles of self-discovery and personal transformation.

BOOK I, STRESS: ADMITTING HURT

She started as a tree struck by lightning. Yet she distrusted help.	She was a twig at the mercy of the elelments.	She was wilted flowers yearning for water and light.	She dreamed of plenty but was immobilized by self-consciousness.	Her world crumbled like a crystal forest. Yet she held the secret of growth in the palm of her hand.	Her cracked crock started healing and could retain some milk.

BOOK II: RESPONSE AND ANXIETY: TAKING RISKS BUT FEELING THREATENED.

Abandonments in her childhood made her feel vengeful towards her adoptive mother.	Her anger blew her into opposite directions.	But her positive energy reconstructed her fragmented self.	A wounded Unicorn worked like a beaver to build a new world.	A horseman straddled the boundary.	Her butterfly was threatened by her predatory fish.

BOOK III: DEFENSE: PASSION IS FRIGHTENING AND MAKES BOUNDARIES DESIRABLE.

Therapy was the birth canal that delivered her from a world of conflicts into one of resolutions.	But her anger like a fire-breathing dragon was in her way.	She knew she had to restrain this dragon and put its fire out.	Therapy was a one-way mirror that made her feel naked and vulnerable.	Her passion scared her like a demon that possessed her body. She escaped to the safety of her husband.	With relief her twin opposites hatched a cooler identity.

BOOK IV: ROLE REVERSAL: TRAPPED BUT RECONCILED

She was a spider in the spotlight	She buried the past by draping a cross.	An angel by an ornate gate unlocked an orderly world.	She was in control like Jack-in-The -Box, like a spider darting on the web.	In a dream she was surrounded by spiders. She had made peace with them.	The spider was her creativity hidden in her hand.

BOOK V: COMPROMISE: FEELING ACCEPTED, RESPECTFUL AND INSPIRED

She grew new roots and found the keys to happiness. Her obscure past yielded her new innocence.	Art and Science, Love and Restraint bridged the alienated individuals of her family.	Enlightenment transformed her from an old fossil into a live embryo.	With tears she buried the dinosaur of her anger into a bed of waterlillies.	Her dinosaur eggs hatched playful monkeys and she could be vulnerable to her husband.	She could accept the four seasons of her life.

MURAL XII. MONITORING THE HEALING PROCESS OF A SUBMISSIVE BULIMIC, 50-year-old Gladys, through the repeated use of only one protocol - the *Animal Metaphor Test.*

PHASE I: GLADYS EVOLVED FROM A CHILD CHASTISED BY HER GRANDMOTHER TO A FIRE-BREATHING DRAGON AFRAID OF HURTING HER LOVED ONES.

PHASE II: IN THE MOAT SERIES. THE PROBLEM WAS CLARIFIED AS A POWER IMBALANCE AS SHE EVOLVED FROM A DUMB BUNNY TO A FREE, SOARING EAGLE.

PHASE III: IN THE SNAKE/VULTURE SERIES THE PROBLEM SHIFTED TO AN EATING DISORDER AS SHE RESPONDED TO STRESS, CONTROLLING AND LOSING CONTROL OF FOOD. She evolved from a snake hissing at a vulture to a jaguar destroying both snake and vulture.

PHASE IV: IN THE FINAL PHASE OF THERAPY SHE RECTIFIED POWER IN A NUMBER OF RELATIONSHIPS. She evolved from being rejected from her mom's kangaroo pouch to admitting to her husband her need for a true partnership.

Stress (RO)	Response (RA)	Anxiety (APR)	Defense (CPRA)	Reversal (RR)	Compromise (CRA)
Memory: "You are a bad girl." Grandma: You can't bring that stupid sandwich to your sick mother.	**Mask I:** "Perpetual Smile" Shutting out sadness with a smile and outrageous makeup.	**Mask II:** "Blackout" Unable to express emotions she was also unable to stop eating.	**Animal Metaphor:** "Who will listen, will you?" Cat: You can't really hear me can you? Dog: Why should I hear what you do have to say?	**Dream:** "Running Late" Can't find clothes that fit...but I can hide my fat body in a submarine.	**Short Story:** "Dove or Demon" I'm reliable, considerate, dull; she turned into a fire breathing dragon, hurt those around her. Then wept.
"Run Rabbit Run" Gilla: Rabbit, you are the proverbial dumb bunny. You are gullible, inane and spineless.	"A Ray of Sunshine" Hey ostrich, it's nice to see you without your head in the sand. You say others don't hear you, but you never listen to ME, your inner self.	"Mermaid and Centaur" (M) : I am nothing. I am vulnerable, unclothed. (C): I care not to hear you speak of sadness, I don't want to hear such things. I am a centaur/you a fish.	"Lamb and Bull" Why don't I know you? Why have you fenced me in? Why do I have my back to you? Why can't I ever figure out how I feel about you?	"The Feckless Fawn", Deer: Your big teeth and claws scare me, You might hurt me. Bear: You're making me mad. Get over here before I lose my temper and bite you.	"Feathers & Claws" 'Here I am soaring upward. Why haven't I been here before? The eagle flew beyond the mountains and the bear waved good-bye.'
"Feast or Famine" Snake: I can hiss at you and, if I choose, bite you with my venom-filled fangs.	"Venom for the Vulture, Feathers For The Snake" Vulture: I am not sure I am ready to die... I can still fly away. A failed attempt to become a whole.	"Dealing with a stressor A Storm Approaching." Snake: You have me up against the wall in a storm. Am I safe in the eye of the storm?	"After the Storm." The vulture won the battle. She ran amok and ate... the snake grew weary and weak.	"Now or Never." Snake: If you keep feeding me the way you are, I'll die. Rabbit: The only thing I know to do is cry.	"Life is Not Binge or Purge" Jaguar destroys snake and vulture. And says, 'I'll win. My patience has run out. The snake and the vulture must die.'
"No Room For Two" Mom Kangaroo: Why are you eating so much? Soon you'll be fat and ugly. Child: I eat for solace so you'll be aware of me.	"Wake up and Live" Armadillo says to Porcupine: You are not bound by convention. You can color outside the lines.	"Jaguar vs. Hippo" Jaguar: You're so obese and ugly. You must stuff food and drink in your cavernous mouth all day and night.	"How very dull." Bobcat self says to bighorn sheep husband: You never wanted to change anything nor do you want me to change. There is no joy to look forward to.	"An unveiling" Girland to Girpoise: Neither of us express anger. We have to tell each other when, why we're angry. People can have disputes and be friends again.	"Who Am I ?" Dolphin: I enjoy companionship. What are you? Pigasu: A "we" and not an "I." The pig eats too much, the jaguar desires control and the seagull wants freedom.

|2|

Clinical Delivery Case Studies:
The Submissiveness Relational Modality
About Being Non-Asservative

Introduction and Definition of Submissiveness

Psychiatric Versus Relational Diagnoses
The relational modality diagnoses depart from the traditional clinical-symptom-oriented focus of DSMs by identifying instead the psychodynamic RELATIONAL and SYNDROMAL nature of the unconscious. This approach examines the formal organization of emotions and behaviors and entails a completely different approach to diagnosis and related psychotherapeutic interventions.

In the following case studies we identify the subordinacy syndrome, the relational modality diagnosis, as underlying a variety of symptom-based disorders. Submissiveness is a wellness condition that under stress may manifest as multiple symptoms misdiagnosed as clinical psychiatric diagnoses. Diagnostic categories of wellness identify two items: first the person's relational modality and second how this unfolds syndromally psychodynamically along the six role process.

Here we must understand that the subordinacy modalities under stress may decompensate from wellness to illness. The diagnosis of these conditions as clinical symptom categories represents misdiagnoses stigmatizing the sufferer while inflicting on them improper diagnoses entailing ineffective treatments. The clinical diagnoses of relational modalities as 'chemical imbalances' or cognitive impairments entailing focused cognitive behavior modification programs accompanied by medication-regiments prescribed for depression and anxiety are improper and ineffective treatments. These therapies seek to suppress emotions rather than to extinguish them by modifying the underlying communicational difficulties that evoke them. Stigmatizing labels and chemotherapies with their side effects reinforce the patients' sense of helplessness and worthlessness.

The relational wellness diagnoses entail understanding clinical symptoms as generated by behaviors that are corrigible by making the appropriate psychodynamic relational changes. Several conditions in the following pages have been addressed successfully with relational insights and power management patient-identified interventions. The diagnoses of wellness, dominance and submissiveness, and the assessment instruments help the patients to identify their problems as relational modality generated symptoms and to address them with power management interventions. In the case of submissiveness the intervention is assertiveness improving the communication of feelings. In the cases of dominance the intervention is the opposite, self-restraint, admission of vulnerabilities and the reduction of dominant aggressive cover up behaviors.

The significance of the relational diagnoses is in providing the client/patient with insights that s/he identifies through the completion of the self-assessment guiding the test taker to the needed therapeutic power management relational changes. The test taker with the help of the assessment recognizes one's relational modality and its syndromal repercussions as a pattern organizing one's life experiences and intuitively suggesting the needed changes.

The therapist only needs to reinforce the client's spontaneously articulated insights and directives for change. The therapist can clarify the relational diagnosis syndrome/pattern and encourage the patient to adhere to the identified changes. There is benefit in the analysis of transference and of resistance in pursuing the identified changes. These classical additional therapeutic interventions can be helpful as needed.

About Submissive Relational Modalities
The relational modality syndromal diagnosis of submissiveness entails the psychodynamic treatment of assertiveness. This diagnosis is a preferable alternative to attributing the problems to a clinical stigmatizing and alienating illness that is beyond the patient's control. Power Management Therapy addresses relational psychodynamic restructuring of behaviors and emotions, attitude changes, as the means to combat the clinical symptoms.

Submissive people have difficulty expressing their feelings out of consideration of other people's feelings. They have difficulty pursuing social power positioning that is being assertive. They keep their feelings to themselves rather than expressing them. Consequently they suffer of a sense of powerlessness translated into feelings of self-doubt and worthlessness.

To compensate for this deficit of power they seek approval and attention by readily conforming to authorities. The submissive individual is vulnerable to authority figures; s/he feels easily respect and dependence to powerful secure people. They may become depressed if they do not get this support or recognition. Alternatively they may seek escapes and also assume antagonistic defiant, self-defeating negative attention-seeking behaviors.

Thus while these individuals give in to parental and marital authorities rather than express their feelings appropriately they may silently defy their partners by tenaciously escaping them seeking secret pleasures, multiple escapes or self-defeating patterns. But they also may become resentful and hostile, negative, depressed, and self-destructive inflicting harm to themselves

Some of the secret ways for achieving pleasure and some negative attention getting behaviors are illustrated in this cohort of seven patients: self-indulgence with food, sexual escapades, active phantasies like foot-fetishism, and alternatively expressing anger through self-mutilation and self-destructive patterns. At some point these patterns of escapism fail. The submissive persons get overwhelmed with the consequences of ineffective adjustments going out of control as patterns and fantasies backfire and these individuals loose control over their behaviors with ensuing anxiety, guilt, depression, embarrassment, hopelessness and alienation. Their fears of worthlessness are self-fulfilling.

Therapeutic Interventions
Unlike Cognitive Behavioral Therapy focusing on the clinical symptoms the focus in CPM is the underlying relational modality deviation. The following case studies reflect the effective use of

Power Management as the means to restoring wellness. The therapy combines the administration of the self-assessment battery with the cognitive component, explanations on the syndromal nature of the relational diagnoses. Gradually through the insights generated by the therapeutic evaluation, alternatively through long-term individual or group therapy utilizing creativity for self-discovery, these patients are relieved of their symptoms through relatively short-term therapeutic interventions. Recoveries have occurred in the span of six sessions, varying from 3 to 16 sessions, though two long-term therapy cases are also recorded here.

The treatment of choice has been consistent in the following seven studies: The diagnosis is established with the inventory test, reinforced with the metaphor therapeutic tests, generating insights about one's relational modality. Personal empowerment is facilitated through improved communication of feelings both through encouraging creativity for self-discovery and through relational guidance. The evidence of the effectiveness of this treatment is in the swift reduction of protracted symptoms upon utilizing the self-assessment.

The seven case studies illustrate the range of conditions that have benefited from learning to cope with communicational-relational difficulties and as a result recovering self-confidence, self-esteem and wellness. The studies demonstrate how the submissive patients' problems are offset by expressing thoughts and feelings and by understanding their wellness diagnoses and these diagnoses' decompensation.

Diagnostic Criteria
Relational modality scores of the inventory of submissive individuals are diagnostic. It clearly reflects the deviation along the submissiveness scales coinciding with negative scores along the dominance scales. Elevation in the submissive antagonism scale coincides with elevated psychic tension, reflecting the disabling consequence of holding feelings in. Frequently the submissive cooperative and submissive antagonistic scales are both elevated at the same time.

The relational diagnoses are also identifiable through the patients' Animal Metaphor choices. It is of significance that the patients in this study are given names based on their animal metaphor tests.

These names derived from the animal metaphor test reveal their problematic relating and entail their therapeutic changes:

1. 'The caribou falling behind the herd and the predatory wolf' is about a man who suffered from a chronic dysfunctional marital relationship and who experienced symptoms of chronic depression.

2. 'Trying to survive as a dog' is a man suffering of gastrointestinal symptoms secondary to stress experienced in a multiple relationships.

3. 'The anteater and the lion' is about depression and personality damage caused to a young vulnerable woman by a protracted incestuous relationship with her grand father.

4. 'The horse that wanted to jump a fence' is about a woman suffering of panic attacks, anxiety, depression and an eating disorder, symptoms activated following her marital infidelity.

5. 'The wolf and the bird with the broken wing' is a about a submissive antagonistic self-mutilating and suicidal woman.

6. 'The vulture and the snake' is about a woman with a serious chronic eating disorder.

7. 'The foot fetish' or 'The explosive Lion and the withdrawn Dog' is the story of a young submissive man with a compulsive conduct disorder.

The animal metaphor below shows his relational diagnosis:

Type of animal: Lion
Age in human years: 24
Sex: Female
Describe the animal's personality using 3 or more traits:
Unpredictable, explosive, distraught.

Animal #2
Type of animal: Dog
Age in human years: 26
Sex: Male
Describe the animal's personality using 3 or more traits:
Withdrawn, uncomfortable, confused.

Step 6: Give a title to the story. "The Rock Meets Hard Place"

Note what these case studies' metaphors have in common: the identity animals are victims of powerful counterparts. Submissiveness is about feeling overpowered and victimized.

Review of the Seven Case Studies

Case Study 1: *The Caribou Falling Behind the Herd and the Predatory Wolf*

'The caribou falling behind the herd at the mercy of a wolf'-*a simple evaluation without therapy* is the story of a submissive judge, who could not stand up for his rights. He was compelled into a marriage by a manipulative and demanding girlfriend, who 'had gotten herself pregnant'. He stayed married feeling like a prisoner, avoiding relations with his wife, while she was unfaithful and unabashedly promiscuous. He did not have the courage to either confront his wife or the freedom of starting his life again without the church's approval. He was evaluated utilizing the CAB workbook to examine if he qualified for the Catholic Tribunal's criteria for terminating a marriage.

The submissiveness of the judge shows throughout his testing. His pattern determined his lifetime adjustment. The memories included early life self-sacrifice, a shotgun wedding, and recently an attack in public by his new girlfriend. The mask portrayed a judge, an authority; behind the mask was a scared and innocent lamb. In his Animal Metaphor Test he is a caribou falling behind the herd at the mercy of a wolf. The insight on the caribou's conduct was that he 'was willing to accept this fate of being sacrificed in the service of improving the species'. In his Fairy Tale Metaphor he was the pig relating to the proverbial wolf. The wolf is trying to reassure the pig, 'Trust me', while we see a knife up his sleeve. In this case study we see the dysfunctional social adjustment of submissiveness. The evaluation was completed and the judge added his personal letter to the Tribunal explaining his submissive personality's difficulties dealing with a very difficult dominant spouse.

Case Study 2: *Trying to Survive as a Dog*

Surviving as a dog with a lion biting his head off' was the metaphor of a 57 year old professor of art. He was consulting me for protracted gastrointestinal problems. In an 8 sessions therapy he managed to produce a lengthy testing record recognizing his submissiveness successfully addressing a better management of feelings. The professor emerged to become self-aware and more confident. He was able to correct many perceptions and become secure in relationships. He completed therapy and was more comfortable with people and feelings and less preoccupied by his gastrointestinal complaints.

Case Study 3: *The Anteater and the Lion*

'The Ant Eater and the Lion' is the evaluation protocol of a 23-year-old woman, who had been victim of sexual abuse by her grand father for many years. She had submitted to his demands until she confided to a girl friend, then she finally protested at the abuse. 'The Ant Eater and the Lion' completed a self-evaluation, without any therapist interpretation or intervention; the inventory revealed the young woman was a very submissive cooperative person. She illustrated the abuse by her grand father in her conflictual memory. In her Animal Metaphor she is disfigured into an anteater admiring a lion. In her quest for recovery she had great aspirations and wished to become herself a lion, at least pretend being one. She concluded her book of self-revelations with a metaphor of assertiveness as a unicorn battling a dragon. The letter to herself discusses her new insights.

Case Study 4: *The Horse That Wanted to Jump a Fence, also identified as The Wise Oak*
'The horse that wanted to jump a fence' was a submissive cooperative married woman in her thirties. She had rebelled by having an extramarital relationship and upon that she experienced multiple anxiety attacks followed by medical interventions. She was trying to escape a controlling cruel very dominant husband, while she did not have the strength of seeking divorce. She completed three workbooks. Two of them derived from an initial period in therapy and then a third book many years later. Her conflicts are depicted across her several workbooks. The books were her therapy. She was very creative and used the creativity to unfold her troubled youth and complicated adult emotional life.

Her Conflictual Memories Tests portray that she was abusively punished and intimidated by her father. She is helpless presented without hands in the images. She was the 'blondie, the child that was an accident, and who did not fit'. In her marriage she was physically abused and manipulated by her husband. Her mask hides her emotions. In her Animal Metaphor she was a horse that wants to jump the fence. In other metaphors her animals got predictably in trouble with authorities, or alternatively sought to please authorities. They are consistently punished. In her early dream experience she had fallen in a pit full of snakes being ridiculed by her family standing on the rim of the pit. In her short story she is enjoying an escapade but is threatened by a ghost with open jaws in the distance emerging from a cave.

In therapy she learned how to manage her husband. As she grew confident she saw her cruel husband with compassion but set limits to his cruelty. Her final essay was accompanied by the image of an oak, encompassing all her metaphors instead of completing the conflict resolution six-cycle poster. She accommodated her metaphor animals in the branches of an Oak tree feeling reconciled with all her feelings; she made peace with her self, she felt loved and respected without escapist relationship. The tree presented her rootedness in the marriage. She compromised staying put in her difficult marriage content with her cruel but reliable husband.

Case Study 5: *The Wolf and the Bird with the Broken Wing*
This very troubled woman was bent to self-destruct. 'The wolf and the bird with the broken wing', also identified from another metaphor as the 'Troll burned by the Sun' was a 35 year old teacher, married for second time, with a long term history of self mutilations and suicidal attempts; she was a 'cutter', who had been hospitalized multiple times for suicidal attempts, without therapeutic success. She was unstoppable in cutting herself upon any frustration. She kept a journal of incidents in parallel with taking multiple medications.

She completed in 16 sessions two workbooks, stopped cutting herself, stopped using medications and progressed to social adjustment. She represents a stunning rapid recovery after years of in and out patient therapeutic failures. The recovery because of the treatment is reflected in art work generated upon the end of her initial two sessions in which she contrasted how she felt before and after these two sessions. The cause effect connection of therapy and healing is also reflected in the rapid reduction of self-mutilation episodes between weekly sessions.

Her relational modality diagnosis was clearly that of a submissive antagonistic person. The pattern manifested across the personality inventory and all her creativity tests. The conflictual memories present punishments and losses. The family portrait shows feelings of lack of status suffered in her divided family. The masks reflect cover-ups of many bad feelings. Her original metaphor was that of a bird with a broken wing in front of a wolf's open mouth. The wolf thought she was not even worth eating.

In her dream we see a glimpse of her hoped for recovery: she was portrayed successful running a special education musical class. The first book Short Story Metaphor is of a troll burning up in flames at the sight of the sun.

The second sequence of metaphors reflects evidence of her recovery. Her metaphors present transformation across the same themes as in the first book. Transformation is evident by contrasting the new set of metaphors with the original set. Her many improvements, are summed up in the same symbolic choices reconfigured: reflected in memories, masks, animal metaphors etc. In the second book the principle metaphor presents her as a turtle on the way of a lion and moving on as fast as she can. Finally the short story presents the theme of the sun and the burning troll transformed to the Sun and the Moon. Her skittish troll in flames becomes the self-sufficient moon lighting the sky at night. She was the princess of the night, the moon, instead of feeling downtrodden and antagonistic she had become collaborative.

The transformation of a self-mutilating woman from a scared fragile troll hiding from the Sun to a luminous moon was associated with her complete rehabilitation from her obsessive self-mutilation to functioning in the real world at home and in an upstart family business. In 16 sessions, she had completed her therapy. She had been able to stop completely hurting herself. Her recovery is recorded with the gradual cessation of her cutting episodes. Upon termination of therapy, she had stopped her multiple medications, and had assumed responsibilities in real life challenges. She also composed a short essay confirming her recovery.

Case Study 6: *The Vulture and the Snake*
Gladys was a 50-year-old married woman in a long-term therapy with myself. Her case study is recorded as multiple animal metaphors. Clearly a submissive antagonistic person, the record of her therapy is shown as a series of phases consistently evolving to resolutions as the convoluted path of her finding her identity and her voice. She summed up her transformation, as how the "we" becomes an "I" overcoming inner conflicts and addressing the interpersonal relations.
She ended her long journey of many soul searching bold poems asking in a metaphor: 'Who am I?' She answered it with the Pijasu: the "we" that becomes an "I": The pig that eats too much, the jaguar, who desires control and the seagull, who wants freedom. In another metaphor these multiple identities are united to become a Dolphin that enjoys companionship and is not embarrassed to talk of feelings, argue and be friends again.

Case Study 7: *The Foot Fetish Youth*
A young married man was referred for an evaluation by his therapist. He completed the workbook. All his documents reflected his deep preoccupation with women's feet. The record explained the history of the development of his obsession, which manifested in the daytime but also was troubling him at night in his dreams. The assessment identified his relational modality as submissive cooperative. Fetishism had evolved as a pattern of misdirected assertiveness. The problem was that he lost control of his escapist conduct. He experienced guilt and embarrassment reinforcing his feeling of worthlessness and furthering his social withdrawal.

The assessment was therapeutic in the sense that he recognized his vulnerability to approval by his parents, who were deceased, and that he could feel good about himself without their approval since he had achieved certain accomplishments that attested his being successful along their criteria.

The assessment helped him: first, by understanding his problem as one of a relational modality diagnosis; he developed insights about the logical connection of his personality pattern of submissiveness, compensated by his aggressive attention-getting escapism, which elicited his embarrassment as reversals as loosing control to overpowering rejecting women. Second, he experienced cathartic release from guilt by revealing his secret preoccupations.

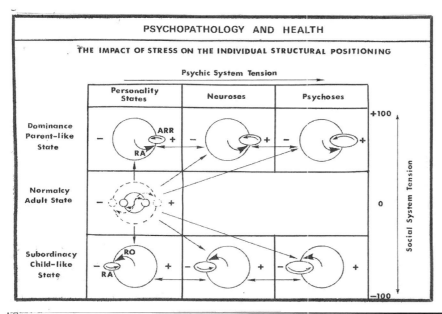

PSYCHOPATHOLOGY AND HEALTH

THE IMPACT OF STRESS ON THE INDIVIDUAL STRUCTURAL POSITIONING

SOCIAL SYNDROMES				
	Subordinacy		**Dominance**	
	Cooperative	Antagonistic	Cooperative	Antagonistic
	RA RO	RO RA	RA ARR	ARR RA
Diagnosis	Passive Dependent	Passive Aggressive	Active Dependent	Active Aggressive
Transactional Analysis	Child	Adapted Child	Nurturing Parent	Critical Parent
Formal Relating	RO-Accommodating RA-Trusting	RO-Withdrawing RA-Hostile	RA-Demanding CPRA-Nurturing	RA-Controlling ARR-Distrustful
New Situation	Looks forward to	Resigned to	Afraid of	Paranoid in
Degrees of stress:				
Degree 1	Happy Follower	Reluctant Follower	Social Leader Fights for Oppressed	Individualistic Leader. Limit-tester
Degree 2	Blames self. Holds negative feelings in. Apologetic.	Blames the leader.	Blames others. Portrays self as victim.	Blames everybody. Denies hurt feelings.
Degree 3	Seeks help	Is tense but helpless	Manipulates Threatens to abandon system	Abandons system

119

Characteristics Of Submissive Persons' Artwork, Animal Metaphors And The Transparent Mask Sequence

Submissiveness Demonstrated by the Animal Metaphor Tests
We recognize substantial polarization between animal choices with asymmetry of the animals' power positions. The asymmetry reflects severe conflicts where one animal is presented as a victim of a violent partner, i.e. one is a hunter the other is hunted.

- The test taker identifies with the weak vulnerable animal, usually being neglected, and occasionally abused.

- The identity animal features signs of defect or injury, handicap, like a broken wing, his head being in the mouth of the dominant animal, his face deformed like that of the ant eater.

- The underlying difficulty in communications is reflected in the positions and the placement of the animals, such as turning their backs to each other and the viewer.

- The identity animal is usually positioned on the right side of the field reflecting the stance of depression, guilt and introspection rather than impulsivity and extroversion.

Case Title	Picture	Who Do You Identify With?
Case Study 1 *A Caribou Falling Behind the Herd and the Predatory Wolf*		"[I identify with] Caribou: his world exploits his weakness. He is naïve and bewildered…as a young man, I was 'behind the herd' of my peers in areas of self-esteem and self-confidence as well as sexual sophistication."
Case Study 2 *Trying to Survive as a Dog*		"[I identify with] the dog – all he needs to do is to learn to live the life he has been given. He's never going to be a tiger! [This is] simply just a scenario between me and the strong people in my life."
Case Study 3 *The Anteater and the Lion*		"[I identify with the] Anteater, because I want to run a lot, [and] believe that [the] ony way to deal is to run…I'm afraid of what others think of me…I want to be powerful and beautifull like the lion."

Case Study 4 *The Wise Oak*		"[I identify with] both. I am the little bunny, because as a child I missed getting loved and whenever I was getting attention, it was usually because I had done something wrong. The tree fairy is…my conscience."
Case Study 5 *The Wolf and the Bird with the Broken Wing*		"I want to fly away from my problems, but can't. I feel I can't help myself…I feel like my problems will not go away, leaving me helpless to defend myself from those who don't accept me."
Case Study 6 *The Vulture and the Snake*		"[I identify with] the dog…perhaps I'm bored/lonely since husband started working in the city…when under pressure, or feeling sorry for myself, I plan on over-eating and drinking as a reward.

Submissiveness' Transparent Mask Test

While the first mask presents power and strength, the second mask reflects the true feelings of helplessness, failure, sadness, guilt and some hostility. The third mask, the heart encompasses the duality of feelings as the prevalent conflicts and resolutions.

The first mask may present deceptive symbols of power and authority, like the Judge, or defenses, like a wall, and also a warrior attitude or anger, like Mr. Dynamo.

The second mask presents hurt feelings, images of traumas, and words identifying hurt feelings. It presents the weaknesses of a person's identity, like behind the powerful judge we have a vulnerable lamb, confusion, lack of identity, and the loss of control.

The third mask, the heart encompassing the totality of conflicts, is presented traumatized and encapsulated, hiding the hurt feelings reflecting alienation and social withdrawal. The submissive person shows more attention to inner feelings than outward interpersonal conflicts. It shows also the difficulty communicating feelings, like the impediment of a moat dividing the heart in halves. The heart is empty; it has a hole, another is totally encased in a jar, 'completely unrevealed'.

Case Title	Mask	Feelings	Heart's Inner Conflict
Case Study 1 *The Caribou Falling Behind the Herd and the Predatory Wolf* *The Judge and the Lamb*	*Judge in a Wig* Power, authority vs. insecurity. [This mask represents a] hiding place...[a] vehicle to project controlled images to the world – an image of power and control.	*Lamb in the Meadow* Vulnerability. [An] actor without costumes or props.	*My Heart* Everything is pushed in, encased from the world...[a] bubbling cauldron of conflicts that is hidden from everyone.
Case Study 2 *Trying to Survive as a Dog*	*Mr. Dynamo* Artistry, confidence, boldness, trust...stability, immunity, firmness.	*Who Is This Man?* Confusion. I'm not sure who is behind the smiling mask...it seems to be the start of conflicts. The always happy face I thought was my true face is removed.	*Heart Under Siege* Threats to the heart, confusion...this represents a heart that is in danger.
Case Study 3 *The Anteater and the Lion*	*Unknown* Power, strength, no fear, tough...need to be powerful instead of being weak. Don't let anyone get close to me.	*Unkindly Thoughts* Pain, anger, rage, fear, hate, rejection, failure, hurt, relief, shame. Let down walls and show what's there.	*Completely Unrevealed* A lot of times I feel that I am not okay. Anger, hate, failure, wanting to stay alive but bothered by suicidal thoughts."

Case Study 4 *The Wise Oak*	*The Warrior* Strength, fearlessness, power, free to scream…[but] someone other than the warrior is holding her mask.	*Seeking Control* Peace, no anger, no control, emotions, sadness, happiness someone else is controlling her mask…this person needs help making decisions for herself.	*Mixed Emotions* Most of the heart is full of love, a small portion is anger, then confusion…on how to feel, and when.
Case Study 5 *The Bird with the Broken Wing*	*Put a Bag Over Your Head* Embarrassment, worthlessness, ugliness. I don't want the world to see my bad characteristics. I'll come out when it's safe	*My World* Fear of: danger, ridicule, jealousy, hurt, sadness, mistrust. I can't deal with conflicts, real or imagined – I fear confrontations [and[negative feedback.	*Hole in My Heart* I feel incomplete, unfinished, not a whole person. I need to find what I am missing.
Case Study 6 *The Vulture and the Snake*	*Perpetual Smile* False happiness. Self-deceit, mockery. Shutting out sadness with a smile.	*Blackout* Dejection, rejection, unwillingness [and] inability to express her feelings, and being preoccupied with eating.	Double Image. Discord Two facets are separated: happiness on one side; hidden feelings, anger, sadness, fear [and] shadows are there, but they are constantly being repressed.

Submissiveness Case Study One

Psychiatric Evaluation of a Judge, "The Sacrificial Lamb"
Alternatively, "The Caribou that Falls Behind the Herd"

Introduction and Discussion

This is the evaluation of a judge, referred to me by his priest regarding annulment of his marriage to be granted by the Tribunal based on his entering the marriage using his free will versus being coerced. I saw the judge for five sessions and evaluated him using the Conflict Analysis Battery. His case is reviewed here because it illustrates very clearly the profile of the submissive personality across the range of the battery testing. This study also illustrates the educational, diagnostic and therapeutic value of the assessment as demonstrated in the patient's self report.

The submissiveness relational profile is equally pronounced across all the projective tests. To the question of '*How do you relate with others, and how do you get yourself in trouble?*' He responded saying: "I surrender my own wants and needs to avoid conflicts. To avoid making the other person mad or upset, I give in. Later I resent the other person and hate myself."

The Personality Inventory

The personality inventory scores present his relational modality as both submissive cooperative and antagonistic. The metaphor testing is integrated along the conflict resolution template of six emotions, reflecting his choices along the syndromal sequence of passivities and activities leading him to the resolution of his conflicts showing the end of his marital relationship.

His RMES scores were uniformly -3 across the dominance items and +3 across the submissive scales informing us that his relational modality was clearly submissive. He scored high on both the submissive cooperative and the antagonistic scales. The judge's inventory choices reflect consistently the submissive relational modality. The scores are less consistent in the subscale of hostility. He is angry but he has difficulty communicating it, consistently holding his feelings to himself and experiencing the need to avoid conflict rather than confront his counterparts. There is elevation of psychic tension in the area of depression.

Projective tests confirm the inventory's findings of submissiveness.

124

Summary of the projective tests:

- The drawing of his parental family shows that he felt manipulated by his powerful mother like a puppet.

- His childhood conflictual memory is about not protesting when he wasn't treated equally with his siblings.

- His later life memory is about his shotgun wedding; he is getting married reluctantly, wearing a prisoner's striped outfit, ball and chain on his feet, next to the church is a jail.

- The image behind the mask of a judge is a lamb.

- His two metaphors are about being a victim of a misleading wolf. In the animal metaphor he is the caribou that falls behind the herd and in the fairy tale metaphor he is the pig being reassured by a wolf with a hidden knife.

- He reports a significant dream about getting shot by a disgruntled criminal whom he had given a sentence; and,

- His short story is about a voyage with a selfish partner that ends with parting company.

The record confirms the submissiveness relational pattern clearly across all his metaphors: The projective material, the autobiographical tests, family portrait, memories and dream test confirm this as the relational pattern that affected his decisions throughout his life. His metaphor stories corroborate this deviation by presenting a consistent preference for self-sacrifice out of concern for the welfare of others.

- *Stress* **is presented with the family portrait and three conflictual memories**

- The Family Portrait reveals that while his father is sitting in a chair slumped over a table with a bottle of wine at a distance, his mother is portrayed as a puppeteer of her children. Unlike his siblings cutting off the puppet strings held by his mother the judge is going off into the world still controlled by his mother holding on to his strings. Strings still attached to his image show the ease of his being manipulated and his powerlessness in making decisions in relationships.

- His Childhood Conflictual Memory presents an episode of self-sacrifice: the judge recalls a time that his father sent him to buy ice cream with only enough money for three rather than four ice cream bars. He recalled not asserting himself; he rationalized his reaction by deciding that he simply did not desire to have any ice cream.

- In the Conflictual Memory from his adult life, he presented his wedding. It reveals a shotgun held at his head. Behind the church is a jail. The bride is presented as pregnant. His father in law was an officer, his warden. He wore a striped suit like a prisoner and was held in place by a ball and chain. He explained that he was coerced by a manipulative, willful and selfish promiscuous woman into marriage against his will by her deliberately getting pregnant. He was not ready for marriage. He had wanted to go to law school but when she got pregnant he consented to marry her. He did not tell any of his college friends about getting married, and did not invite any of them to the wedding and later to his home. He recalled getting drunk the night before and having an accident on the way to renting his tuxedo. He avoided his bride during their honeymoon and there was little interest in sex in their relationship; in fact, he chose to have vasectomy after a few years of marriage. His wife was unfaithful but he did not confront her. She undermined his authority with their children, sabotaged his finances, and competed with his professional interests.

Response and *Anxiety* is presented in the triple mask test

- He drew a mask of a judge, but when the mask becomes transparent we see the client's true identity that of a lamb. His heart is well-encapsulated identifying only positive feelings. In his third mask he portrayed love--no hostility or anger at the suffering he experienced over the years. He indicated love for his new lady friend, and his children and duty for his profession.

Defense is illustrated in the animal and fairy tale tests

- In both his Animal and Fairy Tale metaphors, his counterpart appears to be a willful and deceptive wolf.

- In the Animal Metaphor he identified with a caribou falling behind the herd. In his comments he accepts surrendering without fight as the predicament of improving the species. He yields cooperatively, sacrifices his interests and avoids fighting or attempting to defend himself, and these choices show his lack of assertiveness.

- In the Fairy Tale metaphor the proverbial pig seeks to erect a house to protect himself from the deceitful wolf knocking on his door saying: 'trust me', while carrying a knife in his sleeve.

Reversal is presented in the dream metaphor:

- He suffers of a recurring nightmare in which he is haunted by the image of a gunman targeting his shotgun at him. He is afraid for his life and safety. The conflictual memory of his shotgun wedding also featured a gun like his recurring nightmare. One may connect the two and conclude that the judge is suffering from guilt, which inhibited him from speaking his mind and from asserting his rights as a person and as a judge.

Compromise is illustrated in the short story metaphor

- The Short Story exercise presents him upon the end of a dangerous journey by boat. His companion has betrayed him and as soon as the voyage ends, the two companions will part ways forever. The test reflects his bitterness toward his wife and his deep-seated desire to extricate himself from his spouse of many years.

Information on a Second Workbook

I asked the judge to repeat the assessment with another workbook to detect an evolution in his disposition following the completion of the evaluation. The judge misunderstood my instructions and instead copied the testing, using colors and a more legible handwriting. He used a pen instead of a pencil. In the second set of images he presented more clearly his mother's powerful manipulation of the family. He presented the Judge and lamb masks, but altered the symmetry of the animal metaphors, making the caribou into a dot in the distance, the little pig was eclipsed while the wolf stands up alone in the picture obviously hiding a knife in his sleeve saying 'trust me'.

This censorship reinforced the impression that the judge's subordinacy is problematic deferring to dominant, inconsiderate, and manipulative partners in his life in a consistent manner, censoring his own image and interests while attending to the demands of others. Indeed in the first book he related a recent conflict pertaining to his current relationship; the new lady in his life had recently physically attacked him in public in a fit of rage over his supporting his son's education. In the second book he left this memory out of the book altogether. His suppressing his thoughts and feelings and unpleasant emotions reflected the problematic dimension of his relational modality.

Diagnostic Impression

The clearly submissive pattern of the inventory test, corroborated by the projective tests, confirms his vulnerability to being coerced. He consistently presented himself as a person willing to be intimidated, manipulated, and abused. This relational pattern determined his lifetime decisions and it was the factor leading him to his wedding. This information leads us to conclude that coercion, not free will, was the reason he entered into his marriage of 24 years.

The battery findings and his self-assessment report reveal a consistent pattern of extreme submissive cooperation, which under moderate stress transforms into submissive antagonism, his default modality in resolving conflicts. His testing reveals this submissive way of relating prior to, during, and after his marriage. This approach to resolving conflict has led him to yield to authorities or circumstances in his life without expressing any resistance. His submissiveness has magnified external factors in making decisions out of a sense of moral obligation to conform by surrendering his own interests to societal expectations. He experienced this submissive disposition toward many authority figures, in particular his mother and his father. Completing his duties as a judge was one of the items in the drawing of his heart. Finally this submissiveness is demonstrated in his compliance to the requirements of Church's authority.

There is no doubt that the judge, not having the capacity to express his feelings, was compelled to make concessions and suffer in a Christian manner. Deprived of the skill to communicate his feelings effectively and identifying with Christian values he did not have the means to be directed by personal choices. This deferential approach deprived this devout person of the freedom to choose.

But this pattern of surrender did not serve him right in his relationship with his ex-wife as resentments increased. He felt victimized and coerced into the marriage. He felt manipulated by her from the outset of their relationship. He perceived her during their marriage as consistently abusing power at his expense. He defended himself from her by withdrawing since the inception of their relationship. He was willing to be a lamb led to slaughter, a caribou that had to be sacrificed to the wolf, to be the pig trusting the words of a wolf knocking on his door. Thus he built resentments like the helpless pig whose house is going to be blown away by the calculating wolf. In his marriage, resentments ran his life rather than love. It was a miserable relationship and it was terminated as untenable. At some point in his life's journey he decided to seek a divorce for lack of a meaningful and fair partnership. His divorce was a preferable alternative to living at home behind a brick wall protecting him from a wife whom he perceived as a wolf constantly threatening him with emotional extinction.

This development in a relationship is not unusual, except in its intensity. Frequently through a pattern of spousal self-selection, opposites often attract and marry. But couples displaying extreme relational power management modalities often fail in their relationships for two reasons:

First, the submissive person, like the judge, holds his feelings in, experiences excessive resentments, and instead of seeking to actively repair the relationship, chooses to avoid further conflicts building defenses/walls to protect himself from abuse. The battery findings reveal a consistent pattern of extreme submissive-cooperative relating which, under stress, has been transformed into submissive-antagonistic relating as the default modality of resolving conflicts.

His excessively submissive mode of relating led to his being oppressed and feeling exploited and betrayed. The judge's submissiveness, reinforced culturally by his being a devout Christian embracing the spirit of self-sacrifice, manifested upon the inception of this marriage conceived because of an unwanted pregnancy. External social and internal psychological factors forced him to yield to a union in spite of his own preference. He experienced this marriage as serving a sentence. With this disposition he has been feeling resentful towards his partner and justified in seeking termination of this relationship.

Second, concurrently his dominant wife expressed anger, and engaged in limit testing, self-righteous and sometimes unconscionable acts. His withdrawal facilitated his wife's taking liberties and testing the limits of the marriage, which in turn intensified his perception of her as selfish and self-righteous, demanding and controlling, judgmental and dismissive. His submissiveness and her dominance led to mutual suffering and the failure of their relationship.

This pattern of alienation compounded their marital strife and led to psychopathology and incompatibility. This course of events has been the scenario of this marriage.

The psychological profile of the judge and the alleged social profile of his wife should have been considered enough of a justification to annul the marriage on the basis of incompatibility and well established alienation. The church's tribunal considered his report and mine but rejected his application.

I recommended therapy for the judge to specifically develop self-confidence and skills to effectively express his feelings. This skill could help him avert his being a victim and his becoming resentful and self-loathing in future relationships.

Patient Insights: Personal Essay

The Judge Composed The Following Letter To The Tribunal At The End Of The Brief Evaluation

To: The Tribunal

Please consider this letter as a supplement to the marital summary that I provided as part of my application for annulment.

I am asking this Tribunal to declare my marriage to T. T. on June 21, 1972 a nullity because the evidence proves, to a standard of moral certitude, that the "marriage" was the result of a gross defect in consent. I realize that there are many forces working against me in this effort. These include:

1) A general disapproval by the Church hierarchy in Rome to the number of annulments granted in the United States.

2) The 24 year length of my marriage

3) The opposition by my spiteful ex-wife

4) The New York Tribunal's conclusion that they could not conclude to a nullity in my case.

Despite these obstacles, I intend to persevere with my petition now pending. I am doing this because:

1) I firmly believe in the rightness of my cause and know in my heart that my marriage was not bound by God;

2) I do not wish to live my life as an "outlaw" in the eyes of the Church but rather as a full member of the mystical body of Christ; and

3) I want to remarry within the Church and in that way have a good and holy marital relationship with my new wife.

Given the realities of my situation, I have endeavored to learn about myself and about human personality and behavior so as to present the most complete and persuasive case to the Tribunal.

In this regard, I offer the following:

The modern approach groups human personality types into generally two categories: dominant and submissive. Within these basic groups there can be antagonistic and cooperative features. So a person may be dominant antagonistic, dominant cooperative, submissive antagonistic or submissive cooperative. Or, have a combination of traits from the various groups. While, from a scientific point of view, no one group is "good" or "bad", personality profiles that are strongly dominant or submissive create problems for the person in interpersonal relationships. These problems can, in turn, result in coping strategies that are undesirable and destructive.

In my case, the above information on human personality is of more than mere abstract academic interest. Indeed, I gave up a quarter century of my life because of my inability to surmount the barriers to happiness imposed by my personality. Psychological testing has demonstrated quite clearly that I am a submissive personality type. As such, there is a strong feature of my personality that is willing to subvert my own interests in order to avoid conflict. This subversion results in behaviors that at the same time:

a) Adopt positions inimical to my happiness but are perceived as necessary to avoid stress and conflict; and,

b) Allows the unfulfilled feelings to fester within creating resentment, unhappiness and despair.

The experience of the psychological testing has also shown me that my former wife is very much a dominant personality. As such she thrives on conflict, insists that her feelings be accepted, exalts her wants and needs over everything else, is prone to anger and uses anger as a behavioral response to get her way. As detailed in the Marital Summary, my account of the circumstances of my wedding and marriage are replete with examples of this dominant behavior. A few instances are as follows.

a. T. T. tumultuous and rebellious relationship with her father that involved her violent arguments with him as a young teenager and his corresponding several efforts to tame his wild daughter [this stands in stark contrast to my experience of being an overly dutiful and conforming son for my parents].

b. T. T.'s experiences with sex. She started dating GI's when she was 13 and continued in numerous relationships ever since. She was sexually promiscuous as a teenager in part to satisfy her own sexual interests and in part to disrespect her father. This promiscuity continued even after her marriage as evidenced by her numerous extra marital affairs. [Again, this is just the opposite of my experience, which involved no dating whatsoever as a teenager, no sexual experience before T. T. and no significant experience with women at all].

c. T. T.' s reaction when faced with the certain prospect that our relationship would end when I entered law school in the fall of 1971. Her dominant personality and desire to get married and get away from her tyrannical father was responsible for her getting herself pregnant so as to trap me into marriage. This was accomplished by her aggressively making our relationship sexual when it had previously not been that way. For my part, once she became pregnant with the attendant scandal, I felt I had no choice but to marry her despite the fact that I did not love her.

d. Her slothful behavior during the marriage as manifested by her refusal to work in the face of economic need. Her anger, which flared regularly when she would not get her way. Her extra marital affairs that fed her sexual needs that were unsatisfied in our loveless marriage.

e. Finally, her conduct during our divorce as shown by her mercenary and greedy attempts to destroy me, because I had finally rejected her. Her purchase of a new dining room set, new car, credit card purchases and house all were efforts to aggrandize her lifestyle at my

130

expense. She further demanded that I am fully responsible for the educational needs of our two children.

The benefits of these personality insights are two fold:

First, they show quite clearly why and how I could be forced into a loveless marriage. I saw my options through the prism of my submissive personality that refracted away any self-interest in favor of avoiding scandal to my family at all costs. On her side, it shows the ends that she would go to get what she wanted- a ticket out of her dysfunctional home and a meal ticket for life.

Second, the personality insights provide a measure of self-knowledge that will inform my future conduct and relationships so as to avoid the destructive decisions I've made in the past. I look to the future with clarity I never had before.

Thank you for considering the above,

Very truly yours, Judge ABC

Relational Modality Evaluation Scale

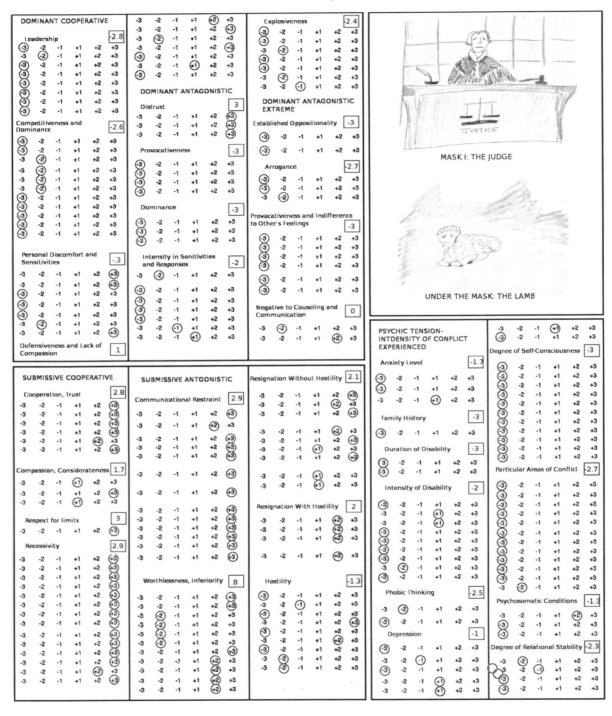

MASK I: THE JUDGE

UNDER THE MASK: THE LAMB

DOMINANT COOPERATIVE

Leadership -2.8

Competitiveness and Dominance -2.6

Personal Discomfort and Sensitivities -.3

Defensiveness and Lack of Compassion .1

DOMINANT ANTAGONISTIC

Distrust 3

Provocativeness -3

Dominance -3

Intensity in Senitivities and Responses -2

Explosiveness -2.4

DOMINANT ANTAGONISTIC EXTREME

Established Oppositionality -3

Arrogance -2.7

Provocativeness and Indifference to Other's Feelings -3

Negative to Couseling and Communication 0

SUBMISSIVE COOPERATIVE

Cooperation, Trust 2.8

Compassion, Considerateness 1.7

Respect for limits 3

Recessivity 2.9

SUBMISSIVE ANTGONISTIC

Communicational Restraint 2.9

Worthlessness, Inferiority .8

Resignation Without Hostility 2.1

Resignation With Hostility 2

Hostility -1.3

PSYCHIC TENSION- INTDENSITY OF CONFLICT EXPERIENCED

Anxiety Level -1.7

Family History -3

Duration of Disability -3

Intensity of Disability -2

Phobic Thinking -2.5

Depression -1

Degree of Self-Consciousness -3

Particular Areas of Conflict -2.7

Psychosomatic Conditions -1.3

Degree of Relational Stability -2.3

132

Transcription of the Judge's Metaphors

STRESS

CHILDHOOD CONFLICTUAL MEMORY

Step 1: Draw a conflictual childhood memory:

Step 2: Describe the incident: I was about 9 years old. We went to hockey game with my two cousins. My father sent me to an ice cream vendor to buy 4 ice cream bars (two for my brother and me and two for my two cousins.) I ordered four bars from the vendor, but only had enough money for three. I was not sure my father had more money and did not want to embarrass him. I bought three bars and told everyone that I did not want any ice cream. It was very embarrassing.

Step 3: How did you feel about this person? I was angry at my father but also felt bad for him. I did not want him to look bad in front of my uncle. **How did this person feel about you?** My father had no idea I was short of money.

Step 4: What were the conflicts? [left blank]

Step 5: What happened before? [left blank]

Step 6: After? [left blank]

Step 7: Your share in this conflict? Not talking about the problem.
Note: Remainder of questions in this test are left blank.

ADOLESCENT CONFLICTUAL MEMORY

Step 1: Draw a conflictual adolescent memory:

Step 2: Describe the incident: Shotgun marriage. I did not assert my own interests. My tuxedo is the stripes of a convict--front door church, back door jail.

Step 3: Effect on life: It ruined my life for 24 years.

RECENT CONFLICT

Step 1: Draw a recent conflictual memory:

Step 2: Describe the incident: Fight with girlfriend, she ripped my shirt in a public dispute.

Step 3: Effect on life: Introduced doubt that I can maintain a loving and happy relationship.

BALLOON PORTRAIT AND STORY

FAMILY ORIGIN

Step 1: Draw a balloon portrait of your family of origin:

Step 2: Identify each individual:
Father, postal clerk, distant insular, silent passive.
Mother, extrovert, domineering, control, distant.
Me, intelligent, first-born, hardworking, withdrawn.
J., brother, extrovert, rebellious, drives Mercedes Benz.
M., sister, kind, scatterbrained
J., brother, even-tempered

Step 3: What are they saying? The balloons do not talk together.

Step 4: What happened before? [left blank]

Step 5: After? [left blank]

Step 6: Title: "Trailblazer."

Step 7: What are the conflicts? I have to forge my path in the world alone. Brother is cutting the strings of control.

RESPONSE

Mask I

Step 1: Draw a mask:

Step 2: Answer the following questions:

Title: "Judge in a Wig."

Age: 48   **Sex:** Male

Emotions conveyed: Power, authority.

Step 3: Conflicts represented: Power vs. Insecurity.

Step 4: Resolution of conflicts represented: Hiding Place

ANXIETY

MASK II

Step 5: Draw what is behind the mask:

Step 6: Fill in the blanks and answer the questions:

Title: "Lamb in a Meadow"

Age: ? **Sex:** ?

Emotions conveyed: [left blank]

Step 7: Conflicts represented: Vulnerability.

Step 8: Resolution of conflicts: None.

Step 9: Draw what is in the heart:

Title: "My Heart."

Step 10: Items and themes represented: A witches brew of love, guilt and duty.

Step 11: Feelings and conflicts represented: Everything is pushed in, encased from the world.

Step 12: Resolution of conflicts? Handle these things yourself in your <u>own</u> way.

Step 13: Title of the sequence: "Free to the World; Face; Gut."

Step 14: Summarize the sequence of transformations:

Mask = vehicle to project controlled image to the world – an image of power and control.
Transparent Mask = actor without costume or props.
Heart = bubbling cauldron of conflicts that is hidden from everybody.

Step 15: Conclusions about the way this person resolves conflicts: Internalizes everything.

Step 16: Does this relate to how you handle feelings: All things are directed inward.

Step 17: What changes should be made: Although changes are desirable, they are possible.

Step 18: What changes are you willing to make: I am not sure.

DEFENSE

ANIMAL METAPHOR TEST #1

Step 1: Draw two animals

Step 2: Fill in the blanks

Animal #1

Type of animal: Wolf
Age: 20   **Sex:** Female
Personality: Ruthless, cruel, survivor.

Animal #2

Type of animal: Caribou
Age: 20   **Sex:** Male
Personality: Peaceful, kind, friendly.

Step 3: What are they saying?

> **#2:** "Wolf, why must you attack me? I will do you no harm, I just want to live in peace with my herd."
>
> **#1:** "I need to eat in order to live. You are weak and unable to keep up with your herd. I make the herd stronger by hunting the weak members. There is nothing personal in this – but I need to survive."
>
> **#2:** "Wolf, why can't you survive on the grass and plants like I do? Why must you kill me? I want to live too. I may be weak and slow, but I do not want to die. I cannot survive your attack, but you can find other kinds of food."
>
> **#1:** "I do not want to debate this. It is not a matter of logic or fairness, it is survival!"

Step 4: What happened before? The wolf was chasing the herd and the caribou fell behind and was about to be attacked.

Step 5: After? The wolf attacked and killed the caribou.

Step 6: Title: "Improving the Herd."

Step 7a: Conflicts between themselves: "Improving the Herd."

Step 7b: Conflicts between them and the world: The wolf's world required her to be ruthless and exploit the weakness of others. The caribou's world provides him peace and community, but exposes him to a violent death.

Step 8: What changes should they make to resolve their conflicts? The wolf should "look outside the dots" to find a way of survival that does not involve killing. The caribou should be more wry and wily and protect itself more and not submit to death. He must see the world as it is-- dangerous and hostile, and act accordingly.

Step 9: Which animal do you identify with: Caribou: his world exploits his weakness. He is naive and bewildered. **Other animal:** Ex-wife: She is shallow and ruthless, selfish and domineering.

Step 10: How does this pertain to you? As a young man, I was behind the "herd" of my peers in areas of self-esteem and self-confidence as well as sexual sophistication. My ex-wife got herself pregnant and trapped me into marriage. She "hunted" me and devoured me. I, like the caribou, did not assert my rights effectively.

Step 11: What changes should you make? I must assert my own wants in situations where others are trying to infringe on those rights.

Step 12: Present a similar incident: Shotgun marriage; student loan for son.

Step 13: How do you relate with others, and how do you get yourself in trouble? I surrender my own wants and needs to avoid conflicts. To avoid making the other person mad or upset, I give in. Later I resent the other person and hate myself.

Step 14: What changes are you willing to make? Although I understand the problem from an intellectual point of view, I am not sure that I can make the needed changes. I usually prefer to withdraw than to engage in conflict. It is not worth it to me.

Step 1: Draw two fairy tale characters:

Step 2: Fill in the blanks

Character#1: Pig **(not presented in the drawing)**

Age: 20   **Sex:** Male
Personality: Industrious, cautious, vulnerable.

Character#2: Wolf

Age: 20   **Sex:** Male
Personality: Cruel, aggressive, persistent, smooth, attractive, persuasive.

Step 3: What are they saying?

> **#2:** So pig, I see that you are going to build a brick house, why are you doing that?
>
> **#1:** Well, I'm not saying that you would do me harm, but a pig cannot be too careful these days.
>
> **#2**: Oh pig, I'm disappointed. Don't you trust me? If you were any kind of a decent pig, you would not think so badly of your fellow creatures. What have I ever done to you?
>
> **#1:** You blew down the straw house of my younger brother and the stick nose of my older brother. So, I'm not taking any chances!
>
> **#2:** Who said I did those things? Don't believe everything you hear. I never blew down anybody's house. Trust me. Now, put away those bricks and let's take a walk and have dinner together.

Step 4: What happened before? The pig was building a brick house to protect himself from the wolf. The wolf was stalking food.

Step 5: After? I'm not sure. If the pig believed the wolf, then maybe they went for a walk and the pig felt guilty for mistrusting the wolf. If the pig did not believe the wolf, then the pig kept building--fast.

Step 6: Title: "Trust?"

Step 7a: Conflicts between themselves: The pig wants a barrier between himself and the threats, the wolf wants to remove barriers to achieve his wants and needs.

Step 7b: Conflicts between them and the world: The pig feels vulnerable and needs protection from a dangerous world. The wolf needs to dominate resisting world.

Step 8: What changes should they make to resolve conflicts? Sincerity that leads to mutual trust. The pig must protect himself first, <u>then</u> open his heart to maybe trusting someone. He cannot run the risk of blind trust.

Step 9: Which character do you identify with? I am the pig, attempting to protect myself from a hostile world. **Other character:** [left blank]

Step 10: How does this pertain to you? I see myself as naive. I see the world as hostile. I want a "brick wall" around me.

Step 11: What changes should you make? Unsure. Maybe this is a conflict that should not be "resolved". It may be that a state of conflict simply exists and one must accept it.
Note: Remainder of questions in this test are left blank.

REVERSAL

DREAM ANALYSIS

Step 1: Choose a dream: Past dream.

Step 2: Draw the dream:

Step 3: Describe the dream: I am walking from the courthouse--am shot and killed by a gunman inside the car.

Step 4: Describe the participants:
Me: working, trusting, naïve.
Gunman: brazen, angry, killer.

Step 5: What are the conflicts? Life/Death.

Step 6: What occurrences preceded the dream? Not sure.

Step 7: Explanation of the dream: Death may be the final escape from the pains of life.

Step 8: Do you dream a lot? No.

Step 9: Other dreams: I rarely recall dreams.

Step 10: Connections or patterns in dreams: My job makes me the object of people's frustration and anger.

COMPROMISE

SHORT STORY

Step 1: Write a short story:
Jack and Tom were sailing around the world in a 40' sailboat. When they reached the southern tip of South America they encountered a terrible storm. Help was over one thousand miles away, so they had to manage the problem themselves.

Jack wanted to abandon ship but Tom insisted that they stay. Jack felt that the lifeboat would have a better chance of making it to the rocky shore. Tom did not want to abandon the both because he had a lot of money invested in it.

Jack agreed to stay. By reefing the sails and staying awake for 30 hours they rode out the storm and continued on their voyage. But Jack resented the fact that Tom put the value of the boat over Tom's safety.

Step 2: Illustrate the story:

Step 3: Fill in the blanks:

Character#1

Character name: Jack
Age: 30   **Sex:** Male
Personality: Sensible, considerate, submissive, naïve, silent.

Character#2
Character name: Tom
Age: 35   **Sex:** Male
Personality: Mercenary, selfish, aggressive, materialistic, verbal.

Step 4: What happened before? The two had bought the boat and planned the trip for years. They thought themselves to be close friends.

Step 5: After: They continued to finish the voyage, then parted together.

Step 6: Title: "Lifeboat."

Step 7: Conflicts between themselves: Jack values his safety over money. Tom values money over safety.

Step 8: What changes should they make to resolve conflicts? Consider the others views; understand the value system each is operating on.

Step 9: Which character do you identify with: Jack. **Other character:** Ex-wife.

Step 10: How does this pertain to you? I want to escape the stormy seas of my life.

Step 11: What changes should you make? Not sure.

Step 12: Present a similar incident: [left blank]

Step 13: How do you relate with others, and how do you get yourself in trouble? Too submissive.

Step 14: What changes are you willing to make? [left blank]

Summary with the Metaphor Profile

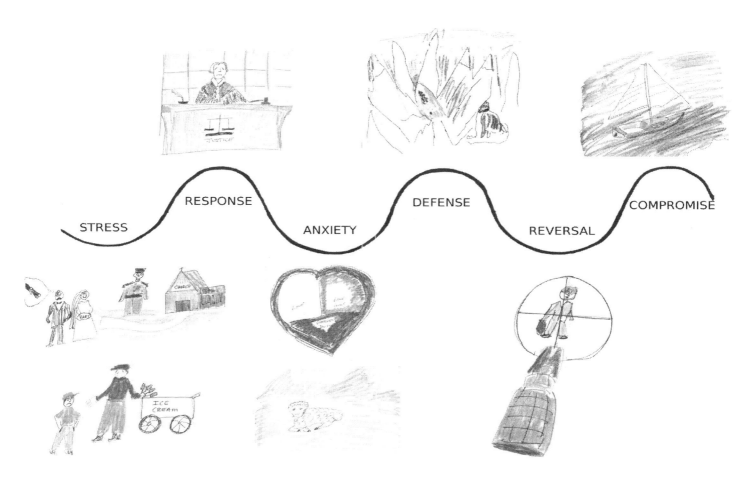

Stress:
Told to buy
ice cream he
sacrifices his
own share.
Trapped in
shotgun
marriage to
dominant
wife.

Response:
Judge as a
mask.

Anxiety:
Under the
mask is a
scared meek
lamb.
His heart is
full of love
for kids and
fiancé.

Defense:
Caribou
falling
behind the
herd doomed
to become
prey to
ruthless wolf

Reversal:
Being shot at
by criminal
outside the
courthouse

Compromise:
Boat drifting in
high seas in
conflict with
materialist
companion.
They survive
to go their
separate ways

Submissive Case Study Two
Trying to Survive as a Dog

Introduction and Discussion: The patient's complaint

The patient was a 55-year-old professor of art education, who came to therapy requesting training in self-hypnosis. He sought help to deal with a gastrointestinal disorder; he had been losing weight and had failed to find a diet to agree with his system. Initially, he did not complain about a number of other difficulties in his life, such as dealing with his daughter, grandchildren and difficulties in dating women. Though an artist, he was reluctant in completing the CAB testing, but after complying, he saw that it revealed to him much about himself. He opened up and shared the intense conflicts of his life. He eventually practiced art exercises with his grand children and became more comfortable with them.

"I act, calm; this has always permitted me to either avoid or solve potential conflicts. I have always felt that avoiding or removing anger was the best course to prevent escalation of conflicts."

This case study illustrates several points:

1. Diagnostically it is of interest by illustrating dynamics of a submissive cooperative person responding to the stress of a threatening exploitive family environment. He repressed his anger, felt depressed and socially withdrawn, developing psychosomatic preoccupations. He was frustrated seeking to overcome the symptoms with self-disciplined hypnotic relaxation.

2. Therapeutically the case study illustrates the effectiveness of the testing in providing emotional catharsis, but also insights on the origin of problems as a relational diagnosis. The therapy was of short duration. It was transformative without being completed with very deep self-awareness, yet it was adequate for substantial psychodynamic growth, interpersonal changes, and effective symptom relief in several aspects of his adjustment.

3. The case is of interest illustrating the outcome monitoring using the simple technique of graphically presenting changes of before and after therapy in the areas of the original conflicts.

The Evaluation

The testing evaluation revealed the syndromal connection of his emotions at a number of levels. Each metaphor confirms his relational choices but the synthesis of metaphors integrates parts into the syndromal totality of his particular conflict resolution.

Stress was presented as his being caught between his conflicted parents illustrated in both his memories and family of origin balloon portrait. He is a victim exposed to their fights and his responses were to run away. His mother liked him because he was no trouble, but she was portrayed as exploitive and manipulative, while his father was threatening him with his manly vocational choices disparaging his proclivity for the arts.

His response reflected in his mask test is in the identity of Mr. Dynamo, a pleasant care-taking guy, eager to please, who wears a smile.

Anxiety, the face behind the mask, is a sad person presenting worry and failure in coping. His Defense is a striking animal metaphor: a lion biting a dog's head off.
"Why do you have to bite my head off?"

"Because you're so much trouble. You simply can't get your ducks all in a row and I can't depend on you to fulfill my needs."

Two other metaphors Jack and Jill, and a grasshopper and a spider present his problematic marital relationship and his submissive coping mechanism. He failed and finally withdrew from his dominant wife, perceiving her as a manic-depressive.

Reversal still presents him threatened by a dominant woman taking over his reading a book. "this woman came and sat on me. She took over and started reading the book at her own pace. She insisted in reading the book the way she wanted to, disregarding my need to read the book." The dream shows his feeling used and imposed upon.

His Compromise in the Short Story presents a wise person enlightening a younger person and passing the torch. He identified with both characters. We see how he has an elaborate spiritual way of helping others. He is a perfect caring educator, but he is also obsessive and controlling in his pursuits.

Therapeutic Outcome: a brief illustrated essay
The therapeutic experience was helpful. Upon termination of the therapy the patient completed a set of before and after therapy images reflecting the change in his feelings toward four issues. Four images reflect improvements in dealing with food tolerance, hypnosis, his relationship with women and that with his grandchildren. Having uncovered his held in feelings he became comfortable with his relationships and less preoccupied with his GI physical symptoms.

Patient's Essay
Clarifying Changes

Anxiety about Food Symptoms
I don't seem to have anxieties anymore. That is why I went to Dr. Levis in the first place. What we did has greatly alleviated my anxieties. I can't put my finger and say this made the change. I had a floating anxiety. I couldn't attribute it to anything. This floating anxiety has dissipated.

Meditation
When I meditate I am thinking of the valley of peace and a pine forest; I am washing my body with brush of magic waterfall; blue light from heaven--I float on the pond--I don't have need to go to the bottom of the pond anymore. It means I don't have a need to hide. I can be in the sunlight appreciating being me. Blue light is healing. Before I used to swallow a golden eel--It'd go through my digestive system and go out with a black cloud, the toxins in the water.

Problems with Women
My ex-wife was manic-depressive; she was incapacitated--when she was high she was great--four weeks high and low with menstruation. I should have realized that if I didn't cut the ice nothing could be done--I was angry and resentful. I'd starve myself physically and mentally. I'd hide in a room. I didn't realize I was angry. I was doing art.

Relationship with Grandchildren
My daughter had complained that I was a delinquent grandfather. I didn't want to be with them.
I usually have been doing art as an escape. What I have been doing in therapy is retrieving information through art. I have been doing art with my grandchildren. I've set up a cabinet with art supplies and art projects with them.

Relationship with Daughter
My daughter is like me--she becomes intolerant--she has tight imagery about what life is like. When she's not feeling good she's up a wall. She has marital problems. I am working with her to calm her down--She has always talked to her mother and not me--now she talks to me about these things, rather than her mother--I don't ask her why --I don't want to put her on the spot. She says I have been more relaxed. I didn't know I was angry— hostile--children mind when their parents get into fights--I didn't realize how angry I was until we did the testing about my anger. The testing showed that I am not dominant but submissive. The marriage forced me to be hostile, I saw it as being dominant.

146

Before and After Images Contrasting How He Changed in Four Problem Areas in the Course of His Therapeutic Experience

Food Symptoms:

Meditation:

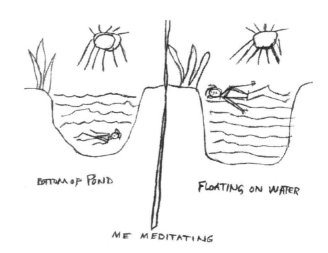

Relationship with Women:

Relationship with Grandchildren:

Transcription of the Case: The Relational Modality Evaluation Scale

Transcription of the Metaphors

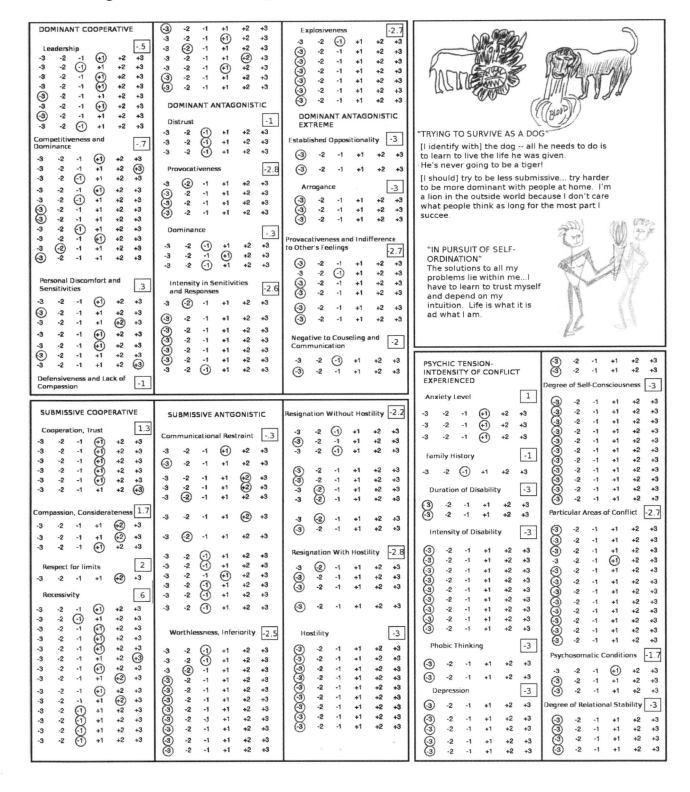

"TRYING TO SURVIVE AS A DOG"

[I identify with] the dog -- all he needs to do is to learn to live the life he was given. He's never going to be a tiger!

[I should] try to be less submissive... try harder to be more dominant with people at home. I'm a lion in the outside world because I don't care what people think as long for the most part I succee.

"IN PURSUIT OF SELF-ORDINATION"
The solutions to all my problems lie within me...I have to learn to trust myself and depend on my intuition. Life is what it is ad what I am.

CHILDHOOD CONFLICTUAL MEMORY

Step 1: Draw a conflictual childhood memory:

Step 2: Describe the incident: Mother and Father. They were arguing over my father coming home late--very late after work. He had stopped in to a grill for a few beers with the guys after his late shift.

Step 3: How did you feel about this person? I was scared. **How did this person feel about you?** Mother didn't love me.

Step 4: What were the conflicts? Don't remember.

Step 5: What happened before? Don't remember.

Step 6: After? She accused him of playing around. Also he would rather be with the boys than with her.

Step 7: Your share in this conflict? None that I know of!

Step 8: Effect on life: There were many such experiences. I had to become very insular just to survive in that kind of volatile environment.

Step 9: Have you been repeating yourself? Yes.

Step 10: Has this conflict been resolved in your mind? No.

Step 11: Resolved in this relationship? No.

Step 12: What changes should be made? Try to be less insular? Try to become more liberated?

Step 1: Draw a conflictual adolescent memory:

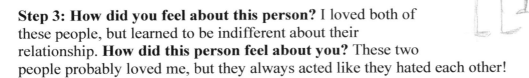

Step 2: Describe the incident: Mother, Father, Son. Both of
these people were always at each other's throats. They fought
like cats and dogs. What really happened to me is what is more
important. I was constantly being torn apart. I became oblivious
to what they did to each other. All I knew is that I was in the
middle of a war zone.

Step 3: How did you feel about this person? I loved both of
these people, but learned to be indifferent about their
relationship. **How did this person feel about you?** These two
people probably loved me, but they always acted like they hated each other!

Step 4: What were the conflicts? The conflicts were mostly petty, trivial incidents. The power
struggle was all that mattered. It was constantly a no-win no-lose situation. It was simply one
disaster after another, again and again.

Step 5: What happened before? There is no before and after. Every day was the same. They
seemed to almost enjoy the battle. After every battle there I was left in no-man's land. I learned to
dread the quiet spaces because of the fear of the next battle. I never knew how bad it was going to
get.

Step 6: After? [see step 5]

Step 7: Your share in this conflict? None that I know of, I simply sat on the sidelines seeking not
to get crushed in the heat of the battle. Getting out of the line of fire became a major
preoccupation.

Step 8: Effect on life: No doubt this is the basis of my floating anxiety. I'm also very shy of close
relationships, and not very trusting.

Step 9: Have you been repeating yourself? Of course I have.

Step 10: Has this conflict been resolved in your mind? Probably not.

Step 11: Resolved in this relationship? Never.

Step 12: What changes should be made? I have to learn that this is not the way people normally
get along. People can get along by compromising over difficult issues. Of course, it's easier if you
can find someone who has the same value system as you do. In our materialistic society it is
difficult to find people who are spiritually oriented without being religiously deterministic.

FAMILY OF ORIGIN

Step 1: Draw a balloon portrait of your family of origin:

Step 2: Identify each individual:
1. **Father:** easy going, happy-go-lucky, outgoing.
2. **Mother:** bitchy, eccentric, cranky.
3. **Son:** quiet, eager to please, solicitous.

Step 3: What are they saying?
#2 – "He's a good boy. Always does what I tell him, and he never causes any problems."
#1 – "Yeah, the kid is really ok, but is he really going to be able to survive in the real world?"
#2 – "As long as he doesn't cause me any difficulty I really don't care!"
#1 – "Well I'll take him to the steel foundry and show him around a man's world."
#3 – "The steel foundry scares the hell out of me. I don't want to do that the rest of my life.'
#1 – "Well that's a real man's job, not something for sissies."
#3 – "There's got to be another way to make a living, and I'll find it."

Step 4: What happened before?
#2 – "I need to buy my new furniture; that's the most important thing in my life."
#1 – "You deserve it baby, you've worked all your life."
#3 – "But I need to go to college after high school."
#2 – "You need to get a job so I can buy new furniture."

Step 5: After?
#2 – "This kid's got some idea that he's got to go to school for the rest of his life. When is he going to make some real money and contribute to my income?"
#1 – "He's just a kid, he'll get it together and realize that he's going to have to work for a living."

Step 6: Give this story a title: "Surviving in the Real World."

RESPONSE

MASK I

Step 1: Draw a mask:

Step 2: Answer the following questions:

Title: "Mr. Dynamo."
Age: 33   Sex: Male
Emotions conveyed: Artistry, confidence, boldness, trust.

Step 3: Conflicts represented: Conflict between what you see and what you hear. See one thing and hear another.

Step 4: Resolution of conflicts represented: Stability, immutability, firmness.

ANXIETY

MASK II

Step 5: Draw what is behind the mask.

Step 6: Fill in the blanks and answer the questions:

Title: "Who Is This Man?"
Age: 51   Sex: Male
Emotions conveyed? Confusion.

Step 7: Conflicts represented: I'm not sure who is behind the smiling mask.

Step 8: Resolution of conflicts? None. It seems to be the start of some conflicts.

Step 9: Draw what is in the heart.

Title: "Heart Under Siege."

Step 10: Items and themes represented: Threats to the heart, confusion. Pins, dark cloud, fears of heart attack, threats to my physical being, diabetes.

Step 11: Feelings and conflicts represented: This represents a heart, which is in danger. Someone, something is threatening the heart.

Step 12: Resolution of conflicts? [This question was left blank]

Step 13: Title of the sequence:
"The Unmasking."

Step 14: Summarize the sequence of transformations: The smiling, always happy face I thought was my true face was removed. The face beneath it, my actual face is now confused, not sure what to feel or what to express.

Step 15: Conclusions about the way this person resolves conflicts: I usually avoid all forms of conflict. Whenever I encounter conflict, I analyze the situation and deal with it logically, unemotionally. Where authority is concerned, I comply with all that is asked of me, but if I feel I am being wronged, I work within the system guidelines to solve the conflict.

Step 16: Does this relate to how you handle feelings: Tact, calm, mutual respect have always permitted me to either avoid or solve potential conflicts. I have always felt that avoiding or removing anger was the best course to prevent escalating of conflicts.

Step 17: What changes should be made: I'm not sure. Recently, I told one of my principals that I was suffering from the effects of 3 years of work problems. I calmly told her (even though my heart was racing and my hands were trembling) that I could not cope with her. I was respectful, did not yell, the way I feel one should treat an administrator.

Step 18: What changes are you willing to make: I'm not sure. I have used all of the methods in my "medicine bag" to cure the wound. I thought removing myself from the pain and risk (despite financial aid and social and professional stigma risks) was my only sure solution. I've been told that is not the best course.

153

ANIMAL METAPHOR TEST #1

Step 1: Draw two animals.

Step 2: Fill in the blanks

Animal #1
Type of animal: Lion
Age: 34 **Sex:** Female
Personality: Angry, forgetful, demanding.

Animal #2
Type of animal: Dog
Age: 60 **Sex:** Male
Personality: Docile, teachable, gentle.

Step 3: What are they saying?
#2 "Why do you have to bite my head off?"
#1 – "Because you're so much trouble. You simply can't get your ducks all in a row and I can't depend on you to fulfill my needs."
#2 – "But I try!"
#1 – "But that's not good enough. You're always too uptight. You're just not worth all the trouble you cause."

Step 4: What happened before?

#2 – "You got such a nice back yard and being on a cul-de-sac is also good for the kids."
#1 – "Yeah, I like this house. It's not bad for this stage in my life."

Step 5: After? Nothing much, the conversation went sort of dead at that point.

Step 6: Title: "Trying to Survive as a Dog."

Step 7a: Conflicts between themselves: The dog #2 has to get his act together in order to please the important people. The lion #1 is hungry and is going to eat up everything in sight.

Step 7b: Conflicts between them and the world: #2 wants too much to please. #1 is too demanding.

Step 8: What changes should they make to resolve conflicts? #1 has to learn to accept the dog for what he is. #2 has to learn to be satisfied with just being a dog.

Step 9: Which animal do you identify with: #2--all he needs to do is to learn to live the life he was given. He's never going to be a tiger! **Other animal:** #1 is my daughter. Very much like my ex-wife--she plays the mother role well and wants the men in her life to fight the world for supremacy.

Step 10: How does this pertain to you? It's simply just a scenario between me and the strong people in my life.

Step 11: What changes should you make? Try to be less submissive.

Step 12: Present a similar incident: Basically the same happened with my ex-wife. She was very demanding but could not face the world outside to get what she wanted. So she used me as a means to an end, then became dissatisfied with that end.

Step 13: How do you relate with others, and how do you get yourself in trouble? I'm a lion in the outside world because I don't care what people think as long as, for the most part, I succeed.
Step 14: What changes are you willing to make? To try harder to be more dominant with people at home.

REVERSAL

FAIRYTALE METAPHOR

Step 1: Draw two fairy tale characters.

Step 2: Fill in the blanks

Character#1: Jack
Age: 50's   **Sex:** Male
Personality: Assiduous, persistent, self-reliant.

Character#2: Jill
Age: 50's   **Sex:** Female
Personality: Tempestuous, moody, contentious.

Step 3: What are they saying?
Jack says to Jill, " Jill why do you keep running up and down the hill all of the time? You're very active, but you never bring any water up the hill in your pail. You're always up and down. I have a very hard time understanding you. When you're up, you do everything in a frenzy, which, by the way is very exhausting for me. But, when you're down, nothing I do seems to help you.

Jill says, "When I'm up, I'm very excited about everything and so I want to get as much water in my pail as possible. But, when I'm down, I simply have no ambition to do anything and all I want to do is sleep.

Jack says, "But life can't be carried out in spurts of frenzy. You have to be more consistent in what you are doing in order to get anywhere.

Step 4: What happened before? Jill was lying in bed not wanting to get up this morning. She said, "Just leave me alone; I want to sleep all day. Jack said, " But there's so much that has to be done. The kids have to be cared for and I have to go to work. Somebody has to stoke the home fires while the breadwinner is out making a living. Jill says, "But I don't feel like doing anything today."

Step 5: After? Jill stayed in bed. Jack said, "Dammit Jill, this is the way things always go. You seem to be either flying so high that I have to peel you off the walls. Or, you're so low that you can't seem to function at all. Can't you find some happy medium?

Step 6: Title: "Just Another Day in the Life of Jack and Jill."

Step 7a: Conflicts between themselves: Jack resents the fact that Jill doesn't want to do her part in the family scheme of things. Jack gets angry because Jill thinks that she has a choice in whether she will or will not function normally in life. She does only what she likes to do and not what she has to do. So Jack is angry when Jill is down and doesn't want to roll up her sleeves and complete her day's responsibilities. Yet, on the other hand, when Jill is flying high, Jack is simply overwhelmed by her hyperactivity. And so, he gets angry because he just can't keep up with the mania that surrounds him.

Step 7b: Conflicts between them and the world: Jack is trying to make things work, but gets frustrated with Jill's highs and lows. Jack says to Jill, "Nothing is going to fall in your lap in this life, you have to conscientiously pursue your goals in order to make things work out." Jack grew up in a time when the men made their way in the world in order to support their family and women stayed home to take care of the family and stoke the home fires. The rules of the game were pretty clear for him and his father and grandfather before him. Then, sort of late in the game, the Women's Movement came along and changed the rules of the game in mid-stream. Women were supposed to not only have and rear a family, but also pursue a career! Women seem to be in a double-bind situation, they're damned if they do and they're damned if they don't. I see it with my daughter all the time. She just loves staying home and rearing the kids, but she also feels that she should be out in the world and have a career.

Step 8: What changes should they make to resolve conflicts? Jack and Jill should have established a game plan and stayed with it. Any kind of significant career takes half of a lifetime to establish. Raising a family should be considered a career. Jill becomes angry because she doesn't want to deal with events as they are. She raised a very difficult child, when even the pros didn't know what to do with this kind of kid. She did the impossible and saved this kid from personal disaster, when even the professionals gave up on him, both teachers and psychologists alike. What more can anyone ask for? It is very difficult to change directions midstream, or to pursue two divergent objectives at the same time.

Step 9: Which character do you identify with? I identify with Jack, obviously. He is doing the best job he knows how. But when the rules of the game change in the middle of the game, he finds it difficult to cope with the new rules, especially when a special child is involved. Other character: Jill is my ex-wife. She's resentful because of the choices she has made in her life and wanted to make changes that were impossible at the time. Having chosen to be a mother, she abandoned her plans to pursue a teaching career. Of course, the fact that the second child was so hyperactive also made family life very difficult. But, when the child grew up, there was no reason why she couldn't go back to school to pursue a career. Ironically, the divorce motivated her to do just that. But at 58 years old, getting a full time teaching job is difficult. Even she realizes that age discrimination is a factor at her age.

156

Step 10: How does this pertain to you? This is the life that was for me and my ex-wife. Because of her manic/depression and the birth of a severely hyperactive child, and also the ideals of the Woman's Movement, life for Jack and Jill became very confusing at best. At the time, no one even knew how to deal with their problem child. And, putting the ideals of the Women's Movement in the mix turned out to be pure hell.

Step 11: What changes should you make? We all make choices in life and these choices determine much of our circumstances. We all have to work with these circumstances in the best way we know how. When people are not willing to simplify their life's operations, they can easily become bewildered. So we have to live with some of the choices we make. There are no simple answers!

Step 12: Present a similar incident: When I was younger, I tended repeatedly to find women who had a hard time getting their act together. I would help them get it all together, thinking that's great, the problems are solved. To my surprise, the same problems would come up again under a different guise. My ex-wife had problem keeping it all together when I met her in college. Soon after we were going together, her grades got much better. I thought that her problems were simple, but little did I know how complex they really were. So with my ex-wife, I always seemed to get myself in a bag that I couldn't get myself out of. In any case, I finally learned that you can't get another person's act together for them. If they can't do it for themselves, nobody else can do it for them.

Step 13: How do you relate with others, and how do you get yourself in trouble? Well, this same pattern carries over into all aspects of my life. I tend to want to help people get it all together so to speak. I even try to help my students get it all together. But all to no avail, I've discovered that those that can, do and those that can't, don't. I can only act as a catalyst to help things happen. I can't do it for them. The same pattern happens with colleagues. I tend to want to get people out of the hole that they've dug for themselves. And, of course, that's not possible. We all make the path we must walk on, and nobody can walk that path for us.

Step 14. What changes are you willing to make? I must be aware that my sole responsibility is to keep my own act together and leave getting other peoples' act together to the professionals who are qualified to do this kind of work. I must not get myself emotionally involved with other peoples' problems.

But since I know that I tend to be attracted to helping people get their act together, I am wary of relationships, because I'm a sucker for people who need crutches to lean on. What I've got to do is find a woman who's even got her act together better than I do. Where are these women? And if they do have their act together, are they going to run over me like a steam-roller?

Though I prefer to be a follower in most things in life, I do have a very decisive inner direction, which can easily be trampled. Though I can appear hardy and stoic on the outside, I'm really very sensitive and susceptible to the least infraction on the inside. In any case, I will just remain open to possibility that some woman who's got it all together could come along and just want to share her world with me without trying to change me into something that I'm not. After all, maybe I've got a lot to bring to a relationship.

Step 1: Draw two animals with an intensified conflict:

Step 2: Fill in the blanks:

Animal #1

Type of animal: Grasshopper Namia
Age: 50's **Sex:** Female
Personality: Animated, fickle, impractical,
restless.

Animal #2

Type of animal: Spider Fayda
Age: 50's **Sex:** Male
Personality: Quiet, sensitive,
impressionable, focused.

Step 3: What are they saying?
Quietly sitting amidst the dewdrops at the heart of its web, Jayda, the spider is carefully watching Namia the grasshopper hopping merrily about in the vicinity. There is no peace for Namia, because her very nature is to hop all about in constant search for sustenance. She hops and hops in her effort to find something new, never staying still unless she is feeding her gluttonous appetites upon some delectable morsel recently acquired.

Jayda, the spider, on the other hand, remains all but immobile in the center of his web waiting for the day's provisions to simply arrive upon his doorstep. Then with a sudden furry, he pounces upon the object of his attention and wraps it in a maze of added webbing.

And so, this is what happens to Namia. She accidentally gets entangled in Jayda's web. Whereas he says, "Welcome my long legged friend, you will make a splendid meal." Namia, the grasshopper, is kicking frantically about trying to free herself from the sticky webbing that entangles all of her six limbs. She says, "please, free me, I need to hop about and to run and play until I drop from exhaustion. I need to hop and play without any concern for where my next meal will come from, nor what will happen tomorrow."

Step 4: What happened before? The grasshopper was hopping all about and the spider was centered in stillness upon his web. Namia says, "Oh, look at that nice spider web, it looks so beautifully symmetrical and well-constructed. Jayda says, " Yes, come and test out its strength for yourself.

Step 5: After? Namia seeks freedom, she says, "There's got to be more to life than is encompassed by this web, and I must find it." Jayda says, "But each of us must construct our own world in order to survive, why did you get yourself stuck in my web?"

Step 6: Title: "Is My Web Not Your Web?"

Step 7a: Conflicts between themselves: Namia thinks she needs the stability and support of the web, but finds that for her it is difficult to settle down and just be satisfied with what the web provides. Jayda, on the other hand, has constructed the full length and width his world and can't understand why Namia must hop around all the time.

Step 7b: Conflicts between them and the world: The conflict comprises two different world-views, or to put it another way, oil and water simply don't mix.

Step 8: What changes should they make to resolve conflicts? Resolution of this basic conflict is a moot question at this time, since Namia has already cut herself loose from Jayda's web.

Step 9: Which animal do you identify with: I see myself as Jayda, the spider. I've built my world and am quite satisfied to stay in the center of it. Other animal:
I see my ex-wife as Namia, the grasshopper. She's still hopping all about trying to find some steady ground to stand on, which continually seems to elude her.

Step 10: How does this pertain to you? The grasshopper and spider metaphors pertain to my ex-wife and I. It seems that she was never satisfied with things as they were and was always seeking greener pastures. I seemed to have a clear vision of the path I wished to follow from a very young age. And, I simply pursued my goals step-by-step without hesitation. I made decisions and I was willing to live with those decisions. My ex-wife also made decisions, but always wanted to change her mind or was unhappy with her choices. Of course, it is a woman's prerogative to change her mind, but it sure doesn't make for a smooth journey.

Step 11. What changes should you make? No changes at this time are needed. It's all water under the bridge now!

Step 12. In life we repeat ourselves. Present an incident, similar to what transpired in you metaphor story, to illustrate your particular pattern. I seem to be quite determined to make my way in the world. I'm not inflexible, however. If I can't reach the peak of the mountain from one side, I'll go around the other side and try to see if there is another way up. If anything, I am persistent.

Step 13: Present a similar incident: Well, some people don't like to deal with persistent individuals. They feel that they're a pain in the butt. But, I find that persistence compensates for a lot of other inabilities. Most people fail in securing their goals just because they won't go the extra mile. In any case, if there's a way to get to one's goal, I've got the tenacity to continue.

Step 14. What changes are you willing to make? Well, I try to camouflage my persistence as best I can so as not to ruffle other peoples' proverbial feathers. But, if a little ruffling of feathers has to take place, well so be it. In short, I try to smile while getting to my goal, but get to my goal I must.

Step 1: Choose a dream: Recent dream.

Step 2: Draw the dream:

Step 3: Describe the dream: I was sitting in a living room chair reading a book and this woman came and sat on me. She took over and started reading the book at her own pace. She insisted in reading the book the way she wanted to, disregarding my need to read the book. So an argument started over the pace at which the book was to be read. I wanted to read at a more leisurely pace and she wanted to read at a faster pace to get done with the book.

Step 4: Describe the participants:
Me: Quiet, calm, peaceful.
Woman: Excited, hyper, obstinate.

Step 5: What are the conflicts? The conflict seemed to be over how fast or slow the book should be read.

Step 6: What occurrences preceded the dream? I got out of bed to go to the bathroom. Otherwise nothing that I know of happened before this dream.

Step 7: Explanation of the dream: This is a classic power struggle for control. Reading the book is probably incidental. The power struggle is over me having control over my life. There is a woman taking over control over what I can and cannot do.

Step 8: Do you dream a lot? Probably, all I remember is bits and pieces.

Step 9: Other dreams: A car trying to run me down, falling out of buildings.

Step 10: Connections or patterns in dreams: Do you see any pertinent connection or patterns in your dreams? Possibly being overcome by the people in my life?

COMPROMISE

Short Story

Step 1: Write a short story:
This is a story about how Yarmel introduced his young friend Xebec to the concepts of the Angelica Brotherhood. The moon was radiating its full evening splendor throughout the pine forest where Xebec and Yarmel were slowly walking up the crest of a hill towards the summit.

Yarmel says to Xebec, "It is time, my young friend, that I introduce you to the concepts of the Angelica Brotherhood." This was Xebec's 21st birthday, and he was wondering were he was going in this life. Xebec had graduated from college and was indeed capable of making a place for himself in the world. But as he confided earlier to his elder friend and mentor Yarmel, "This everyday world seems to hold no meaning for me. I seem to find little satisfaction in competing with my contemporaries and in perpetuating the idiocies of their world."

Yarmel had listened attentively to his young friend's misgivings about his life in this contemporary society, and decided it was time to introduce the boy to the concepts of the Angelica Brotherhood.

"Xebec, my young friend, this life, as you know it, is only a matrix into which you are born so that you can construct a viable destiny that will bring you closer to the reality of Eternal Flight. Once you've sprouted and developed the Wings for Eternal Flight, you will live forever, destined to spending an endless existence helping others develop their Wings for Eternal Flight. You must, however, persevere in the practice of the precepts of the Angelica Brotherhood throughout this life and maybe many more lives in order to promote the full development of the Wings for Eternal Flight."

Xebec, looking quite surprised says, "You mean this world is not at all what it appears to be? We are all fated to do something more important? By the way, what is this so-called Angelica Brotherhood and what does it have to do with my disdain for my present plight?"

Yarmel turns to him and says, "My son, you have not even begun to understand the nature of the reality of which we all partake. First of all, to explain what the entire Angelica Brotherhood is all about would take me much more time than is available to us this evening. And, I can only give you this coveted information in bits and pieces as they become more palatable to you over a period of time. This information is so deep and abstruse that you will be able to consume only selective portions of this weighty material at any one time. So let's start with the basic concept of Eternal Flight."

"Xebec," Yarmel continues, "you are well positioned at this time to become a Good Householder. In other words, you can fit into this society very nicely, make a living, and pursue a normal life. You've woven yourself into the fabric of our social system and are now equipped to pursue the higher goal of Self-Ordination. And this is really much of what the Angelica Brotherhood is all about. They are a group of men and women who, having succeeded in placing themselves very strategically into the ordinary life of this planet's human bipeds, can now begin the process of Self-Ordination in order to initiate the sprouting and development of the Wings of Eternal Flight, which will eventually take them to the heights of Total Union with the Great Spirit."

"Once Self-Ordination is achieved, and the Wings of Eternal Flight are fully formed and activated," Yarmel emphasizes, "these anointed ones shall then join forces with the rest of the Angelica Brotherhood to help the Great Spirit in His efforts to admit all human bipeds to the Sacred Realm. Once these human bipeds are admitted to this holiest of realms, they, in turn, spend the rest of their everlasting existence guiding others in their quest for greater awareness, which in turn abets the efforts of the Mother Planet that fostered and nurtured their exquisite development."

Xebec looks at Yarmel with astonishment and says, "My goodness, you mean that we are all destined to serve as patriots of the Sacred Realm?"

Yarmel grins slyly and says, "What other destiny could we as human bipeds possibly envision beyond the ultimate serving of this our Mother Planet for the glory of the Great Spirit. This organism we term our Mother Planet is the only ship in the sea of spatial eternity upon which we have chosen to set sail. It is through our best efforts upon this grand organism, our Mother Planet that we pursue the development of that greater awareness granted to us by the Father for the continued development and expansion of His glory. Indeed, we are all part and parcel of That Is. And so, we must pursue these higher goals in order to complete our necessary evolutionary development."

Xebec ponders his mentor's comments for a moment and says, "Yarmel, please initiate me into the Angelica Brotherhood as soon as possible. Now that I know my purpose for living, I haven't a moment to waste. Besides, I always wondered what those two little protrusions were behind my shoulder blades!"

Step 2: Illustrate the story:

Step 3: Fill in the blanks:

Character #1

Character name: Yarmel
Age: ? Sex: Male
Personality: Authoritative, gentle, supportive.

Character #2

Character name: Xebec
Age: 21 **Sex:** Male
Personality: Sensitive, inquisitive, impressionable

Step 4: What happened before? Before Xebec had met Yarmel, he had been seriously searching for a way to make some sense out of his life. He was searching for meaning since he was a boy. He knew that the traditional, orthodox expressions of purpose provided by his birth family were sadly lacking. So he started looking in every which way for a safe harbor in which to anchor his very soul. When he found Yarmel, he knew that this was the beginning of something special. And from that day on, he was able to find meaning.

Step 5: After: After he had met Yarmel, Xebec felt that he had found something that would last the rest of his life. He knew instinctively that though Yarmel may only be able to provide

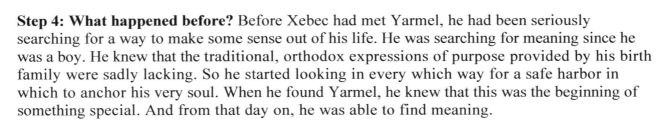

fragments of the sacred path he had so long sought to follow, this, nevertheless, would be his life's pursuit from that day forward. And so it was, as the journey continued, Xebec knew deep in the fiber of his being that having the grace to enter the Sacred Realm before his demise would comprise his primary preoccupation in this lifetime.

Step 6: Title: "In Pursuit of Self-Ordination."

Step 7: Conflicts between themselves: Yarmel and Xebec are like two sides of the same coin. Yarmel was actually Xebec in his youth. Since Xebec was dissatisfied with life as it is, he continued looking for direction outside of himself, not realizing, of course, that the journey is always a solitary undertaking. He found direction in Yarmel's world view, but didn't understand that it takes a lifetime just to develop an appreciation for the potential development of man's destiny. Yarmel recognized Xebec's impatience and wished he could accelerate the youth's personal development. The tension created between the two men was due to Xebec's impatience with the length of time any real spiritual growth must take. Since Yarmel was patient with the youth, conflict was held at a minimum.

Step 8: What changes should they make to resolve conflicts? The conflict between Xebec and Yarmel was inevitable simply because they view the world from different perspectives. We can't expect a 20 year old to view the world like a 60 year old. Yarmel must be patient with Xebec, as all things evolve accordingly. We simply must recognize that the Xebecs in our lives are meant to keep the Yarmels of this world active and sensitive to the needs of the novice. We are all both novice and accomplished adept at every stage of our development. We are always the means to our own metamorphosis. At each cocoon stage, we beget flights of fancy, which almost always lead us to new discoveries within the Sacred Realm.

Step 9: Which character do you identify with: In my youth, I identified exclusively with Xebec. As I grow older, I identify more with Yarmel.

Step 10: How does this pertain to you? As I indicated above, Yarmel and Xebec are two sides of the same coin. I see myself as both of these characters combined. Each of us pass through these same stages, in our quest for meaning. The nature of that meaning, however, must not be determined by the particular culture that spawns us. We should try to rise above our meager beginnings to find a new dawn every day. This is where the practice of an art form for its own sake is useful. It provides me with the necessary materials of self-exploration.

I must also try to help others (my students in particular) to find a direction beyond just making a living. The artist (music, theater, dance, poetry, painting, etc.) is seeking to contact a level of being above and beyond his/her everyday existence. Yet, this everyday existence is what we must stay in touch with in order to develop a better understanding of what needs to be achieved as we continue on the spiral path upwards towards the Sacred Realm.

Step 11: What changes should you make? I must cease trying to solve the various problems that come up in my life and keep my eye on the greater meaning that I seek. Problems can be resolved without solutions necessarily occurring. Trying to change what can be changed, accepting graciously what can't be changed and learning to live with it.

Step 12: Present a similar incident: Well, I often look outside of myself for solutions to my problems and so repeatedly set myself up for disappointment. I have to learn to trust myself and depend upon my intuition. Life is what it is and I am what I am. There are no simple answers. I have to stop looking for and expecting panaceas.

Step 13: What changes are you willing to make? I must confront my fears and realize that they are not reality. I must remember that one of the best remedies for fear when it does occur is to breathe deeply. What more is there need for? Out of the boy grows the man. The seeds we plant in our youth shall be harvested in our old age. I am not, however, any longer the boy. I need not carry the baggage of my youth any further.

Summary: Metaphor Profile

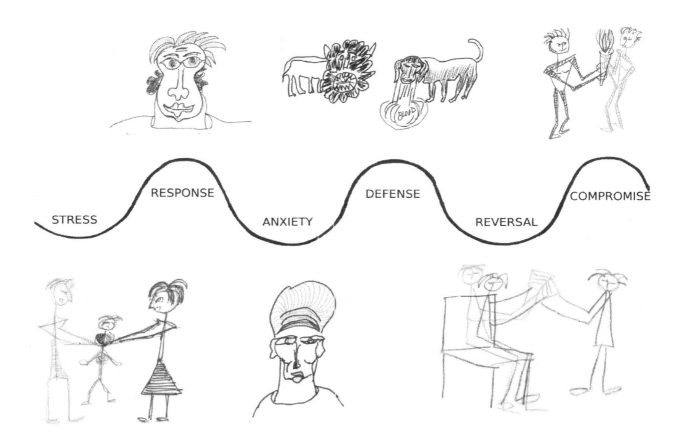

Stress:
Throughout his childhood, he watched from the sidelines as his parents constantly fought.

Response:
His mask, titled "Mr. Dynamo," is bold and confident.

Anxiety:
Underneath the mask, the face is confused about its true identity.

Defense:
A lion bites off a dog's head. He identifies himself with the dog and his ex-wife with the lion.

Reversal:
A dream, in which a woman prevents him from reading at his own pace.

Compromise:
The experienced character teaches the inexperienced character.

Submissive Case Study Three
The Anteater and the Lion

Introduction And Discussion

The following paragraph delivers the summation of the self-assessment as completed by a young woman, 25 years old, who was referred for an evaluation by her therapist, who had a problem with her fabricating lies rather than telling the truth about her thoughts and feelings. The balance of this report is the transcription of the statements of the self-assessment as completed by the patient without any initial coaching and interpretation following the testing.

Patient's responses to reconstructing the six role process by completing a questionnaire:

The initial stress: Being sexually abused by grandfather.

Indicate your response to the stress: Initial response was secrecy. I had to be very secretive about what was happening between my grandfather and I.

Identify here your fears about others' responses to your experience: My fears were that I believed that they would blame and hate me for what I had done. They didn't love me anymore.

Identify your defensive thinking, or how you dealt with your fears: Dealt with fears by building walls around myself so that no one could get at me. If no one could get close to me then no one could hurt me.

Indicate your role reversal, the outcome of your defensive behaviors: Had a heated argument with my girlfriend where I told her that I hated my grandfather. My exact line was that "He looks like he could rape somebody."

Indicate your compromise along the lines of settling your conflict: Started to talk to my girlfriend about my being abused by my grandfather. She advised me to get help.

Identify how you feel now. Has this exploration of a past conflict offered you any relief of

166

tension?

Yes, it definitely has given me a relief of the tension inside, for now. I am able to look at my situation and see what to do instead of staying stuck.

Formal Analysis

Could this evolution of thoughts and behaviors have any relevance for you toward resolving conflicts? Could help me in that in the future I can handle conflicts on my own. I can understand where and why I feel the way that I do sometimes.

The completion of the record and then of its analysis represented a certain accomplishment for the patient; it generated insights and then corrective responses. It was a useful exercise in putting the facts out and looking at her life in a masterful manner.

> The metaphors in sequence provide information about her submissive relational modality pattern and its syndromal unfolding.
>
> **Stress:** the test is a report on the initial rape incident. The other tests reveal subsequent traumatic experiences
>
> **Response:** Her unique mask as that of a brick wall covering her feelings, blocking others, hiding behind it
>
> **Anxiety:** Reflected as keeping the lid on a jar containing all her traumatic experiences and her escapes, use of drugs, alcohol and suicidal ideation, for fears of self-incrimination leading to her blocking all communications.
>
> **Defense:** Feeling like a sperm eating ant-eater as an ugly and self-pitying person, yet regarding highly and respectfully her tormentor and rapist.
>
> **Reversal:** Feeling her life out of control as the merry-go-round spinning out of control with her child on it as she was pulled away by her grandfather.
>
> **Compromise:** The story presents self-empowerment and healing in a healthy rescue fantasy.

This record reflects on the effectiveness of the self-assessment as a diagnostic and therapeutic intervention.

This record is significant for the following two reasons:
It is diagnostic. Her relational profile was of a submissive cooperative and antagonistic person allowing others to command her behaviors. In complying, she had the tendency to blame herself rather than rebel, protest or get angry with the abuser.

The experience was therapeutic: She was able to recognize how her self- image and her relation to the world had been damaged by her incestuous experience. She was able to see the big wall she built around herself. She was able to see how badly it made her feel about herself, and how much she was impressed and intimidated by authorities, how she felt inadequate, ugly and suicidal. She accepted being honest rather than lie and tell people what they wanted to hear. In her Short Story Metaphor she was a unicorn with a short horn but achieved a level of self-acceptance, in spite of her past experiences and her marked sense of inferiority.

The workbook generated a clear and accurate clinical profile. It uncovered the conflict but also elicited a healthy resolution from the testee. The process generated emotions, insights and personal healing; she was able to achieve distance from the experience and relief from the agony of self-incrimination. It helped her to become comfortable with facing reality. She identified the walls as her identity and was able to go beyond them; she revealed the full extent of her traumas and her defenses. She took the walls down and was able to be true in expressing herself.

The metaphors helped her to face and talk about her emotional reality without hiding and lying about the experiences and her feelings, as she usually had in the past. Honesty had been a key problem in her therapy. The process of graphically portraying facts and feelings had the effect of personal growth entailing resolution of cathartic value.

Reflecting on her animal choices and her dream, she saw how profoundly the experience had affected her life and had become the core issue of her concerns. The evaluation clarified her damaged identity but also her need for rehabilitation. With the insights generated by the testing, she was able to complete the construction of a metaphor establishing self-acceptance and complete the following letter to herself reviewing her impressions about the experience.

Patient's Essay
Know Thyself Letter

Step #1: Correspond with a good old friend of yours, someone you truly trust, and review confidentially your feelings about your testing experience. Review what dramatic material has emerged about yourself through your metaphor stories, and confide if this experience has touched you and why.

Dear B.,

Hello! How are you? Hopefully, you're doing well. I'm writing to you because something different happened to me today and I thought you'd be interested too. Well, it's no surprise to you that I'm seeing a therapist, but today it was different. Today I chose to participate in taking several tests at the center. No, nothing to worry about. The test consisted of a drawing and then questions about it. Simple, right? Wrong! It took a lot out of me to draw what was inside me and then write about what was going on. I learned a lot today. I wrote a story about a lion and an ant-eater and damn, wouldn't you believe that I would really like to be the lion but am actually the ant-eater. It seems that in most of my testing I was an underdog. I couldn't come out on top for nothing! This really bothers me!

Anyway, I also took a part of the test where I had to answer over 100 questions about whether or not I agreed or disagreed with whatever it was asking. I guess I mostly enjoyed this part because some of the questions that were there I've asked myself before. I mean a lot of what the examples were I could relate to, meaning that at one time or another I've felt or acted in that way. I'm really excited today because I really feel I learned a lot about myself. Most of the thoughts I have aren't so weird, you know? Yes, this is true – 'tis I speaking! Well, I hate to end here but I have to get back to my other assignments. Talk to you soon!

Step #2: Share your overall reflections about how you wish to modify your way of relating or communicating so that you can be better adjusted.
I wish to modify my way of relating by trying to deal with people honestly. By that I mean not giving them what I think they want to hear. Instead, try to let them know more about me and why I am the way I am. I also intend to structure my life according to how I wish to live it, not according to whatever others' wish me to do. Have to open up and tell people more about me and where I come from. Tell people how I feel, regardless of how I think they'll take it.

Step #3: Have you been honest in your communication with your friend? If not, why not? I've been somewhat honest with my girlfriend because I really find it hard to believe that she would be interested in the total picture. Not sure about how she will respond towards me.

Transcription of the Case: The Relational Modality Evaluation Scale

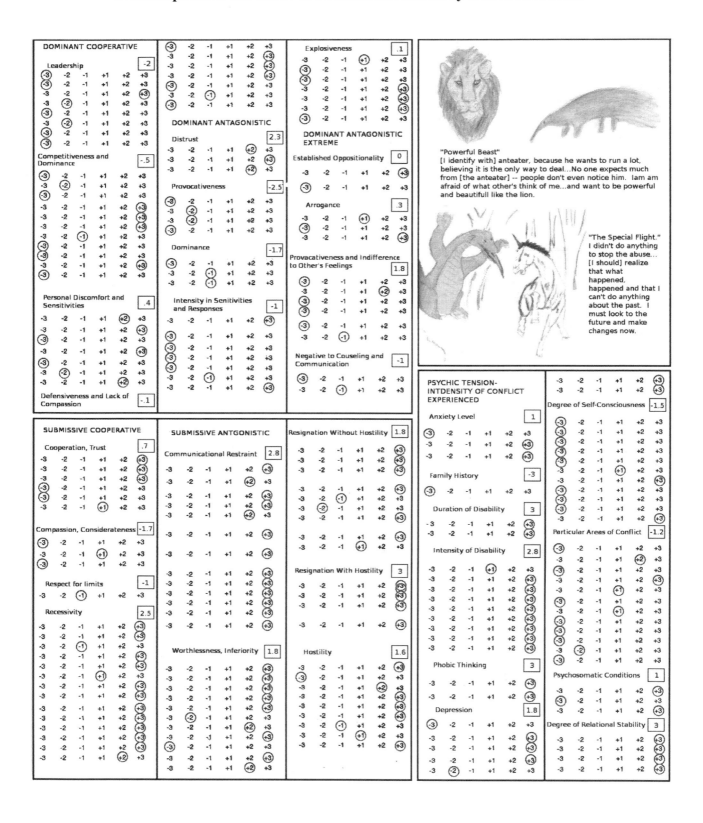

DOMINANT COOPERATIVE

Leadership: -2

Competitiveness and Dominance: -.5

Personal Discomfort and Sensitivities: .4

Defensiveness and Lack of Compassion: -.1

DOMINANT ANTAGONISTIC

Distrust: 2.3

Provocativeness: -2.5

Dominance: -1.7

Intensity in Sensitivities and Responses: -1

Explosiveness: .1

DOMINANT ANTAGONISTIC EXTREME

Established Oppositionality: 0

Arrogance: .3

Provocativeness and Indifference to Other's Feelings: 1.8

Negative to Counseling and Communication: -1

"Powerful Beast"
[I identify with] anteater, because he wants to run a lot, believing it is the only way to deal...No one expects much from [the anteater] -- people don't even notice him. I am am afraid of what other's think of me...and want to be powerful and beautifull like the lion.

"The Special Flight."
I didn't do anything to stop the abuse... [I should] realize that what happened, happened and that I can't do anything about the past. I must look to the future and make changes now.

SUBMISSIVE COOPERATIVE

Cooperation, Trust: .7

Compassion, Considerateness: -1.7

Respect for limits: -1

Recessivity: 2.5

SUBMISSIVE ANTGONISTIC

Communicational Restraint: 2.8

Worthlessness, Inferiority: 1.8

Resignation Without Hostility: 1.8

Resignation With Hostility: 3

Hostility: 1.6

PSYCHIC TENSION- INTDENSITY OF CONFLICT EXPERIENCED

Anxiety Level: 1

Family History: -3

Duration of Disability: 3

Intensity of Disability: 2.8

Phobic Thinking: 3

Depression: 1.8

Degree of Self-Consciousness: -1.5

Particular Areas of Conflict: -1.2

Psychosomatic Conditions: 1

Degree of Relational Stability: 3

170

CHILDHOOD CONFLICTUAL MEMORY

Step 1: Draw a conflictual childhood memory:

Step 2: Describe the incident: I was asleep in my uncle's bedroom. My grandmother had been taken to the hospital because she had been ill. My cousin was asleep in other bedroom--my grandfather stayed with us. While I was asleep my grandfather put his hands on my breast and between my legs. I awakened, alarmed, disoriented. He entered me--very painful--wanted to get away.

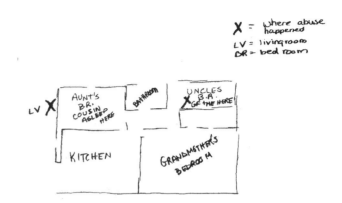

Step 3: How did you feel about this person? Felt he was the only one that really loved me. Trusted him. **How did this person feel about you?** Obviously, he didn't give shit about me because he raped me several times. If he loved me he wouldn't have done the things he did to me.

Step 4: What were the conflicts? Secrecy--no one could know--would tell me not to tell anyone. Fear-about anyone finding out, blame, people hating me.

Step 5: What happened before? Before this incident much the same would occur. He would tell me to touch him and suck him and he would do the same to me.

Step 6: After? Afterward, the fear became more in me. I thought that people would hate me if I told--wanted to protect him from others. Hated him too.

Step 7: Your share in this conflict? I never told anyone. Couple or more times I initiated what happened.

Step 8: Effect on life: Drastically in a way that I don't trust people, and men in particular. Very hard for me to even contemplate even having sex. Believe that I am dirty--that sex is dirty. Don't let people get close to me--very insecure.

Step 9: Have you been repeating yourself? Yes.

Step 10: Has this conflict been resolved in your mind? No.

Step 11: Resolved in this relationship? Insofar as he doesn't call me anymore.

Step 12: What changes should be made? Could talk about everything and empty myself out. Realize it wasn't my fault.

Step 1: Draw a conflictual adolescent memory:

Step 2: Describe the incident: Entire class--I got up and walked out--felt like my insides had been ripped out.

Step 3: Effect on life: Didn't tell anyone--very secretive about my whereabouts and about my friends.

Recent Conflict

Step 1: Draw a recent conflictual memory:

Step 2: Describe the incident: Doctor, myself, nurse, counselor. My fault because I went to bed without birth control.

Step 3: Effect on life: Can't erase it. Bothered a lot.

FAMILY OF ORIGIN

Step 1: Draw a balloon portrait of your family of origin:

Step 2: Identify each individual:

#1: (green): Mother, unfeeling, unnatural, fake.
#2: (yellow): Father , puppy dog led around easily, powerless, bum.
#3: (blue): Brother, smart, easy-going, very loyal.
#4: (red): Brother , funny, laid back, open.
#5: (black): Me, quite boring, angry, chicken.

Step 3: What are they saying?

#2 – "I don't know why you still have therapy--with that money you could be enjoying yourself."
#5 – "Right, dad, whatever you say."

Step 4: What happened before? Watching TV.

Step 5: After? Nothing. #5 left room, annoyed.

Step 6: Title:. "Just Passing Through."

Step 7: What are the conflicts? #5 doesn't want to be bothered with #1 and #2. Feels they didn't protect her as a child, hates them, at times she wishes that they were dead. Doesn't want to understand them. Hates #2 because he didn't do anything.

Step 8: What changes should be made to resolve these conflicts? #5 should either die or move out by herself. #1 and #2 should try loving #5. #5 should attempt to trust #1 and #2.

RESPONSE

Mask I

Step 1: Draw a mask:

Step 2: Answer the following questions:

Title: "Unknown"
Age: 23   Sex: Female
Emotions conveyed: Power, strength, no fear, tough, loner.

Step 3: Conflicts represented: Need to be powerful instead of being weak. Need to be strong.

Step 4: Resolution of conflicts represented: Truth.

ANXIETY

MASK II

Step 5: Draw what is behind the mask.

Step 6: Fill in the blanks and answer the questions:

Title: "Unkindly Thoughts."
Age: 23   **Sex:** Female
Emotions conveyed? Pain, anger, rage, fear, hate, rejection, failure, hurt, relief, shame.

Step 7: Conflicts represented: Problems with parents and grandfather, wanting to kill, sexual hang-ups that I have.

Step 8: Resolution of conflicts? Deal by doing drugs-- cocaine or pills, drinking Jack Daniels--or simply killing myself.

MASK III

Step 9: Draw what is in the heart.

Title: "Completely Unrevealed."

Step 10: Items and themes represented: Grandfather, sex, pains, blades, knives, school failures, isolation, alcohol and drugs.

Step 11: Feelings and conflicts represented: A lot of times I feel that I am not okay--there's something wrong with me. Anger, hate, failure, wanting to stay alive but often bothered by suicidal thoughts.

Step 12: Resolution of conflicts? Deal by doing drugs and alcohol, if that doesn't work then kill myself. Only way out--I can't admit to anyone my past.

Step 13: Title of the sequence: "Incredible Con-Job."

Step 14: Summarize the sequence of transformations:

Image 1: don't let anyone get close to me--very thick walls surround me.
Image 2: let down walls and show some of what's there.
Image 3: more of image two, except don't tell all of what is there.

Step 15: Conclusions about the way this person resolves conflicts: Conclusions: person runs instead of dealing--afraid to be hurt therefore doesn't trust anyone--only way to deal when she feels bad is to kill herself.

Step 16: Does this relate to how you handle feelings? Progression relates to me in that I do those things I always pretend that everything is okay. I never talk about the pain--too busy being the comedian.

Step 17: What changes should be made: Open up more-- realize that services are available and utilize them. Make others fully aware of what and how I feel.

Step 18: What changes are you willing to make: Open up more. Stop trying to satisfy people. Try to accept myself for who I am. Realize that there's more ways of dealing than negative ones.

DEFENSE

ANIMAL METAPHOR TEST #1

Step 1: Draw two animals:

Step 2: Fill in the blanks

Animal #1
Type of animal: Lion
Age: 30 **Sex:** Male
Personality: Powerful, loyal, beautiful.

Animal #2
Type of animal: Anteater
Age: 23 **Sex:** Female
Personality: Insecure, needy, ugly

Step 3: What are they saying?

#1 – "What's the matter with you?"
#2 – "Go away! Leave me alone."
#1 – "Well, you know I didn't get to be king of the jungle by walking away from other people's needs."
#2 – "Well you can rest your head about this one because even you can't do anything about it!"
#1 – "What! Don't you know that I can help-- just try me."
#2 – "I'm ugly."
#1 – "What?"
#2 – "Just what I said – I'm ugly!"
#1 – "What brought this on?"
#2 – "I just want to be beautiful."
#1 – "Anty, you are beautiful inside! It doesn't matter what you look like on the outside."
#2 – "Thanks."

Step 4: What happened before? Lion: resting in the shade.
Anteater: crying and attempting to hide face in a bush.

Step 5: After? Both began to play and hang out together.

Step 6: Title: "Powerful Beast."

Step 7a: Conflicts between themselves: Different type. #1 must be powerful, strong, everyone expects him to be king. #2 no one expects much from him-- in fact, a lot of people don't even notice him.

Step 7b: Conflicts between them and the world: Beauty vs. Ugliness--many people are hung up on what a person looks like physically. They don't realize that what matters is inside.

Step 8: What changes should they make to resolve conflicts? Try to be open and honest and live lives freely without interactions with others.

Step 9: Which animal do you identify with: Anteater only because I want to run a lot. Believe that only way to deal is to run and either get high or drunk. **Other animal:** Anyone who has a degree because they are the "Kings of the Jungle."

Step 10: How does this pertain to you?

1) I'm afraid of what others think of me.
2) I want to be with the elite, because I am not happy where I am.
3) I want to be powerful and beautiful like the lion.

Step 11: What changes should you make? Try to change my way of thinking. Realize that I'm okay, and move on.

Step 12: Present a similar incident: Instead of telling the truth I lie because I don't want to hurt anyone or bring down expectations. Must be the best of all every time. Not satisfied with being average--become very depressed then think about failures which then bring on suicidal thoughts.

Step 13: How do you relate with others, and how do you get yourself in trouble? I set things up by first lying to people because it is easier than disappointing them. I believe that they really don't care about me-- really aren't interested in me or what I have to say.

Step 14: What changes are you willing to make? Any that will help me be in control of my life, to feel secure; be independent; start to live my life.

FAIRYTALE METAPHOR

Step 1: Draw two fairy tale characters:

Step 2: Fill in the blanks:

Character#1: Wellington (wolf)
Age: 28 **Sex:** Male
Personality: Bold, strong, powerful.

Character#2: Patience (pig)
Age: 28 **Sex:** Male
Personality: Accommodating, happy, average.

Step 3: What are they saying?

> **#1** – "Hey, stupid! What are you rolling around in the mud like an idiot for?"
> **#2** – "Having fun, Wellington. You should try it sometime."
> **#1** – "You should be ashamed of yourself. Don't you realize that you're locked up in this pen and you can't do anything. I mean I would be furious."
> **#2** – "Wellington, sometimes you just can't have whatever you want so you have to go along with it.
> **#1** – "Not me, I'm not going to settle for anything."
> **#2** – "Wellington, you have to. Otherwise you will be miserable."

Step 4: What happened before? Wellington was sitting on a fence watching Patience play in her pen.

Step 5: After? Patience continued to play while Wellington withdrew totally.

Step 6: Title: "Miserable Wellington."

Step 7a: Conflicts between themselves: Wellington--mad at life because he wants Patience to feel the same way he does, and to stop feeling so good.

Step 7b: Conflicts between them and the world: Patience is satisfied with life the way it is. Wellington is not-- he wants to be the best--if he can't, he doesn't want to go on.

Step 8: What changes should they make to resolve conflicts? Wellington should start to realize that while he's upset, life is continuing. You have to take charge of your life, because if you don't life takes a hold of you.

Step 9: Which character do you identify with: Wellington, because I have to be the best all the time --I am not satisfied with where I am. **Other character:** Therapist, because she tries to deal with life one day at a time--she enjoys each day, but I'm not able to. I get bored. I'm too average.

Step 10: How does this pertain to you? It pertains to me in that I'm not satisfied with where I am. I need to be number one-- if I'm not, depression sets in.

Step 11: What changes should you make?

    1) talk more about my feelings.
    2) do positive things so I'll feel better.
    3) realize that although I may feel rotten at times, the days will eventually get better.

Step 12: Present a similar incident: Afraid to say what's there--I keep all inside, then I get very depressed; suicidal thoughts enter my mind.

Step 13: How do you relate with others, and how do you get yourself in trouble? Don't tell anyone how I feel – keep everything inside until finally I just want to die. I believe the only way to deal with failures is to die.

Step 14: What changes are you willing to make? Any that will help me get ahead and be in control.

REVERSAL

ANIMAL METAPHOR TEST #2

Step 1: Draw two animals with an intensified conflict:

Step 2: Fill in the blanks:

Animal #1

Type of animal: Wolf
Age: Male   **Sex:** 38
Personality: Strong, stable, powerful, sly.

Animal #2

Type of animal: Rabbit
Age in human years: 23
Sex: Female
Personality: Insecure, soft, naïve.

178

Step 3: What are they saying?

#1 – "Here you are!"
#2 – "WH-WHAT DO YOU WANT?"
#1 – "I want to look at you. I want to study every part of your body, little bunny."
#2 – "Why-why would you ever want to do something like that, Mr. Wolf?"
#1 – "Because I like to see what I am going to be eating!"
#2 – "No, don't!"

Step 4: What happened before? Wolf was looking for rabbit in woods.

Step 5: After? Wolf ate the rabbit and kept going.

Step 6: Title: "Wolf's Victory."

Step 7a: Conflicts between themselves: Wolf is dominant and strong compared to the rabbit.

Step 7b: Conflicts between them and the world: Wolf is strong while rabbit is weak. People expect the wolf to act that way, so he does. Rabbit brought it to himself because he could have fought more.

Step 8: What changes should they make to resolve conflicts? Wolf should stop spreading his weight around. Rabbit should have gotten more power.

DREAM ANALYSIS

Step 1: Choose a dream: Recurring dream.

Step 2: Draw the dream:

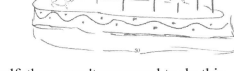

Step 3: Describe the dream: I'm a bystander looking in, I guess. There's this merry-go-round. My daughter and I are on this when suddenly my grandfather appears. I jump off the merry-go-round and forget my daughter. I can hear her crying for me. But when I try to get on, the merry-go-round starts going really fast. I can't get on.

Step 4: Describe the participants: Grandfather: evil, sly, mean. Daughter: innocent, carefree, scared. Me: scared, selfish, powerless.

Step 5: What are the conflicts? The fact that I can't get back on the merry-go-round. I left my daughter on it. Grandfathers aren't supposed to do this.

Step 6: What occurrences preceded the dream? Earlier that evening I had read an article on incest.

Step 7: Explanation of the dream: Not feeling well about myself or others around me. Maybe feel that my mom left me with my grandfather--maybe underneath I blame her.

Step 8: Do you dream a lot? No.

Step 9: Other dreams:

    1) Grandfather having sex with me (cause pain.)
    2) My child on merry-go-round. I can't get to her.
    3) Having him yell at me.
    4) Death scenes-- I'm dead and no one cares.

Step 10: Connections or patterns in dreams: Always powerless, inferior, never feel good about self in dreams, always in trouble, can't come out on top.

COMPROMISE

SHORT STORY

Step 1: Write a short story:
Once upon a time there were many dragons and unicorns. For many years they lived together in peace. But then the dragons grew jealous of the unicorns' magic horns. One day a dragon killed a unicorn and stole its horn. In the dragon's hands the unicorn's magic turned evil and made the dragons hate the unicorns. The dragons tried to kill the unicorns, but the unicorns fought back. They fought terrible battles, and many dragons and unicorns died. Since then, both dragons and unicorns have struggled to survive. The dragons attack the unicorns because they are still filled with a lot of evil powers. The unicorns didn't fight back because there were only a few of them left.

The dragon crept up to the house and looked inside. Uratuma heard and felt its hot and hungry breath. She saw a dragon paw reach in through the window and withdraw. The dragon then left. "Was that dragon after me?" Uratuma asked the bird that had flown in. "Sure thing," answered Aero. Uratuma wasn't feeling good because she noticed that her horn wasn't very long. Uratuma flopped down on her bed and felt angry. She was mad at the dragons, and mad at her horn. You see, in order for Uratuma's horn to grow, she would have to do an act of bravery. Aero started to tell Uratuma about how the dragon had captured her parents in a cave that was next to a waterfall. Uratume escaped from the house that was holding her and rushed through the woods after Aero who was leading the way. Then Uratuma arrived at the cave. A unicorn popped his head out of the cave entrance. "It's father!" said Uratuma. She and Aero flew up to him. Inside the cave were five other unicorns. The cave was holding the last unicorns in the world. "How fine you look with your horn" said Uratima's father. But Uratuma could see the disappointment in his eyes. Her horn wasn't fully grown, so she couldn't help him break the dragon's spell. Uratuma just shut her eyes to keep the tears back.

Just then, she heard a terrible noise and felt a terrible heat. Opening her eyes, she saw the huge dragon creeping into the cave. "Silly, stupid unicorns," said Damien. "You think you're smart, but you're really stupid. You just ran into a cave with no way out. I have you trapped here!" The dragon crept closer. It was awful how hot its fiery breath made the air in the cave. Uratuma felt her skin tighten with the heat.

180

"Stop where you are!" she cried, jumping in the air and landing closer to the dragon.

The dragon, who was surprised that a baby unicorn had jumped at him, stopped moving, and for a moment, held all the hot air. Just then Uratuma's horn grew all the way.

"Turn!" said her father.

Uratuma turned and let the other unicorns touch her horn with theirs. At that moment when all points touched, a spark flashed in the air, and the dragon sat back on his haunches. The unicorns stared at the dragon. The spell had helped the dragon become friendly--he helped the unicorns leave the cave.

Step 2: Illustrate the story:

Step 3: Fill in the blanks:

Character#1

Character name: Uratuma
Age: 23 **Sex:** Female
Personality: Innocent, honest, inexperienced, naïve.

Character#2

Character name: Damien
Age: 60 **Sex:** Female
Personality: Hostile, wicked, evil, powerful.

Step 4: What happened before? Dragon had taken apart Uratuma's house and captured her parents.

Step 5: After: Uratuma became very strong and courageous.

Step 6: Title: "The Special Flight."

Step 7: Conflicts between themselves: Innocence vs. Experience.

Step 8: What changes should they make to resolve conflicts? Damien should stop hurting innocent people. Uratuma should realize that there is nothing wrong with her.

Step 9: Which character do you identify with: Unicorn--didn't know what was happening in beginning, but let it go on, then at 19 stopped it. **Other character:** Grandfather, because he is so wicked, evil, and hurts innocent people.

Step 10: How does this pertain to you? In the way that I let my grandfather do whatever he wanted with me. I didn't do anything to stop the abuse.

Step 11: What changes should you make? Realize that what happened, happened and that I can't do anything about the past. I must look to the future and make changes.

Step 12: Present a similar incident: An incident where I was an innocent child and my grandfather took that away. I guess I keep it alive because I believed it. I just can't forget it.

Step 13: How do you relate with others, and how do you get yourself in trouble? I tend to give people what I think they want to hear. I hardly ever express the way I feel out in public. I try to accommodate the other person even if at times it means losing part of me. Always careful because I don't want to let anyone down, or rather their expectations of me. To give you an example of this:

> I had been seeing another counselor. Before and during our course of therapy she had prescribed imipramines to help me deal with depression. I wasn't taking these pills and since there had been no improvement she wanted me to have a blood test to check the level. Well needless to say I took about 7 because I wanted her to find it in my blood.

Step 14: What changes are you willing to make? Any that are required so I will be better.

Formal Analysis Protocol

CYCLE 1: Explore the 6-role process by seeking to resolve a conflict or conflictual relationship. Start by identifying a current unresolved conflict that is of significance to you. The conflict's intensity will determine the intensity of all the exchanges that follow. Proceed by describing this conflict and then follow its course of the six logical steps towards its resolution.

Role #1 RO: The first cycle consists of the initial stress or suffering, the role oppression state, and of the first mastery response, labeled role assumption, which deals with the suffering. Indicate in detail the stressful experience.

Being sexually abused by grandfather.

Role #2 RA: Indicate your role assumption or response to the initial stress.
Initial response or RA was secrecy. I had to be very secretive about what was happening between my grandfather and I.

CYCLE 2: The first cycle of stress and mastery response does not resolve the conflict but shifts the social energy to the psychic realm where the conflict generates anxieties and defenses. Formal analysis shows that anxieties are unrealistic fears related to the initial mastery behaviors. Anxieties amount to anticipations of role reversal, e.g., being attacked, criticized, or whatever the initial role assumption conduct was. These irrational fears lead one to related defensiveness. They alarm a person to take precautionary and preemptive measures and protect himself from the anticipated trouble.

Role #3 ARR: Identify here your anticipated role reversal, your fears about others' responses to your original initiative in the context of your particular conflict.
My fears were that I believed that they would blame and hate me for what I had done. They didn't love me anymore.

Role #4 CPRA: Identify your defensive or counter-phobic role assumptive actions or thinking, or how you dealt with your fears.
Dealt with fears by building walls round myself so that no one could get at me. If no one could get close to me then no one could hurt me.

Cycle 3: The first cycle of initial stress and mastery behaviors was followed by the second cycle, that of fears and defensive conduct. This second cycle of anxieties (or anticipations) and defensive (or counter-phobic) activities did not resolve the original conflict but shifted its energy to the interpersonal realm. The third cycle consists of a setback, the passivity, and a compromise, the activity state. Conflict resolution is attained in this cycle. The setback is called role reversal. It corresponds to the fulfillment of one's prophesies or one's irrational fears. The ensuing true resolution of conflict is called compromise role assumption.

Role #5 RR: Indicate your role reversal, the outcome of your defensive behaviors.
Had a heated argument with my girlfriend where I told her that I hated my grandfather. My exact

line was that "He looks like he could rape somebody."

Role #6 CRA: Indicate your compromise disposition or attitude upon experiencing the above setback by explaining what you did along the lines of settling your conflict.
Started to talk to my girlfriend about my being abused by my grandfather. She advised me to get help.

Role 6b, Insight Feedback on the Experience of Conflict Resolution: In this section we review this exercise to become aware of its value in bringing about resolution of conflict.
Step #1: Identify how you feel now. Has this exploration of a past conflict offered you any relief of tension?
Yes, it definitely has given me a relief of the tension inside, for now. I am able to look at my situation and see what to do instead of staying stuck.

Step #2: Could this evolution of thoughts and behaviors have any relevance for you toward resolving conflicts?
Could help me in that in the future I can handle conflicts on my own. I can understand where and why I feel the way that I do sometimes.

Summary

Stress: the test is a report on the initial rape incident. The other tests reveal subsequent traumatic experiences

Response: a brick wall as covering her feelings, blocking others, hiding behind it

Anxiety: fear of self-incrimination by keeping the lid on her communications.

Defense: aspiring to be a lion; the lion and the ant eater presented her respect of authority identified with the abuser and how this affected her self-image as an ugly and self-pitying person.

Reversal: Her merry-go-round spinning out of control presents her sense of loss of her child, her youth, herself, her childhood, for attending to her grandfather.

Compromise: The story presents self-empowerment and healing in a healthy rescue fantasy.

The Metaphor Profile

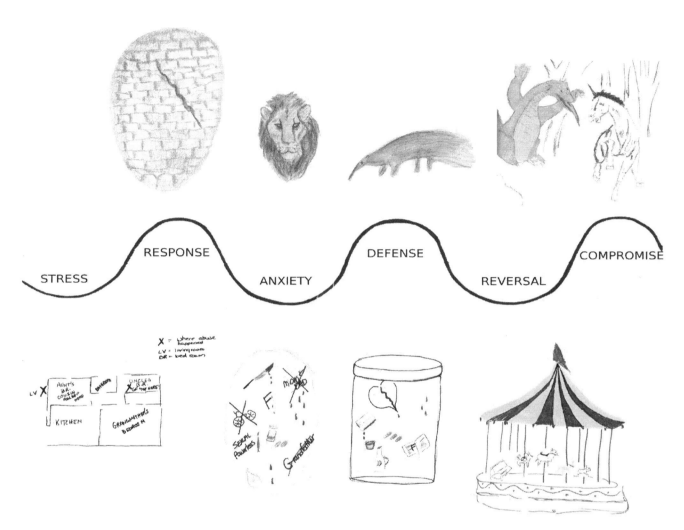

Stress:
She relates the first time she was sexually abused by her grandfather.

Response:
Her mask is a brick wall.

Anxiety:
Under the mask, the face and heart are filled with pain, rejection, failure, shame, self-mutilation, and anger at her grandfather.

Defense:
A submissive anteater wants to be beautiful, and confides in a "Powerful Beast."

Reversal:
Dream in which she encounters her grandfather and forgets to bring her daughter on the merry-go-round.

Compromise:
A Unicorn and a Dragon fight: Innocence versus Experience.

185

Case Study Four
Three Workbooks: A Trilogy

Act One: The Horse That Wants to Jump a Fence, The Wise Oak

Introduction And Discussion

Wise Oak was a 36-year-old married woman, mother of two with multiple emotional and behavioral diagnoses: panic disorder, anorexia and bulimia, depression with suicidal thoughts, occasional alcohol abuse, domestic difficulties complicated recently by an extramarital relations. Her panic attacks were related with her getting involved in an extramarital relationship and feeling overwhelmed with guilt.

This study presents her evaluation through the power management protocols and the evolution of her condition captured in three workbooks completed over a long period of time. The two workbooks represent the evaluation and recovery phases of the treatment respectively. The third was a follow up study ten years later. The first book was the evaluation. It captured her developmental history and integrated her feelings and behaviors into a meaningful submissive antagonistic adjustment pattern. The insights from the first book helped her to understand her relational modality of submissiveness, and her escapist behaviors satisfying her need for attention and love, which she was not receiving at home either with her family of origin or with her husband.

The second book, the recovery profile, presents her dealing with her conflicts by asserting herself in her relationship with her very dominant husband enabling her to reduce her need for attention from extramarital relations. As she became assertive in her relation with her abusive husband and she stopped her escapades she was freed of her clinical symptoms.

Her multiple metaphors document her pattern and her progress in therapy. She enjoyed creativity and consistently gained insights and self-awareness. She completed her therapy organizing her metaphors in an original way: not as the tests connected by the template of six-role states but by finding a home for all her metaphor story animals perched in a well rooted oak tree. She was reconciling all her feelings, all her conflicts, the different aspects of herself, into her well grounded conciliatory identity. She was protective of all creatures, had respect of all her feelings, and recommitted herself to her marriage; the wise oak was not going to be uprooted. The horse was not going to jump the fence. Instead it grew in friendliness to accommodate as positive all her growth experiences.

Formulation of the Case

Her RMES is clearly pointing to a submissive profile. The projective tests confirm her submissive relational modality. Symbolism from her metaphors reinforce the diagnosis of submissiveness: many choices and comments validate the inventory findings, consistently presenting a personality pattern of submissive cooperative to mildly submissive antagonistic profile.

Characteristics of submissiveness:

- Graphically this state of mind in her case is illustrated with the consistent absence of hands, her eyes and mouth are shut, the low placement of her balloon among the family constellations, her identity animals are low on the totem pole of the animal kingdom, her acceptance of the victim role and the characterization of animals as sneaky.

- Text wise we see this state as her need for love, sex, and food as a means of gratification and seeking social approval.

- Clinically we see her willingness to be punished as deserved for her escapism in the intensity of her anxiety and depression, her suicidal thinking.

- Socially we see her submissiveness in her allowing her husband to torment her emotionally and physically by inflicting pain on her during moments of intimacy.

The conflicts of the series of animal metaphors:

Her first metaphor was of horse with a bull. The horse wants to jump the fence and find freedom from the secure pasture controlled by the bull. This metaphor was inserted in her metaphor poster. It reflects the patient's need to escape the restrictions imposed by her husband and her very strict parents.

The snake and rat metaphor reflects animal choices that are low on the totem pole of the power hierarchy; they are clever unwanted animals; their feelings are antagonistic and the outcome was a huge self-punishment for the selfish rat. Their conflicts were over a piece of cheese. They remained unresolved signaling the lack of cooperation and mutual respect. The rat does not cooperate; the snake curses it to choke; the rat gets punished for his selfishness as the cheese is poisoned.

The bunny and hawk story reflected the feminine escapist choices and the repeated failures of these choices as the bunny gets in trouble and gets flattened or punished. The hawk identity shows some sense of success in her adventures, but the end is not fulfilling. The pattern is self-destructive and the patient tore up the protocol disowning her attempts at assertive escapism.

The story of the fox and the owl reflects a pattern of seeking love and attention but failing to gain it and being a victim of the selfish, dominant character of the owl. She makes progress as she is able to confront the unyielding respected wise owl. The owl returns the attention as alternative to affection and we see here a happy ending, a successful conflict resolution.

I requested at the completion of the therapy that she compose an essay and a mural integrating the artwork of the metaphor exercises meaningfully on the template of the process, the six role states of the personal drama. Instead she composed an original poster, representing an oak tree lovingly sheltering all her metaphor dyads, summing up her evolution to wellness through her metaphorical states. She also completed an essay that reflects her insights.

Her oak poster revealed the synopsis of her therapeutic experience in a very original manner bypassing the template's rigid structuring of events; yet it reflected her evolution of metaphors starting with her remarkably painful Conflictual Memory Test. She presented herself, physically abused by her father, drawing herself with severed hands. In the left side of the tree the conflictual memory girl without hands, and further down the dreams of her being in a pit of snakes her family laughing at her. The tree then grew hands like leaves. And the metaphors are reflected as the growth into an oak tree. The images became more meaningful with one liner explanations reflecting continuity in her reconciliation with herself and her family of metaphors, her sensitive emotional states.

The tree statement reflected her growth, departing from her original suffering and despair, the handlessness and powerlessness of an unloved, child ridiculed in a pit of snakes by her family. She grew tall and strong, with nurturing hands and multiple nests; this world in peace included her imaginative escapist kite and the flying carpet anchored at the tree. The tree was anchoring her at one place, she was no longer jumping the fence. She completed her journey of self-discovery and became self-confident. The oak tree choice, her new sense of self, reflected her deep rooted and long term healing transformation. Her depiction of the tree as a home for all her metaphor animals reflected her making peace with her past, with her many split identities and with her conflicts and resolutions bound in a playful progression.

The conflictual memory of no hands and the dream of being unloved in the bottom of a pit of snakes led to the self-accepting hands growing as leaves of the Wise Oak providing shelter to all her metaphor creatures. The Oak tree features hands, which had been consistently missing in her likable but helpless girl.

The text shows that the rootedness of the Oak is self-acceptance and emotional growth; she became the wise oak. She recognized her intelligent and sensitive qualities and her gradual evolution from the victim of a menacing, threatening husband to someone with the willingness to respect him as a hardworking partner. The positive behaviors are rewarded. Honesty generated mutual positive feelings. Cooperation is established in the fox and owl story but it is a long stretch before the fox confronts the owl for mutual respect.

It had taken a long time for Wise Oak to stand up to her husband, to whom she had been bringing her paychecks and from whom she only received little cash for her week's expenses.

She gained insights from reviewing her metaphors recognizing her initial denial of being like the snake and the rat; she laughed at herself for denying these identities and admitted that her life was like that of these two creatures. She recognized how she delegated these identities in conflict to her husband and her son. Testing the insightfulness of the metaphor assessment process she chose to construct a metaphor between her two darling dogs. She was very cheerful in admitting her consistent pattern of seeking attention projected in their games.

Personal Essay

It all started one year ago, I woke up standing in my kitchen in the middle of the night, fully dressed except for one missing sock, holding the hand of a teddy bear. When I woke, I was confused and scared. Questions began to run through my head. How did I get there? Where was I going? And what would have happened if I got outside and wandered off to an unknown place? I had sleep-walked before, but never woke up fully dressed or confused. Usually I woke in my living room wearing whatever I went to bed wearing. The week before was also confusing and scary for me. A family member had visited for the week and it brought back a lot of forgotten memories that I had wished to keep forgetting.

Shortly after the sleepwalking incident, I was suffering heaviness on my chest and had trouble swallowing. At first I thought it was just heartburn or some kind of indigestion problem, but after several attempts on my own to relieve the discomfort, I went to see my family doctor. I was really nervous because my mother had a triple bypass and I was thinking something was going wrong with my heart too. My doctor asked questions and did an EKG and my heart was fine. Physically I was great; it was mentally I was not so good.

She explained to me that I was suffering from anxiety. That was shocking to me because I could never imagine a mind causing so many symptoms to my body all at once. So, the doctor's first response to this was to give me three prescriptions, one for xanax, one for Prozac, and one for Wellbutrin. I left the doctor's office not feeling any better and drove immediately to the drugstore. I filled all my prescriptions and ran home to start taking them to feel better. That was not the conclusion.

After one hour or more I crawled into my bed and covered my head and tried to forget the world around me. After 2 days of taking these medications, I had the hardest time passing my bed and trying not to crawl into it to forget the world around me. I had stopped eating because I was paranoid that I was going to have some allergic reaction to food that was going to make me feel worse or create more hives that I was getting from the side effects I was experiencing from the medications. I had all the side effects and was beginning to feel worse every day I was taking the medications. It was the worse time of my life and all I wanted to do was end it all by suicide.
I felt worse for my family, they were also having a tough time watching me fall apart. Then I took matters into my own hands and began researching anxiety on the internet and all the drugs I was taking. I stopped taking the Wellbutrin because I was experiencing all the side effects of that drug. Then the Xanax because it was making me sleepy all the time. I continued with the Prozac because it did make me feel a little okay. After researching anxiety, I tried to fix it on my own by trying exercise.

I woke up and told myself this was going to be a new day for me and I wasn't going to let this get me down. I took my kid to school and parked my truck in the grocery store parking lot and started to walk, but I did not get far when I began to break. I got scared for some reason and began to panic, then came the hyperventilating. It was awful. I went back to my truck and called Doctor Levis. He told me to come to see him. This was when recovery was about to begin and I didn't even know it at the time…

Dr Levis gave me a workbook and there I wrote a lot of stories.

I was driving up the road with my window down and music loud. It was a cold March morning, but the cold seemed to help me and the music seemed to distract me a little bit. Then I began telling a story out loud and this is my story.

'Little bunny Lou Lou was running up the street. When she came to the end she never stopped at the stop sign. Along came a big truck and there was little bunny Lou Lou flattened in the road. Then a tree fairy came out of the forest nearby and flew over little bunny Lou Lou's flattened, mangled haired body. She said, " oh little bunny Lou Lou, you beautiful creature, look at what has happened to you. You are too precious to be like this, so, I am going to fix you." The little tree fairy scooped up the little bunny's body in her tiny hands and took her to the edge of the forest and laid the bunny on the warm forest floor. She raised her magic wand above the lifeless body and said, " Little bunny Lou Lou I am going to fix you. Under one condition, you must stay out of trouble. If you decide to be in trouble, it will only bring you bad luck." Then the little tree fairy waved her wand into the air and spoke of a magical spell. `POOF' there was a loud bang and it echoed through the forest and across the valley. When the smoke cleared, there sat little bunny Lou Lou dazed and confused. She looked around and there was nobody there but she could hear a tiny voice in her head saying, " little bunny Lou Lou you must stay out of trouble." Little bunny Lou Lou stood up and shook out her ruffled fur and ran away.'

Now this story goes on, in and out of trouble and in and out of being killed and coming back to life with the help of a little tree fairy. Which now I see representing my anxiety and thoughts of suicide. The little bunny gets trapped in deep dark holes, which for me represents depression. But in each tragedy there is a compromise, which is the tree fairy that always brings me back to life or the old gopher, who tries to protect me and show me the errors of my ways.

After doing the metaphors several times and a few drawings here and there, I have been able to reflect on myself in a positive way. I see my conflicts, my defense mechanism, my compromises, but I also see few resolutions. I know now what I need to do is to make more resolutions and how to keep myself out of trouble. I have learned how to use power management to my advantage instead of letting someone else's power ruin me. I am growing again and understanding myself better than I have ever known myself before. I am learning about myself.

The workbook is a little scary for me because I never realized it was all about me, until looking back after 3 years on my workbook. I was amazed at how correct the workbook really was about me.

"I am a better person now. I can and will stand my ground, and I will stay and talk it over, no matter how long it takes."

A Graduation Poster, Summing Up the Evaluation and Outcome of the Metaphor Therapy

Stress	*Conflictual Memory*	Punished by father, her image has no hands.
Response	*Mask*	Warrior mask
Anxiety	*Behind the Mask II*	Mask held by a hand presenting sadness and hope
Defense	*Animal Metaphors serving as the monitoring device of her progress*	Horse jumping corral fence vs. bull, reflecting her eagerness to test the boundaries of her marriage Snake versus selfish rat. The selfish rat eats the poisonous cheese and dies. Bunny versus hawk, always in trouble
Defense	*Fairy Tale*	Feeling victimized; beauty versus the beast dominating her decision making
Reversal	*Childhood Dream*	In a pit of snakes laughed at by family; was she an accident? She the blond kid, must have been adopted; she did not feel loved by her family.
Compromise	*Short Story*	Finding love in a cave but being in danger of a monster. Finding a way for Jack and Jill to effectively solve conflicts.

March 5th 2007

Transcription of the Case: The Relational Modality Evaluation Scale

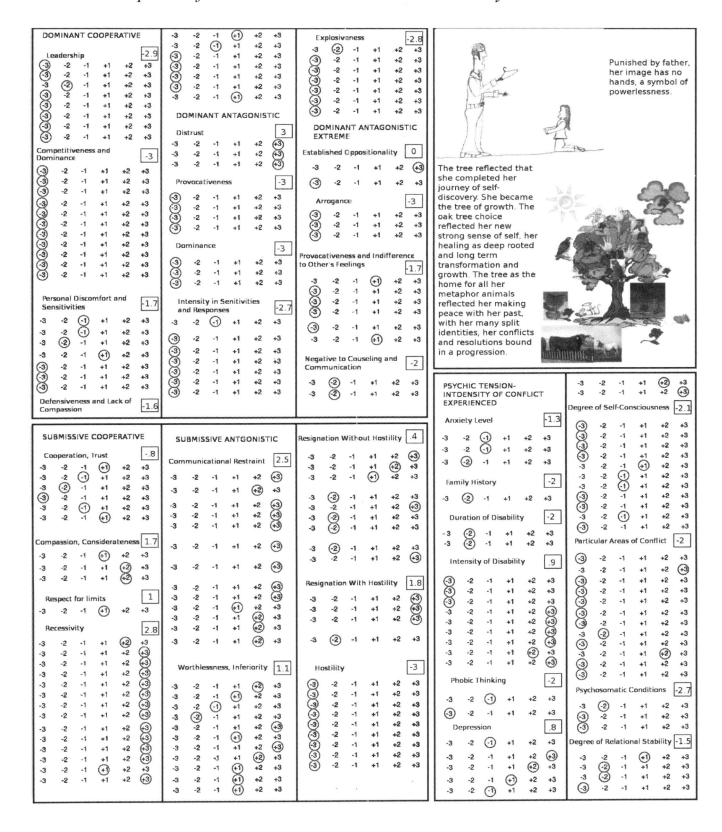

Book One: Rejected and seeking love

CHILDHOOD CONFLICTUAL MEMORY

Step 1: Draw a conflictual childhood memory:

Step 2: Describe the incident: My brother and I were home from school. We were playing, my dad said to be quiet, but we still played and laughed. He warned us and sent us in our rooms to kneel in the corners. We sneaked out of the corners and made faces at each other. My father caught us and slapped our hands with a metal coat hanger several times. My brother wouldn't cry, so my dad hit him harder and longer.

Step 3: How did you feel about this person? I think he was sick and needed help about his drinking and child abusing, but I still loved him very much.

How did this person feel about you? I was a burden and shouldn't have been born.

Step 4: What were the conflicts? We were not quiet when asked.

Step 5: What happened before? My dad was watching TV and my mom was sick in bed.

Step 6: After? I cried until I fell asleep in the corner. My brother did the same after he ran his hands under cold water. We went without dinner that night.

Step 7: Your share in this conflict? I kept laughing while my brother acted funny.

Step 8: Effect on life: I will <u>NEVER</u> hurt my children. I will always tell them I love them and that I am happy they were born.

Step 9: Have you been repeating yourself? No.

Step 10: Has this conflict been resolved in your mind? Yes.

Step 11: Resolved in this relationship? Yes.

Step 12: What changes should be made? It can't be resolved for my father is dead, but I forgive him and still love him. He is my father.

194

ADOLESCENT CONFLICTUAL MEMORY

Step 1: Draw a conflictual adolescent memory:

Step 2: Describe the incident: My mother and I. My mom was sick in bed. The school called because I didn't show up for the field trip to Boston.

Step 3: Effect on life: I should have grown up to be a doctor, because my whole childhood consisted of taking care of my family.

RECENT CONFLICT

Step 1: Draw a recent conflictual memory:

Step 2: Describe the incident: Everybody. They ALL want me in one way or another and I go CRAZY trying to accommodate them to keep them happy and content.

Step 3: Effect on life: I am getting sad and I tend to eat more.

BALLOON PORTRAIT AND STORY

Family of Origin

Step 1: Draw a balloon portrait of your family of origin:

Step 2: Identify each individual:
Father, (deceased), strict, drunk, funny.
Brother, (deceased), awesome, depressed, loving.
Mother, naive, sick, uneducated.
Brother, snob, jerk, selfish.
Sister, depressed, sexually active, lonely.
Brother, crazy, creative, lonely.
Myself, confused, naïve, happy.

Step 3: What are they saying? Well, my father and brother are at peace.

> #5 – "My tattoo represents our brother as a panther."
> #7 – "You don't even know him and if you did it would be an eagle."
> #3 – "You shouldn't remember him that way."
> #6 – "You are all stupid and don't know anything."
> #4 – "You should just cut off your arm."

Step 4: What happened before? Crying over the death of our son/brother.

Step 5: After? Fighting/arguing.

Step 6: Title: "No Tattoo"

Step 7: What are the conflicts? A disagreement.

Step 8: What changes should be made to resolve these conflicts? Let whoever do whatever they want and let them think whatever they want. Maybe, that person saw her brother in a different way than anybody else.

MARITAL BALLOONS

Step 1: Draw a balloon portrait of your marital family:

Step 2: Identify characteristics:

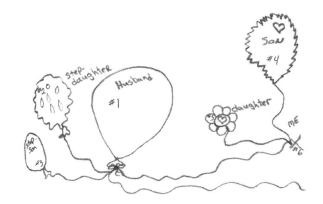

> #1: Powerful, insecure, possessive.
> #2: selfish, demanding, mentally unstable.
> #3: need of attention, lazy, abusive.
> #4: strong minded, selfish, greedy.
> #5: my self: caring, moody, loving.
> **Step 3: What are they saying?**
> #1 – "where is your mother? She is 3 minutes late!"
> #5 – "Dad, she is working, unlike you!"
> #3 – "Yeah!"
> #2 – "She is probably out cheating on you."

Step 4: Title: "Mom is Out!"

Step 5: What are the conflicts? Jealousy.

RESPONSE

MASK I

Step 1: Draw a mask:
Step 2: Answer the following questions:

Title: "The Warrior."
Age: 50   **Sex:** Female
Emotions conveyed: Strength, fearless, power, free
to scream.

Step 3: Conflicts represented: Someone other than the warrior is holding her mask.

Step 4: Resolution of conflicts represented: "Let Go!"

ANXIETY

MASK II

Step 5: Draw what is behind the mask:

Step 6: Fill in the blanks and answer the questions:

    Title: "Seeking Control."
    Age: 50   **Sex:** Female
    Emotions conveyed? Peace, no anger, no
    control, a lot of emotions, sadness, happiness,
    etc.

Step 7: Conflicts represented: Someone else is
controlling her mask. When it should be removed or when it should stay.

Step 8: Resolution of conflicts? Take control of her own life.

MASK III

Step 9: Draw what is in the heart:

Title: "Mixed Emotions."

Step 10: Items and themes represented: Most of the heart
full of love, a small portion is anger, then confusion, and no
limits.

is

Step 11: Feelings and conflicts represented: Confusion of how to feel, and when.

Step 12: Resolution of conflicts? Don't let your heart interfere with your mind.

Step 13: Title of the sequence: "Talking Heads."

Step 14: Summarize the sequence of transformations: This person needs help making decisions for herself.

Step 15: Conclusions about the way this person resolves conflicts: She only resolves them in her mind and heart, but never resolves them outside of that.

Step 16: How do you handle feelings? I like to keep my feelings to myself.
Step 17: What changes should be made: "Maybe" try talking more to whomever I have conflicts with or problems. May be not.

Step 18: What changes are you willing to make: Put my head between my legs and wish it all away.

DEFENSE

ANIMAL METAPHOR TEST #1

Step 1: Draw two animals:

Step 2: Fill in the blanks:

Animal #1

Animal #2

Type of animal: snake
Age: 36   **Sex:** Female
Personality: Sneaky, witty, self-confident, smart.

Type of animal: Rat
Age: 20   **Sex:** Female
Personality: Sneaky, careless, unkind, greedy.

Step 3: What are they saying?

  #1 – "What are you going to do with that piece of cheese?"
  #2 – "Eat it, of course."
  #1 – "Are you going to share it?"
  #2 – "Why should I? You have nothing to share with me."
  #1 – "I don't have anything to share, but my mind."
  #2 – "What good is you mind to me? I am already the smartest in the world. I was able to get into a home and steal a piece of cheese without being caught."
  #1 – "You do not have to be smart to steal!"
  #2 – "Enough of your criticizing, I am going to enjoy my cheese without you!"
  #1 – "I hope you choke!"

Step 4: What happened before? The snake was basking in the sun. The Rat was pooping all over someone's house before he stole some cheese.

Step 5: After? The snake slithered away completely annoyed. The Rat ate the cheese (which was poisoned) and died shortly after.

Step 6: Title: "Life is Short."

Step 7a: Conflicts between themselves: GREED.

Step 7b: Conflicts between them and the world: The snake and the Rat are from two different worlds and cultures, but they have a lot in common--such as greed--and they both feel they are better than one another, which alone creates a lot of conflicts.

Step 8: What changes should they make to resolve conflicts? The Rat should share without expecting something in return. The snake shouldn't be so blunt about how smart he is.

Step 9: Which animal do you identify with: Neither. **Other animal:** Not sure.

Step 10: How does this pertain to you? It really doesn't exactly, but if I had to give two people, then it would be my husband and son.

Step 11: What changes should you make? Well, for one they should both just compromise their issues instead of always trying to win a fight that never ends.

Step 12: Present a similar incident: My son is always trying to be good enough for his father, but never succeeds so now he has an "I don't care" attitude. He does something wrong and his father will yell and he just doesn't care if he is yelling.

Step 13: How do you relate with others, and how do you get yourself in trouble? Whenever my son and husband are fighting, I always get in the middle of it because I think they should just talk it out and try to come to a resolution. But instead, I end up losing it and they turn on me. I wish they were not so stubborn.

Step 14: What changes are you willing to make? Keep out of it!

FAIRYTALE METAPHOR

Step 1: Draw two fairy tale characters:

Step 2: Fill in the blanks:

Character#1: Beauty
Age: 34   **Sex:** Female
Personality: Naïve, caring, moody, sensitive, understanding.

Character#2: Beast
Age: 50   **Sex:** Male
Personality: Moody, insecure, caring, protective, possessive, selfish.

Step 3: What are they saying?

#2 – Come away with me to a land I love so much,
a place, where I feel free to express myself without being judged.
#1 – "I love it here where I feel grounded."
#2 – "But you love me, yes?"
#1 – "Yes, I love you and I want you to be happy."
#2 – "I am not happy here, I want to start a new life for me."
#1 – "We will be leaving everything behind – family, friends, and precious memories."
#2 – "That is okay. We have one life. We need to have more change and make new memories and friends."
#1 – "I am scared of change. I won't go."
#2 –"Then I will stay too! I won't be happy, but if that is what you want, then okay."

Step 4: What happened before? Traveling on horseback through a peaceful kingdom admiring how everybody seemed so free and relaxed.

Step 5: After? The beauty was very sad and felt very guilty for making the Beast unhappy. She knew he had an unhappy childhood in these surroundings and felt he deserved to be happy. So, she sat and thought about a change. The beast sulked back to his home and said nothing more.

Step 6: Title: "Go Or Not To Go."

Step 7a: Conflicts between themselves: They can't agree on their future happiness.

Step 7b: Conflicts between them and the world: The beast feels that in the kingdom he lives now, the people are always judging him and his family. The beauty feels opposite and comfortable with her surroundings.

Step 8: What changes should they make to resolve conflicts? Maybe a compromise would be the right thing to do, or a good/bad list to weigh out options.

Step 9: Which character do you identify with: The beauty because I finally feel content in my life and I don't want to lose that feeling when I have spent my whole life searching for it. **Other character:** My husband, because he has not found contentment in his life and he wants more.

Step 10: How does this pertain to you? My husband wants to move to N.H. because it is a beautiful place. I am afraid if we lived there, I might not have the same attitude.

Step 11: What changes should you make? I am not sure.

Step 12: Present a similar incident: Insecure husband + insecure wife = always an incident.

200

Step 13: How do you relate with others, and how do you get yourself in trouble? He always makes me feel guilty and I always give in to his feelings.

Step 14: What changes are you willing to make? I am not sure, I don't want to make waves.

REVERSAL

ANIMAL METAPHOR TEST #2

Step 1: Draw two animals with an intensified conflict:

Step 2: Fill in the blanks:

Animal #1

Type of animal: Heart
Age: 30's   **Sex:** Female
Personality: Moody, sensitive, shy.

Animal #2

Type of animal: Lips
Age: Late 40's   **Sex:** Female
Personality: arrogant, pushy, but yet very sensitive.

Step 3: What are they saying?

#1 – "Why do you feel you have to be so bossy with me?'
#2 – "Because I know you can do more."
#1 – "But I can't do more than what I am already doing. Remember I have feelings too.'
#2 – "Yes, I do know you have feelings. I too have feelings and you're always hurting them."
#1 – "I don't mean to hurt your feelings, but sometimes I get so frustrated because you won't listen to me. It seems like you care about everybody else instead of being my true friend. You want everything for you and nothing for me. I always feel like I was put here for you. I want to explode and die."
#2 – "I'm sorry you feel that way, but I have so much to do in my life and you are only a tiny-tiny bit of it. I am important and I can't keep wasting my valuable time trying to make you feel better. You need to grow up and stop acting like a baby and do what is expected of you without feedback."
#1 – "You are right. What has become of me--I am sorry. I will continue my job without grief and I will be more careful about hurting your feelings. I truly am sorry."

Step 4: What happened before? They were working together.

Step 5: After? #1 went back to work without further comments, and did as she was told. #2 did the same except she gave the orders.

Step 6: Title: "The Heart Vs. The Lips."

Step 7a: Conflicts between themselves: Each feels that their feelings are being hurt by one another.

Step 7b: Conflicts between them and the world: Too much chaos and not enough communication.

Step 8: What changes should they make to resolve conflicts? Respect each other's feelings.

DREAM ANALYSIS

Step 1: Choose a dream: Significant childhood dream, recurring from time to time.

Step 2: Draw the dream:

Step 3: Describe the dream: The dream consists of me digging a hole so deep I can't get out. Snakes emerge from the walls of the hole and slither all over me. I am crying, yelling for help. My family comes and stands around the top of the hole, laughing and pointing at me. They won't help me. I am dying in this hole and nobody will help.

Step 4: Describe the participants: My mother, father, sister, three brothers, myself.

Step 5: What are the conflicts? The snakes are killing me because I can't breathe. They are slithering all over me, even in my mouth.

Step 6: What occurrences preceded the dream? Panic attack--waking up in sweat, crying myself back to sleep. Sometimes I wake up someplace other than my bed.

Step 7: Explanation of the dream: When I need my family the most, they are not there for me. I feel if I died today, I would not be missed.

Step 8: Do you dream a lot? Yes.

Step 9: Other dreams: My other dreams consist of sexual fantasies. Occasionally I will have dreams about my death and how other people react to it and how they move on with their lives and how each day goes by, I am forgotten once again.

Step 10: Connections or patterns in dreams: I guess: sex, need attention, death, sex, need attention, Death, yeah, I guess you could say there is a pattern.

COMPROMISE

Step 1: Write a short story: The girl and the boy stepped out of the cave into the bright sunlight. They stood for a moment until their eyes adjusted to the brightness. Their bodies were covered in sweat. The girl sat on a rock nearby and the boy leaned against the cave entrance. They both seemed out of breath and distraught.

Finally after what seemed like hours, the girl began to speak, "Wow! So what did you think of that? We were almost caught by that thing. Did you see it?"

"Yeah, it was something else. Where did it come from? It surprised me," answered the boy.

The girl thought for a moment and answered the boy, "I think it came from under the ground, like a cave beneath us. Whatever it was, it didn't seem very mean, just a little scary looking. "
"Do you think it was just as afraid as us?" said the boy. "I don't know, let's go back," the girl said as she stood up and stretched. "No way, it could catch us and kill us!" the boy answered anxiously. "We are fast runners and it is too large to get us," said the girl. "Okay, you're right, and you are the leader," the boy answered with a lot of doubt.

The girl and boy stretched for a moment and then entered the cave. It was dark inside the cave, except for a few small tunnels of light that came from the ceiling above. It gave them enough light to lead them down the cave path without getting hurt. As they held hands tightly, they came across the place where they were lying previously embraced in each other's arms. They slowed down their pace and approached cautiously. In the corner they could see two eyes, quivering slightly. As they moved closer, the eyes raised up out of sight. Now, all the boy and girl could see were several mouths inside one another. It was acting as if it were screaming, but not a sound left its mouths. The boy and girl stood and stared at the thing helplessly. The thing did just the same. Nobody moved for a slight moment in time, then suddenly with no notice, the thing vanished out of sight without a sound. The girl and boy paused for a moment and they walked slowly to the corner where the thing once was and there was nothing, not a trace of it anywhere.

"Where did it go? What is it?" they thought together. They sat on the long, flat, cold rock silently and wait for an hour or more for its return, but it never came back. Neither the boy nor the girl spoke. They both felt that maybe it was just their imagination playing tricks on them during their climaxes of their sexual encounter in the cave. They went their separate ways and never spoke about the thing to no one, or themselves. They took that secret to their graves, some fifty years later.

Step 2: Illustrate the story:

Step 3: Fill in the blanks:

Character#1

Character name: Boy and Girl
Age: 34/35 **Sex:** M/F

Personality: The boy: powerful, smart, sensitive. The girl: naïve, sensitive, daring.

Character#2

Character name: Thing
Age: ? **Sex:** ?
Personality: Quiet with a sense of loudness, shy, very insecure, hiding/lurking.

Step 4: What happened before? The boy and girl were experiencing foreplay.

Step 5: After: They stayed together forever because they had a special secret that nobody could take away. They lived happily ever after.

Step 6: Title: "What Lies Beneath."

Step 7: Conflicts between themselves: The fear of what lingers in the shadows.

Step 8: What changes should they make to resolve conflicts? Use a little more common sense.

Step 9: Which character do you identify with: Girl and Boy. **Other character:** The monster of my imagination.

Step 10: How does this pertain to you? It's a secret! (nothing really).

Step 11: What changes should you make? Use a little more common sense and not play with someone's heart because if I am too careless, it might get broken.

Step 12: Present a similar incident: I love too much and I fall in love too easily and someone always gets hurt in the end.

Step 13: How do you relate with others, and how do you get yourself in trouble? Same as above.

Step 14: What changes are you willing to make? I don't know how to change this pattern. If I do change it, I will hurt a lot of people and end up living in a cave away from everybody. I will die alone.

Act 2: Learning to Feel Good About Herself and Setting Limits to Her Limit Testing and Attention Seeking Behaviors

STRESS
CHILDHOOD CONFLICTUAL MEMORY:
Testing the limit and getting severely punished

Step 1: Draw a conflictual childhood memory:

Step 2: Describe the incident: My parents told me to get out of the kitchen and go back to my room. I was sad because my siblings got to stay but I couldn't. I heard them laughing and snuck out of my room. They were looking out the window at something and I wanted to see too, but I was too small. I tried anyways, and burned my arm on the sauce pot. My father was furious and threw me to the kitchen sink. Then my mom spanked me with a wooden spoon because I left my room.

Step 3: How did you feel about this person? I hated them both.

How did this person feel about you? I think they wished I was never born.

Step 4: What were the conflicts? I wasn't doing what I was told to do and I got hurt because of it.

Step 5: What happened before? I was playing in my dad's chair because my siblings had told me it was okay. My dad's chair was forbidden to the kids.

Step 6: After? I went to bed without dinner and cried myself to sleep.

Step 7: Your share in this conflict? I should have done what I was told to do and stayed out of my dad's chair and stayed in my room.

Step 8: Effect on life: I have a difficult time making decisions for myself. I sometimes wait for someone to tell me what to do.

Step 9: Have you been repeating yourself? Yes.

Step 10: Has this conflict been resolved in your mind? Yes.

Step 11: Resolved in this relationship? Yes.

Step 12: What changes should be made? I talked to my mom. I forgave my parents.

ADOLESCENT CONFLICTUAL MEMORY

Step 1: Draw a conflictual adolescent memory:

Step 2: Describe the incident: My best friend and I were raped by two older men. I always felt it was my fault because I may have led the men on by being too nice or friendly and they took it differently.

Step 3: Effect on life: I feel I need sex to make men like/love me. Confusing getting attention with sexual escapades complicating relations and self image.

RECENT CONFLICT
Which is her position between her husband and her son?

Step 1: Draw a recent conflictual memory:

Step 2: Describe the incident: It was me, my husband, and my son. They always argue. It starts out with something recent and ends up with everything from the past. I should try supporting my husband more.

Step 3: Effect on life: I always get upset and walk away.

BALLOON PORTRAIT AND STORY

Family of Origin

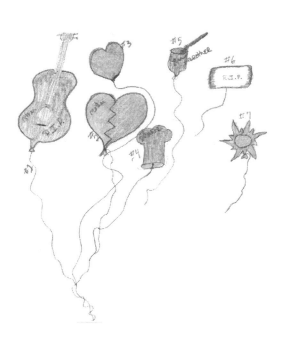

Step 1: Draw a balloon portrait of your family of origin: The patient is distancing self from the family shining on her own by feeling good, rather than seeking to to attach her string to theirs.

Step 2: Identify each individual:
Father, strict, unhappy, abusive.
Mother, unhappy, tired, ill.

Sister, simple, depressed, naïve.
Brother, snob, selfish, greedy.
Brother, crazy, anxious, angry.
Brother, suicidal, scared, naïve.
Myself, warm, scared, naïve.

Step 3: What are they saying?

#1 – "Go to bed or you'll all get it again!"
#2 – "Snore."
#3 – "Stop crying or he'll come back."
#4 – "Make her shut up or we'll get it again."
#5 – "I'll make her shut up! I'll put my fist in her mouth!"
#6 – "It's okay. I will tell you a story if you stop crying."
#7 – "Ok."

Step 4: What happened before? They had just all got spanked and sent to bed, I was still crying and we needed to be quiet.

Step 5: After? #6 was telling #7 the story about the cave people.

Step 6: Title: "Silence."

Step 7: What are the conflicts? They need to control anger in an angry environment.

Step 8: What changes should be made to resolve these conflicts? The father needed to stop drinking and show more patience to his children, so in return the children would learn patience as well.

RESPONSE

MARITAL BALLOONS
Her identity is a hart, she is close to her husband but separate in her affiliation with her children.

Step 1: Draw a balloon portrait of your marital family:

Step 2: Identify characteristics:

#1: Husband, sensitive, strong, insecure.
#2: Myself, caring, weak, scared.
#3: Son, stubborn, caring, strong.
#4: Daughter, sensitive, caring, stubborn.

Step 3: What are they saying?

#1 – "I do everything for my family and all
I get treated like is shit!"
#2 – "We are not mind readers, you need to tell us what's on your mind."
#3 – "Thank you, dad, for all you have done for me, but whatever I say to you is causing an

argument, so what do you want me to say?"
#4 – "Can we go for a ride?"

Step 4: Title: "It's All About Feelings"

Step 5: What are the conflicts? Lack of communication and listening skills.

MASK I
Recognizing her positive qualities, happiness, and expressing herself creatively; whistling.

Step 1: Draw a mask:

Step 2: Answer the following questions:

Title: "The Whistling Clown."
Age: 45   **Sex:** Female
Emotions conveyed: Happiness, silliness, pleasure, mischief

Step 3: Conflicts represented: Hiding behind sadness/mask

Step 4: Resolution of conflicts represented: It's ok to be sad sometimes, but it's even better to enjoy life and be happy.

ANXIETY

MASK II
Feeling beautiful

Step 5: Draw what is behind the mask:

Step 6: Fill in the blanks and answer the questions:

Title: "Whistling Fool."
Age: 36   **Sex:** Female
Emotions conveyed? Happiness, fear, hiding, adjusting.

Step 7: Conflicts represented: She is trying to cover up her anxiety with happiness. It's like a false appearance.

Step 8: Resolution of conflicts? Let the anxiety out and get over it and be happy for real.

Step 9: Draw what is in the heart:
Title: "Heart Burn."

Step 10: Items and themes represented: The 1 ton weight = anxiety; heart = love; sun = warmth; peace sign = peace.

Step 11: Feelings and conflicts represented: My heart feels love and warmth for the people and pets that cause anxiety. Then I feel at peace when all is okay.

Step 12: Resolution of conflicts? I need to stop trying so hard to be the best mother.

Step 13: Title of the sequence: "Growing Up Again."

Step 14: Summarize the sequence of transformations: The clown is hiding behind a mask of true feelings. It's all about growing up again.

Step 15: Conclusions about the way this person resolves conflicts: Once again, hiding behind conflicts. Not really realizing them but trying very hard to understand the conflict and make compromises.

Step 16: Does this relate to how you handle feelings: Right now, I am beginning to accept anxiety as or part of my life. I try hard to control it and resolve the cause of the anxiety.

Step 17: What changes should be made: I do not communicate my feelings to the right people. I should just take a deep breath and let it out and realize nothing is going to happen to me.

Step 18: What changes are you willing to make: Not create the conflicts in the first place. And if I do come to a conflict, I will face it and confront it until it's resolved. I won't walk away until I can resolve it or at least make a compromise.

DEFENSE

ANIMAL METAPHOR TEST #1

Step 1: Draw two animals.

Step 2: Fill in the blanks

Animal #1

Type of animal: Tree Fairy
Age: 1 million **Sex:** Both

Personality: Smart, helpful, caring.

Animal #2

Type of animal: Bunny
Age: 30   **Sex:** Female
Personality: Sweet, naïve, mischievous.

Step 3: What are they saying?

> #2 – "Oh little bunny, you are too beautiful to be flattened here on the roadside. I will change you back if you promise to stay out of trouble. POOF!"
> #1 – "Thank you, tree fairy. I will try really hard to be good."
> #2 – "Okay then, be off with you."
> #1 – "I think I will go to the school of mice and pick up the little field mice and "bop" them on the head."

Step 4: What happened before? The little bunny was running up Union Street and did not stop at the stop sign. She ran out onto the main road and was hit by a truck. The tree fairy was appointed her guardian and was watching from the rooftop of the courthouse.

Step 5: After? The tree fairy went to look for the bunny from a nearby tree. The bunny headed for more trouble.

Step 6: Title: "The Great Adventures of Little Bunny Lou Lou."

Step 7a: Conflicts between themselves: The tree fairy just wants the bunny to behave and stay out of trouble and to keep her safe. The little bunny wants attention and feels she can only get it by getting into trouble.

Step 7b: Conflicts between them and the world: All the things around the little bunny in her world are things that get her in trouble. The tree fairy wants to take her out and put her someplace safe.

Step 8: What changes should they make to resolve conflicts? The bunny needs to realize the attention she is seeking is not the kind of attention she really wants. She also needs to know that if she does good things and stays out of trouble, she will get all the right attention she truly deserves. The tree fairy should never give up on the bunny and always have patience with her, because she will figure this all out and she will be okay.

Step 9: Which animal do you identify with: Both. I am the little bunny because as a child I missed getting loved and whenever I was getting attention, it was usually because I had done something wrong. But I was getting the wrong attention. The tree fairy is my right state of mind, my conscience. **Other animal:** The world around me, it's the trouble I seek.

Step 10: How does this pertain to you? I am always looking for attention. I am always looking for love. I am always trying to get some kind of feeling of being cared about.

Step 11: What changes should you make? Stop looking for love and attention, because you have all you need right here at home. No need to be greedy.

Step 12: Present a similar incident: Well, when I was young, I used to sit on a stone wall and wave to all the people driving by, but it only led to men stopping and giving me the wrong attention.

Step 13: How do you relate with others, and how do you get yourself in trouble? As an adult I have found I tend to play a victim. I put myself in victim situations.

Step 14: What changes are you willing to make? Stop being a victim.

FAIRYTALE METAPHOR

Step 1: Draw two fairy tale characters.

Step 2: Fill in the blanks

Character#1: Alice in Wonderland
Age: 18 **Sex:** Female
Personality: Curious, naïve, simple.

Character#2: Mr. Caterpillar
Age: 25 **Sex:** Male
Personality: Wise, mellow, happy.

Step 3: What are they saying?

> #1 – I was following Mr. Rabbit and I lost him and now I'm lost. Can you help me?
> #2 – Come sit with me and have a smoke.
> #1 – Um, I don't smoke.
> #2 – Oh, come on. A little won't hurt you.
> #1 – But what if I like it so much I want more?
> #2 – It's okay to have or want more.
> #1 – No thank you. Did you see Mr. Rabbit?
> #2 – Ok, your loss. Yes I did see him. He is late for tea. He went that way through the hedges.
> #1 – Thank you.

Step 4: What happened before? Alice was chasing a muttering Mr. Rabbit. Mr. Caterpillar was relaxing and smoking pot on top of a mushroom.

Step 5: After? Alice traveled through the hedges to find the Rabbit and Mr. Caterpillar smoked some more and drifted off into a trance.

Step 6: Title: "Finding Mr. Rabbit."

Step 7a: Conflicts between themselves: Alice was experiencing peer pressure and the feeling of being lost in a new environment. Mr. Caterpillar was not really having any conflict.

Step 7b: Conflicts between them and the world: There was really no conflict between them. Alice was lost and looking for direction and Mr. Caterpillar was looking for a little companionship. The world around Alice was unfamiliar and scary and around Mr. Caterpillar it was at ease and comfortable because he was in his own environment.

Step 8: What changes should they make to resolve conflicts? Alice should take a deep breath and step back to take in the new wonders and beauty of the new world she is in. Mr. Caterpillar should quit smoking and get off his mushroom and do something a little more with his life, such as making a cocoon to become a butterfly. Then he can fly away to different lands. (Which he eventually does because nature will not allow him to stay a caterpillar forever.)

Step 9: Which character do you identify with: I identify with Alice, because I am starting a new life and the road not taken is a long, scary looking road. **Other character:** Myself as well, because I've been so used to sitting high on my mushroom in my own little world, I was so comfortable and content, that I was afraid to leave.

Step 10: How does this pertain to you? I have been in one place for so long that I have felt I would never know anything else, but nature has pushed me off my mushroom and forced me to grow wings and fly away to explore better worlds.

Step 11: What changes should you make? I feel I should take in my new world and enjoy the scenery and stop chasing the rabbit/bunny (trouble).

Step 12: Present a similar incident: When I was 13, I was sent away for the whole summer to babysit on a farm. I was scared to be away from home. My stomach was ill for the whole summer

Step 13: How do you relate with others, and how do you get yourself in trouble? Several times in my life I was pulled from what makes me comfortable, and I end up making myself very anxious, which in turn makes me feel awful and ruins any kind of fun for the people around me. So once I feel uncomfortable, I try doing things to make my situation better but instead I get in trouble.

Step 14: What changes are you willing to make? I am willing to put myself into more different environments besides my own and learn to enjoy and appreciate where I am and what I am doing, taking a lot of deep breaths.

REVERSAL

ANIMAL METAPHOR TEST #2

Step 1: Draw two animals with an intensified conflict:

Step 2: Fill in the blanks:

Animal #1

Type of animal: Red Oak

Age: 150   **Sex:** Female
Personality: Well-rooted, strong and sturdy, wise.

Animal #2

Type of animal: Pine Sapling
Age: 25 **Sex:** Female
Personality: Scared, weak, unsure.

Step 3: What are they saying?

> #2 – "Oak, may I ask you something?"
> #1 – "Sure, sapling. I will try to answer any question you may have for me."
> #2 – "Will I live as long as you?"
> #1 – "Oh little sapling, I cannot predict the future. But I will say, you may not live as long as me."
> #2 – "Why, Oak? Why won't I live as long as you? You are already old and I am a young sapling."
> #1 – "I am old, but my roots are planted deep into the earth below. I am strong and sturdy. The wind and I are good friends."
> #2 – "It shouldn't matter who your friends are, right?"
> #1 – "Well, in my case it does."
> #2 –"Ok, I don't want to argue."
> #1 – "Look sapling, Mother Nature puts us all here for a reason. You will provide shade and food for all the creatures and you will drop seeds to make more of you. You will grow taller faster than me. You will not lose all your needles either."
> #2 – "I understand, I guess."
> #1 – "Also, my roots are deeper than yours, and that means the wind has a harder time knocking me down. Maybe you should try digging your roots a little deeper."
> #2 – "I will try."

Step 4: What happened before? Just standing around shading the creatures of the forest.

Step 5: After? The wind began to blow and the sapling tried really hard to push the roots down deeper. The oak watched and grinned.

Step 6: Title: "Let the Wind Blow."

Step 7a: Conflicts between themselves: One being better than the other.

Step 7b: Conflicts between them and the world: The thought of dying.

Step 8: What changes should they make to resolve conflicts? The oak should help the sapling with more encouraging words of wisdom.

Step 1: Choose a dream: Recent dream.

Step 2: Draw the dream:

Step 3: Describe the dream:

Step 4: Describe the participants:
Young me: scared, helpless, lost.
Older me: Brave, learning, not to be so scared.

Step 5: What are the conflicts? The snakes are the conflicts in this dream.

Step 6: What occurrences preceded the dream? I woke up and had a great day.

Step 7: Explanation of the dream: I used to have a recurring dream about being trapped in a pit of snakes with no help from my family to get out. [*note: this is the dream described in book 1*] I feel my new dream is saying, I don't need help, I can do this on my own and by that I mean live life happily and free.

Step 8: Do you dream a lot? Yes.

Step 9: Other dreams: All of my other dreams are too sexually explicit for me to feel comfortable explaining. Basically they are all sexually related in one way or another.

Step 10: Connections or patterns in dreams: Yes, the snake pit is a place where I would go to be punished. Punished for acting out sexually.

COMPROMISE
Short Story

Step 1: Write a short story: Jack and Jill went up the hill and down the other side one late summer's night. Once they were on the other side of the hill, they came across a cottage made from chocolate and gumdrops. They stood and stared at the house for a few minutes before they went closer.

"Let's knock on the door ," said Jack. "Okay, but what will we say if someone answers?" asked Jill. "We will ask for directions. Then we will be friendly so the person will invite us inside," responded Jack. "I am not sure this is a good idea. Maybe we should go back home," said

Jill in a nervous voice.

Jill stood for a minute and thought. "No, Jack! No more games! If you want to do this, then you can do it alone. I am going home," said Jill and she turned around and head back over the hill.

Once she got to the top of the hill, she turned round to see where Jack was and to her disbelief, he was only several steps behind. He looked angry at Jill and walked past her and down the other side of the hill to home. Jill followed slowly. Jack was only angry for that evening. By next morning Jack and Jill were best friends again and off on a new adventure.

Step 2: Illustrate the story:

Step 3: Fill in the blanks:

Character#1

Character name: Jack
Age: 13 **Sex:** Male
Personality: Curious, adventurous, caring

Character#2

Character name: Jill
Age: 14 **Sex:** Female
Personality: Smart, loving, considerate.

Step 4: What happened before? Jack and Jill talked about going berry picking on the other side of the hill.

Step 5: After: They weren't talking to each other.

Step 6: Title: "Berry Picking Gone Bad."

Step 7: Conflicts between themselves: Jack wanted to do something out of greed. He wanted to trick the owner of the candy house so he could eat some of the house. Jill stood her ground and refused to go along with it.

Step 8: What changes should they make to resolve conflicts? They should have talked a little more instead of Jill just walking away. Communication is important between friends, family, anyone.

Step 9: Which character do you identify with: Jill, because whenever there is a conflict in front of me I will argue for a minute and then I will go, walk away without resolving anything.
Other character: My husband, because he tries to get me to do things I am not comfortable doing. We argue and I end up walking away without resolving anything.

Step 10: How does this pertain to you? I am a better person now. I can/will stand my ground and I will stay and talk it over, no matter how long it takes.

Step 11: What changes should you make? Deep breaths and a lot of patience. I can do this and be strong and understanding.

Step 12: Present a similar incident: My brother and I went to an old house. He wanted to break in and explore the house, but I was too scared. He threatened me and I got scared and ran home. He was really angry with me and wouldn't talk for days.

Step 13: How do you relate with others, and how do you get yourself in trouble? I am a person who will do whatever it takes to keep everyone happy, even if it is wrong or right. I do not like conflict. I avoid it whenever possible.

Step 14: What changes are you willing to make? Face the conflicts and bring them to a resolution, no matter how long it takes.

ADDITIONAL METAPHOR TEST

The Fox and the Owl

The Fox
Female: 10 years
Sly, swift, playful

The Owl
Male:13 years
Wise, proud, knowledgeable

The fox crossed the road to the other side and entered the dark forest. In his mouth he carried a field mouse by the tail. The mouse knew his own fate as he swung in mid-air. The fox gallantly trotted through the forest over dead trees, which laid upon the forest floor and through bramble bushes with ease. He came to an old oak tree that stood tall and straight, as if to reach the full moon that lit up the night sky, along with the bright shining stars. The fox came to a stop at the base of the tree. He placed the frightened field mouse on the ground and before it could run, the fox placed his front paw on top of the mouse and held it to the ground firmly, unable to escape.

The fox looked up the tree to the first long branch and said, "Do you want to come to the field and play with me tonight?" Sitting tall and straight on the branch sat an owl.

This owl was not your ordinary owl; it was a great horned owl, the most clever and wise of all forest animals. Before answering the fox he had to turn his head all the way around to face the fox. He looked down and with a slow strong voice, he said, "What will you give me to play with you?" The fox sat down and thought for a brief second and before thinking anymore and using a little common sense, he said, " I have a nice fat field mouse under my paw that just might suit you ." The field mouse quivered with more fear than before, at the thought of the owl picking him to pieces and eating him with his sharp beak. The owl said with pleasure, "A fat field mouse, huh? That sounds absolutely delightful."

216

The owl swooped down to the nearest sturdy bush and looked anxiously for the field mouse. The little field mouse saw the owl and began to struggle with all its' strength. The more it struggled, the more pressure the fox placed upon its back. The ground beneath the mouse began to cave in a little. The owl stared at the mouse and said, "well, is this the fat mouse you were referring to, fox?" The fox looked at his paw and the mouse was not there. He looked around frantically for the field mouse that had escaped his doom. "I had a mouse here, really I did!" The fox began to pace searching for the field mouse. The owl lost his patience and said, "fox, give up, I believe you, you had a fat field mouse. But now it is gone and do you still want to play?" The fox stopped searching and excitedly replied, "oh yes, can we? Can we? I love to play!" The owl shook his head at the dancing fox and thought, "what am I getting myself into?"

The fox stopped dancing and looked at the owl and asked, "what do you want to play first? I like to play hiding go seek or maybe we could play catch me if you can? What do you like to play?" The owl thought for a moment and said, " I like to play catch the field mouse or bunny. Whichever one we can catch first is the winner and the winner has to give it up to the loser." The fox did not even think about this game at all, he was just so happy to play any game with the owl that he responded too fast before thinking, " yes, yes, that sounds like so much fun!" So, the owl flew to the nearby field across the road and the fox followed with excitement, dancing and jumping the whole way.

Once the fox and the owl arrived at the field, the owl began to recite the game rules, "This rock that lays in the middle of the field is home base. You will take the right side of the field and I will take the left side of the field. Whoever catches a mouse or bunny first will bring it back to the rock and yell 'I got it' really loud. There will be a time limit. Once the full moon has shifted to the forest edge above the old maple, your time will be up and if no one has caught anything, the game will be over and I will go home, because I can't play all night, for I need to hunt for my dinner." The fox said the rules were fair and wanted so hard to catch something because he wanted to play all night. The owl counted, " 1-2-3- Go !" and off they went to catch a mouse or bunny.

My Resolution:
My first animal metaphor was a rat and snake. I felt that both animals were sneaky, greedy, and somewhat unkind to each other. I finished the workbook and did a second animal metaphor with a short story. My animals went from a rat and snake to an owl and fox. The new animals are basically still unkind, but yet they play games of using each other for each other's needs. Once they realize what they are doing, they understand that they are just hurting each other's feelings and they learn to forgive and share and move on to a happy ending. They become best of friends for life.

The Kite: A dreamer, light, whispering
The Flying Carpet: Loud, magical, fast.

#2 – "Hey Kite, where are you headed?"
#1 – "Well, Flying Carpet, I am going wherever the wind shall take me."
#2 – 'That could be anywhere."
#1 – "You know, I am anxious to see what my future has in store for me."
#2 – "Don't be ridiculous, kite. What happens if the wind blows you into a tree and you are stuck forever?"
#1 – "Don't worry, if that should happen, then that is my fate. I am sure Wind won't leave me there forever, he will slow me down eventually."
#2 – "But what if you are torn into shreds? Wind won't be able to help you then!"
#1 – "Flying Carpet, please do not worry, my future is secure on the air. Whatever my future is, then it is."
#2 – "Look Kite, I like you a lot and I think you are beautiful. Please hook your kite string to me and we will travel with the wind together."
#1 – "Ok."

Book 1: *Testing the normative limits in the pursuit of love and experiencing anxiety*

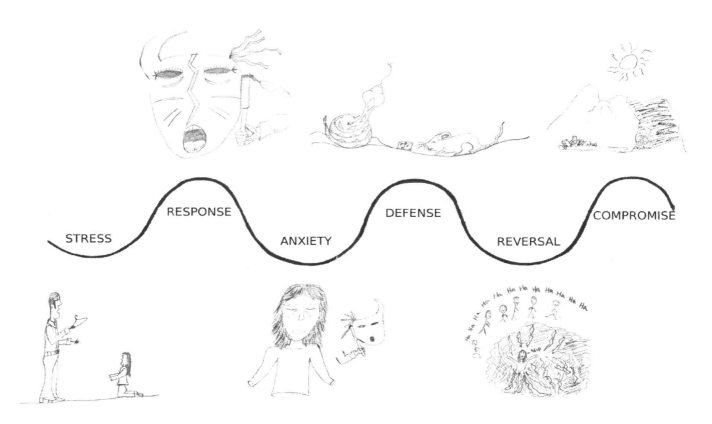

Stress:
Helpless, handless physically abused by her father.

Response:
A hand holding a Warrior mask in front of her face.

Anxiety:
Girl without hands, helpless.

Defense:
Snake curses selfish rat for not sharing his cheese. The rat eats poisoned cheese and dies.

Reversal:
Dream of being in a pit of snakes being laughed at by family up top.

Compromise:
Making love but threatened by cave monster.

Book 2: *Finding happiness by setting limits to her self*

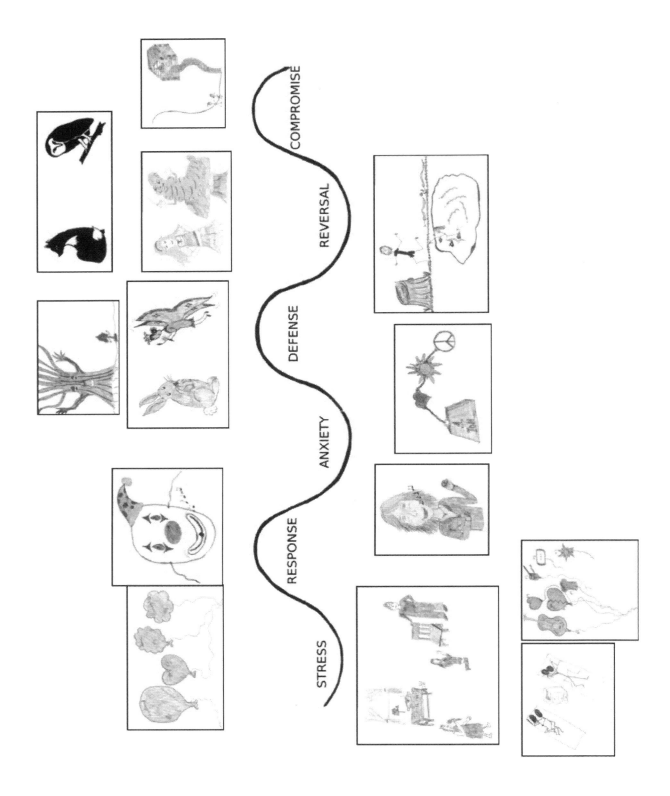

Power Management
Books One & Two

Testimony of the healing of anxiety symptoms by insightfully reducing acting out behaviors
First book: Evaluation

Stress: She was an unloved, rejected, punished child
Response: Behind the warrior mask is a helpless girl without power of her own.
Anxiety: She was looking to find love outside of her family.
Defense: She was the selfish rat that gets the cheese and is poisoned for her transgression.
Reversal: In her dream she was reminded of being unloved rejected in the pit of snakes, not belonging in the family.
Compromise: Resolution finding love, sexual acceptance, but being haunted by eyes, her self consciousness, guilt and anxiety.
Insights: She was escaping depression by finding love; this created anxiety; it was the cause of her illnesses; her guilt made her feel self-conscious, scared. Her fears emerged as anxiety symptoms.

Second Book: Therapy Outcome

Stress: The girl who was seeking attention that was not given to her by the family, sought to find love by passers by. She and her friend got raped, were taken advantage of by older men.
Response: She learned early to distance herself from her family, holding her feelings of hurt and anger inside but kept a positive outlook and her mask shows her as a whistling not speaking clown.
Anxiety: The hidden face now is a beautiful person weighted down by a ton of depression but inspired by uplifting peaceful feelings.
Defense: A number of stories now tell her to stop seeking attention to not get in trouble and not get flattened by traffic. The oak tree tells the sapling to trust growing and developing roots and branches caring for creatures.
As Alice she knows how to resist the temptations of the wonderland.
Reversal: She is rewarded and she has a dream of emerging from the pit of snakes and walking out of feeling rejected by her family and friends.
Compromise: Indeed she is able to have attention without bribing the owl. The two are engaged now to catch a mouse to feed each other.
The errant flying kite is no longer victim of the winds about to be ruined but is tethered to a magic carpet bound to success.
Remarkable keeping herself at a distance from the playful owl and also use of dark colors to connote sobering reality as power and limits without dangers and fun escapes.

Act #3: Wise Oak's Third Book Several Years After the Course of Therapy

Understanding the symbolic continuum exploring balance in her emotional turmoil

Introduction and Discussion

This is the third book of Wise Oak. She completed this book years after the termination from therapy for panic and anxiety issues generated by her extramarital conflicts. Her current family's circumstances had changed: Her mother was sick and needed daily care and Wise Oak was her caretaker. Her husband was diagnosed with terminal cancer and she was taking care of him as well. Her son's divorced wife wished to move close to her family located in a far way state along with her children, Wise Oak's grand children. Oak felt very threatened as she loved taking care of them.

In the first book she identified her childhood lack of love and her pursuit of loving relationships backfiring for her. She identified similar oppressive experiences that had led her to rebel to find love through escapades, conduct that had caused anxiety as fears of death and illness.

In her second book she was learning to restrain her dependency needs, set boundaries to her attention seeking guilt evoking behaviors. Her self-restraint, a spontaneous power management approach, had given her relief from her anxiety symptoms. I labeled her the Wise Oak because of a poster she had composed upon termination presenting an Oak Tree harboring lovingly all her animal metaphors.

The art and content of the third book reflects meaningful changes in having overcome her own dependency needs but being troubled for not being able to provide for the dependency needs of others. This document demonstrates the new phase of conflicts in the same symbolic system as the earlier books: anticipating and providing for the dependency needs of her grandchildren projecting to them her own need for love as a child.

This study is useful in understanding the nature of role systems. It clarifies the evolution from anxiety symptoms generated by her dependency needs, to anxiety concerns about the anticipated needs of her grand-children. The passivity of her needs had been satisfied by affairs and then controlled by self-restraints. The new passivity, anticipated needs of the grand children, was dealt by the need to provide for them and fears of being handicapped in doing so.

Providing for others' needs was the complementary aspect of her role-continuum. A person who needs a lot of love also feels the needs of others for love or caring and has the readiness to support these needs. At another level she expressed this need for caring intensely not only by taking care of the members of her family but also by adopting distressed cats and dogs. She had three dogs and a wild hostile cat. While complaining for demanding partners she was also acknowledging and denouncing her own need for love: She was seeking to temper her 'being greedy'.

She completed this workbook using the symbolic image of a tree by placing herself in the 'house tree person' exercise as an old person in front of a tree as her final rest state. She concluded, "Every nail/ screw was placed by her hands" she also "had planted one tree in the front of the house for her children and grand children to play. One day the woman was old and alone. She hobbled out to this magnificent tree. She sat at the base of the tree, closed her eyes and let the sun warm her old, achy body. The base of this tree is the aging woman's resting place. The end." The tree metaphor tells us about her coming to find peace of mind. The unloved child having come of age had built a loving reality for her family and herself with her hard work.

The current sequence of metaphors completes a therapeutic trilogy transforming conflicts as passivity, antagonism and alienation to resolution as activity, cooperation and mutual respect. The journey that began with feeling unloved, rejected and ridiculed, alienated from her family, recreated in her conflictual memory as a bed-wetter punished cruelly by her mother, is completed with the cycle of loving, caring stories, multiple accommodations of others with patience and a persistence in caring in spite of the odds.

The new book begins from the theme of feeling rejected and deprived of love as a child, to metaphors presenting the state of resolution in her adulthood. She is nursing her mother, husband and grand-children. These are her compromises, the resolution state. She is no longer pursuing temptations and getting punished; she is actively seeking to care and at the end find the object of her affection, the lost grand-children; she is relieved of pain as she becomes able to nurse them.

The set of books is an art statement like a retrospective or a three-act play worth analyzing. The first book was colorless and replete with sad stories. The second was alive with colors and consistent in moral lessons.

The third book of essays is very different from the initial in aspects of art-work and emotional disposition. The art-work is elaborate, very different from the black and white drawings that expressed pain, escapism and fears of death. It evolved from colorless pictures of her suffering as a handless girl, to depict detailed colorful close ups of faces crowding the art-space allowing the expression of emotions. Her species are bold and expressive animal-heads of equal size.

The theme of the images is matched by the texts differing from the second book, which was colorful but pertained to setting limits to herself to avert anxiety. The focus is on close-ups of mutuality in relationships. The content of her metaphors matches the focused art as she analyzes relationships with maturity and self-awareness. The conflicts are not inner but interpersonal. They pertain to dealing with the needs of others but also insightfully looking at her self.

STRESS
The sense of stress as rejection surfaced again in her three conflictual memories: in childhood as a bed-wetter dealing with her unloving punitive mother, in adolescence dealing with a rapist, and in her adulthood dealing with her husband's insensitivity to their children. Her stressful experiences clearly depict her as victim of abusive relationships.

RESPONSE
Her new response is reflected in her masks. It is revealing her capacity to have courage and heal: her first Mask is about the state of courage; she presents cracks that need repair; the second mask anxiety is about the opposite, hope. She reveals the strengths of the repair as her healing. The inner heart shows strengths as reality and fantasy combined visually in showing a heart in full detail prepared for a loving life.

The Mask reflects her conflicts as the snake of temptations and the rat, her yearning for love getting her in trouble. *Snakes and Rats are Arch Enemies. But yet they both can make you feel weak in the knees. Broken. Courage- MisNeACH Let them go and patch the cracks.*

Underneath the mask we see the healing in her new identity: ***Emotions conveyed?*** *The feeling of change, peace, and happiness;* ***Conflicts represented:*** *The Pain in Progress of change.*

Step 8: Resolution of conflicts represented: *Change can be scary and good all at the same time.*

> *"Metamorph"*
> ***Age:*** *42* ***Sex:*** *female*
> *"THE TRUE HEART"*

Step 10: Items and themes represented: *The key to future opportunities. A party to be worth celebrating. Reaching for freedom. Love/ Fire.*

Step 11: Feelings and conflicts represented:
This heart is stressed about many outcomes due to arise in the future.

Step 12: What resolution of conflicts does it convey? *Patience is the resolution, for those who wait.*

Step 13: Title of the sequence: *"Getting what the heart needs."*

Step 14: Summarize the sequence of transformations.
Patience and freedom are the main aspects of these images.

Step 15: Conclusions about the way this person resolves conflicts:
This person does not resolve anything. They just dream about a wanted future. They spend more time organizing their future instead of the present.

Step 16: How does this relate to how you handle feelings?
I push my feelings aside to focus on what lies ahead. I tell myself to compromise every time because it's easier. I look forward to my future.

Step 17: What changes should be made?
I should keep my feelings up front and center.

Step 18: What changes are you willing to make?
Be honest with myself so I can be honest with others.

DEFENSE
Her Defense state is illustrated in a number of metaphors.
In the first metaphor the loving partner, a gorilla whom she has difficulty trusting, crushes her; this gorilla is her mother.

In the Fairy Tale Metaphor: Red Riding Hood seeks to negotiate with the Wolf but surrenders to the demanding wolf the entire basket; ***Which character do you identify with?*** *Both. I have greed in my mind like the wolf and compromise in my heart like little Red Riding Hood.*

REVERSAL

It is not surprising that the emotionally deprived bedwetting girl punished by her cruel mother, protected by her older sister wakes up at night sleep walking with a teddy bear seeking desperately to love children.

In the intensified conflictual metaphor she is a dog finding passage through a Cape Buffalo's turf guarding her youngsters.

Age: 80   Sex: female
Personality: Aggressive, tough, arrogant.
The age and traits refer to her mother's personality but could also describe her daughter in law's personality.

Type of animal 2: Dog,
Age: 30   Sex: Female,
Personality: Faithful, nervous, shy.
These traits pertain to herself. The Beefalo is uncompromising in granting privileges to the dog.

COMPROMISE

In the Short Story metaphor a Satyress pursuing the cries of children is in pain to provide for them. The metaphor related to her concern of loosing contact with her two grand children upon her son's divorce from his wife; the divorcing daughter-in-law wished to move closer to her family in the South. The Satyress is guided by a Centaur, a 'non lover', to the lost children, which satisfies her need to care. Her hero I suspect represents her son and the father of her beloved grand-children.

The reversal of being a caregiver is a theme underlying her metaphors. In spite of her mother's insensitivity, or just because of awareness of this rejection she is now caring for her. This conflictual relationship surfaces continuously in her metaphors. The powerful individuals in her metaphors are not men but women. The gorilla figure is identified as her mother. In the fairy Tale the wolf is her selfish mother whom she is taking care of on a daily basis.

The wolf's Age: 80   Sex: female.

First animal Metaphor, Step 10: *How does this pertain to you?* I am my mother's caregiver. I do everything for her happiness. She says she trusts me but is always lying to me. She uses guilt and illness as tools to get what she wants from me. She says she loves me but she is selfish.

Step 11: *What changes should you make?* I need to stop trying to get love from a mother who doesn't know how to give it freely.

Step 12: Present a similar incident: My mom is alone. She waits for my arrival everyday. Twice a day. If a day comes when I can't make it and I want to spend it with my grand babies, she will make herself sick and make me feel guilty.

Step 13: *How do you relate with others, and how do you get yourself in trouble?* I am always sacrificing my happiness to please everyone. I don't like it when people are mad, sad, or displeased with me. I just want everybody to be happy so I can be happy too. This means feeling sorry for people and giving them what they need even though it's wrong.

Step 14: What changes are you willing to make? Stop Playing The Victim Role.

In her Fairy Tale Metaphor the dog needs to be more convincing and not give in too quickly. In the intensified metaphor the Cape Beefalo is another woman, protective of her children keeping her children at a distance from the passer by dog. She recognizes the problems of all partners as dominant individuals and her own problems as those of a submissive cooperative individual.

SHORT STORY METAPHOR

Step 8: *What changes should they make to resolve conflicts?* Satyress needs to calm her mind and ignore the infant cries. She can't calm all the cries. Apollo should stick to what he knows best- the hunt.

Step 9: *Which character do you identify with*: Satyress, because sometimes I just want to help anyone/ everyone and it drives me crazy to think I can't do it all. **Other character:** Apollo reminds me of a Non-lover who thinks I can just find my way with his guidance, but he doesn't understand my heart.

Step 10: *How does this pertain to you?* Because all stories I write somehow pertain to me.

Step 11: *What changes should you make?* Get help!! Find my way on my own.

This third book reflects her strength in dealing with demanding dominant people in a number of relationships giving in spontaneously, selflessly, but resenting their selfishness. She gives love, but protests at their behaviors. She is critical of her mother, the gorilla, her husband, the selfish wolf, and her daughter in law, the obstinate beefalo protective of her children.

Her choices as illustrated in her metaphor tests show herself as a bunny dealing with a crushing insensitive demanding gorilla; as a Red Riding Hood meaning well with a selfish Big Bad Wolf who is greedy and untrustworthy, in her intensified metaphor she is a Dog trespassing in the turf of an aggressive, tough, arrogant Cape Beefalo. She is trying to please and care for her mother and husband but she is able to be critical of them rather than feeling helpless and victimized. In the insights from the metaphors she does not just blame others; she admits her own dependency, her greed for love, the need for attention. While critical of others she is also self-aware.

The resolution presents her submissiveness as a choice; she enjoys the life of a submissive person: being available to love and service others. She cares, has feelings and can make concessions not because of weakness but because of maturity and inner strength. Her current conflicts center in her need to give love but she also admits she needs to manage her own need for love, her concern for the future. She declared the means to cope with a positive attentive attitude. She has now a healthy heart, which is manifested across all her metaphors. In them she accepts responsibility for her share of the conflicts; she is critical of her own neediness and admits responsibility for generating problems.

The book sheds light to the patient's conflicts and strengths; she is a cooperative submissive individual yearning for love by others and concerned for the needs of others. She is learning to be appropriate in her neediness but also in the measure of caring for others. She is setting limits to herself and to the demands of others. This position decreases her original symptom of anxiety and fears of dying. This attitude is the strong root system of the Wise old Oak.

Transcript of her metaphors

STRESS

CHILDHOOD CONFLICTUAL MEMORY

Step 1: Draw a conflictual childhood memory:

Step 2: Describe the incident: I was 4 years old. I wet the bed. My mom was furious with me. She pulled me out of bed and put me in a cold shower with my night-clothes on. I am not sure how long I was there; my sister came and took me out. I remember being so cold. My sister stripped me and wrapped me in a blanket and held me until I stopped shivering; then she dressed me and we changed my bed together. I don't know where my mom went.

Step 3: How did you feel about this person? I felt confused. I felt like she was mad at me. **How did this person feel about you?** I was a burden to her.

Step 4: What were the conflicts? I woke up in a wet bed. My first time and apparently it was not allowed ever.

Step 5: What happened before? I was sleeping. I woke up wet and cried.

Step 6: After? My mom came into our room. She asked me what was wrong. I told her and she yelled and took my arm and pulled me out of bed and put me in a cold shower.

Step 7: Your share in this conflict? I was 4 years old. I wet the bed in the middle of the night.

Step 8: Effect on life: Accidents Happen!

Step 9: Have you been repeating yourself? No

Step 10: Has this conflict been resolved in your mind? ? Yes

Step 11: Resolved in this relationship? Yes

Step 12: What changes should be made? It's the past. Leave it there

Step 1: Draw a conflictual adolescent memory:

Step 2: Describe the incident

Age 13 my best friend and I were raped. The man "Bruce" took me home; before dropping me off he showed me his gun. He told me if I said anything he would come for my family first.

Step 3: How has this affected you?

I think about my friend often. I never saw her again.

RECENT CONFLICT

Step 1: Recent Conflict: Draw the most conflictual recent memory

Step 2: Describe the incident: Me and my husband. Our daughter was expressing anger toward some unfairness in her childhood. I wanted to resolve the issue, but he thought it was bullshit.

Step 3: Effect on life: I feel like I have really screwed my kids out of a lot of enjoyment in life.

FAMILY OF ORIGIN

Step 1: Draw a balloon portrait of your family of origin.

Step 2: Identify each individual, his/her relationship, his/her age, and personality, listing three characteristics.

1. Mother- 69: selfish- guilt master- weak
2. Father- died when he was 50: strict- abusive- strong
3. Sister- 52: emotionally unbalanced- weak- sad
4. Brother- 50: arrogant- self-centered- careless
5. Brother- 49: anxious- big dreamer- smart
6. Brother- 24: sad- insecure- GONE
7. Myself- 42: insecure- anxious- COMPASSIONATE

Step 3: The balloons are having a conversation. What are they saying?

1, mom: I'm helpless and ALL ALONE.
4, oldest brother: I'm too busy building my own life.
3, sister: I can't help. I work too much.
5, Brother: I would help but I don't like drama.
2 + # 6 Dead;
7, myself: It's okay I will take care of you MOM. My life can wait. Really it's okay. I know I owe you, cause you gave birth to me.

Step 4: What were the balloons saying or doing before the conversation you just recorded?
Making excuses why they can't help care for their mother.

Step 5: What were the balloons saying or doing after the initial conversation?
Going on with their lives and doing what makes them happy.

Step 6: Give a title to the story.
Family ties.

Step 7: What conflicts are these balloons experiencing?

7, myself: is the only one with the conflict. The others have their resolutions- moving on with their lives knowing their little sister is caring for their mother.

Step 8: What changes should be made to resolve these conflicts?

 # 7: Should let her mother be more independent.

RESPONSE

MARITAL FAMILY BALLOON PORTRAIT

Step 1: Draw a balloon portrait of your marital family.

Step 2: Identify three characteristics of each member of the family:

 Balloons:
 # 1, husband: Insecure- angry- selfish

 # 2: Self, Silent: invisible- unsure

 # 3: daughter, strong willed- smart- creative

 # 4: son, inner sunshine- confused- itchy feet

Step 3: The individuals are conversing. Record their exchanges

 #1: "My way! No! Because I say so!"
 #2: "It's my fault. I'm sorry!"
 #3: "Stop! I can handle this!"
 #4: "AARGH!!""

Step 4: Title: Cutting The Air with a Knife

Step 5: What conflicts are these individuals experiencing? If#1 is not Happy- Then NO ONE will be HAPPY. #2 takes everything she has to keep #1 happy not realizing she is destroying #3+ 4's happiness.

TRANSPARENT MASK TEST I

Step 1: Draw a mask:

Step 2: Answer the following questions:

 Title: "SNEAKS and Squeeks"
 Age: 21   **Sex:** female

What emotions does this mask convey? Broken. Courage- MisNeACH

Step 3: Conflicts represented: Snakes and Rats are Arch Enemies. But yet they both can make you feel weak in the knees.

Step 4: Resolution of conflicts represented: Let them go and patch the cracks.

ANXIETY

Step 5: Imagine that the mask you drew has become transparent. Make a drawing of what you see through the mask, reflecting true feelings.

Step 6: Fill in the blanks and answer the questions:

>   **Title:** "Metamorph"
>   **Age:** 42   **Sex:** female
>   **Emotions conveyed?** The feeling of change, peace, and happiness

Step 7: Conflicts represented: The Pain in Progress of change.

Step 8: Resolution of conflicts represented: Change can be scary and good all at the same time. In the place of snakes and rats we see flowers and a butterfly emerge.

MASK III

Draw what is in the heart.

Step 9: Title: "THE TRUE HEART"

Step 10: Items and themes represented: The key to future opportunities. A party to be worth celebrating. Reaching for freedom. Love/ Fire.

Step 11: Feelings and conflicts represented:
This heart is stressed about many outcomes due to arise in the future.

Step 12: What resolution of conflicts does it convey? Patience is the resolution, for those who wait.

Step 13: Title of the sequence: "Getting what the heart needs."

Step 14: Summarize the sequence of transformations.
Patience and freedom are the main aspects of these images.

Step 15: Conclusions about the way this person resolves conflicts:
This person does not resolve anything. They just dream about a wanted future. They spend more time organizing their future instead of the present.

Step 16: Does this relate to how you handle feelings?
I push my feelings aside to focus on what lies ahead. I tell myself to compromise every time because it's easier. I look forward to my future.

Step 17: What changes should be made?
I should keep my feelings up front and center.

Step 18: What changes are you willing to make?
Be honest with myself so I can be honest with others.

DEFENSE

ANIMAL METAPHOR TEST #1

Step 1: Draw two animals.

Step 2: Fill in the blanks

Animal #1

Type of animal: Gorilla
Age: 40, **Sex:** Male
Personality: Powerful, strong, dominant.

Animal #2

Type of animal: Rabbit
Age: 16 **Sex:** Female
Personality: Weak, timid, submissive.

Step 3: What are they saying

> #1 – "Hi Rabbit. I'm going to call you bunny."
> #2 – "My name is Grace."
> #1 – "Ok. Hello Grace. My name is Ralph."
> #2 – "Nice to meet you."
> #1 – "Come with me to the jungle."
> #2 – "I can't. The jungle is not a good place for me."
> #1 – "Don't be a chicken and come with me. It will be fun I promise"

#2 – "We can have fun here."
#1 – "Stop playing games and come with me. Trust me."
#2 – "Will you carry me? And keep me safe?"
#1 – "I am your friend. I will carry you and keep you safe."
#2 – "Ok, I will go."
#1 – "Come into my arms and I will carry you"
#2 – "OK"
#1 – "My arms are big and strong you will be safe."
#2 – I feel safe. Thank you.
#1 – That's what friends are for- you're welcome.

Step 4: What happened before?
They were at the zoo. The jungle was a man made jungle. The Rabbit is free to roam, but the Gorilla is in a pen. The Gorilla was sitting on a grassy Knoll when the Rabbit came along to eat the grass.

Step 5: After? Rabbit climbed into Ralph's strong hands. He headed for the jungle when he heard the zoo keeper yell. Ralph got scared and without thinking he put both strong hands to the ground. Grace was smashed into nothing. Ralph felt horrible and never was the same. He loved Grace.

Step 6: Title: "Jungle Talk."

Step 7a: Conflicts between themselves: No real conflicts, except stepping out of their comfort zone. The Gorilla was a little over confident.

Step 7b: Conflicts between them and the world: The Rabbit does not belong in the jungle. The Gorilla should have respected the rabbit's fears. The zoo can be a scary place.

Step 8: What changes should they make to resolve conflicts? The Gorilla should not be so pushy and respect the fears of the Rabbit. The Rabbit needs to learn to speak up and stand her ground, without feeling obligated to make everyone happy.

Step 9: Which animal do you identify with: The Rabbit, because I never speak up for myself. I prefer everyone else's happiness, over my own.

Whom do you identify with the counterpart animal? Elaborate.
The Gorilla. I feel the need for people to trust me with their lives and then I feel I failed them when it doesn't work out for them.

Step 10: How does this pertain to you? I am my mother's caregiver. I do everything for her happiness. She says she trusts me but is always lying to me. She uses guilt and illness as tools to get what she wants from me. She says she loves me but she is selfish.

Step 11: What changes should you make? I need to stop trying to get love from a mother who doesn't know how to give it freely.

Step 12: Present a similar incident: My mom is alone. She waits for my arrival everyday. Twice a day. If a day comes when I can't make it and I want to spend it with my grand babies, she will make herself sick and make me feel guilty.

Step 13: How do you relate with others, and how do you get yourself in trouble? I am always sacrificing my happiness to please everyone. I don't like it when people are mad, sad, or displeased with me. I just want everybody to be happy so I can be happy too. This means feeling sorry for people and giving them what they need even though it's wrong.

Step 14: What changes are you willing to make? Stop Playing The Victim Role.

FAIRYTALE METAPHOR

Step 1: Draw two fairy tale characters.

Step 2: Fill in the blanks

  Character#1: Little Red Riding Hood
  Age: 18 **Sex:** Female
  Personality: Shy, scared, negative.

  Character#2: Big Bad Wolf.
  Age: 39 **Sex:** Female
  Personality: Fierce, brave, smart.

Step 3: What are they saying?

  #2 – Give me your basket!
  #1 – No- it's for my sick friend.
  #2 – What's in the basket?
  #1 – Chicken, biscuits and apple pie.
  #2- I like it. Now give it to me!
  #1- No! it's to make my friend feel better.
  #2- I don't care about your friend. I am hungry. Give it to me!
  #1- Please go away.
  #2- Not until you give me that basket.
  #1 How about I give you a ¼ of what's in my basket?
  #2-No- I want half! Or all.
  #1- Ok, Ok, Ok- here is half.
  #2- Good!

Step 4: What happened before? #2 was hiding in the bushes waiting. #1 was taking a short cut to her friend's house to feed her sick friend.

Step 5: After?
  #2 Grabbed the basket and ran to a nearby hole and ate everything in the basket. #1 was shocked at first, then, she became sad. She continued on the path crying all the way.

Step 6: Title: The Story of Greed

Step 7a: Conflicts between themselves: The lack of compromise from the wolf. Little Red Riding Hood compromised too much.

Step 7b: Conflicts between them and the world: There is greed all around them… Everyone wants more. More Money- More Food- More Elaborate material possessions. Greed stomps out the good in their heart.

Step 8: What changes should they make to resolve conflicts?
Be happy for what you have in life. Not what you want.

Step 9: Which character do you identify with: Both. I have greed in my mind like the wolf and compromise in my heart like little Red Riding Hood.

Step 10: How does this pertain to you? I am greedy when it comes to love + sex. I compromise everything for everyone.

Step 11: What changes should you make? Grow a 'mean' bone in my body and stop pleasing everyone and start being greedy toward myself.

Step 12: Present a similar incident: My mom + husband always want more time with me. I give them all my time. I never take time for myself. When I ask for time for myself, I have to compromise for it- give them what they want so I can get what I want- Time!

Step 13: How do you relate with others, and how do you get yourself in trouble? I am always looking to be loved without having to compromise for it. I also want to feel respected and appreciated without guilt.

Step 14: What changes are you willing to make? Stand up! Just say, "Enough is enough!" "Get you own damn pills!" "Wash your own damn dishes!"

REVERSAL

ANIMAL METAPHOR TEST #2

Step 1: Draw Two Animals with an Intensified Conflict

Step 2: Fill in the blanks

Animal #1

Type of animal: Cape Beefalo
Age: 80 **Sex:** female
Personality: Aggressive, tough, arrogant.

Animal #2

Type of animal: Dog
Age: 30 **Sex:** Female
Personality: Faithful, nervous, shy

Step 3: What are they saying?
  #1 – Get away from my babies!!
  #2 – I'm only passing thru, I won't hurt your babies.
  #1 – I will kill you if you don't get far away from my babies!
  #2 – Listen, Buffalo, it's too long and far to go around and I need to get home to my pack before dark. I promise I will not hurt your babies. I know how aggressive you are and protective of your babies, so I won't take the chance of pissing you off.
  #1—I've warned you twice- I will NOT say it again. Now make your move!!
  #2—Fine! You win. I will go around!

Step 4: What happened before? #2 was walking toward a herd of Buffalo. #1 was grazing on sweet grass as her twin calves were nursing.

Step 5: After?
#2 took the long way around with her tail between her legs. #1 continued to graze at peace.

Step 6: Title: So far away- Yet so close

Step 7a: Conflicts between themselves: They are conflicted.

Step 7b: Conflicts between them and the world: The Buffalo trusts no one and the dog makes promises that she never keeps and somehow the buffalo knows this and refuses to trust the dog.

Step 8: What changes should they make to resolve conflicts? The Buffalo should understand that not every dog is the same. Learn to trust. The dog needs to be more convincing and not give in too quickly.

Step 1: Choose a dream: Recurring
dream.

Step 2: Draw the dream:

Step 3: Describe the dream: I sleep
with a teddy bear. I always have slept
with a teddy bear. In my dream I'm
always doing something wrong with the
feeling of being caught. When I wake up
I'm standing at door half dressed holding
the hand of my teddy bear.

Step 4: Describe the participants:
Myself: anxious- curious- nervous
Male stranger- loving- caring- sweet
Parent figure- strict- demanding- angry

Step 5: What are the conflicts? I am always getting into trouble. Always afraid of getting caught.
Whomever I'm in trouble with is encouraging me to move on with it. The parent figures are
always angry with me.

Step 6: What occurrences preceded the dream? I don't know.

Step 7: Explanation of the dream: So I have this dream that reflects my life. Getting in trouble.
Looking for love and always wanting to run away.

Step 8: Do you dream a lot? Yes.

Step 9: Other dreams:
1. I'm trapped in a cave surrounded by puppies. I never want to leave. I laugh a lot in this
   dream.
2. My mother and husband pass away. I feel lost in freedom and don't know what to do.
3. Reflecting on good childhood memories.

Step 10: Connections or patterns in dreams: I don't know.

238

COMPROMISE

Step 1: Write a short story

Satyress was walking through the woods one day. She was searching for the lost infants. Only she could hear them cry. As she searched she came across a Centaur- his name was Apollo. "What are you searching for?" he asked Satyress. "I am searching for the infants. They cry to me for the milk from my breast." She answered.

Apollo looked confused. "I don't hear it. How can you?"
Saryress began to sob and with her head hanging low, she said, "I hear them cry. I never find them and my breasts respond to their cries by giving milk. I can't stop the milk from coming as long as I hear them cry."

Apollo felt sorry for her and said, "How can I help?"
Satyress responded, "My heart tells me they are Northeast past the woods, but my mind has no sense of direction."

Apollo says, "I have a great sense of direction, if you tell me the way by your heart, I will lead you to the crying children."

Satyress's eyes widened and promise filled her heart and her breast weeped more milk than ever before. She accepted the offer. Apollo and Satyress set out at sunrise thru the woods, heading northeast. By sunset that same day they came to a waterfall and Satyress's breast poured down like the waterfall. Tears flowed from her eyes and her heart weeped in pain.

"Are you alright Satyress?" asked Apollo. "The infants are here! But I can't see them! She replied. The infants' cries got louder and louder.

Apollo raced around to search all the options. Then he stopped at the bottom of the waterfalls and yelled to Saryress, "Come quick!!! I found them!" Satyress ran as fast as her hooves could take her to the waterfalls. The cries were so loud in her ears; it was almost painful to her. Apollo grabbed Satyress by the hand and took her thru the waterfall to a cave. Inside the cave there were two small infants crying. Satyress scooped them both up and they instantly latched onto her breasts. She smiled and was happy again. The infants stopped crying and Apollo left her and moved on to another adventure.

Step 2: Illustrate the story:

Step 3: Fill in the blanks:

Character#1

Character name: Satyress
Age: 20 **Sex:** female
Personality: Motherly, Caring, Naïve

Character#2

Character name: Apollo
Age: 30 **Sex:** Male
Personality: Smart, brave, adventurous.

Step 4: What happened before? Satyress was walking around in circles confused in which direction to go. Apollo was hunting for food.

Step 5: After: Apollo left Satyress and returned to the hunt. Satyress stayed at the waterfalls and let the infants feed until they were full.

Step 6: Title: Infant cry.

Step 7a: Conflicts between themselves: Satyress was conflicted by the cries of infants. Apollo was not conflicted. May be by the hunt.

Step 8: What changes should they make to resolve conflicts? Satyress needs to calm her mind and ignore the infant cries. She can't calm all the cries. Apollo should stick to what he knows best- the hunt.

Step 9: Which character do you identify with: Satyress, because sometimes I just want to help anyone/ everyone and it drives me crazy to think I can't do it all. **Other character:** Apollo reminds me of a Non-lover who thinks I can just find my way with his guidance, but he doesn't understand my heart.

Step 10: How does this pertain to you? Because all stories I write somehow pertain to me.

Step 11: What changes should you make? Get help!! Find my way on my own.

Step 12: Present a similar incident:

Step 13: How do you relate with others, and how do you get yourself in trouble? No comment.

Step 14: What changes are you willing to make? I don't know. I will keep searching to find the

240

path that leads me to good Karma.

SCRIBBLE METAPHOR

Step 1: Make a scribble

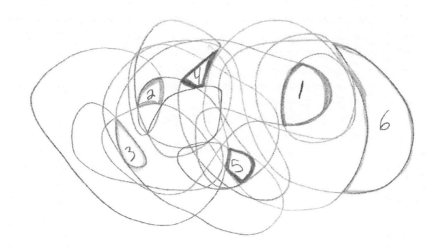

Describe the items you identified in this process:

1. Reminds me of a balloon
2. The nose of a soft bunny
3. Teardrop
4. Blood diamond
5. Lavender flower petal
6. A leaf from a flowering tree/ bush.

Elaborate on the significance of these items to you:

1. Balloons are fun and bright. They make people happy.
2. Bunny noses are sweet and I like the way they wiggle.
3. Teardrops are universal. They can represent sadness and happiness.
4. Blood diamond: a.k.a. a conflict diamond/ war diamond
5. Lavender is a natural stress reliever. It's my scent.
6. It's a leaf! Leaves represent new birth in the spring- shade in the summer- beauty in the fall- and death in the winter.

Draw a house:

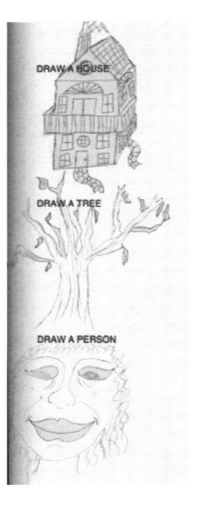

> **Things you like about the house:**
> Style, Space; The second floor deck lots of windows
>
> **Things you don't like:**
> Payments, No trees, It's non-existing

Draw a tree:

> **Things you like about the tree:**
> It's big, Strong, Beautiful
>
> **Things you don't like:**
> It's dying, The wood is in high demand, I'm too old to climb it

Draw a person:

> **Things you like about the person:**
> Happy, Bright, Positive
>
> **Things you don't like:**
> False, Bad hair, Tired

Compose a short story using the house-tree-person information:
The man worked hard and built the house of his dreams. Every nail/ screw was placed by his hands. He planted the tree in the front of the house. His children played in this tree. Then his grandchildren played around this tree. One day the man was old and alone. He hobbled out to this magnificent tree. He sat at the base of the tree, closed his eyes and let the sun warm his old, achey body. The base of this tree is the old man's resting place. The end.'

The emotionally deprived child because a grandmother concerned about her grandchildren's emotional needs. But as a wise oak se found peace of mind. Books was like composing a three act, completing the three acts of lifetime drama. "Happy bright and positive" but a bit tired she was ready to make more sacrifices.

Case Study Five

The Sun and the Troll Transformed into the Sun and the Moon
The Record of the Healing of a Therapy Resistant Cutter

Introduction and Discussion: Six Criteria in judging therapy outcome
This case study is different from other cases in the sense that it focuses on observing the outcome of the therapy. There are several measurable criteria that we may use to compare progress in therapy in this case study.

1. Comparison of the effectiveness of Power Management versus prior Cognitive Behavior Modification Therapy that was available for three years.

2. The length of the period of treatment from the inception of therapy to its termination upon the state of recovery and the 16 session duration of this recovery for at least a year without a relapse.

3. The monitoring of episodes of symptomatic behaviors, here, episodes of self-mutilation, which in this case diminished gradually to total elimination within a ten-week period.

4. The before and after session drawings reflecting the emotional impact of the first two sessions.

5. The comparison of the equivalent tests of two consecutive workbooks.

6. The patient's statements after the completion of the two workbooks and the end of therapy

The patient was a 32-year-old, married woman, in her second marriage, mother of a 6 year-old step-daughter, special ed schoolteacher, referred for an evaluation and therapy. She had a long psychiatric history, with multiple hospitalizations and she was currently in outpatient therapy prescribed multiple medications. In spite of several years of state of the art treatments at the local University inpatient and outpatient services she was still suffering of the same disabling disorder. She was suicidal and had been cutting herself compulsively. She showed me the daily record of the episodes of cutting herself. The record also indicated what triggered the episodes and the medications she was taking during that period of time.

The major trigger was that she had lost her job and the hope to return to teaching. She had been unable to work for a couple of years. She had given up hope of ever getting better and returning to work again. She had been repeatedly hospitalized for suicidal behaviors, for cutting herself obsessively, for crippling depression, anxiety, and low self-esteem. In spite of prolonged psychotherapy, multiple hospitalizations, and several antidepressant medications, she continued to obsessively cut herself and talk of suicide. She was resigned; she admitted feeling like a failure as a teacher, wife, and mother, "I am a total failure".

Upon her first visit she showed me with embarrassment her body-cutting pattern. She had been cutting herself carefully in parallel lines like a loaf of sliced wonder bread across her entire body. Scars and fresh cuts lined not only her arms, but her torso, thighs and legs.

Her therapy lasted 16 outpatient sessions during which she completed two workbooks of the Conflict Analysis Battery. The weekly insights generated from them helped her to recover from her depression and her compulsive self-destructive pattern. She was discharged from therapy without medications. She was able to handle life as usual assuming running a store business and living at home with her husband and child. She was referred to a therapist for follow up spaced out monitoring sessions. Her recovery continued for the next year.

This case study examines the therapy outcome by comparing the equivalent tests of the two workbooks a month and a half apart. The first book served as the evaluation and the base line. It revealed her relational modality as a submissive cooperative and antagonistic personality. The second or recovery book completed in the course of two months showed her progress as modifications in the respective tests reflecting her emotional growth. Upon the completion of each workbook she composed a brief review essay. The first integrated her responses along the six-role process but did not address her feelings. The essay upon termination of therapy describes her symptomatic recovery and attitude change as well as her successful emotional social adjustment.

Her prior cognitive therapy trained her in monitoring the episodes of cutting, along with the meds she was taking when she started working with me. I asked her to continue monitoring these cutting episodes and other behaviors. I also asked her to compose artwork regarding her impressions about how she felt before and after the first two sessions.

This case study is unlike other case studies as its focus is on contrasting the corresponding tests of the two consecutive workbooks illustrating her emotional growth and the change of her relational attitude. The Short Story tests of the two workbooks reflect her transformation as how the patient evolved from feeling like an ugly Troll hiding from the sun to feeling like the wise Moon looking forward to a bright day.

Patient Relational Modality Inventory provides a clear diagnostic profile of a submissive person. She scored +3 across both the cooperative and antagonistic submissive modalities, with elevated scores in the realm of psychic tension. I 'brood about things that bother me' and 'do not let others know when I am angry'. Her submissive antagonism made her helpless and resentful. The Psychic Tension was elevated and did change mildly in the second workbook. There were only subtle changes in her relational inventory from Book One to Book T. Her metaphor testing confirmed her inventory relational scores of a very polarized Submissive Cooperative and Antagonistic modality.

There are striking changes reflected in her projective tests. She completed one workbook (the evaluation record) and few weeks later she completed a second workbook (the therapy outcome record). She terminated therapy having attended the totality of 16 sessions, with full recovery from her depression and her compulsion to cut herself. She discontinued medications and returned to a well functioning state of mind. She did not return to her favorite profession, being a teacher, but she was able to assume the responsibility of running a new store and resume her life as a wife and mother in a new location.

Upon the completion of each of her two workbooks she also completed a short essay about her state of mind. So we have an accurate record of her progress following the Power Management psychodynamic therapy and can compare the effectiveness of this therapeutic modality to the prior CBT she received at the inpatient and outpatient facilities of the university hospital.

Her first essay was about her relational modality diagnosis and detecting the syndromal unfolding of her emotions along the six role-state process. At the end of a few sessions she completed the first workbook and composed the following summation of insights.

'Writing Assignment'

Essay on the Conflict Resolution Process Following, the Completion of the Evaluation

1/15/97 (client essay after third visit)

> **Stress:** The stressors I have identified through my drawings and writings center on themes of intensity, worthlessness, insignificance, and fear.

> **Response:** I have identified my typical response to stress as running away from, hiding from, or otherwise eluding stressful confrontations.

> **Anxiety:** The anxiety I feel comes in several forms, but all relate to fear, 1) guilt (fear of having done the wrong thing), 2) death (fear of dying), 3) shame (fear of social "death", anger, fear of my inability to make appropriate responses).

> **Defense:** The defenses I have identified are two-fold: one is a very hostile and aggressive reaction to a perceived threat, the other is to just give up and admit my worthlessness and inability to help others.

> **Reversal:** In the reversal exercise, some positive elements are apparent, including the ability to help myself and show love.

> **Compromise:** The compromise aspect revealed a duality of personality – the ability to exhibit traits, which are in direct conflict with one another. One side is a dark, worthless, troublesome entity, while the other is a caring, giving, responsive entity. I must learn to reconcile this duality and find a balance, which is psychologically healthy in order to reclaim my mental health.

Essay following the completion of the second workbook, end of March, 97.

'Towards recovery', four months later. Looking back at the past few years of my life, it seems as if I were a different person from who I once was, and almost the opposite of who I would hope to be.

The horrible things I have done to myself have reinforced my self-loathing and have left emotional scars on my family. I am sickened and embarrassed by my behavior: screaming tantrums, cutting and scarring my skin, biting myself, hitting myself, suicide scenarios and quasi-attempts to kill myself, fleeing and hiding from my family, swearing, throwing knives at the wall, tying my hair in knots, refusing to bathe. Who was that person, and how did she get that way?

During my therapy, I have been able to identify contributing factors to my state of emotional distress. Some of these were: a controlling mother, a critical father, self-perceived guilt for the death of my aunt, an uncommunicative step-father, a criticizing grandmother, a marriage of false pretense, a series of rapes, a severely mentally ill

246

mother-in-law, failure to attain the job I had planned for and an extremely stressful work environment.

The feelings arising from my responses to these factors in my life have created the horrible monster I became. If asked to describe myself, I would say bad, stupid, lazy, ugly, fat, mean, bitter, unwanted, worthless and a burden to those around her – better off dead.

So, after five hospitalizations for suicide, a series of medications and countless therapy sessions, has anything changed?

Yes – in degrees. I have not cut myself in a while, and think of it infrequently. I do not believe that I would actually kill myself, nor seriously threaten to, again. I am becoming more involved in my daily family life and responsibilities. I am able to take care of my young step-daughter, niece and nephew. I am not becoming overwhelmed by the major changes in my life – moving to a new home and opening a store. I am looking forward to my new job.

I am still learning to live with myself, but I think I can, I think I can, I think I can…

Before and After Images

Images about how she felt before and after her first evaluation session
Following the first session, she completed an evaluation of the impact of the session by drawing images of how she felt before and after regarding four topics: therapy, herself, her relationship with her mother, and the future. These images illustrate a dramatic change in a very short period of time. The images for her own self before the session are negative, showing conflicts with no resolution. In comparison, the pictures representing how she felt afterwards display a positive state of mind. She has become aware that there is hope and the potential of a satisfactory resolution.

Therapy:

Before: Same behaviors – no resolution.   **After:** May begin to resolve issues.

HOW CLIENT FEELS ABOUT
THERAPY

THERAPY

same behaviors –
no resolution

may begin to
resolve issues

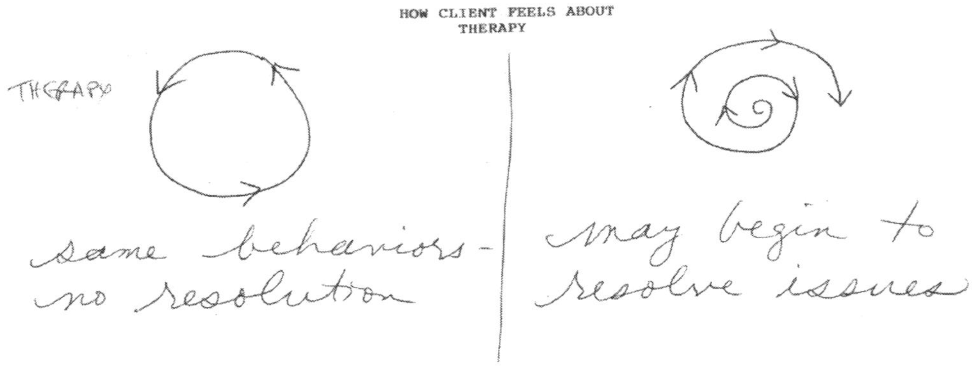

Herself:

Before: Suicidal, worthless, off the edge.   **After:** Still perilous, but somewhat grounded.

HOW CLIENY FEELS ABOUT
HERSELF

Self

suicidal, worthless,
off the edge

still perilous, but
somewhat grounded

248

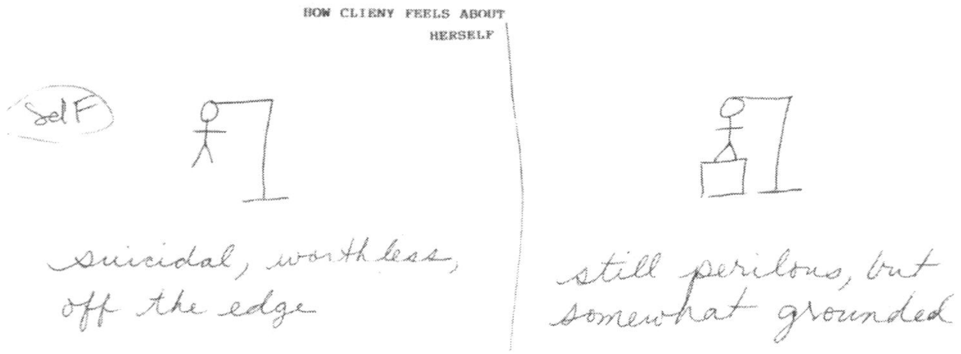

Relationship with Mother:

Before: Overpowering.

After: May be able to stand up to her with help.

HOW CLIENT FEELS ABOUT
HER RELATIONSHIP
WITH HER MOTHER

FIRST SESSION

MOTHER

overpowering

may be able to
stand up to her
with help

The Future:

Before: None.

After: Maybe there is a future.

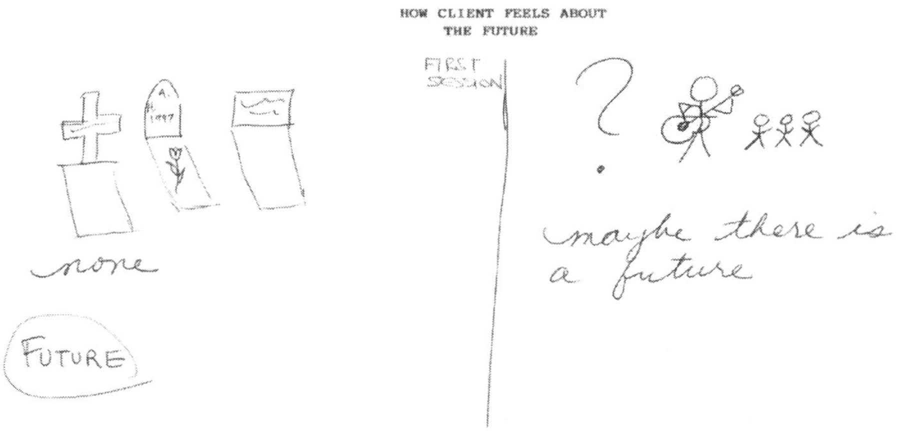

HOW CLIENT FEELS ABOUT
THE FUTURE

FIRST SESSION

FUTURE

?

maybe there is
a future

Images about how she felt before and after her second evaluation session

Therapy:

Before: Intellectual learning.   **After:** Learning I'm a big baby.

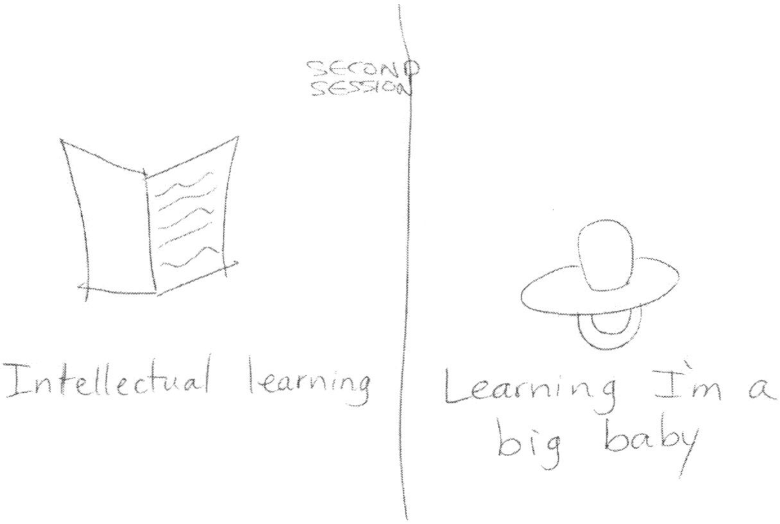

SECOND
SESSION

Intellectual learning

Learning I'm a
big baby

Herself:

Before: Average loser   **After:** Insignificant blob

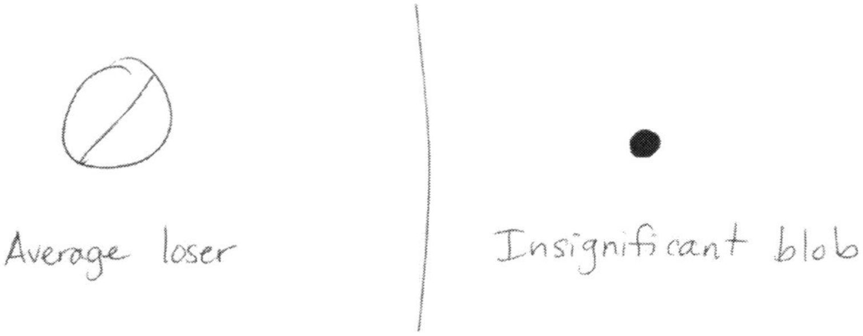

Average loser

Insignificant blob

Relationship with Mother:

Before: Friction   **After:** Friction and distance.

Friction   Friction and distance

Record of Her Episodes of Cutting
Throughout the course of her therapy, her episodes lessened dramatically. The following is a brief summarization of her episode record.

Week 1:
   Six episodes in six days. Symptoms included panic attacks, swearing, increased heart rate, drinking, screaming, cutting and urge to cut.

Week 2:
   Four episodes. Drinking, swearing, verbal tics, increased heart rate, screaming, and cutting.

Week 3:
   Two episodes. Anxiety attack, swearing, drinking, biting self, cutting.

Week 4:
   One episode. Anger at self-anxiety and feeling of dread, verbal tics, screaming, cutting.

Week 5:
   Two episodes. Stabbed self, urge to cut, verbal tics, yelling.

Week 6:
   Two episodes. Anxiety attack, **crying,** verbal tics, heavy breathing.

Transcript: Relational Modality Evaluation Scale
The profile of a submissive antagonistic relational modality diagnosis

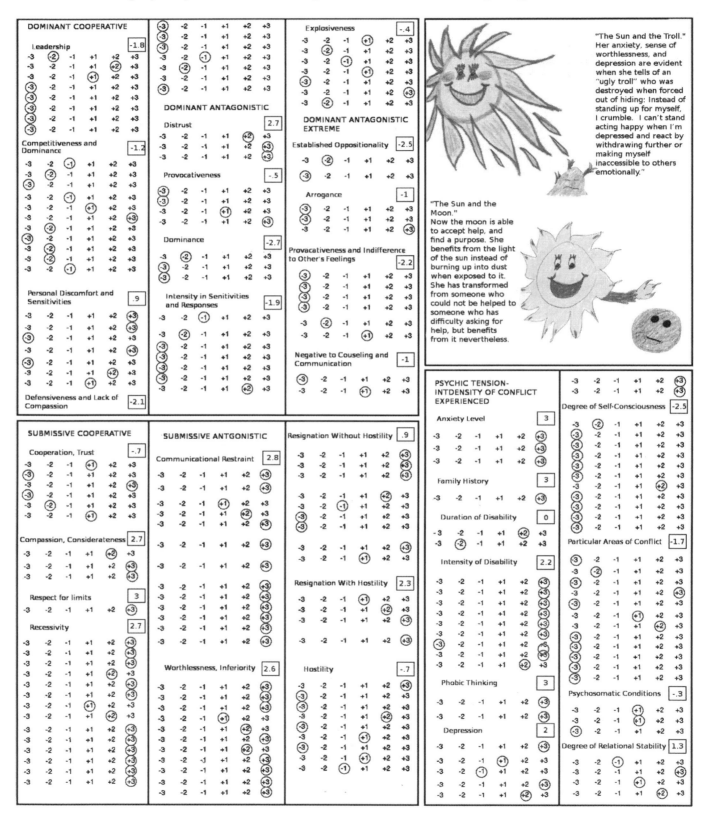

Comparison of Two Consecutive Workbooks
The Evaluation and Therapy Outcome Records

STRESS

The state of stress is presented with two tests: and the Balloons of the Family of Origin and the three Conflictual Memory Tests. These highlight the source of conflicts within her formative years.

The Family Balloon confirms that the patient saw herself as worthless and damaged. Unlike the balloons of her family members, her minuscule balloon lays helpless, popped, black, and abandoned at the bottom of the page underneath the umbrella balloon, representing her father, while her mother is presented as the counterpart, a stormy cloud unleashing rain and thunder. It is interesting to see the images of her two sisters represented by their creative works and the happy images of her loving husband and his daughter.

In the analysis of her drawings she explained her feeling controlled by her mother, and that she perceived herself as a burden on her whole family. "They are all upset in their own way and angry at me because I won't get better; I have to get better so everyone can stop worrying about me."

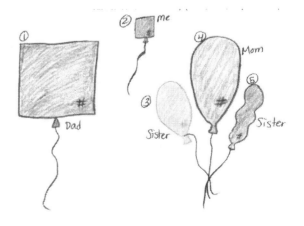

In the second workbook the Family Balloon Portrait has changed dramatically. She has been reconciled with her family. She noted what changes should be made to resolve the conflicts represented in the family: "I should stop worrying about trying to be perfect and just worry about trying to get better and be more productive." Her balloon in this portrait is still small, but undamaged and floating at a higher level that the rest of the family. This reflects her recovery from being popped and ripped apart. But here she is presented as flying high away from her attachments to the rest of the members of her family. Her balloon is square, like her father's. This connection between them is made clear in the dialog:

- Balloon #1 – "I have some responsibility for your depression."

- Balloon #2 – "I'd rather be like Dad, but not so sad and angry."

The balloon drawing reflects a noticeable change in her self-perception. The self-disgust, revulsion, and hatred is much less pervasive; she now has enough self-regard to recognize that she has needs, deserves to address them, and must address them.

Another way of portraying the family dynamics uses the metaphor of zoo animals instead of balloons to portray the family members. In the Zoo Test she presented herself as mouse in the context of her parental family and as a snake creeping away in her marital constellation. Both images reflect herself as a small, worthless, and disliked animal seeking to find an escape. In both cases the animal she identifies with is positioned at the bottom of the page, as was her first balloon.

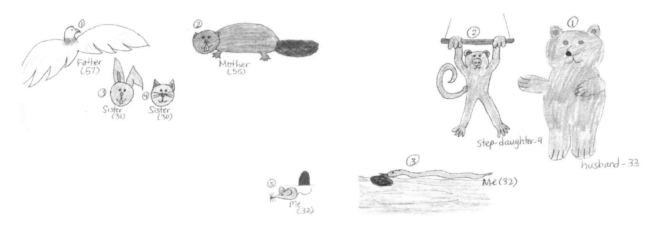

The following two tests, depicting her family of origin on the left and her marital family on the right, are also similar in that in each test she expresses her sadness at having failed the people she loves. Whether she is a mouse alone in an isolated hole, or a snake who doesn't want to play with her family her choices of animals and their lowly positioning are consistent with her worthlessness and alienation. She described herself as a mouse in her family of origin "lowly, sneaky, disliked," and as a snake in her marital family "negative, sad, disliked"

In the text she described her family of origin as "trying to pretend they were a real family," and suggested that "they should learn to spend time together without guilt, anger, and jealousy".

Sources of stress and conflict are clearly visible in

Patient A's **Conflictual Memory Test.**

Her first conflictual memory test reveals a particularly traumatic experience, a memory of loss and alienation, which provides insight into the lack of good communications in her family. She recalls watching her step-father take her sick grandmother away and then never seeing her again, parting with her without getting to say goodbye, or receiving any closure whatsoever.

Her second conflictual memories reveal several other losses compounded with self-blame. In the first, she describes an incident in which her aunt died on the way to her graduation party.

"I had changed the date of my 8th grade graduation party, selfishly – to go to a friend's party. On the day of my party, my aunt and her three children were rear-ended by a drunk driver and their car pushed into a concrete overpass headfirst. I was on the upstairs phone when my uncle told my mother what had happened to her only sister and her children. She died several days later. I killed her with my selfishness." In response to the question 'How did you feel about this person, and how did they feel about you," she writes: "I loved my aunt very much. She always treated me like a grown-up and was fun to be with. She loved me, too. She respected and liked me as a person."

The patient blamed herself for the death of her favorite aunt: "I felt totally responsible for her death--still do. If I had not been selfish, she and the kids would not have been in that accident."

This incident was not mentioned in the first book. The fact that she was able to discuss this memory is a testimony to the effectiveness of the workbook. By this point, she was more willing and comfortable with looking inside herself. In a later conflictual memory she related the strong impact of this experience: "I was wearing a cross, [and] a high-school peer asked "what does that mean?" I said "Jesus died on the cross!" He said "If your mother died in a car accident, would you

wear a car on your neck?" She did such a drawing stating: "I feel I should wear a car to remind me of my Aunt's death." A recent memory of conflict illustrated a bloody hand. "I cut my wrist on what I thought was a vein," she writes. "I wanted to die, but I was afraid. It scares me to know how desperate I can become."

RESPONSE

MASK 1

The response to the stress is illustrated in the mask metaphor.

The first mask is a paper bag over her head with two small eye-holes. It represents her worthlessness.

The second book's mask's is a tapestry divided into positive and negative sides. It shows her transformation. She goes from being stuck inside a conflict, to realizing that there may be a way to find a resolution. The paper-bag mask changed to a tapestry with an eye peeking through, someone who is willing to acknowledge the positive alongside the negative, as opposed to only the negative. Her response is split between hiding and revealing a funny side.
\

Book 1, Mask 1, RESPONSE   **Book 2, Mask, RESPONSE**

ANXIETY

Masks II and III in her first book show the conflict she carried inside. The face under the mask is represented by various negative images, e.g. a skull-and-crossbones labeled 'DANGER,' and band-aid labeled 'HURT.' Her heart is drawn with a hole in the center, clearly displaying her feelings of being empty and feeling the void. She writes: "The hole is the missing piece of my life. I feel incomplete, unfinished, not a whole person. I need to find what I am missing. I allow outside influences and inner weakness to destroy me. I run and hide from the bad, but make my life worse in the process…[I should] try to stop feeling so jealous and useless."

In the second book her Transparent Mask completed in January of 1998, the mask, titled "Peeking Through the Tapestry", shows a tapestry (the mask) with two "dark", "evil eyes", and a single round, searching eye, peeking out from behind the tapestry. She underscores the drawing with this: "The side with one small eyeball shows a glimmer of hope. The side with 2 evil eyes shows anger, fear, mistrust." In reflecting on this mask further, the patient notes that "more is seen through the negative side, but some things retain a small hope" and states that this mask represents that "both good and evil can exist together." This is a marked change from her mask in her first booklet.

Book 1

Mask 2: *Feelings*   **Mask 3:** *What is in your heart*

Book 2

ANXIETY

The sequence of masks in the second booklet is titled "Pull Back the Curtain", and while she writes that she "does not accept the positive without worrying about the negative" this "pulling back" of the curtain of her pain and self-hatred seems to be a true beginning of change. Presented here is her new-found willingness to acknowledge her ability to perceive small "glimmers of hope", which in turn, yield positive changes in her life. Her portrayals of what is beneath the mask and what is in the mask wearer's heart show similar transformations. These drawings and her interpretation of them still indicate a serious amount of pain and grief, all markedly impacted by "dark" and "evil" shaded in areas, but there is the new component of the hope and the coexistence of good and evil, as opposed to evil's saturation of her world with hopelessness.

THE ANIMAL METAPHOR TEST
The test asks the test-taker to draw two animals, write a story about said animals, and reflect on how the story pertains to the test-taker's own life. Her first Animal Metaphor she created a tale between a "strong, powerful, vicious, confident, sly" wolf that spews verbal insults at a "hurt, scared, stunned, helpless, confused" bird with a broken wing. She titles this tale: "Broken Wing-- Broken Heart."

The dialog between the wolf and the bird goes as follows:

> **Wolf** – "You are worthless-- I am more powerful than you."
> **Bird** – "Yes, you are right. I don't deserve to live."
> **Wolf** – "You are very bad and should be punished."
> **Bird** – "Yes, that is true. I have done many bad things and deserve all the bad things that happen to me."

In accordance with her inventory, she identifies with the submissive, hurting disabled bird. Akin to the bird, she feels worthless and broken--unable to fly: "I want to fly away from my problems, but can't. I feel I can't help myself…I feel like my problems will not go away, leaving me helpless to defend myself from those who don't accept me." In her mind, she is "not even fit to be killed." Although she acknowledges that she needs to correct her maladaptive thought patterns, she also communicates the belief that she will always be inferior and that her problems can never be resolved. She is convinced, and reiterates this throughout this initial test that she is beyond help. The story of the wolf and the bird ends when the wolf departs, deeming the bird unfit for consumption.

Her second animal metaphor shows a shift in role-play to a more active role positioning, which, though slight, represents a positive shift from a much more hopeless, wounded bird that cannot fly.

In this metaphor test, titled "The Unwanted Turtle", a "fierce, brave, and strong" lion bullies a "meek, slow, scared" turtle.

> **Lion** – "Get out of my forest."
> **Turtle** – "Ok, I'm going."
> **Lion** – "Get out NOW."
> **Turtle** – "I'm trying to."
> **Lion** – "Move faster."
> **Turtle** – "I'm moving as fast as I can."
> **Lion** – "You're lazy and a liar."
> **Turtle** – "I'm sorry to upset you. I'm just being myself."

While the turtle in this sequence concedes that she is sorry for upsetting the lion and will indeed get out of his forest, she defends herself somewhat by saying that she is moving as fast as she can and that she is just being herself. She writes that "the lion should stop bossing others around" and that the "turtle should stand up for her rights".

Her animal metaphor reflects the same shift from the passive victim of the anxiety phase to playing a more defensive and active role in her recovery, however slight these role shifts may be.

This seems a fitting metaphor to illustrate a slow but steady journey on the path to recovery. The turtle is progressing slowly, and though others may not like it, she is doing the best she can. The inclination to "hide" which is very clear in the first booklet still holds true here, but hiding in her own built-in shell seems to be a more adaptive and in-control response than fleeing to remote caves or dying. She begins to acknowledge in this second book that, sometimes, she needs to isolate herself from others. This is a self-protective measure, however, enabling her to stay focused on recovery from self-destructive behavior stemming from her feeling disgusting, hated, useless, and "nasty". For example, in reflecting on a real life event in which her mother shot down some of her hopes, discouraging her from working towards the completion of a project, she notes that it may be better, from now on, if she can "keep [her] ideas to [her]self and just talk to [her husband] about them so [she] won't keep getting hurt and feeling betrayed."

The rejecting lion represents her mother, the dark stormy cloud, and the wolf of the first metaphor.

Book 1

A FAIRYTALE

As in previous tests, when prompted to draw and compose a story with two fairy tale characters, she identifies with the character that is "lonely, desperate, longing and sad…trapped in a secluded place". In her fairy tale metaphor, Prince Charming has come to rescue the trapped and frightened Rapunzel, but the long-haired woman is not certain she wants to be rescued.

The following is the dialogue between this Rapunzel and this Prince:

> **Rapunzel** – "Get me out of here, I'm scared!"
> **Prince** – "I'll try, but you have to help me."
> **Rapunzel** – "How am I supposed to help?"
> **Prince** – Help me up, and don't let me fall."
> **Rapunzel** – "What if I can't help you?"
> **Prince** – "Then you'll have to stay up there forever."
> **Rapunzel** – "Maybe that would be what I need."

Like Rapunzel, she feels isolated and ambivalent about the possibility of rescue and survival outside her secluded fortress. The similarity of their respective situations is very clear. In her answer to step 12, which prompts 'present an incident, similar to what transpired in your metaphor story, to illustrate your particular pattern,' she writes "I was hiding away, cutting myself, making a noose, throwing knives. I kept hanging up the phone when my family called, concerned. I refused help; refused to accept to choose life."

She writes that "Rapunzel is trying to decide to live or die…[she] is afraid of living in the real world--she feels it is a dangerous place." The patient is unsure that she deserves to live a happy life, if such a thing is possible, and even doubts whether she is worthy of living at all. She concludes this test by writing, "[I need to] make a decision/commitment to living and get on with it."

REVERSAL

DREAM METAPHORS

In contrast to the helpless and isolated Rapunzel and Rat characters, the dream analysis in book one reverses some of the negative patterns and presents a much more positive scenario in which she is appreciated and welcomed. This dream takes place at a Kindergarten where she encounters two other teachers and a student. The feelings expressed in this test are markedly different from those enumerated in the other tests. In this dream, she is "happy, relieved, relaxed" because she has obtained a desired vocation and feels appreciated. Perhaps this is an indication that she should return to her profession as a special ed. teacher. She answers the question 'attempt to give an explanation of this dream' by saying: "I plan on getting a job with younger children…I think I will enjoy a new job and will be well-liked by the children."

Her dream as represented in the second workbook harkens back to her first marriage and abusive relationship with her ex-husband. She writes: "I dreamed that my ex-husband was dead. At first I felt scared and sad, then I felt relieved."

In thinking about the significance of the dream, she hypothesizes that its content indicates that "[she] still ha[s] not been able to put [her] first marriage behind [her]… [She] still ha[s] guilty feelings about hurting the family." The intensified animal metaphor and the dream exercise recall memories of being helpless, attacked, and trapped, and remind one intensely of the metaphors of the first book, where she was far more hopeless and self-hating than she seems to be in book two.

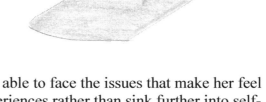

The dreams have a healing, cathartic effect, as she is able to face the issues that make her feel guilty and is able to reconcile herself with those experiences rather than sink further into self-loathing.

The trend of positive shifts in self-perception seem to reverse and regress in her Intensified Animal Metaphor Test, a negative setback which make sense when contextualized in the reversal phase, which prompts the test taker to experience more stress in constructing a metaphor. At this point she failed the 'more stress' test.

In the only intensified metaphor we have, presented in the second book, she composed a metaphor of self defeat: titled "Mercy Killing", the rat has no shell to hide in: she cannot save herself, nor can anyone else save her. The boa constrictor squeezes her to death, taking the rat "out of [its] misery".

Boa – "I've got you now!"
Rat – "Help!"
Boa – "There's no way out: I'm going to kill you!"
Rat – "Can't anyone help me?"
Boa – "You are powerless against me."
Rat – "I give up – do what you will."
Boa – "Any last words?"
Rat – "Thank you for taking me out of my misery."

She writes that "The rat doesn't bother hiding so well, as she is indifferent about her life. The rat feels powerless and gives up when there is no help from others".

COMPROMISE

SHORT STORY

A tone of resolution is illustrated in observing the evolution between her Short Story Test in books 1 and 2. In her first workbook, her short story encapsulates nearly all of her unresolved tension. Her anxiety, sense of worthlessness, and depression are evident when she tells of an "ugly troll" who was destroyed when forced out of hiding.

The following is her short story in its entirety:

Who Needs a Troll?

Once upon a time there was an ugly, evil troll whom everyone hated. Each day, the sun came out and tried to shine upon all the creatures, including the troll.

When the sun shone down, the troll would run and hide – in a dark hole; under a bridge; deep in the forest; anywhere the sun could not touch.

Each day the sun would try to catch the troll before it could hide away. The troll always hid too fast, and avoided the sun.

One day, the sun was desperate to shine its light upon the ugly, disgusting troll. The sun thought it could change the troll into a happier creature.

So the sun rose up early while the troll was sleeping, and shone upon the evil creature.

Touched by goodness, the evil troll caught fire, burned hot and glowing, then all was left was a pile of dingy, grey cinders.

The sun called its friend the wind, who blew the cinders and scattered them to places all over the world.

No one cared and no one missed the nasty troll.

"Who needs a troll?" she asks. This inquiry corresponds with her belief that she is nasty and that no one would miss her if she were to disappear. As Rapunzel was better off living alone in her tower, she too maintains that it would have been better if "The Sun [left]...the troll alone and let it live in darkness." She easily applies this story to her own life. She is frustrated by individuals who demand that she feign cheeriness and wishes that she could "hide better". In answer to the question "how does this short story pertain to you?" she writes, "I cannot endure too much forced cheerfulness. I feel like I will die if forced to act like something I am not."

In further questions, she continues to relate the story and the characters to her own life: "My mother is constantly after me to 'cheer up' and 'snap out of it,' which only serves to make me feel more depressed and guilty…Instead of standing up for myself, I crumble. I can't stand acting happy when I'm depressed and react by withdrawing further or making myself inaccessible to others emotionally." In answer to the question 'What changes should you make to resolve your conflicts?' she suggests "hide better." Thus, the concluding compromise arrived at in her first assessment book is one of defeat, death, and retreat into complete obscurity. This is a compromise that indicates a high level of emotional conflict and need for emotional resolution. She managed to achieve it in the next workbook.

In the second assessment book, which was completed within two months of the first, there are noticeable changes in her self-perception and world perception within the metaphorical exercises outlined in the testing booklet. The major stresses and tensions presented in the first book are still pertinent in the second, but the six step process of conflict resolution worked out in her creative assessment tasks seem one step closer to a healthier compromise.

The compromise and final step of the sequence is a positive one, which seems to bring her out of the darkness again. In the first workbook, she still was having difficulty thinking any change or any positive help was possible. Now she writes: "I don't make my needs known. I wait for others to offer help".. "I should be more direct about making my needs known."

This shift in being able to ask and accept help is the most illuminated and positive change conveyed in this second booklet, which she says is best illustrated in her short story about the sun and the moon. In her initial short story, recall that the sun tries to help the "nasty troll", who cannot be helped and is only hurt further when the sun tries to light up his life. The sun, in trying to help, ends up incinerating the troll, who is then forgotten, lost dust on the wind.

In the second short story she completed, called "Giving the Moon Its Glow" the sun returns as the bright and purposeful figure on the left side of the page. Instead of a slit-eyed, frowning lump of troll in the right corner there now is a wide eyed, sad, and lost looking moon. While the moon is still situated below the sun, its size and position on the page suggests a much closer status or more equal worth. Now the patient as the moon is able to accept help, and find a purpose. She benefits from the light of the sun instead of burning up into dust when exposed to it.

Giving The Moon Its Glow
The Sun and the Moon were sisters. The sun was bright and cheerful and used its powerful rays to greet people to a new day, make the flowers grow, make life on earth possible with its warmth. The moon was cold and dark. It just hung in the sky, watching the glory of the sun. It had no light to shine upon the world, so nobody even knew it was there.

One day the moon was feeling very sad about being unknown and useless. Her sister, Sun, decided to share some of its light when it was resting.

Now the moon shone brightly at night, showing itself in the sky as a promise of a new day to come! It even learned to change its shape so people could use it to measure time! It found that with help from the sun, it had its own purpose.

Conclusion

She draws meaning from the story, saying that "[she is] reluctant to help [her] self and ha[s] no self-worth. [She] can only become someone useful with the help of others." The patient made significant steps in self-acceptance. "I should learn to accept my limitations and be satisfied with who I am.".. "The Moon should start to form its own identity and find ways to be useful...I will try not to depend on others so much."

Book 1
Metaphor Profile

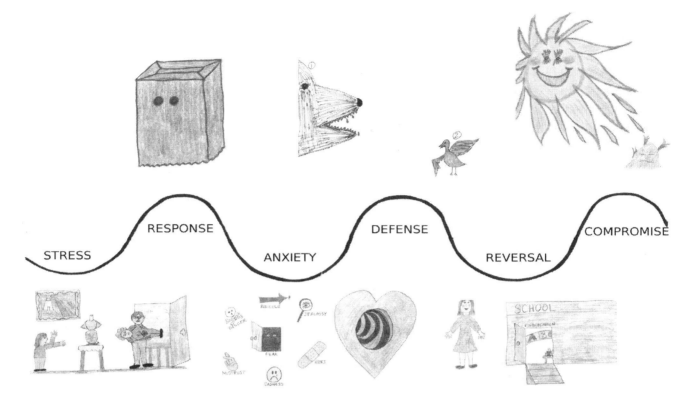

Stress:
Losing her loving grandmother.

Response:
Mask is a bag over her head.

Anxiety:
A list of traumas and negative feelings, followed by an empty heart.

Defense:
Open mouth of a wolf despises helpless, worthless bird with broken wing.

Reversal:
Dreaming of teaching again.

Compromise:
Sun and troll afraid of light, burning with flames over his head.

Book 2
Metaphor Profile

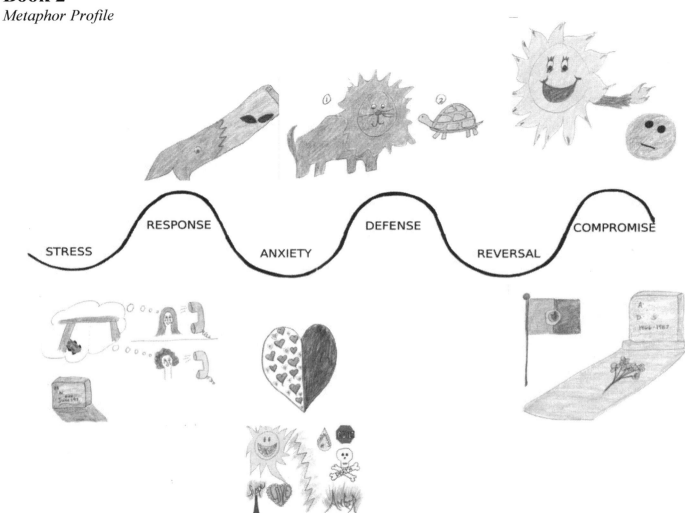

Stress:
Losing loving
aunt in an
accident upon
her
graduation,
and blaming
herself as
responsible
for her death.

Response:
Balance
between
positive and
negative
feelings.

Anxiety:
Heart is
alive but
divided by
pain and
healing.

Defense:
Turtle gets
out of the
way of cruel
lion

Reversal:
Dream about
ex-husbands
death.

Compromise:
Modification of
characters: Sun
and troll now as
moon sharing
control of
universe, moon
shining at night

Submissive Case Study Six
The Vulture and the Snake
Monitoring the Outcome of Long Term Therapy

Introduction, Relational Modality Diagnosis and the Choice of Clinical Symptoms
This case study illustrates the communicational problem of subordinacy relational modalities generating psychopathology, how in this case the blockage of communications is compensated by the development of a secret activity, which eventually becomes an eating disorder. It also demonstrates that the treatment of the specific illness must address the underlying subordinacy disorder as conflict energy channeled to the behavioral pattern that has gone out of control.

The study explores the therapeutic intervention of assertiveness and monitoring the patient's progress utilizing the metaphor process. The observation of one single type of metaphor, the Animal Metaphor Test, delivered periodically during her therapy and the related texts became the measuring rod for the gradual shift of focus away from food and into feelings. We can see her therapy as the challenge of shifting the focus from managing/controlling the eating disorder to correcting the power imbalance in social transactions. The dramatic eating illness was then a problem of subordinacy: a communicational or power management disorder.

Gladys was a smart and gracious pleasant, somewhat giddy, middle aged woman, who came to therapy for an eating disorder that began in her childhood years. She was very self-conscious of her weight. Following the assessment she continued on a routine of completing animal metaphors practically at every session she attended. It was her choice to use the device as a means of sharing her preoccupations. At some point, early in therapy, she brought to our sessions poems she composed in parallel to the metaphors. The poems like the metaphors wrote themselves. The poems amplified the expression of feelings more directly, than the conflicts illustrated in her metaphors. There was though subtle continuity in her metaphors that allowed us at the end of her therapy to look back at the therapeutic experience as a progression of conflict resolutions leading from secret empowerment through defiance by binging to empowerment through effective communication of feelings and the reduction of the preoccupation with food.

Pursuing assertiveness is not easy. The cumulative analysis of her metaphors helps to examine in a retrospective the evolution of the therapy as a progression to assertiveness. The communicational problem was center stage in both the ongoing AMTs and in the content of her poetry. Her art record reflects the struggle in the course of her long-term therapeutic experience from becoming aware of the underlying problem to becoming able to correct it.

Her metaphors represent the accurate clinical record of what occurred in the therapy as a completed story. We distinguish four phases in the dialectic evolution of her metaphors as sequences of conflict resolutions in the course of her therapy. We detect the formal structure of the metaphors integrating her associations as a four phase series: the evaluation is the first, followed by three interrelated conflict resolution phases. The story evolved as having a beginning, recognizing the power imbalance due to her relational modality of submissive antagonism as the moat separating expressed and repressed, a middle, the activation of the eating disorder upon an encounter with an authority figure as the battle between the vulture and the snake, and the end, her developing skills of appropriate power management as the direct and honest exploration of thoughts and feelings.

Phase I the assessment with all the tests, the Evaluation: Binging as personal empowerment through secret defiance of parental authorities

The routine assessment revealed her personality as a submissive cooperative and antagonistic person. Her projectives revealed her preoccupation with food, secret binging, as the means of a very submissive girl defying her forbidding parents, who were very fixated themselves on proper eating controls. In this phase we diagnose not only an eating disorder but its cause as the underlying relational problem: her submissive antagonistic relational modality. The eating disorder was identifiable throughout all her metaphors. But in them we can clearly also identify the relational modality pattern, her difficulty with communicating her feelings, expression of which scared her as the fear of loosing control of her anger and destroying her family.

Her Childhood Conflictual Memory was about valuing food, bringing a triple-decker sandwich to her sick mother, but being criticized about it by her grand mother.

The Transparent Mask Test started with the mask of the perpetual smile. A well made up façade covered her mouth as a black hole. At a deeper level in her heart we see the underlying relational modality communications problem as a divide between smiles and flowers, next to somber feelings, cruel teeth, dark clouds, stormy skies…The divide between the two sets of feelings was a moat. The moat theme illustrated the block in the communication of her feelings. The difficulty morphed in the use of the mouth to eat rather than talk but binging was defiance to authorities and a form of secret empowerment.

The impaired expression of feelings manifested in her animal metaphor as animals turned their backs to each other and to the viewer.

It was also dangerous to express her feelings as presented in her Short Story of a fiery dragon burning little animals to a crisp. She was afraid of losing control of her anger like in one occasion banging her son's head on the kitchen floor.

The evaluation identified the block of communications or power assumption, and its manifestation as an eating disorder, the secret empowerment. The eating disorder then was secondary to a power disorder caused by her innate relational modality. The modality was the impediment for good communications and it was transforming interpersonal unresolved conflicts into activating the focus on the eating pattern as defiance to the parental authorities.

Phase II: Therapy dealing with the theme of the moat, symbolically illustrating her difficulty in communicating feelings.

The counterpart elements became animals representing emotions struggling with each other across the moat. Authoritarian, parental figures on the one side, herself on the other she was transformed from a bunny to a soaring eagle reflecting her subtle personal growth as self-awareness. The discovery of this cover up of feelings reflected in the moat symbolism was addressed by improving her communications at a symbolic level but not in relations in general. These moat metaphors reflected her discreet need for parental approval. She never matured in self-confidence. Her drama was intensified as she sought approval by fasting.

Phase III: The Vulture and Snake period, an interpersonal conflict activating the eating disorder.

Gladys was very impressed by a woman co-therapist in our group therapy sessions. Her response to this new authority was to seek approval through control of her eating. The encounter was dealt by anorexic control of her behaviors. Her anorexic period was followed by uncontrollable binging leading to the escalation of her eating disorder as reflected in her vulture versus snake series of metaphors. She controlled her eating wishing to be thin like a snake and then lost control and binged like a vulture. The disorder precipitated a medical crisis for which she was hospitalized. This led to a turn in her therapy. Her resolution manifested with a jaguar, who killed both the snake and the vulture. The jaguar attitude is the departure for a new quest for assertiveness.

Phase IV: Expressing feelings, Dealing with people effectively, social empowerment as the treatment of choice for the eating disorder

The alternative to binging and purging was dealing assertively with people by voicing her distinct feelings in a succession of relationships from the past and the present. The sequence dealt with hurt feelings in a variety of important relationships. She made strides communicating feelings. First, she dealt with feelings of rejection by her mother, cast out of mother Kangaroo's pouch for her sibling. She resented her mother's favoring her brother. The Centaur and Mermaid metaphor reviews her relationship with her father; Gila Monster and Rabbit, her relationship with her business associate; Sheep and Bull, her relationship with her husband; Ostrich and Griffin, the relationship of her two identities. She created new species of animals integrating her many identities. Achieving honesty coincided with her new identity as a playful dolphin. In this series of metaphors Gladys accepted responsibility for her life, for resolving her relationship with her father, correcting her relationship with her daughter-in-law, dealing with a co-worker at the office and accepting responsibility for bringing her therapy to completion.

Graphically the resolution of conflicts is presented with a number of symbolic changes. The animals of the new metaphors are (1) not separated by a river, (2) they are of similar size, she is attempting to integrate her many identities but she recognizes many irreconcilable aspects of her being, and (3) she addresses issues about daily conflicts. It is remarkable how clearly her statements articulated her need for sharing feelings as well as the acceptance of her multiple identities, the hidden aspects of herself. This development coincided with the end of her therapy. Gladys managed to withdraw successfully from drinking and binging while intercepting the difficulties she encountered in her multiple relationships. From powerlessness she emerged to power through the brave and honest expression of feelings. Her images identified hurtful experiences. This phase squarely addressed the impasse in her marital relationship leading to the integration of her multiple identities and the reduction of her secret preoccupation with food. This coincided with her telling her husband the truth: 'we can fight but be friends again.' Her eating disorder was resolved through her gradual gains in dealing with feelings assertively.

Gladys' eating disorder masked the relational power imbalance. Her therapy had addressed not her symptoms of eating controls but her relational modality as new skills in power management. The origin of the problem was in her disposition to hold feelings in. This had led to an emotional behavioral imbalance and the eating was a conflictual assertion, binging was her compensatory self-indulgence. She could be disobedient by sneaking forbidden food frowned upon by her grandmother and mother. Binging was her symbolic assertiveness that had evolved at an early age to represent her identity. Then controlling her eating predictably led to loosing control. The illness was the loss of control over her favorite escape. Her dreaded anger manifested as parental subterfuge with secret eating habits had become a real illness, an eating disorder. But the pathogenesis and the therapeutic undoing of that hinged on undoing her submissive antagonistic approach to dealing with people.

Wellness coincided with assertiveness as the goal of her therapy, manifested as the honest non-hostile communication of feelings. While the eating disorder was under control she still had difficulty extricating herself from a passive aggressive way of handling communications even in our own relationship. This modality was never dealt clearly with me. She avoided dealing with her antagonism towards me.

This study demonstrates that clinical symptoms are not the illness but the symptoms of the underlying power disorder: the decompensation of the relational modality, a wellness diagnosis; here symptoms were generated by the relational modality of submissive antagonism. This modality inhibits the expression of negative feelings. She was inhibited from an early age; her eating disorder was a fixation formed at an early age as she rebelled by asserting herself through mischievous compensatory behaviors in the conflictual area of binge eating. Her punishment for binging was becoming fat and seeking treatments to undo it.

Because of her submissive modality she functioned in a passive antagonistic mode, depending on approval from others, yet consistently undermining her partners by secretly assuming her independence through self-gratification. Therapy helped her to assert herself by being honest; this was the function of her therapy and of her poetry, her spontaneous healing mechanism. This was the means for her liking herself. This evolution to self-esteem was a tough and slow process.

This power management therapy taught her to communicate her emotions lessening the energy that fueled the eating obsession. Wellness was achieved as she became comfortable in the flow of emotions through the channels of creativity initiated through the metaphor testing. Therapy reduced her eating disorder by encouraging her to express her feelings. She benefited from the use of her spontaneous creativity in the form of poetry. The gift of poetry helped her to articulate her innermost feelings and to gain self-confidence as the alternative to craving parental approval.

Several patients evolved from the workbook of metaphors to sincere interest in the arts. Gladys is a good representative of this development. In her case, poetry became part of her life. It freed the expression of her pent-up feelings. Her poetry was eloquent and meaningful, reflecting the intensity of the unresolved conflicts in parallel with her discussing them in the metaphor testing.

The art, from a means of structured therapy, became the means of the outpouring of her bottled up feelings and self-doubts. The successful expression of her feelings helped her healing. She evolved a sense of self by experiencing the satisfaction of discovering that she was talented. This self-esteem solidified the assertiveness that she learned to value in the course of her therapy. This case study then attests to the role of creativity not only as a vehicle of insights, but as the means of therapeutic change. Through it she challenged the sacrosanct world of her authorities. Creativity manifests often in people with submissive personality. Here we should note the difference between the metaphor testing and creativity as poetry. The metaphors have a healing direction evolving from insight, to accepting responsibility for oneself, to thinking of making changes. Poetry can be problematic as self-indulgence in expression without moral direction. In the case of her favorite poet it had led to a suicide.

Personal Essay
An Autobiography Illustrated by Metaphors

Chapter One

I was not born fat. But I spent most of my life fat. Fat consumed me. Fat made me hide. Fat made me lie. My entire life was ruled by fat with but one desire--to be thin.

It must have happened somewhere in grammar school. I have very few memories of ever being not fat. My Girl Scout uniform was a "Chubette." I looked like a green wave in my camp shorts. Usually a very obedient child, I ran from the classroom that day we were being weighed. How could I live if my classmates knew my weight? Such degradation. Such shame.

Shame was instilled in me early on. (The "toxic" shame that John Bradshaw speaks of.) How do we "learn" shame? By an unthinking mother. My brother (2 1/2 years older) and I had a childhood friend, Billy. In the midst of our playing one day, I said, "Wait for me, I have to go to the bathroom." Mother pounced on that. "You never tell anyone, especially boys, that you are going to the bathroom." To this day, I am still embarrassed, or shamed, to "go to the bathroom" if anyone, especially a male, is about.

Shame was also etched into my psyche by my father. We never locked our back door. Always the front door, never the back door. Alone in that large, old house one night, I was scared. Strange sounds emanated from cellar to attic. Could I be so bold as to lock the back door? I did. I felt safe. Imagine my parents' chagrin upon reaching home and being locked out! None of us carried keys. I was awakened by their knocking and shouting. Father asked me, "Were you afraid of being stolen?" Such shame overwhelmed me. I was unfit to be the brave daughter of this god, my father. On the rare occasion today that I lock the back door, I am still swallowed in a sea of shame. The front door is always locked.

Brothers can activate shame. Again involving our friend Billy. After Billy moved away, my brother and I were invited to spend a weekend with his family. It was late winter. My mother packed my clothes. Eddie, my brother, and Billy were in the bedroom while I unpacked. Eddie drew from the suitcase a pair of woolen, almost-to-the-knee "undies." He held them up (they were peach colored--I still dislike that color) at arm's length and chortled. Billy also chortled. I wanted to evaporate. My mother was still at it even after I was a wife and mother. Mother was an excellent cook. We often "went to Grandma's house" for holidays. The extremely caloric and delicious-looking dessert was always presented with a flourish. Mother would pause, look at her only daughter and proclaim, "You, of course, don't want any." Shame on you, daughter dear, you are fat--you cannot share my offering, was, of course, the message I received. Engulfed in shame, I would eat everything in my house when I got home.

Shame was most insidious when I deposited it on myself. The better part of my life was spent trying to impress and please my father. Although in many childhood areas I think I did this. I was the baseball nut, not my brother. I had a regulation score book and scored the NY Giants games whilst listening to the radio. The Mets get my attention now. Baseball was one of the few topics I could safely discuss with my father. Many of his opinions were drivel to me. But, of course, I could not dissent. That would be shameful.

My grammar school grades were great. Graduated salutatorian. My brother, with his lousy grades, was sent away to prep school. Did I envy him his glamorous military school life away from home? My high school grades plummeted to the ocean floor. My memories of those four years are: fat, shame, rebellion, fat, hate for my parents, hate for me, and more fat and shame.

During my teenage years there was scant exchange with my parents. After dinner, I immediately withdrew to my room, my Maginot Line. It too was violated. After my clandestine visits to the bakery shop, I would stash the empty boxes in a drawer, waiting for a chance to discard the evidence of my eating, my shame. Upon reaching my haven one day, I was stunned by an overwhelming sight. These "binge boxes" were piled on the floor in the middle of the room. My mother did this and never said a word to me about this sin of sins. If shame could kill, I died.

Never let it be said my not-fat mother and father were not in touch with my fat. Many dollars were fed to various doctors in an effort to rid me of my fat. These efforts were all abysmal failures.

Innumerable diets were spawned over the ensuing years. At times I was almost "normal" in weight. But never quite. This was elusive. Many times I nearly grasped it, only to have it slip away with the tide.

I married. A most aloof and uncommunicative person, such as I. He was MAN, I was woman. He now shared the pedestal with my father. There were two gods to please.

As my weight bounced up and down, he never disparaged me. No remarks were ever made about my eating. Of course, most of my eating, and certainly all of my binging, was done in solitude.

As was most of my thinking. We were both unto ourselves. Meaningful, intimate, heart-to-heart talk was rare. Not surprising, it was a continuum of my rearing.

From this lopsided union, three sons were born. The eldest to die before age twenty-and-one in an auto crash. Our third son was born two days before our first son's fourth birthday. I was not child-oriented. My vague, far-off plan had been to someday have two children, a he and a she. It was both shocking and dismaying to be pregnant. I loathed every month. I was misshapen, fat again and again and again. But they were mine and life went on.

Until a clear, cold day in February when our first-born died. The puppy-size rift that existed between my husband and I rapidly matured into mastiff-size. It was as though we had all died. All four of us grieved unto ourselves. Each created their own barrier to pain and disbelief. We accepted not, we shared not.

At the time of the accident, I was relatively thin for me. I was just completing one of the better-known weight loss programs. Seventy pounds were shed. Within the next year or so, I gained ninety. Again, I was fat. Again the travail of losing and gaining and finding the diet that would work. I found it. I became almost-thin. I delighted in it. My husband never said a word during these whopping losses, gains and losses. But I did please the other god. My father was enthused with my thinner body.

Within eighteen months of becoming an almost-thin person, I did something totally out of character. I bought a franchised weight loss business. My husband went along with me, my father was appalled. "You must be dumb to leave your job with all those great benefits." At the same time, he loaned me money to buy the place!

This step toward independence proved to be dangerous. In my new business, I was surrounded by food. Food and fat-people-wanting-to-be-thin pervaded my waking hours. It permeated my dreams. It drove me to eat. It drove me away from the scale. It haunted me. It nearly destroyed me. A weight loss counselor may not be fat. I was becoming fat again. The parent company would slap my hand and say, "Shame on you. You must be thin."

This Is How I Got Where I Was At. It led me to therapy.

Chapter Two
My Mask, My Cloak

My reason for seeking professional help was, you guessed it, my fat. Give therapy a few weeks and I'd be that thin person I always yearned for.

Each passing week brought forth pain, confusion and bleakness, but given at the start of my therapy, no thinness. It became apparent, via the tests given at the start of my therapy, that my fat was but my insulation, my buffer zone, against the world. Of deeper significance, was my perpetual smile and happy mien presented to the outside world. This defense had been in place for many years. Fat and complaisancey were my bed partners. As a fat person I could not draw attention to me. A low profile was essential. Smile, Smile. Anger must be hidden at all cost.

The conflictual memory captured my inner conflict, food as my initiative, my identity versus obedience.

PHASE I
In the evaluation process, Gladys connected being chastised by her grandmother to having a black hole for a mouth, as well as becoming a fire-breathing dragon afraid of hurting her loved ones. In the process she admitted her problem of repression of emotions: 'Express rather than repress.'

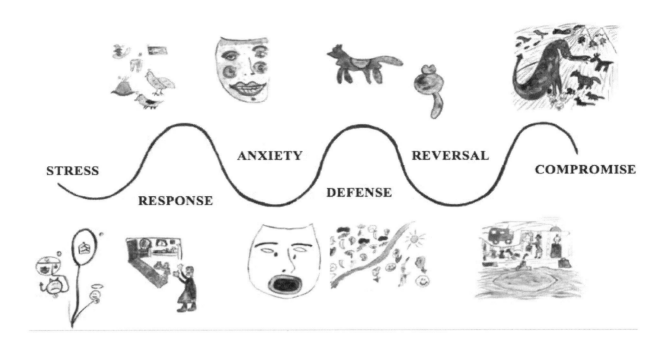

STRESS   ANXIETY   REVERSAL   COMPROMISE

RESPONSE   DEFENSE

FAMILY OF ORIGIN BALLOONS & CONFLICTUAL MEMORY: Grandma: You can't bring that stupid sandwich to your sick mother.	MARITAL FAMILY BALLOONS & Mask I: "Perpetual Smile." Shutting out sadness with a smile and outrageous makeup.	Mask II: "Blackout." Unable to express emotion and being preoccupied with eating. Mask III: The moat separates her feelings of anger and sadness from the happy surface of bunnies and sunshine.	ANIMAL METAPHOR: "Who Will Listen, Will You?" Cat: You can't relly hear me, can you? Dog: Why should I hear what you have to say?	DREAM: "Running Late." Can't find any clothes that fit…but I can hide my fat body in a submarine.	SHORT STORY: "Rage and Fear." I'm reliable, considerate, dull. She turned into a fire-breathing dragon and hurt those around her. Then she wept.

The Evaluation
Phase One

The testing record captured therapy as the unfolding drama. Therapy was concluded upon her rectifying relationships. Wellness was achieved by overcoming fears of rejection and by emerging heroically as an honest, vulnerable, brave, powerful and self respecting adult.

The Role System

Stress: Being hurt about her interest in food.

Response: Perpetual Smile, pretty face but only a façade.

Anxiety: The open mouth covering up the anger by favoring secret binging. Fears of losing control of the cover up recognizing the sequestering of bad feelings.

Defense: Controlling anger but losing control of binging.

Reversal: Being fat and fearing being exposed.

Compromise: The alternative manifested: Expressing her anger and hurting her family. Insight: She is holding her feelings in, tenaciously becoming hostile and sarcastic at the cost of her body image, which betrays her mischief.

STRESS

The Conflictual Memory Test (CMT) addresses the symbolic role choice of her obsessions, food. Her interest in food was intensified upon her grandmother's disapproval. She rebelled at the lack of approval with secretly binging. The configuration of the family balloons (Balloon Test) without strings corresponded to denial of dependency needs and avoidance of dealing with feelings.

RESPONSE AND ANXIETY

The Mask Test (TMT) reveals her identity of a perpetual smile as controlling feelings and concealing the inner voice manifested as insatiable binging, illustrated with an open mouth that she identified as the black hole. This image represents her obsession with the mouth. The heroine's anger was satisfied with food rather than the expression of her feelings; risk taking and setbacks in terms of alternatives between eating and spiting fire as a dragon. Her heart reflected a moat separating her two identities, her perpetual smile covering up the reality of her unexpressed well-guarded angry emotions.

DEFENSE

The Animal Metaphor Test (AMT) revealed her secret binging consoling her for her loneliness, the lack of communication with parents, husband and children. Her animals turn their backs to each other and also the viewer of the test. The playfulness of the animals and her binging and drinking, were the effort to overcome loneliness, her husband was periodically away from town.

REVERSAL

Her dream reflected her fear of losing the cover up of cloths, she had to hide her fat body, not fitting in her clothes. She was seeking refuge in a submarine.

COMPROMISE

The Short Story revealed the compromise as a dragon burning her dear helpless ones, a squirrel, a mouse, and other animals, representing her family. The patient explained the terror of losing control of her held in anger. At one occasion she found herself banging her son's head on the floor. Submissive antagonism is about controlling one's feelings but also occasionally losing control.

CONFLICTUAL MEMORY TEST

Who was there? (Age, relationship, your age then). Mother in bed, me on staircase. Grandmother at bottom. Age about 7 to 9 perhaps. **How do you think this person felt about you?** Extremely irate at that moment. In general, I don't know.

How did you feel about this person? Did not like her.

What happened and what are they saying? My mother is ill. I have made her a sandwich (about a foot tall with nothing but lettuce and American cheese). I'm bringing upstairs to Mother. Grandmother is ranting and raving that I can't, the premise being, I imagine, that it was not edible.

What happened before this incident? In a child's manner, I was attempting to do something for my sick mother with my grandmother breathing fire and telling me 'no'.

What happened after this incident? My mother was appreciative. Have no memory of grandmother's after reactions or my father's reaction to the event.

What were the conflicts involved? My wanting to do something for my mother and being told not to.

What was your share in the conflict? Making a silly sandwich.

How has this experience affected your life? Perhaps by not doing things I'd really like to for fear of censure.

Have you been repeating yourself? Yes.

Has this conflict been resolved in your mind? In mind, no. In relationship, grandmother died a few years later.

Has this conflict been resolved in this relationship? To not be overwhelmed by thinking beforehand of possible reactions of others to actions I would like to undertake.

I was asked to draw a mask, the Transparent Mask Test. I did. It was my perception of the face I presented to the world. A clown's face. A smiling face. I dubbed it "Perpetual Smile". The emotion conveyed was my way of self-deceit and mockery. I shut out my sadness with a smile and outrageous make-up -- like a clown.

The underside of this mask, the transparency, I called "Blackout". It showed my dejection and feelings of rejection. The eyes were closed but they wept. The mouth a blank, a black hole. Communication was nil. Nothing came forth. But everything went in. Anger, food, hate, food, hostility, food, guilt, food.

With my eyes closed, I could ignore all that was hurtful. My mother's illness and death; my five-year old niece's illness and death. Conversely, no one, even those closest to me, could see my inner emotions, both good and bad.

Next up was my drawing depicting what I saw in my heart. It was called "Double Image". A moat separated two sets of feelings. On the one side there were the sun, flowers, smiling faces. My mask to the world. On the other side of the moat was my inner self: tears, black clouds, a broken heart, grim faces, and the ears to show that no one ever listened.

My title for the sequence: "Deceit, Reality and Discord". Through this soul-searching test, I concluded that I was constantly running away from life; I relegated conflicts to the rear of my mind. It became obvious that I had to express rather than repress. My two fragmented selves had to be integrated into a whole.

MASK I
Title: Perpetual Smile (female)

What emotions does this mask convey? False happiness.

What are the conflicts represented in this mask? Self-deceit, mockery.
What resolution of conflicts does this Mask represent? Shutting out sadness with a smile and outrageous makeup.

MASK II
Title: Blackout (female)

What emotions does this mask convey? Dejection, rejection.

What are the conflicts represented in this mask? Unwillingness, inability to express her feelings and being preoccupied with eating.

What resolution of conflicts does this Mask represent? Admission, if eyes were open.

MASK III
Title: Double Image

Indicate items and themes represented in the drawing.
(1) Black clouds/lightning, ears, fangs, eyes/tears, unsmiling faces broken heart. (Avoiding to face the storm); (2) sun, flowers, smiling faces, **Elaborate on what feelings and conflicts this drawing represents.** Two facets are separated, happiness reflected on one side; hidden feelings, anger, sadness, fear, shadows are there, but are constantly being repressed.

What resolution of conflicts does it convey? There is none with the separation between the two facets.

Sequence title: Deceit, Reality and Discord

Summarize here the sequence of transformations of these images. From bad to worse

What are your conclusions about the way this person resolves conflicts? [left blank]

How does that progression relate to your feelings and choices you have in handling feelings? She doesn't, she runs away. Conflicts have been relegated to rear of mind.

Revealing to patient: Very accurate

What changes should you make in the way you communicate your feelings? Express rather than repress.
What changes are you willing to make in order to reduce the intensity of these conflicts? Ascertain why I'm so lopsided and thence to integrate the two into a whole.

> To express my feelings, both hateful and loving, would only draw attention to me. People would see me -- and my fat. Create no waves, be a good child, be a good wife. True anger was only expressed as a mother. I could yell and scream when my children substantially aroused my ire. In all my life, I only exploded, publicly, in front of my children.
>
> My children suffered due to my taciturnity. They were often left undefended. I could never allow myself to show emotion or the chutzpah to even speak up for my own children. Only dogs get mad. A daughter and wife do not.

BALLOON PORTRAITS AND FAMILY (MARITAL FAMILY)

Balloon #1: [fish in a tank] Husband, cold, taciturn, uninterested
Balloon #2: [butterfly] Son, carefree, entertaining, lovable. I worry about him, he didn't graduate. He has a terrible temper.
Balloon #3: [star] Son, quiet, kind, caring, deep, sensitive; my star, my stability. I resent him getting married.
Balloon #4: [elliptical] Me, stubborn, quiet, considerate.
Balloon #5 explosive daughter in law
Balloon #6 Son, died.

I care inordinately about them.

The balloons are having a conversation. What are they saying to each other?

#4: We seem to be far apart. Balloons should be in a bunch, together. I wonder why things have gotten like this.
#1, 2, 3: Who knows, what does it matter?
What were the balloons saying or doing before the conversation you just recorded? Each doing their own thing

What were the balloons saying or doing after the initial conversation? Each drifted away since there was no desire to pursue a conversation.

Title: Each Unto Himself

What conflicts are these balloons experiencing? The inability to ascertain, or the desire to ascertain, a means of becoming a "bunch".

280

What changes should be made to resolve these conflicts? More "meeting" of bodies and minds. Conflicts cannot be resolved if people do not communicate.

One of my high school teachers referred to me as imperturbable. My favorite aunt would make unseemly statements in an effort to break through my coat of calm. A neighbor once stated he'd like to be with me during an atomic attack -- I was always so placid. The caption in my high school yearbook: "As merry as the day is long." I was indeed a fortress. Nothing could erupt this volcano. Total control. So important to me. Present a smile to the world, be unflappable and I would be safe.

In 34 years of marriage I can recall but one verbal argument -- this only a year or so ago. My feelings were never let know, I ate them. My life was a constant binge not only with food, but emotions as well. My outside grew larger, my inside shriveled.

In the AMT my animals turned their backs to each other and the viewer of the images. In the story I recognized a pattern. When under pressure, or feeling sorry for myself, or lonely I plan on over-eating, drinking as a reward. It seems to be something to look forward to.

ANIMAL METAPHOR TEST

Animal #1: German Shepherd dog, age 28, female; loving, dedicated, happy.

Animal #2: Persian cat, age 6, male; regal, friendly, cool.

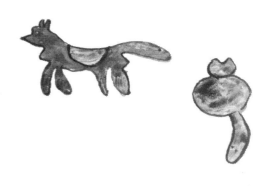

The animals are conversing, what are they saying?

> #1: Hi, Shah. We're alone again. What shall we do?
> #2: Well, Magnum, we can run around the house, with you chasing me; or I can sleep on the microwave and you can sleep on the bed.
> #1: Let's play chase. You get on the coffee table, I'll pull you off and then chase after you.
> #2: OK, but don't grab my whole head in your mouth. Try to do it gently from my neck.
> #1: That's agreeable. Let's go!

What were the animals doing and saying just before the conversation was recorded? They were commiserating with each other that the humans were gone again and they did not know what to do.

What did you animals do and say after the initial conversation: They went into the living room and started their playing, Magnum being careful not to grab Shah by the head. After the chase, usually not lasting too long, they returned to their rest areas.

Title: The Animals Alone At Home

What conflicts are these animals experiencing between themselves? They are experiencing loneliness due to the humans leaving the house. They don't know what to do until they converse with each other.

What changes should these animals make to resolve their conflicts? Just to continue their "together" activities when they are left alone.

Which animal do you identify with most? Elaborate. Dog

How does this animal drama pertain to you? Perhaps I'm bored/lonely since husband started working in Chicago. In the face of diversity, if not on a diet, to find solace in eating and drinking.

Pattern: When under pressure, or feeling sorry for myself, I plan on over-eating, drinking as a reward. It seems to be something to look forward to.

What changes should you make to resolve your conflicts? Find an activity of interest on weekends/days off to become involved in.

What changes are you willing to make? Any necessary.

Disclosure of self was incomprehensible to me. No one was allowed to see the shriveled inner me, not even I. I was a Dorian Gray. This made therapy extremely painful and slow-paced. How could I reveal my innermost feelings and fears to another being? A psychiatrist, fine, but still a body with two ears. These ears would listen and hear, not like others in the past. These ears would know me for what I was. A nothing. A sham. A mask with a perpetual smile. A chunk of ice. So painful. My principal fear was being seen for who I am. A dream as a metaphor reflected my fears of being seen as fat. The dream gave me the perfect hideaway, a submarine.

DREAM
"Running Late"

"Can't find clothes that fit...but I can hide my fat body in a submarine."

This test was generated early in therapy, at the evaluation period, and presents the dragon encountering a group of animals representing Gladys' family.

Here is the dragon with fire out of his mouth. The test presents her fear of losing control of her anger and burning her own family to a crisp.

Animal# 1:
Dragon; fierce, overbearing, dangerous, irate, expressive.

Animal #2:
Mouse; timid, quiet, downtrodden.

Dialogue:

> **Dragon:** If you don't get out of my way I'll burn you to a crisp! Now!
>
> **Mouse:** Please don't. It will hurt me.
>
> **Dragon:** So? You're an inconsequential, useless, rather inane animal. I don't know why God put you on this earth. You're stupid, your only function is to scare silly women. I might even step on you rather than wasting my breath.
>
> **Mouse:** If you must, you must.

Before: Staring at each other in silence.

After: The dragon slayed the mouse.

Title: "Rage and Fear."

Conflicts: The dragon is enraged since the mouse is in its way. The mouse is worried about being hurt and would like to take flight.

Changes: The dragon must realize other creatures also exist and have rights. The mouse must speak up more and learn to outwit the dragon by intellect since it certainly can't do much else due to its size.

Identification: Mouse. **Other animal:** Many people, not me.

Pertinence: In matters of giving in to others' wishes even if I did not want to do something or go someplace.

Change/resolution: Communicate with the dragons about how I feel and what I would like.

Incident: Have ever so often gone somewhere or done something I didn't want to do since it was easier than expressing my needs.

Pattern: My pattern over the years has become established and ingrained, ergo, others continue to expect me to go along with their desires.

Will to change: Anything ??

Dragon / Mouse

A modicum of self-destruction is appearing through the pen. This was an early statement of self-hate. I didn't like me, but I had the power to self-destruct me. I also had the power to change me. My wall separating me from humanity showed up in this early AMT, a dragon and a mouse. Needless to say, I am the Mouse -- the rest of the world a Dragon. Such a fierce, colorful, aggressive Dragon. Living in secure and mighty mountains. Someone to be admired. The epitome of control and power. The Mouse existed in a drab, colorless, nothing world.

The Mouse was in the Dragon's way and the Dragon threatened to burn the Mouse to a crisp. Or, being the Mouse was so inconsequential, the Dragon thought it easier to just step on and squash the Mouse. She wasn't worth the Dragon's breath. The Mouse was totally intimidated and in awe of the Dragon. She allowed the Dragon to slay her. She didn't even have the prudence to flee. Here was verification of me, The Mouse. Don't object, don't argue, don't defend myself. Do not open my mouth. Be in awe of the world. Be a willow tree, bend and bend some more. Do unto others, never unto myself. These lessons leak well, came forth via the pen.

Poetry

One day my hand started to write. Sheer gibberish to me, but a less painful avenue to expression. I was mortified and ashamed after presenting my writings. Eventually they were dubbed as "poetry". This I refused to believe since I was a creative-less clod. But the pen had free rein. It wrote what I couldn't say.

Early on in my writings, I discovered Sylvia Plath. Her poetry and life consumed me. I read every book I could find by her or about her. I affiliated with her in so many instances, e.g., "When there is no one around to make you feel wanted and appreciated, it's sort of easy to talk yourself into feeling worthless." "I am obsessed by wanting to escape from that course." (I too had such an obsession.): "Sometimes I feel so stupid and dull and uncreative that I am amazed when people tell me differently." She killed herself. My early readings did not indicate how. I called the library -- gas from her stove. I was mesmerized and infatuated with her life. I admired all she did.

I equated with Sylvia. So many of my thoughts intermingled with hers. Both warped and not so.

My Poem:

> Sylvia
> A mask was her downfall, it was always in place.
> Hostility must remain caned as a beast in the zoo.
> Alas, it crack'd, she fell apart.
> Too gutless for the razor, the sea regurgitated her.
> Forty pretty pills almost did her in
> But the bitch goddess said, "Nay, I shall not die"
> The inner being was strong and won.
> Only for a decade, though.

An Early Poem:

The storm clouds are moving ever so swiftly
I wish they wouldn't go, they are my friends.
They cloak me from my fears
Nay, they reinforce my fears
But they are ever so comforting.
They seem to hide me from the world.
I hide behind them as I hide behind my glasses.
It is said the eyes are the mirror of the soul
I must be hiding my innermost self
Is that self so bad it needs to be held in secret?
Do I fear it will erupt like Dorian Gray?
His soul became warped, his body remained pure
His was a life of duplicity and, yes, fear
Alas, mine is so too.

My fears of being uncloaked show up here.
Breaking up of the clouds alarmed me –
the world would then see me as I truly was -- a sum of nothing:
I'm always worried about what others may think.
I am compulsed to be well-behaved and fall in place
I must please, please, please.
All must be perfect, perfect, perfect.
Do not create waves my dear, Be quiet and demure.
I don't, I am. What a waste.

How did I grow to be a pleaser?
I was brought up to be sweet and kind
You must never be rude - it's not nice
Others always come first,
that must be so I don't remember the lessons,
But I did learn very well
Otherwise, why am I so?

Uselessity
I must have been born docile and pliable
Indelible impressions were cast on me.
Squished and squashed.
Mother was teacher, Father was god
Force did not exist, words did their job
Why must I be perfect? I'm certainly not.
Memories are so rare, is that repression?
Or a defense mechanism to maintain my sanity?
Again an "ity" - mediocrity, stupidity, on and on
Tonight is me - uselessity.

There was no time for me to be me. I spent my life in pursuit of happiness -- other peoples'. My dues for walking this earth were perfection. Nothing else would do. I expressed it so:

286

Perfection Only May Exist

> Mediocrity, you may not, nay, cannot, exist
> You reek with hollowness, you are unfulfilled.
> To be perfect is to be supreme
> You are as trash and not to be stood
> Contamination, putrification, stagnant, imperfect
> You are to be scorned and slain again and again
> Mediocrity, you are death.

Perfection exacts a heavy toll. To be perfect is a state of apartness, aloofness. To a fat person, it's akin to hiding in a tent dress. Should any one see the rolls of fat, I would be imperfect. Not to be allowed. My separation from the world of reality may be likened to the operation that separates Siamese twins. A wall, a moat, a fence always enabled me to keep my distance from others and to pursue my path to perfection.

The building of the wall was exacerbated by non-hearing ears. When I did communicate with others, I was ignored. Pull back, pull back. Don't let them hurt me again. If they shan't listen, I shan't speak. Another binge--stuffing myself with anger:

> Run, rabbit, run.
> Hurry away into the sun.
> Run to the forest, the trees are tall
> The pine needles are soft, the moss is cool.
> They can't hear you when you speak.
> They don't see you when you are there.
> So, hide, rabbit, hide, it's good for you.
> The rabbit's ears are back.
> Hurray, he's getting mad.
> He's not a he, he's a she, he's me.

> But why didn't people hear me?
> Why, didn't they listen to what I said?
> K's burn was treated so lightly
> The vet ignored the poor ill dog.
> Husband never heard me about the meeting place.
> Was it my serenity in the face of adversity?
> Did I not speak loud enough?
> I guess I don't speak since no one hears.

The three references in this poem, my son's burned arm, the vet not hearing me for months about my dog's worsening condition, and my husband's failure to know where to meet me after graduation for my Master's degree, were all meaningful to me. Yet, they were ignored.

> Dogs bark, cat's meow, birds sing, elephants bellow
> They express their anger and their fears.
> People talk softly at times, they also shout at times

They express their love, their anger and their fears.
Why am I mute?

I was even jealous of animals expressing emotions.
Still asking that question: "Why am I mute?"

> I love you, I hate you
> You are mine, do I want you?
> I can throw you away
> I can keep you if I want
> I despise your weakness
> I hate your quietness
> You are mute, you are dull
> I don't like you, you are me.

A modicum of self-destruction is appearing through the pen. This was an early statement of self-hate. I didn't like me, but I had the power to self-destruct me. I also had the power to change me.

Bravado

> The rain is on the windshield all blotchy and dull
> It softens the light.
> Turn on the wipers, clear it away.
> You are a raindrop on my soul.
> I love you not, I think tonight.
> If you were to die, I'd miss you not.
> I know your secret.
> You are bravado, a machine programmed well
> Once taught, that is the end
> You could not change, can you now?
> A pile of putty you were born
> Thence molded into a piece of quartz.
> A free thinker not, once taught, cast in concrete
> You should be pitied, your brain was stifled
> Parenting was poor, it ruined a soul
> No free thinking, no creativity, imagination none.
> You were programmed and that was that
> The spark was squashed, she ruled your head
> You might as well be dead.

My Anger, My Moat, My Quiet:

As downtrodden and mouse-like as I felt, it became obvious that anger seethed beneath my mask. But anger was undesirable. To be angry was naughty. An awareness of my anger cropped up in a very few lines:

> It must be easier as well as safer
> To wear an almost constant smile.

288

It's a mask to hide me from the world
If I smile I can't be angry
At least not so anyone knows
However, I know.

I was also in deep fear of expressing my anger:
I cannot cry, I cannot rage
To cry is uncontrollable, why can't I?
To rage is controllable, and had always been
 If you learn to control an emotion entirely
Why can't you learn to give it leeway?
Is rage too strong a word?
Rage must be over-expressed anger
If anger has been so long suppressed
Will rage run rampant and just explode?

Anger, and especially rage, were almost never allowed to surface through my mask. Indeed, I created a river, a moat. One side was cool and calm – the other ferocious and furious. This dichotomy was so rigid, I often didn't even know when I was angered:

It's not just a matter of expressing anger
Although that I don't know how to do
More important than expression of anger
Is knowing indeed when you are angry.

Anger scared me. Anger awed me. Oh, to be angry. I was overwhelmed when someone, anyone, expressed anger. I was jealous. Why didn't the world cast aspersions on these people. How could they not alienate those who received their outbursts of anger? How could anyone still like them? Anger terrified me to such an extent that I overcame it. I made it surrender to my power. The power of control. I imprisoned it so deep in my soul that it couldn't erupt. This dung heap was nurtured over the years. It fed upon itself. A cancer dissipating my spirit. As it intensified, it warped my mind.

When my first son was five years old, my anger unloosed itself. To a proportion unknown to me. My child did something to upset me (I remember not what). He was on the floor. My hands seized his shoulders. I pounded his head on the floor. The scene is as vivid today as it was that day thirty years ago. I must never allow my anger to take control ever-again. What had I done? This was my son. I, no, my anger, was a monster. It was omnipotent. It attacked with fearsome speed. Something snapped in my head. It was me. The horror of what I was capable of immobilized me. Shame and fear espoused one another. Guilt was spawned.

Guilt and shame intermingle such as the tendrils of a morning glory. The longer they are allowed to flourish, the more difficult they are to untangle:

Guilt comes in many shapes and forms. It is most tremendous when people die:

My grandmother died -- I didn't like her, but I caused her demise
My mother died -- I was impatient with her.
My son died -- did I cause it?

It also attacks in other ways
It builds up and almost envelops me.

My guilt for these past offenses hung heavy. It impacted on my present existence -- it clouded the future. More from Sylvia Plath: "The hardest thing, I think, is to live richly in the present without letting it be tainted and spoiled out of fear for the future or regret for a badly damaged past."

Guilt was heaviest regarding the death of my son. We had lived in a small village in Westchester County during K's growing up years. He loved the village, he loved the house, he loved his friends. He loved life. While he was going to college, a local school, we moved to Connecticut. The main reason being the company I worked for relocated to CT. Everything considered, we deemed it beneficial to leave our home of twelve years for another in CT. None of the boys were ecstatic! K. was outraged! He ultimately found an apartment, went to school and worked at three jobs to support his apartment. When one or two of his jobs petered out, he was forced to move back to CT. He commuted to NY school and to see his friends.

One Friday night he almost made it home. He died in a car crash a scant ten minutes from home. K. was dead. My twenty-year-old son lay dead on a road. I was the cause. Because of me, we moved. Guilt wrapped itself around each convolution of my brain. It's message oozed from each tentacle as it grew: "Bad mother", and grew "Bad daughter", and grew "Bad granddaughter", and grew "Bad wife."

A bird flew into my car years after my son died. Guilt surged through my being. I had killed the bird.

A Poem:

They fly in the air so free
Their colors are lovely to see
They create happiness with their song
They are a joy to behold as they soar
Then they go thump and are dead.

I began to equate the myriad of dead animals I passed every day on the parkway with my son who had died:

I cry for the animals dead on the road
I cry for the animals forsaken and lone
They affect me in a manner untold
It is as though my heart is broken
Words cannot explain the effect
It is like the night Kevin died.
It is desperation
It is frustration
It breaks my heart
It is a weight so heavy I want to die.

In the moat series, the problem was clarified as a power imbalance as she evolved from a dumb bunny to a soaring eagle.

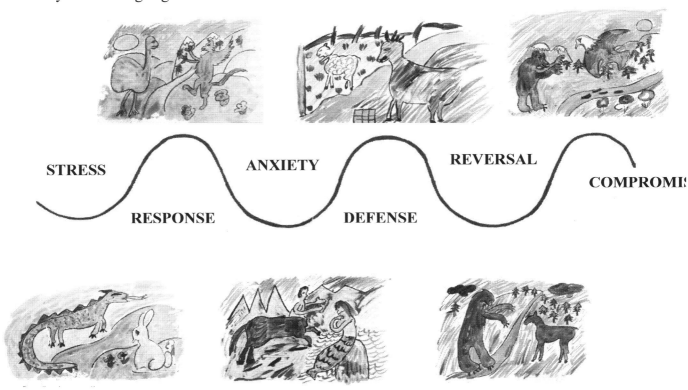

STRESS   ANXIETY   REVERSAL   COMPROMI

RESPONSE   DEFENSE

"Run, Rabbit, Run"
Gila: Rabbit, you are the proverbial 'dumb bunny.' You are gullible, inane and spineless.

"A Ray of Sunshine"
Griffin: Hey, ostrich, it's nice to see you without your head in the sand. You say others don't hear you, but then you never listen to me, your inner self.

"Mermaid and Centaur"
(M): I am vulnerable, I am unclothed. (C): I do not want to hear such things. I am a mighty centaur. You are nothing but a fish.

"Lamb and Bull"
Lamb: Why don't I know you? Why have you fenced me in? Why do I have my back to you? Why can't I ever figure out how I feel about you?

"The Feckless Fawn"
Deer: Your big teeth and claws scare me. You might hurt me. Bear: You're making me mad. Get over here before I lose my temper and bite you.

"Feathers and Claws" Eagle: Here I am, soaring upward. Why haven't I been here before? The eagle flew beyond the mountains and the bear waved goodbye.

Rabbit and Gila Monster

Animal #1: Gila monster, female; avaricious, amoral, nasty, selfish, unsympathetic.

Animal #2: Rabbit, female; scared, shy, running and hiding, afraid, fearful, worrier.

Dialogue:

#1: Really, rabbit, you are the proverbial "dumb bunny". You are gullible, inane and spineless. I've already stomped allover you once and I can do it again. My reputation is fierce so you'd best watch out

#2: Silence.

#1: Are you sick, why do you sit there like a clod? With one swish of my tail I can knock you down. The stream will not protect you. I do what I want, I say what I please and I get what I want.

#2: Silence, tears and flight.

Before: The Gila monster wanted the flowers and had laid claim to them. She wanted almost everything in the rabbit's territory. She took what she wanted. The rabbit sat there and hid behind a bush.

After: The Gila monster shook her head over the dumb bunny and made off with the flowers. The rabbit couldn't speak since her voice would crack and the tears would flow. She retreated.

Title: "Run Rabbit, Run."

Conflicts: The Gila monster has no conflict, whatever she does is right in her eyes. The rabbit should stay and fight, but runs away in panic.

Conflicts/world: Others realize the Gila monster is greedy and nasty. She doesn't. The rabbit realizes she can't face conflict and tries to run from the world.

Identification: Rabbit.

Other: Business associate. Pertinence: It depicts an actual happening in my office.

Changes/resolution: Stop being a gutless wonder.

Incident: Aforementioned office incident.

Pattern: Cannot fight back; when I become emotional I run.

There is asymmetry, irreversibility, which implies on the surface she is a limited rabbit, running, fearing being destroyed, innocent, helpless. The flip side is the angry monster that is being controlled by the barrier, boat, river, and the fear of losing control of the anger always there, attributed to partners: boss, husband, father, children.

Ostrich and Griffin

Animal #1: Ostrich,
Sex: female; speedy, ignorant, shameful, cheerful, suppressive, useless, dull, weak.

Animal #2: Griffin:
Sex: female; strong, purposive, free, daring, proud, expressive, protective.

Dialogue:

#2: Hey, ostrich, it's nice to see you without your head in the sand. You tend to ignore so many things and be embarrassed so often you rarely allow me to talk to you. You say others don't hear you, but then you never listen to me, your inner self.

#1: I admire you, griffin, but never knew you are indeed me. Why have I never allowed you to surface before and when I did, never heard you?

#2: Because you have always chosen to ignore the impurities and imperfections in life. You are ashamed to cry as well as yell. You are forever smiling and cheerful in front of the world, that's not life. You can't accept the bad and unhappy situations. You suppress by running and ignoring. You never face up to reality. In short, you are useless and exceedingly dull. You are weak, spineless. Are you going to run and hide your head in the sand again?

#1: I don't understand. I admire you. You possess strength to do what you want. You dare try everything. You don't worry over what people will say. You can express your thoughts, be they bad or good. And, yes, you are proud of this. You are what I want to become. You are in the cool mountains amid the trees and flowers. I am in the hot sun stuck in the sand. It is drab, it is a waste of time. I don't know how to set you free.

#2: Then rot!

Before: The ostrich was alone with her thoughts. She was sick of her head always being in the sand. She was annoyed and depressed with her dullness and reputation for always being happy. In this abysmal state of mind, the griffin suddenly appeared.

After: The griffin receded to the inner recesses of the mind as the ostrich hid her head in the sand, again.

Title: "A Day of Sunshine."

Conflicts: Being one, the griffin and the ostrich are experiencing inner turmoil.

Conflicts/world: They are true opposites: One is dull, one is exciting; one is proud, one is humiliated; one is strong, one is weak; one is free, one is imprisoned.

Resolution: A balance needs to be struck.

Identification: Ostrich.

Pertinence: I am the ostrich personified, totally one-sided. I want to be more the griffin.

Incident: Do not face up to rotten side of life, e.g., mother. Try to appease everyone all the time, goes on and on.

Pattern: Even if I feel I'm right, will always soften statements, or add a qualifier or ask a question.

Centaur and Mermaid

Animal #1: Centaur
Sex: male
Traits: opinionated, vociferous, selfish

Animal #2: Mermaid
Sex: female
Traits: embarrassed, reticent, frightened, dejected, ineffectual

Dialogue:

#1: I am mighty. I am strong. I have four strong legs and two mighty arms. I roam the countryside at large. You should look up to me. I am your creator. You are as nothing. You have no legs. What good is a fin? You are confined to water. Who looks up to you? I know who I am. Who are you?

#2: I am nothing. Are you, though, not the cause of my nothingness? I am vulnerable, I am unclothed, but then so are you. I cannot leave the water to come to you, but you can come to me.

#1: I care not to come to you. I care not to hear you. You speak of sadness. I do not want to hear such things. I am, after all, a mighty centaur. You are nothing but a fish.

Before: The mermaid was trying to get the centaur's attention by calling. She could not wave her arms since that would bare her nudity. The centaur finally heard her soft voice and started above conversation first, not giving her a chance to say what was on her mind.

After: Since the centaur did not want to hear the mermaid's troubles, he galloped away. The mermaid wept into the sea around her.

Title: "I Am Nothing."

Conflicts: Inability to communicate. The Centaur speaks but will not hear matters of import to the mermaid. The mermaid cannot make herself heard; she must weep alone.

Conflicts/world: There is a void. The centaur wants his creation to be happy so will not hear otherwise. The mermaid wants to share and please the centaur but everything she does is never right and the bad news is ignored.

Identification: Mermaid, she is isolated on a rock in the ocean. Other: father, he is unapproachable, impossible to please or impress.

Pertinence: The mermaid is truly a nothing, she cannot make herself heard. The centaur has always given her whatever she asked for materially, but not emotionally. Although she finds it difficult to ask for material things, it is not possible for her to ask for love and understanding, cannot discuss inner feelings, especially unhappy situations.

Changes: Should open my mouth at the time of displeasure, frustration, aggravation, anger, sadness.

Incident: Took me years (and mine) to finally ask my father why he married Mary, his second wife. Have not discussed recent fight with my brother. My father has not asked, either.

Pattern: Never show concerns with pertinent people, clam up and smolder. Do not vent feelings.

Lamb and Bull

Animal #1: Lamb
Sex: female
Traits: docile, weak, gentle, leery, stunted, repressed

Animal #2: Bull
Sex: male
Traits: quiet, overpowering, squelching, dominant, dismal, glowering

Dialogue:

#1. Why have you fenced me in? Why do I have my back to you? Why can't I ever figure out how I feel about you? The word I seek is elusive. You squelch me. I'm leery of you. I'm not afraid of you per se. You don't awe me, but there is something I can't grasp that stunts me. It's so damned annoying. I've known you for over 30 years and I don't know how to explain what you do to me. I'm fenced in. I'm unnatural. I'm cold. I can't talk to you in a sensible, coherent state. Why can't I react to you? You must be one of my elusive shadows. I think you must be like my father. Two bulls and one lamb. A lamb is an immature sheep. Too bad you're not a wolf. Why a wolf? A wolf in sheep's clothing.

#2: I do love you. You never let me get close to you. You hide, you run, you ignore. Your body and mind are unknown to me. Perhaps that's why I never hear you. My mother was fenced in and liked it. You never liked my mother. She was my all.

#1: Perhaps she was the stream that always separated us. That stream became a river after K died. But you always repressed me. The fence was always there. I can't get away from your aura. Can I and do I want to jump over the fence?

Before: Absolutely nothing.

After: They spoke no more.

Conflicts: They don't know each other, nor how to.

Conflicts/world: The lamb can't understand herself, no less the bull.
[No indication for changes]

Identification: Lamb, has been docile but is now seeking answers so she can become a sheep.

Other: Husband, can't understand what he does or doesn't do to me.

I feel like I'm on a far-off mountain
Removed from everything – isolated
I am cold and aloof and yet a frenzy exists
I feel helpless, I feel inert, I am in turmoil. (08-20-85)

Rumblings of self-hate began to appear out of my anger, my moat, my guilt:

Love is another four-letter word nicer than most
It connotes deep feeling, pure and kind
Some love you take for granted --
You love your children, you love your dog
To be silly, you love your shoes
The word is often misused like so many others
You hate this, you hate that
Do I truly hate myself? (08-22-85)

Was this self-hate generated by years of unspoken anger, distancing myself from the rest of the world and my cancerous guilt? Menacing dread was creeping into my life:

The lights are all on, the radio too.
The air cleaner drones as I sit here alone
An eerie feeling is covering me like a shroud
There is something to be feared out there
Rather, it is something to be met
But it is a fearsome thing
I have put it off so long -- forever it seems
Am I able to bring it forth in a normal way
Or will it encompass me and blow me apart? (08-22-85)
Was the fat attack that had brought me to therapy indeed born from my anger, my moat, my guilt?

PHASE III:

In the Snake / Vulture series, the problem of the eating disorder reemerged as she responded to stress, controlling and losing control of food. Her metaphors evolved from snake hissing at a vulture to a jaguar destroying both snake and vulture.

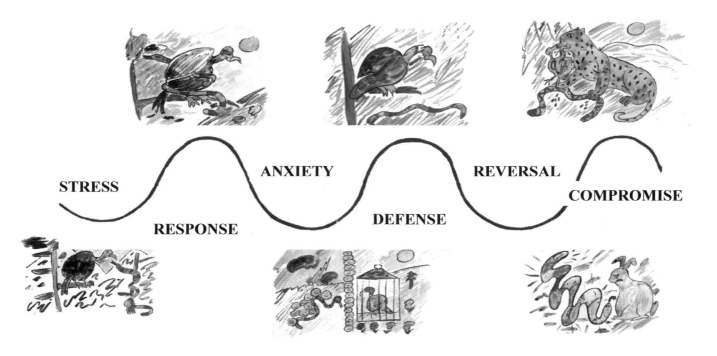

STRESS   ANXIETY   REVERSAL

RESPONSE   DEFENSE   COMPROMISE

"Feast or Famine"	"Venom for the Vulture, Wings for the Snake"	"Dealing with Stress, or, a Storm Approaching"	"After the Storm"	"Now or Never"	"Life is Not Binge or Purge"
Snake: I can hiss at you, and if I want, bite you with my venom filled fangs.	Vulture: I am not sure I am ready to die. I can still fly away. A failed attempt to become a whole.	Snake: You have me up against the wall in the storm. Am I safe in the eye of the storm?	The vulture won the battle. She ran amok and ate...the snake grew weary and weak.	Snake: If you keep feeding me the way you are, I'll die. Rabbit: The only thing I know how to do is cry.	Jaguar destroys vulture and snake, and says, "I'll win. My patience has run out. The snake and vulture must die!"

298

Patient's Analysis of the Relapse

In the midst of my turmoil -- my anger -- my guilt and the on-going fat, I met Sue. Sue was the psychodrama leader in a group I was invited to attend. I hesitantly agreed to go, but not to speak. I intended to blend into the background and watch and listen. Not easy to do when you are fat. Sue fascinated me -- she was bright, attractive Sue, outgoing, just nice – and thin. Everything I ached to be. As much as I scrunched into my chair, found me. Not strange, since you can't hide fat. She asked why I was in the group. My reply: "I'm fat." Sue's reply: "You're not fat." How could this pinnacle of excellence not see I was fat? It shouted out from every roll: "Fat, fat, this is fat! How could I make her see the fat? Such a simple solution! I would become thin -- then Sue would know I had been fat. Pure logic. I was pleased with myself. I was determined. I was powerful. I could do it.

My expression of these feelings:

    You don't seem to understand my need
    I am not trying to please you
    I but want to make your eyes
    See me as my eyes see me -- fat.
    Fat is indeed not the main problem
    That I now know is so
    But since my anger remains hidden deep and will not surface
    The only thing I know to do is attack the fat. (08-22-85)

Sue was all-important to me. I not only needed her approval, I needed her empathy. There was no other way to make Sue's eyes see me. More significantly, to make Sue's ears hear me. This became my mission. My burning desire, my life. Sue must see me thin to appreciate that I was fat.

To be thin, you may not eat. But being highly skilled in matters of nutrition, I knew I had to eat something. Due to his job, my husband was living in Chicago at this time. He came home two or three weekends a month. I did not have to cook for another. There was no one to interrupt my plan. Although, I could eat everything in sight or absolutely nothing at all without any reaction or comment from my spouse. But it was easier being alone. My "diet" consisted of cauliflower, mushrooms, tomatoes and an occasional peach. Very occasional -- fruit is partly composed of sugar! To add a bit of variety, I'd sometimes use dietetic blue cheese salad dressing on the tomatoes. Eating was confined to dinner. Copious amounts of coffee filled my stomach throughout the day. My counseling to my dieters however was never compromised and right on target. If only I could listen to my own good advice.

    The Vulture appeared shortly after my anorexic behavior sprouted:
    I'm running scared -- it's the rabbit again.
    Or is it a dragon trying to emerge?
    Perhaps it's the Vulture wanting to consume
    Vultures eat carrion - - that I don't want
    I want to be a dragon to do as I please
    I want to be someone who will be seen and heard (09-02-85)

I was so intent that Sue would see and hear me. Whilst working on an AMT at this time my cast of characters emerged.

The rotund Vulture was lazy and taciturn. The slender Snake was sharp-tongued and forward. The Vulture was surprised to see the slinky, thin Snake slither up the tree so fast. The Snake told the Vulture she had been hiding under rocks for a long time. She was growing old and fat and found it hard to slither at all. But her newly-gained thinness brought her pleasure, attention and agility. She warned the Vulture that she could kill her with her venom-filled fangs. The Vulture queried the Snake as to why the Snake would want to harm her. The Snake replied that the Vulture was the epitome of a big blob. She did nothing but perch in a dead tree looking for dead things on the ground to pick at and snake added that the Vulture only attacked those dead and rotting -- no one who would fight back.

The Vulture declared that the Snake was no better -- slithering along the ground and in trees to attack those living. The Vulture deemed it better to remain as she was -- silent and calm.
I was both the vulture and, down deep, the Snake. The Vulture sat and wait never acted, never allowed herself to express feelings -- a big blob. She ate and ate and became sadder and sadder. The Snake said what she wanted. But me, the Snake, was still mostly under a rock. The Snake was the me I wanted to be. She was stretching and stirring from my depths. She would be living proof for Sue. The Snake was winning the battle with the Vulture. I was losing weight. Sheer delight! Thinness was within my grasp.

But the Vulture was not annihilated! She too stirred. She came out through my pen:

> I'm afraid to eat
> I'm afraid not to eat
> I'm obsessed with the scales
> I weigh at least twice a day
> I now look in all mirrors rather than running away It seems as though I'll lose control
> Should I eat as I know I should
> I've been adept at excuses for almost three weeks
> It's time to stop this nonsense, so why can't I? (09-85)

More:

> Am I doing this to prove a point?
> Or is it much more than that?
> The point has been made -- I am indeed somewhat thinner
> So why do I persist in this silliness? (09085)
> Something strange was happening. I was losing weight and should have been ecstatic. I was not:
> Sunrise is a thing of beauty
> The pinks, the dusty mauve are a delight.
> These gentle colors diminish ever so fast In their stead appears a magnificent orb
> It's brightness and magnitude overwhelm the eyes
> There was no sunrise today (09-85)

and:

I am hurting today. I know not why.
Sadness pervades like a dismal shroud
I yearn to be caressed and cared for.
Loneliness is all about me and I despair. (09-85)

At this time the Vulture and Snake made their second appearance:

The Snake was now the star of the cast. She was forward, angry, in control, assured, powerful and still sharp-tongued. The Vulture was self-recriminating, an escapist, non-expressive, distant, out of control and weak.

In the final phase of therapy she rectified power in a number of relationships. She evolved from being rejected from her mom's kangaroo pouch to admitting to her husband a need for a real partnership, seeking acceptance for all parts of her many hidden identities.

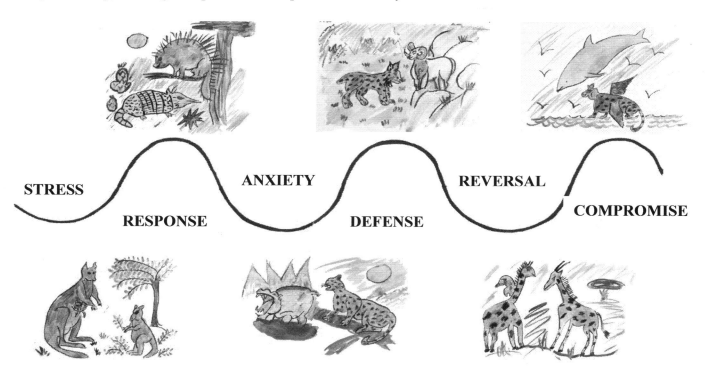

STRESS   ANXIETY   REVERSAL

RESPONSE   DEFENSE   COMPROMISE

"No Room For Two"	"Wake Up and Live"	"Jaguar vs. Hippo"	"How Very Dull"	"An Unveiling"	"Who Am I?"
Mother: Why are you eating so much? Soon you'll be fat and ugly. Child: I eat for solace. I eat so you'll be aware of me.	Armadillo says to Porcupine: You are not bound by convention. You can color outside the lines.	Jaguar: You're ugly and obese. You must stuff food and drink in your cavernous mouth all day and night.	Bobcat self says to bighorn sheep husband: you never wanted to change anything nor did you want me to change. There is no joy to look forward to.	Girland to Girpoise: Neither of us express anger. We have to tell each other when, why we're angry. People can have disputes and be friends again.	Dolphin: I enjoy companionship. What are you? Pigagu: A "we" and not an "I". The pig eats too much, the jaguar desires control and the seagull wants freedom.

Mother and Child Kangaroo

Animal #1: Mother Kangaroo

Animal #2: Child Kangaroo, age 8, female; reserved, overly sensitive and reactive, suffers in silence. [Note: No room in the pouch for me]

Dialogue:

> **#1:** Why are you eating so much? Look how pudgy you're getting. Soon you'll be fat and ugly. As it is I have no room in my pouch for you, your brother is more than I can handle.

> **#2:** I eat for solace. I eat so you'll be aware of me. It doesn't matter how big I get since you have no room for me. Food gives me comfort, it makes me feel warm. You don't do that.

> **#1:** I can only do so much, your brother is always getting in trouble. My energies have to go to him. Don't forget that I have cared for you. I have taught you many things. I even taught you how to eat.

Before: The child kangaroo wanted to jump in the mother's pouch, but there was no room there. She was lonely and bewildered. She needed warmth and love. She ate and ate more leaves to get her mother's attention. The mother kangaroo was preoccupied with her son and had no time for her daughter. The daughter spoke no more.

After: The mother continued to look after her son and keep him warm and safe. The daughter ate and ate and ate. Her one attempt at dialogue was fruitless so she became mute.

Title: "No Room for Two"

Conflicts: The mother wants to help her daughter but is too busy with her son. The daughter doesn't know how else to get attention and love of her mother and suffers in silence.

Conflicts/world: The mother's capabilities are limited, her first child overwhelms her. The daughter lets this depress her rather than overcoming it.

Changes: In later years it was said the mother did too much for the daughter and ignored the son. The daughter should grow up.

Identification: Child.

Other: Mother.

Pertinence: I still let the lack of love and attention overwhelm and depress me. However I can

303

now do a reversal of behavior, e.g., under-eat rather than overeat. I still overreact.

Change/resolution: Get the attention I seek by letting my needs and desires be known, even if not possible to attain them, just to vent them.

Concluding Comments

What do we learn from this study?

This record attests to the diagnostic and therapeutic use of the metaphor analysis technique and its relevance in monitoring long-term therapy outcome.

The Power Management therapy accomplished its objectives by assisting the patient in understanding the eating disorder as an emotional behavioral problem originating in her difficulty in communicating her feelings. The case study confirms the two aspects of relational analysis: the notion of relational modality diagnosis and the notion of the syndromal organization of emotions proceeding predictably along the six role state syndromal organization from a conflict to its resolution. We witness this dialectic organization in each sample metaphor, also in the organization of metaphors in each phase of the therapy and also in the order of the succession of phases in the course of her therapy. The evaluation phase is in formal relation to the final phase as a conflict defined as passivity, antagonism and alienation to resolution as mastery, cooperation and mutual respect. The case is a study in communications as conflict resolution leading to personal empowerment.

The beginning of her therapy presented this communications problem in relational terms: 'One of my high school teachers referred to me as imperturbable. My favorite aunt would make unseemly statements in an effort to break through my coat of calm. A neighbor once stated he'd like to be with me during an atomic attack -- I was always so placid. The caption in my high school yearbook: "As merry as the day is long". I was indeed a fortress. Nothing could erupt this volcano. Total control. So important to me. Present a smile to the world, be unflappable and I would be safe. In 34 years of marriage I can recall but one verbal argument -- this only a year or so ago. My feelings were never let know, I ate them. My life was a constant binge not only with food, but emotions as well. My outside grew larger, my inside shriveled. In the AMT my animals turned their backs to each other and the viewer of the images. In the story I recognized a pattern. When under pressure, or feeling sorry for myself, or lonely I plan on over-eating, drinking as a reward. It seems to be something to look forward to'. The last metaphors present the resolution to this withdrawal; they attest comfort in talking about her feelings: 'We have to tell each other when, why we're angry. People can have disputes and be friends again'.

This case study attests that emotions are formally related sequence of ideas as energies, which progress obligatorily from conflict to resolution seeking power balance. Pathology consists in the manifestation of imbalance, manifested symptomatically as unresolved conflicts, leading to cycles of acting out and related guilt ridden consequences. The case study attests that behaviors and emotions, a vicious cycle, may be interrupted as emotions are expressed and the person achieves a sense of self-respect. It is important to understand the psychodynamic nature of pathology in order to intervene appropriately to achieve wellness. The solution is not in antidepressant medications to overcome the depression but in self-awareness and the development of appropriate coping skills.

Resolution occurred gradually as Gladys recognized her capacity to express her feelings by eloquently writing poetry. She had fun rechanneling her energy, redirecting emotional charges into creativity, which helped her to be honest and to feel good about herself. Poems are metaphors, miniatures of the personal daily drama. The emotional release coincides with a sense of empowerment as the resolution. The energies processed through creativity are like waters channeled into a generator producing useful electricity rather than as wild self-destructive imploding behaviors. The patient was aware of the original pattern of defiance of authority, compliance and rebellion. The poetry surpassed the limits of the metaphor testing. It served her in venting her feelings spontaneously. Creativity as art helped Gladys beyond dependency on the approval of a parent or the therapist. Artfully presented thoughts surpass science in expressing emotions. "With poetry I am coming out of hiding. I am free. I don't want to ever be accused of being a logical person. That is my doctor's bag." Her hostile criticism represents a sign of healthy expression of feelings. It is a welcome assertion.

Rebelling from her 'doctor's bag' she offered me her art to chronicle the science of her therapeutic experience as a dramatic totality with a beginning, middle and a moral end. Dramatic plays resolve power issues with justice. Weak characters, victims, become protagonists as strong characters, while their counterparts as villains are weakened. In plays like Ibsen's "Doll's House", we witness the heroine's dramatic exit with resolutions of the empowerment of the oppressed as she walks out on her cruel dominant husband. The "doll-wife" who was once considered dishonest walks away from her judgmental husband Torvald and her children, accusing him of dishonesty. How could the tender, thoughtful wife of yesterday be so heartless to her husband, for whom she was committing a crime? In this play, the heroine, the victim, seeks empowerment without compromise and without easy resolutions. In that sense she acts negatively, or in an over-compensatory way, selfishly. She resolved her personal conflicts by compounding the social one, as lack of respect for the marital union. In therapy the desirable resolution is in a compromise, a reconciliation that reduces personal and social conflicts; therapy seeks a happy ending. Here it achieved non-dramatically personal adjustment as establishing mutual respect saving the marital union by leading to a happy end.

Therapy, like theater, seeks resolutions as compromises between the opposites of the hero's conflicts. Therapy seeks to accomplish personal transformation following the principles of correcting both inner and outer systemic justice, restructuring relationships, beginning with the analysis of the metaphors as a circumscribed dramatic totality. Her characters across the moat started communicating and eventually the moat disappeared. Then they became the opponents of the eating disorder, the vulture and the snake in a direct combat. After the inner tiger killed both of them the parties of the metaphors became symmetrical partners talking honestly and kindly to each other.

Gladys did not abandon her husband and home. She was able to reconcile her two selves, the vulture and the snake, and enjoy a dignified integration as a jaguar and then as a dolphin staying at home hurt as a bereaved mother, but liking herself and her husband. She interrupted the cheating game of hiding her feelings and sneaking food, as she did when she was a girl chastised by her mother and in vain seeking to please her father. Instead of hiding her feelings and binging she was enjoying talking to her husband and no longer needing escapist outlets.

She completed therapy and enjoyed her flower garden project, loving her picket fence covered with climbing roses. She was proud of getting angry with her husband for his messing up her knife to clear a bush. She was able to converse with her son about his feelings and to critically review her deceased mother's disposition. She was able to deal with relations openly and honestly rather than be mad and sneak food, then pay the price by being obsessed by her looks, her image and her diet. She organized her poetry in a book. This was the desirable conclusion to her long despair. She completed her drama and the curtain fell on a happy ending.

Case Study Seven
The Foot Fetish Obsession,
The Explosive Lion and the Withdrawn Dog

Introduction

This case study was inserted into this volume at a late point in the research project. The relevance of this evaluation is in that it clearly demonstrates the diagnostic and therapeutic function of the self-assessment. It was chosen as a very meaningful evaluation, in spite of missing the usual patient insights and the tabulation of the relational modality.

Theo was a 26 year old married man employed as a manager of a large organization, who sought help for a failing marital relationship. His wife wanted to proceed with divorce. He had been in therapy for several sessions but the therapeutic work was inconclusive so he was referred for a psychological evaluation to me.

The evaluation consisted in completing the Conflict Analysis Battery self-assessment, which proved to be informative about a secret adjustment pattern. In detecting the pattern, foot fetishism, the evaluation was educational, diagnostic and therapeutic. This evaluation reframed his therapy, which he continued in the original setting.

The assessment illustrated the psychodynamic genesis of the foot fetish obsession. It also clarified empowerment as the path to breaking the pattern. His relational modality was clearly submissive cooperative. Like most submissive people he was extremely dependent of parental approval. The battery revealed his dependency disposition being frustrated and leading to acting out behaviors. Because of his successful older siblings and favored younger sister he also sought attention in the classroom. His antiques had the reverse effect: rejection by his siblings and failure in getting love from his parents. His teacher disapproved of his behaviors as well. She had punished him placing him in front of the class. He had responded with a sexually stimulating secret phantasy. Rejections had led to his social withdrawal and retreat to intense fantasy life, the obsessive pattern of foot fetishism. This pattern had gotten out of his control.

The assessment helped him in several ways. He identified his relational modality diagnosis, his submissive cooperative disposition. He experienced cathartic release from guilt caused by revealing his many secrets. He developed insights about the logical connection of his personality pattern of submissiveness, compensated by his aggressive attention getting escapism, which elicited his embarrassment and fears of loosing control to overpowering women. The metaphor tests confirmed the diagnosis of submissiveness and helped to reconstruct the pernicious pattern as the six-role sequence. Fetishism offered him inner assertiveness but was again followed by guilt

308

leading to embarrassment reinforcing his feeling of worthlessness and furthering his social withdrawal. At the end of his evaluation he was considering a more open relationship with his wife.

Transcription of the Assessment

STRESS

CONFLICTUAL MEMORY TEST

Childhood memory: rejection by his siblings

Step 1: Please draw and color a most conflictual memory from your childhood. Feel free to be as imaginative as you wish with the portrayal of this conflict to allow your feelings to show through the drawings.

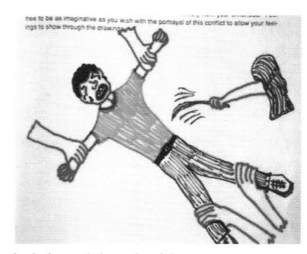

Step 2: Describe the incident. Who was there and what happened? I was about 8-10 years old. I remember my three older brothers used to get my sister and myself to fight. They would make it very difficult for me to win. They on occasion would hold me down so my sister could tickle me until I cried or my parents came to my aid. This was only a once in a while occurrence. Not every day or even weekly!

Step 3: How did you feel about this person? How did this person feel about you? I have always resented my sister in some ways because she was spoiled and stole so much attention being the baby and the only girl.

Step 4: What were the conflicts involved? Accepting humiliation at an early age

Step 5: What happened before? Similar situations

Step 6: What happened after? Similar situations

Step 7: What was your share in creating this conflict? To gain attention I had to be wild and obnoxious so my bigger and more reserved brothers thought nothing about tormenting the brat in the family.

Step 8: How has this experience affected your life? I honestly don't know, but I do know I hated that helpless feeling and continue to fear being helpless to this day

Step 9: Have you been repeating yourself? [left blank]

Step 10: Has this conflict been resolved in your mind? [left blank]

Step 11: Has this conflict been resolved in this relationship? [left blank]
Step 12: What changes could be made to resolve your conflicts, to free yourself from re-experiencing them? [left blank]

310

CONFLICT OF ADOLESCENCE

Step 1: Draw the most conflictual memory of your adolescence (see next page).

Step 2: Describe the incident. (Who was there, what happened? What was your share in creating the conflict?) Early childhood saw bedwetting as a daily occurrence. Still bed wetting once a week or so going into high school
Step 3: How has this affected you? I don't know, but it had to have a big effect on my self-esteem.

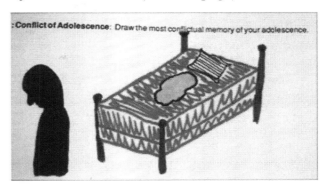

RECENT CONFLICT

Step 1: Draw the most conflictual recent memory:

Step 2: Describe the incident. (Who was there, what happened? What was your share in creating the conflict?) After 4 months of marriage my wife moved out of the bedroom because, bed too small, my sweating, etc…

Step 3: How has this affected you? It hurt because I knew that there had to be more to it

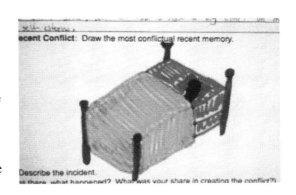

BALLOON PORTRAITS AND STORY

Step 1: Please make a portrait of your family of origin by drawing and coloring balloons to depict each member of the group. Allow your feelings about the members of your family to show through these drawings.

Step 2: Identify each individual, his/her relationship, his/her age, and personality, listing three characteristics.

    Balloon #1: Father, 43, cold, explosive and quiet.

    Balloon #2: Mother, 43, proud, kind and very maternal

    Balloon #3: Sister, 7, spoiled, selfish and traitorous

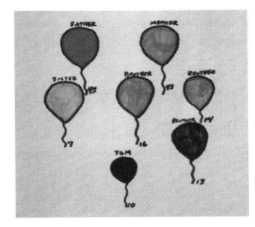

Balloon #4: Brother, 16, gifted, determined and reserved

Balloon #5: Brother, 14, practical, quiet and perceptive

Balloon #6: Brother, 13, smart, meek and compliant

Balloon #7: self, 10, energetic, careless and creative

Step 3: The balloons are having a conversation. What are they saying?
#2 is talking to #1 "I knew he could do it. #4 was just offered a full scholarship to an Ivy League school. Now if only we can get our other four to follow in his footsteps

Step 4: What were the balloons saying or doing before the conversation you just recorded?
#4 was considered the best track athlete in the state and was being recruited by all the top schools in the country.

Step 5: What were the balloons saying or doing after the initial conversation? #7 knew that athletics and scholarships were the way to go to gain recognition within the family

Step 6: Give a title to the story. "Follow the leader"

Step 7: What conflicts are these balloons experiencing? Basing love on merit. Creating incentives for acceptance.

Step 8: What changes should be made to resolve these conflicts? Love and praise your children equally. Do not set standards by which every child should feel obligated to achieve.

RESPONSE

TRANSPARENT MASK TEST

Step 1: Draw a mask

Step 2: Answer the following questions:

Give the mask a title: "In Search of acceptance"

Age: 10
Sex: M

What emotions does this mask convey? Confusion, jealousy, recklessness.

Step 3: What are the conflicts represented in this mask? Why can't you be like your brothers? We kept trying until we got a baby girl.

Step 4: What resolution of conflicts does this mask represent? Conform and be loved.

Step 5: Imagine the mask you drew has become transparent. Make a drawing of what you see through the mask, reflecting true feelings.

Fill in the blanks and answer the questions:

Step 6: Name or title: "Conform on the outside, hide what's inside"

Age: 13
Sex: M

What emotions does this mask convey?
Cleverness, deceit, freedom

Step 7: What are the conflicts represented in this mask? J is smart but fools around too much in class! I just wish he could get grades like his brothers!

Step 8: What resolution of conflicts does this mask represent? My thoughts couldn't be controlled like everything else in my life

Step 9: Make a drawing of what you see in this person's heart. Indicate this figuratively, portraying conflicts or using colors reflecting this person's emotions .

Answer the following questions:

Title: "Learning to Juggle"

Step 10: Indicate items and themes represented in this drawing. Cloud/Fantasies, horn/getting noticed at home, Shadow/shyness developing, Books/school, Shoe/sports, cross/Religion, lock/rules, stairs/striving for goals, balls/different lifestyles

Step 11: Elaborate on what feelings and conflicts this drawing represents. Don't let your family know how shy you are at school. Maybe my friends wont like me if they see how I am at home. Never let anyone know your attracted and turned on by girls' feet.

Step 12: What resolution of conflicts does it convey? Juggling my three distinct lifestyles seemed to keep everyone happy.

Step 13: Give a title to the sequence: How is an adolescent supposed to act?

Step 14: Summarize here the sequence of transformations of these images: when dealt with the problem of not getting enough attention at home I adjusted my life privately and socially to gain more attention. I sacrificed my attention in public to obtain more at home. I created an imaginative fantasy that would allow me to be subjected to anything just to get noticed

Step 15: What are your conclusions about the way this person resolves conflicts? Instead of confronting a problem I chose to alter my entire life to please those around me and avoid dealing with my problem

Step 16: How does that progression relate to your feelings and choices you have in handling feelings? I still deal with everyday problems in a similar way. Although in my job I find it much easier to confront my conflicts

Step 17: What changes should you make in the way you communicate your feelings? Learn to open up and talk about things that bother me rather than suppress them and let them build.

Step 18: What changes are you willing to make in order to reduce the intensity of these conflicts? Better communicate with people around me. Find other releases rather than masturbation or alcohol

314

*A*NIMAL *M*ETAPHOR *T*EST *#1*

This test offers you the opportunity to be imaginative and create a story featuring two animals. To do this, follow these steps:

Step 1: Draw two animal figures in color (see next page).

Step 2: Fill in the blanks

Animal #1

Type of animal: Lion
Age in human years: 24
Sex: Female
Describe the animal's personality using 3 or more traits: Unpredictable, explosive, distraught.

Animal #2

Type of animal: Dog
Age in human years: 26
Sex: Male
Describe the animal's personality using 3 or more traits: Withdrawn, uncomfortable, confused.

Step 3: The characters are having a conversation. What are they saying to each other? Indicate the sequence referring to the characters by their identity number.

#2 – Did you get the time off so we can go to my brothers 30th Birthday party.

#1 – Look, I don't want to go; we need the money so why don't you go to the party and I'll work.

#2 – You can't keep avoiding my family. It'll only make matters worse.

#1 – Your Aunt, your cousin and your sister were rude to me at my wedding and at Xmas –I don't want to deal with it.

#2 – I know that some of what they have done is wrong but can't you understand why they do the things they do.

#1 – I don't want to talk about it, you can go. Just don't expect me to go with you.

#2 – I cant believe you won't try for my sake.

#1 – I've given up trying, it hasn't done me any good up to this point why should I think it will now?

#2 – I can't just turn my back on my entire family because you don't get along with three members. What about the ten or fifteen others that you do get along with?

#1 – They have to learn that I will not stand for that kind of treatment

#2 – Fine. Don't go, you would probably just cause a scene anyway!

Step 4: What were the characters saying or doing before the conversation you just recorded? The animals were going about their business and letting the tension build like they always do. When problems arise it is safe to say that we will ignore each other for hours, sometimes days, until we confront the problem.

Step 5: What were the characters saying or doing after the initial conversation? Continue to ignore each other because we never settle things totally, usually we are just putting it off and making things worse.

Step 6: Give a title to the story. "The Rock Meets Hard Place"

Step 7a: What conflicts are these characters experiencing between themselves? Poor communication skills, selfishness to some degree on both parts, stubbornness.

Step 7b: What are the conflicts between them and the world. Elaborate. The same problems seem to come up repeatedly. We communicate less and less.

Step 8: What changes should these characters make to resolve their conflicts? Respect others' opinion and try to look at different points of view. Be more open in what is expressed and why it is being expressed. Don't let things build up; try to settle them before they become full blown.

Step 9: Which animal do you identify with most? Elaborate. The dog, he is quiet, loyal but confused about his role in life. **Who do you identify with the counterpart animal? Elaborate.** The lion is my wife. She is very unpredictable, explosive and combative.

Step 10: How does this animal drama pertain to you? Our marriage has turned into a trap that we both feel uncomfortable in. We don't communicate because we know it will lead to arguments. When we do communicate we find out how different we are. It seems that the differences that once drew us together are now driving us apart.

Step 11: What changes should you make to resolve your conflicts? Communicate with others to get different perspectives. Evaluate my priorities in life. Stop putting everything off and deal with things as they come.

Step 12: In life we repeat ourselves. Present an incident similar to what transpired in your metaphor story to illustrate your particular pattern. In July of 1982, 3 months after my father died of a massive heart attack, I found out my mother was terminal and had less than six months to live. I refused to believe that both my parents could die in so short a time. Instead of spending every chance I could with Mom. I kept distant. In September I went off to college, 3 weeks later she died with me making no effort to visit or call her.

Step 13: Reviewing this incident, describe your relational pattern, that is, how you relate with other people, and how you set things up to get yourself in trouble. I try to rationalize problems and ignore them rather than confront them. I always choose to allow myself to get hurt rather than hurt anyone around me.

Step 14: What changes are you willing to make? Don't bottle up things that bother me. Confront problems rather than suppress them. Don't be afraid to show real emotions rather than being the person everyone expects me to be.

DEFENSE

FAIRYTALE METAPHOR

This test offers you the opportunity to be imaginative and create a story featuring two characters from your favorite fairy tale. To do this, follow these steps:

Step 1: Draw your two characters in color.
Step 2: Fill in the blanks

Character#1: Joyce
Age in human years: 27
Sex: female
Describe the personality using 3 or more traits: Beautiful, sexy, stern.

Character#2: Theo
Age in human years: 12
Sex: Male
Describe the personality using 3 or more traits: Sheltered, changing, mischievous.

Step 3: The characters are having a conversation. What are they saying to each other? Indicate the sequence referring to the characters by their identity number.

#1: Theo you have got to get on the ball in my class, I won't tolerate your nonsense
#2: But Mrs. Miller, there are others in the class that fool around. How come you don't come down so hard on them?
#1: Theo, your mom is my third cousin. I'm going to be harder on you because I want you to be a good student your parents can be proud of.
#2: Your not going to tell them, are you?
#1: No, but you better shape up in my class or I will have no choice.
#2: Okay, I'll try to be a better student.
#1: Just to be sure; I'm going to move your seat right in front of me in class. This way I can keep a close eye on you.
#2: Whatever you say, as long as you don't tell my parents that I've been bad.

Step 4: What were the characters saying or doing before the conversation you just recorded?
I was fooling around in class, being disruptive, talking to classmates; anything to get some of the attention that I lacked at home. Even the negative attention seemed better than none at all.

Step 5: What were the characters saying or doing after the initial conversation? I would sit directly in front of Mrs. Miller as she would sit on top of her desk and cross her legs. I was developing a crush on her, as many students would have. She almost always wore sandals on her feet and being seated so close I began to stare at them. Having mostly fully clothed nuns in past years I began to establish a keen awareness towards the female foot.

Step 6: Give a title to the story. "The opening of Pandora's box"

Step 7a: What conflicts are these characters experiencing between themselves? One is trying to turn a student around to get him to pay attention and learn more. The other is developing a crush on a beautiful, strict, teacher.

Step 7b: What are the conflicts between them and the world. Elaborate. I began to place myself in a daydream world, one that I perceived as safer. In the next year or so I began to have wet dreams that would involve Mrs. Miller's feet or very similar female feet. Although I knew it was strange, how could I control it or discuss it with anyone?

Step 8: What changes should these characters make to resolve their conflicts? I moved on to Junior High School where I was finding that many girls would dress in sandals and other shoes that would expose their feet. I soon forgot about Mrs. Miller and would fantasize about my most recent foot experience. After staring at a pretty girl's feet in class that night I could draw it almost perfectly and masturbate to my work of art.

Step 9: Which character do you identify with most? Elaborate. Theo
Who do you identify with the counterpart character? Elaborate. My seventh grade teacher (she also would teach some of my eight grade classes).

Step 10: How does this drama pertain to you? This fairy tale shows the point in my life where I began to suppress my need for attention and started to tap into my own thoughts to satisfy my needs. The only problem is that I began to change drastically from an energetic, mischievous boy to a shy and quiet adolescent in Junior High and High school.

Step 11: What changes should you make to resolve your conflicts? This one I let grow rather than resolve. I would masturbate three or four times a week in High school thinking about the sexiest feet I saw in class that day. The fantasies were starting to take the personality of the girl into consideration. Before High school I was only interested in the appearance of the foot; the shape, the grooming, the shoes worn, etc. During and after High school the personality of the girl was equally or more important. The more bossy or bitchy, the better or the more excited I would become.

Step 12: In life we repeat ourselves. Present an incident similar to what transpired in your metaphor story to illustrate your particular pattern. [left blank]

Step 13: Reviewing this incident, describe your relational pattern, that is, how you relate with other people, and how you set things up to get yourself in trouble. [left blank]

Step 14: What changes are you willing to make? I honestly don't know

REVERSAL

ANIMAL METAPHOR #2

Step 2: Fill in the blanks

Animal #1

Type of animal: Bird
Age in human years: 45
Sex: Male
**Describe the animal's personality using 3 or
more traits:** Distant, cold, explosive.

Animal #2

Type of animal: Bird
Age in human years: 45
Sex: Female
Describe the animal's personality using 3 or more traits: Kind, caring, maternal.

Step 3: The characters are having a conversation. What are they saying to each other? Indicate the sequence referring to the characters by their identity number.

#2 – We are so proud of our oldest, he has become a star athlete and is receiving a full scholarship to an Ivy League school.
#1 – Now if we can only get the others to do the same
#2 – Well, he has certainly set a good example that the others could strive for. If they work hard there is no reason that they can't do the same.

Step 4: What were the characters saying or doing before the conversation you just recorded? Reading me the numerous newspaper clippings that talked about the scholar/athlete that was set an example for all to see!

Step 5: What were the characters saying or doing after the initial conversation?
#2 would be on the phone talking to all the world proclaiming the merits of this mentor sibling. #1 would do similar at his work.

Step 6: Give a title to the story. "Setting the Standards"

Step 7a: What conflicts are these characters experiencing between themselves? No conflict, it was clear what we were expected to achieve and aspire towards.

Step 7b: What are the conflicts between them and the world. Elaborate. Constant praise over one child's achievements. Limited praise to the other children with very little trickling down to me. Pleasing them and making them proud was the dearest way to obtain their love and attention.

Step 8: What changes should these characters make to resolve their conflicts? Love all your children equally no matter how they grow up. Don't put restrictions on your love or goals so unobtainable that constant thought of failure is so certain.

REVERSAL

DREAM ANALYSIS

Step 1: Choose an outstanding dream from the past, a recent dream or a recurring dream. Variation of recurring recent dream.

Step 2: Make a drawing portraying the key transaction captured in the dream.

Step 3: Relate the content of the dream. Most of the dreams I remember are anxiety dreams about work or social problems I am facing or about to face. The dream outlined is the one that pops into my head on a regular basis. It is very generic in that I never can tell who the woman is; she is very attractive but someone I have never met. She flirts with me and gets me embarrassed with her aggressiveness. She tells me that she knows about my secret and starts to remove her shoes. I fall to the ground and start to feverishly kiss her bare feet. Usually I awake at this point with my heart pounding and in a very aroused state.

Step 4: List the participants and attribute three traits to each of them.
Myself: silent, almost lifeless and embarrassed
Female: Sexy, very arrogant and very dominant.

Step 5: What are the conflicts? The struggle between my fantasies and my reality

Step 6: What occurrences preceded the dream? Sometimes it will be in a social setting where this temptress would pick me out of a crowd and be able to look right through me, steal my inner most thoughts and bring them out in the open.

Step 7: Attempt to give an explanation of the dream. Sexual Frustration

Step 8: Do you dream a lot? No.

Step 9: Please outline other dreams. Any stress or tension will be dreamt about and magnified in the dream. Usually these dreams have nothing to do with sex or feet. I would say 75% of my dreams are of this nature and 25% are the sexual fantasies. On the whole I only remember one or two dreams a week and that is usually only for a minute or two when I first awake. I remember the sexual ones more vividly because I awake so abruptly and so excited.

Step 10: Dreams are related to each other. Do you see a pertinent connection or patterns in your dreams? They all seem to be on the negative side in that they all pertain to something that is bothering me. The frustration of sex, work and social problems seems to be magnified in my dream state.

COMPROMISE

SHORT STORY

Step 1: Choose two imaginary characters and write a short story about one of their adventures.
Mr. X and Mrs. X are riding off into the sunset and are reflecting on their parenthood. We agreed that the oldest will be a great success; Ivy League getting offers from Fortune 500 companies. The 2nd has got a strong position in a local company with a good chance of advancement. The 3rd is off at school, studying accounting and getting great grades. Our youngest gets straight A's in high school. Our only concern is our 4th who has always struggled in school and doesn't take life too seriously. We just hope he's not wasting his time at college and going to parties all the time. Well we can ride off knowing that at least 4 of our offspring will be successful in whatever they do.

Step 2: Make a drawing of the key transaction between the characters.
Fill in the blanks

Character#1

Name: Mrs. X
Age: 53
Sex: Female
Describe the animal's personality using 3 or more traits: [LEFT BLANK}

Character#2

Name: Mr. X
Age: 53
Sex: Male
Describe the personality using 3 or more traits: [LEFT BLANK}

Step 3: What had gone on before the adventure? 25 years of bringing up their children

Step 4: What happened after the adventure? I began to take life very seriously, almost too seriously. My only release from the seriousness was my fantasies.

Step 5: Give a title to the story. "Into the Sunset"

Step 6: What conflicts are these characters experiencing? Trying to figure out how 4 children could be so perfect and how one would fight and rebel every step of the way.

Step 7: What changes should these characters make to resolve their conflicts? [LEFT BLANK}

321

Step 8: Which character do you identify with most? Elaborate. Mrs. X, or my mother. **Who do you identify with the counterpart animal? Elaborate.** Mr X, or my father.

Step 9: How does this character drama pertain to you? Sometimes I get mad because my parents left me before I could prove myself. I did make it through college, I did get a good job, I did get promoted and more on to a Fortune 500 company. Yet it all seems so insignificant because they are gone and they left with the feeling that I would become a failure.

Step 10: What changes should you make to resolve your conflicts? Realize that it doesn't matter how they feel or anybody feels at this point and start enjoying life in spite of all the difficulties.

Step 13: What changes are you willing to make? Try to enjoy life more, not take things too seriously. Communicate my problems with others and be more open.

Discussion of the Case

The assessment was effective at multiple levels:

1. It was educational. At the end of the evaluation he could understand what had happened at an intellectual level by sharing his secret experiences. He was understanding the nature of his problem as that of a submissive disposition, a wellness relational diagnosis. He evolved insights into the development of his fetishism explaining rationally his adjustment reactions as the connection of his seeking desperately approval. He detected his problems by himself, identified what changes he needed to make to correct it and came full circle on his own to the realization that he may start to feel good about himself. Enabled to communicate his feelings he realized that he could turn from fantasy to reality. He identified by himself his problems and that he needed to assert himself and be sad but also proud of himself without parental recognition. He did not deal with the reality of lack of communication with his wife leading to his alienation from her and his related escaping to phantasies rather than a fulfilling love relationship with her. He was aware of needing to be honest with her and of the need to share his problematic pattern with her.

2. The testing had been diagnostic. Reason connected his dependency needs to his acting out behaviors, his feelings of inferiority, sibling rivalries, lack of communications, non-assertiveness, which had led to his seeking attention through mischief. His fetishist obsessiveness was due to seeking self-gratification secretly rather than seeking attention overtly, which he was not allowed to do. The problem currently was perpetuated by his failure in establishing an honest relationship with his wife.

3.The experience was therapeutic. The assessment presented the emotional aspect of his problem behaviors. The sharing relieved a huge emotional burden. The composition of the metaphors represented a cathartic emotional experience. His sharing his secret life enabled him to question this type of adjustment. Through the metaphors he was able to deal with his depression and hurt feelings. He realized he needed to accept himself. Mortified he was able to find conflict resolution through self-acceptance. In his Short Story Metaphor he was able to deal with his lack of recognition from his parents, who had died before he proved himself socially. His conflict's resolution was presented there. He realized that he could feel good about himself without parental approval, through self-acceptance. Also he realized that he needed to be honest, communicating his feelings and admitting failures. He became conscious of the unconscious and became aware that he had to confront his counterproductive submissive relating. The relationship with his wife was one to explore with the help from a professional.

The Metaphor Profile Established by Reconstructing the Six-Role Pattern

The grammar of his symbolic language
One key word ties all role states in a continuum. The key word is humiliation.

Stress: Feeling powerless, *humiliated and unloved, alienated, antagonistic*

Response: seeking power with fantasies, the hammer and the anvil.

Anxiety: He feels self conscious for *acting out in secrecy. He is afraid of being caught* in mischievous pleasure of indulging self; he is self-conscious.

Defense: *seeking approval* and failing with wife but finding pleasure in his secret life.

Awareness of the *shift from seeking approval to experiencing arousal with feet fantasies.*
Reversal: In dreams, *Humiliated by being discovered in self indulgence.*
This feeling of defeat is associated in his Intensified Metaphor where he admits *feeling aware of being a failure* in the eyes of his parents.

Compromise: finding pride as his vocational success as his vindication. Proceeding to mastery, cooperation and mutual respect: *accepting his predicament, being a success yet without the possibility of being* praised by his parents, enjoying life now free from the need of approval. *Compromise as pride for self without getting approval from anybody; facing reality by communicating his feelings assertively*

The evolution of feelings across the six role states follows the transformation from conflict as passivity, antagonism and alienation to the conflict's resolution as a state of mastery, cooperation and mutual respect, indeed of self-respect.

Stress: The Conflictual Memory Tests and the Family Portrait defines his formative role choice experience as suffering rejection and self doubts, humiliation by his siblings at an early age.
All his conflictual memories point to the failures in his need for recognition as stressors leading to a sense of humiliation. He felt humiliated in the key memory his being pinned down by his three brothers and titillated by his younger sister. This state of helplessness is associated with his sense of inferiority and powerlessness compared to his successful siblings.
Another painful memory is that he was a bed wetter, a problem protracted into his adolescence.
The recent memory compounded his sense of being a looser. It portrays him sleeping alone in the conjugal bed feeling rejected by his wife.

The Response identifies his identity as phantasies of forbidden pleasures shaping his symbolic system
The Mask Test reveals his identity as a row of shoe making anvils. The parents are the hammer. A gold bar stands out among the rods of steel. The picture of his strange mask reveals his awareness of the hierarchical nature of his world. He is aware of sibling rivalries and feels humiliated comparing himself to his successful siblings.

His Anxiety, revealed hidden behind the mask, is the vulnerability of his secret preoccupations.

What about if he were discovered in his preoccupations?
He was able to rebel and satisfy his needs for love by seeking sexual gratifications secretly. But he experienced anxiety about being exposed. He craved power in the realm of feet related fantasies, forbidden thoughts that made him vulnerable. In his heart he was juggling his several identities: reaching for love and excitement, but feeling again like a failure.

Step 6: **Name or title:** "Conform on the outside, hide what's inside"
What emotions does this mask convey? 'Cleverness, deceit, freedom'

Step 7: **What are the conflicts represented in this mask?** T. is smart but fools around too much in class! I just wish he could get grades like his brothers!

Step 8: **What resolution of conflicts does this mask represent?** My thoughts couldn't be controlled like everything else in my life. Don't let your family know how shy you are at school. May be my friends wont like me if they see how I am at home. Never let anyone know your attracted and turned on by girls' feet.

Step 12: **What resolution of conflicts does it convey?** Juggling my three distinct lifestyles seemed to keep everyone happy.

Step 14: **Summarize here the sequence of transformations of these images:** when dealt with the problem of not getting enough attention at home I just adjusted my life privately and socially to gain more attention. I sacrificed my attention in public to obtain more at home. I created an imaginative world, a fantasy that would allow me to be subjected to anything just to get noticed.

Step 15: **What are your conclusions about the way this person resolves conflicts?**
Instead of confronting a problem I chose to alter my entire life to please those around me and avoid dealing with my problem.

Step 16: **How does that progression relate to your feelings and choices you have in handling feelings?** I still deal with everyday problems in a similar way. Although in my job I find it much easier to confront my conflicts

Step 17: **What changes should you make in the way you communicate your feelings?:** Learn to open up and talk about things that bother me rather than suppress them and let them build up.

Defense: in his two metaphors, he presents the failure of his marriage and his success in phantasies offsetting his sense of failure.
The Animal Metaphor presents a masterful lion and a timid dependent dog. The animal metaphor is about the current preoccupation, seeking approval from his wife struggling with her in his interest to visit his parents to find parental approval; instead he is failing to gain her cooperation thus loosing power in his marriage.

His Fairy Tale; explaining the theme of Cinderella and the prince with the golden slipper in his hand retraced the history of his preoccupation with feet. Comments provide explicit information on his phantasy life. It started seeking attention in the classroom. The teacher confined him in the front seat. There he stared at the teacher's feet. This led him to act out foot fantasies of secret behaviors that shaped his adjustment day and night as pleasures and fears of exposure.

Reversal is about loosing control of the secrecy of his foot-fetish pattern in his dreams.
Dreams fulfill fears, the dreaded anticipations of the anxiety role state.
The Dream is of being discovered in his pursuit of feet, he is caught surrendering to the overpowering feminine feet. Revealed in this weakness he feels powerless, a failure once again in the eyes of the world; the world will see him as a pervert. The dream exposes his sexual excitement and related pleasurable activity pursued in daily life. His secret aggression is exposed. Exposure, revelation is felt as powerlessness and humiliation. This dreaded state is the content of his nightmares. He is caught. This state rekindles the dreaded original role state of his childhood feelings of humiliation.

Compromise: The Short Story Test is autobiographic and presents his family related compromise attitude changes; this test reveals his own recovery as conflict resolution insights.

The story has a healing cathartic effect as he becomes aware, as he admits to himself, the significance of his deep-seated yearning for parental approval, his dependency needs; and as he is also mourning the loss of his parents before he could prove to them his successful social adjustment. But at the same time he recognizes his own sense of pride and self-respect.
'Sometimes I get mad because my parents left me before I could prove myself. I did make it through college, I did get a good job, I did get promoted and more on to a Fortune 500 company. Yet it all seems so insignificant because they are gone and they left with the feeling that I would become a failure'.

The compromise is reconciling himself with reality, first by recognizing the need for love and approval from his prematurely deceased parents, before they recognize his successful adjustment. Then he is admitting sense of loss but recognizes the need for self-confidence.

He also articulates the corrective attitude: independence of others' approval: ' I realize that it doesn't matter how they feel or anybody feels at this point and start enjoying life in spite of all the difficulties.'

The personal injunction frees him from the sense of powerlessness and alienation; communications are valued as self-empowerment: 'Try to enjoy life more, not take things too seriously. Communicate my problems with others and be more open'.

Metaphor Profile Summation of the Conflict Resolution Process

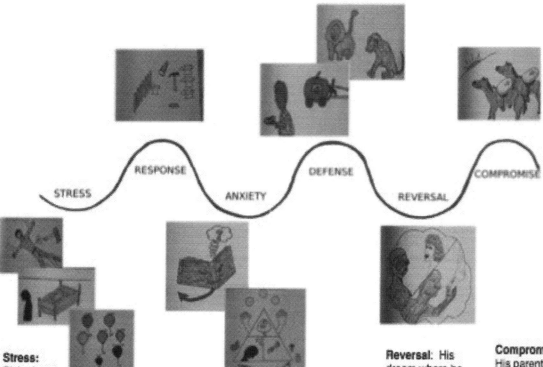

Stress:
Picked on
by brothers
and sister
who
teamed up
on him,
tickling him
to tears.
Wetting the
bed at an
old age.
Saw
himself as
the outcast,
the black-
sheep of
the family

Response:
Confusion,
Jealousy,
Why can't
you be like
your
brothers.
We kept
trying until
we got a
baby girl.

Anxiety:
Under the
mask is a
devilish
book who
"Conforms
on the
outside,
hide whats
inside." His
heart is
segmented
into the
different
aspects of
his life;
fantasies,
school,
religion,
sports. The
shadow
represents
shyness

Defense:
The
cowardly
dog and the
strong lion.
Views
himself as
the dog and
his wife as
the lion who
is stronger
and must
be
submitted
to.

Reversal: His
dream where he
is confronted by
a strong,
powerful woman
who
embarrasses
him with her
aggressiveness.
This Temptress
is able to "look
right through
me, steal my
inner thoughts
and bring them
out in the open."

Compromise:
His parents
tombstones
being carried
off into the
sunset as he
realizes that
he was a
successful
person and
that he
doesn't need
his parents for
validation. He
realizes that
he can accept
himself.

Drama Reconstructed as a Role Relational Continuum

1.STRESS CMT Position of powerlessness, antagonism, alienation	2. RESPONSE MASK Power in competing with siblings in symbolic domain, of a hammer and anvils possible shoe anvils while sister as precious gold.	3. ANXIETY SECOND MASK Afraid of humiliation of being caught in forbidden escape, juggling identities. Power combined with guilt about his foot fetish	4. DEFENSE AMT. Actively seeking approval from family but with wife resisting. He is again in powerless position. Fairy Tale secretly seeking approval by teacher and escaping in phantasy empowerment, through foot fetish.	5. REVERSAL DREAM Caught in mischief, helpless in surrendering to humiliating powerful need, embarrassed. INTENSIFIED AMT rejected by family as a failure.	6. COMROMISE: SHORT STORY Admitting his need for approval and recognizing his own self worth. Finding, achieving, resolution in dealing with loss of approval through self-acceptance.

|3|

Clinical Delivery Case Studies
The Dominance Relational Modality
All About Lions

Clinical Delivery Case Studies
The Dominance Relational Modality
All About Lions

Introduction

In this chapter we focus on the clinical delivery of Power Management to patients of my psychiatric practice diagnosed with dominant relational modalities. We examine the wellness syndromal characteristics of this diagnosis and its decompensation to illness. The patients in these case studies illustrate the psychodynamic genesis of clinical symptoms and the psychotherapeutic value of the power management intervention. They demonstrate the effectiveness of the self-assessment battery in helping to develop insights and to generate directives for behavior modification. The studies demonstrate the diagnostic and therapeutic effectiveness of the assessment in eliminating or at least diminishing psychopathology.

Relational Modality Scores

The dominant individuals' relations scores are consistently elevated while their submissiveness scores are consistently low. The psychic tension is elevated in the areas of anxiety and sself-consciousness. The online delivery scores reflect the spectrum of relational modalities with figures varying from one to six. Elevations of four are diagnostic of the dominance relating.

Traditional DSM 5 psychiatric diagnoses focus on symptoms and overlook the psychodynamic origin of pathology. Each of these dominance cases would have been ascribed a clinical symptom focused diagnosis. The study observes psycho and socio-pathologies in the seven cases in exclusively psychodynamic terms. The clinical symptoms for dominance include a whole range of psychopathology. Anxiety is pervasive, manifested through a variety of clinical diagnoses and social dysfunctional adjustments. Dominance is experienced as phobias, panic disorders, paralyzing emotions that can be disabling in many aspects of one's life, such as performance anxiety, but also discretely as insidious emotional resistance, a defense to vulnerability and a pervasive lack of trust reinforcing one's readiness to overreact.

There are two types of pathology: The first is generated by experiences of anticipation of role reversal: relational psycho-anxiety conditions, reaching the intensity of panic attacks, or alternatively as paranoid fears, emotional apprehension. The second is generated by defensive role assumptions causing social problems. Behavior of aggressiveness: counterphobic provocative or defensive activities lead to conflicts in all relationships, domestic and professional potentially escalating to suicidal and homicidal thinking and actions. Two individuals in this study of seven patients got in trouble and were fired from their employment positions. One upon being fired and also rejected by his wife was close to murdering his wife and two children and also committing suicide. The other upon being fired experienced psychosomatic symptoms.

The relational wellness diagnosis of dominance entails recognizing the pathogenetic role of aggressiveness, anger, uninhibited expression of feelings as the normative deviation towards power positions. This may be graphically portrayed with vectors towards the power polarity in the concentric circles power field diagram. Antagonism is portrayed with counterclockwise vectors, while cooperation with clockwise ones. The response to the power positioning induces in the person psychic tension experienced as anticipations of role reversal; the person anticipates becoming the recipient of her/his aggressiveness.

Freud identified the state of anticipation of role reversal as 'projection'. The projected emotions may be graphically portrayed in the peripherally positioned ellipse representing the psychic system of the individual as vectors, forces, countering the social system power displacements. These forces in the aggressive person induce the ensuing escalation of defensiveness, which leads to escalation of social conflicts and, which eventually leads to the social role reversal of the individual.

About Lions and the Chain Reation
In the metaphorical language of the Wizard of Oz the dominant antagonistic modality is illustrated in the image of being a lion that is cowardly. Examining the feelings of the Lion or the aggressive individual we may recognize the evolution of the dominance syndrome along the six-role process:

Stress is the position of personal disturbance.

Power as role assumption is the response state as aggression depicted by being a lion.
This response generates anxiety as anticipations of role-reversal; this is reflected in the lion becoming anxious or cowardly.

In turn anxieties elicit defensiveness as counterphobic responses. The lion roars and shows his teeth.

Defensiveness eventually leads to role reversals; the lion looses control to the hunters; s/he is in panic; s/he is rescued by the proverbial mouse.

The reversal elicits compromises; the lion is grateful to the mouse, who rescued him. The mouse is the lion's submissive partner. Lions seek out mice; these are the only persons lions are comfortable with. Dominant individuals marry submissive partners.

Therapeutic Intervention: Restrains on Aggressive Behavior
The dominance diagnosis entails the therapeutic intervention of realizing one's own transgressive display of power as the origin of fears, anxieties, and disabilities. With this realization the patient becomes aware of the need of power management as reduction of his / her anger. The case studies reflect this consistent psychodynamic pattern: intense power positioning, be it cooperative or antagonistic, as

responsible for the generation of paralyzing emotional and social, personal and interpersonal states of discomfort. The patient realizes that the restraint of power is the secret in healing oneself from the disabling symptoms.

Note that five of the seven patients in this cohort chose in their animal metaphors the identity of a lion, while most of their metaphors are power plays between the two metaphorical figures.

Review of the Seven Case Studies

Case #1: *Holocaust Survivor, Lion Versus Lion*
Two lions in conflict over an antelope, the spoils of the hunt, was the Animal Metaphor title of a 65-year-old **dominant cooperative** woman, whose problems were related with having been a Holocaust survivor. She was troubled by her unresolved relation with the past.

In a single workbook completed in a three-session therapeutic evaluation she presented her dominance pattern. Her aggressiveness was illustrated in her Animal Metaphor Test, 'two lions in conflict over a dead antelope' reflecting her need for control. Her mask labeled 'Inscrutable' reflected on her emotional defensive stance. This seeming coldness covered up her deep sense of self-doubt, illustrated in a tree with poison fruit revealed underneath the mask. She was able to admit her self-blame for the sense of relief she had experienced as a seven-year old girl upon the deportation of her overprotective grand-parents. The dream metaphor illustrated her reunion with her beloved grand parents. She was also able to check her transgressiveness manifested in a number of metaphors like her Short Story.

The healing effect of the experience was in her being able to emote and mourn the loss of her mother and of her grand parents upon the celebration of an anniversary of the creation of Israel. She sent me a letter containing art and text of a metaphor test that she constructed herself to thank me for making progress in her emotional life. In this letter she informed me of her making a fool of herself, breaking down and crying in a pubic setting. She was no longer 'inscrutable' or emotionally frozen.

Case #2: *The Lame Ant And The Damaged Flea*
The Flea and the lame Ant, was a 45-year-old male pianist, with performance anxiety. With the help of four workbooks completed in as many sessions, the performance phobic pianist was freed from his anxiety by recognizing the role of his dominant personality. He identified his arrogance in his conflictual memory as defiance of his mother. He had been self-pleasuring obsessively, in spite of his mother's reproaching him of this conduct. His early sexual rebelliousness reflecting his dominant disposition had caused him to feel worthless and self-conscious. The guilt for arrogant perfectionism leading to self-consciousness was the underlying factor in his performance anxiety. His metaphors evolved from his diminished self-identity as a lame ant and a damaged flea into his final image of a rehabilitated lion and high flying wounded eagle, coinciding with the cure of his performance anxiety.

Case Study #3: *Captive as a Circus Elephant versus Free Like a Butterfly*
A 28-year-old artist was referred to me by her mother to consider administering an antidepressant. She was angry with her mother and had chosen to live far way from home. A two-session single workbook evaluation provided insights into her well-established dominance. This manifested in her scales and also in her metaphors.

The dominance pattern had determined her abrasive family interactions. The workbook helped her to understand her sensitivities and anger manifested across her metaphors: She identified many conflictual memories of anger at others. The anger at her mother was illustrated in the jagged family balloon of her mother, the anger at her step-father was depicted in a recent conflictual memory upon him trying to embrace her. Her phobic sensitivities showed in her two metaphors as the dilemmas of a bride: the first was captured in her Animal Metaphor between a captive circus elephant versus feeling free like a butterfly, the second was captured in the Fairy Tale Metaphor as Beauty loving the Beast versus Cinderella looking for a prince.

The young woman suffered of general apprehension, anxiety and depression manifested in hesitations to getting married lasting several years for fear of trusting her boyfriend. In the third mask, presenting what is in your heart, she made sure that her heart is very well defended; the heart had three layers of protective encapsulations. In her Dream image, a nightmare, her heart is broken in two halves. Her fears of his breaking her heart caused her to resist getting married. Her counter-phobic defensiveness resolved itself in her Short Story Metaphor with the image of a couple trusting each other and kissing.

The insights into her pattern of dominance enabled her to look at her self, identify her anger at her relationships starting with her mother and also manifesting in her relationship with her boyfriend of three years. She got married soon after the evaluation. I heard from her mother that the marriage lasted only three months. Her hopes of happiness soured, as she soon perceived her husband as the hurtful beast. Fears are self-fulfilling. The dominant person is guided by her fears rather than by reality. She divorced the husband and returned to being the Butterfly-Cinderella looking for a prince.

Case Study #4: *The Dragon and the Unicorn*
The dragon and the unicorn, a 22-year-old college student, married woman, experienced panic elicited upon her anticipation of delivering a paper in her literature class. An eight-session therapy helped her to comprehend her performance anxiety by understanding her dominance syndrome. Her limit testing behavior had caused her self-consciousness, which manifested clinically as performance anxiety.

Her extraordinary dominant personality was the origin of the anxiety as anticipations of role reversal. She identified her dominance as the cause of her social phobia and tried to learn to contain her over-reactions. Her art work helped her to realize this anger manifested in all her very beautiful images: these included her conflictual memories as an intense need for reassurance, her intense responses at being left out of a family funeral, her devastating responses at feeling neglected, her acting out with young people prior to her marriage. She realized that her identity was that of a Lion. Indeed her mask was that of a lion. It covered a very angry lion underneath. Her heart was tethered illustrating her anxiety as unacceptable restraints to her intense emotions.

Insights in her pattern of angry responses led to restraining her emotionality that successfully resolved her anxiety and fears of performance. Her paranoid, and paralyzing fears dissipated and she was able to prepare herself for the presentation. She completed therapy with a lengthy Short Story illustrated in a massive drawing. The story reflected her anger transformed into leadership and commitment for success: A brave unicorn rescued her father's nation by single handedly battling the enemy, a devastating dragon. Her winged unicorn, probably presenting her passion for success and recognition, overpowered the fiery demonic dragon threatening her father's kingdom; the dragon, her tethered personal powerful anger was harnessed in the service to her family as caring leadership. In the story she was triumphant rescuing her clan and her brother who was defeated in the battle with the dragon. She saved the kingdom and her sense of safety in the leadership position thus also dealing with her sibling rivalry feelings.

Case Study #5: *The Turkey and the Mountain Lion*
The Turkey and the Mountain Lion was a 35-year-old attractive woman experiencing severe anxiety around her boy friend's three children. She composed in four sessions her first workbook, the evaluation. This was followed up with two months of group therapy during which she completed a second

workbook. She understood how her dominant relational pattern caused anxiety and chronic depression.

In her first workbook's Short Story Metaphor, she was the humbled greyhound upset by three alley cats; she realized the connection between her fear of her boy friend's three children as the anticipations of a role reversal: she had projected her aggressiveness directed against her own stepmother to her boyfriend's children. Because of these fears she was intolerant of his three kind children. This insight helped her to moderate her defensive responses. Her anxiety and depression diminished. She recovered her self-confidence. Self-aware she was able to settle down and get married to her friend after a six-year long engagement. This marriage lasted several years.

In the second workbook she found comfort recognizing the source of her feelings in her relationship with her father. She had reacted angrily at experiencing abandonment by her father who had left home abruptly. She resolved her agitation at him as she composed a story between 'a nervous terrier upsetting a beefalo'. She was the nervous terrier circling around a beefalo driving him dizzy with her antiques. She recognized in the big animal her annoyed father and became emotionally ready to be reconciled with him.

Case Study #6: *The Cheshire Cat and the Pit-bull*

Cheshire Cat versus Pit-bull was the story of a 40 year-old male teacher, a cooperative dominant person, who was very depressed for being fired from his school for insubordination. In a six-session therapeutic evaluation he completed two workbooks, which he then used to sum up his life episodes meaningfully explaining the pattern of his dominance. In his self-evaluation he clearly explained his dominant pattern evoking social and emotional conflicts.

His dominant cooperative personality diagnosis manifested in his mask as the Cheshire Cat's ear to ear grin. In the first book the individual recognized the significance of his defense and how the crisis at his school system reflected a reversal for his controlling pattern, identified with the smiling Cheshire Cat. In his Animal Metaphor his cat was pinned down by a Pit Bull. His self-confidence collapsing led him to cry in his Short Story Metaphor. He was able to recognize his Cheshire Cat smile as a defense to being hurt and was able to let himself feel good for breaking down and crying for the first time in his life. But his compromise illustrated in the first book did not change his dominant personality; he swiftly recovered from his depression fighting back the school system and winning the battle of his dismissal.

The second book portrayed his recovery from the state of depression as he used his wit to outsmart the school system. Instead of being fired for insubordination he was able to get out of the school system with a compensable disability. His humor was a powerful defense but also the key factor in his social conflicts, which led to his reversal of fortune; it had precipitated insubordination and the end of his career, accompanied by an emotional breakdown. His faulty survival tactic reflected his self-defeating power struggle; he was trying to change the system rather than himself. His dominance resisted therapy but he was able to become self aware of his troubling emotional dynamic. He admitted that he could also be a pit-bull.

Case #7: Pathology of Couples, *The Bull and the Cow Versus the Lamb and the Bear*

This middle-aged dominant man was fired because of stealing an article from the place of his employment. His dominant antagonistic behavior manifested in both the work environment and his domestic relations. He was very mad at being fired from his work and at being rejected in his advances by his easy-going wife. This loss of standing almost led him to the ultimate abuse of power; he came close to murdering his family and committing suicide. Awareness of his being out of control drove him to seek help.

Therapeutic Insights Power Management entails a shift in interventions from cognitive focus on controlling irrational emotions to the simpler alternative of managing behaviors.
Therapeutically it is important that the test taker realize the syndromal relational nature of the process as the cause effect relation between aggressiveness and the experience of anxiety. Anxiety manifests as anticipations of aggression from others. Evolving insights into the anxiety as secondary to one's own aggressive conduct is the first step to making relational attitudinal corrective changes. This connection has been the key interpretation throughout the dominance case studies. Following up on these insights with personal self-restraints has led the ensuing excellent therapy outcomes. We observe rapid recoveries in the seven clinical case studies presented under dominance.

Unlike cognitive behavior therapies the focus in Power Management is not in dealing with distressing emotions like anxiety and depression, but in dealing with the *behaviors* responsible for the generation of the unpleasant *emotions*. One can readily experience relief of these emotions, be those anxiety, depression or paranoid distortions, defensiveness and real social setbacks handicapping one's adjustment by addressing one's own inappropriate aggressiveness.

Therapy begins with education on the syndromal nature of relational modalities and ends with identifying one's modality diagnosis. The diagnosis of dominance is made in the metaphor tests by the test taker and so is the insight for making concessions. It helps to understand the condition of the Cowardly Lion as the aggressiveness projected to others eliciting anxiety and more defensiveness. Once a person understands the price of being a lion s/he will modify one's behavior. Thus learning about the psychodynamic origin of anxiety, as a relational modality diagnosis and recognizing its manifestation in one's inventory and metaphors, the person becomes comfortable in making changes. Knowledge delivers reassurance and the testing delivers insights. These are the tools for the individual to identify the problem and to moderate power behaviors, which in turn diminish the level of apprehensiveness, floating anxiety, and reduce the need for defensive aggressiveness.

The insight on the relational diagnosis goes hand in hand with understanding the difficulty of a dominant person to respect the two problematic aspects of this relational modality:
First, restraining one's tendency to abuse power.
Second, the difficulty the dominant person has in listening to criticism, hence surrendering power.

Characteristics Of Dominant Persons' Artwork

Below one can see the images reflecting the profiles of dominance in both the Animal Metaphor Tests and also the three Masks; we recognize there the conflicts of the dominant modality and the insights generated by the metaphors.

The images frequently present fights and conflicts. The metaphor identity animal frequently is that of a lion. It is so in five of the seven patients including the Animal Metaphor and the Mask Test.

- Two equally powerful animals confront each other.

- The test taker identifies with the most powerful animal when there are differences between the two.

- The identity animal has difficulty accepting responsibility.

- The test taker realizes the pattern of dominance and suggests changes by restraining one's controlling tendencies.

- The test taker accepts restraining one's power, becoming more receptive in other people's feelings thus making changes or compromises.

A reminder of the images reflecting the submissive individuals' metaphor choices.
In submissiveness we detect substantial polarization between animal choices. The portray one animal as a victim of the other as a violent partner: one is a hunter the other is hunted.

Asymmetry of power positions: the person identifies with the weak animal. An animal will feature signs of damage, defect or injury, handicap, like a broken wing, a ring around one's neck where one's head is being bitten off. The positions and the placement of the animals show lack of communication between them.

The animal of choice is in a posture showing remorse, guilt and quest for forgiveness.

Case Title	Picture	Who Do You Identify With?
Case #1: *Holocaust Survivor Lion Versus Lion*		"[I identify with Lion] #1, since he did the killing and the spoils belong to him. However, he is not willing to share even a small piece with the other lion, who is also needy."
Case #2: *The Ant and the Flea*		"[I identify with the] llama – out of place, lonely, sad and worthless – so much and yet so little. Unlike her, though, I don't 'take it as it is.'"
Case #3: *The Elephant and the Butterfly*		"I can move like [the elephant] in terms of analyzing feelings and emotions and understanding how one needs to deal with responsibilities. You can't just keep on flying."
Case #4: *The Dragon and the Unicorn*		"[I identify with] Piglet. When I was young, I'd always blame somebody else for my wrongdoing. I denied my own responsibility."
Case #5: *The Turkey and the Mountain Lion*		"[I identify with] the Turkey. My modus operandus is 'flight, not fight'…it's a manifestation of a scenerio I know well: myself being weaker than a more controlling dominant person."
Case #6: *The Cheshire Cat and the Pit-bull*		"I am the Cheshire Cat. I used to be the happiest 'cat' I know. I really wish I could dissapear from my current situation, or at least use my climbing ability to climb out of the pit I'm in. I want my ear-to-ear smile back."

Dominance Case Studies' Three Masks

Dominant Masks

The first mask presents one's powerful emotions as an authority, experiencing resistance to weakness and emotions. The feelings mask presents self-portraits realistically and with feelings of determination and defiance. The heart mask shows the nature of conflicts as with external forces rather than internal ones. The heart is suffering in alternative ways it clearly displays be those of guilt, anger and depression.

Reminder of submissive masks

There are distinct differences for the dominant and submissive sets of masks.
The first mask may present power and authority, or defenses, like a wall, and also a warrior attitude or anger, like Mr. Dynamo; these are deceptive symbols of power.

The second mask presents images of traumas, and enumeration of hurt feelings and mishaps. It presents the weaknesses of a person's identity: like behind the powerful judge we have a vulnerable lamb, confusion, lack of identity, and the loss of control.

The heart is traumatized and encapsulated, harboring the hurt feelings or illustrating the difficulty communicating them, like the impediment of a moat, a hole in the heart, encasement, a state of being 'completely unrevealed'.

Case Study	Mask	Hidden Feelings	Total Picture What Is In Your Heart
Case #1: *Holocaust Survivor*	"'Inscrutable.' Some worry, but well controlled…a non-committal posture."	"'Perfect Looking Poison Fruit.' Suspicion, impulse … take things at face value… flawless fruits which are poison, things are not what they seem."	"'A Heart Full of Good Intentions, and What it Paves the Road To.' Laughing at emptiness, pain, confusion…humor helps in the solutions of difficult problems."
Case #2: *The Ant and the Flea*	"'Venetian	"'"	"'Bleeding Heart with

	Rendezvous.' Expectation, anxiety. Lust vs. spirituality, fear vs. confidence. "	Determined.' Persistent determination [and] absence of doubt.	Halo.' Deep sadness and despair. Helplessness and great goodness of spirit."
Case #3: *The Elephant and the Butterfly*	"'Infinity.' An eternal sense of being strong, hiding any conflict that may be in this person. [The mask represents] truth."	"'Jillian' Motion, Beauty, Intensity, Mystery. Seeing the beauty and strength, insecure person who wears the mask. "	"'Amazing Grace.' Abnormality [and] sensitivity – not a perfect heart. The heart is complicated…[it] has layers for protection. What is really inside the person."
Case #4: *The Dragon and the Unicorn*	"'Phoenix the Cat.' This mask became handy…whenever she got angry, upset, suspicious. Learn to control your emotion."	"'Phoenix the Mad Cat.'[This is] the girl's true color. The girl could get aggressive when the mad cat was let out of his cage. Two cats lived inside her."	"'Heart in Chains.' She restrained herself to avoid getting in trouble…she could not express her love."
Case #5: *The Turkey and the Mountain Lion*	"'Block of Worry.' Stress, confusion, sadness, frustration, fear, indecision."	"'Fragmenting of the Perfect Jewel.' Fragmenting of energies, dissipation of	"'Hope and Fear.' The struggle to maintain my own goals against other desires, biology, etc…maybe there will be

		dreams. Not knowing where to focus."	time for all in its due course?"
Case #6: *The Cheshire Cat*	"'The Ever-Smiling Cheshire Cat.' Perpetual happiness…I want to return to this face/mask…I thought [it] was my true face."	"'Who Is This Man?' Confusion…I'm not sure who is behind the smiling mask."	"'Heart Under Siege.' Threats to the heart, confusion. This represents a heart, which is in danger.

Dominant Masks

The first mask presents one's powerful emotions as in authority, resistance to weakness and emotions.

THE FIRST IMAGE

"'Inscrutable.'
Some worry, but well controlled…a non-committal posture."

"'Venetian Rendezvous.'
Expectation, anxiety. Lust vs. spirituality, fear vs. confidence"

"'Infinity.'
An eternal sense of being strong, hiding any conflict that may be in this person. [The mask represents] truth."

"'Phoenix the Cat.'
This mask became handy…whenever she got angry, upset, suspicious. Learn to control your emotions."

"'Block of Worry.'
Stress, confusion, sadness, frustration, fear, indecision."

"'The Ever-Smiling Cheshire Cat.'
Perpetual happiness…I want to return to this face/mask…I thought [it] was my true face."

The Second Image Presents the Hidden Feelings

The second mask reveals one's real persona, mostly as one's face and identifies the person's feelings of strength. The dominant person's face features clearly delineated features, such as open eyes, clear features of the face, the nose and the mouth. The characteristic feelings are attributes of power such as determination, beauty, mystery, madness, and perfection. They may also present powerlessness such as guilt, fragmentation, confusion, wonderment, anxiety and self-accusations, but unlike the submissive person's second mask they do not present exclusively weaknesses and multiple traumas.

"'Perfect Looking Poison Fruit.'
Suspicion, impulse … take things at face value… flawless fruits which are poison, things are not what they seem."

"'Determined.'
Persistent determination [and] absence of doubt.

"'Jillian'
Motion, Beauty, Intensity, Mystery. Seeing the beauty and strength, insecure person who wears the mask. "

"'Phoenix the Mad Cat.'[This is] the girl's true color. The girl could get aggressive when the mad cat was let out of his cage. Two cats lived inside her."

"'Fragmenting of the Perfect Jewel.'
Fragmenting of energies, dissipation of dreams. Not knowing where to focus."

"'Who Is This Man?'
Confusion…I'm not sure who is behind the smiling mask."

The Third Image: The Heart, Illustrates Feelings Clearly and Social Conflicts

The image of the heart reveals the combination of strengths and weaknesses. The shell of the heart is reinforced so the heart cannot be easily broken; it can be multilayered to protect itself from being hurt. The contents of the heart combine feelings of strength, deceptiveness and possibly malevolence, sometimes it is full of despair and self-contempt. Instead of internal turmoil the dominant heart may be the object of external attacks as 'a heart under siege'.

"'A Heart Full of Good Intentions, and
What it Paves the Road To.'
Laughing at emptiness, pain, confusion…humor helps in the solutions of difficult problems." ,

"'Bleeding Heart with Halo.'
Deep sadness and despair. Helplessness and great goodness of spirit."

"'Amazing Grace.'
Abnormality [and] sensitivity – not a perfect heart. The heart is complicated…[it] has layers for protection. What is really inside the person."

"'Heart in Chains.'
She restrained herself to avoid getting in trouble…she could not express her love."

'Hope and Fear.'
The struggle to maintain my own goals against other desires, biology, etc…maybe there will be time for all in its due course?"

"'Heart Under Siege.'
Threats to the heart, confusion. This represents a heart, which is in danger.

Case Study One
Hannah, A Holocaust Survivor

A Case Study Illustrating the Diagnostic Value and the Therapeutic Effectiveness of the Self-Assessment Battery

Introduction

This study illustrates the diagnostic and therapeutic effectiveness of the self-assessment. It delivered a healing outcome through a modest professional intervention, a three-session therapeutic evaluation. The success of the intervention is confirmed by the observations of the patient. The emotional nature of the self-assessment helped Hannah to resolve conflicts, and to understand herself in the context of her dominant personality.

This study is of a 62-year-old Holocaust survivor, who visited my office requesting a psychological evaluation regarding her childhood experiences as a displaced person. I asked her to complete the Conflict Analysis Battery as the means to generate a record of her memories of the War years and their impact on her mental health. She presented me with the completed workbook and subsequently with extensive comments about its healing impact.

She was born in 1933 to a Jewish mother and a German father; her parents were divorced when Hannah was only 6 years old. Her father was killed in action on the Russian front; her mother attempted suicide after being gang raped by German soldiers; she was then hospitalized, subsequently deported, and upon her release from a concentration camp succeeded in committing suicide. Hannah's maternal grandparents became her guardians until they were themselves deported. She narrowly escaped deportation, first by being placed in a foundling home and subsequently by living with her paternal grandparents. Due to her mixed ethnic background, she and her persecuted paternal grandparents escaped from Austria to Switzerland.

One of the causes of her distress was guilt concerning the childlike sense of relief she had experienced when her Jewish grandparents were deported to an alleged labor camp. She later found out that they were killed. Evidence of this guilt and of her damaged sense of self was clearly illustrated in her Transparent Mask Test, in which she depicted herself as 'inscrutable' hiding underneath this mask her feelings of being a mutilated tree bearing poison fruit.

Hannah's relational modality generated assertive thoughts and also related guilt feelings. Her childhood responses of seeking independence had generated guilt about her defiant thoughts. She was able to understand her responses instead of holding them against herself feeling that she was a terrible and cruel person, as portrayed in her Transparent Mask Test as the broken tree with the poison fruit.

The evaluation had a therapeutic impact. It changed her defensive detachment; it removed her emotional guard. It freed her from her guilt feelings as a survivor. The release from this guilt is documented in two protocols: one was a dream experienced during the evaluation period in which she was reunited with her grandmother. Another was about an emotional experience that followed the termination of her evaluation. Hannah mailed me record; it reconstructed the format of a recent memory test, including art and questions of this experience. In it she described her loosing her composure, breaking down, 'making a fool of myself in public', a very significant experience for 'an inscrutable' person, upon listening to an Israeli singer during a celebration of the anniversary of the creation of Israel.

Hannah gave me a release to publish the record of her case study also insisting that I could use her full name. The transcript of her workbook follows including her essay recounting the impact of the evaluation.

This is a fascinating case as this woman was a child of a Jewish mother and a German father, who was indeed a pilot killed in action. It is of emotional significance as the child lost the Jewish grand parents and was rescued by the German family, who escaped with her into Switzerland. In her Family Zoo Portrait she has these two identities in a dialogue, which is of great emotional relevance as it reflects her own sense of identity as a little mule. The experiences between the two ethnic identities were personalized as she rescued her mother from a suicide attempt following her being gang raped by German soldiers.

❖   ALBERT LEVIS' PARALLEL CULTURAL CONFLICTS   ❖

Here we have a personal drama that is of significance to myself as I too was a child in hiding during the Holocaust. I too as an adult sought to understand the turmoil of the cultural conflicts of that War, which I experienced as the devastation of Europe and of my neighborhood. The war exterminated the Jewish community of Greece. I too had to deal with the traumatic experiences of my childhood and the ideologies of the times: The communist uprising that killed my grand father was also inspirational to myself as a youth of the times. My quest for meaning led me into developing insights into a new conceptualization of behavior. I found Hannah's Fairy Tale Metaphor story of Joshua and Cerberus, the dog guardian of Hades, as very relevant an explanation of the relativity of values as normative realities. Her thinking of an explanation parallels mine as a response to understanding and healing from the traumas of the world manipulated by the ideologies of the times.

Another aspect of this case study is its significance beyond my focus of insights based on the relational modality. The experience here documents the significance of the structural therapeutic value of the art therapy without insights on one's relational modality.

The case study is important in its documenting a relational diagnosis of dominance exemplified here with the metaphor of two lions struggling over a kill. The two lions could be the two identities in her self: the Judaic and the Germanic. But what is more important in this case study is illustrating the significance of the diagnostic interpretation. The patient/client here recovered from her defensive stance with insights into her relational diagnosis. She praised the experience in her essay for the insights generated by the assessment.

Personal Essay
My '$5 Psychotherapy Sessions'

"The original purpose of my examination by Dr. Levis was the existence or non-existence of leftover psychological scars caused by my childhood experiences during the Nazi times. I was uncertain that any concrete proof of them could be established at all, and it appeared even more unlikely that it could be done within a short period of time. But that was before I knew of Dr. Levis's method of completing several creativity exercises. I was allowed to take the first part of the Conflict Analysis Battery with me as homework since I live some distance away.

Sitting at my kitchen table (a familiar non-threatening environment) I confronted a series of tests (in many ways similar in format to tests I had faced at school except that the only preparation I needed was having lived my life). The tests are about memories from my childhood, portraits of the family, dreams, animal and fairy tale metaphors. They started with a drawing and continued with a series of thought provoking questions. The tests led me to painful memories, and to thinking of how to represent them. The questions about them (i.e. who was there? How did you feel about that person?) helped me to be analytical rather than to relive them alone. I had to keep my concentration within that experience quite clinically for a longer period of time than I think I ever had before. I was led through the series of questions to a solution of my own. I began to enjoy the unfolding stories and final answers. I found that I could not predict them; they wrote themselves, one reply leading to another. I began to understand what I had heard writers say, 'that characters behaved as they wished to, once they were conceived.'

Dreams had always been difficult to analyze on my own; I have tried. They reminded me of onions, one layer uncovered another, until I got quite confused. Suddenly a dream I had attempted to unravel for the past 53 years, whenever I thought of it, became a simple matter when subjected to Dr. Levis' method. Perhaps the act of creating a physical image gave it a more concrete reality in my mind. Whatever... it worked! Whenever I finished my assignment, the doctor received it asking additional questions or helping me see a missed clue. After three sessions he knew more about me than long-time friends and I had gained valuable insights, an unexpected bonus for me. I feel more secure now, because I know that my own mind can provide the answers to all my problems. I can follow the method of dealing with them.

As a member of an organization called Holocaust Child Survivors of Connecticut, Inc., I attend commemorative services for the slaughtered Jews during the reign of terror of the Third Reich. This is the first year I could look at it calmly as something like the honoring of veterans of wars or tortured prisoners and not as an invitation to relive a terrible time. (See the attached recent memory drawings and process). The healing fall-out of my therapy is not in yet.

Had the high school psychologist, who called me into his office after I became a student in America put a Conflict Analysis Battery of tests in front of me, I could not have gotten away with a simple "yes" to his question of "Are you happy?" when I was not at all.

My husband had abdominal pains, which doctors believed to be psychological during the early years of our marriage, which sent him to a psychiatrist. He was very uncommunicative in his sessions; he terminated therapy. His symptoms ceased altogether within two years. He probably would have completed Dr. Levis' tests (he told me when I showed him the ones I did) since they fitted into the pattern of testing he was used to from school rather then his image of a lunatic who is asked strange personal questions by a man he hardly knew.

I feel that the fact of having to reveal highly personal data in Dr. Levis' tests is masked by having to perform an introspective solitary task first with you alone as a witness. When the doctor reads back your material, he is telling you your story, and you make corrections or additions only, distracted from the realization that you have just confided in him.

As a person who recently completed a testing series with Dr. Levis, I am greatly impressed by the possibilities of his system. Judging from my experience it is a superior vehicle for screenings, such as for kids in a school and for conflict in the work place. The testing can be used for a fast, accurate psychological assessment or for a self-assessment at any point in time of a person's life. It reflects clearly one's state of mind. In psychotherapy or psychoanalysis it can be taken to whatever detail is desired or necessary, greatly reducing the time required for the completion of therapy and the hours spent with a professional. This in turn reduces the cost providing a larger population with access to therapy.

In my last job as a budget analyst for the State, my boss had the belief that all problems presented could be reduced to asking what? why? and how? Dr. Levis's final process question is "how will I use this experience to change my behavior?" To my knowledge this question is absent from much of modern therapy. My New York City College roommate was still having weekly sessions, 15 years after I left the city, when our correspondence ended. Each test included in the battery I took, ended with the question "How will I change my behavior to avoid a conflict of this nature in the future?" The answer is that I have made peace with myself. One big burden, hate and guilt have been lifted from my mind. I feel better about myself, resolved with my experiences. I am more spontaneous in my emotions and more open in my expressions.

In conclusion I can only say that I can glimpse a wide highway of uses for Dr. Levis' tests and that it travels a long way towards my generations' cry of "What the world needs now is a $5.00 psychoanalytic session."

Addendum
Appended to the letter; a recent memory, drawing and process

"I want to share an example of being spontaneous in my emotional expression.
"Chava Alberstein sang Israeli and Yiddish songs including the plaintive theme from Schindler's List which I know every note of but I only remember the often repeated "Kinderle" from the words. Her powerful responsive voice resounded through the Bethel Temple and I was aware of little else but that wonderful noise. I remember thinking how excellent her singing was, when I realized that I was crying and I didn't really know why. My emotions were rising and ebbing with the music that pervaded me and I stopped caring that I was making a spectacle of myself. Lest you think that I am always that emotional, let me hasten to say that I only did that once before, and that was at home listening to a record many years ago in my twenties. Though I don't know Yiddish, I knew the melodies of many of the songs. Did my mother or grandmother sing these songs when I was little? Or grandfather play them on his violin? The answer to this question will have to be added to the many mysteries of my early childhood."

CHAVA ALBERSTEIN

husband M   4th cousin F   Abba in law M   3rd cousin M   2nd cousin-in-law F   3rd c

Celebration of Israel (#2) Independence Day
May 4, 1995

Transcript of the Case Study

STRESS

CHILDHOOD CONFLICTUAL MEMORY #1

Step 1: Please draw and color a most conflictual memory from your childhood. Feel free to be as imaginative as you wish with the portrayal of this conflict to allow your feelings to show through the drawings.

Step 2: Describe the incident. Who was there and what happened?
Mother, neighbor's daughter at 18 years old who worked in Terezin but was permitted to sleep in an old apartment and me --- 8-9 years old. Grandparents are substitute parents, scene of Labor Camp where she thought her grandparents were sent to. We lived with them after my parents were divorced.

He and Grandma were sent to Terezin. They aren't saying anything. From there to the 'East' as I just explained. The last time I heard from Prague, they still said, 'destination unknown' at the Red Cross right after W.W. II. We spoke to people in D.P. camps, freed from concentration camps. Not one of them remembered either one of my grandparents.

Step 3: How did you feel about this person?
When I was asked as people do, 'Whom do you love best?' My answer was always my Grandfather, then long, long nothing, then my Grandmother and Mother. He had recently retired and spent much time with me, going for walks, helping with homework, etc.

How did this person feel about you?
From the courtyard which abutted the inside kitchen window, our neighbor's daughter handed me a post-card which was signed by my Mother's parents. It read, 'We are going towards the East.' This was the last I ever heard of them. I loved my Grandmother and Grandfather and I think they did, me

Step 4: What were the conflicts involved?
After W.W.II, I learned that as far as anyone knew, they were killed somehow or perished somehow.

Step 5: What happened before?
My grandparents were deported to Terezin. At that time I thought they went to a work-camp. My Grandpa had said, 'I worked most of my life, I can work a little more.' I believed it and since I believed it to be temporary, some part of me felt glad to be rid of the loving control I always complained about. Like being followed when I went to school—a walk of one block. The answer to this has become terribly true, 'Someday you will wish that one of us could follow you.'

Step 6: What happened after?
During W.W. II many rumors abounded about concentration camps. What was true? I did not know! Anyway, my information was limited.

Step 7: What was your share in creating this conflict?
Whenever I thought of my mother's parents, I remember our neighbor's daughter saying that my grandfather was in the hospital. I remembered hearing that old and sick people were those who could not work and they were killed first.

Step 8: How has this experience affected your life?
It's a haunting memory of terrible endings including cannibalism (which I hear happened in some instances), cars left on the railroad tracks for them to starve, suffocate or what have you. The poison gas showers in the death camps create other scenarios.

Step 9: Have you been repeating yourself?
Probably.

Step 10: Has this conflict been resolved in your mind?
No.

Step 11: Has this conflict been resolved in this relationship?
I know they must be dead.

Step 12: What changes could be made to resolve your conflicts, to free yourself from re-experiencing them?
I am not sure. I know I am trying to forgive myself and not feel like a terrible person for feeling a slight feeling of freedom, at first. I wasn't old enough to know any better, and, I did not know that I would never see them again. Sometimes I think someone shot them, the best of the possible horror stories. Whatever happened, it's done and no matter what I do I can't change it. Very true and neat in theory. My mind can still spin haunting horror stories, especially when some movie or story brings me back to that time.

Step 1: Please draw and color a most conflictual memory from your childhood.

Step 2: Describe the incident. Who was there and what happened?
Nuns, (Sisters of Charitas), many children, foundlings. I am 8-9 years old. Foundling home... I used to throw up my breakfast until I complained. I hated going to the bathroom; cockroaches as big as mice.

Step 3: How did you feel about this person?
I liked the nun who wanted me to be Mary in the Christmas play and I liked the girl with the book. Often other boys and girls. I disliked twins who constantly ran around the day-room and were reputed to be full of lice and were constantly noisy.

How did this person feel about you?
Many different relationships. One nun liked me, one appeared to dislike everyone. Don't remember the others well... though they seem okay or okay in asking me in retrospect. Friendly, especially one girl (who hid a book about Rio de Janeiro in her mattress).

Step 4: What were the conflicts involved?
One morning at breakfast throwing up for no apparent reason I am out into the infirmary. Cannot keep any food down. The unfriendly nun gives me many painful enemas and keeps slapping and scolding a strange little girl in the only other bed in the large room. The 4-year-old girl I realize today masturbated almost constantly. Eventually the nuns in charge decided that I had appendicitis and I am transferred to a hospital run by other nuns. I was not used to the conditions I had to live with, and developed physical symptoms to cope with it. Luckily I could escape the situation.

Step 5: What happened before?
At night I wait as long as I can in my bunk bed before I tackle the dark to the bathroom where there is light, which reveals water bugs as large as mice and big European cockroaches. I hate to think what made that crunchy noise as I walked through the dark. Usually I leave a light path of urine because I waited too long. Every morning some nuns with large aprons comb each child one after the other with narrow teethed lice-combs. I had long hair and I am afraid to catch lice.

Step 6: What happened after?
In the hospital, a sympathetic nun feeds me broth and I can keep it down. I confide in her and tell her that all mail in the foundling home is censored and that I cannot contact my mother. She smuggles out a letter to her. Whatever the chain of events this started, I don't know, but it landed me in Bodenbach at my father's home.

Step 7: What was your share in creating this conflict?
I was a spoiled brat, who was suddenly immersed in previously unknown reality situations and found myself unable to cope with them.

Step 8: How has this experience affected your life?
Perhaps made me less sure that I can handle whatever comes my way -- though I would be loath to admit it.

Step 9: Have you been repeating yourself?
I don't think so.

Step 10: Has this conflict been resolved in your mind?
Yes, a long time ago.

Step 11: Has this conflict been resolved in this relationship?
I don't think any relationship other than mine at the foundling home was involved.

Step 12: What changes could be made to resolve your conflicts, to free yourself from re-experiencing them?
I am not aware of these same conflicts in my present life.

Step 1: Please draw and color a most conflictual memory from your childhood.

Step 2: Describe the incident. Who was there and what happened?
My mother hanged herself on the bathroom doorknob with a towel. I just woke up... I don't know who is saying what. I am frantic trying to get her off the handle and in my excitement choke her more before she falls down.

Step 3: How did you feel about this person?
Loved her.

How did this person feel about you?
Loved me most of the time.

Step 4: What were the conflicts involved?
Before we went to sleep, a few German soldiers forced the door to our partially sealed off apartment. They were noisy and laughing. The man who held me between his knees, laughingly but firmly— smelled of beer. My mother was in the only other room with some of them. I heard strange noises, yelling and my mother crying and shouting which for the most part I did not understand.

Step 5: What happened before?
After what seemed like a long time—two men or three entered the kitchen and one said, 'Wir Mussen Gehen' (we must go). In the other room my mother was crying, her head buried in the couch. To my anxious questions I got no answers except finally, 'it's alright now, don't worry.' Then she took a shower and we went to bed.

Step 6: What happened after?
I was afraid my mother was hurt and that in the awkward way I tried to help her, I hurt her even more. She lay on the floor bleeding from her mouth and was unconscious for some time.

Step 7: What was your share in creating this conflict?
I did not create it, but I was of little help, I may have made matters worse.

Step 8: How has this experience affected your life?
The memory haunted me for a long time and is still a sad, unpleasant memory.

Step 9: Have you been repeating yourself?
At first—I am sure.

Step 10: Has this conflict been resolved in your mind?
As much as something like that can be resolved.

Step 11: Has this conflict been resolved in this relationship?

The relationship is not a live one.

Step 12: What changes could be made to resolve your conflicts, to free yourself from re-experiencing them?

The years have taken the fear, guilt and immediacy from the memory, but it will remain a bad memory.

FAMILY ZOO PORTRAIT AND STORY

Step 1: Please make a portrait of your family of origin by drawing and coloring animals in a zoo to depict each member of the group. Feel free to be imaginative with the configurations, the shapes, the colors, and the placement of the animals. Allow your feelings about the members of your family to show through these drawings.

Step 2: Identify each individual, his/her relationship, his/her age, and personality, listing three characteristics.

#1 – Unicorn, Maternal grandfather, 1942 was age 63, honest, trusting, patient

#2 – Owl, Maternal grandmother, 1942 was age 62, enterprising, clever, people-oriented.

#3 – Mule, Myself, age 62, analytical, polite, try to keep my feelings private.

#4 – Song-bird, Mother age 36 in 1946, emotional, wonderful mezzo-soprano, vegetarian

#5 – Porcupine, Aunt T., age 87 Mother's sister, adored husband, critical, protective

#6 – Griffin Uncle R.', age 56 in 1956. (T.'s husband) keen, scientifically oriented mind, versatile, loving

#7 – Coyote, Father, age 25 in 1936, athletic, liked garlic, threw me into the air then caught me.

#8 – Parrot, Uncle G. (father's brother) age in 1943 was 17, indoctrinated, enthusiastic, idealistic. (Nazi shot in air-crash)

#9 – Ostrich, Paternal grandfather age in 1949 was 67, strict, fair, strong work ethic.

Step 3: The animals are having a conversation. What are they saying?

#6 – "If this were possible we would hardly be in one group."

#1 – "More than 50 years ago - hardly, but shouldn't we have learned something since?

#2 – "These lessons are too cerebral, the wounds are not only physical, many are emotional too."

#4 – "Don't I know that!! Mine haven't healed yet and I doubt they ever can completely!"

#3 – "I am glad anyway. I didn't think I would ever see any of you. If I wish real hard maybe, I can take what I see at face value and erase the tearing and killing of WW II and of sick ideologies."

#8 – "Before I died, I began to question all that stuff they taught me. I still can't let go completely of it after all they made it part of my being and I was growing around it. My ideals are colored by it and when I tear it out it's difficult to not tear everything." 'He was a kid who believed wonderful things for Germany and he told me terrible things like Jews were sabotaging Germany-- machinations with money. I felt sorry for him but I did not like what he was saying. He was parroting all the stuff he'd learned.'

#7 – "What can I say it's not a time I am proud of."

#9 – "And to think that I may have inadvertently encouraged it. In my day, patriotism was a virtue and not something to be used."

#5 – "Aren't those lame excuses for murdering 12 million people; 6 of them Jews and crippling and maiming more?"

Step 4: What were the zoo animals saying or doing before the conversation you just recorded?
The last I know #1 and #2 were missing 'destination unknown'. #3 was answering "Step 2", #4, committed suicide in an insane asylum. #5 died of compression pneumonia in a rest home. #6 Died of complications following a heart attack in Hartford Hospital. #7 was missing in action at the battle of Stalingrad WWII. #8 burned in a plane in WWII. #9 must have died in Austria--I broke off all contact with Father's family after leaving Europe.

Step 5: What were the animals saying or doing after the initial conversation?
They finally decided that it is very unlikely that any court in this world could find planned, promoted murder of people excusable for any reason. Sometimes in a murder mystery one understands the forces that compel the murderer (he may be a victim too) but, it still makes him responsible.

Step 6: Give a title to the story.
"Can We Understand Some of Our Persecutors and If So, Are They Innocent?"

Step 7: What conflicts are these animals experiencing?
One side is judging the other. The others try to explain their motivations.

Step 8: What changes should be made to resolve these conflicts?
They should concentrate on their area of agreement rather than past assessments of guilt. What happened is done and cannot be changed. I interrupted this to watch 60 Minutes on T.V. I cannot continue my sophistry and "know-it-allness." The first segment was on Argentine death planes in 1986. They compared it with the Holocaust, but then that is vague right now. Never the less whether death planes or Yugoslavian or Iraqi atrocities somewhere in the world the song is 'People who kill people... what or who are they?'

RESPONSE

MASK I

Step 1: Draw a mask.

Step 2: Answer the following questions:

Give the mask a title: "Inscrutable."

Age: 40 **Sex:** Female

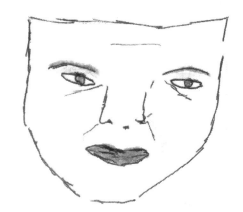

What emotions does this mask convey? Some worry, but well controlled.

Step 3: What are the conflicts represented in this mask? No conflicts, but then it is just a mask.

Step 4: What resolution of conflicts does this mask represent? I can handle crisis situations, but have difficulty with daily normal living.

ANXIETY

MASK II AND MASK III

Step 5: Imagine the mask you drew has become transparent. Make a drawing of what you see through the mask, reflecting true feelings.
Fill in the blanks and answer the questions:

Step 6: Title: "Perfect Looking Poison Fruit."

Age: 62 **Sex:** Female

What emotions does this mask convey? Suspicion, impulse to be gullible and take things at face value.

Step 7: What are the conflicts represented in this mask? Cannot judge things by casually noticing appearances.

Step 8: What resolution of conflicts does this mask represent? Digging deeper, learning more. Scene from a dream: ripe beautiful fruit, but the fruit was poisoned and all the beauty did not mean much.

Step 9: Make a drawing of what you see in this person's heart. Indicate this figuratively, portraying conflicts or using colors reflecting this person's emotions.

Answer the following questions:

Title: "A Heart Full of Good Intentions and What it Paves the Road To." ...hell

Step 10: Indicate items and themes represented in this drawing: It is not very serious, though there is some truth to it.

Step 11: Elaborate on what feelings and conflicts this drawing represents: Laughing at your emptiness, pain, confusion, whatever!

Step 12: What resolution of conflicts does it convey? That it helps sometimes to not take yourself too seriously. To good intentions the way to hell is paved!

Step 13: Give a title to the sequence: "Going Inside."

Step 14: Summarize here the sequence of transformations of these images:

Mask 1: A non-commital posture.
Mask 2: A beautiful scene with flawless fruits which are poisonous; things are not the way they seem.
Mask 3: Humor helps in the solutions of difficult problems.

Step 15: What are your conclusions about the way this person resolves conflicts? Does not take him/herself too seriously.

Step 16: How does that progression relate to your feelings and choices you have in handling feelings? I often take things too seriously and myself too, and I have to remind myself that is always necessary. Humor breaks the tension, and often allows more creative solutions.

Step 17: What changes should you make in the way you communicate your feelings? Everything is not a life and death struggle.

Step 18: What changes are you willing to make in order to reduce the intensity of these conflicts? When I get too tense or frustrated, I will remember to let humor lighten the scene.

DEFENSE

ANIMAL METAPHOR TEST #1

This test offers you the opportunity to be imaginative and create a story featuring two animals.

Step 1: Draw two animal figures in color:

Step 2: Fill in the blanks:

Animal #1:
Type of animal: Lion
Age in human years: 20's   **Sex:** Male

Describe the animal's personality using 3 or more traits: Fierce, determined, persistent.

Animal #2:
Same as #1.

Step 3: The characters are having a conversation. What are they saying to each other? Indicate the sequence referring to the characters by their identity number.

> #1 – "Get away thief, the catch is mine."
> #2 – "No way, by right it's mine."
> #1 – "We shall see about that!"
> #2 – "Roar, growl, Grrr!!"
> #1 – "Grrr, grrr." They continue to growl and fight.

Step 4: What were the characters saying or doing before the conversation you just recorded? #1 killed an antelope. #2 saw it from a distance and galloped to the kill and the fight began.

Step 5: What were the characters saying or doing after the initial conversation? They continue to fight, each insisting that the spoils are his. #1 says he and his pride need the food. #2 insists that he saw the antelope first and anyway it was from a herd he was stalking, but #1 killed the antelope while he was resting.

Step 6: Give a title to the story: "The Lions and the Antelope."

Step 7a: What conflicts are these characters experiencing between themselves? Conflicts of hunger-survival--ownership.

Step 7b: What are the conflicts between them and the world? Elaborate. They must kill to live. They are also territorial animals so one of them encroached on the others territory.

Step 8: What changes should these characters make to resolve their conflicts? Ideally they should each take half of the antelope."

Step 9: Which animal do you identify with most? Elaborate. Perhaps #1 since he did the killing and the spoils belong to him. However, he is not willing to share even a small piece with the other lion, who is also needy. I really identify with neither, but think it to be the way of the world. **Who do you identify with the counterpart animal? Elaborate.** A nation or person who thinks he or she should have something another has.

Step 10: How does this animal drama pertain to you? It goes on constantly and I have to join if I want to survive.

Step 11: What changes should you make to resolve your conflicts? I am not sure, but if these two lions represent my conflicts I would be willing to share at least part of my catch, but in the real world that is most often unacceptable and/or impossible.

Step 12: In life we repeat ourselves. Present an incident similar to what transpired in your metaphor story to illustrate your particular pattern. I was thinking more of nations than myself. I.E. the Gulf War, but it is probably true of most wars if not all. But at any time I am part of a nation and must take part willy-nilly in conflicts they have...without any regard to my personal feelings.

Step 13: Reviewing this incident, describe your relational pattern that is, how you relate with other people, and how you set things up to get yourself in trouble. According to this, by not being an agreeing member of a nation in conflict.

Step 14: What changes are you willing to make?   From what I've got so far, I don't believe this to pertain to any present conflict, except in too general terms for me to recognize it.

FAIRYTALE METAPHOR TEST

This test offers you the opportunity to be imaginative and create a story featuring two characters from your favorite fairy tale. To do this, follow these steps.

Step 1: Draw your two characters in color:

Step 2: Fill in the blanks:

Character#1: Joshua
Age in human years: 10 **Sex:** Male
Describe the animal's personality using 3 or more traits: Adventurous, curious and trusting.

Character#2: Cerberus--a flying dog that talks
Age in human years: ageless
Sex: no sex

Describe the animal's personality using 3 or more traits: Changeable but almost always wise, accommodating, instructive.

Step 3: The characters are having a conversation. What are they saying to each other? Indicate the sequence referring to the characters by their identity number.

#2 – "A strong belief of enough people propelled me into being again."
#1 – "Cerberus, will you take me to the land that never ends?"
#2 – "Yes...it's a wondrous realm where we also have many problems." He flew closer to the ground and Joshua saw continents almost constantly appear and vanish again. It gave a flickering sensation of a neon light.
#2 – "That happens when believers and naysayers are just about even. The same thing is true for individuals and you can see it happening over there." He pointed it out with one paw shaking up Joshua quite a bit when he did it.
#2 – "Then also strange and evil philosophies sometimes gain ascendance, so we also have our share of devils and dictators and we often are afraid that they will destroy some gods or heavens. But as

upsetting as that may be, at the time, it's all part of the scheme of things like having to have darkness in order to know what light is. Do you understand? The guiding principles in force have to have both; it is the balance that is important. One cannot destroy the other side completely for humanity to function."

Joshua nodded thoughtfully as he watched the interplay those differences created and from his high perch it looked like waves in the ocean.

Step 4: What were the characters saying or doing before the conversation you just recorded? Cerberus did not exist for a time, since only a formula, which calculated the belief and its strength humans had in his existence against the disbelief and its strength determined his appearance or disappearance. At the right balance he automatically appeared or vanished. Joshua was walking through the meadow planning to go fishing.

Step 5: What were the characters saying or doing after the initial conversation? They were leaving the fantastic land that never ends and #2 deposited #1 in the meadow where he found him. Then he flew to a shady tree to take a nap. As he lay down he started to fade, but #1 knew that he did not do it for he believed in him more than ever. And even if #2 disappeared for now, he would be back to teach #1 new things.

Step 6: Give a title to the story: "Joshua's Second Trip to the Land That Never Ends."

Step 7a: What conflicts are these characters experiencing between themselves? The conflicts of the existence of good and evil and of other polarities

Step 7b: What are the conflicts between them and the world? Elaborate. #2 has to live with the problem of a cyclical existence and non-existence he has no control over. #1 is challenged to see good and evil from a new perspective.

Step 8: What changes should these characters make to resolve their conflicts? The trip was made in the hope of gaining new insights and if #1 understood #2, many of his conflicts should be solved.

Step 9: Which character do you identify with most? Elaborate. Both, but Joshua more than Cerberus perhaps because though the concepts aren't new by any means, I am surprised they emerged and that they did so without my conscious volition.

Who do you identify with the counterpart animal? Elaborate. Myself, to a lesser degree.

Step 10: How does this character drama pertain to you? It mirrors my basic opinions, except that I have not applied it in just that way...or at least not consciously.

Step 11: What changes should you make to resolve your conflicts? Accept them as a perhaps unpleasant but necessary part of living.

Step 12: In life we repeat ourselves. Present an incident similar to what transpired in your metaphor story to illustrate your particular pattern. Accepting my MS as a part of living. I have done that to a very large degree. My pain however, I am working on, but I have been less successful since it disrupts my current pattern of living. My investigation into a hospital bed as a possible help is a step in the right direction. It might allow me more sleep without having to change the pain itself.

Step 13: Reviewing this incident, describe your relational pattern, that is, how you relate with other people, and how you set things up to get yourself in trouble. I cannot change anyone but myself so as long as it doesn't affect my personal integrity, I will attempt to do that, if necessary.

Step 14: What changes are you willing to make? Hospital bed, if after investigation it improves the situation.

REVERSAL

DREAM ANALYSIS

Step 1: Choose an outstanding dream from the past, a recent dream or a recurring dream. Significant childhood dream, 9 years old.

Step 2: Make a drawing portraying the key transaction captured in the dream. *(See next page).*

Step 3: Relate the content of the dream: A large black-bird, raven or crow sat on a makeshift wooden fence with three sunflowers in foreground. The bird was sinister, but the real horror was that I could see both the moon and the sun at the same time. It meant the end of the world. Mother and I were on the path walking towards the sunflowers and the birds.

Step 4: List the participants and attribute three traits to each of them.

> **Sun:** life giving, hot, represents day.
> **Moon:** night, cold, death.
> **Bird:** untrustworthy, foretells doom, death.
> Sunflowers: blooming life, food, sunflower seeds- growing.
> **Mother:** likes sunflower seeds, going on outings with me, grandparents. I like to go with mother, like sunflower seeds, don't like crows much.

Step 5: What are the conflicts? I know it is the end of the world and I am terrified. The bird signifies evil to me and fills me with foreboding.

Step 6: What occurrences preceded the dream? Don't remember whether grandparents left for Terezin yesterday or recently.

Step 7: Attempt to give an explanation of the dream. My world as I knew it ended. I look towards the future with much distrust. The sunflowers represent my mother and there is a chance that somehow she'll save me from the worst consequences of the end of the world.

Step 8: Do you dream a lot? (Hannah's note: question corresponds to other more recent dream).

Step 9: Please outline other dreams.

Step 10: Dreams are related to each other. Do you see any pertinent connection or patterns in your dreams? I thought of the dream many times without being able to get a handle on this context. I looked at the picture and I did! This is why I am so impressed. I told my mother of this dream and she said she had the same dream. The fact that supposedly she did see it scared me even more.

DREAM ANALYSIS

RECENT DREAM

Step 1: Choose an outstanding dream from the past, a recent dream or a recurring dream. Check your choice in the appropriate category. Recent dream.

Step 2: Make a drawing portraying the key transaction captured in the dream.

Step 3: Relate the content of the dream:
Relating at least part of my life to someone (don't know who).... and my grandmother is still alive in Prague in a government shelter, a man who was there recently told me. Of course she doesn't like the regimented life she has to lead. The meaning of my words is becoming clearer to me and it is as if I heard it for the first time. The other person asks why hasn't she written to you or you to her? As I consider this I am puzzled as to indeed why not? Then the answer comes to me and I say that I don't know her address or she mine! In my dream I think she is alive! I didn't know that!"

Step 4: List the participants and attribute three traits to each of them. The listening
　　1) questioning other person, I hear but do not see.
　　2) curious, logical, attentive- puzzled, glad, frustrated--should I consider grandmother as present? If yes, then…
　　3) alive, uncomfortable, far away.

Step 5: What are the conflicts? Even though I am happy that grandmother lives, I cannot see her or communicate in any manner. It also detracts from my joy that she dislikes the way she has to live.

Step 6: What occurrences preceded the dream? Fell asleep in front of the T.V. Was there any input from the story on the screen? When I woke up there was some supernatural music and a hovering female presence visible. A man sat up in bed awakening evidently puzzled. A bell boy entered his bedroom and asked if everything was alright. The man answered, 'yes'.

Step 7: Attempt to give an explanation of the dream. It may be somewhat of a resolution of some of the nightmares I've had about grandmother's and grandfather's fate. Or was it something spawned by a combination of my mind and T.V.? It has happened before like when someone asks questions when I doze off, I will supply people some action but the questions are from the T.V. for my mini-dream. However, up to now I was always aware of this happening. The only time I remember dreaming that grandma is alive.

364

Step 8: Do you dream a lot? Yes, when I sleep normally, which has happened seldom in the last 10 years.

Step 9: Please outline other dreams. In childhood from 4-7 years old or so I had reoccurring dreams of wailing sirens (a sound which terrified me). Someone grabbing my leg in or under water and pulling me down, boa-like snakes wrapping around me. The dreams were different, but the mentioned occurrences repeated themselves.

During and after W.W.II dreams about planes and bombs. Nightmares or close to it about mother, grandparents, father. About getting caught by SS or Gestapo. Only once do I remember being dead (dream was about 20 years ago). I know I was killed but don't know how and I was waiting for something to happen and nothing did. I told myself so there is nothing after death after all and kept watching preparations for my funeral, etc. and didn't realize until after I woke up that this was something sometimes I know I dreamed about but can't remember the dream.

Step 10: Dreams are related to each other. Do you see a pertinent connection or patterns in your dreams? Yes, in general terms it deals with problems I want to solve, even though it may not be obvious. Sometimes it hints at solutions. Problems I cannot solve will keep repeating themselves, sometimes in different guises until they are solved, if they are solved. They will also include wishes and fairly unimportant "stuff" of which my mind will clear itself."

COMPROMISE

SHORT STORY

Step 1: Choose two imaginary characters and write a short story about one of their adventures.

Ava – "I have never been away from Plonington."
Allan – "Me neither."
Ava – "My niece was on a farm this summer and when they wanted milk--they went to Bessy the cow instead of the store."
Allan – "Neato and I bet that Bessy had no cash register in her stall!"
Ava – "I know, hardly!"
Allan – "This is the day I want to meet my first cow! You too?"
Ava – "Okay, but how?"
Allan – "Let's start with the C-train to Tottersville."
Ava – "How much is the fare?"
Allan – "Let's ask?" He walks down the stairs of the nearest subway station and walks to the booth.
Allan – "How much to Tottersville?"
Attendant – "$19.30 round trip."
Allan – "Thank you. I thought it was less." Ava has caught up to him and hears the answer.
Ava – "More than I've got!" Somewhat dejectedly.
Allan – "Ditto but there are always a lot of dames with cash!" He swaggers.
Ava – "You would not dare, not what after happened to Don! There are no cows in jail!"
Allan – "I would not bet on it!" He laughs and changes his pose.
Ava – "We are young, there will be other weekends for cows. We'll just have to see Robotman at the Elm Theater like we wanted to in the first place."
Allan – "You'll buy the popcorn?" He smiles.

Ava – "Alright."
Together they walk towards the theater.

Step 2: Fill in the blanks:

Character#1
Name: Ava **Age:** 12 **Sex:** Female
Describe the character's personality using 3 or more traits:
adventurous, funny, a dreamer

Character#2
Name: Allan **Age:** 12 **Sex:** Male
Describe the character's personality using 3 or more traits:
Same as above for traits.

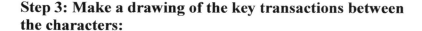

Step 3: Make a drawing of the key transactions between the characters:

Step 4: What had gone on before the adventure? Ava and Allan both live in the same tenement house of a large city. They go to school together and are friends."

Step 5: What happened after the adventure? They save for the trip to Tottersville and eventually see the country and a cow. It does not live up to their expectations. The country is not the problem as the place they dreamt of.

Step 6: Give a title to the story: "Ava and Allan's Saturday"

Step 7: What conflicts are these characters experiencing between themselves? They think of country life as innocent and uncomplicated. Later they learn they were wrong. In the meantime they enjoy themselves.

Step 8: What changes should these characters make to resolve their conflicts? They are joking and playing rather than being serious. I meant to make it a bit of a caricature of the stereotypical city child who longs for the country, looking at it seriously they should try to learn to appreciate the advantages of city life. What it offers instead of only being aware of problems.

Step 9: Which character do you identify with most? Elaborate. Probably Ava. **Who do you identify with the counterpart character? Elaborate.** No one. I had a boy-chum in school, but that was much earlier (younger age) for a short time only (moved away), etc. etc. The only similarity that remains is that he was a boy.

Step 10: How does this character drama pertain to you? At that time, (during WWII), I could have no friends because we were in "hiding". Wishful thinking? Possibly in this case although 'Allan' appears to be another facet of my personality, which is bolder and less bound by conventions than the one 'Ava' represents. Even though 'Allan's solutions' may be more creative and offbeat, Ava keeps me honest and out of jail.

Step 11: What changes should you make to resolve your conflicts? I don't see a conflict between the two (Ava and Allan) except that Ava may at least temporarily make action mental only (lack of money = reality of situation).

Step 12: In life we repeat ourselves. Present an incident similar to what transpired in your metaphor story to illustrate your particular pattern. It appears Allan would accept things at face value while Ava would be plucking them apart for consistency and safety.

Step 13: Reviewing this incident, describe your relational pattern, that is, how you relate with other people, and how you set things up to get yourself in trouble: Ava has a tendency to keep somewhat to herself, but she also guards my safety. Neither Allan nor Ava's aspect will upset my relationships as long as they keep each other in the proper balance. They are both necessary.

Step 14: What changes are you willing to make? Be more attentive as to which aspects of my personality are propelling me and whether the balance they maintain is equilibrium.

Discussion

Diagnostic impression

Below I am presenting some observations reconstructing the testing record as resolving conflicts along a dominant syndromal scenario corresponding to her relational modality, evident in her inventory. This diagnostic impression is reinforced by several metaphor tests.

Insights changed the pattern. She was able to come to terms with the past. Facing her own stories her feelings changed from guilt and apprehension. She had a dream of finally meeting her grand mother. She was able to experience innocence that's being vulnerable and break down in public. The metaphors conveyed her dominance that entailed her anxiety

STRESS

Her Conflictual Memories reflect her capacity to take initiatives: seeking independence from her grand parents supervision.

Associated with guilt feelings for a sense of relief for feeling freed from their supervision and controls, she also experiences guilt upon her mother's attempted suicide and her inadvertent participation as she was suffocating hanging from a doorknob.

Another memory portrayed the dramatic scenes of being in a foundling home and experiencing her own set of controlling childhood responses, like not going to the bathroom until she almost lost bladder control, resisting food, thinking independently and critically about her German grand parents and relatives. The family portraits reflect positive figures toward the Jewish and negative feelings for the German members of her family.

RESPONSE

In her family portrait she is a mule and she describes herself as a brat. A "little mule" reflects a willful, independent, stubborn, domesticated but youthful concept of her personality.

Her Mask identity is a face resisting scrutiny, resisting openness by being *inscrutable*; this attribute of her Mask pertains to her capacity of resisting weaknesses.

ANXIETY

The image behind the mask presents three broken trees. Two with broken branches (her parents) a third (herself) just green and growing but bearing poisonous fruit. In her heart we see "good intensions leading to hell."

The middle tree represents her sense of guilt as the poison fruit, between her ravaged parents. The third picture shows the emotional pains of her childhood still in her heart. "The road to hell with good intensions is paved" reflecting her identifying her ambivalence in thinking about her grand parents. She felt guilty for experiencing some relief when her grand parents were deported. Did she feel Germanic like her father's side of the family? Their intensions brought the Jews to hell, to the concentration camps. Was she one of them? She tried to distance herself from them though they had rescued her from the Nazis. Through the artwork of the family portrait, she was able to distance herself from them.

368

DEFENSE

In the first metaphor the issue is aggression for survival as the struggle between two lions reflecting her need for power in conflict with others.

The Fairy Tale Metaphor about the trip to the land that never ends reconciled her with the reality of normative paradoxes that we live in a world of alternative values. She is questioning illusions and reality. This story shows her seeking to reconcile this divided world ruled by Cerberus, the keeper of the underworld, who is stoic in facing the world of differences as beliefs and disbeliefs.

REVERSAL

Her reversal illustrated losing control by experiencing the end of the world in her childhood dream of the crow in front of the sun and the moon. While the sunflowers reminded her of her mother, the sun and the moon close together reflected her fears of death, hopelessness, the loss of her dear ones, grand parents, mother and father, the end of her feelings of security that she had enjoyed around her loving family. Reacting to the sense of impending end, her recent dream provided her with a wish fulfillment: reencountering her grand mother.

COMPROMISE

Her Short Story is about wanting a free meal, milking a cow in the country, complicated by considering robbing a rich lady. She decided not to use violence, but to work hard to visit the country legitimately. The insight was to check her aggressiveness and stay out of trouble. The inner emotional release was in self-acceptance, feeling good about herself. Indeed she was able to feel better and allowed her emotions to manifest; she could be vulnerable, let her guard down. She released her self from her own cruel criticism. Did this story have to do with her hopes for reparation money from the Germans, represented as a free meal?

The testimony of her recovery was conveyed in her supplementary protocol, of breaking down and crying. In that sense she was absolved from guilt and found her self as emotionally alive. She was able to release her guard upon the Israeli singer's performance reminding her of her mother, a 'song bird' in the Zoo family portrait. She was freed from associating herself with her violent guilt-ridden self. She could feel pleasure and sadness. She could be a child enjoying the music of her lost culture, her dear grandparents and of her beloved mother, she was an innocent no longer blaming herself for surviving.

9. THE METAPHOR PROCESS IS A COST-EFFECTIVE VEHICLE FOR SELF-DISCOVERY AND SELF-HEALING. THE WORKBOOK GUIDED HANNA, A 62 YEAR OLD HOLOCAUST SURVIVOR TO RECOGNIZE AND RESOLVE HER CONFLICTS.

IN ONLY THREE SESSIONS SHE WAS ABLE TO MAKE PEACE WITH HERSELF TO GET RID OF HER MASK AND TO FEEL ALIVE, VULNERABLE AND PASSIONATE AGAIN.

1a. STRESS. Three MEMORIES OF CONFLICT reveal a proneness for power and guilt.

a. German soldiers forced the door, they took my mother to another room. I heard her crying and shouting. The next morning my mother had tried to hang herself. I felt guilty.

b. My grandparents were deported to Auschwitz. I thought to a "work-camp". Some part of me felt glad to be rid of their loving control. Later, when I realized they went to a "death-camp", I felt like a terrible person for enjoying a slight feeling of freedom.

c. I was taken to a founding home. At night I tackled the way to the bathroom past waterbugs and cockroaches. Every morning the nuns combed each child for lice. Every day I got sick. I was a spoiled brat unable to cope with the new reality.

1b. STRESS. In her ZOO FAMILY PORTRAIT she contrasted her Jewish mother's and her German father's families and wondered "Can we understand some of our persecutors and if so are they innocent?"

Owl - Maternal Grandmother: Enterprising.
Mule - Myself: Analytical, polite, private.
Songbird - Mother: Emotional, mezzo-soprano, vegetarian, clever, outgoing.
Porcupine: Aunt, critical.
Parrot: Uncle G., indoctrinated, idealistic, Nazi.
Coyote-German Father: Liked Radio, teased me.
Lion-Maternal Grandfather: Honest, posing, patient.

They made lame excuses for murdering 12 million people. Ostrich: Grandfather, in denial. I may have inadvertently encouraged it. Before I died, I began to question all the stuff they taught me.
If I wish real hard maybe I can erase the Holocaust and take what I see at face value.

2a. RESPONSE. In her MARITAL BALLOON PORTRAITS she admits anger in her marital family.

My husband agreed to forgo his share so that his sisters could get more of the inheritances; we were all very angry.

2b. RESPONSE. She hid her emotions behind strength. "Inscrutable", is the face of a 40-year-old woman who does not want to admit to weakness; this face is a well controlled mask.

3a. ANXIETY. In her TRUE FEELINGS MASK she denounced herself as deceptive. She was a "Perfect Looking Poison Fruit"

3b. ANXIETY. In WHAT IS IN YOUR HEART DRAWING she denounces her good motives but then dismisses these concerns.

My heart is full of good intentions that pave the road to hell. I take things too seriously. It helps to laugh at your pain and confusion.

4a. DEFENSE. Her ANIMAL METAPHOR TEST reveals her emerging from victimization by identifying with the aggressors' dominant behaviors.

#1 "We shall see about that!"
#2 "No way, by golly, it's mine."
#1 "Get away thief, the catch is mine."
#2 "No way, by golly, it's mine."
#3 "Roar, growl, Grrr!"
#4 "Grr, Errr. They continue to growl and fight."

One lion killed an antelope. Another one reached on his territory. They must kill to live, they are territorial. I identify with the lions. The lions could be nations or persons who think they should have something somebody else has. It goes on constantly and I have to join it if I want to survive.

4b. DEFENSE. Her FAIRY TALE METAPHOR reconciles her with an unpleasant reality. This fairytale is about Joshua, a 10-year-old boy. His friend Cerberus, an adventurous, trusting, wise, changeable, flying age-old dog is guiding him to the land that never ends. The boy is myself. The dog represents my grandfather.

Joshua: Will you take me to the land that never ends?
Cerberus: A strong belief of enough people propelled me into being again.

Cerberus: It's a wondrous realm, continents appear and vanish. That happens when believers and naysayers are just about even. Evil philosophies sometimes gain ascendancy and destroy gods and heavens. The guiding principle is to have balance.

5a. REVERSAL. Three DREAM METAPHORS reveal her fears of the impending destruction of her universe and of herself.

5b. REVERSAL. In a memorable DREAM AT AGE 40 she finally met her fate, death: I remember being dead. I was killed but don't know how, and I was waiting for something to happen and nothing did. I told myself there is nothing after death afterall and kept watching the preparations for my funeral.

5c. REVERSAL. A RECENT DREAM gave her relief, her grandmother had not died in Auschwitz. She was alive and well.

Grandmother is still alive in Prague in a government shelter. She has not written me because she doesn't know my address.

A CHILDHOOD DREAM: 9-years-old. A large black sinister crow sat on a wooden fence next to three sunflowers. Above the moon and the sun shone at the same time. This meant the end of the world the way I knew it. I was terrified. The sunflowers represent my mother and hope.

6a. COMPROMISE. Her SHORT STORY METAPHOR reveals her successfully restraining dominant and anxiety provoking strivings.

Ava: My niece was on a farm this summer and when they wanted milk they went to Bessy the cow instead of the store.
Allan: This is the day I want to meet my first cow!
Ava: How much is the fare to the country? It is more than I've got.
Allan: There are alot of dames with cows!
Ava: You would not dare! There will be other weekends for cows.

Allan appears to be the bold unconventional facet of my personality. Ava keeps me honest and out of jail.

6b. COMPROMISE. In a THANK YOU NOTE she shared her losing control and experiencing a profound emotional release.

A mezzo-soprano sings to celebrate the Israeli Independence Day. I broke down sobbing and made a fool of myself, but I did not care. Her voice filled me with peace. I felt alive again.

Mural Transcript

STRESS
Memories of Conflict reveals a proneness for power and guilt.

German soldiers forced the door; they took my mother to another room. I heard her crying and shouting. The next morning my mother had tried to hang herself. I felt guilty.

My grandparents were deported to Auschwitz, I thought to a "work-camp". Some part of me felt glad to be rid of their loving control. Later when I realized they went to a "death-camp", I felt like a terrible person for enjoying a slight feeling of freedom. I was taken to a foundling home. At night I tackled the way to the bathroom past waterbugs and cockroaches. Every morning the nuns combed each child for lice. Every day I got sick. I was a spoiled brat unable to cope with the new reality.

Zoo Family Portrait She contrasted her Jewish mother's and her German father's families and wondered "Can we understand some of our persecutors and if so are they innocent?"

Unicorn - Maternal grandfather: Honest,trusting, patient
Owl - Maternal grandmother: Enterprising, clever, outgoing
Ostrich - Paternal grandpa: Strict, fair, strong work ethic. Mule- Myself: Analytical, polite, private.
Songbird - Mother: Emotional, mezzo-soprano, vegetarian Porcupine- Aunt : Critical, protective
Griffin - Uncle : Scientific, versatile, loving. Coyote-German Father: Liked garlic, tossed me up into the air
Parrot - Uncle G.: Indoctrinated, idealistic, Nazi

Unicorn: Shouldn't we have learned something since?
Owl:The wounds are emotional.
Mule: If I wish real hard maybe I can erase the Holocaust and take what I see at face value.
Porcupine: They made lame excuses for murdering 12 million people.
Ostrich: I may have inadvertently encouraged it.
Parrot: Before I died, I began to question all the stuff they taught me.

RESPONSE
In her *Marital Balloon Portraits* she admits anger in her marital family. My husband agreed to forgo his share so that his sisters could get more of the inheritance; we were all very angry.

She hid her emotions behind strength. "Inscrutable", is the face of a 40-year-old woman who does not want to admit to weakness; this face is a well-controlled mask.

ANXIETY
In her *True Feelings Mask* she denounced herself as deceptive. She was a "Perfect Looking Poison Fruit".This image reflected my being suspicious, alternatively gullible, that is taking things at face value.

In her *What is in Your Heart* drawing, she denounces her good motives but then dismisses these concerns. My heart is full of good intentions that pave the road to hell. I take things too seriously. It helps to laugh at your pain and confusion.

DEFENSE

Her *Animal Metaphor Test* reveals her emerging from victimization by identifying with the aggressors' dominant behaviors.

> #1 "Get away thief, the catch is mine."
> #2"No way, by right, it's mine." #1"We shall see about that!" #2"Roar, growl, Grrr!"
> #1" Grrr, grrr. They continue to growl and fight."

One lion killed an antelope. Another encroached on his territory. They must kill to live, they are territorial. I identify with the lions. The lions could be nations or persons who think they should have something somebody else has. It goes on constantly and I have to join it if I want to survive.

DEFENSE

Her *Fairytale Metaphor* reconciles her with an unpleasant reality. This fairytale is about Joshua, a 10-year-old boy. His friend Cerberus, an adventurous, trusting, wise, changeable, flying ageless dog is guiding him to the land that never ends. The boy is myself. The dog represents my grandfather.

> **Cerberus:** A strong belief of enough people propelled me into being again.
> **Joshua:** Will you take me to the land that never ends?
> **Cerberus:** It's a wondrous realm, continents appear and vanish. That happens when believers and naysayers are just about even. Evil philosophies sometimes gain ascendancy and destroy gods and heavens. The guiding principles to have balance.

REVERSAL

Three *Dream Metaphors* reveal her fears of the impending destruction of her universe and of herself.

A *Childhood Dream* 9-years-old. A large black sinister crow sat on a wooden fence next to three sunflowers. Above the moon and the sun shone at the same time. This meant the end of the world the way I knew it. I was terrified. The sunflowers represent my mother and hope.

In a memorable *Dream at Age 40* she finally met her fate, death: I remember being dead. I was killed but don't know how, and I was waiting for something to happen and nothing did. I told myself there is nothing after death after all and kept watching the preparations for my funeral.

A *Recent Dream* gave her relief, her grandmother had not died in Auschwitz. She was alive and well. Grandmother is still alive in Prague in a government shelter. She has not written me because she doesn't know my address.

COMPROMISE

Her *Short Story Metaphor* reveals her successfully restraining dominant and anxiety provoking strivings.

In a thank you note she shared her losing control and experiencing a profound emotional release. A mezzo-soprano sings to celebrate the Israeli Independence Day. I broke down sobbing and made a fool of myself, but I did not care. Her voice filled me with peace.

I felt alive again.

Dominant Case Study Two
How the Handicapped Flea and Ant Became the Disabled Lion and Eagle

Introduction And Discussion:

I treated this 40-year-old musician as a friend. I encountered him playing the piano at a resort hotel; he found out that I came from Greece, where he had a second home. We talked about Greece, then I identified myself as a psychiatrist and he confided to me that he had been treated for performance anxiety for his piano playing without success. I offered him a workbook and invited him to visit me in Vermont, two hours away, to review his compositions. He returned 5 times always bringing me a completed book and taking another. He completed four books in six visits in the course of a year.

I supervised his self-explorations, giving him some insights and advice. The four books reported in this study record his deep emotional problem and its devastating impact on his life, but they also reflect his transformation and healing. They reflect his anxiety that started from childhood experiences. The RMES scales and his metaphors indicate a clear deviation to dominance. My contribution was based on identifying the cause of his performance anxiety founded on his dominant relational modality. I pointed out that his behaviors and his symptoms were determined by this dominance manifested in his oppositionality to his mother as the key factor to his ongoing social anxiety plaguing him throughout the years. His aggressiveness generated self consciousness anxiety and it accounted for his self-consciousness upon performing as a pianist.

The images of his metaphors and his essay inform about the nature of his disabling relational problem and the process of his rehabilitation. From a flea and handicapped ant, he emerged to become two mildly disabled yet well-functioning powerful animals: an eagle and a lion, the leaders of the animal kingdom, reflecting that he was able to play and feel confident and powerful. The simple intervention had relieved him of his performance anxiety.

EXCERPTS

Step 12: Present a similar incident: *Constantly trying to be perfect. When I practice I have trouble focusing if I imagine someone is listening! (That's the whole point of playing).*

Step 13: How do you relate with others, and how do you get yourself in trouble? *I see myself as different. Therefore I must be better and yet I fear they will see through me because I am not perfect.*

Although the objective of his visits was the performance anxiety, the problem was broader. He suffered of a damaged or diminished self-esteem. He had feelings of worthlessness, which manifested across his testing. As these were addressed his performance anxiety was eliminated. The quotations above and below attest the fact of his being relieved of his self-consciousness as he felt less damaged or defective. What helped him was that the workbook generated insights had led him to diminished perfectionism and increased sense of compassionate self-acceptance.

Step 11: What changes should you make?

Step 12: Present a similar incident: *Just talking to you, Doctor, was at times hopeful, despairing, frustrating, filled with jealously, fear, warmth, etc. I should maintain PMA (positive mental attitude) and understand that, though limited, I can still achieve my goals and dreams.*

Step 12: Present a similar incident: *Happiness every time I perform.*

Step 13: How do you relate with others, and how do you get yourself in trouble?

Step 14: What changes are you willing to make? *Wanted things to be perfect.*

Personal Essay

There is a cancer in my soul. It takes the form of a belief system that says I am defective, that there is something intrinsically, organically wrong with me; that somehow the stars and planets were so configured at my birth to preclude my success at anything; that no matter what I do, I will fail – not at first, but ultimately; that my destiny was set for me and is unchangeable. All of these things I know rationally to be absurd. But deep down, unconsciously the cancer has a hold that I have never been able to be free from. It has destroyed most of my life. It has prevented me from taking a realistic look at myself and my achievements – I feel incapable of doing anything even though I know I can do them – this cancer lives not in my conscious mind but in my unconscious. I cannot get to it – this I have tried for years and years. It has me completely in its grip though I do my best to ignore it and always hope someone will be found to save me.

I have felt this way almost my entire life. The bad thing is that all my undertakings prove this to be true – they all ultimately fail. I may reach one level of "success" but the desired outcome is never achieved. Therefore the unconscious belief filters into the conscious, and reinforces the feeling of helplessness and "bad destiny." I fear there is really no hope…"

When I first came to Dr. Levis I was in what might be called neutral position. My self-image although not great wasn't completely negative either. In the animal metaphor I placed a cat and llama in a conversation, which ended positive and with both animals wanting to be friends. The other exercises drew a similar "glass half full" response. However, over the following months my exercises became more and more pessimistic while my view of myself gradually degenerated into self-loathing. I must say here that much of my life (I am 53 years old) has been a struggle to gain some kind of self-esteem.

On and off I have always experienced moods of total despair with thoughts of suicide as being the only viable solution. This is not self-pity but an almost uncontrollable tidal wave that sweeps me into the pit of hopelessness; my only companion in this terrible journey is loneliness. Anyway, the animals in the exercises became more and more incapacitated (a lame lion, a crippled ant, a flea with no friends) while my own metaphors were reduced to dead flowers and finally a piece of dust.

During all this time Dr. Levis worked hard to make me realize that all the failings (both positive and negative) were reflected in how I interacted with my mother when I was very young; that my cycle of despair was the result of unresolved conflicts between those "learned" feelings of "being bad" and my own desire and determination for a life of some satisfaction and success. Of course, all of this was not new to me as I had had many years of therapy.

But I wish to emphasize that in writing and drawing the exercises one is confronted with an active rather than a merely passive pursuit to the coping with one's problems. I use the word coping carefully for I do not believe that deep-seated problems such as I have are ever really "cured" and that a peaceful co-existence with one's antagonistic elements within oneself can be attained. Only a never ceasing vigilance coupled with a will to be healed could save me.

With creating images and metaphors as Dr. Levis instructs, I think a more concrete foundation on which to form a more objective outlook emerges. This of course, takes time and I wish to emphasize again that motivation is the key word. Without it any therapy is merely a crutch.

As I began to explore the relationship with my mother (i.e. my recollections of childhood traumas, feelings of being loved, humiliated, etc) I was unconsciously beginning to build a bridge between a healthy reality and my ambitions, dreams (which often took the form of recognition and great success). Eventually this bridge began to filter in my consciousness as I saw myself as more complete and able to, in fact, cope with the vicissitudes of life and more importantly began to build a genuine success for myself based on a more firmly grounded reality.

This is not always easy and constant vigilance is required. I think the last image I did of myself (in the final exercise book) was of a slightly deformed eagle, which nevertheless was able to soar above the earth with the greatest possible freedom. I cannot say that this feeling of triumph is always my companion as I have relapses into dark territory when I feel overwhelmed and totally without a sense that "anything matters at all." Yet the animal metaphors and other exercises of Dr. Levis are a key ingredient in the unlocking of unconscious (and conscious) problems, at least in my own case. With great effort, former problems can cease to chain the individual to his former life of seemingly unending cycles of despair and hopelessness. One is able to see and experience life itself as the greatest gift and with it the promise of joy will follow."

Transcript of the Case Study
Relational Modality Evaluation Scale

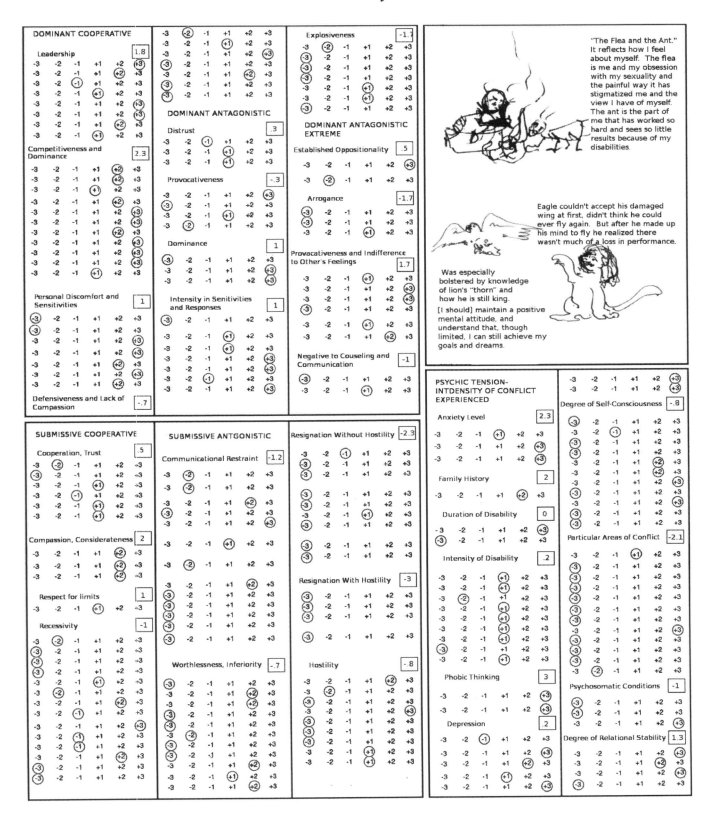

The following is a compilation of the metaphors mentioned in his personal essay, as well as several other relevant segments of his workbooks.

STRESS

CHILDHOOD CONFLICTUAL MEMORY (BOOK ONE)

Step 1: Draw a conflictual childhood memory.

Step 2: Describe the incident. Me rubbing myself to orgasm, which I did habitually since I was 2 or 3 – not knowing why it felt so good and unable to stop doing it even though my mother would berate and humiliate me saying how bad I was for doing it.

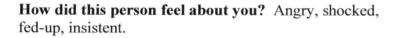

Step 3: How did you feel about this person? Afraid and wanting to please. Not close, but dependent.

How did this person feel about you? Angry, shocked, fed-up, insistent.

Step 4: What were the conflicts? Self-esteem at stake. Not knowing who or what I was at a very early age.

Step 5: What happened before? Feeling good.

Step 6: After? Feeling awful.

Step 7: Your share in this conflict? Being born.

Step 8: Effect on life: In every way.

Step 9: Have you been repeating yourself? Yes.

Step 10: Has this conflict been resolved in your mind? Yes.

Step 11: Resolved in this relationship? More or less.

Step 12: What changes should be made? I don't know.

DEFENSE

ANIMAL METAPHOT TEST #1 (BOOK ONE)

Step 1: Draw two animals.

Step 2: Fill in the blanks

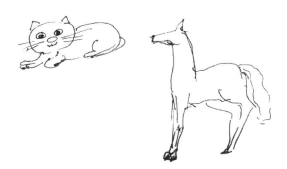

Animal #1
Type of animal: Cat
Age: 3 **Sex:** Male
Personality: Very affectionate, feisty, smart.

Animal #2
Type of animal: Llama
Age: 17 **Sex:** Female

Personality: Hard-working, patient, sensitive.

Step 3: What are they saying?

#2 – "When it's cold, I can take it you need a warm fire to make you feel good."
#1 – "Yes, but I'm good at keeping the mice out--but actually I'm not too good at that either."
#2 – "Yes and not only that, my fur will make beautiful and warm sweaters."
#1 – "I guess I'm what you'd call a pet--next to you I'm not good at much of anything except to keep my master from being too lonely. I know he loves me and I know I do make him smile a lot."
#2 – "Well, I'm not a pet--all that sentimental stuff isn't for me. But I see your point. I often struggle through. It is not easy being a llama in California."
#1 – "Well, since we're both here I'll come out and keep you company more often."

Step 4: What happened before?

#1: sleeping
#2: eating

Step 5: After?

#1: caught a mouse
#2: cried

Step 6: Title: "The Cat and the Llama."

Step 7a: Conflicts between themselves: Some antagonism. But greater conflict with in the llama herself as she realizes that with all the talent she has to offer, that she is, after all, alone and lonely.

Step 7b: Conflicts between them and the world: #1 has few conflicts and is comfortable in his environment. #2 would rather be back in Peru. He is lonely but always puts on a brave face.

Step 8: What changes should they make to resolve conflicts? #1 should try to make friends with #2.

#2 may or may not be willing to accept such a differing level of creature. But she can do more than accept what is.

Step 9: Which animal do you identify with: Llama, who is out of place, lonely, sad and worthless--so much and yet so little. Unlike her, though, I don't "take it as it is"--I hate it and think death is better than the present. **Other animal:** Most people-- though they have their problems, have some security and are well aware of their uses. (I too can be manipulative like the cat).

Step 10: How does this pertain to you? With great exactness. Why on earth would I choose a llama after a cat? Anyone else would choose a mouse. For some reason I felt unable to draw a mouse (!) and the llama was the only thing I thought I could draw. Though the world may want to befriend me, I feel uncomfortable "out of my element", only with my case I don't know what that element is or was.

Step 11: What changes should you make? Adopt a new feeling of self-worth. Somehow acquire a discipline that transcends "feeling" either good or bad. Is this possible??? It seems unattainable to really feel whole any more.

Step 12: Present a similar incident: Just talking to you, Doctor, was at times hopeful, despairing, frustrating, filled with jealously, fear, warmth, etc. When you spoke to the young couple I felt jealous that he was married and remembered how I wanted that desperately once and have never been completely comfortable with my homosexuality.

Step 13: How do you relate with others, and how do you get yourself in trouble? I feel other people are more fortunate than me, (generally.) I sometimes expect that they will not accept me and therefore I behave in a way that sometimes guarantees this result though I desperately want to find peace within myself and fulfillment with my music.

Step 14: What changes are you willing to make? Whatever is necessary. Whatever I am able to do.

REVERSAL

ANIMAL METAPHOR TEST #2 (BOOK ONE)

Step 1: Draw two animals with an intensified conflict:

Step 2: Fill in the blanks:

Animal #1
Type of animal: Lion
Age: 40 **Sex:** Male

Personality: Proud, independent, powerful.

Animal #2
Type of animal: Mouse
Age: 20 **Sex:** Female
Personality: Frightened, hungry, nervous.

Step 3: What are they saying?

#2: Please listen to me.
#1 – "Can't you see I'm taking a nap? Don't bother me."
#2 – "What I have to say is important. <u>Please listen!</u>"
#1 – "No! Go away."
#2 – "If you don't hear me something terrible may happen to you."
#1 – "What?! And be quick about it."
#2 – "I saw hunters nearby. Also the dead body of one of your brothers. If you're not careful you could be next."
#1 – "Are you sure?"
#2 – "Yes. But you don't think I'm worth your time."
#1 – "Wait a moment..."

Step 4: What happened before? #1 sleeping. #2 feeling fretful yet frustrated when he knows he has found something that is very important to say and afraid no one will hear him.

Step 5: After? #1 decided to heed and made a decision not to be "so proud".
#2 was elated that #1 listened. Felt real self-esteem for the first time.

Step 6: Give this story a title: "The Mouse and the Lion."

Step 7a: What are the conflicts between them:
The mouse fears most other animals, especially the lion though he knows he can be of use. The lion looks down on most other animals, especially the mouse, whom he regards with contempt and as something who couldn't possibly have value.

Step 7b: What are the conflicts between them and their world:
The lion, great as he is, can become merely the trophy-object of a hunter. All his strength can be of no use against a rifle. The mouse though fulfilled is quite equipped to survive if he used his head.

Step 8: What changes should they make to resolve conflicts? The lion needs to let his hair down and recognize his need of others. The mouse needs more self-esteem.

COMPROMISE

SHORT STORY (BOOK ONE)

Step 1: Write a short story:
One day it was very cold and a flea couldn't find any warmth. He huddled next to a leaf and started to build a fire. While he was warming his hands he became thoughtful and quite sad. He was misunderstood by everybody--nobody loved him because fleas are no-good blood-sucking parasites.

But he couldn't help it, he was born that way. Why was it so bad to live as nature makes you? As he was close to despair an ant walked by with only four legs. It was quite an ordeal for him yet he was obviously cold and needed to be near the fire. He recognized the flea and wished he could join him.

"Most certainly" said the flea. "But what happened that you only have four legs?"

"A life of constant work," he said. "One leg got caught under a rock and was squashed. Another was crushed under a human foot. It's been a hard life."

"But at least you aren't depressed, like I am. I'm so lonely I sometimes don't think I can go on."

"Don't feel bad. Everyone has something painful in their life. With me it is my mutilated body, all in the service of work. For what purpose I ask?

"Yes, everybody works good but enough is enough. Believe me it is no party."

So the flea reflected on what he said and began to feel better. He decided that as long as he could help a fellow ant from freezing to death he must not be all bad. In fact he grew to accept his lot and the two became inseparable.

Step 2: Illustrate the story:

Step 3: Fill in the blanks:

Character#1
Character name: Flea
Age: ? **Sex:** Male
Personality: Dependent, hungry, strong, well made.

Character#2
Character name: Ant
Age:? **Sex:** Male
Personality: Hard working, independent, resourceful but disabled.

Step 4: What happened before? Flea was cold and afraid, Ant was tired.

Step 5: After: Both said goodbye and agreed to meet every day to talk about their problems and how to solve them.

Step 6: Title: "The Flea and the Ant."

Step 7a: Conflicts between themselves: Flea: unconnected and rejected. Ant: angry, exhausted.

Step 7b: Conflicts between them and the world: [left blank].

Step 8: What changes should they make to resolve conflicts? Both have to find a way to see themselves differently. They cannot change the reality but they can change their attitude.

Step 9: Which character do you identify with: Both.

Step 10: How does this pertain to you? It reflects how I feel about myself. The flea is me and my

382

obsession with my sexuality and the painful way it has stigmatized me in the view I have of myself. The ant is the part of me that has worked so hard and sees so little results because of my disabilities.

Step 11: What changes should you make? I must change my attitude toward what I can't change and learn to see myself as valued although different.

Step 12: Present a similar incident: Constantly trying to be perfect. When I practice I have trouble focusing if I imagine someone listening! (That's the whole point of playing).

Step 13: How do you relate with others, and how do you get yourself in trouble? I see myself as different. Therefore I must be better and yet I fear they will see through me because I am not perfect

Step 14: What changes are you willing to make? I am willing to expose myself as whoever I am.

COMPROMISE

SHORT STORY (BOOK TWO)

Step 1: Write a short story:
A flower grew up alone on a shaded hill. He was not a particularly pretty flower, so no one noticed him. He looked at all the other flowers and wished he could be like them. He looked up to the tall tree, so wise with age and wished he could be like him, too. The shadow of the big tree terrified him--he didn't know why but he knew there was something terribly wrong.

One day a bee came--suddenly the bee stopped and said "You have no pollen. I can't use you. Goodbye."

So it was day after day. Then the rains came and the flower caught a cold and died. His petals were born aloft and made their way to a gardener's hut in the woods.

Somehow in death the petals shone brightly. The gardener noticed them and placed them with his old dead and dried petals. The flower had finally found peace with death.

Step 2: Illustrate the story:

Step 3: Fill in the blanks:

Character#1
Character name: Lonely Flower
Age: 6 months **Sex:** Male
Personality: Sad, frightened, uncomprehending.

Character#2
Character name: Bee
Age: 24 **Sex:** Male
Personality: Hard working, needy, impatient.

"
You have no pollen. I can't use you.

Step 4: What happened before? The flower has just stopped praying for something to happen that would make him feel worthwhile.

Step 5: After?: The bee went to another flower to get what he needed and the flower fell into deep despair.

Step 6: Give this story a title: "The Lonely Flower."

Step 7a: Conflicts between themselves: Flower: terrible feeling of not belonging anywhere and worthlessness. Bee: needs pollen to do his job.

Step 7b: Conflicts between them and the world: [left blank].

Step 8: What changes should they make to resolve conflicts? The flower must recognize and understand that pain will last only a short time and then he will find peace.

Step 9: Which character do you identify with: Flower, and the bee in every way. The tree is the universe whose shadow I feel is cast on me, preventing me from ever attaining any happiness or fulfillment.

Step 10: How does this pertain to you? [left blank].

Step 11: What changes should you make? "Only in death will I find a mirror to the rest of men."

Step 12: Present a similar incident: As I write this I have a strong sense of foreboding and therefore it will become true because I create it in my mind.

Step 13: How do you relate with others, and how do you get yourself in trouble? I don't believe in myself and rely on others to make me feel of any worth at all.

Step 14: What changes are you willing to make? I think I should vacate my space and let someone else take my spot.

DEFENSE

ANIMAL METAPHOR TEST #1 (BOOK FOUR)

Step 1: Draw two animals.

Step 2: Fill in the blanks

Animal #1
Type of animal: Eagle
Age: 45 **Sex:** Male
Personality: Brave, strong, slightly disabled.

Animal #2
Type of animal: Lion
Age: 45 **Sex:** Male
Personality: Lovable, powerful, (also partly) disabled.

Step 3: What are they saying?

#2 – "Hello! I haven't seen you in a while."
#1 – "I've been laid up with a bad wing. The doctor says it's permanently damaged. I was very depressed for a while but I finally realized I had to change my attitude. So here I am and I see that I can fly almost as high and fast as before."
#2 – "I'm glad you're back. You know I've always had one leg shorter than the other-- my left front leg-- it's always been the "thorn" in my paw. It hampers me somewhat, but I realized long ago **that I could still be king without being perfect.** In fact it makes me appreciate your problem better."
#1 – "How nice of you to understand--it's such a beautiful day."
#2 – "Why don't we go for a walk together and have lunch."
#1: "Okay."

Step 4: What happened before? #1: removed himself from his perch after days of inactivity.
#2: just awoke from a nap.

Step 5: After? Go for a walk – talk about themselves as disabled but great anyway.

Step 6: Title: "The Lion and the Eagle."

Step 7a: Conflicts between themselves: No conflicts between themselves.

Step 7b: Conflicts between them and the world: Eagle couldn't accept his damaged wing at first, didn't think he could ever fly again. But after he made up his mind to fly he realized there wasn't much of a loss in performance. Was especially bolstered by knowledge of lion's "thorn" and how he is still king.

Step 8: What changes should they make to resolve conflicts? Have resolved them, but understand that each day new conflicts will arise because of their disabilities and will need to be extra personal in order to maintain their mastery.

Step 9: Which animal do you identify with: Both.

Step 10: How does this pertain to you? Obvious.

Step 11: What changes should you make? Step 12: Present a similar incident: Just talking to you, Doctor, was at times hopeful, despairing, frustrating, filled with jealously, fear, warmth, etc. *I should maintain PMA (positive mental attitude) and understand that, though limited, I can still achieve my goals and dreams.*

Step 12: Present a similar incident: *Happiness every time I perform.*

Step 13: How do you relate with others, and how do you get yourself in trouble?

Step 14: What changes are you willing to make? _Want things to be perfect._

Step 14: What changes are you willing to make? _Be content with what I have._

HOUSE-TREE-PERSON TEST

These four tests illustrate a clear transformation. In the first, the images are somewhat generic and the responses are positive. The second book presents a drastic change: the house, tree and person are all dead, and the responses are negative – the only thing he likes in this sequence is the fact that the man is "dead and free of pain." The images in the third book are very simple and broken down to basic shapes. Lastly, the fourth book presents a positive point of view.

Book One   **Book Two**   **Book Three**   **Book Four**

387

House	**Thing you like about the house:** Fireplace, lots of windows, trees, quiet and cozy. **Things you don't like:** [left blank]	**Thing you like about the house:** [left blank] **Things you don't like:** cold, violated, empty.	**Thing you like about the house:** it's there, gives security. **Things you don't like:** unfinished, not grounded.	**Thing you like about the house:** cozy, beautiful, just right, warm and comfortable. **Things you don't like:** [left blank]
Tree	**Thing you like about the tree:** green, smell, age, shadow. **Things you don't like:** [left blank	**Thing you like about the tree:** [left blank] **Things you don't like:** dead, cut down, unfulfilled.	**Thing you like about the tree:** it's alive. **Things you don't like:** it's crying?	**Thing you like about the tree:** large and stately, green, beautiful, wise. **Things you don't like:** [left blank]
Person	**Thing you like about the person:** nice body, nice clothes. **Things you don't like:** big nose	**Thing you like about the person:** dead and free of pain. **Things you don't like:** no life, can't do any good.	**Thing you like about the person:** [left blank] **Things you don't like:** no hands or face.	**Thing you like about the person:** smart, talented, hardworking, determined. **Things you don't like:** neurotic, lacks focus under pressure, gets too involved with details.

Conclusion — Discussion

What is it that helped this man / person / patient / friend to recover from his depression despondency and find self-confidence? Several hypotheses, several factors that might have all contributed to his recovery from a cancer of the mind:

Explanations

1. Could the major factor actually be the correctness of my interpretation and diagnosis of dominance? This syndromal diagnosis was correct by examining his Relational Modality profile. His scores are clearly dominant and not submissive. The question is did this diagnosis provide him with insights into his relational pattern? Was it dominance that manifested in the past defying his mother pursuing his self-pleasuring in spite of her objections, and was his interest in excellence as a performer a narcissistic and hence aggressive and self-doubt-generating aspiration? Was piano performance as objectionable activity as forbidden self-pleasuring?

2. The paradox in this diagnosis of dominance and antagonism was in the fact that he did not relate along this attitude in our relationship and did not suffer of antagonistic relationships as a problematic issue; his problem was internal: perfectionism on the one side and self doubts, worthlessness, anxiety about his performance as a piano player on the other. The indication of a relational pattern was manifesting in his inner turmoil exposed to social realities that he simply exaggerated and got himself scared of in anticipating failure and disapproval.

3. Experiencing my interest in him as an antidote for his sense of worthlessness in a corrective transferential communication, in which my interest in him and his metaphors as sympathy undid his feelings of worthlessness.

4. What was the value of the art therapy modality? He recognized the cathartic encounter of his self-pitying disposition through the simple art therapy experiences by encountering the irrationality of his self doubts. As the inner thoughts were externalized and manifested the patient was able to reduce their cancerous proliferation. Otherwise stated completing the workbooks helped him to express his inner thoughts and feelings and realize the depths of his extreme and unreasonable sense of worthlessness. Is it possible that this realization was the major factor in his recovery? Did he disown these feelings as pathetic and unjustifiable, as the wounds of his eagle and his lion that he could put in the past and soar to new heights of self-confidence now?

My answer to these questions is to distribute credit to both the relational insights and the cathartic approach of the art-therapy technique.

Case Study Three
The Elephant and the Butterfly

Introduction And Discussion:
This is the story of a 28-year-old artist, referred by her mother, to consider administering antidepressants. The young woman was alienated from her mother. She had chosen to live in Asia. Upon her visit to this country and during a two-session single workbook evaluation we were able to address problems in her life. These were strained family relationships based on a clear pattern of strong angry interactions. This relational pattern was manifested in her inventory scales and also in all her metaphors as dominant antagonism.

The pattern was obvious in her memories of conflict and in the family balloons portrait. It manifested in all her metaphors alluding to her relationship with her boyfriend of many years. Behind her strong mask was a heart that was encapsulated with two thick walls. In spite of the thick walls she portrayed her heart broken in two halves in her dream elicited by her perception of his kissing a girl.

The workbook helped her to understand her anxieties and defenses as a symptom of her dominant personality. Her fears were projections, anticipations of role reversals. Her phobic sensitivities showed in her two principle metaphors in a parallel manner. In the animal metaphor as the dilemmas of feeling like an elephant captured in a circus versus staying free like a butterfly; in the Fairy Tale metaphor her conflict manifested even more sharply as the story of the Beauty making a commitment to the Beast versus being free like Cinderella looking for the prince.
Her fears and defensiveness were suspended in the spontaneity of love away from the confusion of the city in her Short Story Metaphor. The image presents a couple kissing. She realized her aggressiveness and that she needed to make changes.

Her insights of dominance generated from the metaphors elicited her own unsolicited concessions:

Step 13: How do you relate with others, and how do you get yourself in trouble? *Sometime I seem to get myself in trouble by asking too much of someone as well as asking too much of myself – when I have expectations, no one can really live up to them. They do sometimes but it is impossible to do all the time--therefore I set myself up for disappointment. I relate to people in a secure way of who I am but I am always interested to know the life of another.*

Step 14: What changes are you willing to make?
I am willing to not make so many expectations.
I am willing to forgive and really forgive others and myself.
I am willing to listen.
I am willing to take my anger out in other ways rather than on those I love.

The diagnosis of dominance was clear and it enabled her to look at her anger as problematic attitude. She saw it manifesting in all her relationships and she understood that anger also caused fears, her anxiety at getting married as becoming vulnerable to being hurt. **She realized that anxieties and paranoia were related to her dominance and that her angry responses were** the personal emotional problem that she was responsible in contending with. It was the hurdle in settling down in a relationship. She got married soon after the evaluation but her marriage lasted only three months. Her hopes of happiness soured as her prince became the beast. She had anticipated him breaking her heart and indeed was not able to deal with her fears of rejection.

What do we learn from this case study?

1. That we can examine the degree of dominance and the vulnerability of a person to her/his fears or anxieties. In this case the degree of respective dominance was very high as judged by the theme of past performances: her distancing herself from her mother, the incidence of anxieties turned to defensiveness presented in episodes of her three conflicts and also of problems anticipated in all her metaphors as well as her dream. She expressed issues of safety as an elephant captured in a circus, as Beauty victim of the Beast, as a fish that is afraid of being fished and as a wife anticipating being betrayed and her heart being broken.

2. That we can take in consideration the degree of a person's insights and also of her/his willingness and capacity for making changes in dealing with fears before getting so mad that she would simply walk out of a strained relationship.

3. The need for an emotional education and preparing partners in a couple to deal with the respective relational shortcomings and the realistic factors of relational compatibility. This bilateral preparation can alert the parties of their mutual diagnoses and realization of their sensitivities and vulnerabilities. The boyfriend was indeed a submissive person and had a pattern of escaping dealing with conflicts. In recommending marital unions one has to alert the partners of their defenses and the importance of good communications allowing resolution of conflicts in their relationship. The dominant person fears and these fears shape the reality; they are self-fulfilling. She divorced her husband and returned to being the Butterfly-Cinderella looking for a prince.

4. We also learn from this case the limitation of the therapeutic evaluation. It is an accurate diagnostic assessment but two sessions may be adequate for diagnosis. They are not therapeutic enough to help a person to correct patterns. There is another case study in this cohort. It is of a woman phobic of making a commitment into marriage. She had serious past pathology and was medicated for depression. She got married but again this marriage lasted only several years.

Personal Essay

"My name is whatever you would like to name me. A bit of mysteriousness goes well in the beginning of an essay. So I began with doing page 32--the Animal Metaphor Test. And I didn't know what to draw.

I think and think and then as I am looking through a magazine the two animals that seem to draw my attention are a beautiful elephant that seems to be in India and a butterfly flying around flowers. Interesting how I begin this essay because I realize how I am beginning to tell a story that isn't mine. The butterfly came out of my journal, and yes, the elephant did come out of a magazine.

After drawing and writing stories of my drawings for them to come to life--I recognized the patterns from my own life. I noticed my anger and frustration, and how it comes in waves from triggers of past memories and situations. I noticed how I set myself up to be disappointed which in turn leads me to have more emotional controls as balance. I seem to be transient yet want to be stabilized but I don't know if I have the key yet, I didn't know how to unlock the door—I must keep fidgeting with the key, trying to open the door. I turn it left and right and yet I can't seem to unlock the door. Then just like this, I get frustrated and angry but I know some of it is my fault and I turn to putting the guilt on myself, a vicious cycle.

I am 25 years old and still not sure about how to live life happily. Why is it so hard yet of course so simple at the same time? I know how important it is to let go--to be free of my past of disappointments, of sadness--it is amazing how negativity seems to be so sticky, like gum, it just stays and even when you clean it all away there is still a slight stickiness left.

And when one has such happy things in their lives, the grass is still greener in someone else's yard. I just watched a movie--The Hours--and a line is standing out in my mind--a little girl asked why people have to die and Virginia Wolfe responded, "because it is important for those who are all living to see the importance of life--of living life--of not being dead."

I conclude that life is to be lived. It is hard for me to know all of my past, to see the screw-ups and to continually screw up; to have a lack of self-control over the intensity of my feelings and my energy. I am so beautiful and I need to somehow let my anger go or maybe just be okay with it. Although, some days I think I am happy my mood changes and I change my mind within a minute. I conclude that I don't have a conclusion yet."

392

Relational Modality Evaluation Scale

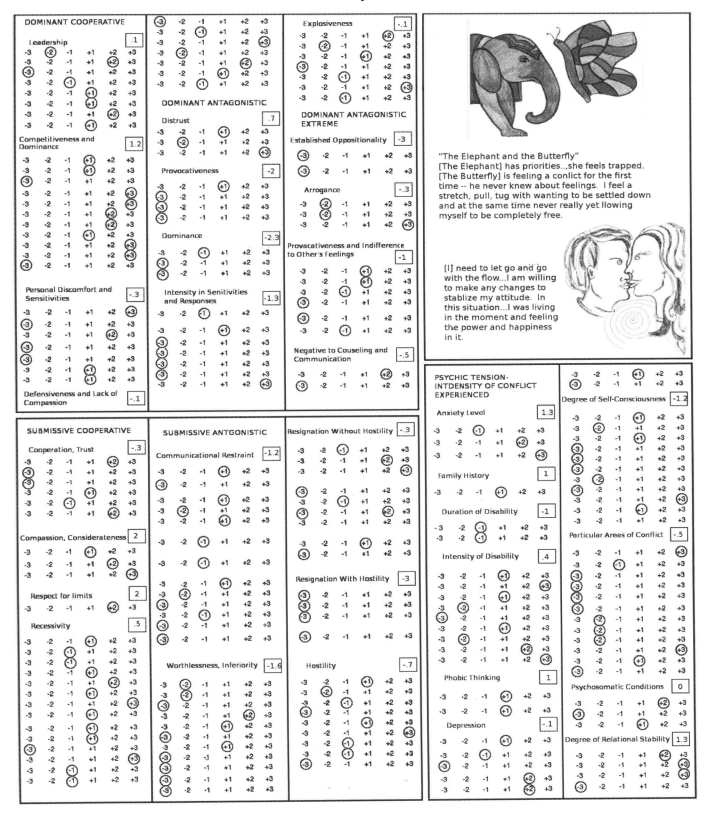

"The Elephant and the Butterfly"
[The Elephant] has priorities...she feels trapped. [The Butterfly] is feeling a conflict for the first time -- he never knew about feelings. I feel a stretch, pull, tug with wanting to be settled down and at the same time never really yet llowing myself to be completely free.

[I] need to let go and go with the flow...I am willing to make any changes to stablize my attitude. In this situation...I was living in the moment and feeling the power and happiness in it.

CHILDHOOD CONFLICTUAL MEMORY

Step 1: Draw a conflictual childhood memory.

Step 2: Describe the incident. Mother, Father, me.

We were all in the kitchen – Mom and Dad were having some kind of argument about something.

Maybe child support money. We were in the first house I remember, which was in Long Island. I don't think I went with him that day. I just remember a conflict with me in the middle.

Step 3: How did you feel about this person? I was angry at both of them.

How did this person feel about you? I don't think they were really paying attention -there was too much energy between them.

Step 4: What were the conflicts? Money, possibly. Probably something to do with seeing me, as well as child support

Step 5: What happened before? Maybe I was getting ready to go to school and spend a weekend or a day with my dad.

Step 6: After? I think he left and maybe I went to my room because it was a safety zone.

Step 7: Your share in this conflict? I didn't have a direct share in creating this conflict. I was a cause of it because I was alive.

Step 8: Effect on life: I was aware of anger and intensity between people who are mad at each other. Maybe I portray a similar way of dealing with conflict, (getting way too angry--not dealing with things rationally.) A frustration of not being listened to and not necessarily mattering because people are going to do what they want anyways.

Step 9: Have you been repeating yourself? Sometimes.

Step 10: Has this conflict been resolved in your mind? Yes.

Step 11: Resolved in this relationship? No, my father passed away.

Step 12: What changes should be made? Understanding anger-- just letting feelings sift through me without taking it personally.

Step 1: Draw a conflictual adolescent memory:

Step 2: Describe the incident: S., Mom, me. I was angry and wanted to take a walk away from the house. They both didn't want me to leave and tried to stop me. Step father wrapped his arms around me and ended up touching my chest. I elbowed him and got away.

Step 3: Effect on life: It used to affect me. Now it is just a memory.

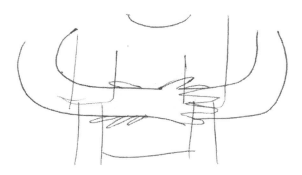

RECENT CONFLICT

Step 1: Draw a recent conflictual memory:

Step 2: Describe the incident: I don't know where the paint swatch was and my mother wanted me to go find it. I didn't want to go and she had one paint swatch already--she got mad at me.

Step 3: Effect on life: It made me mad because she knew where it was if it was anywhere and knew the colors better than me. I also didn't agree with having a new patient of hers--one who has just gotten out of the hospital due to bipolarity--to paint my room.

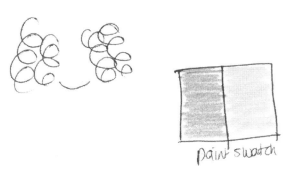

paint swatch

Step 1: Draw a balloon portrait of your family of origin:

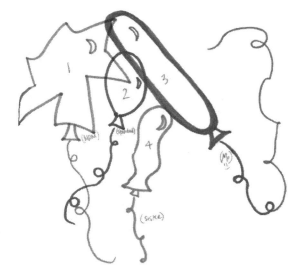

Step 2: Identify each individual:

Mom: strength, caring, core.
Stepfather: quiet strength, supporter, caring.
Myself: loving, caring, hard.
Sister: fun, picking up the pieces, temper.

Step 3: What are they saying? Mom wanting the family to go somewhere. Stepfather is saying that it is best to go and might be fun and if not we should all go anyway. L. is first saying 'no' but then she gives in because otherwise something will be taken away. I am standing my ground and refuse to go.

Step 4: What happened before? Deciding what to do for a family day together.

Step 5: After: [left blank]

Step 6: Title: "Family Day Out."

Step 7: Conflicts: Mom is experiencing the frustration that she knows what will be best for the family to do and no one is interested. Stepfather wants there to be no conflict. L. wants to be listened to and I just am getting angry and sad because I hate having conflict with those I love dearly.

Step 8: What changes should be made? A vote--everybody should put one idea of what they would like to do and then see if we can fit all in it.

Step 1: Draw a balloon portrait of your marital family:

Step 2: Identify each individual:

#1: boyfriend, strong, willing, sensitive, leader, fully independent, loving, thoughtful.
#2: me, strong, weak at times, loving.

Step 3: What are they saying?
Balloon 2 wants balloon 1 to eat healthier.
#1 says we only have one life to live. #2 understands #1 but believes that we also have choices and that what #1 is choosing to eat is unhealthy.
#2 loves #1 and wants what is healthy but also #2 knows half of healthiness is happiness therefore understanding #1 and letting the conflict go.
Step 4: Title: "Healthy vs. Happiness vs. Living"
Step 5: What are the conflicts? Balloon #2 is having a conflict with the way balloon #1 is treating his body in a life he only has one chance at. Balloon #1 wants chicken and fried steak.

RESPONSE

MASK I

Step 1: Draw a mask:

Step 2: Answer the following questions:

Title: "Infinity."
Age: 18 **Sex:** Female
Emotions conveyed: Eternal sense of being.

Step 3: Conflicts represented: Hiding any conflict that might be in the person. Insecurity.

Step 4: Resolution of conflicts represented: Truth.

MASK II

Step 5: Draw what is behind the mask.

Step 6: Fill in the blanks and answer the questions:

Title: "Jillian."
Age: 28 **Sex:** Female
Emotions conveyed?

Step 7: Conflicts represented: None.

Step 8: Resolution of conflicts represented: Relax.

MASK III

Step 9: Draw what is in the heart.

Title: "Amazing Grace."

Step 10: Items and themes represented: Strength, rough and hard (solid) edges.

Step 11: Feelings and conflicts represented: Abnormality – not a perfect heart. Sensitivity (inside of heart)

Step 12: Resolution of conflicts represented: One has layers in order for protection. The heart is complicated.

Step 13: Title of the sequence: "Reality."

Step 14: Summarize the sequence of transformations:
Mask – hiding, yet not because it is not a full-face mask.
Person – seeing the beauty and strength yet insecure person who wears the mask.
Heart – what is really inside the person.

Step 15: Conclusions about the way this person resolves conflicts: Sometimes she puts a protective shield around her feelings but if the conflict is important enough she will dive right in--take control and be sensitive to what she needs to be as well.

Step 16: Does this relate to how you handle feelings: Similar--although I don't think I hide behind anything or anyone. I have insecurities as well as securities and I am not perfect--therefore not a perfect heart.

Step 17: What changes should be made? Sometimes my feelings are too intense and over-dramatic, therefore I'm usually waiting for my feelings to "chill out."

Step 18: What changes are you willing to make: A part of me feels like I seem to be so intense that I probably need to disengage myself from any conflict and release my anger or annoyance in some way and not let it stay inside.

DEFENSE

ANIMAL METAPHOR TEST #1

Step 1: Draw two animals.

Step 2: Fill in the blanks

Animal #1
Type of animal: Elephant.
Age: 32 **Sex:** Female
Personality: Sensitive, trapped, comfortable.

Animal #2
Type of animal: Butterfly
Age: 20 **Sex:** Male
Personality: Free, scared, beautiful.

Step 3: What are they saying? Animal 1 is telling 2 about her life. She works as a circus performer and does stunts. She feels a little trapped but in general she is happy. She is given fun costumes and gets to travel and because she is large, traveling is hard by herself. She has a baby back in the tent waiting for her so she needs to keep the conversation short.
Animal 2 is very intrigued by this large animal because Animal 2 can never stay in one place too long purely because he always needs to use his wings otherwise they get stiff and uncomfortable. Animal 2 lives a life of color and freedom; he has no children and never knew the difference of being happy or unhappy. He just lives his life every day. He flies from place to place, rests, eats, and plays with his fellow butterfly friends.

Step 4: What happened before? They were each doing their own thing-- not noticing each other until they were completely up close almost touching each other. Animal 1 was finding some peanuts on the ground for her baby and animal 2 was flying to another destination when Animal 1's garb of beautiful colors attracted him to stop.

Step 5: After? Animal 1 was ready to go back to the circus tent and Animal 2 still wanted to talk. Animal 1 asked animal 2 to come back to the tent and meet her baby and then she would have more time to talk to him about life.

Step 6: Title: "Animalives."

Step 7a: Conflicts between themselves: Animal 1 has priorities and has to continue her way to life – she feels trapped but is secure with the responsibilities that she has chosen in her life and which have shaped her life to be the way it is now. Animal 2 all of a sudden is feeling a conflict for the first time. He never knew about feelings.

Step 7b: Conflicts between them and the world: Animal 1 is large and cumbersome. It is hard for her to get around. The world seems to be made for much smaller animals. She gets frustrated much. Animal 2 has no conflict until now; he was always just flowing with where his wings seemed to want to take him or not take him.

Step 8: What changes should they make to resolve conflicts? Animal #1--she can't really do anything about her size, she said she was content with being in the circus life. If she wanted to be happier she would have to make different priorities in her life important.

Step 9: Which animal do you identify with: I think animal #1, but I also identify with animal #2. I can move like #1 in terms of analyzing feelings and emotions and understanding how one needs to deal with responsibilities…you can't just keep flying.

Other animal: Some of my boyfriends--a little with my immediate boyfriend. Also young kids. Other kids--never myself--I never did not have my thoughts stop ringing in my head.

Step 10: How does this pertain to you? I feel a constant stretch, pull, tug. With wanting to be settled down and at the same time never really yet allowing myself to be completely free. Although I have traveled to so many places in the world, I have also gone through really tough times of being left alone. For some reason I feel like I live too much in my head and I can't stand it. I get angry and frustrated and cry. I want to be more like animal # 1 in terms of knowing where I stand in life, but animal #2 seems so much happier--first being free and expanding on his freedom --now he actually understands he is free.

Step 11: What changes should you make? I need to let go--I need to get all my thoughts out -but that isn't possible because all I do is keep thinking. I feel like I am who I am – I have realized that since I was twelve. I have accepted who I am but still I seem to drive myself crazy – especially when I care too much about a situation or conflict.

Step 12: Present a similar incident: I repeatedly travel and still I feel like I don't know what I am doing here in life. I see all the beauty one minute, feeling all the wonderfulness that life has to offer, and then the next minute I might get disappointed by someone or something or by myself and then I go to the opposite extreme--not knowing what the point is if everyone is going to die anyways.

Step 13: How do you relate with others, and how do you get yourself in trouble? Sometime I seem to get myself in trouble by asking too much of someone as well as asking too much of myself – when I have expectations, no one can really live up to them. They do sometimes but it is impossible to do all the time--therefore I set myself up for disappointment. I relate to people in a secure way of who I am but I am always interested to know the life of another.

Step 14: What changes are you willing to make?

    I am willing to not make so many expectations.
    I am willing to forgive and really forgive others and myself.
    I am willing to listen.
    I am willing to take my anger out in other ways rather than on those I love.

FAIRYTALE METAPHOR

Step 1: Draw two fairy tale characters.

Step 2: Fill in the blanks

Character#1
The Beauty (and the Beast)
Age: Sex: Female
Personality: Sensitive, caring, intuitive.

Character#2
Alice (in the wonderland)
Age: 18 **Sex:** Female
Personality: Insecure, searching, bewildered.

Step 3: What are they saying? Character #1 is telling #2 about this animal that she has just met. He is a beast, but seems to be a man trapped in a beast. She is telling #2 how interesting and intriguing this beast is. How at first she was scared of him but now she seems to be growing in love with him. She knows it is strange because he is different and he is not a man but her intuition is telling her to "go for it" – not to think so much but rely on her feelings. #2 is listening to #1 and is amazed. Even though she has had so many adventures in wonderland with talking, disappearing cats, and smoking caterpillars she never once thought that it was possible for a human girl to fall in love with an animal. Here she thought she had seen everything! And although she really could never imagine falling in love with a beast she was very happy for character #1. She even felt a little jealous although #1 was a few years older than #2, so #2 knew her time to fall in love would come. She had just finished coming out of the wonderland and thinking so much about herself and all of the characters that can be in this world or even another world that us humans don't even know about. She was lucky to have fallen and met the white rabbit, who was always late for an important date. She knew she was a lucky girl soon to be a woman and life would pan out okay if she would just let it be.

Step 4: What happened before? #1 was walking in a park thinking about her love for the beast. How was she going to explain it to anyone and boom she bumped into Alice and then the words just came out. She was able to fully explain her situation to Alice and Alice was wonderful and listened to her. #2 was also walking in the park because she had just finished reading a book with her older cousin about wonderland.

Step 5: After? #1 explained to #2 how she must get going back to the castle. #2 also needed to get going. They both were happy that they ran into one another.

Step 6: Title: "Reality Dreams."

Step 7a: Conflicts between themselves: #1 is having conflict with love. #2 is having a conflict with what to do next.

Step 7b: Conflicts between them and the world: #1's conflicts between her and her world in love seems to be pretty defined in terms of falling in love with a handsome man (because she is a pretty girl) and living up to her father's expectations, the world seems to think that no one can fall in love with a beast. #2's conflicts between her and her world is she is still so young yet she feels she has seen so much in her wonderland--she doesn't know where to go next.

Step 8: What changes should they make to resolve conflicts? #1 needs to speak to her father about her love for the beast. She also needs to tell the beast how she feels. Then she needs to make a decision or not because she is one to follow her intuition and everything turns out okay because she has no regrets with her intuitions. #2 needs to focus on what her intuition is telling her – not what the others in the wonderland have said.

Step 9: Which character do you identify with: I identify with both equally? I follow my intuition some of the time but I question it a lot--sometimes listening to "older, more learned" people or eccentric people's opinions.

Other character: I identify #1 and #2 with things I like and don't like about myself.

Step 10: How does this pertain to you?   The fairy tale pertains to me because I love to love – and for a long time I thought it possible to not let "physical attraction" or lack of it get in the way. I learned that in reality physical attraction does matter to me and that not letting it matter is a fairy tale. Also, I love traveling and meeting people--seeing a "mad hatter tea party" would be so much fun! I used to let people influence me more when I was younger.

Step 11: What changes should you make? I need to follow my own intuition more--give more faith to myself. Not get so frustrated if I don't know the next path I am going on or what the "right" decision is.

Step 12: Present a similar incident: Sometimes I give my love (feel my love, give too much) too quickly, and with that comes expectations that I have subconsciously. Once again, expectations are a difficult thing to be able to live up to.

Step 13: How do you relate with others, and how do you get yourself in trouble? I need to make the change of knowing how to love and yet not give all of myself.

REVERSAL

ANIMAL METAPHOR TEST #2

Step 1: Draw two animals with an intensified conflict:

Step 2: Fill in the blanks:

Animal #1
Type: Ant
Age: 30 **Sex:** M
Personality: aggressive, survivor, smart.

Animal #2
Type: Fish
Age: 30 **Sex:** F
Personality: Scared, trapped, going with the flow (easygoing).

402

Step 3: What are they saying? #2 peeks out of the wave and sees #1 holding food on his back. #2 is inquisitive and asks #1 why he has food on his back, why doesn't he just eat the food and get more when he is hungry. #1 tells #2 that it is important to bring food back to his home where the queen lives. That is what his job is as well as the job of all of his sisters and brothers. He didn't even think about eating it because he eats with the family and they are back home. #1 was surprised to even be seen by #2 because usually animals like #2 aren't observant enough and are usually minding their own lives in the water. So #1 wanted to know more about #2's life as well. #2 just said how dangerous it was for her--how many boats with netting as well as how important it is for her to be careful about random food that is dangling in the water because there might be a hook in it. Basically her whole life entails being cautious and watching her back. #1 understood that as well but he told her that it is important to do whatever you do as best as you can. Since he is a gatherer of food that is what he does best rather than worrying about being stepped on. Ants also have to be careful--as does every animal.

Step 4: What happened before? #2 was seeing if there were any boats or fishermen out. #1 was thinking about how his home is only a few yards away but he should take a rest soon.

Step 5: After? #2 went back into the water and decided to build a home so she would have someplace safe to go for the night, like the ant. #1 kept going back to his home. He thought to himself how nice it is to just live.

Step 6: Title: "Land vs. Water."

Step 7a: Conflicts between themselves: #2 was feeling how annoying life was for herself-- how difficult it was because of people and large fish out to get her. #1 was experiencing tiredness but then he regained his strength and kept moving.

Step 7b: Conflicts between them and the world: #2: being on the low end of the spectrum. #1: getting food back home.

Step 8: What changes should they make to resolve conflicts? #2 needed to make herself a home and be safe. She decided to set out goals in her everyday life. #1 thought that the best idea was to take a little more time with his family. He realized after talking to #2 how precious life is.

DREAM ANALYSIS

Step 1: Choose a dream: Recent dream.

Step 2: Draw the dream:

Step 3: Describe the dream: My boyfriend had told me he kissed someone (basically was unfaithful) and that it doesn't matter because he was with me now. I had this strange feeling of him being unfaithful and it was true. His brother, who has an open relationship with his girlfriend of 8 or 9 years, had given hints, which brought me to ask my boyfriend if he had done anything with anyone.

Step 4: Describe the participants:

Boyfriend: selfish, inwardly horny, sensitive.
Me: paranoid, insecure, sad.

Step 5: What are the conflicts? The conflict is that P. and I had an understanding. If he did anything with anyone he knew I was not okay with that. He had told me that I could kiss someone but what was important was if I still wanted him afterward and if I did, the kiss wasn't important.

Step 6: What occurrences preceded the dream? I woke up and felt sad and extremely angry. I don't agree with the way my boyfriend's brother doesn't believe in monogamy and I was mad at myself for having my intuition be right--also I was just plain mad because my boyfriend knows I would be hurt and yet he did it anyway.

Step 7: Explanation of the dream: My boyfriend and I have been apart for two and a half weeks and I know that before me his time was spent chasing girls--therefore a lot of the people he knew were girls he had hooked up with. Girls are untrustworthy and will go to limits and I had been thinking about these things.

Step 8: Do you dream a lot? No.

Step 9: Other dreams: I used to have a dream that my teeth were falling out.

Step 10: Connections or patterns in dreams: Yes, insecurity within myself. Also paranoia.

COMPROMISE

SHORT STORY

Step 1: Write a short story:
The story begins on a warm summer evening in New York City. A bunch of people are on the rooftop of an apartment building. Most are sitting in chairs, which are set up in a circle. There is one person on her cell phone on the other side of the roof. Lucy and Jack just arrive and sit in the two empty chairs in the circle. Soon all of the friends of Jack and Lucy leave to go to a bar. Jack and Lucy are left alone. The air smells beautifully sweet although they are in the city with all of the smog and pollution.

Lucy gets up and goes to the edge. She looks down at the "little" people--all hustling and bustling still even though it is 10 pm. Cars honking their horns. The streets are still moving and yet everything looks so fake, like pieces in a game. Jake stands next to her, brushing her lightly with his arm; just enough to feel like he is next to her, yet still separate enough to be independent from her energy. He looks down and without conversing with each other, both Jack and Lucy are thinking similar thoughts about how crazy the world can be. Yet here they are together in their own circle of life on a rooftop--away from the hustling and the bustling. Closer to the stars than the cars, or so it seems.

404

They look at each other now and feel the sense of connection --the understanding of vision.

They kiss and the kiss feels as if it is their first--drawing both of them to understand the connection and specialness they have for one another in this crazy world!

Step 2: Illustrate the story:

Step 3: Fill in the blanks:

Character#1	Character#2
Character name: Lucy	**Character name:** Jack
Age: 25 **Sex:** Female	**Age:** 26 **Sex:** Male
Personality: Exotic, searching, questioning.	**Personality:** Solid, knowledgeable, positive.

Step 4: What happened before? Jack and Lucy had had an evening of adventure in the city. Working their way from downtown to midtown, soon to meet friends on the rooftop.

Step 5: After: Jack and Lucy went and had 2am slice of New York pizza and then went back home where they slept side by side knowing that everything in life is meant to be.

Step 6: Title: "The Good Stuff."

Step 7: Conflicts between themselves: Character #1 was having a conflict within herself about life and how she used to be part of the city life. How easily that strange and difficult life changed and you can find yourself in a whole new world. Character #2 isn't having much of a conflict. He is enjoying the time.

Step 8: What changes should they make to resolve conflicts? #1 needs to let go and go with the flow.

Step 9: Which character do you identify with: Character #1. **Other character:** Boyfriend.

Step 10: How does this pertain to you? It was a scene in my own life.

Step 11: What changes should you make? I don't know sometimes because my thoughts get in the way but standing on that rooftop was beautiful. The understanding being part of a crazy life yet finding places to be separate from it as well. LIFE IS WHAT I WANT TO MAKE IT. Sometimes my moods get the best of me and I make life unhappy for myself.

Step 12: Present a similar incident: [left blank]

Step 13: How do you relate with others, and how do you get yourself in trouble? In this situation I didn't get myself in trouble, instead I was living in the moment and feeling the power and happiness of it.

Step 14: What changes are you willing to make? I am willing to make any changes to stabilize my attitude. I need to take control of my imbalance within.

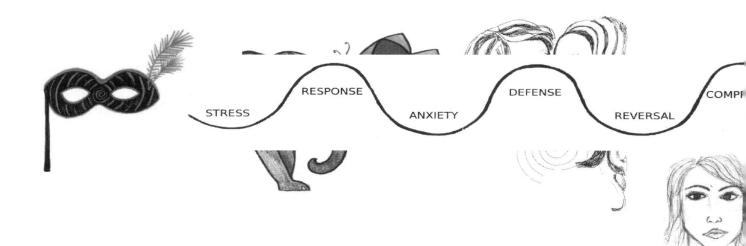

STRESS   RESPONSE   ANXIETY   DEFENSE   REVERSAL   COMPR

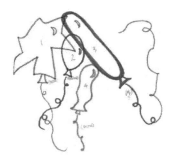

Stress:
Caught between parents' fights Mother as prickly balloon threatening to pop daughter's balloon.

Response:
Ballroom mask.

Anxiety:
Self-portrait presents clear intense feelings. Heart is contained in a series of shells.

Defense:
Trapped circus elephant versus free and scared butterfly.

Trapped as Beauty and the beast vs. free as playful and scared Alice in the wonderland.

Reversal:
Dream in which her heart is broken by lover who betrayed her.

Compromise:
Love story happy ending in a carefree union.

Dominant Case Study Four
The Dragon and the Unicorn

Introduction And Discussion: Before And After Images

Interest of this case is in illustrating the dominance related sense of anxiety or paranoia
A 24-year-old married woman from an Asian country, a student at a local college, sought help because of her disabling social performance anxiety; she was in an utter panic about making a presentation to her college class. I detected her condition as a typical panic attack that could be explained by her relational modality, that of a very pronounced dominant personality. She was the cowardly lion; indeed this was the image of her mask. The aggressiveness of the lion is presented graphically with the angry open mouth of the lion and the consequence to that is revealed in the heart image, a heart bound tightly by a rope, representing how she was expected as an angry child to contain her anger. This relational modality explained the fears, anxiety, stemming from projecting her very aggressive disposition to the environment of her classmates.

Therapy lasted 10 sessions structured by completing the Conflict Analysis Battery, which helped her to identify her massive aggressiveness, manifested in her childhood, continuing into her adolescence and currently in conflicts with her husband. Her dramatic disposition had alienated her mother, a beautiful model, and had generated for her the closeness to a beloved second grandmother. The loss of this grandmother had elicited renewed manifestation of her immense anger.

The patient recognized her angry disposition. She talks about herself in her essay. Her recovery is confirmed in a 'before and after therapy image'. It portrays her with a whip of mastery in the place of the original alienation and panic.

The patient's essay about her therapeutic experience clarifies the benefit contributed by the battery tests as insights in the relational nature of her fears. The Short Story metaphor reflects her turning around by reconciling herself with her family assuming the leadership role in the service of her father though still competing with her brother; it reflects her capacity to feel comfortable in social situations instead of being paralyzed by fears.

Relational Modality Evaluation Scale

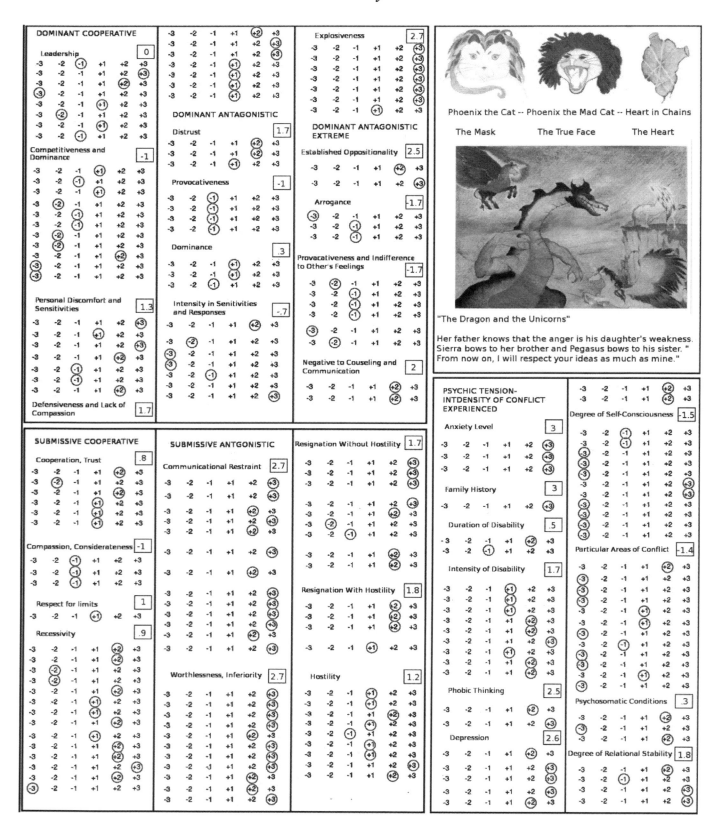

DOMINANT COOPERATIVE

Leadership [0]

Competitiveness and Dominance [-1]

Personal Discomfort and Sensitivities [1.3]

Defensiveness and Lack of Compassion [1.7]

DOMINANT ANTAGONISTIC

Distrust [1.7]

Provocativeness [-1]

Dominance [.3]

Intensity in Senitivities and Responses [-.7]

Explosiveness [2.7]

DOMINANT ANTAGONISTIC EXTREME

Established Oppositionality [2.5]

Arrogance [-1.7]

Provocativeness and Indifference to Other's Feelings [-1.7]

Negative to Couseling and Communication [2]

SUBMISSIVE COOPERATIVE

Cooperation, Trust [.8]

Compassion, Considerateness [-1]

Respect for limits [1]

Recessivity [.9]

SUBMISSIVE ANTGONISTIC

Communicational Restraint [2.7]

Worthlessness, Inferiority [2.7]

Resignation Without Hostility [1.7]

Resignation With Hostility [1.8]

Hostility [1.2]

Phoenix the Cat -- Phoenix the Mad Cat -- Heart in Chains

The Mask   The True Face   The Heart

"The Dragon and the Unicorns"

Her father knows that the anger is his daughter's weakness. Sierra bows to her brother and Pegasus bows to his sister. " From now on, I will respect your ideas as much as mine."

PSYCHIC TENSION- INTDENSITY OF CONFLICT EXPERIENCED

Anxiety Level [3]

Family History [3]

Duration of Disability [.5]

Intensity of Disability [1.7]

Phobic Thinking [2.5]

Depression [2.6]

Degree of Self-Consciousness [-1.5]

Particular Areas of Conflict [-1.4]

Psychosomatic Conditions [.3]

Degree of Relational Stability [1.8]

Before and After Images

Therapy's outcome illustrated with a before and after therapy drawing:

"How I perceived myself when I had to make a presentation
[Before I talked to Dr. Levis]. 'Joker Clown.'
[After]. 'Same Clown, but this time he's holding a whip!'"

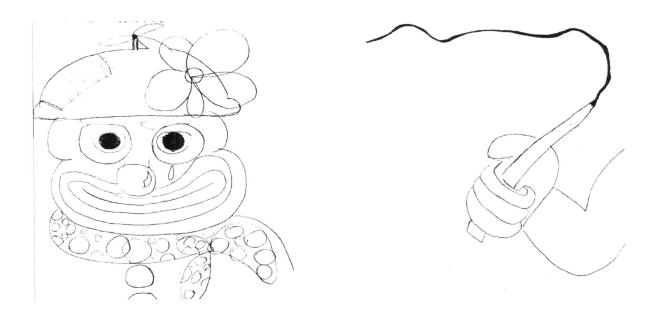

She wrote an essay upon termination, and I integrated her tests around this essay along the six-cycle process.

Transcription of the case study

STRESS

CONFLICTUAL MEMORIES

Childhood Memory

Please sit next to me and listen to a story about a girl who was born with a massive box full of anger. There are several ways to hurt a girl, especially the one with anger in her pocket. Either to smack, to slap, to pinch, or just simply choke her with hurtful words. A stubborn brat deserves occasional painful punishment in which she must accept it silently. There was nothing but the big "ID" coming out of that tiny human being and everyone seemed to have enough for her. She had been told a million times how much everyone loved her and yet they appeared to act in the opposite direction.

Mom kept disappearing every Monday and reappeared like a magician every Friday. How did she manage to be invisible for so long? Dad, too, traveled around and worked very hard with high ambition.

The girl's real grandmother could not walk, so her second grandmother was in charge of looking after her while her parents were away. You see, my mother has a mother and a stepmother because her father had two wives. The second grandma unintentionally became the girl's second mother. Grandma never went away, and besides, she was there when the girl cried. Grandma knew best. She knew things that scared her step-granddaughter. God forgave her for smacking her granddaughter when she was crying. Too bad, the girl loved to cry. What a shame to be born from a beautiful mother who wholeheartedly wished her first child to be as pretty as she was, but her wish has never been granted. It was such disgraceful for her to live with all the criticisms among friends and relatives. "Why don't you look like your beautiful mother?" "Why your mother was so mean that she did not grant you just a speck of her beauty?" "How could she disappoint her loving and caring parents?" However, Grandma never complained. Instead, she even liked having her step granddaughter smile.

When the girl turned 18, her mother took her to see a plastic surgeon. Why? Mom just needed some advice about having a face-lift. However, it all ended up with the girl was asked to see the plastic surgeon and within a couple of weeks after, the girl had her nose reconstructed. The girl was happy. Everyone including grandma were happy. Dad did not notice the change of his daughter until mom told him. Dad made no comment. New nose and what's next? Eyes, yes we almost forgot bout the eyes. No, you cannot have those pair of eyes that look like you are sleeping all the time. Why don't we make them look bigger? Just wee bit bigger. That would do. Why the girl become so self-conscious? Why she hated her looks so much? Why she believed that she was so ugly that she could even stop a clock? You have everything now, my dear. You look fine now. Mom was happy and the girl was happy. The caterpillar had made the transformation.

ADOLESCENT CONFLICTUAL MEMORY

Step 1: Draw a conflictual childhood memory.

Step 2: Describe the incident. Me, my friends, and the temptations of the outside world.

Step 3: How did you feel about this person? I loved them, hated them, and could not live without them.

How did this person feel about you? My friends thought I was crazy.

Step 4: What were the conflicts? We were too wild.

Step 5: What happened before? We flew around the magic garden with 20 unicorns.

Step 6: After? We got bitten by the snake.

Step 7: Your share in this conflict? I was lost.

Step 8: Effect on life: I have a bad attitude for society. It is a sick sad world that we live in.

Step 9: Have you been repeating yourself? No.

Step 10: Has this conflict been resolved in your mind? No.

Step 11: Resolved in this relationship? No.

Step 12: What changes should be made? I would return to my nest and help my mom go through tough times.

Recent episode of intense angry reaction illustrated both in the dark image of this memory and in the story about this reaction.

"The Loss"

Grandma was the first one who cried on the day the girl got married. Later on the girl realized that none of her pictures that were taken with her step grandmother carried the smile. The girl forgot to ask her grandmother to take a photo with her. Grandma waited until most of the guests were gone before she asked the girl for a picture. How could she forget all about her grandma? How did she do that to her beloved grandma? May she burn in hell forever for disregarding her grandma. What the girl forgot to tell her grandma was how she hated being the center of attention and how difficult it was for her to pretend that it was not her wedding day.

It is too late. Grandma died just a year after the girl's marriage. Dad did not want to break the news because he did not want the girl and her husband to travel all the way from the States just for attending grandma's funeral. It's too much of the trouble you see. No, dad would not let the family business interfere with the girl's in-laws. Respect others and always put them first. How well the girl remembered her dad's teaching. Grandma's death was just another sad news that reflected the facts of life. You have to live and learn and try to cope with those facts. You may cry until your eyeballs pop out but it won't bring grandma back. The girl took the next available flight back home. She cried all the way home. It's O.K. Grandma did not suffer. She had been blessed. We respect those who did not suffer before they died. People kept telling the girl that everything was okay. Grandma was very lucky because she passed away in her sleep while she was at the hospital. Did the girl want to hear that fact? Yes she did. Did the girl want to see her grandma while she was alive at the hospital? Yes she did. Why then someone did not inform her? That's the way her dad wanted it to be. No need to tell her. She's too busy and too far away, anyway.

Oh. How angry the girl became. The girl was betrayed. She was disappointed with her family. She hated them all. She hated her in-laws. She hated her husband. They were the reason that kept her dad from telling her, from letting her know that grandma was very, very ill. She wanted her in-laws to die. She wanted them to cry, to suffer, to fall apart.

ZOO PORTRAIT AND STORY

FAMILY OF ORIGIN

Step 1: Draw a zoo portrait of your family of origin.

Step 2: Identify each individual.

> **Dad:** hard working, enjoys good food and wine, plays golf every weekend
> **Mom:** loves animals, has a salty tongue but she is kind, always worries.
> **Me:** likes to argue with Mom, has too many boyfriends, always changes her mind
> **My Brother:** kind, independent, very bright

Step 3: What are the conflicts?
Not sure. May be lack of communication?

Step 4: What changes should be made to resolve these conflicts?
Get together more often. Joke more, and laugh more.

RESPONSE

TRANSPARENT MASK: MASK I

Draw a mask.

"Phoenix The Cat"

It all began from just a minute of uncontrollable urge for attention, together with the rampages power of dominant characteristics; the girl has turned into a baby-sitter's nightmare. To tame this wild creature, physical punishment seemed to speak louder than words. Her father smacked the girl and she was not allowed to cry. She was smacked until she agreed to stop crying. Learn to suppress your anger, my dear child. Learn to control your emotions because there's no room here for such thing. We still love you. The mask became pretty handy for the girl whenever she got angry, upset, suspicious, or hurt. She could not express her emotions. People became too scary especially when she 's angry. She got hurt even if she had no intention to hurting the people. Why is life so complicated?

413

ANXIETY

MASK II

Draw what is under the mask.

"Phoenix The Mad Cat."

Phoenix the mad cat was the girl's true color. Phoenix's hair was red, purple, shocking orange, pink, and maroon. When he spoke, the girl had to cover her ears with her hands because his voice was so loud. The girl could get very aggressive whenever she let the Phoenix The Mad Cat out of his cage. He was amazingly unpredictable. However, things were not as bad as when the girl was very young. Because now, she knew that there were two cats living inside her.

MASK III

THE HEART

Make a drawing of what you see in this person's heart.

"Heart In Chains."

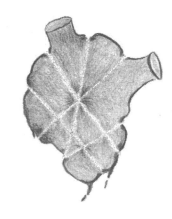

The girl became used to how she restrained herself in order to avoid getting into troubles with her parents and other people. She was upset when she could not express her love to her step grandmother. Once she recalled of bringing home a box of cake for her grandma, but she was told not to let her mother know because she would get jealous. How could she tell her mother not to worry? How could she explain to her mom that her step grandma meant so much to her? How could she stop her step grandma from moving out of her house? How could she tell her not to love her real grandchildren as much as she loved the girl? How to ask a person if he or she really loved her?
What is love anyway?

DEFENSE

ANIMAL METAPHOR #1

Step 1: Draw two animal figures in color.

Step 2: Fill in the blanks

414

Animal #1
Type of animal: Piglet with rainbow tail
Age: 11 **Animal's sex:** Male
Personality: Loves to sing and dance; loves to bake cakes and muffins; does not like thunderstorms.

Animal #2
Type of animal: Owl with eyeglasses
Age: 97 **Sex:** Male
Personality: Very wise and kind; loves to read and experiment; very happy all the time.

Step 3: What are they saying?

#1 – "Hello Owl! How are you today?"
#2 – "Hello, my little one! I am absolutely fine. What can I do for you today?"
#1 – "I 've received a new recipe for Apple Muffin from Grandma yesterday."
#2 – "Then?"
#1 – "You see, last night there was a thunderstorm and I got really scared."
#2 – "Uh-ha. So what does it have anything to do with your Grandma's recipe?"
#1 – "I talked to her on the phone and forgot to write it down on a piece of paper. I thought that I could remember everything easily."
#2 – "Let me guess. This morning you can't remember what your grandma said, can you?"
#1 – "That's correct but it was not my fault. It was the storm's. It made me forget everything."
#2 – "No, no silly little one. It's because you did not write it down on a piece of paper. Don't blame the storm. Come on, let's have a cup of tea."
#1 – "Okay Owl. Can I have some cookies too?"

Step 4: What happened before? The owl was working in his laboratory at his house. The piglet was trying to recall his grandma's recipe for apple muffin

Step 5: After? They both sat down at the owl's green house under the beautiful fig tree and enjoy their cup of tea and cookies.

Step 6: Title: "The Storm, The Piglet, and His Lost Recipe."

Step 7a: Conflicts between themselves: Piglet is too young to accept his own fault, in other words, he does not want to blame himself when things go wrong.

Step 7b: Conflicts between them and the world: Piglet is young and has a lot to learn. Owl is very old. His days are counted. However, he's never stopped learning, discovering, seeking for answers.

Step 8: What changes should they make to resolve conflicts? For piglet only time can help him. Hopefully, when he grows older, he will become wiser and more responsible. Still, he needs a good adviser.
For Owl, he should take some time off from his work and projects because he is getting very old. He has spent all of his life seeking the answers. He did not realize that the more answers he discovers, the more questions will arise.

Step 9: Which animal do you identify with: The owl also represents myself at the present time. I am forever looking for answers for every question that comes into my head. The more I want to know the reason, the more I become puzzled. <u>I also identify with Piglet. When I was young, I'd always blame somebody else for my wrong doing. I denied my own responsibility.</u>

Step 10: How does this pertain to you? There is conflict within myself.

Step 11: What changes should you make? Don't know. Maybe the best solution is to end everything.

REVERSAL

DREAM ANALYSIS

Step 1: Choose a dream: Significant childhood dream.

Step 2: Draw the dream:

Step 3: Describe the dream:
- two-faced monster
- me running away
- voice over
- mysterious woman with no face
- swing chair

The voice over always belongs to a woman. It says "How pity."

The mysterious woman has a kind of wheezy, high pitch voice. She has no face. All I could see was her long, dark hair that covered most of her face. She sat so close to me and bent down to me so that I could hear her voice.

The swing chair in the playground. I used to dream of myself sitting on the swing chair, playing and humming a song. It's very windy. Just like the storm was approaching. But I kept swinging on that chair.

<u>In most dreams I try to run away from things or events that scare me. But I just can't get away from those scary things. It's like running on an exercise mill.</u>

Step 4: Describe the participants: Most of the participants are strangers who I have never met before.

Step 5: What are the conflicts? Arguing over something; threatening to kill me; accussing me of being dumb and ugly.

Step 6: What occurrences preceded the dream? [left blank].

Step 7: Explanation of the dream: No idea.

416

Step 8: Do you dream a lot? Yes

Step 9: Other dreams:

1. Dreams about the death of someone close to me i.e. Dad, Mom, my dog, my brother.
2. Dreams about the death of myself.
3. Dream of taking a shower in the middle of a basketball field.
4. Dream of worms.
5. Dreams of listening to the orchestra but the music was too loud and I could not tell them to stop playing. It always wakes me up.

Step 10: Connections or patterns in dreams: No clue.

Dreams are related to each other.

Do you see any pertinent connection or patterns in your dreams? No clue.

COMPROMISE

The phobic patient completed her therapy presenting me with an oversize illustration of her last test, a short story in which she vindicated herself as a unicorn rescuing her father's kingdom from a dangerous dragon.

She was successful in presenting her work in the classroom without experiencing any anxiety.

Step 1: Choose two imaginary characters and write a short story about one of their adventures.

Once upon the time in the island called Neverland, there was a group of flying unicorns living peacefully with other animals on the lost island. Since there are plenty of food available everywhere for everyone, all the animals are healthy and strong. The strongest flying unicorn in the group has been elected to rule the land and to fight with the dragon that lives in the cave by the sea. On every full moon; he will leave his cave for hunting. The dragon wants to kill all the unicorns in order to overtake the island; therefore, he is the most troublesome of all the unicorns' enemies. There have been fighting events between the Unicorn and the dragon for many decades and the Unicorns have lost so many members of its group.

One day, the King of all Unicorns has called for his daughter and son to discuss about how they would fight against the dragon on the incoming full moon. The King's daughter's name is Sierra. She is a very powerful unicorn that can shoot the fire from the tip of her wings. She has no fear of anything and always wants to go out in the battle with her father on every full moon but her request has always been denied. Her father knows that the anger is his daughter's weakness and is too afraid that he might lose her in the battle. On the other hand the King's son, Pegasus, is more mature and calm even if he is much younger than his sister. Pegasus is not as strong as Sierra, however, he uses his wisdom and intelligence to combat the troubles. Today will be his 20th birthday which in the unicorns' tradition, enables him to join his father in the battlefield.

The King asks Pegasus what he would do if he were to fight with the dragon. Pegasus replies "Father, I would set a trap outside his cave and bait him with fake animals. I would cover those fake animals with raspberry juices and fish blood. Once he sets his feet outside his cave, he would smell the blood and run into the trap. We will dig the trap so deep that he would not be able to climb up and when the tides come in, he will be drowned." The King nods his head and turns to his daughter. "What about you Sierra? What would you do if you were to fight with the dragon?" Sierra stamps her hoof loudly and replies " Father, I am a war-unicorn and I have zero tolerance with that dirty beast. I shall bring my troops and slay him with hundred horns and burn him up with my fire before he even wakes up." The King then asks " Don't you know that the dragon has a very keen nose? What if he could smell you as you enter the cave and there is no room for all of your troops to flee if the dragon wakes up?' The King then adds " My dear daughter, I rather lose my own heart than let you into that cave". The King then decided 'Sierra, would you agree with me if I rather chose your brother's suggestion?' Sierra became so upset once she heard her father's decision that she galloped off into the wilderness.

The full moon is here and every unicorn is ready to capture the dragon according to Pegasus's plan. The wind is so strong and tonight seems to be the perfect night for the end of the beast. The tides crash into the nearby cliff spraying the water all over the rocks. The stars are so bright and seem like they are getting ready to celebrate the victory. Everything is in order, the trap that is so deep, the raspberry juices are so red, and the fish bloods are so rich. All the unicorn troops are waiting on the cliff above the cave's entrance. There is no sign of Sierra and her troops. The wind starts to build up and carry the rich smell of fish blood into the cave. Yes, this will wake up the dragon quicker. Pegasus watches the cave's entrance with unblinking eyes. His wings flapping around with excitement. Suddenly, the ground beneath their hooves starts shaking violently. The dragon is awake.

The dragon's roars sound like thunder. The unicorns start standing on their hind legs and kicking their front legs in the air. " Here it comes!" Pegasus whispers in his throat. He thought he was shouting.

The dragon must have smelt the blood and rushed out of the cave to find the first pray of the night.

"KABLAM!!!" Without delay, the dragon fell into the trap and left behind the echo angry roars in the air. All the unicorns dance around with joy and salute the King and Pegasus." The dragon is dead. The dragon is dead. Hail the King."

But, wait! The trap is too dry. The tides are still too low to reach the trap. The dragon has managed to climb up by digging its claws into the ground. Panic. The King orders his troops to get ready to attack. Pegasus cries out loud. "Oh ! No, the trap could not hold him" He shouts to the King" Father, please call back your troops, I don't want anyone to get killed. "The dragon is extremely angry with us and he is heading for our city." Please send the messengers to tell all animals to evacuate their home and gather around the foothill". The King orders his messengers to carry the emergency message to all animals and orders his troops to try to stop the dragon. "I think I will stop him myself. Pegasus, go to the foothill and guard all the animals". The King left the cliff with his order to his son.

"No, father, you are too frail to fight. Please come with us," Pegasus shouts back but it's too late.

The King tries to stop the dragon by distracting him from heading towards the city. The dragon rises his tail and hits the King. The unicorn soldiers rush to him and protect him with their wings. The land is covered with dead unicorn soldiers and blood is everywhere. The trees catch fire and it spreads out rapidly. The dragon left the King and his unicorn soldiers behind as they head for the city.

Suddenly, the sky is blackened by hundreds of unicorn soldiers and the leader of the troops has a pair of fire wings. Sierra appears from the back of the mountain with her wings ready to fire. She orders her troops to round up the dragon and wound it with their extra sharp horn. The dragon cries in pain and confusion. Sierra flaps her wings and releases the giant ball of fire into the dragon's eyes. The dragon roars for the last time.

The city and all animals are back to normal again but this time everyone seems to look happier than before. The King announces his retirement and proclaims that his son and his daughter shall rule the kingdom together. Sierra bows to her brother and Pegasus bows to his sister. "From now on, I will respect your ideas as much as mines. I know that I would have been dead by now if I had led my troops into the cave". Sierra speaks calmly to her brother and father. And Pegasus replies to Sierra, "I should have thought about having you and your troops stand by because we never know what could possibly go wrong."

The King smiles and says "Use your power wisely and use your wisdom powerfully."

Discussion of the case study

What a beautiful case study in content and also with the artistically perfect illustrations of her dramatically intense emotions! So much need for love and so much sense of pain; so much anxiety and intense defenses; such beautiful healing accepting responsibility instead of being paralyzed. I am very touched by this young woman's need for love and her sensitivity for rejection, her fiery emotions as Phoenix the Mad Cat and the subtle containment of her anger in the tethered heart. What an interesting journey from her paranoid suffering about making a presentation in her college class to her recovery as masterfully leading the unicorns to save her father and collaborate with her brother.

The dynamics of the dominance syndrome:

This case study illustrates well the dynamics of dominance and its treatment. We see here the syndromal nature of the dominance relational modality, as well as its correction with simple proper management of power by transforming passivity to activity, antagonism to cooperation and alienation to mutual respect. This study provides ample evidence on the topic of the dominance relational modality as a disposition that drives a person to express massive anger or to seek power in the system. How sensitive in her experiences of rejection and how intense her responses! The images and the words demonstrate the range of her intense responses to life's stressors. She was aware of these angry and norm testing behaviors and she had awareness of trying to moderate them.

Therapy Outcome:

Therapy started for dealing with the panic prior to a class presentation. It was concluded following her masterful presentation at school and the completion of her Short Story.

Stress: Intense hurt being rejected by her mother, feeling loved by her grand mother.

Response: Her lion with anger contained, for fears of overwhelming her father with her screams.

Anxiety: Loosing control of her anger as the lion unleashed, as thundering anger balanced out by her heart being tethered.

Defense: She was the piglet blaming others unable to accept responsibilities.

Reversal: This is the phase of her panic attack upon performance behavior. Her dreams too show multiple instances of loss of control, fears, running away and being stuck.

Compromise: Her conflict resolution is presented in her Short Story battling the Dragon threatening her community. Her power is now in her fiery wings and horns blinding the overpowering dragon.

She did not talk about her clinical problem that drove her to ask for help other than in her before and after images of how she felt before the therapeutic intervention and after it.

This case illustrates the dynamics of anxiety related to dominance relating. Anxiety as anticipations of reversals handicapped her capacity to deliver a paper, to face the class. Therapy helped her to understand her fears. She developed insights and moderated her behaviors. She processed the power management problems in her life at multiple situations. She recognized her problem of anger. And now she accepted responsibility for modifying it and not blaming others. What a clear evidence of outcome in the images of before and after therapy. She presents here her transformation from a scared clown to a masterful tamer with a whip in hand.

She emerged in reality learning about herself and making a great presentation to her peers. She also healed from her tendency to overreact becoming aware of the need to moderate herself in her family relations. She made changes; she felt less angry and less scared. She concluded therapy with her short story with the statement: "Use your power wisely and use your wisdom powerfully."

Short Story Illustration

Patient Note

"I am screaming for attention, then they give me love and attention. Then I reject it. Why don't you give me love from the beginning?

Last night I had dinner with my husband he said there is improvement. It takes time. When I have anger, I manage it."

STRESS RESPONSE ANXIETY DEFENSE REVERSAL COMPROMISE

Stress:
She had a strong relationship with her grandmother, but wasn't told about her death.

Response:
Her mask is "Phoenix the Cat." She wears it when she is "angry, upset, suspicious, or hurt."

Anxiety:
"Phoenix the Mad Cat" is the true face. Her heart is wrapped in chains.

Defense:
A wise owl teaches a young pig to be responsible for his actions.

Reversal:
Dream: A two-faced monster, a woman with a face obscured by hair, hands reaching out of the ocean, holding a fruit filled with worms.

Compromise:
A unicorn makes peace with its family in order to defeat a dragon, and learns to "use its wisdom powerfully and it's power wisely."

Dominant Case Study Five
The Terrier and the Buffalo

A Case of Mixed Relational Diagnosis

Introduction And Discussion:
This study is of a 33-year-old single woman, who sought help for being very nervous around her boyfriend's three children. She had long history of mental illness and of prior therapies. The patient could qualify for several clinical symptom-based DSM diagnostic labels. The relational modality diagnosis gave her understanding of her emotions and her defenses and these insights were useful in making adjustments in her emotional reactions.

The study is significant for two reasons:

First, it demonstrates the psychodynamic nature of anxiety as paranoid anticipations of role reversal: Here the elicited specific version of fears consisted in projecting to her step-children her antagonism at her own step mother. This insight was generated by a metaphor, (the greyhound and the three ally cats) and helped her to resolve her strained relationship with her boyfriend of six years. Thanks to the insights and the resolution of her fears she was able to proceed after a six-year relationship with getting finally married to him.

Second, the case illustrates the use of retesting to both monitor therapy outcome and to develop more insights and resolutions. The repetition of the assessment helped her to address and resolve her angry stance towards her estranged father as illustrated in the second Short Story metaphor: (the Buffalo and the Terrier.)

First, discussion of the diagnostic therapeutic functions of the assessment
Her relational diagnosis of dominance needs discussion. In all her metaphors she is presented as the smaller and oppressed, threatened animal. How could she be dominant? In her relational scales she scored high on the dominant cooperative scale, and also the dominant antagonistic items. She also scored positive in some submissive cooperative and many submissive antagonistic items.

The justification for dominance is in recognizing her intense anger, but this may be considered a submissive person's hostility. The critical point is that she experienced much anger and many paranoid fears and defensiveness. This set of anxieties and defenses may occur in both the submissive antagonistic and the dominant antagonistic person and she may be seen as having both diagnoses. The smaller animal can also be emotional, explosive and expressive. She was able to be angry toward her

424

father after he and his wife killed her pet goat and offered it to her as tasty dinner. She was able to shut him out of her life for years. She was not holding her feelings back. We could recognize her behaviors as submissive antagonistic, a pattern that manifested in multiple relations. But what is particularly descriptive of this patient is her emotional intensity, which might confuse us in differentiating dominance from submissiveness. Another point that we can make here is that even if she were diagnosed as submissive antagonistic we could understand the nature of her anxieties as based on her hostilities projected on her step-children. Being submissive antagonistic also may generate projections and defenses.

The dilemma of dominance versus submissiveness may be illustrated in the following two metaphors:

Animal #1
Type of animal: *Mouse*
Age: *20* **Sex:** *Female*
Personality: *Kiss-ass, weak, powerless.*

Animal #2
Type of animal: *Hawk*
Age: *50* **Sex:** *Female*
Personality: *Bold, fearless, aggressive.*

As a mouse she was able to make a stand to the hawk:

"Somehow I cope...but I am not strong. I scurry around, trying to avoid predators, and vultures who would pick me dry!". In this encounter she survived, she did not allow herself to be eaten; she was capable to survive abuses.

In her second animal metaphor she is a Turkey versus a Mountain Lion.

Animal #1
Type of animal: *Mountain Lion*
Age: *48* **Sex:** *Female*
Personality: *Vicious, calculating, controlling.*

Animal #2
Type of animal: *Turkey*
Age: *34* **Sex:** *Female*
Personality: *Naïve, gullible, lost.*

Step 3: What are they saying?

#1 – *"You will do just what I tell you--as I tell you."*
#2 – *"Okay, lion--I am only a turkey and you can have me by the throat."*
#1 – *'That's right. Glad you know your place."*
#2 – *"Okay, thank you powerful, almighty lion. Thanks for letting me live--what else may I do for you?"*
#1 – *"Stay out of my sight. Also, you annoy me, you do nothing to serve my purpose."*
#2 – *"May I fly away?"*
#1 – *"No--that gives you too much freedom, pleasure and sense of self. Stay around in fear and hide if you must--but be here for me to kick around or I will eat you!"*
#2 – *"Yes, great lioness."*

On the surface she is compliant and agreeable. But deep down she was a feisty turkey that did not need permission to fly away as she did in her family resentful of the abusive stepmother and the hurtful father. She complied to the Mountain Lion but was ready to explode; alternatively she panicked and attempted to commit suicide twice.

There is a question here: does it make a difference if she were dominant versus submissive? I dare say no. What really matters is understanding the origin of her paranoid fears of her step children and there is no question that these fears were generated by her own negative feelings toward her step mother. Does she have to be dominant for these fears to manifest? The answer is no. So the conclusion is that this case has been placed with this cohort because of the symptom of aggression and paranoia, but it is questionable if one has to be dominant to experience paranoid-nature anxieties.

The first or evaluation workbook addressed and explained the nature of her initial complaint: anxiety related to her boyfriend's children visiting. She understood the relation between her fear of her boyfriend's children and her own intolerance of her step-mother.

The first book, processed upon the four individual session evaluation period, provided resolution to her troubled long term relationship with her boyfriend. She was always sensitive and defensive with his three children: whenever they visited their father, her boyfriend, she felt they were interfering with her relationship with their father. She found out that her anxieties were a projection on these children of her own anger at her step-mother. This insight, which was generated by the Short Story of the greyhound and the three mocking ally cats, relieved her of the anxiety evoked by her step children, which was her principle initial complaint.

Second this study illustrates the therapeutic effectiveness of the repeated use of the assessment.
The second workbook, processed within a three-month-long group therapy experience, helped her to deal with the alienation she had experienced with her father. In the story of the 'buffalo and the terrier' she identified her need for resolution in this relationship by recognizing her own nervousness around him and how her nervousness affected her father. The Short Story of the second workbook of the terrier and the buffalo delivered insights in understanding the anger at her father, and processing these angry feelings helped the healing of that relationship. She could understand her relationship with her father through that metaphor.
It is interesting that both workbooks led to resolution upon the Short Story test; we identify in it the compromise phase in the sequence of tests. It represents the resolution of conflicts.

The case study illustrates the importance of the repetition of the assessment as the two books contributing complementary insights. They both led to emotional catharsis but also the resolution of conflicts in two separate significant relationships. Thus the two books complemented the therapeutic experience; they assisted in understanding and alleviating her clinical symptoms and provided her with a sustainable long-term recovery. Insights were deepened and conflicts were resolved by the psychodynamic understanding of her antagonistic dominant/submissive personality related apprehensions.

The effectiveness of the therapy outcome is documented in the patient's clinical records but also in her two essays upon completion of the two workbooks.
Her impressions attest to the significance of the insights generated. Her assessment is valuable as the critical evaluation of the therapy by an expert patient, one who had been exposed to multiple therapeutic experiences including the use of medications. She was able to connect the testing meaningfully by integrating her metaphors on the template and thus gaining insights on the syndromal organization of her emotions and behaviors allowing her to modify her attitude and experience the relief of her several symptoms, a positive therapeutic outcome:

'During the course of this workbook, I progressed from feeling fractured and stressed with no particular insights as to WHY, to successfully working with identified conflictual patterns towards a resolution. I learned through these protocols that I was carrying around old anger towards my stepmother that would

erupt, causing excessive anxiety whenever my boyfriend's children from a previous marriage would come to visit us. I also learned that I was like a hyperactive terrier that needed to slow down, respect myself and not be so terrified of those in authority roles like my father.

By finally understanding this logical progression of my feelings, insights, and knowledge gained from using the workbook, my anxieties no longer seemed insurmountable. I saw my true colors spread before me in drawings only I could have created in a logical, predictable sequence...I saw the rainbow of my life shining as if after a storm...I now knew where to begin to heal.'

This patient's essays reveal what she gained from therapy. Her essays while explicitly reflecting insights as to the meaningfulness of her experiences, helped her in making changes, they also reflect her intense dependence on authority figures. In her respect for the testing, her strong praise of the intervention I see her dependency needs to my authority but I also marvel at her insights and her rapid response to the standardized delivery of the testing.

The patient following this intervention completed her own personal goals as these were introduced in the images in her heart. She got married with her boyfriend of many years, had a child with him, she also published a book and sustained a good relationship with her father.

Book One

Personal Essay
The User-Friendly Cat

As a 33-year-old female, I decided to go through Dr. Levis' Conflict Analysis Training, (I will refer to as CAT). I needed to find the cause of panic-attacks and severe anxiety I began to experience whenever my boyfriend's children would come to visit him at our shared apartment. I was no stranger to counseling/therapy... in fact for at least 20 years (perhaps more?) I have suffered from depression, two suicide attempts, hospitalizations, fragmented interpersonal relationships, hypochondria, migraine headaches, asthma and a host of other no doubt psychologically related maladies.

CAT proved to be an interesting approach to helping people such as myself suffering from deep conflicts and depressions. It is a unique approach to the mind, allowing the individual to bring forth through a sequence of revealing drawings (these pictures can be analyzed according to shapes and color significance) and statements, their innermost fears, traumas and conflicts. The patient plays an interactive role with the therapist during CAT and perhaps feels more of a sense of mastery over realizing their own conflicts in such a non-threatening way!

In my own case, during the drawing exercises, some of my problematic personality manifested itself vis-a-vis illustrations of a strong predatory animal and one which gets preyed upon, e.g. a hawk and a mouse, the wolf and Red Riding Hood, and most intensely a great white shark and a small sea fish. I examined the implications of my exercises. This scrutiny determined some of the feelings behind my negative 'modus operandi' with my boyfriend and others. It seemed that I was defensive and aggressive because I felt I was always going to be "DEVOURED," preyed upon in relationships. Some of my behavior/s had been touched upon in prior therapy programs--but never as quickly and concisely as in CAT. I surmise that this approach can be construed as a useful tool for a quick, efficient diagnosis if the patient completes the series of simple exercises and consults with the doctor. What I have achieved through this therapy is a clearer, perhaps better springboard from which to either continue therapy or work some conflicts out on my own.

Let me mention that simultaneously while beginning CAT, I began taking antidepressant (.75 mg of Effexor a day). But without the fast diagnostic acumen, which the metaphors provided, I would not have been able to identify current sources of my conflict so easily and begun to try to modify my behavior. Medication alone might have just suppressed the conflicts as opposed to trying to resolve them.

The other thing that this program provided was a review of my past. I depicted my immediate family, their characteristics, strengths, and failings again through drawings and statements. And all this information came to bear on my current interactions with my boyfriend and others. Through the metaphors I was able to review aspects of my past family life in a more logical, rational fashion than previously, as a logical progression of my life instead of solely an emotional outpouring as in some past therapy sessions I have experienced.

Bringing this training into the school system might provide a 'User-Friendly' systematic, psychological avenue in which to diagnose and work towards resolution of conflicts in today's youth. It is a positive program for self-realization and young people need self-realization in order to master themselves early on in life, before their own personality conflicts might cripple or fix them into inescapable life patterns which would sadly follow them into adulthood."

Relational Modality Evaluation Scale

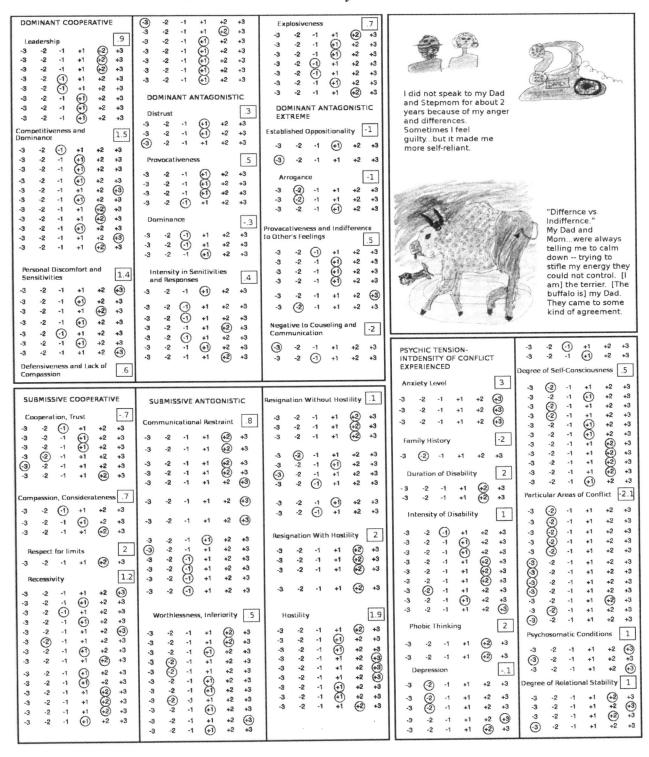

DOMINANT COOPERATIVE

Leadership `.9`

Competitiveness and Dominance `1.5`

Personal Discomfort and Sensitivities `1.4`

Defensiveness and Lack of Compassion `.6`

DOMINANT ANTAGONISTIC

Distrust `.3`

Provocativeness `.5`

Dominance `-.3`

Intensity in Senitivities and Responses `.4`

Explosiveness `.7`

DOMINANT ANTAGONISTIC EXTREME

Established Oppositionality `-1`

Arrogance `-1`

Provacativeness and Indifference to Other's Feelings `.5`

Negative to Couseling and Communication `-2`

I did not speak to my Dad and Stepmom for about 2 years because of my anger and differences. Sometimes I feel guilty...but it made me more self-reliant.

"Differnce vs. Indiffernce." My Dad and Mom...were always telling me to calm down -- trying to stifle my energy they could not control. [I am] the terrier. [The buffalo is] my Dad. They came to some kind of agreement.

SUBMISSIVE COOPERATIVE

Cooperation, Trust `-.7`

Compassion, Considerateness `.7`

Respect for limits `2`

Recessivity `1.2`

SUBMISSIVE ANTGONISTIC

Communicational Restraint `.8`

Worthlessness, Inferiority `.5`

Resignation Without Hostility `.1`

Resignation With Hostility `2`

Hostility `1.9`

PSYCHIC TENSION- INTDENSITY OF CONFLICT EXPERIENCED

Anxiety Level `3`

Family History `-2`

Duration of Disability `2`

Intensity of Disability `1`

Phobic Thinking `2`

Depression `-.1`

Degree of Self-Consciousness `.5`

Particular Areas of Conflict `-2.1`

Psychosomatic Conditions `1`

Degree of Relational Stability `1`

429

Book One

STRESS

CHILDHOOD CONFLICTUAL MEMORY

Step 1: Draw a conflictual childhood memory.

Step 2: Describe the incident. The divorce of my parents is represented here. The two colors represent two divided sides. The lines are cracks in the fabric of reality – the situation.

Step 3: How did you feel about this person? Lots of sadness about this incident. **How did this person feel about you?** N/A.

Step 4: What were the conflicts? Fear, anger, my father's passivity – my mother's wildness and stupidity.

Step 5: What happened before? They continue now.

Step 6: After? They continue now.

Step 7: Your share in this conflict? I'm sure I blamed myself because I was only five.

Step 8: Effect on life: Low self-esteem plus all current problems?

Step 9: Have you been repeating yourself? Yes.

Step 10: Has this conflict been resolved in your mind? No.

Step 11: Resolved in this relationship? No.

Step 12: What changes should be made? I need your advice and help!!!

Step 1: Draw a conflictual adolescent memory:

Step 2: Describe the incident: This deranged moon represents me taking aspirin in overdoses on separate occasions to kill myself.

Step 3: Effect on life: Guilt mainly towards it in regard to my father and stepmother.

RECENT CONFLICT

Step 1: Draw a recent conflictual memory:

Step 2: Describe the incident: Throwing my arms up when partner's kids must come for a visit. Wondering if I wish to start my own family. Passive helpless, vulnerable, "I don't like kids."

Step 3: Effect on life: Angry when his kids come. Can't decide if I want a child?

BALLOON PORTRAIT AND STORY

FAMILY OF ORIGIN

Step 1: Draw a balloon portrait of your family of origin:

Step 2: Identify each individual:

> Father, passive, quiet, thoughtful.
> Mother, impulsive, wild, excitable.
> Brother, gay, intelligent, injured by parents dynamics psychologically.
> Me, blue, confused, like a male.

Step 3: What are they saying? The father says nothing – the mother baits him into an argument. The brother retreats into study, I'm just sad.

Step 4: What happened before? The same. It is a pattern.
Step 5: After? They all go their separate ways.

Step 6: Title: "The Way it Was"

Step 7: What are the conflicts? The parents are mismatched for personality. They don't love each other. The children suffer.

Step 8: What changes should be made to resolve their conflicts? They never should have married – but the mother was pregnant too young. This family construct was artificial.

MARITAL BALLOONS

Step 1: Draw a balloon portrait of your marital family:

Step 2: Identify characteristics:

> Partner, 36 – my "other half" - kind, responsible, growly.
> Me, 33 – blue, conflicted, angry, sad.

Step 3: What are they saying?

> 1: Why do you always fight me?
> 2: I guess I'm just more male than female – competitive!

Step 4: Title: "The Same."

Step 5: What are the conflicts? The female tries to act too much like her male partner.

RESPONSE

MASK I

Step 1: Draw a mask:

Step 2: Answer the following questions:

Title: "The Wart Eye."
Age: 30 **Sex:** Female
Emotions conveyed: An awareness – a realistic knowledge of having an eyelid covered by warts.

Step 3: Conflicts represented: Sadness knowing one isn't perfect – yet unique because of specific ugliness.

Step 4: Resolution of conflicts represented: Living with less than perfection. The face does not have a good side.

ANXIETY

MASK II

Step 5: Draw what is behind the mask.

Step 6: Fill in the blanks and answer the questions:

Title: "Revenge of the Wart Eye"
Age: 30 **Sex:** Female
Emotions conveyed? Sadness at affliction and yet a monstrous feeling of power which could turn evil.

Step 7: Conflicts represented: Wanting to lash out because of a nasty appearance to the world.

Step 8: Resolution of conflicts represented: Realizing that her flaw may be the power and the key/s to success.

MASK III

Step 9: Draw what is in the heart. *(See next page).*

Title: "The Breaking of the Light from the Blackest Heart."

Step 10: Items and themes represented: There is a speck of positiveness within a dark place – a black heart.

Step 11: Feelings and conflicts represented: More depression than happiness.

Step 12: Title of the sequence: "The Emergence."

Step 13: Summarize the sequence of transformations: A person feeling ugly (figuratively and literally.) Anger being resolved – coming out. Beauty = light or positiveness being released from within.

Step 14: Conclusions about the way this person resolves conflicts: They had to be in a dark place before a metamorphosis could occur. Grappling with things.

Step 15: Does this relate to how you handle feelings: Maybe there are two good things to come from my anxiety, depression, etc.?

Step 16: What changes should be made: Try not to be so afraid to let them out. Try not to be so fearful.

Step 17: What changes are you willing to make: Medication and therapy, as long as I can afford it.

DEFENSE

ANIMAL METAPHOR TEST #1

Step 1: Draw two animals.

Step 2: Fill in the blanks

Animal #1
Type of animal: Mouse
Age: 20 **Sex:** Female
Personality: Kiss-ass, weak, powerless.

Animal #2
Type of animal: Hawk
Age: 50 **Sex:** Female
Personality: Bold, fearless, aggressive.

Step 3: What are they saying?

> #2 – "I could eat you for dinner...tear you limb-to-limb."
> #1– "Of course you could. You are bigger and stronger than I by far."
> #2 – "Then how can you possibly survive if you know you can be eaten at any time."
> #1– "[shrugs] Somehow I cope...but I am not strong. I scurry around, trying to avoid predators such as yourself, and vultures who would pick me dry!"

Step 4: What happened before? The hawk was hunting and the mouse was foraging and hiding.

Step 5: After? The mouse was frightened by the hawk's menacing appearance, so it bolted.

Step 6: Title: "Predator and Prey: Two Survival Stories."

Step 7a: Conflicts between themselves: One must avoid the other to survive. In essence the weaker must placate the stronger or run for its life.

Step 7b: Conflicts between them and the world: The mouse is always hiding because it is preyed upon. The hawk has few conflicts--only the storms of nature, bad weather. It is soaring out of reach of enemies.

Step 8: What changes should they make to resolve conflicts? I feel that NATURE is too strong. I guess the mouse is meant to be devoured. The hawk is too proud to EVER show it's weakness.

Step 9: Which animal do you identify with: Although I adore birds, I identify with the mouse. I am always trying to placate angry people in my family and amongst acquaintances. **Other animal:** All of the dominant overbearing people who have been and are involved in my life. mother, stepmother, boyfriend, father, friends.

Step 10: How does this pertain to you? Often I feel I am being devoured by others. Eclipsed-- just as the mouse must feel when the shadow of the hawk falls over her/me.

Step 11: What changes should you make? The mouse should try to fight back? Defend itself more. Assert.

Step 12: Present a similar incident: A boss at a former job dominated and manipulated me for almost three whole years. I let her, I guess, out of fear, etc.

Step 13: How do you relate with others, and how do you get yourself in trouble? I am always presenting my throat to wolves. Trying to survive by placating. No doubt it chips away at my self-esteem.

Step 14: What changes are you willing to make? Anti-depressants. Some therapy. I try to talk to my boyfriend but he is stoical and has antiquated thinking.

REVERSAL

FAIRYTALE METAPHOR

Step 1: Draw two fairy tale characters.

Step 2: Fill in the blanks

Character#1: Red-Riding Hood
Age: 5 **Sex:** Female
Personality: Sweet, charming, innocent.

Character#2: Wolf
Age: 100 **Sex:** Male
Personality: Cunning, wise, vicious.

Step 3: What are they saying?

> #1 – "I'd love to pet you, Wolf. You look furry and soft."
> #2 – "Go ahead and pet me. I'll indulge you.'
> #1 – "You won't bite me – will you?"
> #2 – "Possibly. But you must take that chance yourself."

Step 4: What happened before? Red-Riding Hood was trying to pick flowers in the woods. The Wolf was looking for food.

Step 5: After? The Wolf chased Red-Riding Hood in order to eat her.

Step 6: Title: "The Chat Before the Chase."

Step 7a: Conflicts between themselves: One's nature is innocent. The others is dominant and aggressive--living to devour.

Step 7b: Conflicts between them and the world: Red-Riding Hood much interact in the true JUNGLE of human beings. The Wolf must only follow the laws of the wild; more simple and straightforward.

Step 8: What changes should they make to resolve conflicts? Red-Riding Hood must learn to protect herself. But it is going to be difficult. Her nature, or part of it, is an innocent child.

Step 9: Which character do you identify with: Half and half. Parts of both. I possess elements of both in my nature. **Other character:** All the aggressive and overbearing females (mainly) who have dominated my life.

Step 10: How does this pertain to you? I feel like an "innocent" child constantly being menaced by wolves at every turn.

Step 11: What changes should you make? I fantasize about being the wolf and having power. Others cow-towing to me. I'm not sure how to get power for myself since I have been searching most of my life and it still eludes me.

Step 12: Present a similar incident: Again I reiterate a previous boss for three years. I stayed at the job because of low self-esteem. She totally dominated my life inside and outside of the workplace.

Step 13: How do you relate with others, and how do you get yourself in trouble? I try to placate people who I perceive as more powerful. They manipulate me. Then I resent them because I've lost all power or never had it to begin with.

Step 14: What changes are you willing to make? To keep realizing my destructive patterns and to circumvent them if at all possible!!!

REVERSAL

ANIMAL METAPHOR TEST #2

Step 1: Draw two animals with an intensified conflict:

Step 2: Fill in the blanks:

Animal #1
Type of animal: Great White Shark
Age: 30 **Sex:** Male or Female
Personality: Dangerous, strong, viscous.

Animal #2
Type of animal: Sea Fish
Age: 10 **Sex:** Female
Personality: Sweet, colorful, trusting.

Step 3: What are they saying?

#1 – "What are you doing, little fish? Swimming in <u>my</u> waters. I own the oceanic world. You pathetic little fish – you are not fit to swim here amongst the big fish!"
#2 – "You are right. What am I doing here? I only belong with all the other small fish in the sea".
#1 – "Then get out of my way and sight. Always do what I say. You see these huge teeth? I can do great damage with them, pathetic small fish."

Step 4: What happened before? The Shark was tearing apart a seal. The Little Fish was eating and trying to enjoy the sunshine.

Step 5: After? The small fish scurried out of the shark's way and hid in a deep cave. The shark chased it-- intending a quick meal.

Step 6: Title: "The Shark Factor; Intimidation Backed By Might!"

Step 7a: Conflicts between themselves: Aggression/Intimidation wielded by the larger, meaner fish. The smaller fish is terrified and must always bend to the dictates of the more powerful--or else…

Step 7b: Conflicts between them and the world: Always, it is survival of the fittest. The small fish must always dodge or placate the larger. The large fish must always devour.

Step 8: What changes should they make to resolve conflicts? The large fish (Shark) should mellow. The small one should become more aggressive or assertive.

DREAM ANALYSIS

Step 1: Choose a dream: Recent dream (last 3 years).

Step 2: Draw the dream:

Step 3: Describe the dream: I think the angel represents me rising above intellectual/competitive conflicts. I used to date a fellow in college who was also a creative writer. He was better than I was and I used to feel jealous and filled with rage regarding this. The dream was a peaceful one with the angel ascending towards light and stained glass. The desk is the writing. The couple is myself and this fellow, I guess.

Step 4: Describe the participants:

  Angel: peace, goodness, light
  Desk: writing, academics, achievement.
  Couple: self-acceptance, forgiveness, union.

Step 5: What are the conflicts? Competition, rage, jealousy, repression, inadequacy.

Step 6: What occurrences preceded the dream? The dream was self-contained. It happened out-of-the-blue, but during the course of five years of past therapy.

Step 7: Explanation of the dream: Same as step 3.

Step 8: Do you dream a lot? No.

Step 9: Other dreams: I can't recall a recent or even the last dream I had. [later note]: I had a dream last night. I shot myself in the stomach and then lied and said it was my sister who did it. Then I wondered if the gun had blanks in it. My sister said she was studying and didn't shoot me! Fertility dream? Period?

Step 10: Connections or patterns in dreams: Not really. Only if I am agitated in "real life about an upcoming conscious event. The one last night I believe had to do with menstruation. My periods are difficult.

COMPROMISE

SHORT STORY

Step 1: Write a short story: Dixie the greyhound lives on the street. She was never good enough to be a 'great racing dog' and she was never elegant enough to be an adequate pet. Somehow she became homeless. She has in a sense always been alone – shuffled here and there, and a disassociated loner. Sometimes she howls into abandoned alleyways at night. It is mournful howling.

Casey the tabby cat is also belonging to no one. But she is clever. She socializes and mixes a lot with other cats. She has no problem imposing on other animals. Although she is a cat, Casey has no fear whatsoever of Dixie. Casey watches Dixie constantly – walking atop alley fences, gazing down upon the lonely dog. She gathers her cat friends together and they smirk and laugh at the "has been" greyhound.

Step 2: Illustrate the story:

Step 3: Fill in the blanks:

Character#1
Character name: Casey
Age: 35 **Sex:** Female
Personality: Intelligent, domineering, cunning.

Character#2
Character name: Dixie
Age: 26 **Sex:** Female
Personality: Repressed, SAD, MALLEABLE.

438

Step 4: What happened before? Casey was gathering her friends to spy on Dixie.

Step 5: After: Dixie snarled a lot and then slunk away.

Step 6: Title: "No More--The Ignoring."

Step 7: Conflicts between themselves: Dixie must have the fortitude to ignore all the shit Casey and co. are dishing out. The cats are simply unresolved in themselves and define themselves by being nosy and picking on others.

Step 8: What changes should they make to resolve conflicts? The cats should find something productive and fulfilling to do. Dixie should try to be tougher and feel better about herself.

Step 9: Which character do you identify with: Dixie--but also a little bit of Casey. **Other character:** The bossy and manipulative people all of my life!

Step 10: How does this pertain to you? I feel like a worthless beaten down greyhound, who must fight for every vestige of self-esteem. Conflicted --I constantly feel like snarling. The cats (others) sense low self-esteem. They exploit my sense of powerlessness, etc.

Step 11: What changes should you make? I must feel better about who I am--gain power. I don't like becoming "catty" to feel better about my perceived wretched circumstances.

Step 12: Present a similar incident: My "Monster Boss" dominating me for almost three whole years--both IN and OUT of work. She called me constantly and I was always there for her.

Step 13: How do you relate with others, and how do you get yourself in trouble? I put myself down a lot. People sense I am depressed or that I feel bad about who I am. I always assume I am incompetent at a job, project, my life, everything. I crave structure. I feel powerless when I lose my structure. When I enter a situation, I am so vulnerable, it seems I automatically bend over backwards for complete strangers. This sets a bad precedent.

Step 14: What changes are you willing to make? Therapy and medications.

Book Two

Personal Essay

YOUR TRUE COLORS: An Innovative Palette of Psycho-assessments Boldly Blends The Humanities and The Sciences and Heals as Well

I was bristling with anger until I picked up the crayons! The anger came from my feelings regarding a composite of incidents that happened over my lifetime; both during early childhood and adolescence. I am not describing an art therapy technique...I am referring to a self-discovery, my own just discovered modus operandi.

The bristling style I was not entirely aware of until I began drawing with a box of crayons in a very special workbook developed by Dr. Levis. Now in a sense I have drawn my way towards mental health. Managed to move from anger to reconciliation. Without these drawings linked in a logically proven sequence, I might never have truly discovered that my past is inextricably linked with every moment of my present. And that a very old anger constantly made me uncomfortable generating anxiety, defensiveness and aggression in most of life's situations.

What came out of these drawings was something I already KNEW intellectually but had not necessarily FELT through any other therapies I have tried. I already realized that the breakup of my mother and father when I was about 6-years-old had had a profound effect on my personality. In one particular drawing called a "Conflictual Memory" it was clear that I felt abandoned by my father. Just looking at the picture, my choices of colors, figure positioning and figure expressions SHOWED the impact of this memory. My father was seen as disappearing through a doorway.

A pattern of STRESS therefore began--when I was very young. And like an onion or a callous, other events added other conflictual layers to my character to heighten this stress. Such as a depiction when my father and stepmother butchered a pet goat from the small farm I grew up on and served it to me as a meal to see if I liked the taste, without revealing that it was indeed my pet. I did not speak to my father and stepmother for a few years because of this incident and what I construed as other insensitive events while I was growing up. I would not call them on the telephone or return their calls left on my answering machine: "Conflict of Adolescence".

Still at 34 years old I felt myself to be one big 'Block of Worry' referring to my head and as a RESPONSE TO ALL THE STRESS in my life. The worry was inside me already from childhood, always threatening to come out and it does again and again in these drawings. I drew the fairy tale of Jack Jumping Over the Candlestick and called it "JACK BE QUICKER". Here my life DEFENSES were manifested as Jack who had to escape the powerful lure of the intimidating candle. Jack was me...always feeling pressured to be quicker or better to be able to escape from powerful or construed as powerful authority figures, e.g. my stepmother.

An intensification of this fairy tale was a drawing I did of a mountain lion opposing a

440

turkey. I am of course the turkey: naive, and innocent.

What is revealed as being in my HEART was an interesting composite drawing of the following: a bestselling book (I wish to become a published writer), a parrot head representing my five pet parrots and a ghastly blue infant face representing my fears of becoming a biological mother. All these areas of anxiety were depicted in this heart-shaped drawing "MASK III".

Then there was a picture of myself again drawn as a blockhead showing similarities to the images I had drawn in my heart picture. I called this specific drawing 'Fragmenting of The Perfect Jewel'. I am the jewel and the title expresses the unintegrated aspects of my personality and life, e.g. being torn between the prospect of motherhood, a writing career, my extensive collection of birds and my involvement with my boyfriend in a busy, mail-order business.

The OUTCOME of this composite of feeling torn and stressed was what was underneath those harried feelings manifested in reoccurring, guilty thoughts about having had an illegal abortion while studying in a foreign country 12 years ago. Simultaneously I drew another picture of two more animals depicting another intensification of the current conflicts and scenarios I felt. The animals drawn this time were a large-mouthed basking shark and a minuscule plankton. I was the plankton "ANIMAL METAPHOR II" always on the verge of being devoured or bossed around by a person in a position of power, or an authority figure.

From this stage I composed a SHORT STORY of a COMPROMISE between a high-strung terrier and a sluggish buffalo. I was the terrier trying to run circles around the buffalo, who once again was the representation of a dominating, powerful authority figure. But the dialogue in the story between the two animals was now more tempered with a sense of COMPROMISE--MUTUAL RESPECT.

During the course of this workbook, I progressed from feeling fractured and stressed with no particular insights as to WHY, to successfully working with identified conflictual patterns towards a resolution. I learned that I was like a hyperactive terrier that needed to slow down, respect myself and not be so terrified of those in authority roles. I also learned through these protocols that I was carrying around old anger towards my stepmother that would erupt, causing excessive anxiety whenever my boyfriend's children from a previous marriage would come to visit us. By finally understanding this logical progression of my feelings, insights, and knowledge gained from using the workbook, my anxieties no longer seemed insurmountable. I saw my true colors spread before me in drawings only I could have created in a logical, predictable sequence...I saw the rainbow of my life shining as if after a storm...I now knew where to begin to heal.

CHILDHOOD CONFLICTUAL MEMORY

Step 1: Draw a conflictual childhood memory.

Step 2: Describe the incident. Symbolizes my parent's divorce at age 6. A sense of foreboding and uncertainty as Dad walks through the door to the outside world.

Step 3: How did you feel about this person? I loved him and felt secure when he was around.

How did this person feel about you? I think he liked me but was quietly angry, never expressing much emotion.

Step 4: What were the conflicts? Parents were forced into marriage, because of young mother's unplanned pregnancy.

Step 5: What happened before? Lot of arguing and confusion between the parents.

Step 6: After? Silence and sadness.

Step 7: Your share in this conflict? I think I felt personally responsible. I was young.

Step 8: Effect on life: I think residual fear, uncertainty and sadness.

Step 9: Have you been repeating yourself? Yes.

Step 10: Has this conflict been resolved in your mind? Probably not.

Step 11: Resolved in this relationship? I think and hope so.

Step 12: What changes should be made? Just remind myself it wasn't my fault. I was an innocent!

Step 1: Draw a conflictual adolescent memory:

Step 2: Describe the incident: My dad and stepmom had my pet goat butchered while I visited my grandparents. They asked me to eat it not knowing it was my dead pet when I came home.

Step 3: Effect on life: Anger, fear, distrust, sadness, betrayal, protective feelings of animals.

RECENT CONFLICT

Step 1: Draw a recent conflictual memory:

Step 2: Describe the incident: I did not speak to my dad and stepmom for two years because of my anger and differences and desire to put space between us!

Step 3: Effect on life: Sometimes I feel guilty-- but it also made me more self-reliant.

BALLOON PORTRAIT AND STORY

FAMILY OF ORIGIN

Step 1: Draw a balloon portrait of your family of origin.

Step 2: Identify each individual:

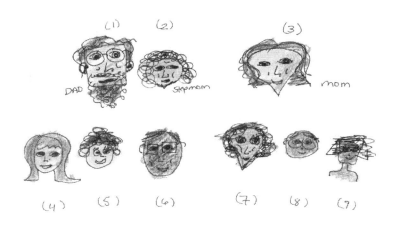

Dad, smart, quiet, contained, cold.
Stepmom, clever, interfering, creative, perfectionist.
Mom, lively, eccentric, witty, intellectual, warm.
A. half-sister, typical, stubborn, judgmental, sweet.
J. half-brother, bright, sporty, boring.
J. full brother, gay, brilliant, stubborn.
Me, blue, conflicted, nervous.
B. half-brother, quiet, ill, tense.
R. half-sister, chatty, brilliant, driven.

Step 3: What are they saying?

Mom: It makes me nervous to see your father again.
Me – "Yeah, I know. I feel your emotions."
Stepmom – "She really isn't a good dresser--your mom?"
Brother J. – "Who cares! It doesn't influence global politics!'
Half-sister A. – "Everyone shut up!"

Step 4: What happened before? Just standing there at a tense family reunion.

Step 5: After?   Relaxing a bit--reconciled to the stress and strain over the years of a broken family.

Step 6: Title: "Settling Into the Cracks; Many Years Gone By."

Step 7: What are the conflicts? The stress of many diverse chaotic personalities bumping against each other. Resonances of the old broken marriage between mom and dad.

Step 8: What changes should be made to resolve their conflicts? None – too late. Two different families. Interactions should be kept apart as always.

MARITAL BALLOONS

Step 1: Draw a balloon portrait of your marital family.

Step 2: Identify characteristics:

Me: lively, cautious, chatty.
Husband: enterprising, funny, controlling
Birds: noisy, messy, clownish

Step 3: What are they saying?

Husband: can you keep the house a little neater?
My kids are coming for another visit!
Me – "It puts enough stress on me. Do they have to stay all summer?"
Husband – "I don't see them much."
Me – "That's true – you see our birds more."
Husband – "You're right"
Me – "I'll try to be understanding, I guess."

Step 4: Title: "Understanding but Resenting."

Step 5: What are the conflicts? I am feeling true fear of my life being intruded on but understand my husband's necessity to see his kids. I will try to quell my fears.

MASK I

Step 1: Draw a mask:

Step 2: Answer the following questions:

Title: "Block of Worry."
Age: 34 **Sex:** Female
Emotions conveyed: Stress, confusion, sadness.

Step 3: Conflicts represented: Frustration, fear, indecision.

Step 4: Resolution of conflicts represented: The head is still on the shoulders in spite of distress!

ANXIETY

MASK II

Step 5: Draw what is behind the mask.

Step 6: Fill in the blanks and answer the questions:

Title: "Fragmenting of the Perfect Jewel."
Age: 34 **Sex:** Female
Emotions conveyed? Fragmenting of energies, dissipation of dreams, longing.

Step 7: Conflicts represented: Not knowing where to focus. Writing? Baby? Business/relationship?

Step 8: What resolution of conflicts does this mask represent?
Perhaps all these things are meant to be in little pieces (aspects) that constitute my whole life?
Mask III

Step 9: Draw what is in the heart:

Title: "Hope and Fear."

Step 10: Items and themes represented: Book, hope regarding writing career, birds give me joy, fear of being a mother.

Step 11: Feelings and conflicts represented: The struggle to maintain my own goals against other desires, biology, etc.

Step 12: What resolution of conflicts does it convey? Maybe there will be time for all in its due course?

Step 13: Title of the sequence: "Rising Above A Mixed Bag.

Step 14: Summarize the sequence of transformations: This person (me) worries. Feels torn apart, then rises from the ashes (broken pieces/fragments) to continue on.

Step 15: Conclusions about the way this person resolves conflicts: Unfortunately, this person is easily agitated and anxious and often is pulled under by fears instead of hopes.

Step 16: Does this relate to how you handle feelings? I often succumb entirely to anxieties.

Step 17: What changes should be made? Try to calm down and make rational choices.

Step 18: What changes are you willing to make? Do some more soul-searching and think in a logical progression.

ANIMAL METAPHOR TEST #1

Step 1: Draw two animals.

Step 2: Fill in the blanks

Animal #1
Type of animal: Mountain Lion
Age: 48 **Sex:** Female
Personality: Viscious, calculating, controlling.

Animal #2
Type of animal: Turkey
Age: 34 **Sex:** Female
Personality: Naïve, gullible, lost.

Step 3: What are they saying?

> #1 – "You will do just what I tell you--as I tell you."
> #2 – "Okay, lion--I am only a turkey and you can have me by the throat."
> #1 – 'That's right. Glad you know your place."
> #2 – "Okay, thank you powerful, almighty lion. Thanks for letting me live--what else may I do for you?"
> #1 – "Stay out of my sight. Also, you annoy me, you do nothing to serve my purpose."
> #2 – "May I fly away?"
> #1 – "No--that gives you too much freedom, pleasure and sense of self. Stay around in fear and hide if you must--but be here for me to kick around or I will eat you!"
> #2 – "Yes, great lioness."

Step 4: What happened before? The lioness was terrorizing some other animal close by. The turkey was picking at bugs quietly.

Step 5: After? The turkey scurried for cover but was careful not to fly. The Mountain. Lion watched, waiting and menacing to pounce.

Step 6: Title: "The Threatening."

Step 7a: Conflicts between themselves: Too much power = lion – grandiosity. Too little power = Turkey + low self-esteem.

Step 7b: Conflicts between them and the world: The lion feels it must always be in control. Turkey feels it must always be vigilant to predators.

Step 8: What changes should they make to resolve conflicts? The lion must loosen its controlling grip. The turkey must stand up for itself more.

Step 9: Which animal do you identify with: The Turkey. My modus operandus is "Flight, not Fight." **Other animal:** My stepmother, pretty much, or other controlling, over-protective, female figures who have cropped up in my life.

Step 10: How does this pertain to you? It is a manifestation of a scenario I know well. Myself being weaker than a more controlling dominant person.

Step 11: What changes should you make? Awareness and then some. I need to know when it's appropriate to be assertive, aggressive or passive.

Step 12: Present a similar incident: An experience for 2.5 years with a tenacious, controlling, personal – life monopolizing female boss.

Step 13: How do you relate with others, and how do you get yourself in trouble? By being too gregarious, naïve and placating as an automatic response.

Step 14: What changes are you willing to make? Awareness and self-control if possible.

REVERSAL

FAIRYTALE METAPHOR

Step 1: Draw two fairy tale characters.

Step 2: Fill in the blanks

Character#1: Jack
Age: 34 **Sex:** Male
Personality: Spry, smart, quick.

Character#2: Candlestick
Age: 50 **Sex:** Female
Personality: controlling, dangerous.

Step 3: What are they saying?

#1 – "I can jump over you and be free of your presence! Escape!"
#2 – "But you will come back because you must--you are drawn to my flame."
#1 – "I won't look at it then."
#2 – "But you will get burned if you don't look!"
#1– "You will force me to become a better jumper!"
#2 – "You'll never make it.'
#1 – "I have to try to break free.'

Step 4: What happened before? Jack was sizing up the candle to jump over it. The candle was sitting there burning and sputtering.

448

Step 5: After? Jack insists that she can break away from the candle's control. The candle tempts, taunts and threatens, insisting Jack is helpless.

Step 6: Title: "Jack Be Quicker."

Step 7a: Conflicts between themselves: One wishes to be free of the others' perceived control. The other wishes to maintain the power of control over another.

Step 7b: Conflicts between them and the world: One wants ultimate control over the environment -- the other wants freedom from total control. Total freedom.

Step 8: What changes should they make to resolve conflicts? One should try to temper (the candle) the need to control. The other (Jack) should feel less intimidated by the stationary candle.

Step 9: Which character do you identify with: Jack. I wanted to escape from my stepmother's constant interference and domination over the family. **Other character:** Stepmother-- controlling/interfering.

Step 10: How does this pertain to you? I replay this scenario with others such as my boss.

Step 11: What changes should you make? Again--awareness, consciousness--trying to be assertive and not placate her and others--that reminds me of her.

Step 12: Present a similar incident: My boss for two and a half years--a demanding, relentless woman, she bugged and dominated me all the time.

Step 13: How do you relate with others, and how do you get yourself in trouble? A people pleaser, submissive placate, rather than resentful and wishing to escape.

Step 14: What changes are you willing to make? Awareness and personal growth. Build confidence – become more assertive without sabotaging relationships within the hostility and aggression.

ANIMAL METAPHOR TEST #2

Step 1: Draw two animals with an intensified conflict:

Step 2: Fill in the blanks:

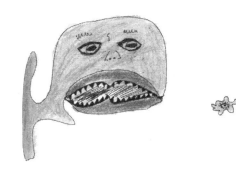

Animal #1
Type of animal: Basking Shark
Age: 22 **Sex:** Female
Personality: Consuming, voracious, dangerous.

Animal #2
Type of animal: Plankton
Age: 7 **Sex:** Female
Personality: Helpless, simple, innocent.

Step 3: What are they saying?

#1 – "I am hungry and it is inevitable that I will eat you!"
#2 – "I know--that's life, and I am resigned to this fact."
#1 – "Good--then we have an understanding. So when I open my moth you do what I say and leap in."
#2 – "Okay, okay...I know I must, but part of me wishes I did not have to."
#1 – "Tough--do it anyway."
#2 – "Okay, I submit."

Step 4: What happened before? The basking shark was eating--the plankton was trying to remain alive, evasively swimming.

Step 5: After? The plankton said nothing--just solemnly jumped into the basking shark's huge mouth, resigned to its fate.

Step 6: Title: "The Way the Void Must Be."

Step 7a: Conflicts between themselves: Too much power (Basking Shark) and too little power (Plankton).

Step 7b: Conflicts between them and the world: By its nature and size the basking shark is powerful. The plankton is miniscule and weak.

Step 8: What changes should they make to resolve conflicts? The Basking Shark should shut its mouth now and again. The plankton should be proud of what it is and stand its ground – stand up to larger predators.

Step 1: Choose a dream: Recurring dream (really a conflictual memory. I think about it a lot.)

Step 2: Draw the dream:

Step 3: Describe the dream: Based on an actual event (age 20). All alone in Scotland having just woken up after an illegal abortion. Wearing a blue flannel nightgown with white angels on it. Felt like NO ANGEL, BUT THE DEVIL OF EVIL.

Step 4: Describe the participants: Self – sad, guilty, dazed.

Step 5: What are the conflicts? Acting too quickly, worried about shame and what my stepmother would think and judge.

Step 6: What occurrences preceded the dream? Walked there to a castle-like structure secretly, by myself.

Step 7: Explanation of the dream: Guilt and maybe maternal stirrings which have lain dormant out of fear?

Step 8: Do you dream a lot? No.

Step 9: Other dreams: Dreamed of getting torn apart and chewed by wolves! Devoured.

Step 10: Connections or patterns in dreams: Devoured by guilt. Maybe the wolves represent guilt?

SHORT STORY

Step 1: Write a short story:
Beefy the buffalo and Tepi the terrier were playing. The terrier was running circles around the buffalo and he grew dizzy.

"Tepi, sometimes you drive me crazy. You circle and circle and bark. Frankly, it makes me nauseous and dizzy!" Spoke Beefy.

"Sorry Beefy--I did not know that--but I'm just a small dog and it is my nature to act this way," said the terrier.

"Can't you stifle yourself ever!? Calm down a little?" asked Beefy.

"Why should I have to?" questioned Tepi. "I am a terrier."

Beefy thought about that for a moment and added, "you should because I am bigger, slower and you are making me sick!" said the annoyed Beefy.

"Alright, I can't change completely, but I will try to temper my behavior to an extent," compromised the little dog.

"Thank you!" said the buffalo.

"But only if you act a little more lively!" said Tepi.

"I'll try!" said the big buffalo.

Step 2: Illustrate the story:

Step 3: Fill in the blanks:

Character#1
Character name: Tepi the Terrier
Age: 4 **Sex:** Female
Personality: Bubbly, friendly, carefree.

Character#2
Character name: Beefy the Buffalo
Age: 40 **Sex:** Male
Personality: Boring, slow, strong.

Step 4: What happened before? Beefy was grazing and Tepi was yipping for Beefy to move and play with him.

452

Step 5: After: They both lay down together and talked quietly about their energy levels/lifestyle differences.

Step 6: Title: "Difference vs. Indifference."

Step 7: Conflicts between themselves: One is trying to control the other and makes demands...the other counters with a demand of her own, however small. They come to some kind of agreement.

Step 8: What changes should they make to resolve conflicts? They came to a polite agreement. One will slow down and one will speed up.

Step 9: Which character do you identify with: The Terrier. **Other character:** Maybe my dad. Calculating and procrastinating.

Step 10: How does this pertain to you? I can be annoying like Tepi. I can learn to compromise, like Tepi, but also assert and have others do some compromising.

Step 11: What changes should you make? Take risks and try to be assertive without being aggressive, needy, or demanding.

Step 12: Present a similar incident: My dad and mom separately were always telling me to calm down--trying to stifle my energy they could not control.

Step 13: How do you relate with others, and how do you get yourself in trouble? I always end up being over-enthusiastic or over energetic and end up with a "lion's share" of things in life dumped on me--yet I may have solicited knowingly or unknowingly.

Step 14: What changes are you willing to make? Awareness and try to curb negative aspects of my behavior; exhibit self-control.

Three types of interpretation of metaphors and integration of the information: A summary of facts and two images. The first image or metaphor profile provided below reflects partial integration of information from both books yielding more information. The second image integrates the metaphors of the second book only.

Balloon Portraits: Marital

Mask I

2. Response:
My *Response* is depict-ed in my dedication to my pets, a flock of parrots which I treat like kids, and in my Mask which presents my identity as that of a "Block of Worry".

Fairy Tale Metaphor

4. Defense:
Perceiving authorities as terrorizing (Mt. Lion), my strategy has been to act as an accommodating Turkey. Similarly in my *Fairytale* "Jack Be Quicker", my small Jack is jumping over a huge candle-stick.

Animal Metaphor Test #1

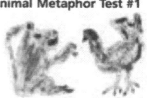

Short Story Metaphor

6. Compromise:
My drama found its resolu-tion as I, the neurotic terrier, could truly renegotiate my relationship with my father as a menacing but talkative Buffalo.

Response: (Role Assumption) **Defense: (Couterphobic Role Assumption)** **Compromise: (Role Assumption)**

Stress: (Role Oppression) **Anxiety: (Anticipated Role Reversal)** **Outcome: (Role Reversal)**

Conflictual Memories Test

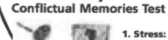

1. Stress:
My Outstanding *Memory of Conflict* was my father leav-ing our home. I was feeling responsible. Two other memories clarify my feelings of hurt and anger. In one, my father and stepmother decided to make my pet billy goat into dinner. In another, I hang up the phone on them for years.

Balloon Portraits: Family of Origin

Mask II

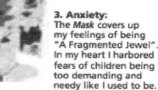

3. Anxiety:
The *Mask* covers up my feelings of being "A Fragmented Jewel". In my heart I harbored fears of children being too demanding and needy like I used to be.

Mask III

Dream Metaphor

Animal Metaphor Test #2

5. Reversal:
My fear of kids was my undoing. This was presented in two metaphors. In a reoccurring dream I was haunted with guilt for an abor-tion. In a story I was a worn-out Greyhound derided by three alley cats (my boyfriend and his children).

454

Stress:
Stress regarding her stepchildren. Memories of her parents cooking her pet goat, and her refusal to speak with her father.

Response:
Mask titled "block of Worry" conveys confusion, sadness, and frustration.

Anxiety:
The true face doesn't know which aspect of life to focus its attention.

Defense:
An aggressive Mountain Lion threatens a submissive Turkey.

Reversal:
Dream/Memory: devoured by guilt and sadness after having an abortion.

Compromise:
The energetic Terrier and the Slow Buffalo come to a positive resolution.

Summary of the Six Roles

STRESS

"My outstanding memory of conflict was my father leaving our home. I was feeling responsible. Two other memories clarify my feelings of hurt and anger. In one, my mother and stepfather decided to make my pet Billy goat into dinner. In another, I hang up the phone on them for years."

RESPONSE

"My response is depicted in my dedication to my pets, a flock of parrots which I treat like kids, and in my mask, which presents my identity as that of a "block of worry".

ANXIETY

"The mask covers up my feelings of being a "fragmented jewel." In my heart I harbored fears of children being too demanding and needy like I used to be."

DEFENSE

"Perceiving authorities as terrorizing (Mt. Lion), my strategy has been to act as an accommodating turkey. Similarly, in my fairy tale, "Jack Be Quicker," my small Jack is jumping over a huge candlestick.

REVERSAL

"My fear of kids was my undoing. This was presented in two metaphors. In a reoccurring dream I was haunted with guilt for an abortion. In a story I was a worn out greyhound derided by three alley cats (my boyfriend and his children.)"

COMPROMISE

"My drama found its resolution as I, the neurotic terrier, could truly negotiate my relationship with my father as a menacing but talkative buffalo."

Case Study Six
The Cheshire Cat and the Pit-Bull
The Dynamics of the Dominant Cooperative Relational Modality

Introduction And Discussion:

This case study is of particular interest in illustrating the dynamics of the dominant cooperative relational modality. The diagnosis of the relational modality is confirmed both by the scoring of the inventory and by the imagery of the metaphor testing. Characteristically this dominant cooperative person, a teacher in his early 40s, like Dorothy defending Toto, got into a power struggle with school authorities defending the interests of his students. His struggle with the school system was captured in two workbooks summarized with a perfect self-report document completed with artistry by the patient in the course of a very short therapy period.

The patient was being dismissed for insubordination because of or his willful handling of school activities. Under the stress of potentially ending his career as an educator this proud man reluctantly sought help. Upon my suggestion he completed two workbooks, which are reproduced in this study. The first was the evaluation of his emotional state: a serious state of depression. The second completed a month later represents the record of his recovery. The two books reflect his dominant cooperative modality in action; the first book presents his depression as a reversal in his power play experiences. The second captures his dominance triumphant. He fought the system, managed to make some changes, and emerged, at least in his view of things, as a winner.

The first book illustrates his defensive pattern as a clown, a dominant cooperative person hiding his feelings behind the mask of the Cheshire Cat smile. The Cheshire Cat was floored by a Pit-bull. The patient was weakened and depressed, had nightmares of loosing control of his classroom. His Short Story portrays him as loosing his composure for the first time crying in front of his family.

The second workbook represents the phase of recovery as his empowerment, as healing by playing a game outsmarting the school system. The patient fought the system and emerged from his depression reversing the outcome of the conflict with the school system. From his perspective he triumphed. Instead of being fired he was let go with a compensable disability, a tinnitus condition, which he had developed exposed to loud music during his school activities. This tinnitus condition could have been of psychological nature, a sign of his emotional tension, secondary to his social conflicts but he used this diagnosis as the principle cause for a disability.

He presented in his second animal metaphor the illness as a hook to catch the school system as a fish. This metaphor is in line with his earlier metaphor of being the pied piper driving the rats, the school administration, out of town. In his final Short Story he resolved his dominance by controlling his antagonism. He chose to be a moth rather than a butterfly so he is less visible, blending with the scenery, rather than standing out.

He illustrated the six role integration of the artwork of his two workbooks into the six-role template identifying the logic of his emotions and behaviors. The patient demonstrated his brilliance and competence as a skilled educator composing the integration of his art-work with the summary of each test.

The therapeutic outcome of this intervention
The intervention may be judged as successful in relieving the patient of his depression, but it might not be qualified as successful in not resolving his conflict generating dominance as a social relational problem. Again we might be content in considering his moderating his antagonistic tendencies as accurately captured in his moth butterfly final metaphor.

This relational modality manifested in his relationship with me as his resistance to making concessions in his attitude to save his career by correcting his relationship with the school system by accepting criticism for his handling the issues at hand. He was happy to be a power player. Instead of saving his career, he exited the school system with the dignity of a disability rather than the stigma of being fired. In line with his pernicious dominance he refused therapy or making compromises both at work and in his relationship with myself. He declined needing any further assistance as he made plans for a new career outside of education.

Findings
This patient's relational inventory in both books presents the clear distinction of cooperative dominance. All items on the dominant antagonism scale are marked negative 3. He also scored high on some submissive cooperative items but negative across all submissive antagonism items. So his diagnosis was that of the dominant cooperative modality.

The first book 'The drama of the clown' duplicates the relational modality scores with his syndromal sequence of emotions.

Stress: The first memory presents him as a student being criticized by a teacher. He felt humiliated in the classroom and adopted the defense of a smile/humor as his shell.
In the adolescent memory he is a circus ring-master, leader of his peers.

Response: His mask portrays accurately his response in the identity of a triumphant Cheshire Cat wearing a broad smile across his face. He used the triumphant smile as a cover up for any hurt feelings. The equivalent power role that of a clown, was his response to stress in his two family portraits.

Anxiety: He perceived himself as attacked. Instead of inner conflicts he perceived all threats as external attacks.

Defense: In his animal metaphor, he is the Cheshire cat floored by a Pit Bull representing his defeat in his struggle with the school authorities. In his Fairy Tale metaphor he is the pied piper. He would like to lead the rats, the school system, out of town.

Reversal: In his dream he presented himself loosing control of his class.

Compromise: His Short Story illustrates his compromise; his conflict resolution was admitting defeat, pain. He felt safe to cry. The image presents him sick in bed holding onto a dog, the new

Dorothy-Toto equivalent, crying in front of his family. The Cheshire Cat defense collapsed to its opposite, an emotional breakdown that he had been fighting off all his life.

In his comments he admitted this breaking down as emotional growth, as a historical breakthrough from his defensiveness. The insight from this evaluation was becoming aware of his identity of a clown as representing avoiding the feelings of powerlessness, the pain of humiliation. The compromise and resolution of his problematic arrogance was the crumbling of his defenses by admitting pain, experiencing the frightening feeling of the helplessness and humiliation of being fired by the school he loved.

In the second book, which we can title as 'the fishing expedition' he demonstrated his empowerment as a Cheshire Cat that becomes a dachshund tunneling through troubles. He is turning things around and has the satisfaction of the last laugh.

Stress: He began this book with the memory of being floored by a bully whom he had made fun of.

Response: His mask, or identity, reinvented the mask of the Cheshire Cat with that of a trickster. He showed his swollen brain and ear identifying his cleverness; the mask of a brain begins his sequence of masterful moves. He assumed the identity of the medical invalid, as bait to catch and defeat the system.

Anxiety: What was in his heart was a big question mark protected by layers of walls of his aorta, revealing his escape route rather than his feelings. The several rings of defense walls allow him a path to escape suffering from the perceived injustices of a hostile world.

Defense: His animal metaphors reflect his clever strategy: he is the 'hook line and thinker' challenging the system by presenting his medical problem as his defense against the disciplinary process. In his Fairy Tale he is the turtle versus the hare, the 'fleet of foot'.

Reversal: There is no pain in this sequence as again he presents himself as a winner in a race.

Compromise: In his Short Story he chose to be a moth blending in the background rather than a butterfly; he was playing Cinderella rather than the step-sisters as butterflies.

The dog tunnel became a multilayered aorta, the shell of a turtle, the scales of a snake, the trunk of the tree where a moth is hardly visible and sheltered from dangers. In this path of the dominant cooperative relating he fought again to win with his cleverness, his good sense of humor. There is no bloodshed. He had no scruples, no guilt in his fighting the system. He had transgressed outsmarting the school system but he justified it morally. He had defied the godliness of Jesus, but placed himself on the moral path, the love of his family, the key to his heart. Confronted by guilt, he asserted his spirituality as a heart with a key covering the cross behind it, restating his virtue as fidelity to his wife; he is a dedicated husband and father.

The second book shows how he morphed out of his depression quietly laughing at the system with witticisms rather than loudly and aggressively. This was the way of the feisty dominant cooperative way of fighting back. His metaphors show his gamesmanship as the ultimate dominant cooperative power-play, tunneling through problems, through adversity with good sense of humor. He claimed victory through disguise and deception rather than through anger and confrontation. He turned around the disciplinary problem and termination from the school system into a medical disability for which he could seek compensation and early retirement as the explanation for leaving the system.

He terminated therapy knowing that he had triumphed again but self-aware of his questionable relational tactics. He was willing to do the work of an educator integrating his metaphors presenting the particular relational modality in its crystal clear dynamics. All could see a dominant cooperative personality disowning aggression, controlling anger, and enjoying a civilized battle of wits, the competitive cooperative way of winning a fight. All his metaphors are intelligent and well controlled battles of wit rather than fiery angry wars and defensive fights. He was floored by 'twinky' but did not strike back at the system. He had the last laugh on them, quietly, cleverly as his relational strategy.

Did he benefit from this brief therapy? He found out about himself but he did not consent to making changes other than lowering his arrogance. He simply played a dominant cooperative game with the bullies of the organization, the pit-bulls and slithered away from the cruelties of life on which he could not prevail.

What more can one expect from a dominant cooperative person other than insight and emotional survival? It is hard to achieve change. I tried to help him save his career as a teacher and to learn to contain his dominance. He contained his dominance but chose instead a new career outside of the constraints of a stifling educational burocracy. I felt sorry for him as he was a gifted educator and he could have learnt to collaborate and compromise. It was nice to see his so educationally perfect integration of a conflict resolution experience.

Patient's Essay

Despondent. Defeated. Desperate.

That was me. For the first time in my life I was unable to solve a problem, avoid pain, ignore diversity. I was at the bottom of a two-year, downward spiral of work-related stress. I needed to be spared the daily humiliation of playing the part of Jean Valjean to an administrator's Jalbert. I was Les Miserables and I was exhibiting so many stress-related illnesses that I feared for my life. I needed out.

I needed Dr. Levis. Fortunately, he was able to squeeze me in on short notice. He had heard my sad saga and agreed that I required some time away from the "firing line." I felt reborn! I even created my own "rebirth announcement" which I later shared with him. He shook my hand.

I was honest with him though. I told him I did not need, did not want drugs or therapy, just someone who could recognize my plight and certify that I could not continue to work under that level of stress. He agreed that he would "treat" me and that I would be away from work for at least two weeks which later became a few more. And, even though I did not want therapy, did not need therapy...at least not in my estimation... I agreed to give his Formal Theory a shot. It was a lot of effort, the equivalent of writing and illustrating a short book. (My wife said she wouldn't have bothered...I said I gave him my word I would put forth the effort.)

I'm a bit torn at this point. Dr. Levis has reached many conclusions about me, some I agree with, some I don't. I've gained some insights into my life and how I've chosen to live it. I've learned that my life, like most people's lives has had two cycles. We go from pain to mastery over the pain. After forty years of utilizing a self-imposed "shell" to avoid letting pain into my being and dealing with it, I experienced pain and broke down in tears in front of my family for the first time. We experienced catharsis. By admitting defeat, I had won.

Dr. Levis thinks I should return to the site of my pain, reach an accommodation with the administration and resume my teaching career. (I know I'm not ready to do that.) He thinks I'll be welcomed, that mutual respect will be re-established, that the torturous level of scrutiny present before my absence will lessen. I don't agree...I also have trouble ignoring the way I've been treated by my administrators for over two years. I'm enough of a crusader to want to change the system so no one else will suffer my fate.

With the conciliatory suggestions from Dr. Levis still "ringing in my ears", I have opted instead to seek a disability benefit related to actual "ringing in my ears." In addition to work related stress, I suffer from "ringing in my ears" stress, the effects of a constant sound from a work-induced condition called tinnitus.

It's been an interesting process, filled with insights, a process I agree would be a very rapid solution to any psychological problem.

My Life as a Play

Where am I? Am I in the pit, in the monster's maw or at the master's end of the leash? Who am I? Am I a victim or a victor? Did I lose or did I win? Am I a Jalvert or Valjean, Road Runner or Wiley Coyote?

All of the above. Some of the above. None of the above. All. Some. None. Also no. Also, no. Confused? Me too.

The curtain rose on this drama while I was engaged in the middle of a saga. I thought I was on the receiving end of a trauma triggered by a vendetta and fueled by a conspiracy. I was desperate to stop the onslaught. Instead I've been advised to take tranquilizers, that I need therapy, that 40 years of a happy life were a lie. I was told I'm a paranoid personality experiencing panic attacks, reliving a "life or death" struggle dredged up from age 10 and re-enacted 40 years later on a stage where "life and death" mean much more. I've been informed that because I defended myself against potential profession-ending accusations (within the system) that I am partially at fault for the escalation of hostilities, as I am difficult to deal with.
Naturally, I'm having difficulty dealing with all that. Truthfully, just like I felt trapped and humiliated in 4th grade (and "won" by developing my "shell") and just like I felt trapped and humiliated by my "pit bull principal" (and "won" by "taking" medical leave),

now I feel trapped and humiliated because <u>I'm the one</u> being trapped and <u>I'm the one</u> being told to apologize when I feel it should be reversed.

In one of my therapeutic stories, I envisioned a scenario where two disembodied people were able to observe me, to see me how I really am. This finally was able to occur within my own family. While discussing my saga with my wife and daughter, I gently mentioned to my wife that she had been very distant lately, that she had been treating me like an outcast. She explained why, ending with, "You're the one who has always been able to remain unaffected by everything. Why can't you do it with this situation?" I broke down (for the first time during my saga), blubbering, "Can't you see?! It's so overpowering that even I can't take it!"

My eyes filled with tears and closed as I began to sob. I didn't see her approach, but I felt my wife's arms, embracing me where I knelt. She had finally joined my daughter in understanding my plight. We joined in a 3-way hug. Rocking side-to-side, in a mother/baby way, as the movie camera zoomed out from the crane shot and the scene faded to credits.

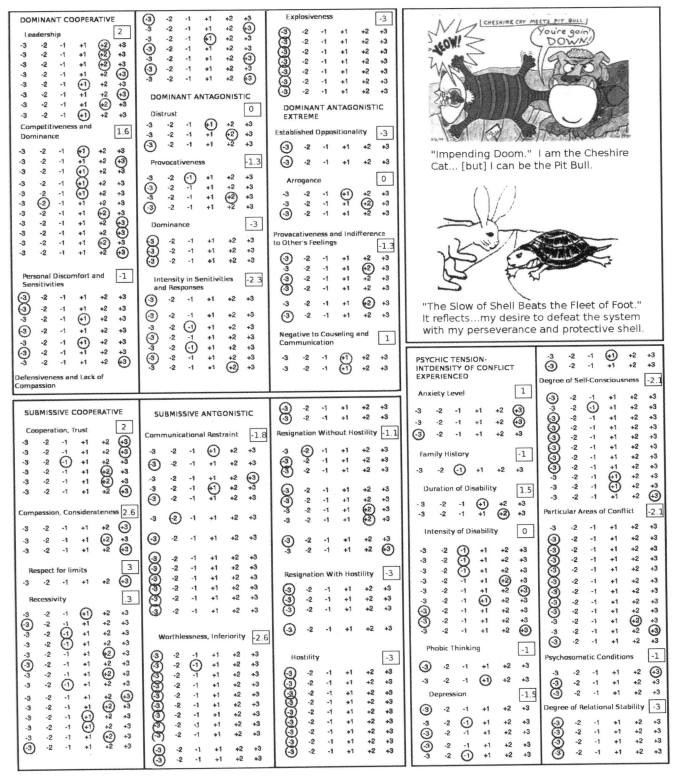

"Impending Doom." I am the Cheshire Cat... [but] I can be the Pit Bull.

"The Slow of Shell Beats the Fleet of Foot." It reflects...my desire to defeat the system with my perseverance and protective shell.

CHILDHOOD CONFLICTUAL MEMORY

Step 1: Draw a conflictual childhood memory:

Step 2: Describe the incident: My 4th grade teacher used to humiliate me in front of m classmates. I used to go home for lunch and cry after these episodes. I felt she would destroy me if I didn't figure out a way to cope. I adopted a shell to keep her negativity from affecting me. In the picture I am tracing a map at the window in class. I said I handed it in. She said I didn't and would not give me another printed map to re-label and re-color. She made me stay after school and trace from the printed map. My Mom came in to defend me. My teacher got my folder and surprise! My map was in it...graded!

Step 3: How did you feel about this person? I felt she was a crabby old teacher who enjoyed humiliating me in front of my classmates and that she was out to break me or destroy me. **How did this person feel about you?** I'm not sure. She definitely did not treat me with compassion.

Step 4: What were the conflicts? An authority figure tried to demonstrate her control over me by "putting me under her thumb" and holding me up as an object of ridicule in front of my peers.

Step 5: What happened before? I was ridiculed before and after this episode. (It was obvious I had handed in the map. It had to be handed in for a grade to appear in her handwriting.)

Step 6: After? I continued to be on her "focal scroll." I managed to survive by creating my "shell."

Step 7: Your share in this conflict? I never did figure out why I and some other classmates were the objects of her scorn. Perhaps she was using the classic method of some authority figures...pick on one of the group, show you can "break" him, and the others will fall in line.

Step 8: Effect on life: I am thankful to my teacher for forcing me to solve my problem by creating my "shell." It allowed me to be the happiest person I know for over 40 years. I bear her no ill will.

Step 9: Have you been repeating yourself? I have used my "shell" repeatedly. I thought it as beneficial.

Step 10: Has this conflict been resolved in your mind? ? I'm glad it happened.
Step 11: Resolved in this relationship? I met her in 1996 and our relationship was quite cordial.

Step 12: What changes should be made? I'm not sure. I'm hoping to learn how the Formal Theory will benefit me. My 4th grade situation and my current situation seem almost exactly the same. My "shell" was working as well as it always had until the flood of illnesses and conditions developed which "upped the ante" from a fear of being destroyed psychologically to a fear of being destroyed physically.

Step 1: Draw a conflictual adolescent memory:

Step 2: Describe the incident: My high school clique was called "the circus" because we were a bunch of clowns always clowning around. I was a ringmaster, but my friend was the "Chief."

Step 3: Effect on life: I wanted total control but never got it. It wasn't an open conflict...we really loved and respected each other until he died a few years ago.

RESPONSE

BALLOON PORTRAIT AND STORY

FAMILY OF ORIGIN

Step 1: Draw a balloon portrait of your family of origin.

Step 2: Identify characteristics.

Brother, quiet, wry humor, angry
Father, quiet, hard-working, giving
Self, confused, likes to make people laugh, creative
Mother, fighter, supportive, giving"

Step 3: What are they saying?

#1 – "Yo! Bro! You look funny."
#2 – "You know your brother was always the class clown."
#4 – "Leave him alone. He likes to make people laugh.'
#3 – "I can't help it. I'm a "kidult" who considers himself a human cartoon character, I'm supposed to be happy all the time and make everyone else happy."

Step 1: Draw a balloon portrait of your marital family.

Step 2: Identify each individual:

Son, reclusive (at home), intelligent, private.
Daughter, open, giving, born teacher.
Self, confused, likes to make people laugh, creative.
Wife, childlike, giving to the point of martyrdom, constantly stressed.

Step 3: What are they saying?

#1 – "Stay out of my life. I'm not going to share how I feel."
#2 – "I'm having trouble accepting what dad is going through and how he is falling apart. It makes me cry and I want to tell these people to stop."
#3 – 'I'm sorry I'm causing you concern and stress. I'm trying to solve this.'
#4 – 'You're afraid you'll have a heart attack! I'm so stressed, I'll probably have one!'

Step 4: Title: "The House of Gags"

Step 5: What are the conflicts? They are all concerned for each other's condition (physical, fiscal, psychological).

RESPONSE

MASK I

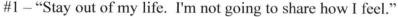

Step 1: Draw a mask:

Step 2: Answer the following questions:
Title: "The Ever-Smiling Cheshire Cat."
Age: 49 Sex: Male
Emotions conveyed: Perpetual Happiness.

Step 3: Conflicts represented: None.

Step 4: Resolution of conflicts represented: I want to return to this mask/face.

ANXIETY

MASK II

Draw what is behind the mask.

Step 6: Fill in the blanks and answer the questions:

Title: "Who Is This Man?"
Age: 51   **Sex:** Male
Emotions conveyed? Confusion.

Step 7: Conflicts represented: I'm not sure who is behind the smiling mask.

Step 8: Resolution of conflicts represented: None. It seems to be the start of some conflicts.

MASK III

Draw what is in the heart.

Step 9: Title: "Heart Under Siege."

Step 10: Items and themes represented: Threats to the heart, confusion. Pins – dark cloud – fears of heart attack – threats to my physical being – diabetes.

Step 11: Feelings and conflicts represented: This represent a heart which is in danger. Someone, something is threatening the heart.

Step 12: What resolution of conflicts does it convey? [left blank].

Step 13: Title of the sequence: "The Unmasking."

Step 14: Summarize the sequence of transformations.
The smiling, always happy face I thought was my true face was removed. The face beneath it, my actual face is now confused, not sure what to feel or what to express.

Step 15: Conclusions about the way this person resolves conflicts: I usually avoid all forms of conflict. Whenever I encounter conflict, I analyze the situation and deal with it logically, unemotionally. Where authority is concerned, I comply with all that is asked of me, but if I feel I am being wronged, I work within the system guidelines to solve the conflict.

Step 16: Does this relate to how you handle feelings? Tact, calm, mutual respect have always permitted me to either avoid or solve potential conflicts. I have always felt that avoiding or removing anger was the best course to prevent escalating of conflicts.

Step 17: What changes should be made? I'm not sure. Recently, I told one of my principals that I was suffering from the effects of 3 years of work problems. I calmly told her (even though my heart was racing and my hands were trembling) that I could not cope with her. I was respectful, did not yell, the way I feel one should treat an administrator.

Step 18: What changes are you willing to make? I'm not sure. I have used all of the methods in my "medicine bag" to cure the wound. I thought removing myself from the pain and risk (despite financial aid and social and professional stigma risks) was my only sure solution. I've been told that is not the best course.

DEFENSE

ANIMAL METAPHOR TEST #1

Step 1: Draw two animals.

Step 2: Fill in the blanks

Animal #1
Type of animal: Cat
Age: 51 **Sex:** Male
Personality: Smiley, climbs well, able to disappear at will.

Animal #2
Type of animal: Pit Bull
Age: 55 **Sex:** Female
Personality: Dictatorial, relentless, two-faced, scary, cruel.

Step 3: What are they saying?

#1 – "Please don't throw me in this pit....I could die!"
#2 – "I don't care! It's what I do."
#1 – "You could change. You don't have to treat me like this!"
#2 – 'I can't change. I'm under orders."
#1 – "I'll disappear if you let me go!"
#2 – "No you won't! I know your type!"

Step 4: What happened before?

Animal #1 – "Please stop chasing me!"
Animal #2 – "Never! I'll catch you. I'll chomp on you. I'll shake you and let you fall to your death!"

Step 5: After? Animal #1 tried to run, tried to disappear. Animal #2 still caught him.

Step 6: Title: "Cheshire Cat Meets Pit Bull."

Step 7a: Conflicts between themselves: Cheshire Cat feels that Pit Bull is his enemy, that once he has been chomped, caught in her jaws, he is doomed.

Step 7b: Conflicts between them and the world: Cat's world was a pleasant, happy world. Pit Bull's world is a world of intimidation and pain.

Step 8: What changes should they make to resolve conflicts? Cheshire Cat should disappear and run away (or at least climb out of the pit if he's not too injured from the fall). Pit Bull should abandon the negative traits of Pit Bulls and become more docile and accepting.

Step 9: Which animal do you identify with: I am the Cheshire Cat. I used to be the happiest "cat" I know. I really wish I could disappear from my current situation, or at least use my climbing ability to climb out of the pit I'm in. I want my ear-to-ear smile back. **Other animal:** Pit Bull is one of my principals, a person who treated me worse than any boss I've ever had, a person who betrays me, who calls me a liar, who will destroy me professionally, psychologically and actually if she is allowed to continue.

Step 10: How does this pertain to you? It is my life right now. I am at the end of a three-year spiral that has changed my life in such a way that even I can't believe, even I can't solve or cope with.

Step 11: What changes should you make? I would allow myself to leave the City and get on with the rest of my life. I fear if I'm forced to continue to be subjected to the level of stress I am under the combination of physical and psychological conditions will do me in.

Step 12: Present a similar incident: I've never been in a situation like this. I've never allowed stress worry and conflict in my life. I've always described myself as the happiest person I know. Now I'm falling apart mentally and physically. I describe myself as desperate, (desperate was never even in my vocabulary!)

(Oops, I forgot. My fourth grade teacher was a pit bull and I felt desperate I felt she would destroy me. I adopted a shell that held of the rest of my life and through two and a half years of this 'til now).

Step 13: How do you relate with others, and how do you get yourself in trouble? I am always mellow, and avoid conflict. I don't usually break down if I feel I'm being attacked, but I always am respectful, calm, and follow the rules of the system I make my case. I feel I conduct myself in a moral and ethical manner in all situations.

Step 14: What changes are you willing to make? I've tried to cope, adapt, knuckle under, do what I had to do to survive and last in my job for the next few years. I can't make any more changes. I feel cornered, the fact that I've had to be subjected to the process to climb out of the pit. The fact that I've been forced to do all I can to cut my hard-earned pension in half indicates, I think, just how desperate I am. I'm concerned for my family. I fear for my life (physical, psychological, and fiscal). I need to end the pain, put this behind me and get on with the rest of my life. Just writing about it like this makes me feel the same trembling, etc., that I feel when I am being pursued and attacked by my principal(s).

FAIRYTALE METAPHOR

Step 1: Draw two fairy tale characters.

Step 2: Fill in the blanks

Character#1: Rapid Rat
Age: 10 **Sex:** Male
Personality: Sneaky, evil, hurtful.

Character#2: The Tried Piper
Age: 20 **Sex:** Male
Personality: Talented, helpful, forceful.

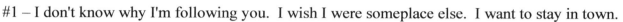

Step 3: What are they saying?

#1 – I don't know why I'm following you. I wish I were someplace else. I want to stay in town.
#2 – The music from my magical flute has you under its spell. You and your kind will follow me and leave the good people of this town alone.
#1 – You may be right, but I'm coming back as soon as you get paid and leave town.
#2 – I don't think so. I'm leading you far away, so unless you're a "homing rat" you won't find your way back.

Step 4: What happened before? The rat was nibbling on corn, exchanging "rat chat" with his friends. The Tried Piper was negotiating the price he would charge for his services with the town fathers. #1 – I love this place. There is food everywhere. #2 – My price is firm. You must pay it or there will be severe consequences.

Step 5: After? The Tried Piper played his tune and the Rapid Rat and his friends followed him out of town.

Step 6: Title: "Get Outta Town!"

Step 7a: Conflicts between themselves: The Tried Piper is repulsed by the rat and wants to remove it. Rapid rat does not like the Tried Piper because he can force Rapid Rat to act against his own will and against his own self-interest.

Step 7b: Conflicts between them and the world: The world detests rats but also tests rats to benefit humanity. The world worships the superstar celebrity "musician" but will turn against him.

Step 8: What changes should they make to resolve conflicts? I'm not sure they can resolve their conflicts. Piper-types will always oppose rat-types...if the price is right and sometimes for no price at all.

Step 9: Which character do you identify with: I'm not sure. I identify with the Rapid Rat and feel like I'm being "led out of town" against my will despite that fact that I love teaching and it does "keep us in food." I identify with the Tried Piper because he performs a valuable service to the community, but he puts children at risk. **Other character:** I see some characteristics of my antagonist administrators in "rats" in general and "rapid" specifically (sneaky, evil, hurtful). I also see their power to lead me against my will and "out of town."

Step 10: How does this pertain to you? I see someone who was "minding his own business" being forced to leave a desirable place. I see people who hold power over me abusing that power, violating the humanist tenets they promote with their clients, the children...treating their other clients, the teachers, oppositely.

Step 11: What changes should you make? ? I would trade a team of antagonist administrators for a team who would at least be objective toward me. I suppose I should feel that I should want to go back and face my accusers, defend myself or admit some wrongdoing, but I still have trouble recognizing what I did that contributed to or caused my problems. I see me trying to cope, survive and compromise while defending myself.

I recently (Monday morning) learned something about one of my many conditions – tinnitus – that it, by itself, can cause stress, poor choice-making, depression and other problems. Since my evaluator and myself have pointed out or questioned some of my choices, I wonder...

Step 12: Present a similar incident: I think my experience with my 4th grade teacher is as close to an exact match as possible in real-life. In art there is a term, symmetry, which applies here.

Step 13: How do you relate with others, and how do you get yourself in trouble? I attempt to make everyone I encounter smile or laugh. I try to be moral, ethical and cooperative, to give more than I receive. I would rather be hurt than hurt someone else. However, if I find myself under attack I do defend myself. I also attempt to change the circumstances, which caused my problems so that others don't have to be subjected to them.

Step 14: What changes are you willing to make? I'm willing to examine my "shell" to see if it is the best way to experience and deal with life's tribulations.

REVERSAL

ANIMAL METAPHOR TEST #2

Step 1: Draw two animals with an intensified conflict:

Step 2: Fill in the blanks:

Animal #1
Type of animal: Lion
Age: 55 **Sex:** Male
Personality: Hungry for meat, relentless pursuer, sharp claws.

Animal #2
Type of animal: Rabbit
Age: 51 **Sex:** Male
Personality: Timid, cuddly, terrified.

Step 3: What are they saying?

#1 – "I'm perplexed and dumbfounded why you've chosen to defy me! My jaws and my claws can rip you asunder! Why are you still here?"

#2 – "I don't know. I'm terrified of your power. I don't want to risk your wrath. I can't believe I'm still here myself."

#1 – "Well, get ready, you tiny buck. I think I'll toy with you one last time before I devour you. What do you think of that?!"

#2 – "I don't think I can handle it. I'm gone."

Step 4: What happened before? The rabbit was grazing in the grass. The lion was sharpening his claws.

Step 5: After? The lion lunged at the rabbit. The rabbit dodged the swipe an escaped down a tunnel.

Step 6: Title: "Lion Wait."

Step 7a: Conflicts between themselves: They are experiencing the age-old conflict of predator and prey.

Step 7b: Conflicts between them and the world: Their conflict is best represented by the characters in "Les Miserables," the relentless lion, Jalvert, forever pursuing the ever-fleeing Jean Valjean. Their roles are pre-determined...the outcome is inevitable unless there is an intervention of some sort.

Step 8: What changes should they make to resolve conflicts? The lion would have to become a vegetarian. The rabbit would have to take out a watch and suddenly realize he was late for an appointment.

DREAM ANALYSIS

Step 1: Choose a dream: Recent dream.

Step 2: Draw the dream:

Step 3: Describe the dream: I recently had a dream (just prior to rising) where I was teaching a class where everything was going wrong. I don't remember too much from it, but I do remember being very uncomfortable and confused over why everything was going wrong. The projects were not coming out right. The words were not coming out of my mouth correctly (which has happened lately in my own presentations). My frustrations in the dream led me to yelling at little kids (something I had done in real life a few times recently, something which is anathema to me, a choice I would hardly ever make).

Step 4: Describe the participants: The teacher was unsuccessful, uncomfortable and confused. The students were unsuccessful, uncomfortable, and upset.

Step 5: What are the conflicts? The teacher wants the students to be successful and produce excellent artworks. The students want to produce excellent artworks. But often do not want to listen to directions or accept alternative ideas.

Step 6: What occurrences preceded the dream? Occurrences in real life classrooms preceded the dream. My principals had been criticizing my methods and results since September. I had been having trouble picking the right words and stumbling over words during instructions. I had also been dizzy and nauseous, almost drunk in both schools. On a few occasions, I found myself yelling (not real loud) and berating kids. I always apologized immediately, but I wasn't even sure myself if I were really angry or just posturing for effect.

Step 7: Explanation of the dream: I assume it was an attempt by my unconscious self to deal with and possibly solve problems I had been encountering in my work, the one arena of my life lately that has begun to invade all aspects of my existence.

Step 8: Do you dream a lot? Yes.

Step 9: Other dreams: I commented just a few hours ago that I was watching TV while reclining on the floor, with my head propped up on my hand and bent arm. My body shut off, I was sleeping immediately and dreaming within a few seconds. (I thought that was impossible, but I've done it often for years. I didn't think REM sleep was possible so soon after entering the sleep state). My dreams are often reality-based. I don't really have fantastic, other-worldly dreams. Since I often fall asleep with the TV on, I often find my dreams paralleling what was going on in the TV show as I awoke.

Step 10: Connections or patterns in dreams: I often see myself attempting to solve things or change things for the better in my dreams. I rarely have negative or nightmarish dreams. I have written them down in a journal I have kept since 1963.

I remember one from about 20 years ago with Barry Goldwater (conservative senator from Arizona and former presidential candidate) and a dinosaur (prophetic?) I also remember a dream from a few years ago when I woke up absolutely terrorized.

While writing this page, the strange coincidence experience I have occurred. I was writing "head" and "senator" when the speaker on TV said the same two words. This happens often to me.

COMPROMISE

SHORT STORY

Step 1: Write a short story:

#1 – "This method that Dr. Brown taught us...it's hard to believe it actually works!"
#2 – "Yeah, I used to try astral projection, but this is so much more real, more vivid!"
#1 – "Where shall we go today?"
#2 – "Well, this guy I taught with is embroiled in a real tug-of-war with the administration. I think I'd like to get some of the behind-the-scenes scoop."
#1 – "Okay, I'll meet you at his house. Where does he live?"
#2 – "He lives in Philadelphia."
#2 – "Wow, there he is, curled up in the fetal position, petting his dog. He doesn't look like the guy I know."
#1 – "I don't know him, but he looks like he's in bad shape. That book he's working on...his art and writing are telling a sad story."
#2 – 'I don't think I want to watch this."
#1 – "Me neither. Let's find a better place to be."

Step 2: Illustrate the story:

Step 3: Fill in the blanks:

Character#1
Character name: Phil
Age: 30 **Sex:** Male
Personality: Curious, open-minded, adventurous.

Character#2
Character name: Jill
Age: 30 **Sex:** Female
Personality: Curious, compassionate, squeamish.

Step 4: What happened before? Both characters had participated in Dr. Courtney Brown's institute, where Distance Viewing is actually taught. #2, Jill, had actually seen and heard about what was transpiring with the "guy," (me).

Step 5: After: They went on to observe a less painful subject. My life was too difficult to deal with, even from the vantage of a disembodied, invisible, only slightly interested observer.

Step 6: Title: "The Brown-Out."

Step 7a: Conflicts between themselves: They have no conflict between each other. They have a conflict between wanting to be an invisible "fly on the wall," and being unable to stand the "visual stench" of what is being heaped upon me.

Step 8: What changes should they make to resolve conflicts? I don't think that question applies in

474

this scene.

Step 9: Which character do you identify with: I identify most with Jill. **Other character:** Phil doesn't remind me of anyone. He is an amalgam of a character.

Step 10: How does this pertain to you? It features me as the one who is observed. However, I think I see in it a subconscious desire on my part, wishing I had taken Dr. Courtney Brown's course and that I could now be able to use Distance Viewing to spy on the group of administrators who have been harassing me.

Step 11: What changes should you make? I have a series of life philosophies which I live by. I call them my "Ten-tenets." Surprisingly, there are 20 or 30 of them. If I had to summarize them and combine them into one "prime directive" (like on Star Trek) I guess it would be "do no harm" (to others or to myself). I don't think I can change that.

Step 12: Present a similar incident: I can't envision anything to relate it to.

Step 13: How do you relate with others, and how do you get yourself in trouble? I don't see how this question fits that scene.

Step 14: What changes are you willing to make? I am willing to drop my shell and be more open. I think that may be part of what got me here. I'm sure it's what led to me crying yesterday when my wife expressed her anger at me, especially because she said I should be able to handle it...I always did before.

SCRIBBLE METAPHOR

Step 1: Make a scribble

Describe the items you identified in this process:

Spiral: a path, which one can follow upward or downward
Fish: an icon with religious implications (on bumpers, the miracle of the fisher, much from little.)
Shark mouth: jaws, danger
Triangle: symbol of a relationship of three people or three groups. It could also mean a shark's triangular tooth.

Elaborate on the significance of these items to you: I've been on a downward spiral for a few years. I now believe I'm on the way up along the same spiral.

I'm not religious, as a matter of fact I often used to joke that I used to be an agnostic, but now I feel so powerful that I might be a 'gagnostic.' (an agnostic isn't sure if there is a God. A gagnostic isn't sure if he is God.) I have not been feeling very godlike/powerful lately. (My name means all powerful and the ascending order of the number of letters in my four names … 6,7,8,9... means great power in numerology.) I see various three-groupings. The Home team, Conspirator's team, Justice team. I see snapping shark jaws on my tail. The fact that I did not put the easily available shark's tooth in the nearby mouth tells me that I see the shark as toothless.

BOOK ONE

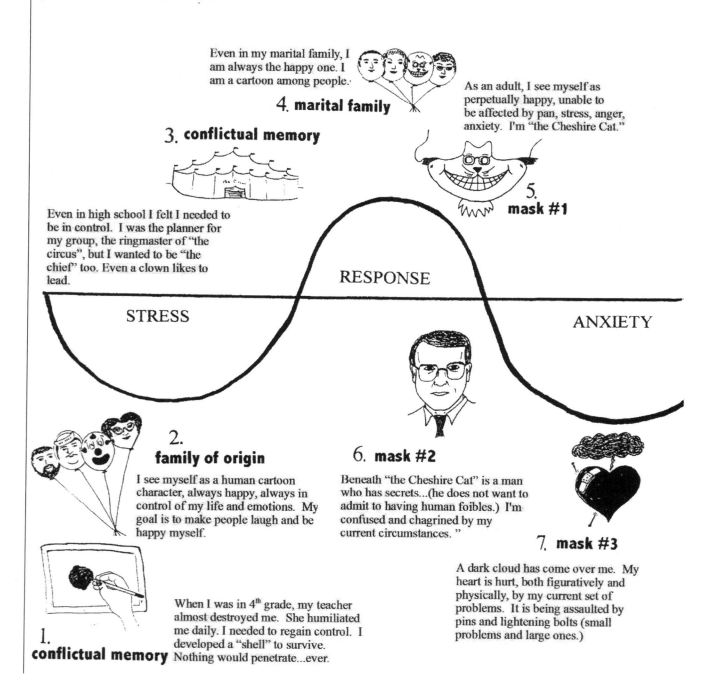

Even in my marital family, I am always the happy one. I am a cartoon among people.

4. marital family

3. conflictual memory

As an adult, I see myself as perpetually happy, unable to be affected by pan, stress, anger, anxiety. I'm "the Cheshire Cat."

5. mask #1

Even in high school I felt I needed to be in control. I was the planner for my group, the ringmaster of "the circus", but I wanted to be "the chief" too. Even a clown likes to lead.

RESPONSE

STRESS

ANXIETY

2.
family of origin

I see myself as a human cartoon character, always happy, always in control of my life and emotions. My goal is to make people laugh and be happy myself.

6. mask #2

Beneath "the Cheshire Cat" is a man who has secrets...(he does not want to admit to having human foibles.) I'm confused and chagrined by my current circumstances."

7. mask #3

A dark cloud has come over me. My heart is hurt, both figuratively and physically, by my current set of problems. It is being assaulted by pins and lightening bolts (small problems and large ones.)

When I was in 4th grade, my teacher almost destroyed me. She humiliated me daily. I needed to regain control. I developed a "shell" to survive. Nothing would penetrate...ever.

1.
conflictual memory

476

Just like in 4th grade, I see myself being threatened again by a pit bull who has sunk her teeth into me and won't let go. Her mission is to dangle me over the pit, to make me feel the fear of impending doom and then to drop me into the pit. I realize that in my reactions to what I consider injustices done to me, that I too can be a "pit bull."

8. animal metaphor #1

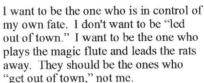

I want to be the one who is in control of my own fate. I don't want to be "led out of town." I want to be the one who plays the magic flute and leads the rats away. They should be the ones who "get out of town," not me.

9. fairy tale metaphor

14. scribble metaphor

I feel confused. I seek refuge in a disability. I don't want to kowtow. I don't want to face them in order to defend myself anymore. I want to start again at a different school. I plan to escape the jaws, swim upstream, against the current, and reverse the downward spiral of the last 2 ½ years. I want to change the system so no one else suffers my fate.

13. short story metaphor

I am the prey. I'm feeling under too much scrutiny. I break down, admit defeat and admit that I am hurt. I break down and cry in front of my family for the first time.

DEFENSE

COMPROMISE

REVERSAL

10. recent conflict

My administrators have been subjecting me to intense scrutiny and stress. I am being punished by "pit bulls." My disabilities, illnesses, make me feel very threatened. I fear for my life.

11. animal metaphor #2

I'm no match for the "King of Beasts." If they want to get you, they will get you.) I challenged, but I lost. I can't handle this losing control over my life, my teaching career, so I want to disappear, run away. I want to hop off, to survive to teach another day.

12. dream analysis

This "torrent of torment" invaded all aspects of my life, waking and sleeping. I had a dream I was teaching a lesson and nothing was going right. It was very upsetting and symbolic of losing control in many areas of my life.

477

BOOK TWO

4. marital family

"Don't Leave
Our Nest"
Our children are
grown now and
ready to go out
on their own.
My response to
this is "please
don't leave the
nest, we love
you, stay with us.

3. conflictual memory

"God Doesn't Measure Up To
My Standards"
This was a major conflict of my
life, the decision to remain a
devout catholic or become a
determined agnostic. God didn't
measure up to my standards for
myself, a mere mortal, so he
didn't come closer to my
standards for my God. I am still
agnostic.

5. mask #1

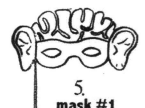

"Brain Sounds...Sound Brain"
My new identity shows the
sound in the ear as the main
problem affecting my mind
and the brain (my wit and
intelligence) as the solution
and my strength.

RESPONSE

STRESS

ANXIETY

6. mask #2

"The Primitive Self"
The mask shows that my
condition affects the primitive
part of the brain, the limbic
system, fight or flight, and
that it is on the right side, the
larger ear. The condition has
transformed my Cheshire Cat
smile into a statement of fear
for my life and primitive
feelings for the system.

1. conflictual memory

"Blinky Says Hello Like a Boxer"
I once used boy's nickname, not
knowing he hated it. I ended up
on the sidewalk. He had punched
me. I don't remember feeling
angry at expressing anger was
something I avoided.

2. family of origin

"Pack a Lunch
For The Pack"
I chose to depict
my family of
origin as dog
balloons. Dogs
are a favorite
animal of mine.
I'm the funny
one, the doxie.
He tunnels in and
out of problems.

7. mask #3

"Aorta Know"
The apple represents education and
the concentric circles represent the
path to my heart (my aorta) as a
tunnel to the unknown Is my
heart/future in education?

Just like in 4th grade, I see myself being threatened again by a pit bull who has sunk her teeth into me and won't let go. Her mission is to dangle me over the pit, to make me feel the fear of impending doom and then to drop me into the pit. I realize that in my reactions to what I consider injustices done to me, that I too can be a "pit bull."

8. animal metaphor #1

I want to be the one who is in control of my own fate. I don't want to be "led out of town." I want to be the one who plays the magic flute and leads the rats away. They should be the ones who "get out of town," not me.

9. fairy tale metaphor

14. scribble metaphor

I feel confused. I seek refuge in a disability. I don't want to kowtow. I don't want to face them in order to defend myself anymore. I want to start again at a different school. I plan to escape the jaws, swim upstream, against the current, and reverse the downward spiral of the last 2 ½ years. I want to change the system so no one else suffers my fate.

13. short story metaphor

I am the prey. I'm feeling under too much scrutiny. I break down, admit defeat and admit that I am hurt. I break down and cry in front of my family for the first time.

DEFENSE

COMPROMISE

REVERSAL

10. recent conflict

My administrators have been subjecting me to intense scrutiny and stress. I am being punished by "pit bulls." My disabilities, illnesses, make me feel very threatened. I fear for my life.

11. animal metaphor #2

I'm no match for the "King of Beasts." If they want to get you, they will get you.) I challenged, but I lost. I can't handle this losing control over my life, my teaching career, so I want to disappear, run away. I want to hop off, to survive to teach another day.

12. dream analysis

This "torrent of torment" invaded all aspects of my life, waking and sleeping. I had a dream I was teaching a lesson and nothing was going right. It was very upsetting and symbolic of losing control in many areas of my life.

Case Study Seven
Marital Complementarity of Relational Modalities

*A Dominant Husband and His Submissive Wife,
the Bull and the Cow, 'Lack of Love' versus the Lamb and the Bear,
'Intimidation'*

Introduction and discussion

A couple's brief evaluation record is inserted here to illustrate the complementarity of relational modalities in marital relations and this configuration's potential for decompensation. The couple came for an evaluation upon his being discharged from a psychiatric hospital. His discharge diagnosis from the hospital was a Schizo-Affective Disorder; his wife's diagnosis was that of an adjustment reaction with depressive features. These traditional clinical diagnoses totally ignored the relational psychodynamic nature of the couple's interpersonal conflicts. Medications had been prescribed but no insight-therapy had been made available.

The significance of this evaluation is in illustrating the relevance of the relational modality diagnoses in couples' relationships.

First, in demonstrating the compatibility of opposite relational modalities attracting each other into love and marital relationships. Indeed marriage of opposite modalities is the prevalent mode of love relations both in heterosexual and homosexual relations.

Second, in illustrating the psychopathology of this type of relationship as decompensation of the relationship because of the flip side of this relational compatibility as the difficulty in dealing with communications between the parties. While love brings opposite relational modalities together such systems do not have the internal flexibility to handle the escalation of tension. Conflicts are not resolved because communications are blocked as the dominant person cannot handle criticism and the submissive person does not have the capacity to express it.

Opposite relational syndromal modalities marry and also evolve to decompensation under stress. Dominant individuals tend to be limit testers, readily frustrated and controlling. They can become too demanding and critical. Submissives are usually receptive and accommodating. They are patient, (passive) and reassuring, but at some point submissive people reach their limit of supportiveness and accommodation. There is a limit on how much dominance, aggression and criticism the submissive person can tolerate before s/he shuts down, and totally withdraw. They tend to hold back anger and reactions. But as pressure rises there is a turning point, a complete communicational breakdown. Submissive people withdraw, and become hostile or passive aggressive fulfilling the fears of the dominant partner.

The case of this couple illustrates the complementarity of modalities and the decompensation scenario. The critical and demanding husband and the submissive wife have reached the end of the capacity to handle inner relational tension. We observe how the dominant husband increases the pressure on his wife and how his wife withdraws rejecting his intense sexual demands. We recognize how this rejection further escalated his dominant responses swiftly evolving from criticizing her to expression of anger leading to violence. He titled his animal metaphor of a bull and a cow as 'lack of love'; she defined it as 'intimidation' between a lamb and a bear.

This study illustrates how the self-assessment provides the needed insights and recommendations for behavior changes helpful to both partners communicating their feelings and thus deescalating the tension of their polarized positions. The evaluations helped the couple to identify the constellation of their relational modalities and to impart insights on the respective needs for individual power management behavioral changes. They realized that their problem was not in chemical imbalances and that medical treatment was not the solution. They became aware of the importance of balancing power in their relationship, diminishing polarization in their power play by improving communications: the dominant husband becoming able to respect his wife and the wife being able to articulate her negative feelings in a firm manner.

The principles for changes were clarified as the rules of good communications: moderation, transforming antagonism to cooperation, and restoring mutual respect. It is very important that couples realize the complementary qualities that each individual has contributed in their loving relationship but also realizing the communicational problems of these modalities.

The evaluation consisted in three visits attended by the patient and his wife and was concluded with the recommendation that they were safe to pursue outpatient therapy to work on their relationship. The brief evaluation diagnosed the underlying problem as the decompensation of communications in a relationship of two opposite relational modalities.

The personality profiles, both the inventory and the projective tests, unequivocally exemplify the typical structure of marital dyads. The evaluation revealed a clear dominance profile for the 49 year-old husband complemented by a subordinacy profile for his 39 year-old wife, illustrating the typical relational constellation of marital dynamics.

The additional stressor compounding the distress in this family system was that the dominant husband had been testing the limit at the workplace and that he had been fired. Upon his vocational failure he had become more demanding at home. His anger had tested the limits of his relationship with his wife. He ended up feeling rejected at work and at home and had become desperate and violent. The escalation of tensions reached the level of maximal polarization. He was ready to commit multiple murders and a suicide. Realizing his potential for violence he sought help and was hospitalized.

Husband's comments about the brief evaluation:

"I would like to comment on the test given by Dr. Levis.

I have seen the doctor three times and when I was working on the test and drawings I found it to be very helpful in dealing with my aggression and the attempted suicide on myself. I did want to harm my family. The Balloon Portraits have helped me deal with my childhood and realize that aggression started in my younger years.

This testing is a much better way in dealing with a patient as one could sit and talk to the doctor and never get to the scope of the problem. This is also a very good way to get to the problem much quicker.

This type of testing will also help decide the exact type of therapy, which will be most beneficial to the patient. I have never had this type of therapy before and have found it to be very helpful in getting to problems quickly. This test also helps one to analyze oneself.

I did feel under pressure with thoughts as I really did not want to release feelings, but the drawings helped even though I do not like to draw. I have been through therapy before and it did not work with just talking to the doctor. I was not able to reveal my true feelings.

I would like to continue using this testing as it has started me to think positive and less negative. This test has also given me a different outlook on life. SUICIDE is not the answer."

Dominant Husband's Versus Submissive Wife's Relational Profiles

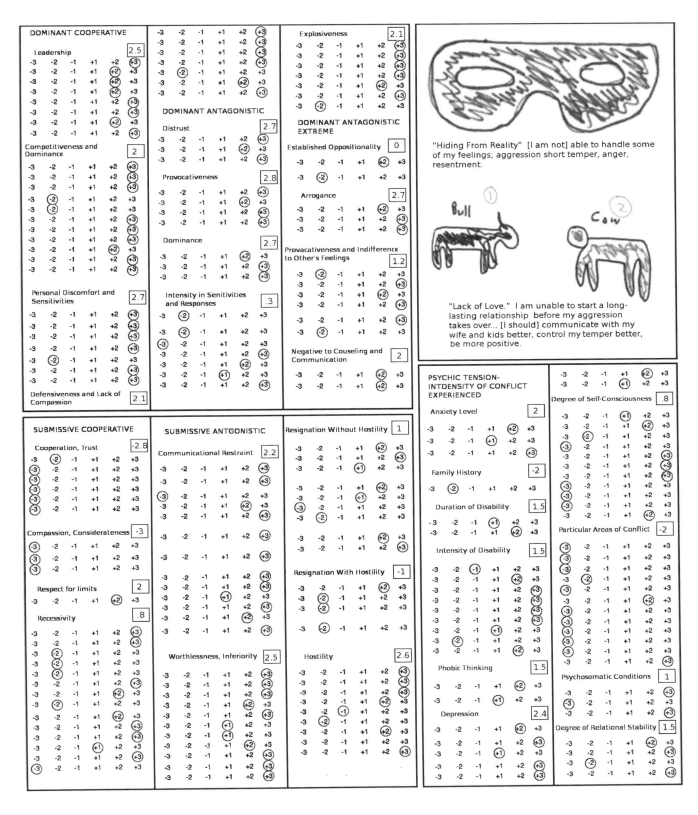

DOMINANT COOPERATIVE
- Leadership — 2.5
- Competitiveness and Dominance — 2
- Personal Discomfort and Sensitivities — 2.7
- Defensiveness and Lack of Compassion — 2.1

DOMINANT ANTAGONISTIC
- Distrust — 2.7
- Provocativeness — 2.8
- Dominance — 2.7
- Intensity in Senitivities and Responses — .3

Explosiveness — 2.1

DOMINANT ANTAGONISTIC EXTREME
- Established Oppositionality — 0
- Arrogance — 2.7
- Provacativeness and Indifference to Other's Feelings — 1.2
- Negative to Couseling and Communication — 2

SUBMISSIVE COOPERATIVE
- Cooperation, Trust — -2.8
- Compassion, Considerateness — -3
- Respect for limits — 2
- Recessivity — .8

SUBMISSIVE ANTGONISTIC
- Communicational Restraint — 2.2
- Worthlessness, Inferiority — 2.5

Resignation Without Hostility — 1

Resignation With Hostility — -1

Hostility — 2.6

PSYCHIC TENSION- INTDENSITY OF CONFLICT EXPERIENCED
- Anxiety Level — 2
- Family History — -2
- Duration of Disability — 1.5
- Intensity of Disability — 1.5
- Phobic Thinking — 1.5
- Depression — 2.4
- Degree of Self-Consciousness — .8
- Particular Areas of Conflict — -2
- Psychosomatic Conditions — 1
- Degree of Relational Stability — 1.5

"Hiding From Reality" [I am not] able to handle some of my feelings; aggression short temper, anger, resentment.

Bull ① Cow ②

"Lack of Love." I am unable to start a long-lasting relationship before my aggression takes over... [I should] communicate with my wife and kids better, control my temper better, be more positive.

Stress: Husband' Metaphor Transcript

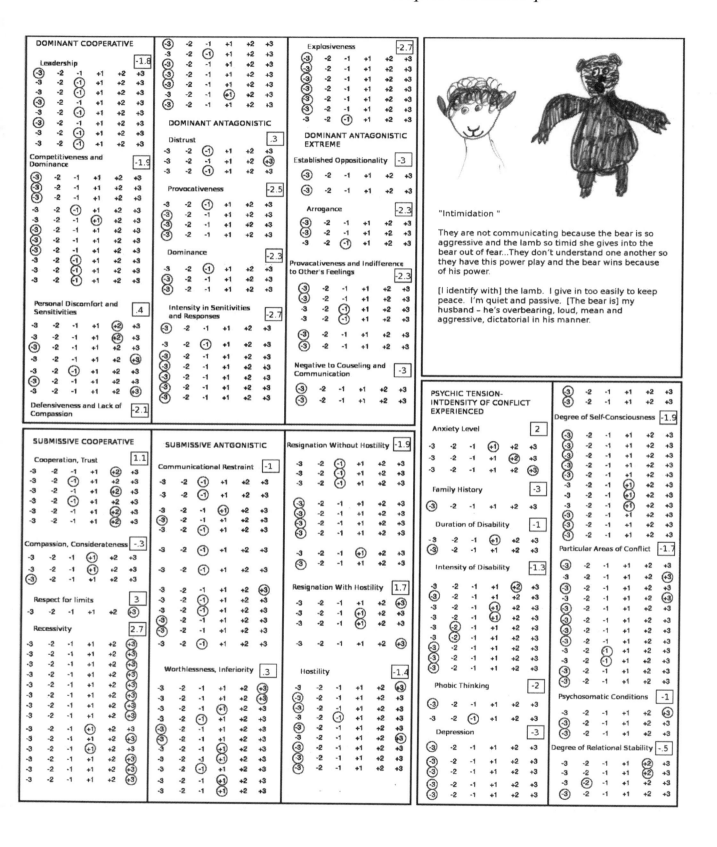

DOMINANT COOPERATIVE

Leadership `-1.8`

Competitiveness and Dominance `-1.9`

Personal Discomfort and Sensitivities `.4`

Defensiveness and Lack of Compassion `-2.1`

DOMINANT ANTAGONISTIC

Distrust `.3`

Provocativeness `-2.5`

Dominance `-2.3`

Intensity in Senitivities and Responses `-2.7`

SUBMISSIVE COOPERATIVE

Cooperation, Trust `1.1`

Compassion, Considerateness `-.3`

Respect for limits `3`

Recessivity `2.7`

SUBMISSIVE ANTGONISTIC

Communicational Restraint `-1`

Worthlessness, Inferiority `.3`

Explosiveness `-2.7`

DOMINANT ANTAGONISTIC EXTREME

Established Oppositionality `-3`

Arrogance `-2.3`

Provacativeness and Indifference to Other's Feelings `-2.3`

Negative to Couseling and Communication `-3`

Resignation Without Hostility `-1.9`

Resignation With Hostility `1.7`

Hostility `-1.4`

"Intimidation"

They are not communicating because the bear is so aggressive and the lamb so timid she gives into the bear out of fear...They don't understand one another so they have this power play and the bear wins because of his power.

[I identify with] the lamb. I give in too easily to keep peace. I'm quiet and passive. [The bear is] my husband – he's overbearing, loud, mean and aggressive, dictatorial in his manner.

PSYCHIC TENSION- INTDENSITY OF CONFLICT EXPERIENCED

Anxiety Level `2`

Family History `-3`

Duration of Disability `-1`

Intensity of Disability `-1.3`

Phobic Thinking `-2`

Depression `-3`

Degree of Self-Consciousness `-1.9`

Particular Areas of Conflict `-1.7`

Psychosomatic Conditions `-1`

Degree of Relational Stability `-.5`

CHILDHOOD CONFLICTUAL MEMORY

Step 1: Draw a conflictual childhood memory:

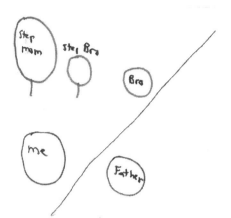

Step 2: Describe the incident: Father remarried. My step-mother then took control of raising us. Father became passive and was hardly home, always working; step-mother very aggressive was punishing and screaming all the time. Step-brother never did anything wrong in her eyes.
Bro: we never got along together.
Me: I related better to step-brother more than brother, even though 8 years difference in age.

Step 3: How did you feel about this person? I felt my step-mother never really loved me all through the years. I was after motherly love, which I never got.

How did this person feel about you? Felt discomfort about raising kids who were not hers.

Step 4: What were the conflicts? Constant punishment and hollering.

Step 5: What happened before? When grandparents had us I was left out as brother looked like lost mother and they had resentment against me.

Step 6: After? After father remarried it seemed that this attitude against me stopped.

Step 7: Your share in this conflict? I was not going to have a woman control me and I started to rebel at the hollering and punishments.

Step 8: Effect on life: This has brought the aggression out of me in two marriages and it just got worse over a long period of time.

Step 9: Have you been repeating yourself? Yes.

Step 10: Has this conflict been resolved in your mind? No.

Step 11: Resolved in this relationship? No.

Step 12: What changes should be made? I love my wife very much and I want to be more assertive in our marriage, stop aggression; ongoing therapy will help me realize my mistakes, regain my family and try to begin a new life with my family.

Step 1: Draw a conflictual adolescent memory:

Step 2: Describe the incident: I was always blamed for things by grand-mother as my brother really never did anything unless I showed him, they claimed.

Step 3: Effect on life: This has made me more aggressive, build defenses to not allow me to lower my guard.

RECENT CONFLICT

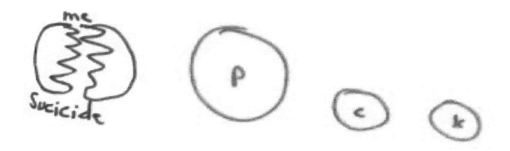

Step 1: Draw a recent conflictual memory:

Step 2: Describe the incident: I tried to commit suicide as I could not take the pressure anymore.

Step 3: Effect on life: By being in the hospital I have been aware that there are people who will help me in the depression through therapy.

BALLOON PORTRAIT AND STORY: MARITAL BALLOONS

Step 1: Draw a balloon portrait of your marital family.

Step 2: Identify characteristics:

> #1 me, (blue): aggressive, dominant, male-things.
> #2: wife, passive, no emotion, no sex.
> #3: son, C. aggressive, hollers at mother, no respect.
> #4: daughter, adorable, loving, innocent.

Step 3: What are they saying? Wife and son are tired of my aggression, swearing and being angry all the time. Since I did not want to go for help, my wife has been mainly concerned about the well-being of the kids, ready to call it quits.

Step 4: Title: "AGGRESSION."

Step 5: What are the conflicts? My family has been breaking up due to my temper and short fuse, my accusing everyone for stupid things that were my fault in the first place; my not asking assertively what I wanted.

RESPONSE

MASK I

Step 1: Draw a mask:
Step 2: Answer the following questions:
Title: "Hiding From Reality."
Age: 53 **Sex:** Male
Emotions conveyed: I am afraid to express my true feelings toward others; I keep feelings inside.
Step 3: Conflicts represented: Short temper, aggression, anger of being myself my whole life.
Step 4: Resolution of conflicts

represented: Not to be able to handle some of my feelings; aggression, short temper, anger, resentment.

ANXIETY

MASK II

Step 5: Draw what is behind the mask.

Step 6: Fill in the blanks and answer the questions:

Title: "Admitting Guilt."
Age: 53 **Sex:** Male
Emotions conveyed? I now see my family slowly moving away from me, as they fear my dealing with life and them.

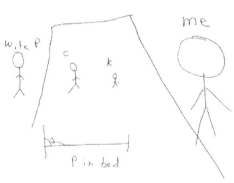

Step 7: Conflicts represented: By my anger I have also lost my wife. My sexual needs, demands, caused trouble for no reason.

Step 8: Resolution of conflicts: I want to regain my family and also to regain the good sex

MASK III

487

Step 9: Draw what is in the heart:

Title: "Losing One's Loved Ones."

Step 10: Items and themes represented:
Losing my family by my refusal to get help.

Step 11: Feelings and conflicts represented:
This is what I have brought to my family
through aggression.

Step 12: Resolution of conflicts: The above
shows that I have lost what I really wanted--
happy home, good sex life, able to talk about
feelings.

Step 13: Title of the sequence: "Regain What
Was Lost."

Step 14: Summarize the sequence of transformations: This is what was before I tried to kill myself, as
I felt there was nothing more to live for. I was alone again with my inner feelings; I was afraid to accept
help.

Step 15: Conclusions about the way this person resolves conflicts: I see P, wife, unable to cope with
my anger. She was only interested in protecting the children and is now ready to leave me.

Step 16: Does this relate to how you handle feelings: It has shown me that I have been unable to relate
to her and the kids and have more aggression than I thought.

Step 17: What changes should be made: Instead of losing my temper, take time out to try to think
taking aggressive action toward others.
S
tep 18: What changes are you willing to make: To go to therapy for myself and family for both of us to save
our marriage…to become less aggressive to all and to regain confidence in myself, self-esteem.

DEFENSE

ANIMAL METAPHOR TEST #1

Step 1: Draw two animals.

Step 2: Fill in the blanks

Animal #1
Type of animal: Bull
Age: 53 **Sex:** Male
Personality: Aggressive, short temper, blames others.

488

Animal #2
Type of animal: Cow
Age: 39 **Sex:** Female
Personality: Passive, sweet and loving, no sex.

Step 3: What are they saying?

#1 – I am coming home and my wife refuses to keep the home clean, and always on the phone. We no longer have sex. No communication.

#2 – My wife is very passive and keeps things inside. She tells me that since I am so aggressive and not cooling my anger, she has lost interest in keeping a clean home and further, she said that the only way to get back at me would be to deny me what I want, a clean house and sex. Now she can control me through passive aggression by not cleaning the apartment and refusing me sex.

My wife has been belittled by me over the years and I was not willing to change. She felt the only way to get back at me was not to do the things I wanted and demanded.

Step 4: What happened before? I had just gotten home from work, tired. My wife was on the phone and the apartment was a mess. The beds were not made and the dishes were not washed. Also she was not taking care of the kids, which she now claims take all of her time. I must realize this, but I could not.

Step 5: After? I still had my aggression and demanded more out of her. My wife was now also being aggressive by refusing me what I wanted and by not having sex was the best way to get back at me.

Step 6: Title: "Lack of Love."

Step 7a: Conflicts between themselves: There has been no communication over the years and both are now aggressive toward each other. I did not want to be dominated by another woman, afraid to lower my guard; meanwhile my wife was building up her guard.

Step 7b: Conflicts between them and the world: Since the aggression has started, their worlds are further apart; unless there is communication nothing will change. Therapy can help them in their lives. I must trust my wife, I realize that she must also trust me but this is very hard for her to do with all the hurt and mistrust over the years.

Step 8: What changes should they make to resolve conflicts? Both should now get therapy if they want the marriage to last. Find out each other's needs to get the marriage back on track. Through therapy this will help to regain the lost love that has taken place over the years.

I must really try to control temper when things are not going my way, think of the consequences that would now become an issue.

Step 9: Which animal do you identify with: The bull is me as I am getting tired of overpowering women. I would not have this happen again. This has happened all through my childhood and adult life, must trust the ones I love, let others help when needed.

Other animal: My wife has been very passive in our marriage and has now taken aggression to get back at me. With all the hurt I have given her, her main concern is to regain some of her self-esteem and protect the kids.

Step 10: How does this pertain to you? I did not realize the wonderful woman I had married has taken on an opposite position in real life. I was afraid to lower my guard, and this has made my life more miserable. I know now I have been taking things out on my family.

I have always been dominated by women, swore I would not let this happen when I got older. I did not want to accept the consequences. I felt I needed the help at times but I really never got rid of my aggression to become more assertive. I have had the fear of going back to the Hospital.

Where I was on my own. NO HELP.

Step 11: What changes should you make? I am willing to go to therapy and want a better way to communicate with my wife. I also need therapy to prevent me from any thoughts of suicide. To be able to communicate with my wife and the kids better, control my temper through med now to help me cope. If I change my ways I truly believe we again can have the sex we once had and to harmonize the relationship.

Step 12: Present a similar incident: During my 1st marriage I realize now that I was the same way. I was treating my 1st wife and kids, the same way I am treating my 2nd wife and kids; the same way aggressive short temper, accusing others for my misdoings and not having trust; while overseas 1st wife had a baby by someone else and I was really hurt; I tried to keep the marriage together, tried swinging as an excuse to keep marriage together, did not work a few years before divorce, wife was seeing another guy while I was home with kids.

Step 13: How do you relate with others, and how do you get yourself in trouble? I am unable to start a long-lasting relationship before my aggression takes over.
By not talking things out with my first wife and by swinging. I truly thought at the time if we got involved in the swinging with other couples it would help. This would help to get my marriage back. I am not able to relate to others as I feel they are truly not my friends but just want to use me. I also have a very short fuse and want things my way; I would get out of control and be very aggressive with others, not really knowing the tone of my voice.

Step 14: What changes are you willing to make? I am willing to go through therapy, and hope over a period of time I'll regain what I've now lost through my aggression, and to bring harmony back into our marriage. By not losing control, to be able to think more positive as there are others like my wife who are willing to help me and themselves regain what we had before we were married. Enjoyed the company of each other both for sex, and the way we danced and enjoyed travel.

TRANSCRIPT OF THE WIFE'S RECORD

We do not have any comments from her about the evaluation other than what is contained in the testing. P was a 39-year-old woman; she was referred to me for evaluation with her husband. She was seeking help and medication management for her depression and domestic relation upon its breaking point.

STRESS

RECENT CONFLICT

490

Step 1: Draw a recent conflictual memory:

Step 2: Describe the incident: Myself, my son. I was blamed for putting his father in the hospital.

Step 3: Effect on life: Dramatically--to the point where I must have harmony in our home for the sake of all of us--especially my son--because he is so confused regarding our relationship.

MARITAL BALLOONS

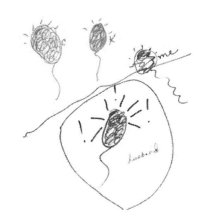

Step 1: Draw a balloon portrait of your marital family.

Step 2: Identify characteristics.

> #1: Son, 6 years, outgoing, bright, temperamental
> #2: Daughter, 17 months, bright, temperamental
> #3: Husband, domineering, vulgar, angry
> #4: Me

Step 3: What are they saying? *[#4 is telling the others what to do, and the others are yelling at her. Conversation involves other family members that were not drawn--step-children.]*

Step 4: What happened before? Arguing, throwing things, utter chaos.

Step 5: After? Tried to get away from husband going outside to play, or watch TV.

Step 6: What are the conflicts? They're having a difficult time dealing with the authority figure (me).

Step 7: Title: Mommy #2

Step 8: What changes should these characters make to resolve these conflicts? Discussion with all involved to discover why these actions occurred--I did the best I could and they resented me.

RESPONSE

MASK I

Step 1: Draw a mask:

Step 2: Answer the following questions:

Title: "Sadness."
Age: 39 **Sex:** Female
Emotions conveyed: A sad person--depressed with the realities of life. Mental anguish and pain.

Step 3: Conflicts represented: Someone stuck in a painful situation not knowing--or afraid to remove herself from it.

Step 4: Resolution of conflicts represented: Finally the "light at the end of the tunnel" is seen and although painful, freedom from the "sadness" eventually occurs.

ANXIETY

MASK II

Step 5: Draw what is behind the mask.

Step 6: Fill in the blanks and answer the questions:

Title: "Liberation."
Age: 39 **Sex:** Female
Emotions conveyed? The words describe the feelings.

Step 7: Conflicts represented: Feelings that love has been laying latent for many years.

Step 8: Resolution of conflicts? Admitting these feelings has given me freedom to deal with them.

MASK III

Step 9: Draw what is in the heart.

Title: "Separation."

Step 10: Items and themes represented: Anger--separation of family--sadness, loneliness--emotion broken into many pieces.

Step 11: Feelings and conflicts represented: All of these emotions have pulled my family apart.

492

Step 12: Resolution of conflicts? It needs quite a bit of mending to be whole and complete.

Step 13: Title of the sequence: "Unity."

Step 14: Summarize the sequence of transformations: Confronting feelings--freedom to express them and realizing the impact on our family unit.

Step 15: Conclusions about the way this person resolves conflicts: Internally--denial, mental anguish, depression.

Step 16: Does this relate to how you handle feelings: I have chosen to ignore some of my problems rather than deal with them.

Step 17: What changes should be made? Be more up front in communicating--more direct and assertive and stuck to my ideals and beliefs.

Step 18: What changes are you willing to make? More honesty and openness regarding my feelings--less internal pain.

DEFENSE

ANIMAL METAPHOR TEST #1

Step 1: Draw two animals.

Step 2: Fill in the blanks

Animal #1
Type of animal: Lamb
Age: 39 **Sex:** Female
Personality: Gentle, kind, quiet.

Animal #2
Type of animal: Bear
Age: 52 **Sex:** Male
Personality: Overbearing, grouchy, nasty.

Step 3: What are they saying?

#1: Please don't hurt me big bear
#2: Why shouldn't I? You're no good to anyone.
#1: But I don't hurt anyone, or bother anyone.
#2: That's your problem--you let everyone walk all over you.
#1: Well I want to stop doing that right now--so leave me alone.
#2: No--I'll drive you crazy before I let you put me in a nuthouse.
#1: That's not my intention--I just want to live harmoniously alongside you.

493

#2: Well if you don't do what I say I'll eat you up--because I'm always right and you don't know anything--so obey me or else.

Step 4: What happened before? The bear was chasing the lamb around trying to scare her because he thought he was being funny and having a good time at her expense.

Step 5: After? The lamb just shut up and listened and obeyed the bear--she didn't feel she had a choice because he was bigger and meaner and couldn't deal with him on his level.

Step 6: Title: "Intimidation."

Step 7a: Conflicts between themselves: They are not communicating because the bear is so aggressive and the lamb so timid she gives into the bear out of fear. No self-esteem, intimidation.

Step 7b: Conflicts between them and the world: They don't understand one another so they have this power play and the bear wins because of his power. Again, misunderstanding and lack of communication.

Step 8: What changes should they make to resolve conflicts? They should have more heart-to-heart talks to release their true feelings in order to be more understanding of one another.

Step 9: Which animal do you identify with: The lamb. I give in too easily to keep peace. I'm quiet and passive. **Other animal:** My husband--he's overbearing, loud, mean and aggressive. Dictatorial in his manner.

Step 10: How does this pertain to you? It's mine and my husband's relationship all the way. Many times I shut my mouth because I'd rather ignore it than deal with his behavior. Instead of discussing things, we both become quiet. Eventually, one starts speaking again without resolving any conflicts. And it starts again the next time.

Step 11: What changes should you make? Again, more emotional communication to understand one another or a deeper level instead of superficial ignorance, which leads to hurt on both parts.

Step 12: Present a similar incident: My husband will come home from work and say "what did you do all day, talk on the phone? The place is a mess." I explain that I did a, b, c, d, e, f, g and the rest, but I'm no good I don't try--he attacks me like the bear. I must have a big flaw in my character because of my cluttered house--I'm worthless.

Step 13: How do you relate with others, and how do you get yourself in trouble? It's a vicious cycle--my house is a mess--he attacks then he wants sex after the attack--I can't talk to him rationally. Maybe I set myself up for it, but honestly sometimes I don't have enough time in the day to do everything with two children, appointments, and depression, which I've suffered with longer than anyone realizes.

Step 14: What changes are you willing to make? I will try my best to make my house neater. What I can't understand how I can be judged as a person because of a cluttered house. If it makes my husband happy I will try as long as I get cooperation and respect.

|4|

Overview of the Case Studies with Comments of the Test Takers about Their Therapeutic and Learning Experiences

INTERN CASES:

The psychic tension scoring was based on the -3 to +3 range where high negative scores reflect wellness, positive scores correspond to illness as high psychic tension

Case Name	Relational Modality	Psychic Tension -3 to+3	Medical Diagnosis	Internship/ Evaluation Duration	Outcome/Patient Comments
The Badger and the Rabbit	Submissive Antagonistic	-2.2	Well	3 month internship	**The Badger and the Rabbit:** "Wisdom and innocence not only coexist in harmony, but actually complement one another. Wisdom alone leads to sadness; innocence alone leads to superficiality. When one becomes capable of experiencing both, true and substantial happiness follows. This is my resolution."
Running Out of Time	Dominant Antagonistic	-2.1	Well	Summer intern Repeated periodic completions of the workbook	**Running Out of time:** "I am innately wired to be dominant and aggressive. I recklessly power through life and get myself in trouble by not heeding the Power Management mantra enough." So, was I less aggressive, I would also be less intense, I would be more peaceful and joyful. If I weren't so competitive, I wouldn't feel like I was always in such a race against time. This test has given me wisdom."
The Elephant and the Fawn	Dominant Cooperative	-.2	anxiety depression ADHD.	2 month internship, family evaluation project	**Elephant and Fawn:** "Completing a CAB workbook and this study of my family has provided me with new perspective on my difficulty with change and anxiety about leaving home, not to mention with a new tool with which to scrutinize my patterns in an imaginative and therapeutic yet remarkably objective and methodical way. Having identified that my fears lie rooted in my anxious-ambivalent attachment to home, I feel more prepared and self-aware and thus more able to envision a path of change…This is a monumental step forward for me, a step very much supported and enhanced by the steps and stories present in my family's workbooks. The similar threads of worry and doubt in our books make me feel less alone in my anxieties, and yet somehow more equipped to tackle my anxieties on my own, for myself."

Case Name	Relational Modality	Psychic Tension	Medical Diagnosis	Therapy/ Evaluation Duration	Outcome/Patient Comments
The Frozen Dinosaur and the Squirrel	Dominant/ Submissive Cooperative	-2.3	Well	6 months	**Dinosaur and Squirrel:** "Being able to put into words the source of your troubles--through the process of creativity--is a relieving and energizing experience. I am currently in a stage of questioning societal norms. Now that my relational pattern has been identified, and my challenges have been brought to light, I feel ready to actively seek out some answers."
The Sun Competing With The Wind	Submissive Cooperative And Antagonistic	-2.5	Well	1 month	**Sun Competing with Wind:** "Essentially, I was unwilling to explore new things because it was easy to live in a sort of stasis instead. This laziness toward discovery held me back though, and I consistently longed for that which I did not give myself…I found that my life was largely a cycle, which I now feel equipped to escape."
Maleficent and the Sleeping Beauty	Dominant Cooperative And Antagonistic	-2.6		3 hours for the completion of the workbook	*This individual was uncomfortable with the amount of information made clear through the evaluation process. He wrote no comments about the experience, outcome, or what he learned about himself through the evaluation.*

DOMINANT CASES:

Case Name	Relational Modality	Psychic Tension	Medical Diagnosis	Therapy/ Evaluation Duration	Outcome/Patient Comments
Holocaust Survivor	(no RMES)	RMES not available	Well	3 Session Evaluation	"I have made peace with myself. One big burden, hate and guilt have been lifted from my mind. I feel better about myself, resolved with my experiences. I am more spontaneous in my emotions and more open in my expressions… I feel more secure now, because I know that my own mind can provide the answers to all my problems."

Name	Type	Number	Problem	Sessions	Quote
Handicapped Flea & Ant / Disabled Lion & Eagle	Dominant Cooperative	.5	Performance Anxiety	6 Sessions Completion of four workbooks	"The animal metaphors and other exercises of Dr. Levis are a key ingredient in the unlocking of unconscious (and conscious) problems…the last image I did of myself…was of a slightly deformed eagle, which nevertheless was able to soar above the earth with the greatest possible freedom. I should maintain positive mental attitude and understand that, though limited, I can still achieve my goals and dreams."
The Elephant and the Butterfly	Dominant Cooperative/Antagonistic	.2	Well	2 Session Evaluation	"I need to somehow let my anger go or maybe just be okay with it…I am willing to make any changes to stabilize my attitude. I need to take control of my imbalance within. I am willing to not make so many expectations, to forgive…others and myself, to listen, [and] to take my anger out in other ways rather than on those I love."
The Dragon and the Unicorn	Dominant/Submissive Antagonistic	1.3	Performance Anxiety	10 session therapy	"I am screaming for attention, then they give me love and attention. Then I reject it…my husband said there is improvement. It takes time. When I have anger, I manage it."
The Terrier and the Buffalo	Dominant Cooperative/Antagonistic	.6	Depression, anxiety, adjustment to domestic relations	4 Session Evaluation 2 months group therapy	"During the course of this workbook, I progressed from feeling fractured and stressed…to identify conflictual patterns towards resolution. By finally understanding this logical progression of my feelings, insights and knowledge gained from using the workbook, my anxieties no longer seemed insurmountable…I now knew where to begin to heal."
The Cheshire Cat and the Pitbull	Dominant Cooperative	-.9	Conflicts within the school system	5 Session Evaluation	"It's been an interesting process, filled with insights, a process I agree would be a very rapid solution to any psychological problem…I've learned that my life, like most people's lives, has had two cycles. We go from pain to mastery over the pain. After forty years of utilizing a self-imposed "shell" to avoid letting pain into my being and dealing with it, I experienced pain and broke down in tears in front of my family for the first time. We experienced catharsis. By admitting defeat, I had won."

Case Name	Relational Modality	Psychic Tension	Medical Diagnosis	Therapy/ Evaluation Duration	Outcome/Patient Comments
The Mad Postal Worker	Dominant Antagonistic	.8	Adjustment reaction, with suicidal and homicidal ideation	3 Session Evaluation	"I found [the CAB] to be very helpful in dealing with my aggression and the attempted suicide on myself and when I wanted to harm my family…[the testing] has shown me that I have been unable to relate to [my wife] and the kids and have more aggression than I thought. I am willing to go through therapy, and hope over a period of time I'll regain what I've now lost through my aggression, and bring harmony back into our marriage. I want a better way to communicate with my wife. This test has also given me a different outlook on life as SUICIDE is not the answer."

SUBMISSIVE CASES:

Case Name	Relational Modality	Psychic Tension	Medical Diagnosis	Therapy/ Evaluation Duration	Outcome/Patient Comments
The Easy-Going Wife	Submissive Cooperative	-1.3	Anxiety	3 Session Evaluation	Regarding the TMT: "Admitting these feelings has given me freedom to deal with them." Relationship with husband: "If [doing the cleaning] makes my husband happy, I will try, as long as I get cooperation and respect."
The Lamb Beneath the Judge's Mask	Submissive Cooperative	-2.3	Well	3 session evaluation	"I surrender my own wants and needs to avoid conflicts. To avoid making the other person mad or upset, I give in. Later I resent the other person and hate myself…I must assert my own wants in situations where others are trying to infringe on those rights."

Title	Personality Style	Score	Issue	Sessions	Outcome
Trying to Survive as a Dog	Submissive Cooperative	-2.2	Gastro-intestinal psychoso-matic distress	10 session therapy	**Anxiety:** [This experience] has greatly alleviated my anxieties." **Relationship with Grandchildren:** "My daughter had complained that I was a delinquent grandfather. I have been retrieving information about art…to do with my grandchildren." **Relationship with women:** "I didn't know I was angry and hostile…I didn't realize how angry I was until we did the testing about my anger. The testing showed that I am not dominant but submissive. The marriage forced me to be dominant. She [my daughter] says I have been more relaxed." **Meditation:** "I float on the pond--I don't have need to go to the bottom of the pond anymore."
The Anteater and the Lion	Submissive Cooperative/Antagonistic	1	Sexual abuse	Psychological Evaluation	"It definitely has given me a relief of the tension inside, for now. I am able to look at my situation and see what to do, instead of staying stuck."
The Wise Oak	Submissive Cooperative/Antagonistic	-1.4	Anxiety	12 session therapy	"I have been able to reflect on myself in a positive way. I see my conflicts, my compromises, my defense mechanism, but I also see very few resolutions. I know now what I need to do to make more resolutions and how to keep myself out of trouble. I have learned how to use power management to my advantage instead of letting someone else's power management ruin me. I am growing again and understanding myself better than I have ever known myself before. I was amazed at how correct the workbook really was about me…I am a better person now. I can and will stand my ground, and I will stay and talk it over, no matter how long it takes."
The Moon and the Troll	Submissive Antagonistic/Cooperative	1	Self-mutilation	16 session therapy	"I have not cut myself in a while, and think of it infrequently. I do not believe that I would actually kill myself, nor seriously threaten to, again. I am becoming more involved in my daily family life and responsibilities. I am able to take care of my young step-daughter, niece and nephew. I am not becoming overwhelmed by the major changes in my life. I am still learning to live with myself, but I think I can, I think I can, I think I can…"

| The Vulture and the Snake | (no RMES) | RMES not available | Eating Disorder | 40 sessions therapy | "It became apparent, via the tests given at the start of my therapy that my fat was but my insulation, my buffer zone, against the world. Of deeper significance was my perpetual smile presented to the outside world. This defense had been in place for many years…I concluded that I was constantly running away from life; I relegated conflicts to the rear of my mind. It became obvious that I had to express rather than repress. My two fragmented selves had to be integrated into a whole. [I should] get the attention I seek by letting my needs and desires known." |

|5|

Discussion: Psychotherapy Versus Psychoeducation

Chapter One
The Impact to Psychotherapy of
Rethinking Psychology as the Moral Science

A Scientific Breakthrough: Understanding the Creative Process
This book of case-studies is about Formal Theory's radical innovations in the realm of the social sciences by introducing the study of the creative process as a scientific conflict resolving entity. This premise changes the conceptualization of the unconscious, the diagnostic categories as relational modalities, and accomplishes their measurement using a self-assessment that is educational, diagnostic and therapeutic.

The new conceptualization clarifies conflict resolution as compelled by an inner need to seek balance, reconciling the individual with her/his culture, and also reconciling her with a broader sense of justice. The motivational forces coincide with those of the three equilibrial operations that balance the trays of a scale; these operations guide the mind to resolve conflict, they represent moral values. The unconscious is shown as a scientific and moral concept since it guides the person to social adjustment, conflict resolution as the adjustment to societal norms or even the change of norms to serve a broader sense of justice or balance.

The new conceptualization of the equilibrial unconscious, both scientifically structured and morality driven radically departs from the current premises and practices of psychology. It reconciles behavior and morality, and places the study of behavior on the scientific foundation of the creative process. This concept totally revamps psychology into the Moral Science.

- The Moral Science refutes the amoral and agnostic unconscious.

- It subsets the current set of clinical non-relational and non-psychodynamic diagnostic categories to the psychodynamic syndromal personality typology.

- It totally departs from current assessment methods and therapeutic approaches introducing the CAB, a self-assessment that delivers insights and direction for changes directly to the test taker.

504

- The new psychology, anchored to equilibrial scientific principles, the laws of nature, regards religions as normative institutions and understands conflict as deviation from their norms. The Moral Science challenges the normative authority of religions by viewing them as partial discoveries of the conflict resolution alternatives and as normatively stagnant.

This is the theoretical context in presenting the case studies of this volume. The unconscious and all behaviors, including religions, are viewed as scientific conflict resolution measurable entities with relational dimensions. The creative process unconscious is shown to be the integrative concept of a totally rigorous humanistic science of behavior. It is very important to comprehend that the unconscious motivation is morality driven. The new psychology is no longer agnostic. On the contrary it is the Science of Conflict Resolution, the Moral Science.

The case studies validate Formal Theory's assumption on the scientific and moral nature of the unconscious. Hence the key human motivation is not libido and thanatos but conflict resolution. This validation transforms the realms of the multiple theories and the many religions into the unified exact Moral Science. While behavior becomes a science, the case studies show the self-assessment delivering emotional psycho-education as a most effective psychotherapy.

The Three Functions of the Conflict Analysis Battery: Educational, Diagnostic and Therapeutic

- **The educational function: understanding the unconscious as a scientific moral order phenomenon**

  The assessment program is educational or cognitive. The online delivery begins with an informational essay. Clinical services begin with explanation on the unconscious as a measurable conflict resolution phenomenon following the four diagnostic categories.

  So therapy begins introducing the syndromal structure of emotions determined by the unconscious sequence of interrelated emotions. We talk about the unit entity that has rigorous constructs and formulas, the formal operations of the equilibrial scale and those of the Simple Harmonic Motion. We do not need to get too deep into the science but it helps to educate people on the unconscious as a natural science entity that has both formal dimensions and a six-part structure as the universal harmonic. This is the object for the scientific and moral study of behavior.

- **Second, the diagnostic function: the process is qualifiable as a set of relational modalities**

  The assessment is diagnostic. The unconscious as a conflict resolution mechanism is qualifiable; we recognize a range of wellness diagnostic categories, four alternative syndromal ways of resolving conflict as wellness diagnoses pertaining to everybody. The diagnostic categories of the Diagnostic Statistical Manual, DSM 5, describe clinical symptoms, illnesses. **The manual does not recognize a wellness personality typology.** The manual's personality diagnoses identify pathological disorders. The professions of psychiatry and psychology do not understand wellness and illness. The fact is that the wellness diagnoses explain the psychodynamic development of most psychopathologies. The case studies present symptoms in the contexts of the relational modalities and direct the elimination of symptoms through relational attitude changes, power management interventions, rather than through chemotherapies.

The relational modalities are syndromal entities. They connect emotions and behaviors explaining wellness and illness as a continuum. These diagnoses applied to one's psychological self-assessment explain the type of pathology experienced, and also how to effectively modify it. Therapy begins educating about the intensity of conflicts leading to distress and that modification in one's power management can effectively eliminate the relational syndromal pathologies.

Conflict Analysis identifies and measures objectively the unconscious as a relational modality with a syndromal psychodynamic unfolding along the six formally interrelated emotions. The mental oscillation predictably evolves from a conflict, the stress state, to its resolution, as the compromise one. Change is in the capacity of the individual to manage her/his power. Power Management is a behavior modification therapy since it always leads the test taker from insights to actions, clarified many times over as responses to the question: 'What changes are you willing to make?'

The theory-based assessment accurately measures the unconscious and identifies the underlying path to conflict resolution.

The diagnostic procedure consists in measuring the formal constellation of one's relational modality and examining the six emotions of the syndromal unfolding of one's relational modality. The modality is determined with the inventory, the syndromal unfolding with the metaphors.

- **The therapeutic function: The assessment detects a pattern's optimal restructuring**

Identifying the unconscious has been traditional psychodynamic therapies' classical diagnostic and therapeutic objective. Therapies have aspired to make the person conscious of the unconscious by identifying the transference relationship between the patient and the therapist. The Moral Science identifies the unconscious using the self-assessment to determine it objectively as the relational modality syndromal diagnosis unfolding as a six-role-state equilibrial process. But it goes further than identifying the unconscious; it directs the person to intervene effectively in modifying it.

CAB's therapeutic effectiveness is due to the testing's capacity to identify the unconscious objectively overcoming the complexities and subjectivity of therapists' interpretations and the need for the therapeutic impersonal relationship required for its accurate determination. Upon recognition the test taker is asked "what are you willing to change?"

The inventory findings are cross-validated by the metaphor tests. They both demonstrate the unconscious as a measurable scientific, qualifiable and quantifiable phenomenon, predictable and readily identifiable as one of the four relational modalities. The CPM is shown to be an effective psychotherapy as well as an effective psycho-education measuring the unconscious as the object for scientific analysis without the need for a therapeutic relationship. But the therapeutic relationship can be useful as a real emotional value supervising and guiding the process of the personal transformation.

The new battery in the context of the educational program changes traditional psychotherapies into a wellness education. The test taker becomes conscious of the unconscious attaining the objectives of insight and potentially changes without being in psychotherapy, without the services of a therapist. The effectiveness of the assessment changes the realm of psychotherapy for most well people into the one of psycho-education.

The assessment reduces the importance of the therapeutic relationship and cancels the diagnostic significance of the transference as this is a misnomer for the relational modality diagnoses. The assessment also facilitates the work of the therapist working with patients. Real troubled, conflicted individuals can use help in finding their way to wellness. The clinical case studies demonstrate transformation in some cases without therapy. The online delivery demonstrates the therapeutic effectiveness of the intervention without any assistance.

The consistent positive insights and identification of needed changes in the online delivery of the assessment validate the new concept of the unconscious, the new diagnostic categories but does not demonstrate effectiveness of the CAB assessment in dealing with serious personal conflicts.

The clinical case studies though are testimonials of the therapeutic relevance and effectiveness of the diagnostic insights guiding a person to wellness with counseling. The consistent positive therapy outcome of the cases and the query responses offered by the online delivery of the assessment validate the new concept of the unconscious, the new diagnostic categories and the effectiveness of the CAB as a therapeutic assessment.

The self-analysis of metaphors reduces the interpretive role of the therapist.
The question emerges of the role of the assessment's effectiveness, speed, objectivity, accuracy in identifying the unconscious, versus the role of traditional therapist, requiring a long-term therapeutic relationship to generate only insights on the patient's/trainee's relational tendencies, a procedure that yet does not measure or qualify the patient's relational distortions.

The patient/student creates the art and interprets his or her metaphors as relational phenomena. The student/patient uses the art, generating imagery, to create the personal symbolic system. The formal theorist as an informed scientist supervises the interpretation of the art. The patient is the artist, the creator, and the analyst and reformer of his/her role. The therapist is merely a facilitator. Therapy is the setting for the pattern to unfold metaphorically and the person to encounter her own narrative tendencies. The individual learns to face the built-in anxieties and counter-phobic mechanisms; s/he is now conscious of the unconscious. In learning to strike a power balance the client embarks on the natural evolution toward health.

Traditional psychodynamic therapy identifies a patient's pattern manifested in the patient therapist relationship as transference.
The self-assessment simplifies the role of the trainer/therapist into that of an educator facilitator. It simplifies the interpretive challenges of the therapist/ educator who simply can guide the student/patient

to organize the testing information to maximize its meaningfulness. The role of the formal analyst for the well person is educational, but for the ill person it remains a more supportive and active reality directed role. As an educator the therapist delivers information on the role of the person in managing power appropriately. She educates the person to understand the consequences of too much or too little power in the syndromal unfolding of interactions. While it is enough to be an educator informing students on how to integrate the testing and extrapolate the findings, this is not adequate in dealing with the emotionally decompensated individual. Yet the art of interpretation is the key in dealing with most psychopathological conditions because behind every decompensation are the syndromal dynamics and the challenge to bring the person out of the emotional intensity to the security of proper responses.

Relational diagnosis diminishes the dependence on the therapist as a diagnostician but empowers her as a transformational consultant.
The scientific knowledge of the process, of the modalities and the testing technology simplifies and changes the role of the analyst into that of an educator and the role of the patient into that of a trainee or student. The testing transforms therapy into an educational experience of self-discovery. The processing of information in each metaphor questionnaire is completed by the test taker. Students become self-aware of their version of resolving conflict as a relational syndrome with its respective strengths and weaknesses. The test taker becomes conscious of the unconscious as a phenomenon of wellness that is manageable.

Traditional therapies are not concerned about delivering systematic knowledge on the unconscious and on the scientific nature of patterns. Unlike the traditional therapies Power Management delivers information on the modalities but also as manifested in the transference distortions in the perception of authority figures. Analysis of patterns accounts for the distortions as innate relational tendencies rather than as due to parental formative experiences. The relational modalities are genetically determined. See the REMS study of twins figure.

The relational modality graph reflects the overlapping relational modality scores of two identical twin brothers attesting to the genetic determination of relational dispositions

RMES Grid

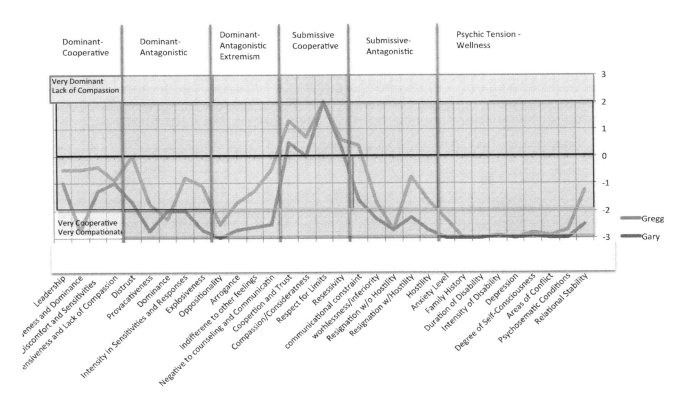

The Heartbeat and the Stethoscope

The relational modalities reflect the underlying orderly process as the mental heartbeat. The battery of tests is the stethoscope for the patient to identify his or her own heartbeat, the predictable six-part process of conflict resolution. The patient/trainee uses it to observe his or her own, the relational modality, to make the diagnosis but also to identify the needed changes. The test taker will consider changes s/he could and is willing to make. The self-assessment's outcome is heightened self-awareness, and clarity on relational changes to be completed over time necessary to reduce any clinical symptoms. A person, who needs help beyond self-help can certainly benefit from traditional therapy. But it is important that the therapist does not get caught in the patient's dependency pattern and become as identified in Alcoholics Anonymous as a "codependent" enabling the client.

The objective of psycho-education is power management as self-awareness and respect of the syndromal and equilibrial nature of relational choices.

Creativity manifests in all arts as the moral of the plot of stories. Movies and dramas, books and poetry, TV shows reinforce optimal power management directives. The assessment works on its own, but it can be assisted by moral traditions enhancing wellness. The assessment promotes self-awareness and evokes coping skills as power management directives. It may also teach wisdom as spiritual rituals reinforcing power management, rediscovering morality as traditional moral strategies to reinforce self-discipline and behavior change. Spirituality embraces creativity as the means of reinforcing correction of one's patterns and leading to emotional empowerment.

Feasibility of introducing the emotional education in the classroom

The question arises if the emotional education, which is effective for the general population, should be integral part of education and administered to school students fulfilling education's mission statement? Education has always promised three objectives:

1. The bridging of the humanities and the sciences,

2. Self-knowledge, in promoting the principle of know-thy-self, and

3. The delivery of moral values.

These three objectives have eluded educators, but these objectives are attainable by the Moral Science. The Power Management program of emotional education can help to achieve the three elusive objectives of education. Should education embrace their delivery as an emotional education suitable for the classroom?

The implication for therapists, educators but also of people managers, be that in an military, prison, or organizational population is that we have a program that can enhance wellness and screen pathology. Everybody needs to understand the science of behavior, to understand oneself, and identify the principles of conflict resolution as moral values. Behavior becoming an exact science, the battery becoming a user-friendly technology, why then would this knowledge and technology not be an integral part of the routine educational experience?

The challenge for clinicians is one of rethinking the unconscious, the DSM 5 diagnostic categories, and assessment procedures. The Moral Science introduces a new set of syndromal diagnostic categories of wellness explaining psycho-dynamically the generation of illness. The new diagnostic categories are relevant in evolving therapeutic changes. Current diagnoses focus on clinical symptoms precluding the psychodynamic generation of symptoms as well as the behavior modification implications necessary to eliminate the symptoms. If we have a new set of wellness diagnostic categories that predict behavior and provide insights readily, it is difficult to understand how we can continue operating in the clinical medical model of diagnoses and fragmented models of therapy.

One thing is clear: since psychology has entered the realm of an exact science the information and its personal relevance are appropriate factual knowledge that should be delivered in the classroom. The scientific and the moral study of behavior should be part of education and training and not considered as the sacrosanct realm reserved for psychology professionals providing clinical services and alternatively for clergy advancing religious normative information as the moral paradigms.

Confidentiality

A problem has to be addressed in the delivery of this emotional education to the classroom, or any educational and organizational setting. This is the issue of privacy and confidentiality. This issue raises the question of how to avoid the revelation of sensitive information in the forum of the classroom where such information could be mishandled by teachers and by students. The solution is in the online delivery of this education totally bypassing the need for a therapist and also of an educator for its effective personalized delivery. The online delivery allows learning through the assessment as the document can remain in the control of the clients, the student and the counsilor. Alternatively this information may be

510

released to a screening third party allowing usage of computer-generated analysis, which could screen the protocols for pathology; in case of pathology the computer generated report can inform the test taker suggesting that s/he seek counseling, while at the same time the report could alert the school to welcome the student/member of organization to counseling services.

The online delivery and processing of information privately could overcome the concerns on the appropriateness of the educational program in the classroom. One can learn through the testing without the concerns of self-revelation compromising one's social status. The feedback to the student/test-taker and limited information to the school/organization could address effectively the issues of professional services serving the needs of the individual and the organization's need for screening the students for serious pathology, while evolving readiness in providing for students' special needs.

Chapter Two
Findings and Validations

The validation of the Formal Theory begins by reviewing its four key hypotheses
The Formal Theory introduces several innovative hypotheses into the field of the social sciences. The case studies represent findings validating these hypotheses, hence transforming the Formal Theory into a brand new psychology, the Moral Science. This science is a totally different psychology from the one we know and practice.

- It changes the epistemic language defining the unconscious as both a natural science and a moral order entity thus bridging the humanities and the sciences.

- It changes diagnostic categories, advancing four well defined relational modalities as diagnoses, a wellness personality typology. These wellness diagnoses are psychodynamic syndromal entities and are predictive of pathology.

- It changes the assessment technology introducing a battery combining an inventory and projective tasks identifying patterns instead of traits. It measures wellness and psychopathology.

- It changes therapy by integrating education and a self-assessment into a manual driven psychotherapy that is didactic, diagnostic, and therapeutic without the need for a therapist.

- As psychology becomes a science it changes the role of the therapist into that of an educator.

These changes represent rethinking the disciplines of psychology. The case studies address the validation of the four disciplines: the new epistemology, the relational modality diagnoses, the effectiveness of the assessment, and its therapeutic function. They present validations for each assumption advanced by the Formal Theory:

1. The introduction of a new epistemology, the scientific study of the unconscious.

   - Can we introduce science in the study of psychology and morality?

   - Is the unconscious a scientific conflict resolving mechanism? Is it governed by the natural laws of the two equilibrial phenomena: the pendulum oscillation and the balance of the trays of the scale?

   - Is the need to conform to norms the ultimate motivational force driving behavior?

   - Is the unconscious a natural science phenomenon with measurable formal and physical dimensions? Is the unconscious a six role state process guided by three formal relational operations?

   - Is the function of resolving conflicts a moral order phenomenon?

- Is this conflict resolving function motivated by normative conformity? Is conflict generated by normative deviations and does the path to resolution follow normative conciliation?

- Is the moral or conflict resolution unconscious based on the homeostatic need for social adjustment as compliance to normative standards?

- Is this unconscious need for conflict resolution the origin of moral order?

- Is morality a scientific psychological rather than a metaphysical phenomenon?

2. The introduction of a new set of diagnostic categories as the wellness relational modalities, non-clinically stigmatizing syndromal personality types.

- Are the diagnostic categories the four relational modalities, determined merely by the two formal operations: reciprocity distinguishing passivity/activity and negation distinguishing cooperation/antagonism distinctions?

- Does the third operation alienation/mutual respect identify the types of psychopathology?

- Are the alternative ways of resolving conflicts syndromal wellness diagnoses?

- Do wellness conflict resolution patterns account also for illness?

3. The introduction of the Conflict Analysis Battery as a didactic, diagnostic and therapeutic self-assessment.

- Does the self-assessment, the Conflict Analysis Battery, identify the relational modalities and their syndromal structure?

- Do the metaphor tests identify the six role states and related emotions correctly?

- Can the assessment be therapeutic without a therapist?

- Can it be delivered under the supervision of a teacher as a concise program of emotional education in the classroom?

4. The introduction of Creativity and Power Management as an effective therapeutic emotional education program clarifying the mental principles that spontaneously resolve conflict: mastery, cooperation and mutual respect as moral values.

- Is the assessment a didactic, diagnostic and therapeutic instrument?

- Does the use of the testing as a manual driven psychotherapy, expedite the clinical outcome of traditional therapies? Does the emotional education therapy lead to good therapy outcomes?

- Does Power Management promote moral values as the path to wellness? Are moral values the scientific principles of conflict resolution?

- Does the orderly and morality driven unconscious inspire respect for a universal moral order?

- Are religions normative restructurings of psychological origin and do they have natural science dimensions like the four personality types?

- Are religions partial and complementary discoveries of the Moral Science?

- Do the attributions of the divine befit the unit unconscious process?

Discussion and Claims of Validation

The case studies validate each assumption advanced by the Formal Theory revising each of the four disciplines considered confirming their integration into the Moral Science.

1. Epistemology: Validations of the Scientific Unconscious

Hypothesis and Evidence: The key formal theoretical assumption is that the unconscious is a natural science entity with a distinct structure and a moral function representing the unit of the science.

- The moral function is demonstrated through the finding that all profiles begin from a conflict and lead to its resolution. The evidence is in each assessment showing the relation of the first role state as characterized by the attributes of conflict: passivity, antagonism and alienation and the last role state, the compromise, characterized by the attributes of resolution: mastery, cooperation and mutual respect. This evidence of the moral function of the unconscious points out that morality is a scientific psychological phenomenon and not a metaphysical one.

- The distinct structure is one determined by two equilibrial natural science mechanisms thus the process is shown to abide by these phenomena's concepts and formulas.

- The inventory findings demonstrate that the mind follows the principles of balance of the trays of a scale the four formal operations. Utilizing the personality inventory we identify the five factors of psychological assessments as coinciding with the five scales of the inventory. Four factors and corresponding scales identify the characteristics of the four relational modalities, while the fifth factor pertains to the psychic tension identifying the degree of wellness versus psychopathology.

- The finding of the universal harmonic integrating meaningfully the metaphors of test takers into conflict resolution harmonics demonstrates that the mind follows three pendulum oscillations and then stops upon a resolution. The evidence on constructs and formulas of the Simple Harmonic Motion is reflected in the reconstruction of the process with samples of creativity as circumscribed six-role process syndromal entities.

The Conclusions: All case studies utilizing the battery assessment provide evidence confirming first, a choice formal relational modality resolution and second that the path to resolution consists of a syndromal six role state emotional dialectic.

514

- The personality inventory identifies the relational modality of a test taker.

- The metaphor tests identify the syndromal six role-state process.

These two measurements may be graphically portrayed in each case study describing the natural science characteristics of the individual unconscious as the dimensions of a harmonic process.

- The relational modality profile is identified in the case studies as a single page image summarizing the inventory scores. The one page image features the scoring of the dominance scales on the top left quadrant and the key metaphor on the top right quadrant. The metaphor is accompanied with a comment illustrating the metaphorical manifestation of the test taker's relational pattern. The lower half of the page comprises the scoring of the submissiveness scales on the left quadrant and the measurement of the psychic tension scale on the lower right quadrant.

- The syndromal sequence of the unit unconscious process is identified in the metaphor profile integrating the metaphors of the test taker along the sine curve of the six-role process.

The combined image of the inventory and of the metaphor profiles validate the unconscious as a relational entity that has a formal and moral or conflict resolution function. The combination of the two graphic reports represents the measurement of the unconscious and validates the hypothesis of the natural science structure of the unconscious. This validation justifies the introduction of the constructs of the two scientific phenomena: the Simple Harmonic Motion and the equilibrial principles of the trays of a scale as the epistemic language of the new science.

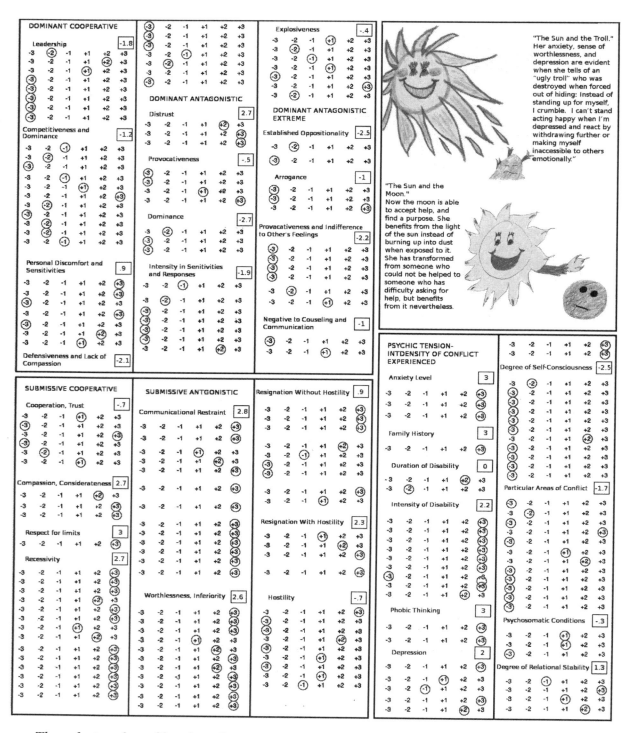

The relational profile of a submissive antagonistic relational modality diagnosis reflecting the low scores in the two dominance scales and the high scores in the submissive both cooperative and antagonistic scales. The psychic tension is elevated in certain symptom areas identifying the patient's depression and suicidal tendencies.

516

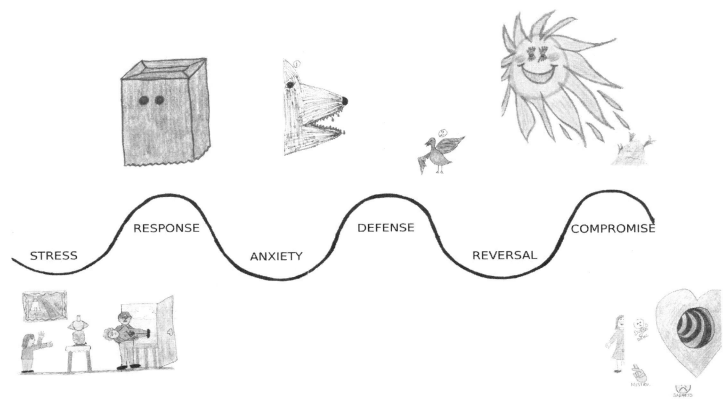

Stress:
Conflictual
memory Losing
her loving
grandmother.

Response:
The transparent
Mask is a bag
over her head.

Anxiety:
A list of traumas
and negative
feelings,
followed by an
empty heart.

Defense:
Open mouth of a
wolf despises
helpless,
worthless bird
with a broken
wing.

Reversal:
Dreaming of
teaching again.

Compromise:
Sun and troll; the
troll is afraid of
light, and exposed to
it burns with flames
over his head.

The metaphor profile as a template of the harmonic process of the six emotions illustrated by the use of the emotion sensitive art work, each test corresponding to one of the six emotions. Stress as passivity, antagonism and alienation begins the syndromal sequence of emotions. Compromise usually reflects mastery, cooperation and mutual respect. The compromise metaphor reflects intensity of conflict and lack of resolution; indeed the patient identifying with the troll sees herself as set on fire by the sun. The resolution occurred in the course of therapy and is illustrated in the second book's metaphor profile (see subordinacy case study #5).

2. Validation of the Relational Modalities as Wellness Syndromal Diagnoses

Hypothesis: The relational inventory identifies the wellness diagnostic categories determined as alternative conflict resolutions following the three formal operations:

- the reciprocal: passivity and activity

- the opposite: cooperation antagonism

- the correlative: alienation versus mutual respect

While the first two formal distinctions lead to four relational modalities, the third is used to quantify conflict resolution as the individual's psychic tension, the measurement of wellness and illness as quantitative variations of psychic tension. The latter distinction accounts for psychopathology as distressed states of wellness.

In parallel to the inventory the metaphor tests integrated as a six role state process identify the process's syndromal psychodynamic connection of emotions and behaviors.

Distinction of Relational Modalities Along the Three Operations

First Along the Operation of Reciprocity: We recognize the dominance and subordinacy relational modalities.

Second Along the Operation of Negation: We distinguish the cooperative and antagonistic variations of the relational modalities.

Evidence: The relational modality inventory identifies a person's relating along the three dichotomies: first the dominance versus subordinacy, second, along the cooperation versus the antagonistic alternatives and third, according to the alienation versus mutual respect distinctions. The latter is reflected in the intensity of psychic tension.

The premise of these formal distinctions is validated in all case studies with the determination of diagnostic features. Dominance is clearly very different from Subordinacy relating as indicated both in the inventory scores and the metaphor profiles. So are cooperative and antagonistic subcategories of both modalities. Thus we identify clearly the four relational modalities and the respective psychic tension in each case study. The cases demonstrate the relational features. Cases are either dominant or submissive. Individuals scoring high in dominance score low in submissiveness and vice versa.

Also the cases are either cooperative or antagonistic. Finally the individuals are either well or they suffer of psychopathology related to the elevation of the psychic tension. There are variations in relating. We identify them as the relations spectrum.

Evidence: All case studies illustrate the identification of the testee's relational modality. There is coincidence between the inventory findings and those of the metaphor tests. The metaphors provide information validating the correctness of the diagnostic categories identified by the personality inventory. The metaphors confirm descriptively social and emotional experiences describing the relational choices.

An example of such correlation: The case studies of two interns Chris, a submissive antagonistic personality, and Melissa, a dominant cooperative one, illustrated in mural 10 of the Murals Exhibit, juxtapose the relational profiles of a submissive and a dominant personality. The behavior patterns of each case study illustrated in their metaphors validate the relational diagnoses measured with the personality inventory. The interns' companion essays clarify insights developed about their very different personality diagnostic categories. The interns' and the patients' essays in each case study confirm the syndromal diagnosis of the identified relational modality.

In more detail and with ample evidence the patients' cohort presents the dramatic differences between the two major diagnostic categories. The patients' cohort is divided in two sections, each section pertaining to the dominance and the subordinacy relational modalities. These sections begin by presenting the artwork of the Animal Metaphors and the Transparent Mask Tests of all cases reflecting the respective relational characteristics of the two opposite relational modalities.

Characteristically submissive individuals have difficulty expressing feelings reflected in the symbolic manifestation of the assumption of power.

- Gladys is an excellent case study of submissiveness identifying symbolically the blockage in the communication of feelings as experienced by submissive individuals. Her case study illustrates, in four phases captured in the aesthetics of metaphor images and companion poetry statements, her difficulty in communicating feelings. The difficulty is shown leading to associated pathology as the energy of conflicts was channeled to a particular preoccupation, food, manifested as the eating disorder of binging and fasting.

- Her long-term therapy illustrates the slow progress in correcting the relational problem, lack of assertiveness, the lack of capacity to communicate her feelings without fear of losing control of her anger. The communicational problem's correction coincided with the healing of her eating disorder.

| Case study #6

The Vulture and the Snake | | "[I identify with] the dog…perhaps I'm bored/lonely since husband started working in the city…when under pressure, or feeling sorry for myself, I plan on over-eating and drinking as a reward. |

Case study #6	*Perpetual Smile*	*Blackout*	*Double Image Discord*
The Vulture and the Snake	 "False happiness. Self-deceit, mockery. Shutting out sadness with a smile."	 Dejection, rejection, unwillingness [and] inability to express her feelings, and being preoccupied with eating.	 Two facets are separated: happiness on one side; hidden feelings, anger, sadness, fear [and] shadows are there, but they are constantly being repressed.

The transparent Mask Test presents the dialectic of a perfect image, the person's identity, contrasted to the imperfection illustrating a person's feelings in the image of the hidden face. A further clarification of the conflicts is brought about in the image of the heart illustrating the tag of war between opposite feelings. While the first mask illustrates a perpetual smile, the second image exposes the problem of the eating disorder, the mouth as the black hole. The third mask illustrates what the underlying difficulty in communicating her thoughts and feelings, reflected in the moat separating good and bad feelings.

- In great contrast to this submissiveness modality we see the artwork of a dominant well individual, the Holocaust survivor, whose approach to life is complicated by the assertive to aggressive expression of emotions. Her related emotional problems had been anxiety and guilt related to her sense of freedom upon the deportation of her grand parents. Her animal metaphors are two lions fighting over spoils of a dead antelope. Her mask reflects difficulty in expressing weakness. Her Short Story is about mischief and self-correction.

Case #1		
Holocaust Survivor Lion versus Lion		"[I identify with Lion] #1, since he did the killing and the spoils belong to him. However, he is not willing to share even a small piece with the other lion, who is also needy."

Case #1	*Inscrutable*	*Perfect Looking Poison Fruit*	*A Heart Full of Good Intentions, and*
Holocaust Survivor			

520

	Some worry, but well controlled…a non-committal posture.	Suspicion, impulse … take things at face value… flawless fruits which are poison, things are not what they seem.	*What it Paves the Road To* Laughing at emptiness, pain, confusion… humor helps in the solutions of difficult problems.

Evidence on the relational operation of negation identifying opposites recognizes the alternatives of cooperation versus antagonism in each major relational modality.

Findings and conclusions: Each relational modality is subdivided by the qualifications of cooperation and antagonism. We see these distinctions in each relational modality cohort. In the dominance section we see these differences represented clearly in two very different dominant persons. The 'Cheshire Cat' is a dominant cooperative person while the 'Postal employee' is a dominant antagonistic individual. The first case is of a teacher, who was fired for being confrontational with the school board by advancing the cause of an educational program of his choice. The second case was of the 'postal employee', who was fired for stealing a pornographic video-tape and who also wanted to kill his family and himself because of feeling rejected and sexually frustrated.

Case #6 *The Cheshire Cat*	*The Ever-Smiling Cheshire Cat* Perpetual happiness…I want to return to this face/mask…I thought [it] was my true face."	*Who Is This Man?* Confusion…I'm not sure who is behind the smiling mask."	*Heart Under Siege* Threats to the heart, confusion. This represents a heart, which is in danger.

In a parallel manner in the subordinacy chapter we see cases of cooperation and antagonism differentiating the respective submissive relational dynamics. The cutter, the 'wolf and the bird with the broken wing', is a submissive antagonistic person. She channeled her aggression to hurting herself; in stark contrast the Wise Oak, was cooperative seeking love and suffering from guilt for having unacceptable extramarital relations. In both cases we see relational profiles of submissiveness with elevated scores with the respective subcategories.

We could arrange the 7 individuals in each relational category as the spectrum starting with cooperative individuals and continued to the antagonistic ones. Similarly we can examine the submissive individuals and detect the cooperation antagonism relating as an incremental qualification.

Along the dichomomy of alienation versus mutual respect, we identify the correlation of elevated scores of psychic tension and psychopathology. Patients' psychic tension is elevated according to the intensity of their psychopathology.

3. Validation of the Conflict Analysis Battery

Hypothesis: The Relational Modality Evaluation Scales (RMES) is an inventory that has four relational scales along the two relational dimensions and a fifth scale along the third polarity, the correlative dimension of the formal conflict resolution process, which measures wellness versus pathology.

Evidence: In statistical studies (The Karas Report) we identify the correctness of the items grouped under the respective scales. The statistical analysis of items led to the identification of five factors four corresponding to a relational scale and the fifth to the psychic tension scale.

The constructs, the dimensions of the items of each scale have been evaluated as highly concordant. The relational personality distinctions were identified as valid and reliable.

Validity of the Scales
All cases show the complementarity of the relational diagnoses derived from the RMES and the manifestation of the modality illustrated by the metaphors. The two types of tests are complementary in the diagnostic faculty but differ in their therapeutic function. The metaphors are emotionally loaded exercises, while the inventory assessment is purely factual, imparting numerical information regarding the relational dimensions, cooperation versus antagonism and passivity versus activity.

Crossvalidation of the Two Instruments
We see the parallels between the two types of psychological measurement in every case study. The metaphors reflect the emotional personal experiences identified numerically by the inventory. The relational inventory assessment is very reliable and does not change during therapy, while the metaphor testing is much more sensitive in reflecting changes.

Second, we identify the correctness of the ten metaphor tests reflecting the syndromal six emotions of the role process. The case studies present evidence correlating the six emotions and the corresponding metaphor tests identifying the corresponding emotions and leading to the reconstruction of the six role process.

- The role of Stress is captured correctly by the Memories of Conflict.

- The role of Response is well illustrated by the choice of the transparent mask test.

- The role of Anxiety is illustrated well by the Feelings Mask, the one hidden behind the response identity mask.

- The role of Defense is well illustrated by the Animal and Fairy Tale Metaphor Tests.

- The state of Reversal is well reflected in the Dreams Metaphors and also in the Intensified Animal Metaphor Test.

- Finally the role state of Compromise is well captured by the Short Stories Metaphor Test as mostly autobiographic and advancing positive solutions.

The similarity in the relational characteristics of a testee's animal metaphors and masks corresponding to the two major modalities is illustrated in the beginning of the two sections of the opposite relational modalities.

Validation of the Six Role Process

The correlation of stress to compromise in each metaphor profile demonstrates the six role process syndromal unfolding of the creative process. The reconstruction of the syndromal conflict resolution process using the metaphors may be readily validated by examining the relation between the tests marking its inception, the stress state, and marking its completion as the state of compromise.

We observe by contrasting the two tests corresponding to the role states of stress and compromise in formal relation to each other. Stress illustrated by the memories of conflict presents the state of passivity, antagonism and alienation, identifying the characteristics of conflict. Compromise, the characteristics of the resolution states are identified by the Short Stories Test presenting the reciprocal operations: mastery, cooperation and mutual respect,

4. Validation of Creativity and Power Management as a Didactic, Diagnostic and Therapeutic Self-Assessment

Hypothesis: The assessment is useful as a therapeutic experience

Findings: We detect positive therapy outcomes with alternative techniques reflecting the changes:

   1.   Observing the record of episodes of pathological behaviors in subordinacy case #5:
We have the record of episodes between several sessions upon the inception of therapy with a cutter. We note the reduction of frequency of cutting behaviors in the course of 16 sessions treatment leading to the complete elimination of the pernicious condition dating several years of unsuccessful therapy.

Record of episodes of cutting herself during the course of the first six weeks of therapy.

Week 1:

Six episodes in six days. Symptoms included panic attacks, swearing, increased heart rate, drinking, screaming, cutting and urge to cut.

Week 2:

Four episodes. Drinking, swearing, verbal tics, increased heart rate, screaming, and cutting.

Week 3:

Two episodes. Anxiety attack, swearing, drinking, biting self, cutting.

Week 4:

One episode. Anger at self-anxiety and feeling of dread, verbal tics, screaming, cutting.

Week 5:

Two episodes. Stabbed self, urge to cut, verbal tics, yelling.

Week 6:

Two episodes. Anxiety attack, crying, verbal tics, heavy breathing.

2a.   Observing the before-and-after-the-first-session drawings reflecting this patient's change of attitude upon the initiation of therapy

After the first session and second session we note an emotional change reflecting the impact of the inception of the Power Management therapy

2b.   Observing the before-and-after-images upon the completion of therapy

The case of the art professor and the Thai princess illustrate the resolution of symptoms.

Therapy

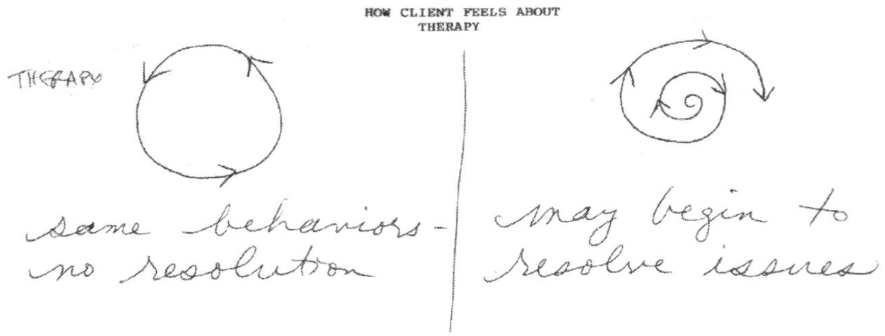

Before: Same behaviors – no resolution.

After: May resolve issues.

HOW CLIENT FEELS ABOUT THERAPY

THERAPY

Same behaviors – no resolution

may begin to resolve issues

begin to

Herself

Before: worthless, edge.

After: Still but grounded.

HOW CLIENY FEELS ABOUT HERSELF

SelF

suicidal, worthless, off the edge

still perilous, but somewhat grounded

Suicidal, off the

perilous, somewhat

Relationship with Mother

Before:

HOW CLIENT FEELS ABOUT HER RELATIONSHIP WITH HER MOTHER

MOTHER

overpowering

FIRST SESSION

may be able to stand up to her with help

Overpowering.

After: May be able to stand up to her with help.

3. Comparing assessments from the evaluation to the termination of therapy

   In one study we contrast the changes of each metaphor test as identified in two consecutive workbooks reflecting the evolution of the patient's self image and attitude to life.

   We have similar comparisons observing the succession of two or more books in several other cases.

4. Personal essays upon the completion of evaluations

Several essays following simple evaluations record dramatic diagnostic and therapeutic impact: The lion and the ant-eater case of sexual abuse, the foot fetish guy, the Holocaust survivor.

Personal essays upon the completion of therapy:
These essays convey in the words of the patients and of the interns the significance of the emotional and learning transformative experience.

Essay following the completion of the second workbook, Case of the Cutter

'Towards recovery', a couple of months later.

Looking back at the past few years of my life, it seems as if I were a different person from who I once was, and almost the opposite of who I would hope to be.

The horrible things I have done to myself have reinforced my self-loathing and have left emotional scars on my family. I am sickened and embarrassed by my behavior: screaming tantrums, cutting and scarring my skin, biting myself, hitting myself, suicide scenarios and quasi-attempts to kill myself, fleeing and hiding from my family, swearing, throwing knives at the wall, tying my hair in knots, refusing to bathe. Who was that person, and how did she get that way?

During my therapy, I have been able to identify contributing factors to my state of emotional distress. Some of these were: a controlling mother, a critical father, self-perceived guilt for the death of my aunt, an uncommunicative step-father, a criticizing grandmother, a marriage of false pretense, a series of rapes, a severely mentally ill mother-in-law, failure to attain the job I had planned for and an extremely stressful work environment.

The feelings arising from my responses to these factors in my life have created the horrible monster I became. If asked to describe myself, I would say bad, stupid, lazy, ugly, fat, mean, bitter, unwanted, worthless and a burden to those around her – better off dead.

So, after five hospitalizations for suicide, a series of medications and countless therapy sessions, has anything changed?

Yes – in degrees. I have not cut myself in a while, and think of it infrequently. I do not believe that I would actually kill myself, nor seriously threaten to, again. I am becoming more involved in my daily family life and responsibilities. I am able to take care of my young step-daughter, niece and nephew. I am not becoming overwhelmed by the major changes in my life – moving to a new home and opening a store. I am looking forward to my new job.

I am still learning to live with myself, but I think I can, I think I can, I think I can...

5. Use of metaphor testing to monitor progress in long-term therapy:
   Gladys evolution of metaphors towards an end goal after several books and long-term therapy

6. Use of retesting to evaluate therapeutic impact of an intervention: Wise Oak's three books.

7. Changes in RMES scores.
   The inventory test is very reliable and as such less sensitive in reflecting outcome changes. The reliability of the RMES test is made obvious with the online retesting, which shows its high

reliability in the minimal numerical score changes as seen in the retesting of individuals.

8. The Query responses for the online delivery of the assessment.
   The elevated scores indicate statistically the effectiveness of the assessment along its three functions: Didactic, diagnostic and therapeutic.

9. The 33 responses in each question of the letter to oneself and the insights derived from the Short Story Test upon the online delivery.

10. Comparison of outcome results and speed with other therapeutic modalities.

11. Research comparing the narrative and mindfulness techniques

12. Contrasting patients' prior lengthy therapeutic experiences versus the PM approach. Table reflecting prior therapeutic experiences.

13. Essays of interns and of patients evaluating the therapeutic and educational experience.

Discussion on the Criteria to Determine Therapy Outcome

1. In cases of illness, clinical outcome is evaluated by the *reduction of pathology, i.e. symptom frequency and severity* as incidents of hurting oneself, bulemic episodes, anxiety attacks, depth of depression, GI symptoms, tension headaches, are measured in the course of therapy to determine changes in the course of therapy.

2. Relational Structural Criteria
   In wellness cases unlike in illness we do not have clear symptoms but *subtle relational restructurings* conveyed accurately in metaphors of consecutive workbooks. Assessment and progress are reflected objectively in relational restructurings of metaphors. The relational criteria do not depend on qualitative external measurement of the state but on quantifiable facts along the measurable criteria of the conflict resolution process.
   The metaphors define the personal unconscious as the dimensions of the three formal operations and the episodes of the unfolding drama. They have clinical and metaphorical measurable dimensions. The object of study being the structure of the unconscious as a transformational totality with the dichotomies of dominance/subordinacy, cooperation/antagonism, alienation / mutual respect are the objectively measurable dimensions. They are measurable through both the inventory and the projectives of the CAB.

Measuring therapy outcome by contrasting consecutive assessments
We compare the initial assessment diagnostic evaluation with subsequent retestings to evaluate therapy outcome.

- Objectivity is conferred by insights generated by the workbook testing in the processing of information. Answers to questions presented in the assessment protocols upon the completion of therapy. Changes are identified in self reporting essays volunteered by the patient or trainee.

- The self-assessment and the additional personal testimonials help to evaluate personal state of mind as insights and hence progress as therapy outcome especially when the patient stops all medications as the alternative factor in causing improvements.

Self-awareness criteria in judging insights are reflected in the testing protocols upon any evaluation. Questions addresses in each test of the CAB explore a number of criteria about insights generated on the nature of one's relational modality.

- Does the patient identify having a diagnosis of power management?

- Does the client admit the animal drama is personally relevant?

- Does the client recognize repetitions of this pattern in his personal life?

- Does s/he accept responsibility for setting things up to get in trouble?

- Does s/he understand the changes s/he needs to make?

- Is s/he willing to make these changes?

- The testee evaluates the personal relevance of the new information.

- Has the analysis helped a person to identify one's relational modality?

- Has he experienced emotional relief, catharsis, the pleasure of resolving conflicts by adjusting one's attitude, finding meaningfulness, enjoyment in the completion of the assessment?

Example in Metaphor Analysis of Consecutive Assessments
We recognize effectiveness in power management as the capacity to identify needed changes and then to fulfill them. The insights entail self-correction changes, self-efficacy.

We review here the evolution in the testing of an educator, who had several episodes of suicide and a condition of self mutilation by cutting herself. This case study is reported under submissiveness in this volume. This study illustrates the progression in therapy by observing it in consecutive metaphors as recorded in two workbooks. The evolution captured in her metaphors attests of her swift recovery from her depression and her cutting episodes.

We see dramatic transformation in the resolution of conflicts from her evaluation set of metaphors to the second book of metaphors illustrating recovery generated in the span of six weeks:

We compare the differences between the two consecutive assessments of this patient in the restructuring of the relationship of her characters in two metaphor tests: the AMT and the Short Story. In the first book we have a wolf with her mouth open menacing extinction and a helpless bird with the broken wing unable to fly. The patient feels rejected by the wolf, who dismissed her as not even good to eat. In her Short Story she is a troll hiding from the sun. Upon her encounter with the sun the troll is set on fire and burns.

In the second set of parallel metaphors: the bird with the broken wing is transformed into a turtle slowly moving past the menacing lion whose mouth is closed. The lion is contemptuous but tolerant, condescending but not humiliating like the wolf. In the Short Story the troll and the sun are transformed into the self-confident moon shining at night as in charge of her domain. This very sick patient, a chronic cutter, recovered from her long term depressive condition and stopped cutting herself in the short span of 16 individual sessions.

"The Sun and the Troll." Her anxiety, sense of worthlessness, and depression are evident when she tells of an "ugly troll" who was destroyed when forced out of hiding: Instead of standing up for myself, I crumble. I can't stand acting happy when I'm depressed and react by withdrawing further or making myself inaccessible to others "emotionally."

"The Sun and the Moon." Now the moon is able to accept help, and find a purpose. She benefits from the light of the sun instead of burning up into dust when exposed to it. She has transformed from someone who could not be helped to someone who has difficulty asking for help, but benefits from it nevertheless.

Recording graphically Power Management restructuring changes in this patient's emotional state.
The testing reported above may be graphically portrayed to reflect the changes reported in her relational state versus others. Her self-esteem as reflected in the first set of metaphor-tests can be plotted on the sociogram. The second set, showing empowerment may be also graphically portrayed to indicate improvement of her self-esteem and of her capacity to deal effectively with authority figures. We can graphically portray changes by plotting her position on the sociogram. We place the individual in the powerless pole indicating the degree of powerlessness in the social system. Another variable is the determination of attitude as reflected in the diagrammatic illustration of antagonism versus cooperation, as her set of feelings recorded in the ellipse on the perimeter of the sociogram. respectively as counter clock wise, antagonism, versus clockwise, cooperation, vectors.

The self-analysis of metaphors by the patient/test taker changes the role of the therapist as an analyst into that of an educator.
The test-taker creates the art and interprets his or her metaphors as relational phenomena. The formal theorist as an informed scientist supervises the interpretation of the art. The patient/client/trainee is the artist, the creator, and the analyst and reformer of his/her role. The therapist is a facilitator and caring observer. The test taking individual faces the pattern of relating. S/he recognizes the relational built-in anxieties and counter-phobic mechanisms. S/he is now conscious of the pattern, assumes responsibility to find a power balance in relations as the path toward health. The setting for the pattern to unfold and the

person to encounter her own relational tendencies is no longer the therapy session but one's guided and facilitated encounter with the creative process.

The relational modalities reflect the underlying orderly process, the mental heartbeat. The battery of tests is the stethoscope for the trainee/patient to identify his or her own heartbeat, the predictable six-part process of conflict resolution. The patient/trainee uses it to observe her own heartbeat, the relational modality, to make the diagnoses but also to identify the needed changes. The test taker will consider changes s/he could and is willing to make. The self-assessment's outcome is heightened self-awareness, and clarity on relational changes to be completed over time necessary to reduce any clinical symptoms.

The objectives of this psychotherapy are self-awareness and respect of the relational choices. The assessment promotes self-awareness and evokes power management directives. It may also teach wisdom as spiritual rituals reinforcing power management, rediscovering morality without dogma, but as traditional moral strategies to reinforce self-discipline and behavior change. Spirituality embraces creativity as the means of reinforcing correction of one's patterns. The person learns to value creativity as the admirable meaningful workings of cultures leading to consensus on norms and emotional empowerment. Creativity manifests in all arts as the morality of the plot of stories. Movies and dramas, books and poetry, TV shows on Law and Order reinforce optimal power management directives. The assessment works on its own, but it can be assisted by traditional methods of enhancing wellness.

Traditional therapies, require a long term therapeutic relationship to generate insights on one's relational tendencies, a procedure that yet does not guarantee therapeutic benefits. The question emerges of the role of the assessment's effectiveness, speed, objectivity, accuracy in identifying the unconscious.

The self-assessment simplifies the role of the trainer/therapist into that of an educator facilitator. It simplifies the interpretive challenges of the therapist/ educator; s/he educates and guides the student to organize the information to maximize meaningfulness for the patient/student. The role of the new therapist is merely educational. S/he is a scientist of emotions. As an educator s/he assists in delivering the information on the nature of relational modalities and on the recognition of individual patterns as the manifestation of the universal harmonic. The educator informs the student on how to integrate the testing and extrapolate the findings.

The scientific knowledge of the process, of the modalities and the testing technology, of the moral and spiritual directedness simplify and change the roles of the analyst as well as the spiritual leader into that of an educator; science transforms the role of a patient into that of a trainee or student. The testing transforms therapy into an educational emotional growth experience. Students become self-aware of their version of resolving conflict as a relational syndrome with its respective strengths and weaknesses. They also understand and study the principles of conflict resolution as the universal guiding moral values. The test taker becomes conscious of the unconscious as a phenomenon of wellness that is manageable and also inspirational.

The Role of the Formal Analyst is Educational
The assessment changes the role of the formal analyst. The interpretations of the tests are conveyed by the test taker as factual information; they are educational, diagnostic and therapeutic communications. Note that there is minimal discussion of each case by the authors as the new role of a therapist has changed from being an interpreter to being a commentator of scientific phenomena; it is the client who amplifies on the meaning of her symbols and related meanings.

The focus of the therapist comments changes in the Power Management training.
Changes in the therapist's comments as didactic:

- Accentuating the insights or serf-discoveries contributed by the patient/testee.

- The diagnosis of a relational modality identifying the syndromal sequencing of emotions and behaviors, sensitivities and responses in the dominance modalities as over valuation of the self, combined with anxiety and defensiveness, in the submissiveness modalities as feelings of worthlessness, depression and hostility.

- The detection of the six role process as manifestation of the pattern in both the RMES and the metaphors.

- Identifying the key role state integrating metaphors: disorders of eating, foot fetishism, depression, sexuality seeking self-esteem.

- Couples relational complementarity as in the postal employee, recognizing the parties' patterns as having respective strengths and weaknesses.

Comments or interpretations focus on the scientific features of the testing:

- Validations of the items of the scales and of the metaphors structure and function.

- As syndromal characteristics and subcategories of scales as a six role syndrome.

- Aesthetic issues and their metaphorical scientific significance, formal sequencing of images transformation in the symbolic language of the test taker Gladys, Wise Oak, Mural 7, 8.

- Sharing self-knowledge with the clients by completing the reconstruction of the tests, exemplified with my Mural # 4, My Metaphors Myself.

- Guidance in identifying changes or lack of progress through retesting and exploring the evolution of the pattern.

    Encouraging changes in the management of power for the elimination of pathology

Validations of the Online Delivery of the Self-Assessment
The query survey below documents the impressions generated by the online delivery of the assessment to a group of 33 test takers. The test takers were asked upon the completion of the assessment to address if the experience was didactic, diagnostic and therapeutic. Their responses confirmed that the test taker learned about the theoretical concepts presented in a lengthy essay provided prior to completing the testing and evolved by oneself diagnostic insights and therapeutic directives.

Q22.3. I felt this program of emotional education was informative on the concept of the unconscious as a natural science conflict resolving mechanism.

#	Answer		Response	%
1	✔ Strongly Disagree		0	0%
2	✔ Disagree		1	3%
3	✔ Neither Agree nor Disagree		5	15%
4	✔ Agree		18	55%
5	✔ Strongly Agree		9	27%
	Total		33	100%

Q22.4. I felt this emotional education program clarified the notion of relational modalities as wellness personality non-stigmatizing diagnostic categories.

#	Answer		Response	%
1	✔ Strongly Disagree		1	3%
2	✔ Disagree		2	6%
3	✔ Neither Agree nor Disagree		8	24%
4	✔ Agree		12	36%
5	✔ Strongly Agree		10	30%
	Total		33	100%

Q22.5. I felt this assessment was diagnostic; it helped me to identify my relational diagnosis.

#	Answer		Response	%
1	✔ Strongly Disagree		1	3%
2	✔ Disagree		4	12%
3	✔ Neither Agree nor Disagree		4	12%
4	✔ Agree		9	27%
5	✔ Strongly Agree		15	45%
	Total		33	100%

Q22.6. The metaphor testing is therapeutic; it helped me to better understand my self and to also think of making changes.

#	Answer		Response	%
1	✔ Strongly Disagree		2	6%
2	✔ Disagree		1	3%
3	✔ Neither Agree nor Disagree		1	3%
4	✔ Agree		12	36%
5	✔ Strongly Agree		17	52%
	Total		33	100%

Q22.7. The combined battery, inventory and creativity based tests offered me both diagnostic and therapeutic information about myself.

#	Answer		Response	%
1	✔ Strongly Disagree		1	3%
2	✔ Disagree		1	3%
3	✔ Neither Agree nor Disagree		7	21%
4	✔ Agree		13	39%
5	✔ Strongly Agree		11	33%
	Total		33	100%

Q22.8. The art work arranged on the six role template integrates the fragmented information into a meaningful conflict resolution process.

#	Answer		Response	%
1	✔ Strongly Disagree		1	3%
2	✔ Disagree		3	9%
3	✔ Neither Agree nor Disagree		3	9%
4	✔ Agree		16	48%
5	✔ Strongly Agree		10	30%
	Total		33	100%

Q22.9. Which one or two of the following relational types do you identify with? A for Dorothy, dominant cooperative, B for the Lion, dominant antagonistic, C for the Scare Crow, submissive cooperative, and D for the Tin Man, submissive antagonistic?

#	Answer		Response	%
1	✔ Type A		10	30%
2	✔ Type B		4	12%
3	✔ Type C		18	55%
4	✔ Type D		8	24%

Q22.10. This didactic self-assessment helped me to identify power management changes to improve my relational pattern.

#	Answer		Response	%
1	✔ Strongly Disagree		2	6%
2	✔ Disagree		1	3%
3	✔ Neither Agree nor Disagree		7	21%
4	✔ Agree		17	52%
5	✔ Strongly Agree		6	18%
	Total		33	100%

Q22.11. I identified with one or both of the animal metaphor characters.

#	Answer		Response	%
1	✔ Strongly Disagree		1	3%
2	✔ Disagree		1	3%
3	✔ Neither Agree nor Disagree		1	3%
4	✔ Agree		16	48%
5	✔ Strongly Agree		14	42%
	Total		33	100%

Statistic	Value
Min Value	1
Max Value	5
Mean	4.24
Variance	0.81
Standard Deviation	0.90
Total Responses	33

Q22.12. Completing the creativity component was an emotional experience.

#	Answer		Response	%
1	✔ Strongly Disagree		3	9%
2	✔ Disagree		2	6%
3	✔ Neither Agree nor Disagree		3	9%
4	✔ Agree		13	39%
5	✔ Strongly Agree		12	36%
	Total		33	100%

Q22.13. I was surprised by the personal relevance of the creativity component.

#	Answer		Response	%
1	✔ Strongly Disagree		1	3%
2	✔ Disagree		3	9%
3	✔ Neither Agree nor Disagree		2	6%
4	✔ Agree		12	36%
5	✔ Strongly Agree		15	45%
	Total		33	100%

Q22.14. I think that this survey would be useful for high school students.

#	Answer		Response	%
1	✔ Strongly Disagree		0	0%
2	✔ Disagree		1	3%
3	✔ Neither Agree nor Disagree		6	18%
4	✔ Agree		13	39%
5	✔ Strongly Agree		13	39%
	Total		33	100%

Q22.15. I think that this survey would be useful for clinical evaluations.

#	Answer		Response	%
1	✔ Strongly Disagree		1	3%
2	✔ Disagree		1	3%
3	✔ Neither Agree nor Disagree		5	15%
4	✔ Agree		10	30%
5	✔ Strongly Agree		16	48%
	Total		33	100%

Statistic	Value
Min Value	1
Max Value	5
Mean	4.18
Variance	1.03
Standard Deviation	1.01
Total Responses	33

Q22.16. After taking this survey, I feel more motivated to make changes in my life.

#	Answer		Response	%
1	✔ Strongly Disagree		2	6%
2	✔ Disagree		2	6%
3	✔ Neither Agree nor Disagree		3	9%
4	✔ Agree		11	33%
5	✔ Strongly Agree		15	45%
	Total		33	100%

Statistic	Value
Min Value	1
Max Value	5
Mean	4.06
Variance	1.37
Standard Deviation	1.17
Total Responses	33

Q22.17. The suggested value for taking this emotional education program should be:

#	Answer		Response	%
1	$25		14	42%
2	$50		11	33%
3	$75		5	15%
4	$100		3	9%
	Total		33	100%

The Online Delivery's Statistical Findings Validate the Theoretical Premise

The responses confirmed that the testing is didactic, diagnostic and therapeutic that hence the testing attained its three objectives.

The reason of the testing's effectiveness is because the creative process has become an intelligible, fathomable entity accurately reflecting the personal psychological make up thus allowing insights and emotional growth. The extraordinary approval of the online delivery of the assessment validates the testing as a program of emotional education. Two of the three test-takers who were critical of the experience did not complete the testing. A third one was a very depressed submissive antagonistic person, whose Short Story presented a suicide. This record as a routine assessment that could have saved his life if the testing were used simply as a screening tool.

As didactic, the experience fulfilled the objectives of education: the integration of the humanities and the rigorous sciences, self-knowledge and clarity on moral values.
As diagnostic it led the participants identify their relational modality diagnoses.
As therapeutic,it fulfilled the objectives of therapy; it guided to making changes, it was emotional, and fincally it provided insights and directives for social adjustment.

- The instrument's essay was didactic: the test takers learnt about the unconscious as a scientific conflict resolving entity and the relational modalities as wellness diagnoses. The testing also revealed psychopathologies and identified numerically and with art imagery their intensity.

- The instrument' relational inventory was diagnostic: The test takers found out through the personality inventory about their wellness relational diagnoses identifying their own diagnosis associating it with the appropriate Wizard of Oz character.

- Many test takers benefited from the meaningful integration of their own metaphors into the six-role states of the template. Revision of the assessment addressed improving the interpretation of the test in a continuum.

- The projective tests were therapeutic: The test taker evolved insights and identified through the assessment changes needed to improve one's wellbeing, emotional and social adjustment.

  Indeed reading the text of the metaphors we realize that the test takers identified the particular type of changes. The distressed dominant individuals experienced need for moderation and the submissive ones expressed need for assertiveness.

- The test-takers were happy with the experience and recommend it unanimously for delivery to high school students and its use for clinical evaluations.

- They ascribed to it a high dollar value reflecting the consensus on its meaningful service to them as consumers.

Validation of Constructs
The query results confirming the effectiveness of the assessment validate the underlying formal theoretical hypotheses on the nature of the unconscious as a natural science conflict resolving measurable process.

The findings validate the hypothesis that the unconscious proceeds resolving conflicts along:

1. The three formal dichotomies leading to the four personality types as alternative diagnostic relational modalities; and,

2. That this process unfolds syndromally along the six role emotional transformative sequence to complete a resolution. This syndromal thinking is present in each metaphor as the dialogue between the characters and also upon the integration of metaphors into the syndromal entity portrayed in the metaphor template of the process.

Conclusions from the Validation of the Process

- The visual inspection alone confirms continuity across the six-role plot of the personal drama. Looking at the images we may detect the troubled beginning of the pattern as stressors and its happy ending as loving compromises.

- The validation on the process is provided visually as the images in the first column of the template portraying the Stress role state illustrated with the Conflictual Memories Tests begins the personal drama with images of suffering; while the sixth column, Compromise, completes the resolution of conflict with images from the Short Story portraying happy couples.

- The records represent an excellent scientific document. The text of the testing represents a useful clinical record documenting an evaluation. Retesting later helps in examining the therapy's outcome.

- Thus the two types of tests validate the thesis of the natural science moral unconscious: it is a conflict resolution process guided by three formal operations that unfolds along a six role state dialectic. The formal syndromal integration of emotions is evidence of the conservation of emotional energy and its upgrading to moral order upon the resolution. This order reflects the unconscious as not only being a natural science entity but also as having a moral function, the social adjustment, or normative conciliation.

- The unconscious is spontaneous in its relational choices but once the person becomes conscious of the unconscious the self-awareness predictably seeks to correct unconscious choices along the three principles of conflict resolution: mastery, cooperation and mutual respect.

- The unconscious is indeed a natural science and moral order unit entity that is measurable.

- The information about one's unconscious can be accessed by the person online without a psychologist or a psychotherapist.

- Therapy does not need a therapeutic relationship to identify the transference relationship. This corresponds to the innate, genetically determined and readily measurable personal relational modality.

- The online delivery demonstrates that the battery is effective along its educational, diagnostic and therapeutic goals on its own.

- The assessment provides to the test taker and to the therapist diagnostic information along three formats: it identifies the relational modalities numerically, processed statistically yielding the accurate measurement of one's relational modality, it provides the integration of the test taker's art in the metaphor profile template visually as the six part syndromal unfolding in the personal experiences and finally it provides a textual transcript as a valuable record. The total report is delivered providing quantitative and qualitative information that can be studied thoroughly but also used for the psychological screening of a big number of test takers. The profile allows identifying the dynamics at a glance.

- This wellness education can be delivered to the general public with great benefit cost effectively online without the use of professional services.

- The case studies illustrate the possibility of delivering the self-assessment to a large cohort, such as a classroom, as an emotional education for the individual students and also as a screening instrument enabling the faculty delivering it to detect psychopathology and to consider addressing it effectively.

- We may conclude that the CAB assessment is an emotional educational program that readily helps the test taker to learn about behavior, to identify her modality and to spontaneously arrive at corrective choices. The program conveys to the test taker and the test deliverer the same report informative of the insights and the identified need for changes. It accomplishes all these services without a therapist's or educator's services but allows the educator and therapist to utilize this information to expedite both evaluations and treatments.

Conclusions: The impact of the Integration of the Social and the Rigorous Sciences for Therapy and Education

The case studies unequivocally confirm the correctness of the Formal Theory's postulations. Science has been introduced into psychology. The new concepts change the study of behavior. The formal unconscious redefines psychology. It introduces rigorous epistemology as the measurable syndromal organization of emotions, new wellness and illness diagnostic categories, a different assessment instrument associated with educational and therapeutic interventions clarifying the importance of moral values as the scientific principles of conflict resolution.

Psychology becomes an exact science. Psychotherapy belongs to the public transformed into psycho-education; sciences are studied in the classroom and tested in the laboratory. The science-based humanities must be introduced in the classroom and tested in the laboratory of creativity for self-discovery. Thus students and the general public may learn about behavior, about morality and also about oneself without being in therapy or in classes of catechism. They may and they should learn about all this knowledge through education on the creative process as a conflict resolving entity. *Emotional and moral literacy should be a civil right equal to the other literacies: reading and mathematical.*

Education versus Therapy
The Moral Science moves humanity forward by making psychology fathomable and intelligible and by demystifying psychology and religions integrating them into one meaningful conceptual continuum of a universal harmonic, the perfect universe. Theories of psychology as well as religions are recognized respectfully as complementary partial discoveries of science. The two separate views of the human condition, psychology and religion, are now integrated and unified but also they are made accountable to science. Religions are reconciled as restructurings of the roles of the family relations increasing fairness in the family system, and redefining the divine by attributing to gods the increasingly abstract traits of the human unconscious. Gods evolved in parallel to the family role-relations from being powerful and punitive to becoming compassionate and benevolent. Now fairness and the most abstract definition of the divine blend with each other as the universal harmonic.

The Formal Theory changes education transforming encyclopedic fragmented information to the meaningful and relevant integration of knowledge. It transforms the student teacher relationship into that of an explorer and his guide, as somebody who knows the nature of meaning. The conceptual and technological innovations attain the three elusive objectives of education: the integration of the humanities and the sciences, self-knowledge, and clarity of moral values. Education with these concepts and technology may become meaningful and personally relevant. Education can integrate psychology and morality.

The Political Significance of the Moral Science
The fact that behavior has become the exact Moral Science, with clear diagnostic categories, user-friendly self-assessment, educational interventions becoming spiritual and therapeutic, and that it identifies moral values as scientific principles has significant political impact. The feuding cultural and religious conflicts are founded on the intransigence of religions as normative institutions. Science softens their rigidity and defensiveness, their resistance to change on the basis of their pre-established

views. It deflates traditional concepts and beliefs. Current psychological concepts and religion-based moralities are neither correct nor moral from the scientific and the normative perspective. Both psychological emphasis on the brain and focus on the medical management of illness, and moral and spiritual reliance on traditional cultural normative systems must be modified as misleading incomplete biased perspectives incompatible with the clarity of emotions and relations as advanced by the Moral Science.

The Moral Science
A New Psychology Integrating Behavior and Morality

The Natural Science Moral Order Process

The Formal Theory was inspired by observing a periodic phenomenon transmitted across the five generations of the Greek Cosmogony. This periodic phenomenon was conceptualized as reflecting the unconscious; the unconscious had a distinct structure: six role states and a distinct moral function: conflict resolution. Creativity as the conflict resolving unconscious was studied as a natural science emotional dialectic abiding by the constructs and formulas of two equilibrial models: the pendulum's simple harmonic motion and the three formal operations of the balancing of the trays of a scale. This entity evolved to become the unit of the social sciences, the common denominator of psychology, creativity, morality and the sciences.

The unit order is the key assumption of the Formal Theory. It is a methodological assumption. It identifies the creative process as the circumscribed object for the study of behavior; we know it as the plot of stories now also as consisting of the interrelation of six emotions in formal relation to each other united in the moral process of a conflict resolution.

This unit can be measured with the self-assessment. The case studies present the measurement of the unconscious and its diagnostic and therapeutic impact. They validate the traditional therapeutic principle of becoming conscious of the unconscious as finding wellness in knowing oneself. The assessment's clinical effectiveness confirmed by the statistical findings of the online delivery of the assessment validate Formal Theory's assumption that the creative process, the projection of the unconscious, is a measurable scientific conflict resolution mechanism.

The significance of this concept is that it bridges behavior's opposite positions: agnostic psychology and dogma-based moralities by delivering clarity to the unconscious as seeking a moral end through an orderly psychological and physiological mental automatism. The conflict resolution concept ushers in the scientific era in thinking about psychology and morality.

The Significance of Norms

Conflict is experienced as psychological discomfort upon a normative deviation. It occurs when a person distances oneself from the position of 'acceptable behaviors', the social gravitational force, the state of rest.

This distancing from the point of moral gravity induces a centripetal force, a motivational force, in the unconscious. This force opposite and reciprocal to the displacement represents the force driving the

541

person to conflict resolution targeting <u>normative compliance</u>.

In the case studies we observe the process manifested along its two dimensions: diagnoses along the four alternative relational modalities and the unfolding of the process along the six role-states. The case studies testing-imagery demonstrates first the clarity of a relational modality diagnosis and it shows the unfolding of the process as a harmonic, a triple dialectic emotional oscillation, progressing from a conflict to its dramatic resolution. The motivation driving this unconscious is the need to reduce psychic tension by reconciling the person within the personal normative structure of her/his symbolic universe. This defines the driving motivational force, morality, as originating in the psychic need to comply to the societal rules. Morality is in the spirit of social or normative compliance originating in the unconscious.

The restoration of balance unfolds as a triple pendulum oscillation manifested in all samples of creativity as the triple cycle harmonic. Returning to the point of rest the mind is released from the discomfort of conflict. But something changes in the process. <u>The energy of conflict is captured into the affirmation of the normative moral order intensifying the normative reference</u>. If the gravitation is religious norms, the impact of the resolution is intensification of the investment in this faith. In this fashion instead of the person learning about psychology s/he becomes more religious.

Knowledge of this unit entity greatly improves psychological services: diagnosis and therapy. The case studies reported in this volume utilizing the Conflict Analysis Battery demonstrate the manifestation of this measurable unconscious. Objectivity of the orderly findings and subjectivity conferred by the test takers concur on the correctness of the measurable unconscious, of the meaningfulness of the relational diagnoses, of the effectiveness of the assessment, and of the therapeutic value of the Power Management approach. These findings validate Formal Theory's assumptions on the scientific and moral unconscious. What is also discovered by observing this mechanism is learning about moral development and the intensification of normative institutions.

This finding places morality on scientific foundation and as originating in the unconscious thinking but also raises the question of the importance and correctness of the normative institutions determining personal behavior.

Religions as Normative Institutions
In the course of the history of civilization religions advanced norms as covenants like the Ten Commandments regulating individual behavior seeking to reduce interpersonal conflicts. Covenants specify the acceptable structuring of family relations as in the father-son covenant. Religions evolved historically changing domestic norms by restructuring gender role relations. They evolved from matriarchy to patriarchy, from the father-son covenant to the messianic mother-child alliance, from alienation in Mexico to mutual respect in Judea and from Greek antagonism between the genders to Indian cooperation of men to women. Religions discovered aspects of the scientific conflict resolution process attributing the qualities of the unconscious to the divine as the responsible moral authority modeling behaviors and attitudes but also regulating the roles of domestic partners.

Religions' conflict resolution models are parallel to personality typology offering to their constituencies alternative sociological or normative injunctions in conflict resolution by identifying different formal operations in resolving conflict. The following cultures advanced three alternative operations and corresponding resolutions:

542

- **Greece in the Homeric Epics discovered the principle of mastery of patriarchy domesticating the wild women of matriarchy**. Patriarchy's men in the Iliad and the Odyssey overpowered matriarchal women: Helen of Troy and Klitemnestra her sister, and the Sirens, Circe and Calypso, and pretty innocent Nausica endangering Odysseus homecoming. Zeus is a role model of male chauvinism in being both powerful and a womanizer. His weapon was the lightning bolt and he showed his prowess attributed 50 recorded extramarital relations, which of course antagonized his wife Hera, who constantly undermined his escapades.

- **India discovered in Hinduism and later Buddhism the formal operation of cooperation.** Men cooperate with women, and respect them as in the relation between Vishnu and his wife Lachsmi. The country still reveres Sacred Cows symbolic of the societal role of women. Hinduism promoted the suppressing of desires by choosing asceticism. Lord Siva steps on the demon of the rebellious child. Buddhism is the philosophy of moderation of asceticism through the eightfold path to inner enlightenment. Self-discipline and detachment from desires reduced the pain or conflict evoked by desires.

- **Judea discovered mutual respect in the Father Son covenant.** The Abrahamic religions discriminated against women. They introduced attires concealing their beauty, their power of attractiveness. The concept of divinity evolved from polytheism to male Monotheism based on a loving but just authority who is fighting temptation. Women became respectful of their husbands trustingly surrendering their offspring to them. Judaism suppressing their political role neutralized the social power of women by reducing their capacity to be seductive socially.

What this analysis introduces is that religions represent normative or acceptable ways in resolving conflicts as alternative conflict resolution modalities. So we note that religions endorse a relational modality as the normative philosophy regulating the lives of the faithful. Religions modeled their relational preferences attributing their choices to their respective divinities. We may then say that religions are deifications of a relational modality as a cultural philosophy. Religions as self-differentiating normative institutions evolved their respective value preferences with multiple stories of their heroes exemplifying virtuous conduct. Thus religions evolved in the history of civilization improving the family relations system usually by over-regulating female sexual conduct.

Formal Theory's contribution to morality is in conferring to the unconscious a scientific motivational force propelling it to conflict resolution as the origin of morality. Second it is in the understanding of normative systems by studying cultural systems and demystifying religions as determining normative compliance to alternative types of conflict resolution.

Science identifies cultural systems as alternative and complementary conflict resolutions and detects continuity in the moral or conflict resolving evolution of religions progressing toward fairness in regulating family relations and in the trend to redefine the divine more abstractly, refining the attributes of the divine as increasingly abstract. One of the descriptions of the Judaic divinity coincides with the conflict resolution process as 'God is he who was, is and will be'.

Thus we consider religions as partial and complementary discoveries of the science of conflict resolution and regard the formal conceptualization of the unconscious as reconciling religions among themselves and integrating them within the calculus of the Moral Science.

Normative Authorities in Transition

Religions evolved in succession to each other in the course of the history of civilization restructuring family relations improving the family institution.

Religions through their ongoing revamping have progressively evolved norms increasing fairness in the structure of family relations and increasing the abstraction on the nature of the divine. Religions, observed in an evolutionary perspective, represent phases and stages in the history of civilization improving family relations and redefining the divine more abstractly. Gods have become less anthropomorphic and more conceptual.

Given society's ongoing normative evolution religions represent humanity's sociological conflict resolutions generated to rectify social conflicts or injustices and bring about peace or conflict resolution to the world. In the process of this evolution each religion is a discovery and also a hurdle to progress. Each religion has innovated and also resisted progress: stronger the convictions, more resistant the faith to yield to reason. So religions resist change to improving relations beyond their sanctified discoveries.

Studying the evolution of religions we observe that norms are time limited social covenants. Religions freezing progress as bound to their sanctified normative beliefs have been replaced by new religions and ideologies with more liberal normative solutions. The Messianic religions, the mother child alliances, were an adjustment response to Judaism's Father-Son Covenant. Religions evolve by upstaging older religions. Generated to rectify social injustices these too became institutions that have frozen society at a set of norms defying changes in the civil rights area. They defend the dated paradigms, even if those are unfair, as representing the ultimate definition of moral order.

This normative battle describes the contemporary conflicts between the Abrahamic religions. Historically Judaism evolved from the Gilgamish epic vilifying women's promiscuity. We see the notion in Eve's surrender to temptation and the loss of paradise. Abraham continued on this theme. He rejected pagan divinities from the start breaking his father's pagan idols to promote monotheism and diminished the role of women by being polygamous.

The Abrahamic religions inherited the master patriarch's gender discrimination. All Abrahamic religions are entrenched in the predicament of resisting criticism and modification. They defend their norms self-righteously as sanctified by their absolute divine moral authorities blocking criticism and societal progress. These religions, while having dramatic inspirational value, are obsolete as prejudicial normative institutions generating normative conflicts with modern civil liberties trends. As usual the originally innovative revolutionary norms gradually become reactionary and unjust by sponsoring inequities in view of societal civil rights progress.

Religions have been ahead of psychology in deliberately guiding behavior morally focusing on the one or the three conflict resolution principles or formal operations in their respective catechisms, their programs of emotional education. But now we have a new reality. The Moral Science catches up with religions by clarifying the nature of the unconscious conflict resolving process as the origin of morality and psychology as the Moral Science.

Science thus respects but demystifies religions. Science recognizes the three principles of conflict resolution as the unified abstract equilibrial principles guiding moral thinking and moral motivation. It is the unconscious that now is the origin of morality. It is a scientific moral mechanism characterized by the qualities of the divine: mastery with moderation, cooperation, and mutual respect; these are the physiologically determined moral values that we must deliberately adopt to effectively resolve conflicts. Morality becomes the essence of the study of psychology. Science integrates psychology and religions into the Moral Science placing them both on the scientific foundation of the study of the nature of the creative process.

Time for Reforms of Psychology and Religion
Science demystifies religions by clarifying morality as a scientific conflict resolution phenomenon. Science by attributing moral order to the unconscious taking it from the divine, and attributing to natural laws characteristic of the mental process questions religions' normative or moral authority. The condition for reconciling religions with science is for them to espouse a new truth in preaching morality: teaching the formal operations as the science based moral values and applying these values in rethinking their normative distinctions. This is indeed a tall order but it is the condition for the world to reconcile its feuding moral paradigms.

Science has the right to overrule religions as they represent only partial discoveries of science promoting them as the total truth. They are misleading the public promoting themselves as representing the total truth. In their obstinacy to prevail along their prejudicial normative determinations they are generating societal conflicts handicapping the social adjustment of the mortals. Prometheus is the science that steals the fire of the gods to give it to the mortals.

Deprived of proper scientific analysis, and legitimized politically by the American Constitution religions have monopolized the concept of morality at the expense of reason and societal normative progress. Morality defined by science becomes totally independent of religions and reclaims moral leadership.

The Moral Science demystifies religions depriving them of their magical metaphysical self-righteousness. Science deprives religions of their entitlement for moral leadership on the basis of dogma as it clarifies the psychological and sociological limitations of these moral orders. Science unmasks the Wizards of Oz as religions manipulating public opinion. In contrast to Toto's unmasking of the Wizard's machinations and manipulations of the public, the Science identifies moral order but reduces religions to natural science psychological phenomena with measurable dimensions. Science reduces moral laws and makes them accountable to natural laws as well as civil rights laws. The significance of this development is that science allows rational people to prevail over both agnostic psychology and also theistically inspired thinkers.

Unlike prior criticisms of faiths the Moral Science clarifies morality rather than cancelling it. It places morality on the foundation of science. It informs the public about the means to find inner harmony and societal peace. We may expect this awareness to moderate religions' self-righteousness and psychology's agnosticism and this way to reach a world wide moral consensus on moral values.

Traditional psychology impervious of the human need for moral order misunderstands the essence of behavior. Ignoring the moral make up of the unconscious is unscientific. Theistic religions relying on dogma based imperatives are misleading the public as well, imposing inequitable gender norms. Such discriminations and their organizational authoritarianism monopolizing wisdom is untenable in our times of globalization of science and technology.

Religions should not be allowed to be divisive politicized institutions expropriating the notion of the divine. They must be made accountable to reason as their self-righteousness threatens peace and ecology in the globalized world. Humans need to be aware of the nature of morality as a science and need to seek to free themselves from dogma in order to find peace and social justice in the world.

The Formal Theory addresses psychology and morality as founded on science and not on neurology and revelation. Morality is not determined by external authorities but by the justice inspired human unconscious seeking fairness in conflict resolutions as defined by civil rights laws.

Civil rights laws determine the contemporary norms of what is socially acceptable. Morality is a psychological sociological scientific phenomenon having nothing to do with metaphysics and biology. It is based on rules of emotional processes determined by the unconscious need to reduce psychic and social conflicts generated as deviations from the normatively acceptable behaviors. The public needs to be respectful only to the norms established by contemporary society's unbiased legislators.

The Scientific Moral Position

The integration of psychology, morality and science is a topic of tremendous clinical, educational and political relevance in our times experiencing an extreme polarization between reason and faith. On the one side the field of psychology is dominated by an agnostic, non-psychodynamic, medicalized view of behavior, on the other side a wide public across several religions is inspired by morality as dogma, as theistic moral paradigms. The science of the process reconciles these fragmented perceptions of the mind and of the divine by understanding the divine as the projection of the process.

The Moral Science addresses solving societal conflicts by shifting the normative authority of religions to the civil authority of science-aware legislators. From this perspective morality is the science of the unconscious conflict resolution process and contemporary psychology and religions are incorrect and misleading partial scientific knowledge.

Science demystifies religions as normative institutions representing partial resolutions of conflict. Religions hence become accountable to science. Science identifies their normative limitations as partial understanding of the process corresponding to dated norms of social order. I.e., the science requires resolutions to end upon establishing mutual respect between the parties in conflict.

The Abrahamic religions discriminate in judging genders placing men as superior to women hence they do not evolve to mutual respect between the genders. Such discriminations are unacceptable from the perspective of contemporary normative civil rights standards, which advocate equality among all people, hence mutual respect. While social norms have evolved from the times of Abraham, the Abrahamic religions are immobilized by abiding to the dated norms, the ones they introduced as normative improvements at the time of their inception.

The problem of religions is that they deify particular conflict resolutions as perfect resolutions espousing normative determinations, which eventually are outgrown as society restructures relations and the companion norms. Gods and norms have evolved from matriarchy to patriarchy, from polytheism to monotheism, from the Judaic father son covenant to the Messianic mother child alliance, from theistic absolutes to philosophical belief systems and social justice inspired ideologies. Accordingly gods have evolved as alternative deifications of the newest role models of conflict resolution. Moral authorities are ascribed with the increasingly abstract attributes of the unconscious. This evolution of concepts of the divine as alternative norms explains the current conflicts between reason and faith.

The volume *Science Stealing the Fire of the Gods and Healing the World* retraces the history of religions. They evolved in succession to each other in the course of the history of civilization restructuring family relations improving the family institution as society's ongoing normative evolution. The sculptural trail in the history of love illustrates paradigm shifts along sociological conflict resolutions generated to rectify social conflicts or injustices. It highlights the accomplishments and limitations of the Abrahamic family. It shows how the Messianic religions, the mother child alliances, were an adjustment response to Judaism's Father-Son Covenant.

The scientific conceptualization of the process clarifies and integrates psychology and morality; it empowers the public redefining morality as based on reason to prevail over theism and over agnosticism. Providing the new insights on morality can free people from clinging to concrete unemotional psychology and to traditional divisive theistic revelation-based beliefs.

It shows how religions were generated to rectify social injustices but also how they become institutions that freeze society at a set of norms in spite of changes in the social political normative landscape, how they defend dated solutions as sacred presenting their partial perspectives as the universal moral order.

Conclusion

The Moral Science is a new psychology. It radically changes the way we conceptualize the unconscious, diagnosis, assessment, therapy, but also morality.

- Instead of an unconscious that is generating conflicts and is non-logical we identify the creative process as a scientific conflict resolving measurable entity.

- Instead of illness based diagnoses we identify wellness relational modality syndromes.

- Instead of multiple atheoretical diagnostic assessments the Conflict Analysis Battery identifies the unconscious as a measurable formal relational modality with the help of the personality inventory and as a six role state syndrome by tapping creativity for self-discovery.

- Instead of multiple divisive moral paradigms we identify morality as the Science of Conflict Resolution where moral values are the three formal operations that guide the process to resolutions. These are: mastery, cooperation and mutual respect.

The formal six-role process is shown to be the unifying order integrating psychology and morality by placing them on the scientific foundation of the creative process. The emotional transformative effectiveness of the training experience validates the formal theoretical assumption. Test takers recognize the conceptual and technological advantages of the Moral Science utilizing the Conflict Analysis Battery. They recognize that the four new concepts rethink psychology, revamp therapy and education, and reconcile religions among themselves as partial and complementary discoveries of the Moral Science.

The Moral Science's concepts integrate psychology, sociology, diagnosis, assessment, morality with science by placing them on the formal analysis of the creative process. The theory provides a meaningful language that translates all private moral languages into a science that can educate the public and heal cultural conflicts as well as individual ones.

The case studies of this volume confirm the educational benefit of implementing this conceptual and technological development. Programs of emotional education, like Power Management, should be used for the education of the public. Education can be improved by delivering in the classroom the integration of the humanities and the sciences, self-knowledge, and clarity of moral values as the scientific principles of the unconscious. This knowledge can also be used to expedite therapy, train workers, political leaders, executives, prisoners, couples in conflict and soldiers involved in cross-cultural warfare.

Conclusions from the Research on
the Creative Process as the Introduction to the Case Studies

Summary of the Power Management Intervention
The unconscious process is identified as the object of scientific analysis. It is a homeostatic physiological mechanism reducing psychic tension through normative conciliation. This mechanism, as the inner need for mastery, cooperation and mutual respect, targets peace of mind and social justice. This emotional syndrome is the origin of all psychological and moral behavior.

Point #1
The Nature of the Unconscious Process

Methodology

- The Formal Theory advances a shift in method from axiomatic propositions on the nature of the unconscious to the formal, relational analysis of emotions in complete stories as syndromal conflict resolution totalities.

- We identify the process manifesting as a syndromal dialectic entity consisting of six emotions: stress and response, anxiety and defense, reversal and compromise. These emotions are guided by three formal operations: passivity is transformed to activity, antagonism to cooperation and alienation to mutual respect.

- This methodological change in the social sciences, amounts to a paradigm shift from stories we believe in that divide humanity, to identifying the universal plot of stories as the paradigm that delivers meaning to all.

Epistemology

- The unconscious is a periodic natural science phenomenon abiding by the formulas of the Simple Harmonic Motion and the operations of the equilibrial scale. It is a natural science six-role state harmonic guided by three formal operations.

- Behavior's object of study is this unconscious formal organization of associations in any sample of creativity.

- The creative process is then a moral, meaningful, directional natural science phenomenon; it is the object for the scientific analysis of behavior.

- The process is both a natural science and a universal moral or conflict resolution phenomenon.

- As both a scientific and moral order entity it reconciles the rigorous sciences with the humanities and transforms psychology into the exact Science of Conflict Resolution, the Moral Science.

- The process is the atomistic unit of a new exact and conflict resolving or moral psychology.

Physiology

- The unconscious process is a homeostatic physiological mechanism reducing psychic tension through the expression of emotions, through actions and through attitude changes. This mechanism is guided by three equilibrial principles: mastery, cooperation and mutual respect.

Conflicts as Normative Deviations, Religions as Normative Institutions

- Normative deviations, aggression or oppression, generate conflicts, psychic tension, to the individual. The motivation to resolution seeks to restore the rest state. By reducing social and psychic tension or discomfort and experiencing relief. This occurs upon normative conciliation. Relief of tension, as resolution, is experienced as pleasure or rest. Conflict energy, or distress, is transformed to order.

- Rest, reduction of psychic and social tension, may be achieved through social change as the restructuring of norms, of social role relations.

- Religions are normative institutions; they seek regulation of conflict resolution by establishing norms. As alternative conflict resolutions they have discovered the principles of formal operations and are forerunners of the Moral Science. They have evolved increasingly fair conflict resolution paradigms by rethinking norms of family role relations and by attributing the characteristics of the unconscious process to the increasingly abstract and ecumenical divine.

Point#2
Diagnostic Categories

- We recognize four formal alternative ways of resolving conflict. They are the four relational syndromes: dominance and subordinacy, both qualified as having cooperative and antagonistic variables. The four relational modalities represent wellness personality diagnoses, which may decompensate leading to corresponding alternative types of psychopathology.

Point #3
The Assessment

- The relational modalities are readily measurable with the use of the personality inventory of the Conflict Analysis Battery.

- The Conflict Analysis Battery is an educational, diagnostic and therapeutic self-assessment; it uses a relational inventory and projective creativity tasks to identify one's relational modality.

- The projective tests identifying six emotions are integrated relationally to reconstruct the syndromal six role state sequence of emotions.

- The diagnosis and its syndromal integration of experiences lead a person to insights, healing and self-corrective changes.

550

- The assessment is diagnostic and therapeutic.

- Compounded with information on the process the assessment becomes a complete emotional education program.

Point #4
Therapy and Psycho-Education

- Creativity and Power Management is a concise and comprehensive program of emotional and moral education that uses the creative process for cognitive study of behavior and for self-discovery. The program delivers insights, enlightenment and wisdom.

- Emotional Education imparts knowledge and insights. It helps managing power by informing the individual about social norms and personal adjustment patterns.

- The scientific principles of conflict resolution: mastery, cooperation and mutual respect, provide clarity on the nature of moral values as the guiding principles for behavior modification.

- For education to become meaningful and relevant it must inform the individual about the universal harmonic in all aspects of behavior, psychology, morality, the arts and make this information personally relevant. It does so by utilizing creativity for self-discovery. Test takers become conscious of the unconscious as their diagnostic entity. They identify themselves changes needed to deal effectively with emotions by deliberately espousing the conflict resolution principles.

The Diagnostic Function of the Assessment

- The two types of assessment, inventory and the projective test, cross-validate each other contributing to the validity and the reliability of the instrument.

- The key application of Formal Theory's unconscious is in recognizing the syndromal organization of emotions predicting the unfolding dialectic of the six role state process guided by three formal operations. The assessment through the battery testing reveals the occurrence of the three alternative formal operations modulating individual responses, the two formal distinctions of passivity activity, cooperation antagonism. The third formal operation, the alienation versus mutual respect corresponding to the psychic tension. It confers quantitative rather than qualitative distinction.

- The key finding from the assessment is diagnostic by identifying one's relational modality, one's category of resolving conflict, along the two formal dichotomies passivity/activity and antagonism/cooperation. This diagnosis is qualified by the third formal operation, the dichotomy between alienation and mutual respect pertaining to the psychic tension. The first two distinctions identify four clinically distinct syndromes, while the third formal operation quantifies the intensity of unresolved conflicts. These are the fundamental wellness diagnostic categories; the third operation, reflecting intensity of alienation as unresolved conflict, corresponds to a level of pathology or illness.

- The online testing automatically delivers scores for the respective relational scales and the psychic intensity. The scores are very significant in terms of identifying wellness and illness. These numbers are also plotted graphically as intensity of each item and each relational modality in a linear fashion.

- Retesting individuals has shown the numbers are 85% the same at the second measurement indicating the reliability of the personality inventory. The metaphor testing duplicate the relational process but also show nuances of change. The metaphors are more sensitive in reflecting personality growth or change.

- The information from the inventory segment serves also in a triage screening of groups of test takers. The relational modalities scores detect pathology. Individuals scoring high on psychic tension and on modality relational either may be referred for further investigation, education or alternatively medical treatment, delivered by appropriate therapists.

- The protocols, as the clinical record, reflect objectively the relational modality as a wellness and or illness diagnosis.

- The tests reveal the intellectual make up of the person and his/her receptivity for growth. This set of tests predicts the person's attitude and capacity to benefit from the more advanced segment of this intervention.

The Therapeutic Function of the Assessment

- The testing combines cognitive, psychodynamic and behavioral therapies integrated within the self-assessment. Utilizing creativity for self-discovery the assessment is not only an intellectual experience but an emotional one, hence the assessment is not only diagnostic but also therapeutic. The questionnaire accompanying each test is constructed as a Socratic dialogue drawing out of the test taker insights and willingness for making changes.

- Students/patients become conscious of the unconscious as a set of personal emotions. They experience them in the course of the testing. They also identify by themselves changes needed to deal effectively with these emotions by deliberately espousing the principles of conflict resolution.

- All educational, clinical and online delivery case studies reflect emotional growth in the evaluation process. The test taker composes stories and always identifies at the end of the exercise with the heroes of the story, thus deriving insights from the compositions as well as references for personal growth.

- The testing identifies the process objectively with its qualifications and quantifications reflecting how a person experiences and responds to stressors.

- Diagnosis identifies a person's relational spectrum, the range of relational modalities characterizing one's personality. Diagnosis identifies the key role state integrating the testee's emotions, life episodes, in a particular symbolic system. Of significance also are the relational and psychic intensity scores of an individual clarifying the difference between wellness and illness.

- It is possible to monitor therapy outcome. The intervention begins with an evaluation assessment followed by a single or repeated use of the workbook. The assessment represents the method of intervention that continues to be diagnostic and therapeutic helping the individual to deal with hidden emotions and also to make behavioral changes. The repetition of the assessment serves monitoring the therapy outcome and reflects the state of resolution in considering termination of the training or alternatively the need to begin therapy.

- The case studies indicate that the educational delivery is therapeutic and that the same intervention can be used for well and for diagnosed individuals.

- The assessment's completeness as a diagnostic and therapeutic intervention indicates the self-sufficiency of the testing process and the reduced need for a highly qualified professional to deliver the psycho-educational objectives.

Wellness Education versus Therapeutic Clinical Use of the Testing

- The cognitive segment of the training informs the testee about the structure and function of the unconscious and the relational modalities.

- The experiential segment informs one of the personal dynamics. The assessment delivers insights to the testee. It also elicits from the testee the identification of attitudinal changes a person needs to make. Hence the assessment by itself is diagnostic and therapeutic.

- This program being wellness education and also therapeutic, may be equally useful for the school as the place to study wellness and for the therapy setting, as the place to treat illness. The difference in the two settings is in the emphasis on the respective alternative segments of the delivery, the cognitive versus the experiential. Education provides a broad cognitive perspective into the nature of the process. Therapy does not need this broad educational information; its objective is reduction of symptoms.

Chapter Three
Therapy Outcome Studies

The studies demonstrate the correctness of the two syndromal distinctions. They demonstrate the predictive value of relational diagnoses as alternative personality types and help in clarifying the appropriateness of changes in the respective modalities: assertiveness for the submissive and emotional restraint for the dominant individuals. The diagnoses are helpful in developing insights and in making changes.

The studies also demonstrate that the assessment works in two types of delivery: in the educational setting without therapy, and in the therapeutic setting without education and that also works for cases of wellness and of illness. The outcomes attest to the value of the assessment process but do not lessen the relevance of the therapeutic relationship for either diagnostic or therapeutic objectives. The credit for the positive outcomes of the Power Management intervention does not refute the value of a personal therapeutic relationship especially in cases of severe psychopathology.

Judging Therapy Outcome and Documenting Changes
In standard outcome research the criteria for judging effectiveness are observing clinical symptoms and setback episodes through self-report questionnaires. Symptom reduction has reflected on the appropriateness of medications, and alternatively attributed credit to the therapist's interventions, representing a therapeutic modality and qualifying the effectiveness of the therapeutic intervention.

In most of our studies we are not concerned with observation of symptoms as we have been dealing mostly with well individuals. Improvements achieved through power management are judged observing personal relational growth. Relational improvements are measured through the repeated use of the battery assessment.

Criteria in Judging the Effectiveness of the Power Management Intervention: Symptom Reduction Versus Relational Personality Changes

By examining outcomes we attribute improvements to the assessment as the common denominator of all interventions. The self-assessment rather than the analysis of transferential dynamics has generated the diagnostic insights as well as the directives for behavioral changes. The outcome studies reported in this volume confirm the effectiveness of the self-assessment as the key component of Creativity and Power Management. Of course the therapeutic relationship is crucial especially dealing with pathology. On the other hand educational work may be considered as therapeutic. We may also question the issue of therapeutic interventions because many of the case studies were evaluations rather than real long-term therapies. But quite a few of the clinical cases represent positive long-term therapy outcomes.

Identifying Outcome Through Comparing Parallel Symbolic Configurations

To measure therapy outcome, to judge the effectiveness of the formal theoretical intervention, we use two relational variables: power position polarizations and attitude, cooperative versus antagonistic disposition; these two variables are reflected in the repeated use of the battery of tests. The two parameters identify progress made and changes still outstanding and required to achieve wellness.

Thus Formal Analysis measures outcome through the observation of relational parameters as these are reflected by contrasting retesting records for parallel metaphor changes. The relational criteria consist in observing the formal restructuring of relations as reflected in the test takers' succession of protocols. We examine the evolution of a person's self-image and interpersonal relations through the formal interpretation of metaphors. Metaphors are judged as reflecting the two variables: power versus powerlessness identified in the choices of conflicted figures and the qualities of attitude reflecting cooperation versus antagonism identifiable in the figures' interactions. The relational diagnosis provides a universal context on pathology. We recognize diagnostic patterns and their pathologies and their therapeutic changes as a spectrum of complementary deviations from the norm with the respective emotional counterbalances.

We identify growth through a number of alternative techniques portraying metaphorically relational changes:

- **We compare the parallel tests in successive volumes of workbooks.**
  The metaphors reflect changes. Formal outcome studies monitor relational progress by comparing equivalent tests in succession of workbooks. These accurately portray the psychosocial relational reality, revealing any personal advances in resolving conflicts. The images and the companion texts in the test taker's words illustrate the formal relational variables connecting one's self in the context of others. The conflict resolution syndromal restructurings reflect the evolution of the 'self versus others' relationships.

- **The key device reflecting changes and emotional growth has been the integration of testing on the six role state template.** This structure integrating the tests meaningfully generates the impression on the psychodynamic evolution of the person through the intervention. The template reflects the power management relational principles of mastery, cooperation and mutual respect revealing how the person changes in resolving conflicts.

- **The personality inventory** usually does not change substantially along the therapy except in reflecting symptom reduction. The restructuring of relations is reflected more sensitively in the identity of animal choices, their qualifying adjectives and their exchanges. Growth is reflected in the insights and willingness to make changes. These changes are quantifiable representing the position of self within the social system and the related intrapsychic emotional responses. The tests correlate image of the self, social conduct choices with the evolution of emotions and related clinical symptoms.

- **Outcome is judged by the clients, students and patients, through their self-report essays required upon the intake evaluation and upon termination of therapy.** The self-report, letter to oneself, may be judged as to the awareness of one's relational diagnosis as the key factor that determines one's emotional adjustment. The wellness relational diagnoses make a person conscious of the unconscious. The conscious trainee identifies needed relational modifications and grows emotionally in the context of relationships. Relational diagnosis acquaints a person with the dynamics of one's actions and related emotions, strengths and weaknesses, as manageable power choices.

- **A simple routine set of before and after drawings contrast one's feelings regarding key issues. Drawings of the before and after states of mind contrast how one feels about issues like therapy, oneself, the future, one's partners, etc,.** Tests of this kind are used to assess the patient's perceptions before and after the initial two sessions. These are also occasionally used for the patient to evaluate the outcome of therapy upon termination. The images identify progress completed as changes in each of the particular areas, such as self, relations with people, the feelings experienced prior to and after the completion of therapy. The art sketches reflect eloquently the progress achieved.

- **The monitoring of episodes of self-destructive behaviors has been used in the case of the 'Wolf and the Bird with the Broken Wing'.** The list of episodes of self-mutilation is monitored along medications used, and eliciting experiences reported by the patient in the course of the therapy. We notice the reduction of incidents of cutting. Sixteen sessions later she was totally free of self mutilations; she was no longer in need of medications and ended therapy, while assuming difficult stressor as responsibilities in her life.

- One of the last pages of the workbook consists of a questionnaire evaluating the testing experience to be completed upon the termination of the assessment process in providing insights and meaning to the testee.

- **Case studies with multiple workbook evaluations: progress reported in both submissive and dominant modalities, both in the cases of interns and of patients.**
There are several case studies, which present repeated workbook evaluations. The first workbook identifies the baseline evaluation, while the second workbook presents the evolution of one's emotions toward recovery. Changes can be also detected in single book therapeutic evaluations. For many cases the second record represents the completion of the therapeutic work. In some cases therapy continues with multiple workbooks but upon the final one we see definite growth and transformation as clearly identifiable deviations from the original format.

❖   PROGRESS RECORDS OF THE INTERNS NON-CLINICAL CASE STUDIES   ❖

NOTE: THESE OBSERVATIONS PERTAIN TO CASES PRESENTED IN
VOLUME 6, THE EDUCATIONAL DELIVERY OF THE ASSESSMENT

Chris, 'Badger versus Rabbit' identified the resolution of his submissive antagonism within the completion of his one book evaluation. He realized his attitude and reversed this through his awareness of arrogance and subterfuge of others. The hostile badger ready to kill the rabbit becomes in his Short Story the amused king respectful of the unpretentious Janitor. Aware of his attitude he dealt with his feelings of rivalry towards his younger brother admitting the need to reduce his tendency of setting himself up to be a resentful victim.

Intern, Melissa, 'Jealous Flowers,' completed five workbooks during a 20-year span as monitoring evaluations without receiving therapy. She observed the evolution of her dominance pattern as a wellness manageable condition. She recognized her dominance and antagonism, her competitiveness and agony for success underlying her time pressures. The span of books began in early adulthood and recorded the manifestation of the pattern into middle age. She learned about herself and managed her needs for power associated with her related reduction of her discomfort and anxieties.

Intern, 'Elephant and Fawn,' completed two books within the context of her educational relationship. The workbooks reflect her resolving her relationship with her mother. She recognized that it was her anger at her mother for her alcoholism, leading to her fears of mother's leaving home. She tested her mother's love by asking her and the rest of the family to do the testing. Her mother's tests confirmed her mother's love. This information led the intern to forgive her mother; this change of attitude released her from her anger, which in turn put an end to her fears of leaving home. In her case we observe the reduction of her fears as directly proportional to the reduction of her anger at her mother. The problem was one of the intern's dominance and related paranoia.

'Wind versus Sun' realized that his submissiveness and resentfulness were going hand in hand.

The 'Squirrel and Dinosaur', recognized dominance as leading him to anxiety, defensive isolation, being voiceless, and in this subtle way he found the courage to express himself.

❖   PROGRESS RECORDS OF THE CLINICAL CASE STUDIES   ❖

The Submissive Individuals Assert Themselves
Submissive patients and interns addressed their powerlessness and their escapist responses.

The Anteater, a sexual abuse victim, upon her evaluation and without therapy came to recognize her submissiveness in her relation with her grand-father and recorded her new set of realizations in the letter to her self. We frequently identify relief of symptoms in the course of the completion of the evaluation.

Wise Oak generated a set of books reflecting a satisfactory resolution of self-image and relations. We note growth in managing power and reduction of symptoms. Dealing with rejection and reactively seeking love generated conflicts, which were resolved through her emotional empowerment. Asserting herself led to relational and emotional stability.

The case of the 'Vulture and the Snake' has several sequences of thematic cycles utilizing a single test, the AMT with ongoing evolution of insights achieved by expressing herself freely with poetry and insightful art. Her seeking approval and having difficulty expressing her anger is reflected in the moat series. Dealing with the eating disorder as her secret compensation by binging and purging eventually led her to become comfortable expressing her feelings. She completed a long-term therapy relationship finding a new identity. Dealing with her hostile feelings and escapist binging tendencies she was able to feel reconciled with her husband.

The 'Wolf and the Bird with the Broken Wing' completed two books. Her healing is reflected in her second book. We see evidence of her healing by contrasting the parallel Short Story Images as well as her other metaphors. We witness her growth from a scared self-hating flammable Troll into became the proud Moon. She found good feelings about herself and stopped hurting herself.

The submissive Judge, who required annulment for his marriage from the Catholic Tribunal completed his self-evaluation writing his insights and explaining to the Tribunal how his submissiveness condition had affected his marital adjustment.

The art teacher 'Surviving as a Dog' understood being self conscious and unable to deal with his anger as underlying his gastrointestinal problems. Comparative images, drawings of the before and after therapy states, reflect his emotional growth. They illustrate his evolution in a number of relationships. He became comfortable with ladies, with his grand children, and with his daughter. He was less preoccupied with his symptoms.

Dominant Individuals Sought to Moderate Their Power Strivings

'Lame Ant and Flea' completed four books reflecting setbacks but also his healing. He recognized his defiance manifested early in his life dealing with his mother related to his being scared of performing. He connected his anger with his phobia. His books reflect how he evolved from depression and self-hate, performance anxiety, and self-consciousness to feeling free of the depression and overcoming his performance anxiety. His identity of a damaged pair of diminutive and defective animals 'The Flea and an Ant' improved substantially as he completed therapy with a metaphor about a ' wounded Lion and an Eagle'. The changes reflect his sense of self as restored.

The 'Turkey and the Mountain Lion' completed two work-books. A big insight occurred as she connected her paranoid fears of her step-children as the projection of her own hostilities at her step mother. Her second workbook recorded emotional growth, as the resolution of angry feelings against her father that had generated interpersonal difficulties in their relationship. She evolved from holding grudges at her father to being able to reconcile herself with him. Her emotional growth allowed her to feel secure with her partner and his children and she proceeded to marrying him after a six year-long conflict ridden relationship.

The 'Cheshire Cat and the Pit-bull' completed two books as well. He realized his fears as a consequence of his own dominance in dealing in a confrontational way with the school system. The second workbook shows his recovery as a compromise in his dominance dynamics; yet his dominance prevailed as his pattern of adjustment. His workbooks reflect moderation, diminution of overt power struggle but the continuation of a power play in his behaviors. He was able to avoid being fired from the school system as he prevailed using a medical handicap and surviving the humiliation of his being terminated for insubordinacy.

The 'Holocaust survivor' dealt with the unresolved guilt for wishing to be alone from her controlling grand parents as she became aware of their deportation. Following therapy she completed artwork on her own, which she delivered confirming her release from her inscrutability, her resistance to emotions.

Sample Evaluation of Therapy Outcome by Comparing Equivalent Tests in Wise Oak's Succession of Workbooks

To appreciate the respective growth we compare the equivalent thematic items: balloons, masks, conflictual memories, animal and fairy tale metaphors, dreams and short stories of two consecutive books. We contrast the equivalent tests in each book and detect the subtle evolution of self and of the modification of psychosocial balance leading to the reduction of personal and interpersonal conflicts. In all her metaphors we see the striking difference between the original set of tests and the subsequent as representing accurately the state of growth and stability of the transformation accomplished through the intervention.

The set of two books convey a resolution of self-image and relations; the set attests to growth in managing power leading to the reduction of her symptoms.

1. Stress: Conflictual memories become more revealing of intense emotional experiences. The testee becomes aware of the conflicts that evoked painful feelings.

2. Response: The mask becomes different. In this case the clown is a new image and role showing her overcoming the helplessness of the first mask.

3. Anxiety: What is behind the mask is a beautiful self in the second version.

4. Defense: Her first AMT reflected her need to escape, a horse jumping the fence in the turf of the bull. This book presents her intense anxiety generated by her escapism. The second set presents her empowerment and her ability to interrupt her escapism. She managed her anxiety evoking tendencies. This pattern of growth manifests consistently across her set of metaphors, reflecting her personal adjustment accompanied with reduction of psychological symptoms such as anxiety, suicidal preoccupation and a sense of futility.

   She was able to stabilize herself emotionally. She also mastered her secret binging. The escapism as a conflictual issue in the evaluation book is corrected in the second book by learning self-restrains. It was her inner growth that decreased the need for attention. Feeling better about her-self preempted the need for seeking approval or attention. Her self-restrain eliminated her anxiety symptoms.

5. Reversal: The dream test is extraordinarily revealing. The original dream presented her trapped in a pit of snakes with the family above laughing at her misery. The recovery dream presented her walking out of the pit.

6. Compromise: In her original short story she is yielding to temptation and experiences anxiety, whereas in the recovery one she is able to avert temptation correcting the distressing behaviors of her husband.

The patient volunteered to complete a third book several years later. This showed a very different set of images. She was much more comfortable in presenting herself and her feelings zeroing into the heads of her animal metaphors. Her problem was being a nurturing grand mother afraid of loosing her beloved grand children to a daughter-in-law moving out of the state. She was projecting her own dependency needs to her grand children and was eager and anxious to provide love for them.

Marital Complementarity of Opposites

A couple presents the complementary dynamics and compatibility of opposite relational modalities but also the pathology evolving in the union of opposites. It is important to highlight the complementarity of opposites in marital relations. A troubled couple exemplifies this very typical configuration and the complication that frequently occurs: under stress such unions decompensate. Examining carefully the relational scales and metaphors we see the relational extreme opposites in this couple. This discrepancy in personalities explains the complex pathology that evolves in such unions. It is important to understand couples' dynamics to correct pathology through relational power management.

He was a very aggressive dominant person. One of his dominant behaviors was his interest in pornography through watching video-tapes. He stole such a tape from the mail at the post-office where he worked and he was fired from his job for this behavior; frustrated from his wife, who had withdrawn under his outbursts protecting herself, he was considering killing her and their ten year old son and committing suicide. In despair upon that critical moment he sought help and was hospitalized.

His relational modality reflected extreme dominance. His animal metaphor was that of a bull and a cow.

Her relational modality scales were clearly submissive. Her animals were a sheep and a bear. She was a vulnerable, dependent person seeking love and safety escapes as a sheep, a needy, vulnerable, defenseless woman.

This marriage of extremely opposite personalities illustrates what is typical of the complementarity of relational modalities in marital relationships. The opposites attract because partners are able to provide for each other the needed support and mutual admiration; same modalities, either dominant or submissive, usually are incompatible; they experience conflicts from the outset. Two dominant individuals fight too much intolerant of each other's need for power and control. They are prone to get frustrated and angry, to test limits and argue, defend, control and walk away. Two submissive individuals fail in their relationships because they are prone to withdraw, to not communicate, and become hostile, depressed or addicted.

This couple dramatizes the decompensation inherent in dominance and subordinacy partnerships. It occurs as the relationship finds itself under a great deal of stress as the dominant person, the limit tester, gets in trouble and puts too many demands on the inhibited and insecure law abiding partner, who withdraws instead of as usual continuing to provide support. This dominant husband was transgressive in a number of ways but she was numb and unable to restrain him or reassure him anymore.

Principles of Power Management

Dominant patients and interns dealt with moderating power to lessen their states of anxiety. Submissive individuals became aware of their need for assertiveness. The key message from the assessment experiences was the same for interns and patients. It has been understanding one's diagnosis as the identification of one's relational pattern delivering insights on how to correct it by making power management adjustments. Learning about one's relational modality has impact on one's life experiences. It leads to identifying changes one should make to avert the conflicts and personal pain caused by paranoid anxieties or repressed urges for conflict generating actions. It is important to realize the psychodynamic nature of behaviors and emotions, recognizing the difficulty making changes but being self aware of the set of needed changes. Personality types do not change; attitudes do. Pathology is a question in the degree of willingness for self-management.

Table Reviewing Outcomes in the Respective Groups of Case Studies

Interns

Case study interns, educational intervention	Length of intervention	Conflicts identified, clinical symptoms	Diagnosis Relational modality	Resolution and outcome
Jealous Flowers	5 books internship without therapy	Competitive relations, anxiety	Dominant cooperative	Self-awareness Effective Power management
Badger versus rabbit	Evaluation and essay on theory during internship	Hostility as a problem	Submissive antagonistic	Insightful self analysis
The frozen dinosaur and the perky squirrel	Evaluation, review analysis work assignment			
The Elephant and the Fawn	2 books	Separation anxiety	Dominant cooperative	Alleviated simply by reviewing her relationship with her mother with a workbook analysis of mother's personality
Wind versus Sun	Evaluation and review	Relationship difficulties, arrogance, isolation	Submissive antagonistic	Made changes in metaphors reflecting change of attitude
Maleficient and the Sleeping Beauty	Evaluation and analysis by Dr Albert L			

Submissive Patients' Clinical work	Number of Sessions			
Wise Oak	Three books 15 sessions	Multiple symptoms, anxiety and depression, eating disorder, Marital difficulties	Submissive cooperative Antagonistic	Intercepted her condition reason for her need for attention and symptoms, developed self esteem and changed escapist need for attention
Wolf and Bird with Broken Wing	Two books/16 sessions	Cutting herself, multiple suicidal attempts	Submissive antagonistic. Understood her need for self punishment	Complete recovery with assumption of responsibilities, stopped meds and therapy
Vulture and Snake	Metaphor evaluation and follow up monitoring, 40 sessions	Eating disorder, escaping parental controls	Submissive antagonistic	Marked recovery with changes in her communication
Surviving like a Dog	10 sessions	GI problems	Submissive	Recovered with relations and feeling good about self, reduction of symptoms
Caribou Falling Behind the Herd	3 session evaluation	Marital conflicts	Submissive cooperative and antagonistic	Insight into his personality and complications for holding feelings back
The anteater	2 session evaluation with out therapy	Victim of sexual abuse by grand father	Submissive cooperative	Developed good sense of self integrating experiences

Dominant Patients				
The Cheshire Cat and the Pit-bull	6 sessions completing 2 books	Conflict with employer about to be fired	Dominant cooperative	Resolved problem by both recognizing defense pattern but also manipulating system
Circus Elephant versus a Butterfly	Evaluation without therapy	Anxiety about commitment, relationship with mother	Dominant	Overcame anger and distrust, married but never changed personal pattern
The Unicorn defeating the Dragon	10 session therapy	Performance anxiety, as a student presenting papers	Dominance	Overcame anxiety and excelled in presenting self, reconciled with family
Lion versus Lion	Evaluation for residual trauma, 3 sessions	Unresolved issues about guilt for surviving	Dominance	Resolved chromic anxiety
Terrier and the Beefallo	2 books, 4 session evaluation and 10 session group therapy	Abandoned by father, domestic anxieties related to intolerance of boyfriend's children		Cured of anxiety understanding her own resentment to stepmother, reconciled with her father
The eagle and the lion	4 books and six sessions	Performance anxiety as a pianist	Dominance and anxiety	Resolved and improved sense of self
Couple Compatibility study	2 person evaluation for attempted murder suicide	Evaluations reflecting the relational complementarity of marital partners	Dominant husband Submissive wife	Satisfactory response to intervention

Chapter Four
The Role of Therapist in the Self-Assessment

About diagnosis and diagnosticians: Is the therapist necessary in making the diagnosis or does the self-assessment deliver the diagnosis on its own?
Many case studies have been presented to highlight the significance of two variables:

First, the distinction on the relational diagnoses by separating the submissive from the dominant case studies.

Second, the distinction of delivery: educational, therapeutic and online as self-directed therapy, which has been the case with several therapeutic evaluations using the workbook; is a doctor necessary or can the person/patient find the diagnosis on her/his own?

The analysis of metaphors validates the inventory findings and simplifies the task of a therapist. Another traditional therapist task has been furthering change by identifying patterns that need to be changed. This role now reverts to the trainee. It is her/his role to identify patterns repeated throughout time as they manifest in one's creativity exercises, and to seek to make changes. Changes follow the innate principles of conflict resolution. The teacher therapist may encourage a thoughtful self examination and articulation of one's goals for change as the student observes one self and sets goals for change.

Interpreting Transference Distortions as Validating Relational Diagnosis
The relational pattern can be identified in the trainee-teacher relationship as well as in that of the patient-therapist one. Awareness of this pattern is critical in the development of insights and in beginning to make changes. It is important for the educator to know that, the student, as in traditional therapy the patient will typically come to distort the perception of the authority figure. This pattern must be identified and diagnosed as evoked by one's role choices, themselves determined by one's unconscious. The particular distortions of reality provide the opportunity to recognize the underlying relational pattern. Of course as with therapists, educators need to be careful to relate correctly with their students, who are prone to follow their innate relational tendencies and related defenses. It is very important that the teacher is appropriate in her/his conduct that is responding with insights, correlating, instead of negating or

reciprocating to the client.

The self-assessment reduces the authoritarianism assumed by the analyst and projected on to the therapist by the patient. The new analyst is not a powerful authority figure and the new patient is not a passive, dependent partner; this therapist/educator is merely a facilitator in the patient's/student's soul-searching journey. The new therapist merely guides the exploration, educates or supervises the trainee to organize the itinerary in the generation and organization of insights. Symptom relief follows reason as attitude changes, increasing responsible self-sufficiency, instead of becoming uncomfortably dependent on the psychoanalytic all-knowing wizard.

The formal-therapist is an educator in that he or she imparts information on relational syndromal patterns and the patient detects the pattern as it manifests itself in the testing as well as in several relationships. The patient/student does not only recognize her personal relational pattern in the testing; s/he rediscovers it articulated again at all real-life relationships, beginning with the relationship with the trainer/therapist.

Therapist/Educator as a Role Model
There is another function of the therapist/educator; s/he is a role model promoting the relational values of conflict resolution: mastery, cooperation and mutual respect. S/he must be the role model of wisdom, of optimal power management in relationships. The model authority should ideally exemplify the conflict resolving process as willingness to accept responsibility for appropriate adjustment of his/her conduct. Alternatively the authority figure may admit his failure in managing effectively his/her life.

The Self-Assessment, a Science-Based Self-Education, and the Role of a Mentor as a Therapist/Teacher/Coach/Clergy Figure to Support Change
The Science of Conflict Resolution clarifies a number of items pertinent to education:

- The unconscious is a scientific and moral order entity.

- Diagnostic categories are wellness syndromal relational modalities.

- The self-assessment, using the creative process, is the means for an effective diagnostic, therapeutic educational/intervention. Analysis of patterns leads to insights and behavior modification.

- The educator/therapist's role is the syndromal interpretation of the test information and the role modeling of the conflict resolution principles as moral values. Teachers introduce the normative rule formative environment.

The assessment technology is useful in therapy but its user friendly nature qualifies it to be delivered within the educational settings. The case studies demonstrate how science changes the traditional tasks of a therapist for diagnosis and therapy. These changes allow the delivery of the assessment and its insights in educational as well as therapeutic settings.

Science and technology change the patient-therapist roles into those of student and teacher. The therapist becomes an educator as s/he teaches psychology as a science and uses a simple assessment to evaluate and to inform about wellness and possibly about illness. Science places education and therapy on a rational cognitive foundation. The message of the therapist educator is not only conveying that the mind is rational, predictable and measurable, but also to impersonate the optimal conflict resolution principles in her/his lifestyle. The self-assessment simplifies diagnosis and therapy. The objective of therapy and education is self-knowledge, which may be easily reached with self-discovery determining a person's relational modality through the self-assessment. Psycho-therapy is transformed into a program of psycho-education. The complexity of the therapist educator's role is bypassed through the online delivery of the assessment.

Science provides education with factual, objective information on the nature of the unconscious identifying its manifestation as a set of relational modalities, scientific phenomena, measurable with the use of the self-assessment. Education pertinent to the interests of the public is the proper forum to present science even if such pertains to psychology and morality. Morality itself must be introduced as a science, the science of cultural conflict resolutions integrating religions as normative institutions, mere partial but complementary discoveries of science. It is possible to educate the public about the scientific and the moral nature of the unconscious providing information about the nature of the process, about the modalities as a science and to apply this information through a simple technology of tapping creativity for self-discovery.

It has been the traditional task of education to compose and analyze essays as well as to educate on matters of science. The additional information contributed by the Moral Science of behavior is the formal structural analysis of essays and the personal relevance of this information. Essays reflect the personal ways of perceiving reality in the context of four alternative relational modalities. Education addresses self-discovery and self-improvement. The Moral Science provides education with the means to achieve its mission in delivering personal insights and enlightenment on values. The testing technology attains education's goals for the integration of knowledge, the bridging of the arts and the sciences, self-knowledge and clarity of moral values.

Chapter Five
Traditional Psychotherapies Integrated into Psychoeducation

The Integration of Psychotherapies Based on Conceptual Revisions
The conceptual and technological advantages of the Creativity and Power Management emotional education program entail changes in the practice of both psychotherapies and education. The effectiveness of the assessment instrument may be explained as representing the integration of the multiple psychotherapies. The traditional therapies are represented in the assessment but their concepts and techniques are modified.

The new integrative approach to therapy redefines the unconscious; it changes the diagnostic categories, and delivers education, diagnosis and therapy combined through the self-assessment. The psychodynamic nature of wellness is reflected in the syndromal organization of emotions and actions.

The six role state syndromal organization of emotions entails targeting actions, power management, to influence the related emotional experiences. The focus on action is different from the current focus on controlling and modifying emotions; emotions as symptoms are viewed as secondary to actions. The name of the intervention is about modifying actions; the therapeutic modality is called Power Management.

Integrating Psychotherapies
The Moral Science's concepts and the technologies of Power Management represent the integrated delivery of multiple but revised psychotherapies. The new concepts may be introduced in psychotherapies to encourage their integration for the compounding of their effectiveness.

1. Power Management has a clear educational/cognitive message equivalent to that of the cognitive therapies; it also has a workbook of activities; this is the battery instrument. This workbook is a diagnostic and therapeutic self-assessment.

2. It also has a strong psychodynamic position: the process connects emotions and behaviors. The Moral Science goes beyond; it changes the psychoanalytic therapies' transference into the

innate wellness diagnosis of the relational modalities.

3. It clarifies behavior modifications choices identified by the test-taker as the needed power management options.

Suggested Adjustments of Cognitive Therapies

Cognitive therapies must be modified to inform on the syndromal integration of behaviors and emotions and to clarify the path to normative conciliation of the individual through power management.

Cognitive therapies must educate on the psychodynamic connection of behaviors and emotions rather than by perceiving emotions as undesirable clinical symptoms. This information may be introduced by comprehending the syndromal nature of behavior and emotions as wellness diagnoses, readily identifiable utilizing the Conflict Analysis Self-assessment as the workbook of choice.

Workbook assignments should be modified in observing the syndromal sequence of emotions and the need to manage one's power behaviors as the means to control one's emotions. The complete self-assessment should help to identify the connection of symptoms and behaviors along the submissive, dominant deviations.

Suggested Adjustments of Psychodynamic Therapies

Psychodynamic therapies need to drop the concepts of the agnostic and irrational unconscious. They need to rethink the concept of transference by adopting the measurable syndromal unconscious as a set of four wellness relational modality diagnoses.

Transference is an innate relational modality readily identified without a therapeutic relationship.

They need to adopt the diagnostic categories of wellness accounting for psychodynamic integration of emotions and behaviors as circumscribed syndromal sequences.

They might want to use the battery of tests in particular the Relational Modality inventory test to measure the nature of the unconscious as a relational modality.

Instead of the structural model, they might consider its equivalent of the six-role conflict resolution process.

Instead of defense mechanisms they might consider relational operations accounting for the transformation of emotions, such as projection as the distinct anticipation of role reversal, sublimation as compromise.

Instead of prolonged study of the unconscious on the couch using free associations they might want to consider the circumscribed use of the creative process with the Conflict Analysis Battery; it leads to insights without developing client therapist dependence.

Suggested Adjustments of Behavior Modification Therapies

Behavior modification therapies may adopt the self-assessment to allow the client to determine her need for changes as power management modifications.

568

Behavior modification programs, assertiveness versus compliance or anger management therapies may be used to reinforce behavior changes clearly spelled by the innate principles of conflict resolution as the definitive moral values.

Meditation, mindfulness focus, reduction of desires may be used to deal with stressors as a series of daily rituals.

Suggested Adjustments to Art Therapies
Creativity is demystified as the means for processing conflicts and developing insights.
Creativity leads to art as a natural science phenomenon that finds simple natural science interpretation.

Suggested Adjustments of Spiritual and Religious Therapies and Counseling
The conflict resolution approach is compatible with all relational conflict resolving traditions recognizing them as endorsements of moral values.

Religions need to educate the public on the history of religions as partial and complementary discoveries of conflict resolution and as thus being forerunners of the Moral Science but with norms that are culturally determined rather than as universal moral paradigms.

Feedback, a Test Taker's Comments
"Dr. Levis' theory puts forth that the unconscious is, in a sense, programmed to resolve conflict and that the phases of this conflict resolution process come to the surface during the creative process. The workbook developed by Dr. Levis, provides a series of creative prompts in which one creates metaphors of one's feelings by formulating characters, drawings, dialogues, stories, evolving both insights and identifying need for changes gradually declaring willingness to accept responsibility for one self and making the needed changes.

"The testing helps to connect one's experiences, emotions, along the interrelated phases of the unconscious conflict resolution mechanism. Each exercise in the workbook corresponds to a particular emotion as a role state in the conflict resolution pattern: stress, response, anxiety, defense, reversal, and compromise. Together, the exercises form a narrative of the patient's drama. The drama is a logical symbolic universe reflecting the mode of relating along four different ways of communicating feelings. The sequence illustrates metaphorically one's feelings and actions along the logical phases of the relational pattern, clarifying that the problem is not a chemical imbalance or innate defect but a simple wellness relational modality diagnosis. One's problems are then ascribed to a curable relational diagnosis. Symptoms are the result of a power imbalance caused by one's relational modality proclivities."

Summing Up the Innovations of the Moral Science
The new science redefines the traditional concepts across the board; we do not have a revision of psychological theories; we usher in the comprehensive integration of psychology and morality bound by the rigorous sciences of physics, logic and math. This new domain is the Moral Science.

- It redefines the unconscious as a scientific and moral order circumscribed periodic phenomenon by studying the creative process as a natural science and moral order measurable entity, the unit of the social sciences.

- It introduces a new set of wellness diagnostic categories as four alternative ways of resolving conflict.

- It hinges on an effective, user friendly self assessment that taps creativity for self-discovery, identifying how a person resolves conflicts. The assessment is didactic, diagnostic and therapeutic.

- It reconciles the religions of the world as partial and complementary discoveries of the Moral Science. The Moral Science completes the mission of religions, the healing of the world, by establishing moral consensus on the nature of the divine.

- It revamps education through the delivery of a concise program of emotional education leading to using creativity for self-discovery and personal power management. It reinforces morality through the insightful integration of religions into the Moral Science and of the arts into meaningful celebrations of the scientific moral order.

Summing Up the Advantages of the Testing Protocol

The application of the concepts manifests in the utilization of the user-friendly psychological assessment; it readily informs the person at a number of levels:

- Clear measurable parameters: relational modality, psychic tension, particular clinical pathologies, identifiable with computer interpretation speed and accuracy

- The personal relevance for the test taker as a didactic, diagnostic, therapeutic experience

- Objectivity of a document for the records of value for the patient and the therapist

- The delivery of information for both testee and observer

- Creation of a valuable record useful as base line to subsequent outcome studies.

- The ease, cost effectiveness of generating the record as a diagnostic and therapeutic experience, with the ability of readily screening a big population

- The REMS inventory as a purely computer software rated assessment, with simplicity and accuracy of its interpretation, with extraordinary validity and reliability

- The Formal Analysis Profile, as criteria available for the scientific analysis of test information

- The at a glance recognition of the relational modality scales and of the art/aesthetic choices of pathology and lack of resolution of conflicts of the metaphor profile.

- The record as meaningful to the client, useful for self-knowledge but also as a record for the screening of several individuals

- Scientific documentation of the diagnostic condition

- Determination of the need for services and

- Knowledge of the receptivity to the client for therapeutic services

- Economy and effectiveness of the didactic, diagnostic and therapeutic evaluation procedure.

- Establishment of normative scores of wellness and illness

34712801R20322

Made in the USA
San Bernardino, CA
05 June 2016